EPA ENVIRONMENTAL ASSESSMENT SOURCEBOOK

Edited by

J. Russell Boulding

Ann Arbor Press, Inc.
Chelsea, Michigan

Library of Congress Cataloging-in-Publication Data

EPA environmental assessment sourcebook / edited by J. Russell Boulding.
     p.   cm.
     Includes bibliographical references and index.
1. Hazardous wastes--Environmental aspects. 2. Hazardous waste sites. I. Boulding, J. Russell.
TD1050.E58E63   1996
628.5--dc20   95-52308
ISBN 1-57504-009-3

ANN ARBOR PRESS, INC.
121 South Main Street, Chelsea, Michigan 48118

PRINTED IN THE UNITED STATES OF AMERICA

ABOUT THE EDITOR

J. Russell Boulding first began working in the environmental field in 1973 when he helped set up the Environmental Defense Fund's Denver Office, and has been a free-lance environmental consultant since 1977 when he established Boulding Soil-Water Consulting in Bloomington, Indiana. He has a B.A. in Geology (1970) from Antioch College, Yellow Springs, Ohio, and an M.S. in Water Resources Management (1975) from the University of Wisconsin/Madison. From 1975 to 1977 he was a soil scientist with the Indiana Department of Natural Resources and mapped soils in southern Indiana on a cooperative program with the U.S. Soil Conservation Service. Since 1984 he has been Senior Environmental Scientist with Eastern Research Group, Inc. in Lexington, Massachusetts.

Mr. Boulding is the author of more than 120 books, chapters, articles and consultant reports in the areas of soil and ground-water contamination assessment, geochemical fate assessment of hazardous wastes, mined land reclamation, and natural resource management and regulatory policy. From 1978 to 1980 he served as a member of the Environmental Subcommittee of the Committee on Surface Mining and Reclamation (COSMAR) of the National Academy of Sciences (NAS) and as a consultant to the NAS Committee on Soil as a Resource in Relation to Surface Mining for Coal. Mr. Boulding is an ARCPACS Certified Professional Soil Classifier and a National Ground Water Association Certified Ground Water Professional. His professional memberships include the Soil Science Society of America, International Society of Soil Science, Association of Ground Water Scientists and Engineers, and the International Association of Hydrogeologists. Since 1992 he has been a member of the American Society for Testing and Material's Committee D18 (Soil and Rock) and active in subcommittees D18.01 (Surface and Subsurface Characterization), D18.07 (Identification and Classification of Soils) and D18.21 (Ground Water and Vadose Zone Investigations). In 1993 he became chair of D18.01's Section on Site Characterization for Environmental Purposes.

PREFACE

The U.S. Environmental Protection Agency (U.S. EPA), through a number of its national research laboratories, publishes several series of relatively short documents that provide up-to-date information on the current state of knowledge about environmental site assessment and remediation of contaminated soil and ground water. Many of these papers have become classics, and widely cited in the literature on environmental site assessment and remediation. Other equally valuable papers have not received the attention they deserve. For several years I have been collecting these documents from EPA's R.S. Kerr Environmental Laboratory (Ada, OK), Environmental Monitoring Systems Laboratory (Las Vegas, NV), and Risk Reduction Engineering Laboratory (Cincinnati, OH)[1], and it occurred to me that it would be nice to make them available in a convenient form for more widespread use. This volume, *EPA Environmental Assessment Sourcebook*, includes papers that focus on contaminant behavior and transport processes and modeling and environmental site characterization and monitoring. The companion volume, *EPA Environmental Engineering Sourcebook*, includes papers and bulletins that focus on remediation of contaminated soils and ground water.

Three types of EPA documents are included in this volume:

1. *Ground Water Issue Papers* (15 chapters). These papers have been developed by the Regional Superfund Ground Water Forum, a group of ground-water scientists, representing EPA's Regional Superfund Offices, organized to exchange up-to-date information related to remediation of Superfund sites.
2. *Environmental Research Briefs* (4 chapters). These papers report theoretical and applied EPA-funded research results. Only research briefs with broad significance for environmental assessment are included in this volume.
3. *Engineering Bulletins* (1 chapter). Engineering Bulletins are a series of documents that summarize the latest information available on selected treatment and site remediation technologies and related issues. Only Engineering Bulletins directly related to environmental site assessment are included in this volume.

Editing of the chapters in this volume include minor editorial corrections, reorganization for consistency, current affiliation of authors (if changed), and updating of references originally cited as in press. Where possible, the NTIS acquisition number for other EPA documents has been added, and some additional annotations may be added, such as the availability of more recent editions of books cited in the original paper. EPA Engineering Bulletins do not list authors at the beginning, as ground-water issue papers and environmental research briefs do, but authors are identified in this volume, if specific authors could be identified. I would like to thank Stephen Schmelling, RSKERL-Ada, and Ken Brown, EMSL-LV for taking the time to help me check and update the current affiliations of authors of the documents included in this volume, and to make sure that the names of EPA contacts and their phone numbers are up-to-date.

---

[1] Recently all of EPA's laboratories were reorganized and renamed. RSKERL and RREL are now part of the National Risk Management Research Laboratory and EMSL-Las Vegas is now the National Exposure Research Laboratory. This volume retains the old names and abbreviations because they are firmly embedded in all the documents included in the volume and because they more clearly differentiate the various sources.

ABBREVIATIONS AND ACRONYMS

CERCLA	Comprehensive Environmental Response, Compensation, and Liability Act (Superfund)
EMSL-LV	U.S. EPA Environmental Monitoring Systems Laboratory, Las Vegas, NV (recently renamed Technical Support Center for Monitoring and Site Characterization)
LESC	Lockheed Engineering & Sciences Company
ORNL	Oak Ridge National Laboratory
OSC	Superfund On-Site Coordinator
RCRA	Resource Conservation and Recovery Act
RPM	Superfund Remedial Project Manager
RREL	U.S. EPA Risk Reduction Engineering Laboratory (recently renamed National Risk Management Research Laboratory)
RSKERL-Ada	U.S. EPA Robert S. Kerr Environmental Research Laboratory, Ada, OK (recently renamed National Risk Management Research Laboratory)
SAIC	Science Applications International Corporation
Superfund	See CERCLA
USCG	U.S. Coast Guard
U.S. EPA	U.S. Environmental Protection Agency
USGS	U.S. Geological Survey

See the end of Chapter 17 for additional abbreviations

CONTENTS

Chapter 1

Overview

J. Russell Boulding, Boulding Soil-Water Consulting, Bloomington, IN

INTRODUCTION

The 22 chapters collected in this volume were developed primarily to serve the needs of the Superfund Program of the U.S. Environmental Protection Agency (EPA), and consequently focus on basic concepts and site investigation methods that are applicable to evaluating soil and ground-water contamination at uncontrolled hazardous waste sites. However, the basic processes that affect contaminant behavior and investigation techniques are equally applicable to a wide range of environmental investigations where prevention, control, or identification of contaminants in air, soil, and ground water are a potential concern. Examples of types of investigations for which the contents of this volume would serve as a useful reference source include:

- Environmental site assessments for real estate property transactions, particularly where a Phase I investigation identifies a known of potential contamination of soil and ground water.
- Site investigations and monitoring at sites with leaking underground storage tanks.
- Site investigations and monitoring at Resource Conservation Recovery Act (RCRA) hazardous waste facilities.
- Site investigations and monitoring at nonhazardous solid waste disposal facilities.
- Site investigations and monitoring at coal and other mineral mining projects.
- Investigations for delineation of wellhead protection areas.

This volume is organized into two parts: (1) contaminant behavior, transport processes, and modeling, and (2) site characterization and monitoring. The contents of each chapter are briefly described below.

PART 1: CONTAMINANT BEHAVIOR, TRANSPORT PROCESSES, AND MODELING

Chapter 2, *Basic Concepts of Contaminant Sorption at Hazardous Waste Sites*, discusses factors and soil characteristics that influence sorption, with emphasis on sorption of organic contaminants, and describes a procedure for estimating the distribution of an organic contaminant between the solid and aqueous phases.

Chapter 3, *Behavior of Metals in Soils*, provides an excellent review of factors and processes that enhance and retard the mobility of metals in the subsurface. It also summarizes information on the behavior of specific metals, and describes methods for metals analysis and evaluating the behavior of metals in soils.

Chapter 4, *Natural Attenuation of Hexavalent Chromium in Ground Water and Soils*, provides an in-depth discussion of the geochemistry of chromium, with emphasis on hexavalent chromium, its most toxic form. The potential for natural reductants in the subsurface to reduce hexavalent chromium to its less toxic trivalent form has resulted in considerable interest in using natural attenuation as part of the cleanup strategy at chromium contaminated sites. This chapter addresses the complex considerations required to determine whether natural attenuation may be feasible at a site.

Chapter 5, *Dense Nonaqueous Phase Liquids*, provides a comprehensive review of the properties of DNAPLs, how they move in the unsaturated and saturated zones, techniques for characterizing their distribution in the subsurface, and methods for remediating DNAPL contaminated sites.

Chapter 6, *Facilitated Transport*, is a classic chapter that describes the mechanisms by which the mobility hydrophobic organic contaminants can be enhanced by cosolvent effects, and how organic and inorganic contaminant mobility can be enhanced by movement of colloids in ground water.

Chapter 7, *Complex Mixtures and Ground-Water Quality*, provides one of the few available detailed discussions of the transport and fate of miscible NAPLs in the subsurface (most of the literature has tended to focus on immiscible NAPLs). The chapter also includes a good discussion of the significance of complex mixtures for remediation of contaminated soil and ground water.

Chapter 8, *Reductive Dehalogenation of Organic Contaminants in Soils and Ground Water*, provides a synthesis of the growing body of recent literature on mechanisms by which microorganisms are able to degrade halogenated organic compounds under anaerobic conditions, and discusses the applications and limitations of these processes for ground-water remediation.

Chapter 9, *Fundamentals of Ground-Water Modeling*, provides, as the title implies, a good overview of the uses and misuses of computer modeling in developing an understanding of the behavior of hydrogeologic systems.

Chapter 10, *Contaminant Transport in Fractured Media: Models for Decision Makers*, is a widely cited chapter that addresses the special difficulties in modeling ground-water flow and contaminant transport in fractured-rock systems. The chapter also includes an overview of techniques for hydrogeologic characterization of fractured-rock aquifers.

PART II: SITE CHARACTERIZATION AND MONITORING

Chapter 11, *Technology Preselection Data Requirements*, provides a useful review of the significance of different contaminants and soil and groundwater parameters for different types of treatment technologies. This chapter can help guide selection of the types of parameters that should be sampled and measured at a site, and also helps evaluate the significance of measured values when selecting candidate remediation technologies (see also Chapter 14).

Chapter 12, *Accuracy of Depth to Water Measurements*, describes the three most commonly used methods for measuring water table elevations: steel tape, electrical methods, and air line methods.

Chapter 13, *Suggested Operating Procedures for Aquifer Pumping Tests*, provides detailed guidance on how to plan and carry out an aquifer pump test.

Chapter 14, *Characterizing Soils for Hazardous Waste Site Assessments*, presents a comprehensive approach to planning, collecting, and using soil data for modeling of water and contaminant transport in the vadose (unsaturated) zone. Numerous useful tables identify primary and ancillary soil characteristics and how they can be measured or estimated, soil characteristics required for vadose zone models, and soil characteristics required for remedial technology evaluation.

Chapter 15, *Soil Sampling and Analysis for Volatile Organic Compounds*, is a seminal chapter that documents the problems with standard techniques for sampling, transporting, and analysis of soils for volatile organic compounds (VOCs), which typically result in measurements that are one or two orders of magnitude lower than actual values. This chapter remains the best single reference source for alternative sampling procedures that can help reduce losses as a result of sampling, transport, and analysis of samples for VOCs.

Chapter 16, *Potential Sources of Error in Ground-Water Sampling at Hazardous Waste Sites*, provides the best-available review of the variety of factors that can introduce errors into sampling results by means of monitoring well design, drilling methods, well development, well and sampling materials, well purging, and sample collection, transport, and analysis. The chapter identifies the types of errors associated with each program element, ease and methods for error avoidance, and ease and methods for error detection.

Chapter 17, *Survey of Laboratory Studies Relating to the Sorption/Desorption of Contaminants on Selected Well Casing Materials*, supplements the previous chapter by providing a more in-depth review of the scientific literature on possible biases to sampling results as the result of sorption and desorption of contaminants on well casing materials.

Chapter 18, *Ground Water Sampling for Metals Analysis*, is another classic chapter which presents recommendations of an EPA-convened technical committee in 1989. These recommendations challenged the conventional ground-water sampling practices of pumping or bailing a well as rapidly as possible to remove "stagnant" water, and routine filtration of ground-water samples to remove particulates. The recommendations in this paper still stand, with some refinements (see Chapters 19, 20 and discussion of recent developments in sampling later in this chapter).

Chapter 19, *Colloidal-Facilitated Transport of Inorganic Contaminants in Ground Water: Part I, Sampling Considerations*, presents results of field investigations at a metals-contaminated site in Arizona which tested and supported the procedures recommended in Chapter 18.

Chapter 20, *Colloidal-Facilitated Transport of Inorganic Contaminants in Ground Water: Part II, Colloidal Transport*, presents results of sampling at three metals-contaminated sites that provide further testing and support for the recommendations in Chapter 18.

OTHER RECENT DOCUMENTS AND DEVELOPMENTS

Environmental Site Assessment Documents

Several EPA documents are useful reference sources for additional information on specific site assessment techniques. *Use of Airborne, Surface, and Borehole Geophysical Techniques at Contaminated Sites* (Boulding, 1993a) covers noninvasive techniques in some detail, and the two-volume *Subsurface Characterization and Monitoring Techniques* (Boulding, 1993b), provides information on more than 280 specific field methods. Both are available from the EPA at no cost (see next section for ordering information). In Boulding (1993b), the first volume covers solids and ground water and the second volume covers the vadose zone and chemical field screening methods.

DNAPL Site Evaluation (Cohen and Mercer, 1993) is another excellent reference that addresses techniques for DNAPL contaminated sites. Finally, the new ASTM D5730 (*Guide to Site Characterization for Environmental Purposes with Emphasis on Soil, Rock, the Vadose Zone, and Ground Water*), approved in August, 1995, provides a systematic framework for any type of environmental site investigation. Especially useful is an Appendix that indexes and lists more than 200 ASTM standard test methods, practices, and guides for use in the field and laboratory that may be potentially useful for environmental site investigations.

Nonaqueous Phase Liquids (NAPLs)

Two recently released EPA Ground Water Issue papers, *Light Nonaqueous Phase Liquids* (Newell et al., 1995) and *Nonaqueous Phase Liquids Compatibility with Materials Used in Well Construction, Sampling, and Remediation* (McCaulou et al., 1995), could not be included in this volume. Both can be obtained from NCEPI (see later section on how to obtain documents from EPA). In contrast to dense nonaqueous phase liquids (DNAPLs; see Chapter 5), light nonaqueous phase liquids (LNAPL) that reach a water table tend to float and spread laterally. A fluctuating water table enhances a process called *smearing*, which spreads residual LNAPL to zones below the seasonal high water table and higher into the unsaturated zone above the seasonal high water table. The LNAPL paper also covers site characterizations techniques and remediation techniques, many of which are similar to those for DNAPLs as covered in Chapter 5. The NAPL compatibility paper includes a table that presents chemical compatibility ratings for 207 organic compounds with 11 types of plastics, 8 types of elastopolymers, ceramic, silica, and 7 types of metals.

Modeling

U.S. EPA (1994) provides a general framework for using ground-water models for a particular project. In recent years there has been a proliferation of computer codes for modeling flow in the unsaturated (vadose) zone. van der Heijde (1994) provides summary information on about 100 such models. Nofziger et al. (1994) evaluated four models (RITZ, VIP, CMLS, and HYDRUS) for application at Superfund sites and found that large uncertainty exists in many model outputs as a result of sensitivity to input values and high parameter variability. Jordon et al. (1995) reviewed six models that are available for evaluating the feasibility, design and performance of soil vapor extraction systems, one of the most commonly used remediation methods for soils contaminated with volatile contaminants.

Sampling

The ground-breaking chapters in this volume on soil sampling for volatile organic compounds-VOCs (Chapter 15), and ground-water sampling for metals analysis (Chapter 18), have stood the test of time. West et al. (1995) found that VOCs concentrations at a former land treatment facility measured onsite using a heated headspace/gas chromatography method were typically 10 times higher than concentration measured at an offsite laboratory using a conventional purge-and-trap/gas chromatography/mass spectrometry method. They concluded that increasing sample density with field analyses was preferable to using complex spatial models to overcome the lack of spatial information from smaller data sets based on offsite laboratory analysis.

The report of an EPA-sponsored workshop on ground-water sampling held in late 1993 (U.S. EPA, 1995) reflects a growing consensus among practitioners that low-flow purging and sampling (as described in Chapter 20) is preferable to earlier practices of purging a well at a high pumping rate or bailing until a fixed number of casing volumes are evacuated. Advantages include: (1) more representative samples, (2) lower volume of purge water, and (3) better spatial resolution for sample collection. However, there is still some resistance by practitioners to this approach mainly due to concern with potential problems with data comparison and interpretation of temporal trends due to differences in sample collection methods. The increased time required for low-flow purging and sampling may also be a matter of concern.

Pohlmann et al. (1994) confirmed the importance of minimizing disturbance of an aquifer during purging in a comparison of filtered and unfiltered ground-water samples collected at landfill sites in Wisconsin and Washington and a site contaminated by industrial waste in Nevada. Bailer-collected samples produced trace metal concentrations in unfiltered samples that were orders of magnitude higher than in 0.45 micron-filtered samples, whereas there were minimal differences in metals concentrations in filtered and unfiltered samples collected using a bladder pump and submersible-centrifugal pump. The difference was attributed to mobilization of aquifers solids by the bailer. Puls and Paul (1995) found that water quality parameters equilibrated faster and initial turbidity levels were lower in dedicated sampling systems (bladder and variable-speed submersible) compared to portable systems using the same pumps.

HOW TO OBTAIN DOCUMENTS FROM THE EPA

EPA publications can be obtained at no charge (while supplies are available) from the following sources:

EPA/625-series documents: ORD Publications, P.O. Box 19968, Cincinnati, OH 45219-0968; phone 513-569-7562, fax 513-569-7562.
Other EPA documents: National Center for Environmental Publications and Information (NCEPI), 11029 Kenwood Road, Cincinnati, OH 45242; fax 513-891-6685.

Other documents, for which an NTIS acquisition number is shown can be obtained from the National Technical Information Service (NTIS), Springfield, VA 22161; phone 800-336-4700, fax 703-321-8547.

REFERENCES

ASTM D5730-95. Guide to Site Characterization for Environmental Purposes with Emphasis on Soil, Rock, the Vadose Zone, and Ground Water. American Society for Testing and Materials, 100 Barr Harbor Drive, West Conshohocken, PA, 19428-2959; 610-832-9585.
Boulding, J.R. 1993a. Use of Airborne, Surface and Borehole Geophysical Techniques at Contaminated Sites: A Reference Guide. EPA/625/R-92/007.

Boulding, J.R. 1993b. Subsurface Characterization and Monitoring Techniques: A Desk Reference Guide; Vol. I: Solids and Ground Water; Vol. II: The Vadose Zone, Field Screening and Analytical Methods. EPA/625/R-93/003a&b.

Cohen, R.M. and J.W. Mercer. 1993. DNAPL Site Evaluation. EPA/600/R-93/002 (NTIS PB93-150217). [Also published by Lewis Publishers as C.K. Smoley edition, Boca Raton, FL, 384 pp.]

Jordan, D.L., J.W. Mercer, and R.M. Cohen. 1995. Review of Mathematical Modeling for Evaluating Soil Vapor Extraction Systems. EPA/540/R-95/513 (NTIS PB95-243051.

McCaulou, D.R., D.G. Jewett, and S.G. Huling. 1995. Nonaqueous Phase Liquids Compatibility with Materials Used in Well Construction, Sampling, and Remediation. Ground Water Issue, EPA/540/S-95/503, 14 pp.

Newell, C.J., S.D. Acree, R.R. Ross, and S.G. Huling. 1995. Light Nonaqueous Phase Liquids. Ground Water Issue, EPA/540/S-95/500, 28 pp.

Nofziger, D.L., J.-S. Chen, and C.T. Haan. 1994. Evaluation of Unsaturated/Vadose Zone Models for Superfund Sites. EPA/600/R-93/184 (NTIS PB94-157675), 188 pp.

Pohlmann, K.R., G.A. Icopini, R.D. McArthur, and C.G. Rosal. 1994. Evaluation of Sampling and Field-Filtration Methods for the Analysis of Trace Metals in Ground Water. EPA/600/R-94/119 (NTIS PB94-201993).

Puls, R.W. and C.J. Paul. 1995. Low-Flow Purging and Sampling of Ground Water Monitoring Wells with Dedicated Systems. Ground Water Monitoring and Remediation 15(1):116–123.

U.S. Environmental Protection Agency (EPA). 1994. Assessment Framework for Ground-Water Model Applications. EPA/500/B-94/003 (OSWER Directive 9029.00), 41 pp.

U.S. Environmental Protection Agency (EPA). 1995. Ground Water Sampling—A Workshop Summary (Dallas, Texas, November 30–December 2, 1993). EPA/600/R-94/205.

van der Heijde, P.K.M. 1994. Identification and Compilation of Unsaturated/Vadose Zone Models. EPA/600/R-94/028 (NTIS PB94-157773).

West, O.R., R.L. Siegrist, R.J. Mitchell, and R.A. Jenkins. 1995. Measurement Error and Spatial Variability Effects on Characterization of Volatile Organics in the Subsurface. Environ. Sci. Technol. 29:647–656.

PART I

Contaminant Behavior,
Transport Processes
and
Modeling

Chapter 2

Basic Concepts of Contaminant Sorption at Hazardous Waste Sites[1]

Marvin D. Piwoni, Laboratory Services Manager, Hazardous Waste Research and Information
Center, Illinois Department of Energy and Natural Resources, Champaign, IL
Jack W. Keeley, Dynamac Corporation, Robert S. Kerr Environmental Research Laboratory, Ada, OK

INTRODUCTION

Processes which influence the behavior of contaminants in the subsurface must be considered both in evaluating the potential for movement as well as in designing remediation activities at hazardous waste sites. Such factors not only tend to regulate the mobility of contaminants, but also their form and stability. Sorption is often the paramount process controlling the behavior of contaminants in the subsurface. This chapter summarizes the basic concepts of sorption in soil and ground water with emphasis on nonpolar organic contaminants.

The Concept of Sorption

Sorption can be defined as the interaction of a contaminant with a solid. More specifically, the term can be further divided into adsorption and absorption. The former refers to an excess contaminant concentration at the surface of a solid while the latter implies a more or less uniform penetration of the solid by a contaminant. In most environmental settings this distinction serves little purpose as there is seldom information concerning the specific nature of the interaction. The term sorption is used in a generic way to encompass both phenomena.

There are a number of factors which control the interaction of a contaminant and the surface of soil or aquifer materials. These include chemical and physical characteristics of the contaminant, composition of the surface of the solid, and the fluid media encompassing both. By gaining an understanding of these factors, logical conclusions can often be drawn about the impact of sorption on the movement and distribution of contaminants in the subsurface. The failure to take sorption into account can result in a significant underestimation of the amount of a contaminant at a site as well as the time required for it to move from one point to another.

In introducing sorption theory it is necessary to define the terms sorbate and sorbent. The sorbate is the contaminant that adheres to the sorbent, or sorbing material. In this discussion the sorbate will usually be an organic molecule and the sorbent will be the soil or aquifer matrix.

FACTORS INFLUENCING SORPTION

The properties of a contaminant have a profound impact on its sorption behavior. Some of these include:

- Water Solubility
- Polar/Ionic Character
- Octanol/Water Partition Coefficient
- Acid/Base Chemistry
- Oxidation/Reduction Chemistry

---

[1] EPA/540/4-90/053.

Contaminant Characteristics

In discussing sorption it is useful to divide chemicals into three groups. Although there are many ways to divide chemicals into subgroups, for this purpose three categories are presented which transcend normal boundaries between inorganic and organic species. These are: (1) ionic or charged species; (2) uncharged polar species and, (3) uncharged nonpolar species.

Most inorganic chemicals in aqueous solution will occur as ionic or charged species. This applies to metals and metalloids, and to other molecules such as cyanide and ammonia. However, in contaminated water, metals and other inorganic constituents can exist as polar or nonpolar neutral species. In any event, the chemical form of a contaminant will have a profound effect on its sorption and, therefore, its environmental mobility.

Organic contaminants have representatives in all three of the sorption categories. Many of the more common organic ground-water contaminants are of the nonpolar species, including trichloroethene (TCE), tetrachloroethene (PCE), the chlorinated benzenes, and the more soluble components of hydrocarbon fuels such as benzene, toluene and xylene. Other important organic contaminants including many of the pesticides, phenols and dyes exist in solution as either charged or polar molecules.

Still other, larger organics, such as surfactants, can have both polar and nonpolar ends within the same molecule. The environmental mobility of contaminants with these distinctive properties has been less thoroughly studied than nonpolar organics; therefore, site-specific investigations may provide the most reliable information for their transport characteristics.

SOIL CHARACTERISTICS

If one avoids the difference between positive and negative charges, a simple rule of sorption might be: for charged species, "opposites attract" and for uncharged species, "likes interact with likes." Likes refers to the three categories of contaminants and to the properties of the soil matrix. Some of the most important characteristics of soil affecting the sorptive behavior of subsurface materials include:

- Mineralogy
- Permeability/Porosity
- Texture
- Homogeneity
- Organic Carbon Content
- Surface Charge
- Surface Area

Soil, in its natural state, is primarily composed of sand, silt, clay, water, and a highly variable amount of natural organic carbon. The latter profoundly complicates a soil's sorptive properties. The combination of these characteristics describes the surfaces offered as sorptive sites to contaminants in water passing through the subsurface matrix. For example, silts and clays have much higher surface areas than sand, usually carry a negative charge, and almost invariably associate with natural organic matter.

It can be deduced that sandy materials offer little in the way of sorptive surfaces to passing contaminants while silts and clays, particularly those having substantial amounts of organic matter, provide a rich sorptive environment for all three categories of contaminants. Even the most porous and highly productive aquifers, composed of sands and gravels, usually have some fine grained material, and a small percent of silts and clays can result in a substantial increase in the sorptive behavior of the aquifer material.

FLUID MEDIA CHARACTERISTICS

Under most contamination situations the primary transporting fluid is water. One of the most important properties of this solvent phase is pH, for it dictates the chemical form and, therefore, the mobility, of all contaminants susceptible to the gain or loss of a proton. As an example, penta-chlorophenol will primarily be an uncharged polar molecule in an aqueous solution whose pH is below about 4.7 and an anion when the pH is above that value, increasing its solubility from 14 to 90 mg/L.

Other characteristics of water that can influence the behavior of contaminants include the salt content and the dissolved organic carbon content. Chlorides, for example, which are not usually of much concern when dealing with organic contaminants, can have an important effect on the mobility of various metals. Dissolved organic matter, at relatively high concentrations found in many leachates, has a significant effect on the mobility of most nonpolar organics (see Chapter 7).

IMPLICATIONS OF THESE CHARACTERISTICS

Although somewhat simplified, it can be assumed for purposes of this discussion, that charged and polar species tend to interact with charged and polar surfaces, and nonpolar compounds interact with nonpolar components of soil, usually the natural organic carbon. In order to make a first estimate of the significance of sorption at a site, it is necessary to determine the polar and nonpolar nature of the material with which the contaminant will come into contact. This is usually done by measuring the cation exchange capacity and the natural organic carbon content, respectively.

The cation exchange capacity (CEC) provides an estimate of the total negatively-charged sites on the surface of the soil. It is determined by measuring the mass of a standard cation, usually ammonia, that displaces another cation held by the soil. Under normal field conditions these sites will be occupied by cations common to the flowing or percolating water, such as Na^+, K^+, Ca^{2+}, and Mg^{2+}. Larger organic cations and highly-charged metal ions like Hg^{2+} or Cr^{3+} will be preferentially retained at these sites by "exchanging" with their normal occupants. Thus large organic cations and heavy metals would not normally be expected to move far through soils with a measurable cation exchange capacity.

At contaminated sites, however, conditions may not be "normal" and Hg^{2+} may be codisposed with high levels of chloride salts. In the complexation chemistry shown in Figure 2-1, Hg^{2+} may be replaced by the neutral complex $HgCl_2$ or the negative ion $HgCl_3$, both of which move through the soil more quickly than the cationic form.

Sorption of Nonpolar Organics

As mentioned above, the chemicals at many contaminated sites are nonpolar organics. It was representatives of these types of compounds (DDT and other chlorinated hydrocarbon pesticides) that first focused attention on the potential hazards of chemicals in the environment because of their widespread use, potential human toxicity, and recalcitrance.

Transport and fate characteristics of these compounds have been well studied, first by the agricultural community and later by environmental scientists. As a result, an understanding of the sorptive behavior of these compounds has evolved which can be used to assess the environmental consequences posed at a waste disposal site.

Many organics of environmental concern have a limited solubility in water because of their nonpolarity and molecular size; that is, the solubility of an organic contaminant decreases with decreasing polarity and increasing molecular size. But even with limited solubilities, many hazardous chemicals at equilibrium are at measurable, and sometimes toxic concentrations in water. Polar molecules, such as ethanol, are compatible with water. Their combination results in a homogeneous solution regardless of the proportions that are mixed.

Nonpolar organic compounds interact with soil organic matter through a process known as "hydrophobic sorption" which can be explained as the affinity of organic compounds for phases other than water. For example, water being a polar molecule is not compatible with other nonpolar molecules, such as DDT, which is immiscible with water.

OCTANOL-WATER PARTITIONING

Organic molecules of increasing size, decreasing polarity and therefore water solubility, are said to exhibit increasing "hydrophobicity" which can be quantified by their octanol-water partition

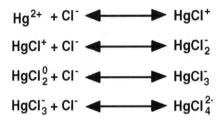

Figure 2-1. Mercury ion complexation in chloride-rich water. The complexation reactions are driven right and down by increasing chloride concentrations, often characteristic of waste waters. Increased complexation produces increased environmental mobility of the mercury.

coefficient. It is a measure of the distribution of the chemical between a water and an organic (octanol) phase with which it is in contact. The more hydrophobic the contaminant, the more likely it is to partition into the octanol phase. The partition coefficient provides a fairly accurate understanding of the sorptive process occurring between water and the soil, more specifically, the soil organic matter.

The octanol-water partition coefficient, expressed as K_{ow} in Figure 2-2, is determined by measuring the concentration of a particular compound in the water and the octanol phases after a period of mixing. It is important to note that the more hydrophobic the compound the less accurate the test, and the results should be viewed accordingly. It is often sufficient to know that an extremely high coefficient means that the compound is very hydrophobic. Since measured K_{ow} values can be in the millions for important environmental contaminants (PCBs, chlorinated pesticides, dioxins and furans), they are often expressed as the base 10 logarithm, Log K_{ow}.

The K_{ow} has two attributes that make it especially useful in environmental assessments. First, it varies in a predictable way within classes of organic compounds. For example, as shown in Figures 2-3 and 2-4, if K_{ow} is known for one member of a class of compounds it can be used reasonably well to estimate a value for other members of the same family. In the examples shown, the K_{ow} can be correlated to the number of chlorine atoms or the number of rings in the molecular structure of classes of contaminants.

The second attribute results from the work of a number of agricultural and environmental researchers who correlated sorption on the organic matter of soils with the K_{ow} of the compounds involved. By using these attributes of the K_{ow}, it is possible to estimate the potential sorption of organic contaminants based on the structure of the compounds and the organic carbon content of the soil or aquifer material.

SORPTION TO SOILS

Thus far it has been suggested that nonpolar organic compounds are sorbed by soils as a function of their hydrophobicity (K_{ow}) and the organic carbon content of the soil. There has been considerable research which suggests that the slow kinetics of the sorption process may be significant in swiftly moving ground water. Sorption studies using flow-through columns produce results sensitive to the flow rate, and batch tests indicate that increased sorption occurs with longer exposure times. The practical implication of these findings may be that sorption is overestimated in aquifer systems with relatively high flow rates.

Sorption is expressed in terms of a partition coefficient K_p, which is defined in Figure 2-2 as the ratio of the concentration of contaminants associated with the solid phase to that in solution, and is, therefore, conceptually similar to K_{ow}. The usefulness of K_{ow} in estimating sorption stems from the fact that the soil organic matter serves the same function as octanol in the octanol-water test. As a result, there have been many empirical relationships developed for estimating sorption from the K_{ow} and the soil organic carbon content. One expression, developed in the laboratory by Piwoni and Banerjee (1989), for the sorption of common environmental contaminants with a low aquifer organic carbon is:

$$\text{Log } K_{oc} = 0.69 \text{ Log } K_{ow} + 0.22$$

Octanol-Water Partition Coefficient:

$$K_{ow} = \frac{Concentration_{Octanol}}{Concentration_{Water}}$$

Almost always presented as Log10 because the numbers are so large for hydrophobic compounds.

Sorption Coefficient:

$$K_p = \frac{Concentration_{Solid\ Phase}}{Concentration_{Solution}}$$

Units are $\frac{mg\ /\ kg}{mg\ /\ L}$ *, which is L / kg.*

Carbon Normalized Sorption Coefficient:

$$K_{oc} = \frac{Sorption\ Coefficient,\ K_p}{Fraction\ Organic\ Carbon}$$

Figure 2-2. Relationships pertinent to nonpolar organic contaminant transport.

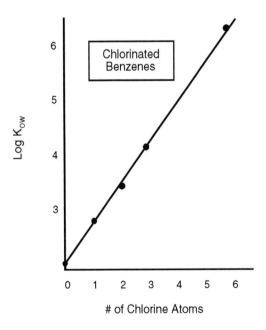

Figure 2-3. Relationship of molecular structure to hydrophobic character.

When applying such a relationship, it is important to select a study in which the compounds used are similar to those of interest at the site under investigation. However, as shown in Figure 2-5, even when applying the empirical relationship to a structurally dissimilar compound such as anthracene, if it is a nonpolar organic, the error of estimate should be less than a factor of five.

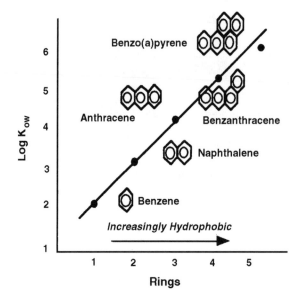

Figure 2-4. Relationship of molecular structure to octanol-water partition coefficient.

These estimates of sorption are based, in large measure, on a good evaluation of the soil organic carbon content at a site which is obtained from the degradation of naturally occurring organic matter. In this regard it is important to realize that soils and aquifer materials are very heterogeneous and the organic carbon content can vary considerably both in the vertical and horizontal dimension. Fortunately, this variability tends to be the greatest in the vertical soil profile while most site investigations are concerned with contaminant movement in the ground water away from the source. While the soil organic carbon content in the horizontal plane usually differs by a factor of ten or less, it can vary by a factor of 10 to 100 in the vertical dimension.

In order to determine the soil organic carbon content at a site, samples are usually obtained using split spoon sampler or other standard soil sampling devices. Representative portions of the soil are then burned in an O_2 atmosphere and the produced CO_2 is measured by IR spectrophotometry. Before burning, soil samples must be acidized to remove inorganic carbon. The accuracy of measuring organic carbon content can also be questionable, particularly at low levels and in carbonate soils. Existing analytical methods for measuring soil organic carbon were developed for the higher concentrations found near the surface. Therefore, at the low levels found in deeper soils and ground water, the same quality assurance procedures used in determining contaminant levels in water should be followed in determining the subsurface organic carbon content.

The processes driving hydrophobic sorption are nonspecific and depend upon small amounts of energy gained by moving contaminants out of the aqueous phase. The extent to which the process proceeds is dependent upon how receptive the soil matrix is to the organic molecule, which is a function of the organic content. But even when the organic carbon content is very low, some sorption of the most hydrophobic molecules continues because of the soil's mineral surfaces.

SORPTION ESTIMATION

In order to use the information provided above in estimating the amount of a contaminant associated with the aqueous and solid phases of an aquifer, it is necessary to develop a contamination scenario. To that end it is assumed that the contaminant at an industrial landfill is 1,4-dichlorobenzene, and there are sufficient data to indicate that: (1) most of the contamination is below the water table; (2) the contaminant concentration in ground water averages 1 mg/L; (3) the measured soil organic carbon is 0.2 percent; and (4) the pore water occupies 50 percent of the aquifer volume. Steps leading to an estimate of the contaminant's distribution between the aqueous and solid phases are:

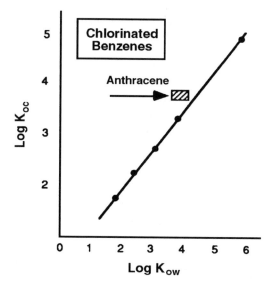

Figure 2-5. Partitioning on soil organic carbon as function of octanol-water partition coefficient.

Field Measurements:

Average contaminant concentration in monitoring wells $Aq_c = 1.0$ mg/L

Soil organic carbon = 0.2 percent, therefore $f_{oc} = 0.002$

Pore water occupies 50 percent of the aquifer's volume.

From the Literature:

Log K_{ow} (1,4-dichlorobenzene) = 3.6

Piwoni and Banerjee Regression, Log $K_{oc} = 0.69\ K_{ow} + 0.22$

Calculated:

Log $K_{oc} = 0.69(3.6) + 0.22 = 2.70$

therefore: $K_{oc} = 506$

$K_p = K_{oc}(f_{oc})/Aq_c = 506\ (0.002)/1.0 \approx 1.0 \approx \underline{\text{Sorbed C}}$
$$\text{Solution C}$$

Conclusion;

The contaminant, equally distributed between each phase, is expressed as mg/kg (soil) and mg/L (water). Since soil is about 2.5 times more dense than water, 2 liters of aquifer would contain 1 liter of water and 2.5 kg of soil. Therefore, 1.0 mg/L of the contaminant would be associated with the water and 2.5 mg (70 percent) would be sorbed to the aquifer's solid phase.

As can be seen from this example, sorption tends to complicate remediation techniques that require pumping water to the surface for treatment. The desorption process has kinetic constraints that can render a pump-and-treat system ineffective. Slow desorption kinetics result in progressively lower contaminant concentrations at the surface, and less cost-effective contaminant removal. It is not uncommon to pump a system until the contaminant concentration in the pumped water meets a mandated restoration level, while the aquifer's solid phase still contains a substantial mass of contaminant. If the pumps are turned off, concentrations in the ground water will soon return to their equilibrium level.

MEASURING SORPTION

It is preferable to obtain the best information possible on which to base an estimate of sorption. Therefore, tests should be made with the contaminants of concern, as well as soils and aquifer material from a specific site. The goal is to obtain a partition coefficient, K_p, for use in the prediction of contaminant movement.

There are essentially two methods for measuring the partition coefficient, those being batch and dynamic techniques. Batch techniques are quicker and easier to perform and, therefore, more amenable to replication and quality control. Dynamic or flow-through techniques offer the advantage of more closely representing processes occurring in the field.

The standard approach to determine the partition coefficient is to generate a sorption isotherm, a graphical representation of the amount of material sorbed at a variety of solute concentrations. The Freundlich isotherm, $S = K_p C^{1/n}$, is the representation most often used for the sorption of nonpolar organics to soils and aquifer materials. In this equation, S is the mass sorbed per mass of sorbent (mg/Kg), C is the solute concentration at equilibrium (mg/L), K_p is the Freundlich partition coefficient, and 1/n is a fitting factor. The equation can be expressed in a linear form for convenience

$$\text{Log } S = \text{Log } K_p + 1/n \text{ Log } C$$

As shown in Figure 2-6, Log K_p can be estimated by determining the intercept of the regression of a Log-Log plot of S and C.

SUMMARY

This has been a discussion of the concepts involved in estimating contaminant sorption, particularly nonpolar organics, at hazardous waste sites. After determining the types of contaminants present at a site, it is possible to estimate K_p using K_{ow} values from the literature, an appropriate sorption coefficient K_{ow} regression equation, and some organic carbon values.

If sorption determinations are within the scope of the project, site representative soil samples and contaminants should be selected from the tests. The measured sorption information is best used to evaluate the validity of preliminary estimates. If the measured partition coefficients differ from the estimates by more than a factor of 2 or 3, it may be useful to select other contaminants from the site and determine K_p values for the same soil samples. A plot of K_p values versus K_{ow} values will provide a useful guide for predicting the sorption characteristics of other contaminants at the site.

EPA CONTACTS

For further information contact: Joe Williams, 405/436-8608; or Dom DiGiulio, 405/436-8605 at RSKERL-Ada.

REFERENCES CITED

Piwoni, M.D. and P. Banerjee. 1989. Sorption of Volatile Organic Solvents from Aquifer Solution onto Subsurface Solids. Journal of Contaminant Hydrology. 4:163–179.

SELECTED ADDITIONAL REFERENCES

Ballard, T.M. 1971. Role of Humic Carrier Substances in DDT Movement Through Forest Soil. Soil Sci. Soc. Am. Proc. 35:145–147.

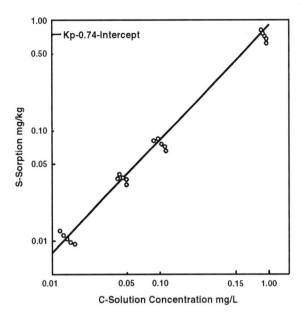

Figure 2-6. Sorption of 1,4-dichlorobenzene.

Banerjee, P., M.D. Piwoni, and K. Ebeid. 1985. Sorption of Organic Contaminants to Low Carbon Substrate Core. Chemosphere 14:1057–1067.

Bouchard, D.C., R.M. Powell, and D.A. Clark. 1988. Organic Cation Effects on the Sorption of Metals and Neutral Organic Compounds on Aquifer Material. J. Environ. Sci. Health Part A 23:585–601.

Bouchard, D.C. and A.L. Wood. 1988. Pesticide Sorption on Geologic Material of Varying Organic Carbon Content. Toxic. Industr. Health 4:341–349.

Briggs, G.G. 1981. Theoretical and Experimental Relationships Between Soil Adsorption, Octanol-Water Partition Coefficients, Water Solubilities, Bioconcentration Factors, and the Parachor. J. Agric. Food Chem. 29:1050–1059.

Brown, D.S. and E.W. Flagg. 1981. Empirical Prediction of Organic Pollutant Sorption in Natural Sediments. J. Environ. Qual. 10:382–386.

Carlson, D.J., L.M. Mayer, M.L. Brann, and T.H. Mague. 1985. Binding of Monomeric Organic Compounds to Macromolecular Dissolved Organic Matter in Seawater. Mar. Chem. 16:141–163.

Carlson, R.M., R.E. Carlson, and H.L. Kopperman. 1975. Determination of Partition Coefficients by Liquid Chromatography. J. Chromatogr. 107:219–223.

Caron, G., I.H. Suffet, and T. Belton. 1985. Effect of Dissolved Organic Carbon on the Environmental Distribution of Nonpolar Organic Compounds. Chemosphere 14:993–1000.

Carter, C.W., and I.H. Suffet. 1982. Binding of DDT to Dissolved Humic Materials. Environ. Sci. Technol. 16:735–740.

Chin Y., W.J. Weber, and T.C. Voice. 1986. Determination of Partition Coefficients and Aqueous Solubilities by Reverse Phase Chromatography-II. Water Res. 20:1443–1450.

Chiou, C.T., R.L. Malcolm, T.I. Brinton, and D.E. Kile. 1986. Water Solubility Enhancement of Some Organic Pollutants and Pesticides by Dissolved Humic and Fulvic Acids. Environ. Sci. Technol. 20:502–508.

Dragun, J. 1988. The Soil Chemistry of Hazardous Materials. Hazardous Materials Control Research Institute. Silver Spring, MD.

Enfield, C.G. 1985. Chemical Transport Facilitated by Multiphase Flow Systems. Water Sci. Technol. 17:1–12.

Enfield, C.G., D.M. Walters, R.F. Carsell, and S.Z. Cohen. 1982. Approximating Transport of Organic Pollutants to Groundwater. Ground Water 20:711–722.

Garbarini, D.R. and L.W. Lion. 1986. Influence of the Nature of Soil Organics on the Sorption of Toluene and Trichloroethylene. Environ. Sci. Technol. 20:1263–1269.

Gamerdinger, A.P., R.J. Wagonet, and M. th. van Genuchten. 1990. Application of Two-Site/Two-Region Models for Studying Simultaneous Transport and Degradation of Pesticides. Soil Sci. Soc. Am. J. 54:957–963.

Gauthier, T.D., W.R. Seitz, and C.L. Grant. 1987. Effects of Structural and Compositional Variations of Dissolved Humic Materials on Pyrene K_{oc} Values. Environ. Sci. Technol. 21:243–248.

Griffin, R.A. and W.R. Roy. 1985. Interaction of Organic Solvents with Saturated Soil-Water Systems. Open File Report prepared for the Environmental Institute for Waste Management Studies, University of Alabama.

Gschwend, P.M. and S. Wu. 1985. On the Constancy of Sediment Water Partition Coefficients of Hydrophobic Organic Pollutants. Environ. Sci. Technol. 19:90–96.

Hassett, J.P. and M.A. Anderson. 1982. Effect of Dissolved Organic Matter on Adsorption of Hydrophobic Organic Compounds by River- and Sewage-Borne Particulate Matter. Water Res. 16:681–686.

Karickhoff, S.W. 1981. Semi-Empirical Estimation of Sorption of Hydrophobic Pollutants on Natural Sediments and Soils. Chemosphere 10:833–846.

Karickhoff, S.W., D.S. Brown, and T.A. Scott. 1979. Sorption of Hydrophobic Pollutants on Natural Sediments. Water Res. 13:241–248.

Landrum, P.F., S.R. Nihart, B.J. Eadie, and W.S. Gardner. 1984. Reverse-Phase Separation Method for Determining Pollutant Binding to Aldrich Humic Acid and Dissolved Organic Carbon of Natural Waters. Environ. Sci. Technol. 18:187–192.

McCarty, P.L., M. Reinhard, and B.E. Rittman. 1981. Trace Organics in Groundwater. Environ. Sci. Technol. 15:40–51.

Morrow, N.R. and I. Chatzis. 1982. Measurement and Correlation of Conditions for Entrapment and Mobilization of Residual Oil. DOE/BC/10310-20.

Mortland, M.M., S. Shaobai, and S.A. Boyd. 1986. Clay-Organic Adsorbents for Phenol and Chlorophenol. Clays and Clay Minerals. 34:581–585.

Page, A.L., R.H. Miller, and D.R. Keeney (eds.). 1982. Methods of Soil Analysis. Part 2. Chemical and Microbiological Properties, 2nd ed. ASA Monograph 9, American Society of Agronomy, Madison, WI.

Poirrier, M.A., B.R. Bordelon, and J.L. Laseter. 1972. Adsorption and Concentration of Dissolved Carbon-14 DDT by Coloring Colloids in Surface Waters. Environ. Sci. Technol. 6:1033–1035.

Rao, P.S.C. and R.E. Jessup. 1983. Sorption and Movement of Pesticides and Other Toxic Substances in Soils. In: D.W. Nelson et al. (eds.), Chemical Mobility and Reactivity in Soil Systems. SSSA Spec. Publ. II, Soil Science Society of American, Madison, WI, pp. 183–201.

Schwarzenbach, R.P. and J. Westall. 1981. Transport of Nonpolar Organic Compounds from Surface Water to Groundwater. Laboratory Sorption Studies. Environ. Sci. Technol. 15:1360–1367.

Thurman, E.M. 1985. Humic Substances in Groundwater. In: G.R. Aiken et al. (eds.), Humic Substances in Soil, Sediment, and Water. Wiley-Interscience, New York, pp. 87–103.

Voice, T.C., C.P. Rice, and W.J. Weber, Jr. 1983. Effect of Solids Concentration on the Sorptive Partitioning of Hydrophobic Pollutants in Aquatic Systems. Environ. Sci. Technol. 17:513–518.

Weber, W.J., Y. Chin, and C.P. Rice. 1986. Determination of Partition Coefficients and Aqueous Solubilities by Reverse Phase Chromatography-I. Water Res. 20:1433–1442.

Wershaw, R.L., P.J. Burcar, and M.C. Goldberg. 1969. Interaction of Pesticides with Natural Organic Material. Environ. Sci. Technol. 3:271–273.

Whitehouse, B. 1985. The Effects of Dissolved Organic Matter on the Aqueous Partitioning of Polynuclear Aromatic Hydrocarbons. Estuarine Coastal Shelf Sci. 20:393–402.

Wilson, J.L. and S.H. Conrad. 1984. Is Physical Displacement of Residual Hydrocarbons a Realistic Possibility in Aquifer Restoration? In: Proc. NWWA/API Conf. on Petroleum Hydrocarbons and Organic Chemicals in Ground Water. National Water Well Association, Worthington, OH, pp. 274–298.

Wolfe, T.A., T. Demiral, and E.R. Baumann. 1985. Interaction of Aliphatic Amines with Montmorillonite to Enhance Adsorption of Organic Pollutants. Clays and Clay Minerals. 33:301–311.

Chapter 3

Behavior of Metals in Soils[1]

Joan E. McLean, Water Research Laboratory, Utah State University, Logan, UT
Bert E. Bledsoe, Retired, U.S. EPA, Robert S. Kerr Environmental Research Laboratory, Ada, OK

INTRODUCTION

The purpose of this document is to introduce to the reader the fundamental processes that control the mobility of metals in the soil environment. This discussion will emphasize the basic chemistry of metals in soils and will provide information on laboratory methods used to evaluate the behavior of metals in soils. The metals selected for discussion in this document are the metals most commonly found at Superfund sites and will be limited to lead (Pb), chromium (Cr), arsenic (As), cadmium (Cd), nickel (Ni), zinc (Zn), copper (Cu), mercury (Hg), silver (Ag), and selenium (Se).

Metals are defined as any element that has a silvery luster and is a good conductor of heat and electricity. There are many terms used to describe and categorize metals, including trace metals, transition metals, micronutrients, toxic metals, heavy metals. Many of these definitions are arbitrary and these terms have been used loosely in the literature to include elements that do not strictly meet the definition of the term. Strictly speaking arsenic and selenium are not metals but are metalloids, displaying both metallic and non-metallic properties. For this paper, the term metal will be used to include all the elements under discussion.

The average concentration of select metals in soils is listed in Table 3-1. All soils naturally contain trace levels of metals. The presence of metals in soil is, therefore, not indicative of contamination. The concentration of metals in uncontaminated soil is primarily related to the geology of the parent material from which the soil was formed. Depending on the local geology, the concentration of metals in a soil may exceed the ranges listed in Table 3-1. For example, Se concentration in non-seleniferous soils in the U.S. ranges from 0.1 to 2 mg/kg. In seleniferous soils, Se ranges from 1 to 80 mg/kg, with reports of up to 1200 mg/kg Se (McNeal and Balistrieri, 1989). Use of common ranges or average concentration of trace metals in soils as an indicator of whether a soil is contaminated is not appropriate since the native concentration of metals in a specific soil may fall out of the listed ranges. Only by direct analysis of uncontaminated soils can background levels of metals be determined.

Metals associated with the aqueous phase of soils are subject to movement with soil water, and may be transported through the vadose zone to ground water. Metals, unlike the hazardous organics, cannot be degraded. Some metals, such as Cr, As, Se, and Hg, can be transformed to other oxidation states in soil, reducing their mobility and toxicity.

Immobilization of metals, by mechanisms of adsorption and precipitation, will prevent movement of the metals to ground water. Metal-soil interaction is such that when metals are introduced at the soil surface, downward transportation does not occur to any great extent unless the metal retention capacity of the soil is overloaded, or metal interaction with the associated waste matrix enhances mobility. Changes in soil environmental conditions over time, such as the degradation of the organic waste matrix, changes in pH, redox potential, or soil solution composition, due to various remediation schemes or to natural weathering processes, also may enhance metal mobility. The extent of vertical contamination is intimately related to the soil solution and surface chemistry of the soil matrix with reference to the metal and waste matrix in question.

---

[1] EPA/540/S-92/018.

19

Table 3-1. Content of Various Elements in Soils (Lindsay, 1979)

Metal	Selected Average for Soils mg/kg	Common Range for Soils mg/kg
Al	71,000	10,000–300,000
Fe	38,000	7,000–550,000
Mn	600	20–3,000
Cu	30	2–100
Cr	100	1–1000
Cd	0.06	0.01–0.70
Zn	50	10–300
As	5	1.0–50
Se	0.3	0.1–2
Ni	40	5–500
Ag	0.05	0.01–5
Pb	10	2–200
Hg	0.03	0.01–0.3

FATE OF METALS IN THE SOIL ENVIRONMENT

In soil, metals are found in one or more of several "pools" of the soil, as described by Shuman (1991):

1) dissolved in the soil solution;
2) occupying exchange sites on inorganic soil constituents;
3) specifically adsorbed on inorganic soil constituents;
4) associated with insoluble soil organic matter;
5) precipitated as pure or mixed solids;
6) present in the structure of secondary minerals; and/or
7) present in the structure of primary minerals.

In situations where metals have been introduced into the environment through human activities, metals are associated with the first five pools. Native metals may be associated with any of the pools depending on the geological history of the area. The aqueous fraction, and those fractions in equilibrium with this fraction, i.e., the exchange fraction, are of primary importance when considering the migration potential of metals associated with soils.

Multiphase equilibria must be considered when defining metal behavior in soils (Figure 3-1). Metals in the soil solution are subject to mass transfer out of the system by leaching to ground water, plant uptake, or volatilization, a potentially important mechanism for Hg, Se, and As. At the same time, metals participate in chemical reactions with the soil solid phase. The concentration of metals in the soil solution, at any given time, is governed by a number of interrelated processes, including inorganic and organic complexation, oxidation-reduction reactions, precipitation/dissolution reactions, and adsorption/desorption reactions. The ability to predict the concentration of a given metal in the soil solution depends on the accuracy with which the multiphase equilibria can be determined or calculated.

Most studies of the behavior of metals in soils have been carried out under equilibrium conditions. Equilibrium data indicate which reactions are likely to occur under prescribed conditions, but do not indicate the time period involved. The kinetic aspect of oxidation/reduction, precipitation/dissolution, and adsorption/desorption reactions involving metals in soil matrix suffers from a lack of published data. Thus the kinetic component, which in many cases is critical to predict the behavior of metals in soils, cannot be assessed easily. Without the kinetic component, the current accepted approach is to assume that local equilibrium occurs in the soil profile. Equilibrium thermodynamic data can then be applied not only to predict which precipitation/dissolution, adsorption/desorption, and/or oxidation/reduction reactions are likely to occur under a given set of conditions, but also to estimate the solution composition, i.e., metal concentration in solution, at equilibrium. This approach relies heavily on the accuracy of thermodynamic data that can be found in the literature.

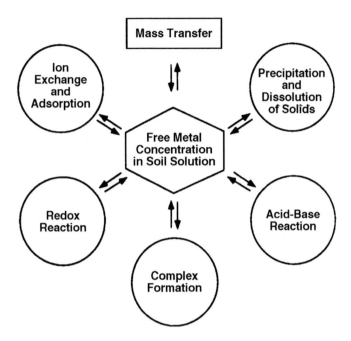

Figure 3-1. Principal controls on free trace metal concentrations in soils solution (Mattigod, et al., 1981).

Soil Solution Chemistry

Metals exist in the soil solution as either free (uncomplexed) metal ions (e.g., Cd^{2+}, Zn^{2+}, Cr^{3+}), in various soluble complexes with inorganic or organic ligands (e.g., $CdSO_4^{\circ}$, $ZnCl^+$, $CdCl_3^-$), or associated with mobile inorganic and organic colloidal material. A complex is defined as a unit in which a central metal ion is bonded by a number of associated atoms or molecules in a defined geometric pattern, e.g., $ZnSO_4^{\circ}$, $CdHCO_3^+$, $Cr(OH)_4^-$. The associated atoms or molecules are termed ligands. In the above examples, SO_4^{2-}, HCO_3^-, and OH^- are ligand. The total concentration of a metal, Me_T, in the soil solution is the sum of the free ion concentration $[Me^{z+}]$, the concentration of soluble organic and inorganic metal complexes, and the concentration of metals associated with mobile colloidal material.

Metals will form soluble complexes with inorganic and organic ligands. Common inorganic ligands are SO_4^{2-}, Cl^-, OH^-, PO_4^{3-}, NO_3^- and CO_3^{2-}. Soil organic ligands include low molecular weight aliphatic, aromatic, and amino acids and soluble constituents of fulvic acids. Formation constants for various metal complexes are available in the literature (e.g., see Nordstrom and Munoz, 1985; Lindsay, 1979, Martell and Smith, 1974–1982). Organic complexation of metals in soil is not as well defined as inorganic complexation because of the difficulty of identifying the large number of organic ligands that may be present in soils. Most of the metal-organic complex species identified in the literature were generated from metal interaction with fulvic acids extracted from sewage sludges (Baham et al., 1978; Baham and Sposito, 1986; Behel et al., 1983; Boyd et al., 1979, 1983; Dudley et al., 1987, Lake et al., 1984; Sposito et al., 1979, 1981, 1982). The soluble metal organic complexes that may form in other waste systems, however, have not been identified.

The presence of complex species in the soil solution can significantly affect the transport of metals through the soil matrix relative to the free metal ion. With complexation, the resulting metal species may be positively or negatively charged or be electrically neutral (e.g., $CdCl_3^+$, $CdCl^-$, $CdCl_2^{\circ}$). The metal complex may be only weakly adsorbed or more strongly adsorbed to soil surfaces relative to the free metal ion. A more detailed discussion on the effect complex formation has on metal mobility is given in the section: Factors Affecting Adsorption and Precipitation. Speciation not only affects mobility of metals but also the bioavailability and toxicity of the metal. The free metal ion is, in general, the most bioavailable and toxic form of the metal.

Several metals of environmental concern exist in soils in more than one oxidation state: arsenic, As(V) and As(III), selenium, Se(VI) and Se(IV), chromium, Cr(VI) and Cr(III), and mercury, Hg(II) and

Hg(I). The oxidation state of these metals determines their relative mobility, bioavailability, and toxicity. For example, hexavalent Cr is relatively mobile in soils, being only weakly sorbed by soils. Hexavalent Cr is also extremely toxic and a known carcinogen. Trivalent Cr, on the other hand, is relatively immobile in soil, being strongly sorbed by soils and readily forming insoluble precipitates, and it is of low toxicity.

Atomic absorption spectrophotometers (AA) and inductively coupled plasma emission spectrometers (ICP) are commonly used to determine the metal concentration in soil solutions. Both techniques measure the total metal concentration in the solution without distinguishing metal speciation or oxidation state. Free metal, complexed metal ion concentrations and concentration of metals in different oxidation states can be determined using ion selective electrodes, polarography colorimetric procedures, gas chromatography-AA, and high performance liquid chromatography-AA (see Kramer and Allen, 1988). While these specific methods are necessary for accurate measurements of metal speciation and oxidation state, these methods are not routinely performed by commercial laboratories nor are these procedures standard EPA methods.

Metal concentrations determined by AA or ICP are often used as inputs into a thermodynamic computer program, such as MINTEQA2 (U.S. EPA, 1987). This program can be used to calculate the speciation and oxidation state of metals in soil solution of known composition. Formation constants are known for many metal complexes. There is, however, only limited information for metal-organic complexes, including formation constants for many naturally occurring ligands and those in waste disposal systems. The required input data for these models include: the concentration of the metal of interest, the inorganic and organic ligands, and the major cations and other metal ions, and pH. In specific cases the redox potential and pCO_2 also may be required. Output consists of an estimation of the concentration of free metals and complexed metals at equilibrium for the specified conditions.

Many predictive methods, based on solution and solid phase chemistry, do not adequately describe transport of metals under field conditions. Solution chemistry considers the interaction between dissolved species, dissolved being defined as substances that will pass a 0.45 µm filter. However, in addition to dissolved metal complexes, metals also may associate with mobile colloidal particles. Colloidal size particles are particles with a diameter ranging from 0.01 and 10 µm (Sposito, 1989). Gschwend and Reynolds (1987) reported that colloidal particles of intermediate diameter, 0.1 µm to 1 µm, were the most mobile particles in a sandy medium. Colloidal particles include iron and manganese oxides, clay minerals, and organic matter. These surfaces have a high capacity for metal sorption. Puls et al. (Chapter 20) reported a 21 times increase in arsenate transport in the presence of colloidal material compared with dissolved arsenate. This increased transport of contaminants associated with mobile colloidal material has been termed facilitated transport (see Chapter 6).

Solid Phase Formation

Metals may precipitate to form a three dimensional solid phase in soils. These precipitates may be pure solids (e.g., $CdCO_3$, $Pb(OH)_2$, ZnS_2) or mixed solids (e.g., $(Fe_xCr_{1-x})(OH)_3$, $Ba(CrO_4,SO_4)$). Mixed solids are formed when various elements co-precipitate. There are several types of coprecipitation, inclusion, adsorption and solid solution formation, distinguished by the type of association between the trace element and the host mineral (Sposito, 1989). Solid solution formation occurs when the trace metal is compatible with the element of the host mineral and thus can uniformly replace the host element throughout the mineral. An example of solid solution formation is the substitution of Cd for Ca in calcium carbonate. Cadmium and Ca have almost identical ionic radii so that Cd can readily substitute for Ca in this carbonate mineral. Mechanisms of retention, whether surface adsorption, surface precipitation, coprecipitation, and pure solid formation are often difficult to distinguish experimentally. Retention involves a progression of these processes. The term sorption is used when the actual mechanism of metal removal from the soil solution is not known (see Chapter 2).

Stability diagrams are used as a convenient technique for illustrating how the solubility of metal compounds varies with soil pH and with metal concentration (or activity). The diagrams also allow some prediction of which solid phase regulates metal activity in the soil solution. Methods for constructing such diagrams are given in Sposito (1989) and Lindsay (1979). Santillan-Medrano and Jurinak (1975) used stability diagrams for predicting the formation of precipitates of Pb and Cd in a calcareous soil. The stability diagrams (Figures 3-2 and 3-3) illustrate the decrease in Pb and Cd solubility with increasing pH, which is the usual trend with cationic metals. Solution activity of Cd is

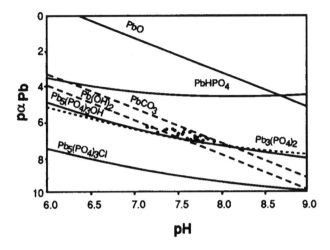

Figure 3-2. The solubility diagram for Pb in Nibley clay loam soil (Santillan-Medrano and Jurinak, 1975).

consistently higher than that for Pb, indicating that Cd may be more mobile in the environment. Lead phosphate compounds at lower pH and a mixed Pb compound at pH>7.5 could be the solid phases regulating Pb in solution. The authors concluded that cadmium solution activity is regulated by the formation of $CdCO_3$ and $Cd(PO_4)_2$ or a mixed Cd solid at pH<7.5. At higher pH, the system is under-saturated with respect to the Cd compounds considered.

The formation of a solid phase may not be an important mechanism compared to adsorption in native soils because of the low concentration of trace metals in these systems (Lindsay, 1979). Precipitation reactions may be of much greater importance in waste systems where the concentration of metals may be exceedingly high. McBride (1980) concluded that calcite ($CaCO_3$) serves as a site for adsorption of Cd^{2+} at low concentrations of Cd, while $CdCO_3$ precipitation, possibly as a coating on the calcite, occurs only at higher Cd concentrations.

Surface Reactions

Adsorption is defined as the accumulation of ions at the interface between a solid phase and an aqueous phase. Adsorption differs from precipitation in that the metal does not form a new three dimensional solid phase but is instead associated with the surfaces of existing soil particles. The soil matrix often includes organic matter, clay minerals, iron and manganese oxides and hydroxides, carbonates, and amorphous aluminosilicates.

Soil organic matter consists of 1) living organisms, 2) soluble biochemicals (amino acids, proteins, carbohydrates, organic acids, polysaccharides, lignin, etc.), and 3) insoluble humic substances. The biochemicals and humic substances provide sites (acid functional groups, such as such as carboxylic, phenolics, alcoholic, enolic-OH and amino groups) for metal sorption. A discussion of the nature of soil organic matter and its role in the retention of metals in soil is given by Stevenson (1991) and Stevenson and Fitch (1986). The biochemicals form water soluble complexes with metals, increasing metal mobility, as discussed in a previous section. The humic substances consist of insoluble polymers of aliphatic and aromatic substances produced through microbial action. Humic substances contain a highly complex mixture of functional groups. Binding of metals to organic matter involves a continuum of reactive sites, ranging from weak forces of attraction to formation of strong chemical bonds. Soil organic matter can be the main source of soil cation exchange capacity, contributing >200meq/100 g of organic matter in surface mineral soils. Organic matter content, however, decreases with depth, so that the mineral constituents of soil will become a more important surface for sorption as the organic matter content of the soil diminishes.

There have been numerous studies of the adsorptive properties of clay minerals, in particular montmorillonite and kaolinite, and iron and manganese oxides. Jenne (1968) concluded that Fe and Mn oxides are the principal soil surfaces that control the mobility of metals in soils and natural water. In arid soils, carbonate minerals may immobilize metals by providing an adsorbing and nucleating

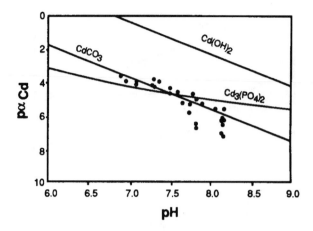

Figure 3-3. The solubility diagram for Cd in Nibley clay loam soil (Santillan-Medrano and Jurinak, 1975).

surface (Santillan-Medrano and Jurinak, 1975; Cavallaro and McBride, 1978; McBride, 1980; Jurinak and Bauer, 1956; McBride and Bouldin, 1984: Dudley et al., 1988, 1991).

Soil surfaces carry either a net negative or positive charge depending on the nature of the surface and the soil pH. The permanent net negative charge on surfaces is due to charge imbalance resulting from the isomorphous substitution of Al^{3+} for Si^{4+} in the tetrahedral layers and/or substitution of Mg^{2+}, Fe^{2+}, etc., for Al^{3+} in the octahedral layers of aluminosilicate clays. The charge on the surface is not affected by changes in soil pH and hence it is termed a permanent charged surface. pH dependent charged surfaces are associated with the edges of clay minerals, with the surfaces of oxides, hydroxides and carbonates, and with organic matter (acid functional groups). The charge arises from the association and dissociation of protons from surface functional groups. Using an iron oxide surface functional group as an example, the association of protons with the functional group results in a positive charge $[-Fe-OH_2^+]$ and dissociation of protons, under more alkaline conditions, results in a negative charge $[-Fe-O^-]$. At the point of zero net proton charge (PZNPC) the functional group is neutral $[-Fe-OH^o]$. For all pH dependent charged surfaces, whether organic or inorganic, as the pH decreases the number of negatively charged sites diminishes. Under more acidic conditions, the majority of pH dependent surfaces will be positively charged and under more alkaline conditions, the majority of sites will be negatively charged. The pH dependent charged surfaces in soils differ widely in their PZNPC.

The structural charge developed on either a permanent charged surface or a pH dependent charged surface must be balanced by ions of opposite charge at or near the surface. The cation exchange capacity is a measure of the negatively charged sites for cation adsorption and anion exchange capacity is a measure of the positively charged sites for anion adsorption. The anion capacity is, however, very small relative to the cation adsorption capacity of soils.

A surface complexation model is often used to describe adsorption behavior (Sposito, 1989). Several types of surface complexes can form between a metal and soil surface functional groups and are defined by the extent of bonding between the metal ion and the surface (Figure 3-4). Metals in a diffuse ion association or in an outer sphere complex are surrounded by waters of hydration and are not directly bonded to the soil surface. These ions accumulate at the interface of the charged surfaces in response to electrostatic forces. These reactions are rapid and reversible with only a weak dependence on the electron configuration of the surface group and the adsorbed ion. These two metal-surface interactions have also been termed exchange reactions because the introduction of other cations into the system, in sufficient concentration, causes the replacement or exchange of the original cations. Metals associated with exchange sites may, depending on the environment, be relatively mobile. Exchangeable metals may be the most significant reserve of potentially mobile metals in soil (Silviera and Sommers, 1977; Latterell et al., 1978).

With inner sphere complexation, the metal is bound directly to the soil surface, no waters of hydration are involved. It is distinguished from the exchangeable state by having ionic and/or covalent character to the binding between the metal and the surface. A much higher bonding energy is

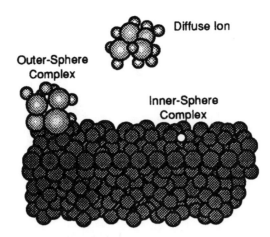

Figure 3-4. The three mechanisms of cation adsorption on a siloxane surface (e.g., montmorillonite) (Sposito, 1989).

involved than in exchange reactions, and the bonding depends on the electron configuration of both the surface group and the metal. This adsorption mechanism is often termed *specific adsorption*. The term specific implies that there are differences in the energy of adsorption among cations, such that other ions, including major cations, Na, Ca, Mg, do not effectively compete for specific surface sites. Specifically adsorbed metal cations are relatively immobile and unaffected by high concentrations of the major cations due to large differences in their energies of adsorption.

At low concentrations, metals are adsorbed by the specific adsorption sites. These adsorbed metals are not removed by the input of major cations. With increasing concentration of the metal, the specific sites become saturated and the exchange sites are filled (Hendrickson and Corey, 1981; Lehmann and Harter, 1984; Garcia-Miragaya et al., 1986; O'Connor et al., 1984; O'Connor et al., 1983). Metals associated with these nonspecific sites are exchangeable with other metal cations and are thus potentially mobile. For example, in an adsorption study using Cd, O'Connor et al. (1984) showed two mechanisms were responsible for metal retention by soil. The authors attributed the first mechanism, active at low concentration (0.01–10 mg/L added Cd), to specific adsorption. At higher concentrations (100–1000 mg/L added Cd), adsorption was attributed to exchange reactions. Desorption studies showed that the added Cd at low concentration was not removed by 0.05 M calcium solutions, whereas at the higher loading rates, the calcium salt removed significant amounts of the adsorbed Cd. These results indicate that the observed affinity of a metal for soil surfaces is concentration dependent. These results also emphasize the importance of using literature or laboratory generated values that cover the range of metal concentration of interest at a specific location. Use of data generated in the wrong concentration range may lead to misinterpretation of the metal binding strength of the soil.

The relative affinity of a soil surface for a free metal cation increases with the tendency of the cation to form strong bonds, i.e., inner sphere complexes, with the surface. The general order of preference for monovalent cations by montmorillonite is $Cs > Rb > K = NH_4 > Na > Li$. For the alkaline earth metals the order is Ba, Sr, Ca, Mg. The preference series indicates a greater attraction of the surface for the less hydrated cations that can fit closer to the clay surface. For transition metals, the size of the hydrated cation cannot be used as the only predictor of adsorption affinity since the electron configuration of a metal plays an important role in adsorption. Table 3-2 reports on results from various researchers on the relative sorption affinity of metals onto a variety of soils and soil constituents. Although there is consistently a higher affinity of these surfaces for Pb and Cu compared with Zn or Cd, the specific order of sorption affinity depends on the properties of the metals, surface type, and experimental conditions.

Anions in the Soil Environment

Common anionic contaminants of concern include: arsenic (AsO_4^{3-} and AsO_2^-), selenium (SeO_3^{2-} and SeO_4^{2-}), and chromium in one of its oxidation states (CrO_4^{2-}). Soil particles, though predominantly

Table 3-2. Relative Affinity of Metals for Soils and Soil Constituents

Soil or Soil Constituent	Relative Order of Sorption	Reference
Goethite	Cu>Pb>Zn>Co>Cd	Forbes et al., 1976
Fe oxide	Pb>Cu>Zn>Cd	Benjamin and Leckie, 1981
Montmorillonite	Cd=Zn>Ni	Puls and Bohn, 1988
Kaolinite	Cd>Zn>Ni	Puls and Bohn, 1988
Soils	Pb>Cu>Zn>Cd>Ni	Biddappa et al., 1981
Soils	Zn>Ni>Cd	Tiller et al., 1984
Mineral soils	Pb>Cu>Zn>Cd	Elliott et al., 1986
Organic soils	Pb>Cu>Cd>Zn	Elliott et al., 1986
Soil	Pb>Cu>Zn>Ni	Harter, 1983

negatively charged, also may carry some positive charges. The oxide surfaces, notably iron, manganese, and aluminum oxides, carbonate surfaces, and insoluble organic matter can generate a significant number of positive charges as the pH decreases. The edges of clay minerals also carry pH dependent charge. These edge sites may be important sites of retention of anions at pHs below the point of zero charge (PZC).

Clay minerals, oxides, and organic matter exert a strong preference for some anions in comparison to other anions, indicating the existence of chemical bonds between the surface and the specific anion. Phosphate has been the most extensively studied anion that exhibits this specific adsorption (inner sphere complex) phenomenon. Selenite (SeO_3^{2-}) and arsenate (AsO_4^{3-}) are adsorbed to oxides and soils through specific binding mechanisms (Rajan, 1979; Neal et al., 1987b). Selenite (SeO_4^{2-}) and hexavalent chromium are only weakly bound to soil surfaces and are thus easily displaced by other anions. Balistrieri and Chao (1987) found the sequence of adsorption of anions onto iron oxide to be: phosphate = silicate = arsenate > bicarbonate/carbonate > citrate = selenite > molybdate > oxalate > fluoride = selenate > sulfate. The adsorption capacity for anions is, however, small relative to cation adsorption capacity of soils.

Soil Properties Affecting Adsorption

The adsorption capacity (both exchange and specific adsorption) of a soil is determined by the number and kind of sites available. Adsorption of metal cations has been correlated with such soil properties as pH, redox potential, clay, soil organic matter, Fe and Mn oxides, and calcium carbonate content. Anion adsorption has been correlated with Fe and Mn oxide content, pH, and redox potential. Adsorption processes are affected by these various soil factors, by the form of the metal added to the soil, and by the solvent introduced along with the metal. The results of these interactions may increase or decrease the movement of metals in the soil water.

Korte et al. (1976) qualitatively ranked the relative mobilities of 11 metals added to 10 soils (Table 3-3) to simulate movement of metals under an anaerobic landfill situation. The leachate used was generated in a septic tank, preserved under carbon dioxide and adjusted to pH of 5. Of the cationic metals studied, lead and copper were the least mobile and mercury(II) was the most mobile (Figure 3-5). The heavier textured soils with higher pHs (Molokai, Nicholson, Mohaveca and Fanno) were effective in attenuating the metals, while sandy soils and/or soils with low pH did not retain the metals effectively. For the anionic metals, clay soils containing oxides with low pH were relatively effective in retaining the anions (Figure 3-6). As with the cationic metals, the light textured soils were the least effective in retaining the anions. Chromium (VI) was the most mobile of the metals studied. Griffin and Shimp (1978) found the relative mobility of nine metals through montmorillonite and kaolinite to be: Cr(VI) > Se > As(III) > As(V) > Cd > Zn > Pb > Cu > Cr(III).

Factors Affecting Adsorption and Precipitation Reactions

Although the principles affecting sorption and precipitation are similar for cationic and anionic metals, for clarity, the following section will concentrate on a general discussion of factors affecting

Table 3-3. Characteristics of the Soils (Korte et al., 1976)

Soil	Order	pH meq/100g	CEC m2/g	Surface Area %	Free Fe Oxides %	Clay	Texture
Wagram	Ultisol	4.2	2	8.0	0.6	4	loamy sand
Ava	Alfisol	4.5	19	61.5	4	31	silty clay loam
Kalkaska	Spodosol	4.7	10	8.9	1.8	5	sand
Davidson	Ultisol	6.2	9	61.3	17	61	clay
Molokai	Oxisol	6.2	14	67.3	23	52	clay silty clay
Chalmers	Mollisol	6.6	26	125.6	3.1	35	loam
Nicholson	Alfisol	6.7	37	120.5	5.6	49	silty clay
Fanno	Alfisol	7	33	122.1	3.7	46	clay
Mohave	Aridisol	7.3	10	38.3	1.7	11	sandy loam
Mohave ca	Aridisol	7.8	12	127.5	2.5	40	clay loam
Anthony	Entisol	7.8	6	19.8	1.8	15	sandy loam

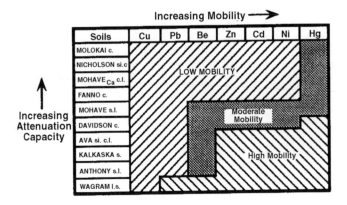

Figure 3-5. Relative mobility of cations through soil (from Korte et al., 1976).

the behavior of cationic metals in soils. Factors affecting anion adsorption and precipitation will be discussed for each individual metal anion in a later section.

Effect of Competing Cations

For specific adsorption sites, trace cationic metals are preferentially adsorbed over the major cations (Na, Ca, Mg) and trace anionic metals are preferentially adsorbed over major anions (SO_4^-, NO_3^-, soluble ionized organic acids). However, when the specific adsorption sites become saturated, exchange reactions dominate and competition for these sites with soil major ions becomes important. Cavallaro and McBride (1978) found that adsorption of Cu and Cd decreased in the presence of 0.01 M $CaCl_2$. They attributed this decrease to competition with Ca for adsorption sites. Cadmium adsorption was more affected by the presence of Ca than Cu. The mobility of Cd may be greatly increased due to such competition. Likewise, Harter (1979) indicated the Ca in solution had a greater effect on Pb adsorption than on Cu. In another study, Harter (1992) added Cu, Ni and Co to calcium saturated soils. The presence of Ca, a common ion in soils with pH>5.6, did not affect Cu sorption but did limit the sorption of Co and Ni. The author emphasized the importance of these results in that standard management practice for metal contaminated soils is to raise the pH to 7, often using a Ca buffered system. The addition of Ca as low as 0.01 M Ca, may increase the mobility of some metals by competing for sorption sites.

Trace metals also will compete with each other for adsorption sites. Although there have been several studies on the relative adsorption affinities of trace metals by soils and soil constituents (see Table 3-2), these studies have compared how much of each metal, added to the soils as individual components, was adsorbed and not whether the adsorption of one metal will interfere with that of another. Few studies have looked directly at the competitive adsorption of metals. Kuo and Baker (1980) reported that the presence of Cu interfered with the adsorption of Zn and Cd. Adsorbed Cu was not significantly affected by added Zn but the presence of Cu, at concentrations as low as 15 µg/L, completely prevented Zn adsorption in one soil with a low cation exchange capacity (Kurdi and Doner, 1983). In contrast, McBride and Blasiak (1979) found that Cu was ineffective in competing for Zn adsorption sites over a pH range of 5–7. The inability of Cu to block Zn adsorption in this study was taken as evidence that Zn and Cu were preferentially adsorbed at different sites. Simultaneous addition of Cd and Zn to Mn oxide lowered the adsorption of both metals (Zasoski and Burau, 1988).

The presence of other cations, whether major or trace metals, can significantly affect the mobility of the metal of interest. Use of data from the literature, generation of laboratory data, or use of computer models that do not reflect the complex mixture of metals specific to a site may not be useful to understand or accurately predict metal mobility.

Effect of Complex Formation

Metal cations form complexes with inorganic and organic ligands. The resulting association has a lower positive charge than the free metal ion, and may be uncharged or carry a net negative charge.

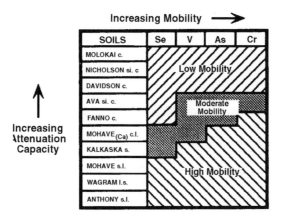

Figure 3-6. Relative mobility of anions through soil (from Korte et al., 1976).

For example, the association of cadmium with chloride results in the following series of charged and uncharged cadmium species: Cd^{2+}, $CdCl^+$, $CdCl_2^0$, $CdCl_3^-$. Benjamin and Leckie (1982) stated that the interaction between metal ions and complexing ligands may result in either a complex that is weakly adsorbed to the soil surface or in a complex that is more strongly adsorbed relative to the free metal ion. In general, the decrease in positive charge on the complexed metal reduces adsorption to a negatively charged surface. One noted exception is the preferential adsorption of hydrolyzed metals ($MeOH^+$) versus the free bivalent metal (James and Healy, 1972). The actual effect of complex formation on sorption depends on the properties of the metal of interest, the type and amount of ligands present, soil surface properties, soil solution composition, pH and redox conditions, as is illustrated by the following research results.

In the presence of the inorganic ligands Cl^- and SO_4^{2-}, the adsorption of Cd on soil and soil constituents was inhibited (O'Connor, et al., 1984; Hirsch et al., 1989; Egozy, 1980; Garcia-Miragaya and Page, 1976; Benjamin and Leckie, 1982) due to the formation of cadmium complexes that were not strongly adsorbed by the soils. Using much higher concentrations of salt than normally encountered in soil solutions (0.1 to 0.5M NaCl), Doner (1978) concluded that the increased mobility of Ni, Cu, and Cd through a soil column was due to complex formation of the metals with Cl^-. The mobility of Cd increased more than that of Ni and Cu, Ni being the least mobile. These observed mobilities are in the same order as that of the stability constants of the chloride complexes of these metals. Within normal concentration of electrolytes in soil solution, Elrashidi and O'Connor (1982) found no measurable change in Zn adsorption by alkaline soils due to complex formation of Zn with Cl^-, NO_3^{2-}, or SO_4^{2-} ions. Under these conditions (anion concentration of 0.1 M), anion complex formation did not compete with the highly selective adsorption sites for Zn. Shuman (1986), using acid soils, observed a decreased adsorption of Zn in the presence of Cl^- at the concentration of $CaCl_2$ used by Elrashidi and O'Connor (1982) but no effect at lower concentrations. McBride (1985), using aluminum oxide, and Cavallaro (1982), using clays, found that high levels of phosphate suppressed adsorption of Cu and Zn. Phosphate did not form strong complexes with Cu or Zn but it was strongly adsorbed to soil surfaces, thus physically blocking the specific adsorption sites of Cu and Zn. Other researchers (Kuo and McNeal, 1984; Stanton and Burger, 1970; Bolland et al., 1977), using lower concentrations of added phosphate, demonstrated enhanced adsorption of Zn and Cd on oxide surfaces. At the concentration of phosphate used in these studies, the adsorption of phosphate onto the oxide surfaces increased the negative charge on the oxide surface, thus enhancing adsorption of the metal cations.

Complex formation between metals and organic ligands affects metal adsorption and hence mobility. The extent of complexation between a metal and soluble organic matter depends on the competition between the metal-binding surface sites and the soluble organic ligand for the metal. Metals that readily form stable complexes with soluble organic matter are likely to be mobile in soils. Overcash and Pal (1979) reported that the order of metal-organic complex stabilities, for the system they studied, was Hg > Cu > Ni > Pb > Co > Zn > Cd. Khan et al. (1982) showed that the mobility of metals through soil followed the order: Cu > Ni > Pb > Ag > Cd. The high mobility of Cu and Ni was attributed to their high complexing nature with soluble soil organic matter. Amrhein et al. (1992) also showed the increased mobility of Cu, Ni, and Pb in the presence of dissolved organic matter. In this study, the Cd leached from the columns was not associated with dissolved organic carbon but was associated with Cl or acetate anions. Metals, such as Cd and Zn, that do not form highly stable complexes with organic matter are not as greatly affected by the presence of dissolved organic matter in the soil solution as metals that do form stable complexes, such as Cu, Pb, or Hg. Dunnivant et al. (1992) and Neal and Sposito (1986), however, demonstrated that dissolved organic matter does reduce Cd sorption due to complexation formation under their experimental conditions.

In systems where the organic ligand adsorbs to the soil surface, metal adsorption may be enhanced by the complexation of the metal to the surface-adsorbed ligand. Haas and Horowitz (1986) found that, in some cases, the presence of organic matter enhanced Cd adsorption by kaolinite. They interpreted these findings to suggest that the presence of an adsorbed layer of organic matter on the clay surface served as a site for Cd retention. Davis and Leckie (1978) found Cu adsorption to iron oxide increased in the presence of glutamic acid and 2,3 pyrazinendicarboxylic acid (2,3 PDCA) but decreased in the presence of picolinic acid. Picolinic acid complexed Cu and the resulting complex was not adsorbed by the oxide surface. The glutamic acid and 2,3 PDCA were adsorbed to the oxide surface, then complexed the added Cu. Using natural organic matter, Davis (1984) demonstrated the adsorption of Cu but not Cd to an organic coated aluminum oxide.

The effect of complexation formation on sorption is dependent on the type and amount of metal present, the type and amount of ligands present, soil surface properties, soil solution composition, pH and redox. The presence of complexing ligands may increase metal retention or greatly increase metal mobility. Use of literature or laboratory data that do not include the presence of complexing ligands, both organic and inorganic, present at the particular site of interest, may lead to significant overestimation or underestimation of metal mobility.

Effect of pH

The pH, either directly or indirectly, affects several mechanisms of metal retention by soils. Figure 3-7 shows the impact of soil pH on the adsorption of Pb, Ni, Zn, and Cu by two soils adjusted to various pHs ranging from approximately 4.3 to 8.3 (Harter, 1983). As is true for all cationic metals, adsorption increased with pH. The author, however, points out that the retention of the metals did not significantly increase until the pH was greater than 7. Figure 3-8 illustrates the adsorption of selenite, SeO_3^{2-}, on five soils adjusted to various pHs. As is true with all oxyanions, i.e., arsenic, selenium and hexavalent chromium, sorption decreases with pH.

The pH dependence of adsorption reactions of cationic metals is due, in part, to the preferential adsorption of the hydrolyzed metal species in comparison to the free metal ion (McBride, 1977; McLaren and Crawford, 1973; Davis and Leckie, 1978; Farrah and Pickering, 1976a,b; James and Healy, 1972; McBride, 1982, Cavallaro and McBride, 1980; Harter, 1983). The proportion of hydrolyzed metal species increases with pH.

Cavallaro and McBride (1980) found that copper adsorption by soils showed a stronger pH dependence than Cd. This finding is consistent with the hypothesis that hydrolysis of Cu at pH 6 increases its retention by soil, while cadmium does not hydrolyze until pH 8. Zinc was shown to be retained in an exchangeable form at low pH in four Fe and Mn oxide dominated soils but became nonexchangeable as the pH was increased above 5.5 (Stahl and James, 1991). The researchers attributed this change in mechanism of sorption as being due to the hydrolysis of Zn and the adsorption of the hydrolysis species by the oxide surfaces.

Many adsorption sites in soils are pH dependent, i.e., Fe and Mn oxides, organic matter, carbonates, and the edges of clay minerals. As the pH decreases, the number of negative sites for cation adsorption diminishes while the number of sites for anion adsorption increases. Also as the pH becomes more acidic, metal cations also face competition for available permanent charged sites by Al^{3+} and H^+.

All trace metal hydroxide, oxide, carbonate, and phosphate precipitates form only under alkaline conditions (Lindsay, 1979). The dissolution of these metal precipitates is strongly dependent on the pH of the system. Jenne (1968) stated that hydrous oxides of Fe and Mn play a principal role in the retention of metals in soils. Solubility of Fe and Mn oxides is also pH-related. Below pH 6, the oxides of Fe and Mn dissolve, releasing adsorbed metal ions to solution (Essen and El Bassam, 1981).

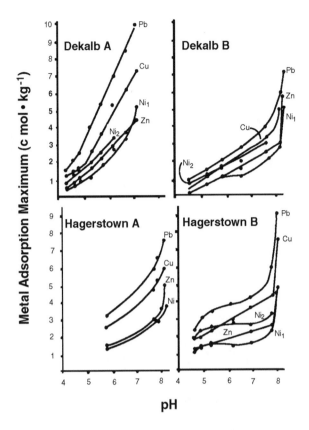

Figure 3-7. Effect of soil pH level on maximum Pb, Cu, Zn, and Ni retention by Dekalb and Hagerstown A and B horizons. Ni_1 and Ni_2 refer to two apparent sorption maxima (Harter, 1983).

Work by McBride and Blasiak (1979) showed increased retention of Zn with increasing pH, as is usual for metal cations. When the pH was increased above 7.5, however, the solution concentration of Zn increased. This phenomenon has been observed in other studies when acid soils were adjusted to pH>7 (Kuo and Baker, 1980) and it has been attributed to the solubilization of organic complexing ligands which effectively compete with the soil surfaces for the metal cation. Most functional groups of complexing ligands are weak acids, thus the stability of the metal complex is pH-dependent with little association in acid media. The degree of association increases with pH. Baham and Sposito (1986) and Inskeep and Baham (1983) demonstrated that the adsorption of Cu to montmorillonite, in the presence of water soluble ligands extracted from sludges and various other organic materials, decreased with increasing pH. This behavior is the opposite of the typical relationship between metal adsorption and pH. Figure 3-9, taken from Baham and Sposito (1986), illustrates that nearly 100% of the Cu added to the clay in the absence of the organic ligands was removed from solution at pH>7. In the presence of the organic ligands, the maximum amount of Cu removed from solution was at pH≈5.5. As the pH was increased above 5.5, adsorption of Cu decreased. The explanation for this phenomenon is that at low pH, H^+ competes with the Cu for complexation with the organic matter. As the pH increases, more of the Cu can be complexed with the organic matter and less is therefore adsorbed by the clay. This phenomenon has important implications with regard to the practice of liming acid soils to raise the pH, increasing metal retention. In soils with significant levels of dissolved organic matter, increasing soil pH may actually mobilize metals due to complex formation.

The pH of the soil system is a very important parameter, directly influencing sorption/desorption, precipitation/dissolution, complex formation, and oxidation-reduction reactions. In general, maximum retention of cationic metals occurs at pH>7 and maximum retention of anionic metals occurs at pH<7. Because of the complexity of the soil-waste system, with its myriad of surface types and solution composition, such a generalization may not hold true. For example, cationic metal mobility has been

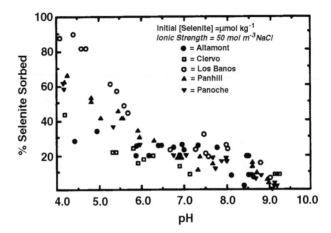

Figure 3-8. Selenite adsorption envelope for five alluvial soils. The initial total selenite concentration was approximately 2 μmol kg⁻¹ (Neal et al., 1987a).

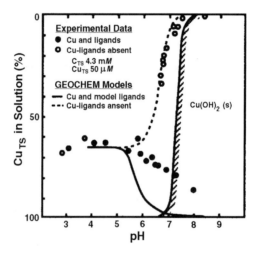

Figure 3-9. Adsorption of Cu [50 mmol m-3 (50 mM)] by Na-montmorillonite in the presence and absence of water soluble extract of sewage sludge (WSE). GEOCHEM simulations were conducted employing the "mixture model" (Baham and Sposito 1986).

observed to increase with increasing pH due to the formation of metal complexes with dissolved organic matter.

Effect of Oxidation-Reduction

Almost half of the metals under consideration have more than one oxidation state in the soil environment and are directly affected by changes in the oxidation-reduction (redox) potential of the soil. The redox potential of a soil system is the measure of the electrochemical potential or availability of electrons within a system. A chemical reaction in which an electron transfer takes place is called an oxidation-reduction process. Metals or elements which gain electrons and lose in valence are undergoing reduction, while those losing electrons and gaining in valence are becoming oxidized. A measure of the redox potential (electron availability) indicates whether the metals are in an oxidized or reduced state.

In soils, reducing conditions are brought about by the absence of oxygen (anaerobic). This is caused by the oxygen being utilized or consumed at a greater rate than it can be transported into the soil system. This can be caused by water-logged soils or soils contaminated with oxygen consuming compounds. The consumption could either be chemical or biological. The biological consumption of oxygen is the result of microbes utilizing the organic contaminant which have entered the soil system. Oxidizing conditions (aerobic) are normally found in well-drained soils as well as soils that have not been subjected to contamination by spills or leaks.

The degree of oxidation or reduction is indicated by the redox potential measurement. The four general ranges of redox conditions which may be encountered in soils at pH 7 are: oxidized soils > +400 millivolts (mv); moderately reduced soils, from +400 to +100 mv; reduced soils, from +100 to -100 mv; highly reduced soils, -100 to -300 mv. The redox state of a soil, as discussed above, usually is closely related to the microbial activity and the type of substrate available to the organisms.

Redox reactions can greatly affect contaminant transport, in slightly acidic to alkaline environments, Fe(III) precipitates as a highly adsorptive solid phase (ferric hydroxide), while Fe(II) is very soluble and does not retain other metals. The reduction of Fe(III) to Fe(II) will bring about the release of ferrous iron to the pore waters and also any metals that were adsorbed to the ferric hydroxide surfaces. The behavior of chromium and selenium also illustrates the importance of redox conditions to metals movement in soils. Hexavalent Cr(VI) is both toxic and a relatively mobile anion while trivalent Cr(III) is far less toxic, relatively insoluble, and strongly adsorbs to surfaces. Selenate (Se(VI)) is mobile, but less toxic than selenite (Se(IV)) which is more toxic, but less mobile. In general, oxidizing conditions favor retention of metals in soils, while reducing conditions contribute to accelerated migration.

Effect of Co-Waste

Most soil-metal interaction studies have been performed using a specific, well characterized background solution, such as an inorganic salt solution (0.01M $CaCl_2$, Na_2SO_4, etc.) or a water soluble extraction of organic matter (leaf litter, sewage sludges, etc.). These studies, as reported above, have led to an understanding of the effects that metal type, metal concentration, solution composition, and soil surface type have on the retention of metals by soils. The behavior of metals associated with various industrial or mining wastes in soil systems has not been extensively studied, however. In such wastes the metal concentration may be much greater than used in studies of native metals and metals associated with the controlled application of fertilizers and sewage sludges, and may be associated with a myriad of inorganic and organic chemicals that have not been characterized but may have a great effect on predicting metal mobility. Below are examples in which investigators have used various waste mixtures for the background solution in sorption studies. In all cases, the results were highly dependent on the waste type used. These examples have been included to emphasize the importance of performing laboratory studies or using literature data that mimic the actual matrix of the waste or soils-waste system being investigated.

The retention of Cd, Cu, and Zn by two calcareous soils using a water extract of an acidic milling waste as the background solution (pH=4.0, dominant major cation was Ca and anion was sulfate) was studied by Dudley et al. (1988, 1991). The presence of carbonate minerals is known to effectively immobilize Cd and Cu by providing an adsorbing or nucleating surface and by buffering pH (Santillan-Medrano and Jurinak, 1975; Cavallaro and McBride, 1978; McBride and Bouldin, 1984). For the soil with a lower carbonate content (0.2% $CaCO_3$), the sorption of Cd and Zn was slow to reach equilibrium (114 hours) due to the complex set of reactions that occurred when the soil (pH 8.6) and acid milling extract (pH 4.0) were combined. The dissolution of carbonates in the acid medium controlled the rate and extent of Cd and Zn sorption. The authors concluded that Cd and Zn were retained by an exchange mechanism only after the pH of the system reached equilibrium (pH 5.5), allowing time for significant transport of these metals. Copper sorption was independent of calcite dissolution. The soil with the higher carbonate content (30%) showed a significant drop in pH (pH 9.1 to 6.6) with the addition of the acid leachate but had sufficient carbonates to buffer the system and sorbed all three metals.

Kotuby-Amacher and Gambrell (1988) studied the retention of Cd and Pb on subsurface soils using a synthetic municipal waste leachate and a synthetic acid metal waste leachate, compared with $Ca(NO_3)_2$ as the background solution. Sorption of the two metals was diminished in the presence of both synthetic leachates. The presence of competing cations and complexing organic and inorganic ligands in the synthetic wastes decreased the retention of Cd and Pb by the soils. Boyle and Fuller

(1987) used soil columns packed with five different soils to evaluate the mobility of Zn in the presence of simulated municipal solid waste leachate with various amounts of total organic carbon (TOC) and total soluble salts (TSS). Zinc transport was enhanced in the presence of higher TOC and TSS. Soil properties considered important for retaining Zn in this study were surface area, CEC, and percent clay content. The authors, however, concluded that the leachate composition was more important than soil properties for determining the mobility of Zn.

Puls et al. (1991) studied the sorption of Pb and Cd on kaolinite in the presence of three organic acids, 2,4-dinitrophenol, p-hydroxybenzoic acid, and o-toluic acid. The acids were selected based on their frequent occurrence at hazardous waste sites and their persistence in soils. Sorption of Pb decreased in the presence of all the acids due to the formation of 1:2 metal-organic complex resulting in an uncharged form of Pb. Sorption of Cd decreased in the presence of two of the acids but increased in the presence of 2,4-dinitrophenol. The authors attributed the increase in sorption as being due to either direct sorption of the acid to the clay with the subsequent sorption of Cd or to the enhanced sorption of the 1:1 complex formed between Cd and the acid.

Sheets and Fuller (1986) studied the transport of Cd through soil columns with 0 to 100% ethylene glycol or 2-propanol as the leaching solution. Soils sorbed less Cd from the ethylene glycol solutions than when the columns were leached with water. The 2-propanol increased sorption in one of the soils tested. The effect on Cd sorption was attributed to the change in soil permeability and surface characterization due to the presence of the solvents.

Metal mobility in soil-waste systems is determined by the type and quantity of soil surfaces present, the concentration of metal of interest, the concentration and type of competing ions and complexing ligands, both organic and inorganic, pH, and redox status. Generalization can only serve as rough guides of the expected behavior of metals in such systems. Use of literature or laboratory data that do not mimic the specific site soil and waste system will not be adequate to describe or predict the behavior of the metal. Data must be site specific. Long term effects also must be considered. As organic constituents of the waste matrix degrade, or as pH or redox conditions change, either through natural processes of weathering or human manipulation, the potential mobility of the metal will change as soil conditions change. Few long term studies have been resorted.

BEHAVIOR OF SPECIFIC METALS

Copper

Copper is retained in soils through exchange and specific adsorption mechanisms. At concentrations typically found in native soils, Cu precipitates are unstable. This may not be the case in waste-soil systems and precipitation may be an important mechanism of retention. Cavallaro and McBride (1978) suggested that a clay mineral exchange phase may serve as a sink for Cu in noncalcareous soils. In calcareous soils, specific adsorption of Cu onto $CaCO_3$ surfaces may control Cu concentration in solution (Cavallaro and McBride, 1978; Dudley, et al., 1988, 1991; McBride and Bouldin, 1984). As reported in the adsorption sequence in Table 3-2, Cu is adsorbed to a greater extent by soils and soil constituents than the other metals studied, with the exception of Pb. Copper, however, has a high affinity for soluble organic ligands and the formation of these complexes may greatly increase Cu mobility in soils.

Zinc

Zinc is readily adsorbed by clay minerals, carbonates, or hydrous oxides. Hickey and Kittrick (1984), Kuo et al. (1983), and Tessier et al. (1980) found that the greatest percent of the total Zn in polluted soils and sediments was associated with Fe and Mn oxides. Precipitation is not a major mechanism of retention of Zn in soils because of the relatively high solubility of Zn compounds. Precipitation may become a more important mechanism of Zn retention in soil-waste systems. As with all cationic metals, Zn adsorption increases with pH.

Zinc hydrolysizes at pH>7.7 and these hydrolyzed species are strongly adsorbed to soil surfaces. Zinc forms complexes with inorganic and organic ligands that will affect its adsorption reactions with the soil surface.

Cadmium

Cadmium may be adsorbed by clay minerals, carbonates or hydrous oxides of iron and manganese or may be precipitated as cadmium carbonate, hydroxide, and phosphate. Evidence suggests that adsorption mechanisms may be the primary source of Cd removal from soils (Dudley et al., 1988, 1991). In soils and sediments polluted with metal wastes, the greatest percentage of the total Cd was associated with the exchangeable fraction (Hickey and Kittrick, 1984; Tessier et al., 1980; Kuo et al., 1983). Cadmium concentrations have been shown to be limited by $CdCO_3$ in neutral and alkaline soils (Santillan-Medrano and Jurinak, 1975). As with all cationic metals, the chemistry of Cd in the soil environment is, to a great extent, controlled by pH. Under acidic conditions Cd solubility increases and very little adsorption of Cd by soil colloids, hydrous oxides, and organic matter takes place. At pH values greater than 6, cadmium is adsorbed by the soil solid phase or is precipitated, and the solution concentrations of cadmium are greatly reduced. Cadmium forms soluble complexes with inorganic and organic ligands, in particular Cl^-. The formation of these complexes will increase Cd mobility in soils.

Lead

Soluble lead added to the soil reacts with clays, phosphates, sulfates, carbonates, hydroxides, and organic matter such that Pb solubility is greatly reduced. At pH values above 6, lead is either adsorbed on clay surfaces or forms lead carbonate. Of all the trace metals listed in Table 3-2, Pb is retained by soils and soil constituents to the greatest extent under the conditions of these studies. Most studies with Pb, however, have been performed in well defined, simple matrices, i.e., 0.01M $CaCl_2$. Puls et al. (1991), and Kotuby-Amacher and Gambrell (1988) have demonstrated decreased sorption of Pb in the presence of complexing ligands and competing cations. Lead has a strong affinity for organic ligands and the formation of such complexes may greatly increase the mobility of Pb in soil.

Nickel

Nickel does not form insoluble precipitates in unpolluted soils and retention for Ni is, therefore, exclusively through adsorption mechanisms. Nickel will adsorb to clays, iron and manganese oxides, and organic matter and is thus removed from the soil solution. The formation of complexes of Ni with both inorganic and organic ligands will increase Ni mobility in soils.

Silver

Published data concerning the interaction of silver with soil are rare. As a cation it will participate in adsorption and precipitation reactions. Silver is very strongly adsorbed by clay and organic matter and precipitates of silver, AgCl, Ag_2SO_4 and $AgCO_3$, are highly insoluble (Lindsay, 1979). Silver is highly immobile in the soil environment.

Mercury

The distribution of mercury species in soils, elemental mercury (Hg°), mercurous ions (Hg_2^{2+}) and mercuric ions (Hg^{2+}), is dependent on soil pH and redox potential. Both the mercurous and mercuric mercury cations are adsorbed by clay minerals, oxides, and organic matter. Adsorption is pH dependent, increasing with increasing pH. Mercurous and mercuric mercury are also immobilized by forming various precipitates. Mercurous mercury precipitates with chloride, phosphate, carbonate, and hydroxide. At concentrations of Hg commonly found in soil, only the phosphate precipitate is stable. In alkaline soils, mercuric mercury will precipitate with carbonate and hydroxide to form a stable solid phase. At lower pH and high chloride concentration, $HgCl_2$ is formed. Divalent mercury also will form complexes with soluble organic matter, chlorides and hydroxides that may contribute to its mobility (Kinniburgh and Jackson, 1978).

Under mildly reducing conditions, both organically bound mercury and inorganic mercury compounds may be degraded to the elemental form of mercury, Hg°. Elemental mercury can readily be converted to methyl or ethyl mercury by biotic and abiotic processes (Rogers, 1976, 1977). These are the most toxic forms of mercury. Both methyl and ethyl mercury are volatile and soluble in water. Griffin and Shimp (1978) estimated that the removal of Hg from a leachate was not due to adsorption by clays, but was due to volatilization and/or precipitation. This removal of mercury increased with pH. Rogers (1979) also found large amounts of mercury volatilized from soils. Amounts of mercury volatilized appeared to be affected by the solubility of the mercury compounds added to soil. Volatilization was also found to be inversely related to soil adsorption capacity. The form of Hg lost from the soil, whether elemental Hg or methylmercury, was not determined in this study.

Arsenic

In the soil environment arsenic exists as either arsenate, As(V) (AsO_4^{3-}), or as arsenite, As(III) (AsO_2^-). Arsenite is the more toxic form of arsenic.

The behavior of arsenate in soil is analogous to that of phosphate, because of their chemical similarity. Like phosphate, arsenate forms insoluble precipitates with iron, aluminum, and calcium. Iron in soils is most effective in controlling arsenate's mobility. Arsenite compounds are reported to be 4–10 times more soluble than arsenate compounds.

Griffin and Shimp (1978), in a study of arsenate adsorption by kaolinite and montmorillonite, found maximum adsorption of As(V) to occur at pH 5. Adsorption of arsenate by aluminum and iron oxides has shown an adsorption maximum at pH 3–4 followed by a gradual decrease in adsorption with increasing pH (Hingston et al., 1971; Anderson et al., 1976). The mechanism of adsorption has been ascribed to inner sphere complexation (specific adsorption), which is the same mechanism controlling the adsorption of phosphate by oxide surfaces (Hingston et al., 1971; Anderson et al., 1976; Anderson and Malotky, 1979).

The adsorption of arsenite, As(III), is also strongly pH dependent. Griffin and Shimp (1978) observed an increase in sorption of As (III) by kaolinite and montmorillonite over a pH range of 3–9. Pierce and Moore (1980) found the maximum adsorption of As(III) by iron oxide occurred at pH 7. Elkhatib et al. (1984b) found adsorption of As(III) to be rapid and irreversible on ten soils. They determined, in this study and another study (Elkhatib et al., 1984a), that Fe oxide, redox, and pH were the most important properties in controlling arsenite adsorption by these soils.

Both pH and the redox are important in assessing the fate of arsenic in soil. At high redox levels, As(V) predominates and arsenic mobility is low. As the pH increases or the redox decreases, As (III) predominates. The reduced form of arsenic is more subject to leaching because of its high solubility. The reduction kinetics are, however, slow. Formation of As (III) also may lead to the volatilization of arsine (AsH_3) and methyl-arsines from soils (Woolson 1977a). Under soil conditions of high organic matter, warm temperatures, adequate moisture, and other conditions conducive to microbial activity, the reaction sequence is driven toward methylation and volatilization (Woolson 1977a, Woolson et al., 1971). Woolson's (1977b) study showed that only 1 to 2 percent of the sodium arsenate applied at a rate of 10 ppm was volatilized in 160 days. The loss of organic arsenical compounds from the soil was far greater than for the inorganic source of arsenic. Arsenite, As(III), can be oxidized to As(V). Manganese oxides are the primary electron acceptor in this oxidation (Oscarson et al., 1983).

Selenium

The behavior of selenium in soils has received great attention in recent years. Studies were stimulated by the high incidence of deformity and mortality of waterfowl at the Kesterson National Wildlife Refuge in California that resulted from the input of agricultural drainage water from the western San Joaquin Valley that was high in Se. Such studies have led to a better understanding of the distribution and movement of Se in soils and ground water.

Selenium exists in the soil environment in four oxidation states: selenide (Se^{2-}), elemental selenium (Se^o), selenite (SeO_3^{2-}), and selenate (SeO_4^{2-}), The concentration and form of Se in soil is governed by pH, redox, and soil composition. Selenate, Se(VI), is the predominant form of selenium in calcareous soils and selenite, Se(IV), is the predominant form in acid soil.

Selenite, Se (IV) binds to sesquioxides, especially to Fe oxides. Balistrieri and Chao (1987) found the removal of selenite by iron oxide to increase with decreasing pH. This study not only demonstrates the effect of pH on selenite adsorption but also the effect of concentration. The decrease in the percentage of selenite adsorbed with increasing concentration of selenite at a given pH indicated multiple sites of selenite retention. At the two lower concentrations, high energy specific adsorption sites were available. As the concentration of selenite was increased these sites became saturated and the lower energy sites were utilized. Griffin and Shimp (1978) found maximum adsorption of selenite on montmorillonite and kaolinite to occur at pH 2–3. Neal et al. (1987a) used five soils from the San Joaquin Valley and found that selenite adsorption by the soils decreased with increasing pH in the range of 4–9. Selenite adsorption to oxides and soils occurs through an inner sphere complexation (specific adsorption) mechanism (Rajan, 1979; Neal et al., 1987b).

In studies of competitive adsorption using phosphate, sulfate, and chloride (Neal, et al., 1987b) and phosphate and various organic acids (Balistrieri and Chao, 1987), selenite adsorption decreased dramatically in the presence of phosphate and the organic acids but was not affected by the presence of sulfate or chloride. Balistrieri and Chao (1987), using Fe oxide, found the sequence of adsorption to be: phosphate = silicate = arsenate > bicarbonate carbonate > citrate = selenite > molybdate > oxalate > fluoride = selenate > sulfate. Precipitation is not a major mechanism of retention of selenite in soils. Manganese selenite may form, however, in strongly acidic environments (Elrashidi et al., 1989).

Selenate dominates under alkaline conditions. In contrast to selenite, selenate, Se(VI), is highly mobile in soils. Benjamin (1983) found that selenate was adsorbed by amorphous iron oxide as a function of pH. Maximum removal was at pH 4.5 and adsorption decreased with increasing pH. Bar-Yosef and Meek (1987) found some indication of selenate adsorption by kaolinite below pH 4. Selenate seems to be adsorbed by weak exchange mechanisms similar to sulfate (Neal and Sposito, 1989), in contrast to selenite that is specifically adsorbed by soils and soil constituents. There has been some evidence that selenate was adsorbed by alkaline soils (Singh et al., 1981), but Goldberg and Glaubig (1988) found no removal of selenate by calcareous montmorillonite. Neal and Sposito (1989), using soils from the San Joaquin Valley, showed no adsorption of added selenate over a pH range from 5.5–9.0. Fio et al. (1991) also observed no sorption of selenate by alkaline soil from the San Joaquin Valley, but did observe the rapid sorption of selenite by this soil. No stable precipitates of selenate are expected to form under the pH and redox conditions of most soils (Elrashidi, et al., 1989).

Similar to other anionic species, selenium is more mobile at higher pHs. Soil factors favoring selenium mobility, as summarized by Balistrieri and Chao (1987) are: alkaline pH, high selenium concentration, oxidizing conditions, and high concentrations of additional anions that strongly adsorb to soils, in particular, phosphate.

Under reduced conditions, selenium is converted to the elemental form. This conversion can provide an effective mechanism for attenuation since mobile selenate occurs only under well aerated, alkaline conditions.

Organic forms of selenium are analogous to those of sulfur including seleno amino acids and their derivatives. Like sulfur, selenium undergoes biomethylation forming volatile methyl selenides.

Chromium

Chromium exists in two possible oxidation states in soils, the trivalent chromium, Cr(III) and the hexavalent chromium, Cr(VI). Forms of Cr(VI) in soils are as chromate ion, $HCrO_4^-$ predominant at pH<6.5, or CrO_4^{2-}, predominant at pH 6.5, and as dichromate, $Cr_2O_7^{2-}$ predominant at higher concentrations (>10mM) and at pH 2–6. The dichromate ions pose a greater health hazard than chromate ions. Both Cr(VI) ions are more toxic than Cr(III) ions. Reviews of the processes that control the fate of chromium in soil and the effect these processes have on remediation are given in Bartlett (1991) and Palmer and Wittbrodt (1991).

Because of the anionic nature of Cr(VI), its association with soil surfaces is limited to positively charged exchange sites, the number of which decreases with increasing soil pH. Iron and aluminum oxide surfaces will adsorb CrO_4^{2-} at acidic and neutral pH (Davis and Leckie, 1980; Zachara et al., 1987; Ainsworth et al., 1989). Stollenwerk and Grove (1985) concluded that the adsorption of Cr(VI) by ground-water alluvium was due to the iron oxides and hydroxides coating the alluvial particles. The adsorbed Cr(VI) was, however, easily desorbed with the input of uncontaminated ground water, indicating nonspecific adsorption of Cr(VI). The presence of chloride and nitrate had little effect on

Cr(VI) adsorption, whereas sulfate and phosphate inhibited adsorption (Stollenwerk and Grove, 1985). Zachara et al. (1987) and Zachara et al. (1989) found SO_4^{2-} and dissolved inorganic carbon inhibited Cr(VI) adsorption by amorphous iron oxyhydroxide and subsurface soils. The presence of sulfate, however, enhanced Cr(VI) adsorption to kaolinite (Zachara et al., 1988). Rai et al. (1987) suggested that $BaCrO_4$ may form in soils at chromium contaminated waste sites. No other precipitates of hexavalent compounds of chromium have been observed in a pH range of 1.0 to 9.0 (Griffin and Shimp, 1978). Hexavalent chromium is highly mobile in soils.

In a study of the relative mobilities of 11 different trace metals for a wide range of soils, Korte et al. (1976) found that clay soil, containing free iron and manganese oxides, significantly retarded Cr(VI) migration (see Figure 3-6). Hexavalent chromium was found to be the only metal studied that was highly mobile in alkaline soils. The parameters that correlated with Cr(VI) immobilization in the soils were free iron oxides, total manganese, and soil pH, whereas the soil properties, cation exchange capacity, surface area, and percent clay had no significant influence on Cr(VI) mobility.

Rai et al. (1987) reported that Cr(III) forms hydroxy complexes in natural water, including $Cr(OH)_2^+$, $Cr(OH)^{2+}$, $Cr(OH)_3^\circ$, and $Cr(OH)_4^-$. Trivalent chromium is readily adsorbed by soils. In a study of the relative mobility of metals in soils at pH 5, Cr(III) was found to be the least mobile (Griffin and Shimp, 1978). Hydroxy species of Cr(III) precipitate at pH 4.5 and complete precipitation of the hydroxy species occurs at pH 5.5.

Hexavalent chromium can be reduced to Cr(III) under normal soil pH and redox conditions. Soil organic matter has been identified as the electron donor in this reaction (Bartlett and Kimble, 1976, Bloomfield and Pruden, 1980). The reduction reaction in the presence of organic matter proceeds at a slow rate at environmental pH and temperatures (Bartlett and Kimble, 1976; James and Bartlett, 1983a,b,c). Bartlett (1991) reported that in natural soils the reduction reaction may be extremely slow, requiring years. The rate of this reduction reaction, however, increases with decreasing soil pH (Cary et al., 1977; Bloomfield and Pruden, 1980). Soil organic matter is probably the principal reducing agent in surface soils. In subsurface soils, where organic matter occurs in low concentration, Fe(II) containing minerals reduce Cr(VI) (Eary and Rai, 1991). Eary and Rai (1991), however, observed that this reaction only occurred in the subsurface soil with a pH<5. The reduction of Cr(VI) occurred in all four subsurface soils tested by decreasing the pH to 2.5.

Bartlett and James (1979), however, demonstrated that under conditions prevalent in some soils, Cr(III) can be oxidized. The presence of oxidized Mn, which serves as an electron acceptor, was determined as an important factor in this reaction.

Industrial use of chromium also includes organic complexed Cr(III). Chromium (III) complexed with soluble organic ligands will remain in the soil solution (James and Bartlett, 1983a). In addition to decreased Cr(III) adsorption, added organic matter also may facilitate oxidation of Cr(III) to Cr(VI).

COMPUTER MODELS

Several equilibrium thermodynamic computer programs are available for modeling soil solution and solid phase chemistry by providing information on the thermodynamic possibility of certain reactions to occur. In addition to calculating the equilibrium speciation of chemical elements in the soil solution and precipitate/dissolution reactions models such as GEOCHEM (Mattigod and Sposito, 1979) and MINTEQA2 (U.S. EPA, 1987) provide information on cation exchange reactions and metal ion adsorption. These models are used to:

1) calculate the distribution of free metal ions and metal-ligand complexes in a soils solution,
2) predict the fate of metals added to soil by providing a listing of which precipitation and adsorption reactions are likely to be controlling the solution concentration of metals, and
3) provide a method for evaluating the effect that changing one or more soil solution parameters, such as pH, redox, inorganic and organic ligand concentration, or metal concentration, has on the adsorption/precipitation behavior of the metal of interest.

These models are equilibrium models and as such do not consider the kinetics of the reactions. These models are also limited by the accuracy of the thermodynamic data base available.

ANALYSIS OF SOIL SAMPLES

Total Concentration of Metals in Soil

Measurement of the total concentration of metals in soils is useful for determining the vertical and horizontal extent of contamination and for measuring any net change (leaching to ground water, surface runoff, erosion) in soil metal concentration over time. The methods do not, however, give an indication as to the chemical form of the metal in the soil system.

The complete dissolution of all solid phase components in soils requires a rigorous digestion using either a heated mixture of nitric acid, sulfuric acid, hydrofluoric acid, and perchloric acid (Page et al., 1982) or a fusion of the soil with sodium carbonate (Page et al., 1982). Both methods require special equipment and special safety considerations. A more commonly used procedure is the hot nitric acid-hydrogen peroxide procedure outlined in SW-846 Method 3050 (U.S. EPA, 1986). This is a partial digestion of the soil solid phase. The method probably releases metals associated with a recent pollution source, i.e., exchangeable, specifically adsorbed to clays, oxides or organic matter, and most precipitates, but would not release metals associated within solid phases that are not dissolved by the hot nitric acid and oxidizing agent, i.e., within the structure of insoluble minerals.

Sequential Extractions of Metals in Soils

Since the potential migration of metals in soil systems is dependent on the chemical form of the metal, extraction procedures have been developed to selectively remove metals from these various geochemical forms. While these procedures cannot be used to identify the actual form of a given metal in a soil, they are useful in categorizing the metals into several operationally defined geochemical fractions, such as exchangeable, specifically adsorbed, and metals associated with carbonates, organic matter, and/or iron and manganese oxides.

Numerous extraction procedures have been developed for metal cations (Sposito et al., 1984; Hickey and Kittrick, 1984; Tessier et al., 1979; Grove and Ellis, 1980; Kuo et al., 1983) and anions (Chao and Sanzolone, 1989; Gruebel et al., 1988). Lake et al. (1984) reviewed a number of the procedures used for cationic metal extraction. The extraction procedures consist of reacting a soil sample with increasing strengths of chemical solutions. Typically, water or a salt solution (KNO_3, $CaCl_2$, etc.) is the first extractant used. These are followed by mild acids, bases, chelating agents, and oxidizing solutions. Table 3-4 illustrates the wide variety of extractants that have been used in the literature for metal cations.

The aqueous fraction and those fractions in equilibrium, i.e., the exchange fraction, with this fraction are of primary importance when considering the migration potential of metals in soils. In theory, mild extractants, such as salt solutions, are more likely to extract metals that could be released to the soil solution with input of water than metals associated with stronger binding mechanisms, such as specifically adsorbed or precipitated metals. Work by Silveira and Sommers (1977) and Latterell et al. (1978) suggests that salt extractable metals represent the potentially mobile portion of the total concentration of metals in soils. Harrison et al. (1981) likewise suggested that the mobility of metals decreases in the order of the extraction sequence. Rigorous evaluation, however, of the appropriateness of any extraction procedure for defining the mobile fraction of metals in soils has not been reported in the literature.

Hickey and Kittrick (1984) used a sequential extraction procedure to separate Cd, Cu, Ni, and Zn in metal polluted soils and sediments into five operationally defined geochemical fractions: exchangeable (1.0M $MgCl_2$), metals associated with carbonates (acetate buffer, pH 5), metals associated with Mn and Fe oxides (0.04M $NH_4OH \cdot HCl$), metals associated with organic matter (0.02M $HNO_3 + H_2O_2$), and residual metals ($HF + HClO_4$). Figure 3-10 shows the average distribution of the metals among the defined geochemical fractions. Approximately 37% of the total Cd and a significant portion of the Zn were in the exchange fraction indicating the potential mobility of these two metals. Only a small portion of the Cu and Ni were in the exchange fraction. A significant portion of the Cu was associated with the organic fraction, in agreement with the known affinity of Cu for organic material. Nickel was mostly associated with the residual fraction and significant portions of Zn and Cu were associated with the oxides. The authors concluded from this study that the relative mobility of the metals followed: Cd > Zn > Cu = Ni.

Table 3-4. Some Bibliographic Data on the Extraction of Heavy Metals Present in Soils and Sediments (Calvet et al., 1990)

Authors	Exchangeable	Fraction associated with carbonates	Fraction associated with oxides	Fraction associated with organic matter	Total amount and residual fraction
McLaren and Crawford[11] (1973)	0.05 N $CaCl_2$	2.5% CH_3COOH	0.1 $(COOH)_2$ +0.175 M $(COONH_4)_2$ pH = 3.5	1 M $K_4P_2O_7$	HF
Stover et al.[12] (1976)	1 M KNO_3 +NaF		0.1 M EDTA pH = 6.5	0.1 M $Na_4P_2O_7$	1 M HNO_3
Gatehouse et al.[13] (1977)		1 M CH_3COONH_4 +CH_3COOH pH = 4.5	0.1 M NH_2OH +1 M CH_3COONH_4 pH = 4.5	30% H_2O_2	HF-$HClO_4$
Filipek and Owen[14] (1979)		1 M CH_3COOH	0.25 M NH_2OH, HCl in 25% (v/v) CH_3COOH	Acidified 30% H_2O_2	HNO_3-HF-$HClO_4$
Tessier et al.[3] (1979)	1 M $MgCl_2$ or 1 M CH_3COONa at pH = 8.2	1 M CH_3COONa + 1 M CH_3COOH at pH = 5.0	0.04 M NH_2OH, HCl in 25% (v/v) CH_3COOH at 96 ± 3°C or 0.3 M $Na_2S_2O_4$ +0.175 M Na-citrate +0.025 M citric acid	0.02 M HNO_3+ 30% H_2O_2, pH = 2 at 85 ± 2°C, 2 h +30% H_2O_2+HNO_3, pH = 2 at 85 ± 2°C, 3 h 3.2 M CH_3COONH_4 in 20% HNO_3	HF-$HClO_4$
Förstner et al.[2] (1979)	0.2 M $BaCl_2$		0.1 M NH_2OH, HNO_3 + 25% (v/v) CH_3COOH + HCl	30% H_2O_2 = NH$_4$OH	HF-$HClO_4$
Schalscha et al.[4] (1980)	1 M KNO_3	0.5 M NaF pH = 6.5	CH_3COOH + HCl 0.1 M EDTA pH = 6.5 double extraction	0.1 M $Na_4P_2O_5$	1 M HNO_3

Reference					
Garcia-Miragaya[15] (1981)	1 N CaCl₂	0.05 M EDTA pH = 7	0.1 N Na₄P₂O₅		HF
Badri and Aston[16] (1981)	1 M CH₃COONH₄ +0.5 M (CH₃COO)₂ Mg	0.25 M NH₂OH, HCl pH = 2	30% H₂O₂ at 180°C + 1 M CH₃COONH₄	HNO₃ at 180°C	
Förstner et al.[17] (1981)	1 M CH₃COONH₄ pH = 7	(1) 0.1 M NH₂OH, ClH +0.01 M HNO₃, pH = 2 (2) 0.2 M (COONH₄)2 +0.2 M (COOH)2, pH = 3	30% H₂O₂, HNO₃ pH = 2 at 85°C extraction with 1 M CH₃COONH₄		
Greffard et al.[6] (1981)	resin-H⁺	(1) (COONa)₂ (2) (COONa)₂ + UV	30% H₂O₂ at 40°C		
Sposito et al.[10]	0.5 M KNO₃	0.5 M Na₂ EDTA	0.5 M NaOH		HNO₃-HF-HCl
Dekeyser et al.[18] (1983)	1 M CH₃COONH₄ pH = 4.5	(1) 0.1 M NH₂OH, HCl (2) 0.2 M (COONH₄)2 (HCOOH)2, pH = 3.3 obscurité (3) same as (2)+UV			
Kuo et al.[7] (1983)	1 M MgCl₂	(1) (COONa)2 (2) Citrate dithionite bicarbonate	6% NaClO₄ at 85°C		HNO₃-HClO₄
Meguelatti et al.[5] (1983)	1 M BaCl₂ +0.6 M CH₃COONa / 1 M CH₃COOH	0.1 M NH₂OH +25% (v/v) CH₃COOH	30% H₂O₂		HF-HCl +0.02 M HNO₃ +3.2 M CH₃COONH₄

Table 3-4. Continued

Authors	Exchangeable	Fraction associated with carbonates	Fraction associated with oxides	Fraction associated with organic matter	Total amount and residual fraction
Shuman[19] (1985)	1 M $Mg(NO_3)_2$ pH = 7		(1) 0.1 M NH_2OH, HCl pH = 2 (2) 0.2 M $(COONH_4)2$ +0.2 M $(COOH)2$, pH = 3 (3) Same as (2) + ascorbic acid	0.7 M NaOCl pH = 8.5	$HF-HNO_3$-HCl
Gibson and Farmer[20] (1986)	1 M CH_3COONH_4 pH = 7	1 M CH_3COONa pH = 5	(1) 0.1 M NH_2OH, ClH +0.01 M HNO_3 (2) 1 M NH_2OH, ClH in 25% (v/v) CH_3COOH	30% H_2O_2 Aqua regia +0.02 M HNO_3 at 85°C	+ HF

Editor's Note: The original Issue Paper did not include references cited in this table. Refer to the Calvet et al. (1990) paper from which this table was developed for full citations.

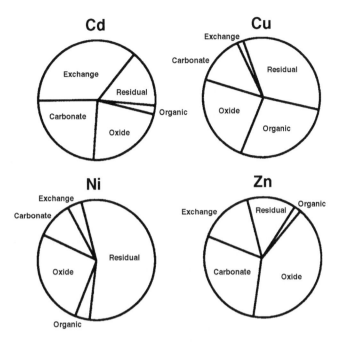

Figure 3-10. Proportions of Cd, Cu, Ni, and Zn in each of the operationally defined geochemical fractions of the experimental samples (Hickey and Kittrick, 1984).

There has been recent criticism of these sequential extraction procedures (Miller et al., 1986; Kheboian and Bauer, 1987 Gruebel et al., 1988; Tipping et al., 1985; Rapin et al., 1986; Calvet et al., 1990). The methods are not entirely specific for a geochemical fraction of the soil and the extractant also may remove metals associated with other fractions. Secondly, readsorption of the extracted metals to the remaining solid phase of the soil may occur leading to artificially low concentrations of the metal being associated with that fraction. Finally, no one extraction procedure would be universally applicable for all metals and all soils. Perhaps the most suitable extractant for defining the mobile fraction of metals in soils under specific site conditions is one that simulates that soil or soil-waste solution chemistry.

TCLP

The Toxicity Characterization Leaching Procedure (TCLP) (U.S. EPA, 1986) is a single extraction procedure, using 0.1M acetic acid, developed to simulate the leaching a waste might undergo if disposed of in a municipal landfill. This method is frequently used to determine the leaching potential of cationic metals in landfill situations where, due to microbial degradation of the waste under anaerobic conditions, acetic acid is produced. While this procedure is appropriate for demonstrating whether an excavated metal contaminated soil is defined as hazardous for disposal at a landfill, its application for evaluating the mobility of metals under field conditions has been questioned (Dragun et al., 1990). Production of acetic acid does not commonly occur in soils. In certain soil-waste systems, leaching tests using acetic acid may be appropriate, but it is not universally representative of the leaching solution for soil-waste systems. The acetic acid leaching procedure was developed for cationic metals. The procedure is not appropriate for extraction of anionic metals. Bartlett (1991) reported that this procedure actually causes the reduction of Cr(VI) to Cr(III) leading to a false measurement of the leachability of Cr(VI) in soil. A more appropriate leaching solution would mimic the specific waste or waste-soil matrix.

Hickey and Kittrick (1984) used an acetate buffer solution in their sequential extraction scheme to remove metals associated with carbonates. This is a similar solution to the TCLP solution except that it is buffered to pH 5. This buffered solution fully dissolves the carbonate minerals in the soil. The unbuffered acetic acid solution used in the TCLP solution cannot maintain a low enough pH in calcareous soils to dissolve carbonates. The metals extracted by the TCLP solution are not related to any definable geochemical fraction and the fraction of metals extracted using this procedure have not been correlated with the mobile fraction of metals in soil.

EVALUATING THE BEHAVIOR OF METALS IN SOILS

Sorption Studies

Soil sorption studies are commonly performed to evaluate the extent of metal retention by a soil or soil constituent. Sorption studies are often used in an attempt to generate the equilibrium distribution coefficient (Kd), the ratio of metal sorbed to metal in solution at equilibrium, which may be utilized in transport models. Sorption studies are also used for comparison of the relative retention of several metals by a soil or the relative retention of a metal by several soils, and are used extensively in correlation studies to determine the relative importance of a soil's chemical and physical properties for metal retention. Sorption studies also can be used to evaluate the effect that changing a soil solution parameter, e.g., adjustment of pH, ionic strength, addition of competing cations, or addition of inorganic or organic ligands, has on metal retention by a soil.

In a sorption study, the soil is reacted with solutions containing varying quantities of the metal(s) of interest for a specified time period using either batch or column techniques. The concentration range used in the study should overlap the concentration of environmental concern. A background electrolyte solution also should be used to simulate normal soil's solution chemistry or the waste matrix and to equalize the ionic strength across all soils. The reaction time should approach thermodynamic equilibrium, usually determined by a preliminary kinetics experiment. After the specified time period the soil and solution are separated by centrifugation and/or filtration. The soil and/or solution phases are then analyzed by atomic absorption spectrophotometry or inductively coupled plasma emission spectrometry. With these techniques it is not possible to distinguish between true adsorption and precipitation reactions. For that reason the term sorption will be used.

Two techniques, batch and column studies, may be used to generate sorption isotherms. The batch technique involves placing the soil and the solutions containing the various concentrations of the metals into a vessel and mixing the samples for a prescribed time period. This is the most commonly used technique because of its ease of laboratory operation and ease of data handling. The disadvantages of the technique are 1) results are sensitive to the soil:solution ratio used, 2) soil:solution ratios in actual soil systems cannot be done in batch studies, so scaling of data from batch studies to soils systems is uncertain, 3) results are sensitive to the mixing rate used, 4) separation techniques may affect results, and 5) many investigators have found that batch generated sorption coefficients are not adequate to describe the behavior of metals in flow through systems.

The column method consists of packing a glass or plastic column with soil. The solutions containing various concentrations of the metals of interest are pumped through the columns and the effluents are collected and analyzed by AA or ICP. Breakthrough occurs when the effluent concentration equals the influent concentration. The advantages of this technique are 1) low soil:solution ratios can be used, 2) separation of the soil and solution phase is not required, 3) mechanical mixing is not required and 4) column studies more closely simulate field conditions than batch methods. The disadvantages are 1) results depend on flow rates used, 2) columns are difficult to set up and maintain, 3) uniform packing of the column is difficult, often leading to channel flow, and 4) fewer columns can be operated at one time compared with the number of batch reactors.

Equilibrium sorption is described by a sorption isotherm. A sorption isotherm is the relationship between the amount of metal sorbed and the equilibrium concentration of the metal or, more correctly, the activity of the free metal in the soil solution. A typical sorption isotherm is shown in Figure 3-11. If the relationship is linear over the concentration range studied then the sorption process can be described by a single coefficient, the distribution coefficient, Kd. For metals, however, the relationship is seldom linear and other equations with two or more coefficients must be used to describe the data.

Equations most frequently used, because of their relative simplicity, to describe the curvilinear sorption behavior of metals in soil are the Langmuir and the Freundlich equations. The Langmuir equation was developed to model gas adsorption on solid surfaces. The derivation of the equation was based on the assumption that adsorption is independent of surface coverage, that there is no

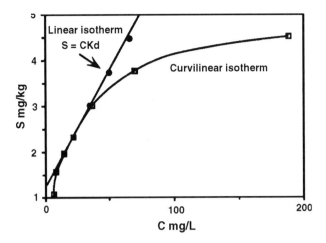

Figure 3-11. Sorption isotherms.

interaction between adsorbed ions, and that only a monolayer of adsorption occurs on the surface. These conditions are not typically met with metals sorption on soils.

The linearized form of the Langmuir equation is:

$$\frac{C}{S} = \frac{C}{M} + \frac{1}{Mb} \tag{1}$$

where C is the concentration or activity of the free metal in solution, S is the quantity of the metal ion sorbed by the soil (i.e., mg metal sorbed/Kg soil), M is the maximum sorption capacity of the soil, and b is the coefficient related to bonding energy. When C/S is plotted as a function of C, the slope is the reciprocal of the sorption capacity, M, and the intercept is 1/Mb.

The Freundlich expression is an empirically derived equation to describe the logarithmic decrease in adsorption energy with increasing surface coverage. The linearized form of the Freundlich equation is:

$$\log S = (N)\log C + \log K \tag{2}$$

where S and C have the same definition as above and N and K are constants fitted from the experimental data. When the slope, N, equals 1, the equation simplifies to:

$$S = CK_d \text{ or } K_d = S/C \tag{3}$$

where K_d is the distribution coefficient. In most studies reported in the literature for metal sorption, the slope of the Freundlich isotherm is seldom equal to 1 and the simplified expression and its single term, K_d, are not appropriate to describe the data.

Figure 3-12 illustrates the use of the Langmuir expression to describe Cu sorption by a soil (Cavallaro and McBride, 1978). The equation describes the behavior of Cu over all concentrations used in this study. Often, however, nonlinear behavior over the concentration range studied is observed with the use of either the Langmuir or Freundlich equations. In Figure 3-13, the Langmuir expression was used to describe the sorption behavior of Cd and Zn by hydrous manganese oxide (Zasoski and Burau, 1988). This non-linear behavior when using the Langmuir equation has been noted by numerous researchers using various metals and soils and soil constituents (Benjamin and Leckie, 1981; Shuman, 1975; Loganathan and Burau, 1973). Non-linearity of metal sorption using the Freundlich equation has also been noted by Zasoski and Burau, (1988); Benjamin and Leckie (1981); Catts and Langmuir (1986); O'Connor et al. (1983, 1984); and Elrashidi and O'Connor (1982). This non-linear behavior has been interpreted to indicate multiple sites of sorption that have different energies of

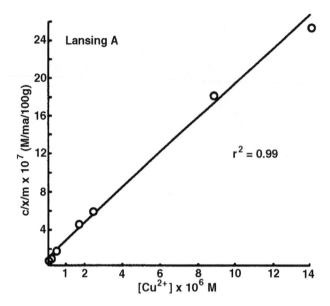

Figure 3-12. Langmuir adsorption isotherm for Cu^{2+} adsorption on the Lansing A soil (Cavallaro and McBride, 1978).

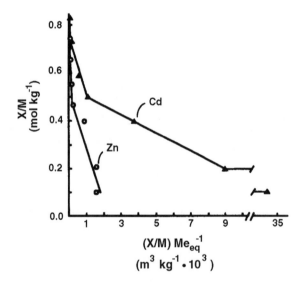

Figure 3-13. Langmuir plot of Cd and Zn sorbed on δ-MnO_2 for the noncompetitive pH 4 data (Zasoski and Burau, 1988).

retention. The mechanisms at low concentrations have been attributed to specific adsorption, whereas the mechanisms at higher concentrations have been considered to be exchange reactions or precipitation. These results illustrate the importance of generating sorption data over the concentration range of interest for a particular application. Large errors in predicting sorptive behavior may result from using data generated in one system and applied to a system with higher or lower metal concentration.

Several researchers have, however, suggested that other equations; for example, the two-surface Langmuir equation (Sposito, 1982; Travis and Etnier, 1981) or the competitive Langmuir equation (Griffin and Au, 1977; Travis and Etnier, 1981), be used to describe the non-linear behavior encountered with the Langmuir equation (Sposito, 1982).

The Langmuir and Freundlich isotherm expressions have proved valuable in interpreting metal behavior in soils. The adsorption isotherm equations were, however, developed for modeling gas adsorption on solids. The sorption of metals by soils violates many of the assumptions associated with these equations. Also, the mechanism described by these equations is adsorption, but it is impossible in a soil system to distinguish between adsorption and precipitation reactions. Adsorption isotherm equations should not be used to indicate adsorption mechanisms without collaborative evidence, but they can be used for an empirical description of the data. Harter (1984) warned against overinterpreting the sorption maximum and "bonding energy" determined using the Langmuir equation. The applicability of adsorption isotherm equations to the interpretation of soil chemical phenomena is a subject of controversy. For further discussion of this controversy see Elprince and Sposito (1981), Griffin and Au (1977), Veith and Sposito (1977), Sposito (1979), Harter and Baker (1977), and Harter (1984).

Desorption

Desorption studies are often performed to determine the reversibility of the sorption reactions. This gives an idea of the strength of the association of the metal with the soil surface. An example of the reversibility of a sorption reaction (Figure 3-14) is taken from Dudley et al. (1988). In this study, two calcareous soils were reacted with various concentrations of Cd. The soils were then desorbed with $CaCl_2$. For the low carbonate soil (Kidman) virtually all of the sorbed Cd was desorbed by the Ca. Only 10–15 percent of the sorbed Cd on the highly calcareous Skumpah soil was desorbed by Ca. These results suggest that Cd was held by the Kidman soil as an exchangeable cation, whereas in the Skumpah, Cd was specifically adsorbed by the $CaCO_3$.

Desorption studies are performed after completion of the sorption study. They can be carried out using either batch or column techniques. For the batch technique the soils used in the sorption are reacted with a salt solution, typically $0.01N$ $CaCl_2$ or a matrix representative of the soil-waste system being studied. Samples are shaken for a specified time period. The soil and liquid are then separated by centrifugation and/or filtration and the solution is analyzed for the metals by AA or ICP. This process is repeated several times. For a column study, the metal equilibrated soil column is flushed with an appropriate solution until the system reaches steady state conditions.

Kinetics

Attention has been mainly given in the literature to equilibrium processes in soils but soil processes are never at equilibrium. Soil systems are dynamic and are thus constantly changing. Most kinetic studies have been performed to establish the proper time interval for use in equilibrium sorption/desorption studies. Most studies assume that ion exchange processes are rapid in soils and that 16 to 24 hours mixing periods, common time periods used in sorption studies, are adequate. This assumption may not be appropriate if other reactions in addition to simple ion exchange, i.e., specific adsorption and precipitation, are involved in metals retention (Harter and Lehmann, 1983). McBride (1980) found that the initial adsorption of Cd on calcite was very rapid, while $CdCO_3$ precipitation of higher Cd^{2+} concentrations was slow. Lehmann and Harter (1984) used kinetics of desorption to study the strength of Cu bonding to a soil. A plot of concentration of Cu in solution versus time indicates an initial rapid release of the Cu followed by a slow reaction. They interpreted these results to indicate that Cu was held at two sites: the rapidly released Cu being loosely held on the soil surfaces and the slowly released Cu being tightly bound.

Each metal-soil system should be tested to determine the time necessary for the individual system to come to equilibrium. Figure 3-15 illustrates the different time periods required for equilibrium for three metals sorbed by a calcareous soil (Dudley, et al., 1988). Copper reached equilibrium within a few hours whereas Cd and Zn did not approach steady state conditions for 144 hours. Use of the time interval appropriate for Cu equilibrium for this soil would mean that only 50 percent of the Cd and Zn adsorbed under steady state conditions would have been determined.

Kinetic studies are being more widely performed because of their importance in determining the transport of metals in soil systems. Many mathematical transport models now allow a kinetic term for sorption. Equilibrium studies predict whether a reaction will occur but give no indication of the time

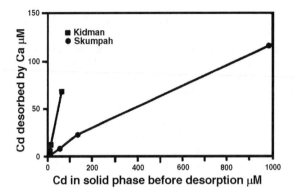

Figure 3-14. Desorption of Cd from Kidman and Skumpah soil by 0.01 M CaCl$_2$ at a soil:solution ratio of 1:25 (Dudley et al., 1988).

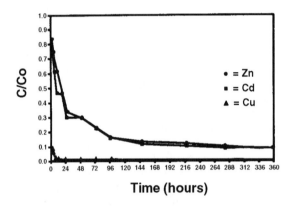

Figure 3-15. Change with time in reduced concentration of metals in suspensions of the Skumpah soils. C$_o$ was the concentration of metal ions at time = 0 (Dudley et al., 1988).

necessary for the reaction to take place. Kinetic studies also contribute to an understanding of reaction mechanisms not discernible from thermodynamic studies (Zasoski and Burau, 1988; Harter and Smith, 1981; Sparks, 1989).

Kinetic studies are similar to sorption procedures, using either batch or column techniques, except samples are collected over time. Several equations have been used to describe the kinetics of sorption reactions of ions on soils and soil constituents. These equations include: first-order, second-order, Elovich equation, parabolic diffusion equation, and power function equation. An excellent review of kinetic processes in soil systems is given by Sparks (1989).

SUMMARY

Metals added to soil will normally be retained at the soil surface. Movement of metals into other environmental compartments, i.e., ground water, surface water, or the atmosphere, should be minimal as long as the retention capacity of the soil is not exceeded. The extent of movement of a metal in the soil system is intimately related to the solution and surface chemistry of the soil and to the specific properties of the metal and associated waste matrix.

The retention mechanisms for metals added to soil include adsorption of the metal by the soil solid surfaces and precipitation. The retention of cationic metals by soil has been correlated with such soil properties as pH, redox potential, surface area, cation exchange capacity, organic mater content, clay content, iron and manganese oxide content, and carbonate content. Anion retention has been correlated with pH, iron and manganese oxide content, and redox potential. In addition to soil properties, consideration must be given to the type of metal and its concentration and to the presence of competing ions, complexing ligands, and the pH and redox potential of the soil-waste matrix. Transport of metals associated with various wastes may be enhanced due to (Puls et al., Chapter 20):

1. facilitated transport caused by metal association with mobile colloidal size particles,
2. formation of metal organic and inorganic complexes that do not sorb to soil solid surfaces,
3. competition with other constituents of waste, both organic and inorganic, for sorption sites, and
4. deceased availability of surface sites caused by the presence of a complex waste matrix.

Because of the wide range of soil characteristics and various forms by which metals can be added to soil, evaluating the extent of metal retention by a soil is site/soil/waste specific. Changes in the soil environment over time, such as the degradation of the organic waste matrix, changes in pH, redox potential, or soil solution composition, due to various remediation schemes or to natural weathering processes also may enhance metal mobility. The extent of vertical contamination is intimately related to the soil solution and surface chemistry of the soil matrix with reference to the metal and waste matrix.

Laboratory methods for evaluating the behavior of metals in soils are available in the literature. Thermodynamic equilibrium computer models are also available to assist with this evaluation. The advantages and disadvantages of some of the available procedures have been presented in this document.

EPA CONTACTS

For further information contact David Burden, 405/438-8606; at RSKERL-Ada.

REFERENCES

Ainsworth, C.C., D.C. Girvin, J.M. Zachara, and S.C. Smith. 1989. Chromate adsorption on goethite: effects of aluminum substitution. Soil Sci. Soc. Am. J. 53:411-418.

Amrhein, C., J.E. Strong, and P.A. Mosher. 1992. Effect of deicing salts on metal and organic matter mobility in roadside soils. Environ. Sci. Technol. 26:703-709.

Anderson M.C. and D.T. Malotky. 1979. The adsorption of protolyzable anions on hydrous oxides at the isoelectric pH. J. Colloid Interface Sci. 72:413-427.

Anderson, M.C., J.F. Ferguson, and J. Gavis. 1976. Arsenate adsorption on amorphous aluminum hydroxide. J. Colloid Interface Sci. 54:391-399.

Baham, J., N.B. Ball, and G. Sposito. 1978. Gel filtration studies of trace metal-fulvic acid solutions extracted from sewage sludge. J. Environ. Qual. 7:181-188.

Baham, J. and G. Sposito. 1986. Proton and metal complexation by water-soluble ligands extracted from anaerobically digested sewage sludge. J. Environ. Qual. 15:239-244.

Balistrieri, L.S. and T.T. Chao. 1987. Selenium adsorption by goethite. Soil Sci. Soc. Am. J. 51:1145-1151.

Bar-Yosef, B. and D. Meek. 1987. Selenium sorption by kaolinite and montmorillonite. Soil Sci. 144:11-19.

Bartlett, R.J. 1991. Chromium cycling in soils and water: links, gaps, and methods. Environ. Health Perspective 92:17-24.

Bartlett, R.J. and B. James. 1979. Behavior of chromium in soils: III. oxidation. J. Environ. Qual. 8:31-35.

Bartlett, R.J. and J.M. Kimble. 1976. Behavior of chromium in soils: II. hexavalent forms. J. Environ. Qual. 5:383-386.

Behel, D., D.W. Nelson, and L.E. Sommers. 1983. Assessment of heavy metals equilibria in sewage sludge-treated soil. J. Environ. Qual. 12:181-186.

Benjamin, M.M. 1983. Adsorption and surface precipitation of metals on amorphous iron oxyhydroxide. Environ. Sci. Technol. 17:686-692.

Benjamin, M.M. and J.O. Leckie. 1981. Multiple-site adsorption of Cd, Zn, and Pb on amorphous iron oxyhydroxide. J. Colloid Interface Sci. 79:209-221.

Benjamin, M.M. and J.O. Leckie. 1982. Effects of complexation by Cl, SO_4, and S_2O_3 on adsorption behavior of Cd on oxide surfaces. Environ. Sci. Technol. 16:162-170.

Biddappa, C.C., M. Chino, and K. Kumazawa. 1981. Adsorption, desorption potential and selective distribution of heavy metals in selected soils of Japan. J. Environ. Sci. Health Part B. 16:511-528.

Bloomfield, C. and G. Pruden. 1980. The behavior of Cr(VI) in soil under aerobic and anaerobic conditions. Environ. Pollut. Ser. A. 103-114.

Bolland, M.D.A., A.M. Posner, and J.P. Quick. 1977. Zinc adsorption by goethite in the absence and presence of phosphate. Aust. J. Soil Res. 15:279-286.

Boyd, S.A., L.E. Sommers, and D.W. Nelson. 1979. Infrared spectra of sewage sludge fractions: evidence for an amide binding site. Soil Sci. Soc. Am. J. 43:893-899.

Boyd, S.A., L.E. Sommers, D.W. Nelson, and D.X. West. 1983. Copper(II) binding by humic acid extracted from sewage sludge: an electron spin resonance study. Soil Sci. Soc. Am. J. 47:43-46.

Boyle, M. and W.H. Fuller. 1987. Effect of municipal solid waste leachate composition on zinc migration through soils. J. Environ Qual. 16:357-360.

Calvet, R., S. Bourgeois, and J.J. Msaky. 1990. Some experiments on extraction of heavy metals present in soil. Intern. J. Environ. Anal. Chem. 39:31-45.

Cary, E.E., W.H. Allaway, and O.E. Olson. 1977. Control of chromium concentration in food plants. II. chemistry of chromium in soils and its availability to plants. J. Agric. Food Chem. 25:305-309.

Catts, J.G. and D. Langmuir. 1986. Adsorption of Cu, Pb, and Zn by MnO_2; applicability of side binding-surface complexation model. Appl. Geochem. 1:255-264.

Cavallaro, N. and M.B. McBride. 1978. Copper and cadmium adsorption characteristics of selected acid and calcareous soils. Soil Sci. Soc. Am. J. 42:550-556.

Cavallaro, N. and M.B. McBride. 1980. Activities of CU^{2+} and Cd^{2+} in soil solutions as affected by pH. Soil Sci. Soc. Am. J. 44:729-732.

Cavallaro, N. 1982. Sorption and fixation of Cu and Zn, and phosphate by soil clays as influenced by the oxide fraction. PhD thesis. Cornell Univ. (Diss. Abstr. 82-10799).

Chao, T.T. and R.F. Sanzolone. 1989. Fractionation of soil selenium by sequential partial dissolution. Soil Sci. Soc. Am. J. 53:385-392.

Davis, J.A. 1984. Complexation of trace metals by adsorbed natural organic matter. Geochim. Cosmochim. Acta. 48:679-691.

Davis, J.A. and J.O. Leckie. 1978. Effect of adsorbed complexing ligands on trace metal uptake by hydrous oxides. Environ. Sci. Technol. 12:1309-1315.

Davis, J.A. and J.O. Leckie. 1980. Surface ionization and complexation at the oxide/water interface. III. adsorption of anions. J. Colloid Interface Sci. 74:32-43.

Doner, H.E. 1978. Chloride as a factor in mobilities of Ni(II), Cu(II), and Cd(II) in soil. Soil Sci. Soc. Am. J. 42:882-885.

Dragun, J., J. Barkach, and S.A. Mason. 1990. Misapplication of the EP-TOX, TCLP, and CAM-WET tests to derive data on migration potential of metals in soil systems. In: Kostecki, P.T. and E.J. Calabrese (eds.), Petroleum Contaminated Soils. Lewis Publishers, Chelsea, MI.

Dudley, L.M., B.L. McNeal, J.E. Baham, C.S. Coray, and H.H. Cheng. 1987. Characterization of soluble organic compounds and complexation of copper, nickel, and zinc in extracts of sludge-amended soils. J. Environ. Qual. 16:341-348.

Dudley, L.M., J.E. McLean, R.C. Sims, and J.J. Jurinak. 1988. Sorption of copper and cadmium from the water-soluble fraction of an acid mine waste by two calcareous soils. Soil Sci. 145:207-214.

Dudley, L.M., J.E. McLean, T.H. Furst, and J.J. Jurinak. 1991. Sorption of Cd and Cu from an acid mine waste extract by two calcareous soils: column studies. Soil Sci. 151:121-135.

Dunnivant, F.M., P.M. Jardine, D.L. Taylor, and J.F. McCarthy. 1992. Cotransport of cadmium and hexachlorbiphenyl by dissolved organic carbon through columns containing aquifer material. Environ. Sci. Technol. 26:360-368.

Eary, L.E. and D. Rai. 1991. Chromate reduction by subsurface soils under acidic conditions. Soil Sci. Soc. Am J 55:676-683.

Egozy, Y. 1980. Adsorption of cadmium and cobalt on montmorillonite as a function of solution composition. Clays Clay Min. 28:311-318.

Elkhatib, E.A., O.L. Bennett, and R.J. Wright. 1984a. Kinetics of arsenite sorption in soils. Soil Sci. Soc. Am. J. 48:758-762.

Elkhatib, E.A., O.L. Bennett, and R.J. Wright. 1984b. Arsenite sorption and desorption in soils. Soil Sci. Soc. Am. J. 48:1025-1030.

Elliott, H.A., M.R. Liberati, and C.P. Huang. 1986. Competitive adsorption of heavy metals by soils. J. Environ. Qual. 15:214-219.

Elprince, A.M. and G. Sposito. 1981. Thermodynamic derivation of equations of Langmuir-type for ion equilibrium in soils. Soil Sci. Soc. Am. J. 45:277-282.

Elrashidi, M.A. and G.A. O'Connor. 1982. Influence of solution composition on sorption of zinc by soils. Soil Sci. Soc. Am. J. 46:1153-1158.

Elrashidi, M.A., D.C. Adriano, and W.L. Lindsay. 1989. Solubility, speciation, and of selenium in soils. In L.W. Jacobs (ed.), Selenium in Agriculture and the Environment. American Society of Agronomy. Madison, WI.

Essen, J. and N. El Bassam. 1981. On the mobility of cadmium under aerobic soil conditions. Environ. Pollut. Ser. A. 15-31.

Farrah, H. and W.J. Pickering. 1976a. The adsorption of copper species by clays: I. kaolinite. Aust. J. Chem. 29:1167-1176.

Farrah, H. and W.J. Pickering. 1976b. The adsorption of copper species by clays: II. illite and montmorillonite. Aust. J. Chem. 29:1649-1656.

Fio, J.L., R. Fujii, and S.J. Deveral. 1991. Selenium mobility and distribution in irrigated and non-irrigated alluvial soils. Soil. Sci. Soc. Am. J. 55:1313-1320.

Forbes, E.A., A.M. Posner, and J.P. Quick. 1976. The specific adsorption of divalent Cd, Co, Pb, and Zn on goethite. J. Soil Sci. 27:154-166.

Garcia-Miragaya, J. and A.L. Page. 1976. Influence of ionic strength and complex formation on sorption of trace amounts of Cd by montmorillonite. Soil Sci. Soc. Am. J. 40:658-663.

Garcia-Miragaya, J., R. Cardenas, and A.L. Page. 1986. Surface loading effect on Cd and Zn sorption by kaolinite and montmorillonite from low concentration solutions. Water, Air, and Soil Pollution 27:181-190.

Goldberg, S. and R.A. Glaubig. 1988. Anion sorption on a calcareous montmorillonite soil-selenium. Soil Sci. Soc. Am. J. 52:954-958.

Griffin, R.A. and A.K. Au. 1977. Lead adsorption by montmorillonite using a competitive Langmuir equation. Soil Sci. Soc. Am. J. 41:880-882.

Griffin, R.A. and N.F. Shimp. 1978. Attenuation of pollutants in municipal landfill leachate by clay minerals. EPA-600/2-78-157.

Grove, J.H. and B.G. Ellis. 1980. Extractable chromium as related to soil pH and applied chromium. Soil Sci. Soc. Am J 44:238-242.

Gruebel, K.A., J.A. Davies, and J.O. Leckie. 1988. The feasibility of using sequential extraction techniques for arsenic and selenium in soils and sediments. Soil Sci. Soc. Am. J. 52:390-397.

Gschwend, P.M. and M.D. Reynolds. 1987. Monodisperse ferrous phosphate colloids in an anoxic groundwater plume. J. Contaminant Hydrol. 1:309-327.

Haas, C.N. and N.D. Horowitz. 1986. Adsorption of cadmium to kaolinite in the presence of organic material. Water, Air, and Soil Pollution 27:131-140.

Harrison, R.M., D.P.H. Laxen, and S.J. Wilson. 1981. Chemical associations of lead, cadmium, copper, and zinc in street dust and roadside soils. Environ. Sci. Technol. 15:1378-1383.

Harter, R.D. 1979. Adsorption of copper and lead by Ap and B2 horizons of several northeastern United States soils. Soil Sci Soc. Am. J. 43:679-683.

Harter, R.D. 1983. Effect of soil pH on adsorption of lead, copper, zinc, and nickel. Soil Sci. Soc. Am. J. 47:47-51.

Harter, R.D. 1984. Curve-fit errors in Langmuir adsorption maxima. Soil Sci. Soc. Am. J. 48:749-752.

Harter, R.D. 1992. Competitive sorption of cobalt, copper, and nickel ions by a calcium saturated soil. Soil Sci. Soc. Am. J. 56:444-449.

Harter, R.D. and D.E. Baker. 1977. Application and misapplication of the Langmuir equation to soil adsorption phenomena. Soil Sci. Soc. Am. J. 41:1077-1080.

Harter, R.D. and R.G. Lehmann. 1983. Use of kinetics for the study of exchange reactions in soils. Soil Sci. Soc. Am. J. 47:666-669.

Harter, R.D. and G. Smith. 1981. Langmuir equation and alternative methods of studying "adsorption" reactions in soils. In R.H. Dowdy, J.A. Ryan, V.V. Volk, and D.E. Baker (eds.), Chemistry in the Soil Environment. American Society of Agronomy. Madison, WI.

Hendrickson, L.L. and R.B. Corey. 1981. Effect of equilibrium metal concentration on apparent selectivity coefficients of soil complexes. Soil Sci. 131:163-171.

Hickey, M.G. and J.A. Kittrick. 1984. Chemical partitioning of cadmium, copper, nickel, and zinc in soils and sediments containing high levels of heavy metals. J Environ. Qual. 13:372-376.

Hingston, F.J., A.M. Posner, and J.P. Quick. 1971. Competitive adsorption of negatively charged ligands on oxide surfaces. Faraday Soc. 52:334-342.

Hirsch, D., S. Nir, and A. Banin. 1989. Prediction of cadmium complexation in solution and adsorption to montmorillonite. Soil Sci Soc. Am. J. 53:716-721.

Inskeep, W.P. and J. Baham. 1983. Competitive complexation of Cd(II) and Cu(II) by water-soluble organic ligands and Na-montmorillonite. Soil Sci. Soc. Am. J. 47:1109-1115.

James, B.R. and R.J. Bartlett. 1983a. Behavior of chromium in soils: V. fate of organically complexed Cr(II) added to soil. J. Environ. Qual. 12:169-172.

James, B.R. and R.J. Bartlett. 1983b. Behavior of chromium in soils, VI. Interaction between oxidation-reduction and organic complexation. J. Environ. Qual. 12:173-176.

James, B.J. and R.J. Bartlett. 1983c. Behavior of chromium in soils. VII. Adsorption and reduction of hexavalent forms. J. Environ. Qual. 12:177-181.

James, R.O. and T.W. Healy. 1972. Adsorption of hydrolyzable metal ions at the oxide-water interface: III. thermodynamic model of adsorption. J. Colloid Interface Sci. 40:65-81.

Jenne, E.A. 1968. Control of Mn, Fe, Co, Ni, Cu, and Zn concentrations in soils and water—the dominant role of hydrous manganese and iron oxides. Adv. in Chem. 7:337-387.

Jurinak, J.J. and N. Bauer. 1956. Thermodynamics of zinc adsorption on calcite, dolomite, and magnesite-type minerals. Soil Sci. Soc. Am. Proc. 20:466-471.

Khan, S., D. Nonden, and N.N. Khan. 1982. The mobility of some heavy metals through Indian red soil. Environ. Pollut. Ser. B. 119-125.

Kheboian, C. and C.F. Bauer. 1987. Accuracy of selective extraction procedures for metal speciation in model aquatic sediments. Anal. Chem. 59:1417-1423.

Kinniburgh, D.G. and M.L. Jackson. 1978. Adsorption of mercury (II) by iron hydrous oxide gel. Soil Sci. Soc. Am. J. 42:45-47.

Korte, N.E., J. Skopp, W.H. Fuller, E.E. Niebla, and B.A. Aleshii. 1976. Trace element movement in soils: influence of soil physical and chemical properties. Soil Sci. 122:350-359.

Kotuby-Amacher, J. and R.P. Gambrell. 1988. Factors Affecting Trace Metal Mobility in Subsurface Soils. EPA/600/2-88/036 (NTIS PB88-224829).

Kramer, J.R. and H.E. Allen. 1988. Metal Speciation: Theory, Analysis and Application. Lewis Publishers, Chelsea, MI.

Kuo, S. and A.S. Baker. 1980. Sorption of copper, zinc, and cadmium by some acid soils. Soil Sci. Soc. Am. J. 44:969-974.

Kuo, S. and B.L. McNeal. 1984. Effect of pH and phosphate on cadmium sorption by a hydrous ferric oxide. Soil Sci. Soc. Am. J. 48:1040-1044.

Kuo, S., P.E. Heilman, and A.S. Baker. 1983. Distribution and forms of copper, zinc, cadmium, iron, and manganese in soils near a copper smelter. Soil Sci. 135:101-109.

Kurdi, F. and H.E. Doner. 1983. Zinc and copper sorption an interaction in soils. Soil Sci. Soc. Am. J. 47:873-876.

Lake, D.L., P.W.W. Kirk, and J.N. Lester. 1984. Fractionation, characterization, and speciation of heavy metals in sewage sludge and sludge-amended soils: a review. J. Environ. Qual. 13:175-183.

Latterell, J.J., R.H. Dowdy, and W.E. Larson. 1978. Correlation of extractable metals and metal uptake of snap beans grown on soil amended with sewage sludge. J. Environ. Qual. 7:435-440.

Lehmann, R.G. and R.D. Harter. 1984. Assessment of copper-soil bond strength by desorption kinetics. Soil Sci. Soc. Am. J. 48:769-772.

Lindsay, W.L. 1979. Chemical Equilibria in Soils. John Wiley and Sons. New York.

Loganathan, P. and R.G. Burau. 1973. Sorption of heavy metals by a hydrous manganese oxide. Geochim. Cosmochim. Acta 37:1277-1293.

Martell, A.E. and R.M. Smith. 1974-1982. Critical Stability Constants, 5 Vols., Plenum Press. New York.

Mattigod, S.V. and G. Sposito. 1979. Chemical modeling of trace metals equilibrium in contaminated soil solutions using the computer program GEOCHEM. In E.A. Jenne (ed.), Chemical Modeling in Aqueous Systems. ACS No. 93, Am. Chem. Soc., Washington, D.C.

Mattigod, S.V., G. Sposito, and A.L. Page. 1981. Factors affecting the solubilities of trace metals in soils. In R.H. Dowdy, J.A. Ryan, V.V. Volk, and D.E. Baker (eds.), Chemistry in the Soil Environment. American Society of Agronomy, Madison, WI.

McBride, M.B. 1977. Copper (II) interaction with kaolinite factors controlling adsorption. Clays and Clay Miner. 26:101-106.

McBride, M.B. 1980. Chemisorption of Cd^{2+} on calcite surfaces. Soil Sci. Soc Am J 44:26-28.

McBride, M.B. 1982. Hydrolysis and dehydration reactions of exchangeable Cu^{2+} on hectorite. Clays and Clay Miner. 30:200-206.

McBride, M.B. 1985. Sorption of copper(II) on aluminum hydroxide as affected by phosphate. Soil Sci. Soc. Am. J. 49:843-846.

McBride, M.B. and J.J. Blasiak. 1979. Zinc and copper solubility as a function of pH in an acidic soil. Soil Sci. Soc. Am. J. 43:866-870.

McBride, M.B. and D.R. Bouldin. 1984. Long-term reactions of copper(II) in a contaminated calcareous soil. Soil Sci. Soc. Am. J. 48:56-59.

McLaren, R.G. and D.V. Crawford. 1973. Studies on soil copper: II. the specific adsorption of copper by soils. J. Soil Sci. 24:443-452.

McNeal, J.M. and L.S. Balistrieri. 1989. Geochemistry and occurrence of selenium: an overview. In L.W. Jacobs (ed.), Selenium in Agriculture and the Environment. American Society of Agronomy. Madison, WI.

Miller, W.P., D.C. Martens, and L.W. Zelazny. 1986. Effect of sequence in extraction of trace metals from soils. Soil Sci. Soc. Am. J. 50:598-601.

Neal, R.H. and G. Sposito. 1986. Effects of soluble organic matter and sewage sludge amendments on cadmium sorption by soils at low cadmium concentrations. Soil Sci. 142:164-172.

Neal, R.H. and G. Sposito. 1989. Selenate adsorption on alluvial soils. Soil Sci. Soc. Am. J. 53:70-74.

Neal, R.H., G. Sposito, K.M. Holtzclaw, and S.J. Trania. 1987a. Selenite adsorption on alluvial soils: I. soil composition and pH effects. Soil Sci. Soc. Am. J. 51:1161-1165.

Neal, R.H., G. Sposito, K.M. Holtzclaw, and S.J. Traina. 1987b. Selenite adsorption on alluvial soils: II. composition effects. Soil Sci. Soc. Am. J. 51:1165-1169.

Nordstrom, D.K. and J.L. Munoz. 1985. Geochemical thermodynamics. U.S. Geol. Surv. Benjamin Cummings Publishing Co., Menlo Park, CA.

O'Connor, G.A., R.S. Bowman, M.A. Elrashidi, and R. Keren. 1983. Solute Retention and Mobility in New Mexico Soils: I. Characterization of Solute Retention Reactions. Agric. Exper. Station Bulletin #701. New Mexico State University, Las Cruces, NM.

O'Connor, G.A., C. O'Connor, and G.R. Cline. 1984. Sorption of cadmium by calcareous soils: influence of solution composition. Soil Sci. Soc. Am. J. 48:1244-1247.

Oscarson, D.W., P.M. Huang, W.K. Liaw, and U.T. Hammer. 1983. Kinetics of oxidation of arsenite by various manganese dioxides. Soil Sci. Soc. Am. J. 47:644-648.

Overcash, M.R. and D. Pal. 1979. Design of Land Treatment Systems for Industrial Wastes--Theory and Practice. Ann Arbor Science Publishers, Ann Arbor, MI.

Page, A.L., R.H. Miller, and D.R. Keeney (eds.). 1982. Methods of soil analysis. Part 2. Chemical and Microbiological Properties. American Society of Agronomy. Madison, WI.

Palmer, C.D. and P.R. Wittbrodt. 1991. Processes affecting the remediation of chromium-contaminated sites. Environ. Health Perspectives 92:25-40.

Pierce, M.L. and C.B. Moore. 1980. Adsorption of arsenite on amorphous iron hydroxide from dilute aqueous solution. Environ. Sci. Technol. 14:214-216.

Puls, R.W. and H.L. Bohn. 1988. Sorption of cadmium, nickel, and zinc by kaolinite and montmorillonite suspensions. Soil Sci. Soc. Am. J. 52:1289-1292.

Puls, R.W., R.M. Powell, D. Clark, and C.J. Eldred. 1991. Effect of pH, solid/solution ratio, ionic strength, and organic acids on Pb and Cd sorption on kaolinite. Water, Air, and Soil Pollution 57-58:423-430.

Rai, D., B.M. Sass, and D.A. Moore. 1987. Chromium (III) hydrolysis constants and solubility of chromium (III) hydroxide. Inorg. Chem. 26:345-349.

Rajan, S.S.S. 1979. Adsorption of selenite, phosphate, and sulphate on iron hydrous oxides. J. Soil Sci. 30:709-718.

Rapin, F., A. Tessier, P.G.C. Campbell, and R. Carignan. 1986. Potential artifacts in the determination of metal partitioning in sediments by a sequential extraction procedure. Environ. Sci. Technol. 20:836-840.

Rogers, R.D. 1976. Methylation of mercury in agricultural soils. J. Environ. Qual. 5:454-458.

Rogers, R.D. 1977. Abiological methylation of mercury in soil. J. Environ. Qual. 6:463-467.

Rogers, R.D. 1979. Volatility of mercury from soils amended with various mercury compounds. Soil Sci. Soc. Am. J. 43:289-291.

Santillan-Medrano, J. and J.J. Jurinak. 1975. The chemistry of lead and cadmium in soils: solid phase formation. Soil Sci. Soc. Am. Proc. 29:851-856.

Sheets, P.J. and W.H. Fuller. 1986. Transport of cadmium by organic solvents through soil. Soil Sci. Soc. Am. J. 50:24-28.

Shuman, L.M. 1975. The effect of soil properties on zinc adsorption by soils. Soil Sci. Soc. Am. Proc. 39:454-458.

Shuman, L.M. 1986. Effect of ionic strength and anions on zinc adsorption by two soils. Soil Sci. Soc. Am. J. 50:1438-1442.

Shuman, L.M. 1991. Chemical forms of micronutrients in soils. In J.J. Mortvedt (ed.), Micronutrients in Agriculture. SSSA Book Series #4. Soil Science Society of America, Madison, WI.

Silviera, D.J. and L.E. Sommers. 1977. Extractability of copper, zinc, cadmium, and lead in soils incubated with sewage sludge. J. Environ. Qual. 6:47-52.

Singh, M., N. Singh, and P.S. Relan. 1981. Adsorption and desorption of selenite and selenate selenium on different soils. Soil Sci. 132:134-141.

Sparks, D.L. 1989. Kinetics of Soil Chemical Processes. Academic Press, San Diego, CA.

Sposito, G. 1979. Derivation of the Langmuir equation for ion exchange reactions in soils. Soil Sci. Soc. Am. J. 43:197-198.

Sposito, G. 1982. On the use of the Langmuir equation in the interpretation of adsorption phenomena: II. the "two surface" Langmuir equation. Soil Sci. Soc. Am. J. 46:1147-1152.

Sposito, G. 1989. The Chemistry of Soils. Oxford University Press, New York.

Sposito, G., K.M. Holtzclaw, and C.S. LeVesque-Madore. 1979. Cupric ion complexation by fulvic acid extracted sewage sludge-soil mixtures. Soil Sci. Soc. Am. J. 43:1148-1155.

Sposito, G., K.M. Holtzclaw, and C.S. LeVesque-Madore. 1981. Trace metal complexation by fulvic acid extracted from sewage sludge: I. determination of stability constants and linear correlation analysis. Soil Sci. Soc. Am. J. 45:465-468.

Sposito, G., F.T. Bingham, S.S. Yadav, and C.A. Inwye. 1982. Trace metal complexation by fulvic acid extracted from sewage sludge. II. development of chemical models. Soil Sci. Soc. Am. J. 46:51-56.

Sposito, G., C.S. LeVesque, J.P. LeClaire, and N. Senesi. 1984. Methodologies to Predict the Mobility and Availability of Hazardous Metals in Sludge-Amended Soils. California Water Resource Center. University of California, Davis, CA.

Stahl, R.S. and B.R. James. 1991. Zinc sorption by B horizon soils as a function of pH. Soil Sci. Soc. Am. J. 55:1592-1597.

Stanton, D.A. and R. Du T. Burger. 1970. Studies on zinc selected Orange Free State soils: V. mechanisms for reaction of zinc with iron and aluminum oxides. Agrochemophysica. 2:65-76.

Stevenson, F.J. 1991. Organic matter-micronutrient reactions in soil. In J.J. Mortvedt (ed.), Micronutrients in Agriculture. SSSA Book Series #4. Soil Science Society of America, Madison, WI.

Stevenson, F.J. and A. Fitch. 1986. Chemistry of complexation of metal ions with soil solution organics. In P.M. Huang and M. Schnitzer (eds.), Interactions of Soil Minerals with Natural Organics and Microbes. SSSA Special Publ. No 17. Soil Science Society of America, Madison, WI.

Stollenwerk, K.G. and D.B. Grove. 1985. Adsorption and desorption of hexavalent chromium in an alluvial aquifer near Telluride, Colorado. J. Environ. Qual. 14:150-155.

Tessier, A., P.G.C. Campbell, and M. Bisson. 1979. Sequential extraction procedure for the speciation of particular trace metals. Anal. Chem. 51:844-850.

Tessier, A., P.G.C. Campbell, and M. Bisson. 1980. Trace metal speciation in the Yamaoka and St. Francois Rivers (Quebec). Can. J. Earth Sci. 17:90-105.

Tiller, K.G., J. Gerth, and G. Brummer. 1984. The relative affinities of Cd, Ni, and Zn for different soil clay fractions and goethite. Geoderma. 34:17-35.

Tipping, E., N.B. Hetherington, and J. Hilton. 1985. Artifacts in use of selective chemical extraction to determine distribution of metals between oxides of manganese and iron. Anal. Chem. 57:1944-1946.

Travis, C.C. and E.L. Etnier. 1981. A survey of sorption relationships for reactive solutes in soils. J. Environ. Qual. 10:8-17.

U.S. Environmental Protection Agency (EPA). 1986. Test Methods for Evaluating Solid Waste, 3rd edition. EPA/530/SW-846 (NTIS PB88-239223); First update, 3rd edition. EPA/530/SW-846.3-1 (NTIS PB89-148076). Current edition and updates available on a subscription basis from U.S. Government Printing Office, Stock #955-001-00000-1.

U.S. Environmental Protection Agency (EPA). 1987. MINTEQ2, an Equilibrium Metal Speciation Model: User's Manual. EPA/600/3-87/012. Athens, GA.

Veith, J.A. and G. Sposito. 1977. On the use of the Langmuir equation in the interpretation of adsorption phenomena. Soil Sci. Soc. Am. J. 41:697-702.

Woolson, E.A. 1977a. Fate of arsenicals in different environmental substrate. Environ. Health Perspect. 19:7381.

Woolson, E.A. 1977b. Generation of allsylarsines from soil. Weed Sci. 25:412-416.

Woolson, E.A., J.H. Axley, and P.C. Kearney. 1971. The chemistry and phytotoxicity of arsenic in soils. I. contaminated field soils. Soil Sci. Soc. Am. Proc. 35:938-943.

Zachara, J.M., D.C. Girvin, R.L. Schmidt, and C.T. Resch. 1987. Chromate adsorption on amorphous iron oxyhydroxide in presence of major ground water ions. Environ. Sci. Technol. 21:589-594.

Zachara, J.M., C.E. Cowan, R.L. Schmidt, and C.C. Ainsworth. 1988. Chromate adsorption on kaolinite. Clays and Clay Miner. 36:317-326.

Zachara, J.M., C.C. Ainsworth, C.E. Cowan, and C.T. Resch. 1989. Adsorption of chromate by subsurface soil horizons. Soil Sci. Soc. Am. J. 53:418-428.

Zasoski, R.J. and R.G. Burau. 1988. Sorption and sorptive interaction of cadmium and zinc on hydrous manganese oxide. Soil Sci. Soc. Am. J. 52:81-87.

Chapter 4

Natural Attenuation of Hexavalent Chromium in Ground Water and Soils[1]

Carl D. Palmer, Department of Environmental Science and Engineering, Oregon Graduate Institute of Science & Technology, Beaverton, OR

Robert W. Puls, U.S. EPA, Robert S. Kerr Environmental Research Laboratory, Ada, OK

INTRODUCTION

This chapter focuses on the natural attenuation of hexavalent chromium in soil and ground water. Much of the interest of natural attenuation of chromium stems from the great expense of remediating chromium-contaminated sites. Some of the issues discussed include the conditions that must be present for the necessary processes to occur, changes in toxicity, the time required for target concentrations to be reached, and assurances that chromium in the reduced state will remain immobile.

Chromium is an important industrial metal used in diverse products and processes (Nriagu, 1988a,b). At many locations, Cr has been released to the environment via leakage, poor storage, or improper disposal practices (Palmer and Wittbrodt, 1991; Calder, 1988). Within the environment, Cr is found primarily in two oxidation states: Cr(VI) and Cr(III). Cr(VI) is relatively mobile in the environment and is acutely toxic, mutagenic (Bianchi et al., 1984; Beyersmann et al., 1984; Bonatti et al., 1976; Paschin et al., 1983), teratogenic (Abbasi and Soni, 1984), and carcinogenic (Mancuso and Heuper, 1951; Mancuso, 1951; Waterhouse, 1975; Yassi and Nieboer, 1988; Ono, 1988). In contrast, Cr(III) has relatively low toxicity (van Weerelt et al., 1984) and is immobile under moderately alkaline to slightly acidic conditions.

Concerns about the impact of chromium on human health and the environment require an evaluation of the potential risk of chromium entering the ground water flow system and being transported beyond compliance boundaries. At sites where such potential exists, active remedial measures such as excavation or pump-and-treat have been undertaken. Experience at sites where pump-and-treat remediation of chromium-contaminated ground water is currently under way suggests that, although it is feasible to remove high levels of chromium from the subsurface, as concentrations decrease it becomes more difficult to remove the remaining chromium (Wittbrodt and Palmer, 1992). While several new remedial technologies are being investigated, there is still concern about the cost of such remediation technology; and, at many sites, there is a debate about the need for expensive remediation.

Researchers have identified natural reductants that can transform the more toxic hexavalent form of chromium to the less toxic trivalent form. Under alkaline to slightly acidic conditions, this Cr(III) precipitates as a fairly insoluble hydroxide, thereby immobilizing it within the soil. Such "natural attenuation" of hexavalent chromium is of great interest because it suggests that strict water-quality standards do not have to be attained everywhere within and beneath the site. If natural attenuation does occur, pump-and-treat remediation could desist after the most contaminated ground water has been removed, even if the maximum contaminant level (MCL) has not been achieved. Under certain circumstances, expensive remedial measures may not even be necessary.

In this chapter, what is known about the transformation of chromium in the subsurface is explored. This is an attempt to identify conditions where it is most likely to occur, and describe soil tests that can assist in determining the likelihood of natural attenuation of Cr(VI) in soils.

---

[1] EPA/540/S-94/505.

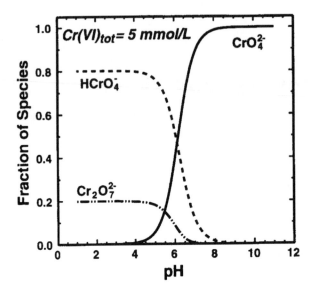

Figure 4-1. Distribution of Cr(VI) species as a function of pH.

THE GEOCHEMISTRY OF CHROMIUM

Chromium exists in oxidation states ranging from +6 to -2, however, only the +6 and +3 oxidation states are commonly encountered in the environment. Cr(VI) exists in solution as monomeric ions $H_2CrO_4^o$, $HCrO_4^-$ (bichromate), and CrO_4^{2-} (chromate), or as the dimeric ion $Cr_2O_7^{2-}$ (dichromate) (e.g., Palmer and Wittbrodt, 1991; Richard and Bourg, 1991). The monomeric species impart a yellow color to the water when the [Cr(VI)] is greater than 1 mg/L. Water that contains high levels of $Cr_2O_7^{2-}$ has an orange color.

The monomeric chromate species are related through a series of acid dissociation reactions

$$H_2CrO_4^o \rightleftarrows HCrO_4^- + H^+ \quad ; K_1$$

$$HCrO_4^- \rightleftarrows CrO_4^{2-} + H^+ \quad ; K_2$$

the pK values are -0.86 and 6.51, respectively (Allison et al., 1990). The dichromate is the result of the polymerization of the monomeric bichromate ions to form the dimer, $Cr_2O_7^{2-}$,

$$HCrO_4^- + HCrO_4^- \rightleftarrows Cr_2O_7^{2-} + H_2O \quad ; K_d$$

where pK_d is -1.54 (Allison et al., 1990). The relative concentration of each of these species depends on both the pH of the contaminated water (Figure 4-1) and the total concentration of Cr(VI) (Figure 4-2). Significant concentrations of $H_2CrO_4^o$ only occur under the extreme condition of pH < 1. Above pH 6.5, CrO_4^{2-} generally dominates. Below pH 6.5, $HCrO_4$ dominates when the Cr(VI) concentrations are low (<30 mM); but $Cr_2O_7^{2-}$ becomes significant when concentrations are greater than 1 mM, or it may even dominate when the total Cr(VI) concentrations are greater than 30 mM.

In the Cr(III)-H_2O system, Cr(III) exists predominantly as Cr^{3+} below pH 3.5. With increasing pH, hydrolysis of Cr^{3+} yields $CrOH^{2+}$, $Cr(OH)_2^+$, $Cr(OH)_3^o$, and $Cr(OH)_4^-$ (Rai et al., 1987). At high concentrations, these ions impart a green color to the solution. Under slightly acidic to alkaline conditions, Cr(III) can precipitate as an amorphous chromium hydroxide.

Amorphous $Cr(OH)_3$ can crystallize as $Cr(OH)_3 \cdot 3H_2O$ or Cr_2O_3 (eskolaite) under different conditions (Swayambunathan et al., 1989). In the presence of Fe(III), trivalent chromium can precipitate as a solid solution. If the pH within the contaminant plume is between 5 and 12, the aqueous concentration of Cr(III) should be less than 1 µmole/L (<0.05 mg/L) (Figure 4-3).

There are several mineral phases that contain Cr(VI) that may be present at chromium-contaminated sites. Palmer and Wittbrodt (1990) identified $PbCrO_4$ (crocoite), $PbCrO_4 \cdot H_2O$ (iranite), and K_2CrO_4

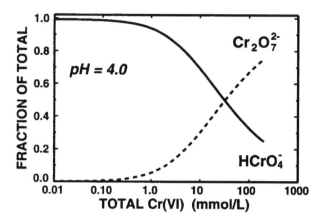

Figure 4-2. Fraction of bichromate ($HCrO_4^-$) and dichromate ($Cr_2O_7^{2-}$) at pH 4 as a function of the total Cr(VI) concentration.

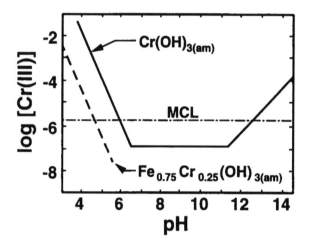

Figure 4-3. Cr(III) concentration in equilibrium with $Cr(OH)_{3(am)}$ and $Fe_{0.75}Cr_{0.25}(OH)_3$, based on data from Rai et al. (1987) and Sass and Rai (1987), respectively.

(tarapacaite) in chromium sludge from a hardchrome plating facility. $CaCrO_4$ was found at a seepage face in a drainage ditch where there was high evaporation. Most of the contaminated ground water was at equilibrium with $BaCrO_4$ (hashemite). $BaCrO_4$ forms a complete solid solution with $BaSO_4$ (Rai et al., 1988) and can be a major impediment to the remediation of chromium-contaminated sites by pump-and-treat (Palmer and Fish, 1992; Wittbrodt and Palmer, 1992).

REDUCTION OF HEXAVALENT CHROMIUM

Cr(VI) is a strong oxidant and is reduced in the presence of electron donors. Electron donors commonly found in soils include aqueous Fe(II), ferrous iron minerals, reduced sulfur, and soil organic matter.

The reduction of Cr(VI) by ferrous iron can be written as

$$HCrO_4^- + 3Fe^{2+} + 7H^+ \rightarrow CR^{3+} + 3Fe^{3+} + 4H_2O$$

This reaction is very fast on the time scales of interest for most environmental problems with the reaction going to completion in less than 5 minutes even in the presence of dissolved oxygen (Eary and Rai, 1988). Only when the pH is greater than 10 or when PO_4 concentrations exceed 0.1 molar does the rate of oxidation of Fe^{2+} by dissolved oxygen exceed the rate of oxidation by Cr(VI) (Eary and Rai, 1988). When the pH of the ground water is greater than 4, Cr(III) precipitates with the Fe(III) in a solid solution with the general composition $Cr_xFe_{1-x}(OH)_3$ (Sass and Rai, 1987; Amonette and Rai, 1990). If the reduction of Cr(VI) by Fe(II) is the only source of Fe(III) and Cr(III), a solid solution with the composition $Cr_{0.25}Fe_{0.75}(OH)_3$ forms via the reaction

$$HCrO_4^- + 3Fe^{2+} + 3H_2O + 5OH^- \rightarrow 4Cr_{0.25}Fe_{0.75}(OH)_3$$

(Eary and Rai, 1988; Sass and Rai, 1987). The solubility of $Cr_xFe_{1-x}(OH)_3$ decreases as the mole fraction of Fe(III) in the solid increases. Therefore, if the pH is between 5 and 12, the concentration of Cr(III) is expected to be less than 10^{-6} molar.

Numerous minerals in geologic materials contain ferrous iron that is potentially available for the reduction of hexavalent chromium. These iron-containing minerals may be silicates, oxides, or sulfides. Common ferrous iron-containing silicates include olivine; pyroxenes such as augite and hedenbergite; the amphiboles hornblende, cummingtonite, and grunerite; micas such as biotite, phlogopite, and glauconite; chlorites, and the smectite nontronite. Iron oxides such as magnetite ($Fe^{2+}Fe_2^{3+}O_4$) contain iron as a major constituent; however, hematite ($Fe_2^{3+}O_3$) can contain small amounts of (FeO). In sulfide minerals such as pyrite (FeS_2), both the ferrous iron and the sulfide are active in reducing hexavalent chromium.

Lancy (1966) suggested that pyrite could be used for treating spent cooling waters that contain Cr(VI) as a corrosion inhibitor. He stated that the reduction of Cr(VI) occurs at the pyrite surface rather than in solution. Lancy (1966) found that reduction by pyrite occurred even in slightly alkaline solutions; however, the pyrite had to be continuously abraded to remove surface coatings. Blowes and Ptacek (1992) conducted batch tests in continuously agitated reaction vessels containing a solution of 18 mg/L Cr(VI) and pyrite both in the presence and in the absence of calcite. In the experiments that used both pyrite and calcite, 50% of the Cr was removed in less than 6.5 hours. Concentrations were < 0.05 mg/L after 20 hours. Experiments conducted without the calcite attained 50% removal in 1 hour and concentrations were < 0.05 mg/L in less than 4 hours.

Cr(VI) reduction in the presence of iron oxides has been observed in several experiments. White and Hochella (1989) found that magnetite and ilmenite reduced Cr(VI) to Cr(III). The reduction of Cr(VI) in the presence of hematite (Fe_2O_3) was demonstrated by Eary and Rai (1989). They attribute the reduction to the presence of a small amount of an FeO component in the hematite. They suggest that reduction occurs in solution after the FeO component has been solubilized.

Reduction of Cr(VI) by ferrous iron-containing silicates has been reported. Eary and Rai (1989) suggest that the reduction of Cr(VI) in the presence of biotite occurs in solution rather than at the mineral surface. They observed an increase in the rate of reduction when their suspensions were spiked with Fe^{3+}. They explain their results with the mechanism proposed by White and Yee (1985) in which Fe^{3+} is reduced at the mineral surface by the reaction

$$[Fe(II), K^+]_{biotite} + Fe^{3+} \rightarrow [Fe(III)]_{biotite} + K^+ + Fe^{2+}$$

where the ions in the brackets denote ions within the crystal structure of biotite. To maintain charge balance, K^+ is released to solution as the iron in the crystal structure is oxidized. The Cr(VI) in solution is then reduced by the Fe^{2+}. The Fe^{3+} resulting from this reduction reaction is then adsorbed to the surface of the biotite where it is again reduced to Fe^{2+}, thus setting up a cycle that ultimately results in the reduction of more Cr(VI) than is stoichiometrically possible for the amount of iron that is in solution.

There are some key experimental difficulties in studying ground water/mineral interactions such as those just described that have some bearing on the transfer of knowledge to the field. Although the processes can in some cases be interpreted from the data on mineral reactions, the rates themselves may be quite useless. A key difficulty in studying mineral reactions in the laboratory is that the rate of the reaction depends on how the solid phase was prepared. For example, if the samples are ground and simply washed before use, microparticles can adhere to the larger grain surfaces. These microparticles have greater specific surface area and can react at a much faster rate than the larger

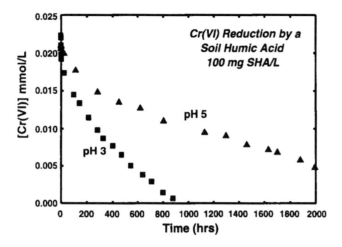

Figure 4-4. Reduction of Cr(VI) in a suspension of 100 mg/L soil humic acid (SHA) at pH 3 and 5 (Wittbrodt and Palmer, 1995).

size particles. Such experimental artifacts were observed in weathering studies of pyroxenes (Schott et al., 1981).

Another important reductant in soils is organic matter. In fact, dichromate reduction has been used as a wet combustion method for the determination of soil organic carbon (Walkley and Black, 1934). Dichromate can react with soil organic carbon according to

$$2Cr_2O_7^{2-} + 3C^\circ + 16H^+ \rightarrow 4Cr^{3+} + 3CO_2 + 8H_2O$$

The Cr^{3+} may hydrolyze and precipitate as Cr-hydroxide or it may bind to the remaining soil organic carbon. Much of the soil organic carbon is present as soil humic and fulvic acids. Redox reaction with these materials has been demonstrated for several redox reactive species. Reduction of Cr(VI) by soil humic and fulvic acids has been demonstrated by Bartlett and Kimble (1976), Bloomfield and Pruden (1980), Goodgame et al. (1984), Boyko and Goodgame (1986), and Stollenwerk and Grove (1985). The rate of reduction of Cr(VI) decreases with increasing pH (Figure 4-4), increases with the increasing initial Cr(VI) concentration, and increases as the concentration of soil humic substance increases. At neutral pH, many weeks may be required for the Cr(VI) to be completely reduced to Cr(III).

In addition to these abiotic reduction pathways, Cr(VI) can be reduced by microbes in the subsurface (Martin et al., 1994). Both aerobic and anaerobic reduction by microbes have been observed; however, the latter is more common. The mechanisms for Cr(VI) reduction by these microbes are not well known. It may be part of a detoxification mechanism that occurs intracellularly. Alternatively, the chromate may be utilized as a terminal electron acceptor as part of the cell's metabolism. A third possibility is that reduction is an extracellular reaction with excreted waste products such as H_2S. In addition to two strains of Gram-positive bacteria, Martin et al. (1994) found a fungus in contaminated soil that was capable of reducing Cr(VI) under anaerobic conditions.

OXIDATION OF CR(III)

Any evaluation of the natural attenuation of Cr(VI) must consider the potential oxidation of the Cr(III) to the toxic Cr(VI) form. In contrast to the numerous pathways for the reduction of Cr(VI), there are very few mechanisms for the oxidation of Cr(III). Only two constituents in the environment are known to oxidize Cr(III) to Cr(VI): dissolved oxygen and manganese dioxides (MnO_2) (Eary and Rai, 1987). Studies of the reaction between dissolved oxygen and Cr(III) revealed very little (Schroeder and Lee, 1975) or no (Eary and Rai, 1987) oxidation of Cr(III) even for experiments conducted at pH as great as 12.5 for 24 days. Therefore, the transformation of Cr(III) by dissolved oxygen is not likely to be an important mechanism for the oxidation of Cr(III).

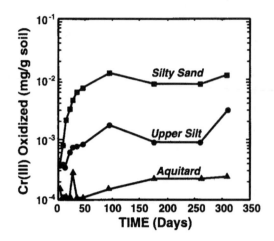

Figure 4-5. Cr(III) oxidized to Cr(VI) in a suspension of Willamette silt loam.

Oxidation of Cr(III) has been observed in several soils and sediments. The oxidation of the Cr(III) can be relatively slow requiring several months (Figure 4-5). For example, Palmer and Wittbrodt (1990) monitored Cr(VI) concentrations in batch tests using three different geologic media from a site in Corvallis, OR. They observed increases in Cr(VI) concentrations over a 300-day period with Cr(VI) concentrations becoming as great as 7 mg/L in one experiment. Bartlett and Kimble (1976) did not observe oxidation of Cr(III) in their dried soils but Bartlett and James (1979) and James and Bartlett (1983a) did observe oxidation in soils that were maintained in a moist state.

Bartlett and James (1979) observed a correlation between the amount of Cr(III) oxidized by soils and the amount of hydroquinone-reduced manganese in soils and suggested the oxidation of Cr(III) is the result of interaction with manganese dioxides. This hypothesis has been experimentally verified using β-MnO$_2$ or pyrolusite (Eary and Rai, 1987) and δ-MnO$_2$ (Fendorf and Zasoski, 1992; Riser and Bailey, 1992). There is an increase in the rate and amount of Cr(III) oxidation as pH decreases, and the surface area to solution volume increases. Experimental results indicate that the oxidation follows the reaction

$$CrOH^{2+} + 1.5 \; \delta\text{-}MnO_2 \rightarrow HCrO_4^- + 1.5Mn^{2+}$$

Significant oxidation of Cr(III) was observed in less than 1 hour (Fendorf and Zasoski, 1992) and continued for more than 600 hours (Eary and Rai, 1987). Eary and Rai (1987) developed an empirical rate law for the oxidation of Cr(III) by β-MnO$_2$; however, the zero point charge for this phase is quite different than birnessite which is more commonly found in soils. Therefore, this rate law may not be applicable to manganese dioxides in soils.

PERSPECTIVE ON THE NATURAL ATTENUATION OF CR(VI)

If hexavalent chromium can be reduced and immobilized in the subsurface as a result of interaction with naturally existing reductants, then expensive remedial measures may not be required at certain sites. In principle, the natural attenuation of Cr(VI) in the subsurface is feasible. There are several natural reductants that can transform Cr(VI) to Cr(III). If the pH of the contaminant plume is between about 5 and 12, Cr(III) precipitates as Cr(OH)$_3$ or as part of a solid solution with Fe(III), thereby keeping Cr(III) concentrations below 1 mole/L (0.05 mg/L). Whether or not natural attenuation at a particular site is a viable option depends on the characteristics of both the aquifer and the contaminant plume under investigation.

The potential reductants of Cr(VI) include aqueous species, adsorbed ions, mineral constituents, and organic matter. When a contaminant plume containing hexavalent chromium enters the subsurface, it displaces the ground water containing the dissolved reductants. There is little mixing of the waters containing the reducing agents and the Cr(VI)-contaminant plume. What mixing does occur will be driven by molecular diffusion at the front of the plume or from the edges of the plume and diffusion from lower permeability lenses containing relatively immobile water. Thus, aqueous reductants such as Fe^{2+} are not going to be important in reducing hexavalent chromium. Mixing of reductants and Cr(VI) in the plume is going to occur primarily through the interactions of the plume with the immobile soil matrix. Such interactions include desorption of reductants such as Fe^{2+} from mineral surfaces, direct and indirect surface redox reactions between Cr(VI) and the mineral surfaces, and reduction by soil organic matter. Thus, it is the soil matrix that is most important with regard to redox transformations of chromium in the subsurface. This argument is further supported by studies that clearly demonstrate that ground water contributes less than 1% of the oxidation capacities (equivalents of Cr oxidized per gram of soil) and reduction capacities (equivalents of Cr reduced per gram of soil) of aquifer systems while the soil matrix contributes the remaining fraction (Barcelona and Holm, 1991). Thus, any discussion of redox transformations of chromium in the subsurface must focus on the soil matrix.

Three key factors must be addressed in considering the potential use of natural attenuation of Cr(VI) in the subsurface. Firstly, the reduction capacity of the aquifer, R_c, must be great enough to reduce all of the Cr(VI) that passes through it. If x_c is the distance from the source to the point of compliance (Figure 4-6), the total mass of Cr(VI) from the source, M_0, must be less than the total mass of Cr(VI), M_r, that can be reduced by the aquifer material between the source and x_c:

$$M_o \leq M_r = x_c A \rho_b R_c \tag{1}$$

where A is the cross-sectional area of the plume normal to the direction of around water flow and $_b$ is the dry bulk density of the aquifer. As x_c increases, the mass of Cr(VI) that can be reduced increases. A key difficulty in applying this criterion is in providing a reasonable estimate of M_0. In the absence of other reactions such as adsorption or precipitation, the minimum rate of movement of the Cr(VI) front through the aquifer, v_{min}, computed by assuming the reductant reacts instantaneously with the Cr(VI), is

$$v_{min} = \frac{v_w}{1 + \dfrac{\rho_b}{\theta_v} \dfrac{R_c}{C_o}} \tag{2}$$

where ρ_b and θ_v are the dry bulk volumetric water content of the porous medium, v_w is the velocity of the ground water, and C_0 is the concentration of the chromium in the contaminant plume.

The second key factor in the application of natural attenuation of Cr(VI) is the rate of reduction relative to the rate of advective transport in the subsurface. The time for the reduction reaction to decrease the concentration from its initial concentration, C_0, to some target concentration, C_s, such as a drinking water standard, should be less than the residence time of the contaminated water in the portion of the aquifer between the source of the Cr(VI) and the point of compliance. For example, if the rate of reduction of Cr(VI) follows a first-order rate equation

$$\frac{dC}{dt} = -kC \tag{3}$$

the time for the concentration of Cr(VI) to decrease from C_0 to C_s must be less than the residence time of the contaminated parcel of water within the aquifer:

$$\frac{\ln(C_o / C_s)}{k} \leq \frac{x_c}{v_w} \tag{4}$$

If natural attenuation is to be a viable option, this criterion must be met. Difficulties in utilizing this criterion arise in applying the appropriate rate equation and obtaining the pertinent rate coefficients.

A third factor concerning the natural attenuation of Cr(VI) is the possible oxidation of Cr(III) to the more toxic hexavalent form. While contamination is actively entering the subsurface, conditions

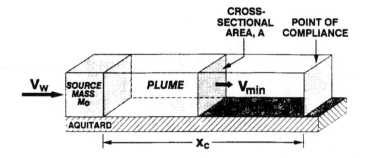

Figure 4-6. Cr-plume moving from the source area to the point of compliance. The initial Cr(VI) concentration in the source area is M_0, V_w is the ground water velocity, v_{min} is the velocity of the Cr(VI) front assuming instantaneous reduction of the Cr(VI), and x_c is the distance from the source area to the point of compliance.

may favor the reduction of Cr(VI) to Cr(III). After the source of the active contamination is removed, however, chemical parameters within the aquifer, particularly pH, may be altered. Under the new conditions, oxidation of Cr(III) may be favored. Thus, soil containing Cr(III) formed during the active contamination phase may become a source of Cr(VI).

Both oxidation and reduction of chromium are occurring simultaneously within the subsurface as part of a geochemical cycle. As the Cr(III) is oxidized to Cr(VI) by manganese dioxides in the soil, Cr(VI) can be reduced to Cr(III) by some reductant such as soil organic carbon or pyrite. The rate of change in [Cr(VI)] (d[Cr(VI)]/dt) is the sum of the rate of reduction of Cr(VI), R_{red}, and the rate of oxidation of Cr(III), R_{ox}:

$$\frac{d[Cr(VI)]}{dt} = \left[\frac{[Cr(VI)]}{dt}\right]_{red} + \left[\frac{[Cr(VI)]}{dt}\right]_{ox} = R_{red} + R_{ox} \tag{5}$$

If a soil initially contains both Cr(VI) and Cr(III), then [Cr(VI)] increases when $R_{red} + R_{ox} > 0$ and decreases when $R_{red} + R_{ox} < 0$. Ultimately, the [Cr(VI)] will reach a steady state; i.e., d[Cr(VI)]/dt = 0. At this time, the rate of loss of Cr(VI) via reduction is balanced by the rate of production by the oxidation of Cr(III):

$$-R_{red} = R_{ox} \tag{6}$$

Wittbrodt and Palmer (1995) suggest that the reduction of Cr(VI) by soil fulvic acid can be represented by

$$R_{red} = -k_{red} \, X_e^{-1} \, [HCrO_4^-][SHS][H^+]^p \tag{7}$$

where [SHS] is the concentration of soil humic substance and X_e denotes the equivalent fraction of the humic substance that has been oxidized. Fendorf and Zasoski (1992) suggest that $CrOH^{2+}$ is the reactive species in the oxidation of Cr(III) by MnO_2. For illustrative purposes, assume that the oxidation reaction follows a rate equation of the form

$$R_{ox} = k_{ox} \, [CrOH^{2+}][A/V]^m \, [H^+]^n \tag{8}$$

where (A/V) denotes the surface area of the MnO_2 per unit volume of solution. If we further assume that the solution is equilibrated with $Cr(OH)_{3(am)}$, then

$$R_{ox} = k_{ox} \, (K/K_w^2)(A/V)^m \, [H^+]^{n+2} \tag{9}$$

where K_w is the dissociation constant for H_2O and K is the equilibrium constant for the reaction

$$Cr(OH)_{3(am)} \rightleftarrows Cr(OH)^{2+} + 2(OH^-)$$

Equating R_{ox} with $-R_{red}$ and rearranging the terms yields

$$\left[HCrO_4^-\right] = \frac{kox}{kred} \frac{K}{K_W^2} Xe \frac{(A / V)^m}{[SHS]} [H^+]^{n+2-p} \tag{10}$$

Although some of the specific points of rate equations presented here are debatable, equation 10 does illustrate aspects of natural attenuation in soils that contain both a reductant and MnO_2. The key point is that as long as the supply of reductant and MnO_2 have not been significantly depleted, $[HCrO_4^-]$ does not converge to zero with increasing residence time within the aquifer as one would expect for a first-order reaction that only considers reduction of Cr(VI). Rather, $[HCrO_4^-]$ converges to some steady-state concentration that is > O that may or may not be above the MCL. This steady-state concentration increases with increasing k_{ox}/k_{red}, and $(A/V)^m/[SHS]$ and it varies with pH. Thus, in principle, if the rate equations are correct and all of the parameters are known, one could calculate the steady-state Cr(VI) concentration and determine if natural attenuation could achieve compliance goals. Studies of the kinetics of these coupled processes need to be done to verify the general forms of the rate equations and to determine the appropriate rate coefficients.

DETERMINING THE POTENTIAL FOR NATURAL ATTENUATION

If "natural attenuation" is to be considered an alternative to expensive remediation efforts, additional characterization is required to demonstrate that the expectations are likely to be met. There is no single test that can tell us if natural attenuation of Cr(VI) will occur at a particular site. Several tests are briefly described which have been utilized to address key factors affecting Cr(VI) transport in the subsurface and describe how the results can be utilized in determining the potential for the natural attenuation of Cr(VI) in the subsurface.

Ideally, it must be demonstrated that 1) there are natural reductants present within the aquifer, 2) the amount of Cr(VI) and other reactive constituents does not exceed the capacity of the aquifer to reduce them, 3) the rate of Cr(VI) reduction is greater than the rate of transport of the aqueous Cr(VI) from the site, 4) the Cr(III) remains immobile, and 5) there is no net oxidation of Cr(III) to Cr(VI). Some of these criteria are relatively simple while others require additional tests and interpretation. Additional tests that will be required include tests of the oxidizing and reducing capacities of the aquifer.

Mass of Cr(VI) at the Source

It must be demonstrated that the amount of Cr(VI) in the aquifer does not exceed the capacity of the soil for reducing this chromium. Therefore, an important first step in evaluating the potential for natural attenuation is to determine the mass of Cr(VI) in the soil. Chromium exists in the subsurface either in solution or in association with the solid phase. Cr(VI) in solution can be determined by the diphenylcarbazide (DPC) method (APHA, 1989). Aqueous samples are most often obtained from monitoring wells. Alternatively, water separates from the soil matrix either by centrifugation or by squeezing. The pH of these waters should be measured to determine if it is within the proper range (5.5 to 12) to ensure the Cr(III) concentrations are less than 1 μM (0.05 mg/L).

Cr(VI) associated with the soil matrix may be adsorbed to mineral surfaces (particularly iron oxides) or precipitated as chromate minerals. There is no precise method for determining each of these fractions of Cr(VI); nonetheless, determinations have been made using sequential extractions. An initial water extraction serves to remove remaining pore water and dissolve highly soluble chromium minerals present in the soil or that may have precipitated as the result of evaporation during sample handling and storage. This water extraction also removes some adsorbed ions.

Following the water extraction, a phosphate extraction is used as a measure of the "exchangeable" chromate in the soil (Bartlett and James, 1988). The test is conducted by adding phosphate to the soil and equilibrating for 24 hours. The water is then separated from the slurry and Cr(VI) is measured by the DPC method (Bartlett and Kimble, 1976; Bartlett and James, 1988). The increase in the chromate concentration is the amount of "exchangeable" chromate. Amacher and Baker (1982) found optimal extraction using 0.01 M monobasic potassium phosphate (KH_2PO_4). James and Bartlett (1983b) used a solution of 0.005 M KH_2PO_4 and 0.05 M K_2HPO_4 to yield a pH of 7.2. James and Bartlett (1983b) stated that doing the extraction at pH 7.2 is preferred because there is less likelihood of chromate reduction than at lower pH. However, decreasing the pH of the soil slurry can result in dissolution of $BaCrO_4$ from the soil. Moreover, if the pH of the soil water was initially low, then increasing the pH to 7.2 can cause precipitation of $BaCrO_4$, thereby complicating the interpretation of the results. When the soil water is not equilibrated with $BaCrO_4$, the phosphate extraction method of James and Bartlett (1983b) primarily measures the amount of adsorbed Cr(VI) in the soil. The phosphate removes chromate by both directly competing for the adsorption sites in the soil and indirectly (in some cases) by increasing the pH.

BaCrO_4 is a likely chromate mineral phase that can be a source of Cr(VI) in contaminated aquifers. There is no direct test for $BaCrO_4$ in soils, however, when the ground water is equilibrated with this phase and the source of the Ba^{2+} is entirely from the clays in the natural soil, the maximum amount of $BaCrO_4$ in the aquifer is equal to the ammonium acetate exchangeable Ba^{2+} (Thomas, 1982) in background soils. For example, Palmer and Wittbrodt (1990) found that the amount of exchangeable Ba^{2+} was useful in estimating the number of pore volumes required to flush Cr(VI) from soil columns.

At many sites, the total Cr(VI) associated with the soil matrix is the sum of the $BaCrO_4$ and the PO_4-extractable Cr(VI). This sum, S, is often reported in units of mass per gram of soil. The total concentration of Cr(VI) in the soil, $Cr(VI)_{tot}$ is the sum of the aqueous Cr(VI) and the matrix associated Cr(VI), S, which can be reported in common units of mass per unit volume of water by

$$Cr(VI)_{tot} = [Cr(VI)] + \frac{1000\rho b}{\theta_v} S \qquad (11)$$

where the dry bulk density of the soil, ρ_b, is in $g\text{-}cm^{-3}$. The total mass of Cr(VI) in the site soils can then be estimated by integrating the concentrations over the volume of contaminated soil.

Mass of Cr(III) in the Subsurface

If all of the chromium that entered the soil was Cr(VI), then demonstrating the presence of Cr(III) in the soil would prove that reduction is occurring. The mass of Cr(III) in the soil can provide a measure of the amount of reduction that has occurred. Although proof of chromate reduction is necessary, it is not sufficient for demonstrating that natural attenuation will adequately protect the environment.

The total amount of Cr(III) present in the soil is the sum of the mass in solution as well as mass associated with the solid phase. Total chromium in solution can be determined by atomic absorption spectrophotometry (AAS) or inductively coupled plasma spectroscopy (ICP). When total chromium is statistically greater than Cr(VI), Cr(III) can be simply determined by difference.

The amount of Cr(III) associated with the soil matrix has ostensibly been determined using several techniques. An ammonium oxalate (0.1 M) extraction serves to remove amorphous hydroxides of Cr, Fe, and Al (Ku et al., 1978; Borggaard, 1988). Bartlett (1991) suggests that a K_2H-citrate extraction provides a measure of the Cr(III) that is potentially removable by low molecular weight organic molecules. A dithionate-citrate-bicarbonate (DCB) extraction is conducted by adding 0.3 M sodium citrate and 0.1 M sodium bicarbonate to the soil sample and heating to 80°C for 20 minutes. One gram of sodium dithionate is then added and the soil slurry is stirred for another 15 minutes. The DCB extraction removes the crystalline forms of the Cr-, Fe-, and Al-oxyhydroxides (Ku et al., 1978; Borggaard, 1988). The dithionate reduces crystalline iron (goethite) in the soil and Cr, Fe, and Al are complexed by the citrate. In addition to the Cr(III) oxyhydroxides, the DCB method also extracts sparingly soluble Cr(VI) mineral phases such as $BaCrO_4$, thereby complicating interpretation of the results. Bartlett (1991) uses 40 mL per gram of soil of 0.7 M NaOCl solution (undiluted laundry bleach) at pH 9.5 to extract chromium. The slurry is placed in a boiling water bath for 20 minutes before the liquid is separated and Cr is determined by AAS or ICP. This method is useful in determining total chromium in the soil because it readily oxidizes and removes Cr(III) that is not removed by other methods.

Identification of Potential Reductants

The presence of Cr(III) in the soil may be indicative of active reduction in the soil, or it may be the result of the neutralization of acidic waters containing Cr(III) with subsequent precipitation of chromium hydroxides. Therefore, identification of specific reductants within the aquifer is warranted. The identification of some potential reductants at a site can be fairly simple in some cases. For example, pyrite (FeS_2), a common constituent in many geological materials, is readily identifiable by its visual characteristics. Other mineral phases capable of reducing Cr(VI) can be identified using classical petrographic techniques or powder X-ray diffraction. Scanning electron microscopy (SEM) can be utilized to identify crystallite morphology. SEMs equipped with energy dispersive X-ray spectroscopy can also provide information about the elemental composition of these crystallites. Electron diffraction patterns obtained from transmission electron microscopes provide crystallographic information. Such electron microscopy methods can, however, be relatively expensive. A fairly simple and inexpensive test for organic carbon can provide a measure of the amount of carbon available for reduction of Cr(VI). Knowledge of the specific reductant within the aquifer is useful in determining the time scale for the reduction of Cr(VI) based on studies that are reported in the literature. Soils containing iron sulfides or organic matter are more likely to reduce Cr(VI) on the time scales of interest than soils containing ferrous iron silicates.

Reduction Capacity of the Aquifer

Adequate protection of the environment by natural attenuation of Cr(VI) requires that the soil possess a large enough reducing capacity to reduce all the hexavalent chromium in the source area. Several measures for predicting reduction of Cr(VI) in soil are presented by Bartlett and James (1988) and Bartlett (1991). A measure of the maximum amount of Cr(VI) that can be reduced per unit mass of aquifer, the "total Cr(VI) reducing capacity," can be obtained using the classical Walkley-Black method for determining soil organic carbon (Bartlett and James, 1988). In this method, 2 to 3 grams of soil are reacted with a mixture of $1N$ $K_2Cr_2O_7$ in $1N$ H_2SO_4 for 30 minutes (Walkley and Black, 1934; Nelson and Sommers, 1982; Bartlett and James, 1988). The Cr(VI) concentration is measured using the diphenylcarbazide (DPC) method (APHA, 1989) and the decrease in the mass of Cr(VI) in the reaction vessel per gram of soil used in the test is the reduction capacity. Although this method of determining soil organic carbon has its limitations (e.g., Nelson and Sommers, 1982), it is a direct measure of how much Cr(VI) can be reduced by a soil at extreme acid concentrations. Variations on this method use heat or a combination of heat and pressure (Nelson and Sommers, 1982). Barcelona and Holm (1991) used a modified closed-tube chemical oxygen demand procedure (U.S. EPA, 1979) to determine reduction capacities.

The extreme conditions of pH and temperature used in the total Cr(VI) reducing capacity test may yield a greater reducing capacity than would be available under most environmental conditions. The "available reducing capacity" test of Bartlett and James (1988) determined the reduction capacity by reacting about 4 to 5 grams of moist soil in a solution of 10 mM H_3PO_4 and $K_2Cr_2O_7$ for 18 hours. The H_3PO_4 is added to buffer the pH and to compete with the Cr(VI) for the adsorption sites. When KH_2PO_4 is used Bartlett and James referred to it as the "reducing intensity." These tests are designed to determine the reducing capacity at pH values more likely to be encountered in the field. However, in long-term reduction tests at near neutral pH, Palmer and Wittbrodt (unpublished data) observed reduction occurring after 250 days (Figure 4-7). Such long-term reduction tests are not practical at most waste sites.

Oxidation Capacity

A potential limitation to the use of natural attenuation of Cr(VI) in soil is the oxidation of the Cr(III) to Cr(VI) by MnO_2. If the oxidizing capacity of the soil is greater than the reduction capacity, then as the chromium is cycled in the soil it could exhaust the soil reductant and be oxidized and ultimately mobilized in the soil. It is important, therefore, to determine the capacity of the aquifer to oxidize Cr(III).

Bartlett and James (1988) suggest a relatively simple test for the amount of Cr(III) that can be oxidized by a soil. The method involves adding 2.5 grams of soil to a solution containing 25 mL of 1 mM $CrCl_3$. After shaking for 15 minutes, a solution of $KH_2PO_4 \cdot K_2HPO_4$ is added to the reaction

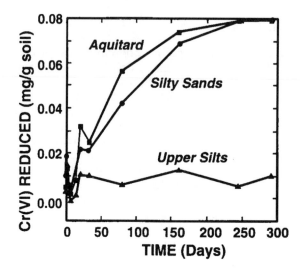

Figure 4-7. Cr(VI) reduced to Cr(III) in Willamette silt loam.

vessel, the slurry centrifuged or filtered, and the Cr(VI) measured using the DPC method. Moist soils should be used in these tests. Drying the soils alters the surfaces of the manganese dioxides, making them less reactive (Bartlett and James, 1979).

Barcelona and Holm (1991) used a solution of chromous (Cr(II)) ion to measure the oxidation capacity of soils. They added about 1 g of soil to cuvettes containing the Cr(II) solution. The work was performed in a glove box to prevent oxygen from reacting with the Cr(II). The cuvettes were sealed, shaken, and allowed to react for 2 hours. The samples were centrifuged and the Cr(II) measured spectrophotometrically. The loss of Cr(II) is then used as a measure of the oxidation capacity of the soils.

Each of these methods has some problems. Palmer and Wittbrodt (unpublished data) conducted oxidation tests similar to the Bartlett and James (1988) method except that the concentration of Cr(VI) was monitored over nearly a year. Cr(VI) concentrations in these tests continued to increase up to 100 days and may have been continuing after 300 days. For one soil, the short-term oxidation test of Bartlett and James underestimated the amount of oxidation obtained in the long-term tests by more than an order of magnitude. It is not clear in the Barcelona and Holm method whether the Cr(II) is being oxidized to Cr(III) or Cr(VI) or some combination of the two. If both products are forming, the results are more difficult to interpret.

If the only mechanism for the oxidation of Cr(III) in soils is oxidation by manganese oxides, then using extraction methods specifically designed for this purpose may be a good way of determining the oxidation capacity of the soils. One very simple extraction technique (Chao, 1972; Gambrell and Patrick, 1982) utilizes 0.1 M hydroxylamine hydrochloride ($NH_2OH \cdot HCl$) in 0.1 M HNO_3. About 0.5 g of soil is added to 25 mL $NH_2OH \cdot HCl$ of the solution and shaken for 30 minutes and the Mn concentration is measured. The number of moles of Cr(III) that can be oxidized is then computed by dividing the number of moles of Mn^{2+} per gram of soil obtained in the extraction be 1.5. The hydroxylamine hydrochloride test is fast, easy, and specifically targets the phase that promotes the oxidation of Cr(III).

Rates of Oxidation and Reduction

Key factors in the suitability of natural attenuation as an option for chromium-contaminated soils are the rates of oxidation and reduction of chromium. This information is the most difficult to obtain. Scientists are only now learning about the form of the applicable rate equations and the appropriate rate coefficients that may apply. Such kinetic studies are an area where research has lagged behind the practical need for the information. While rates can be obtained from the technical literature, one must be careful to use rates of reduction for materials that are most likely controlling the Cr(VI) reduction in the site soil. In addition, because the rates depend on the concentration (surface area per liter of solution) of the reductant and pH, it is important to obtain rate coefficients that were acquired under conditions similar to those at the site. Many rate studies have considered only a limited set of conditions such as a single pH value or one reductant concentration. Consequently, the reported rate coefficients are apparent values that are strictly valid only under the conditions of the experiment. Thus, the experimental factors must be taken into account before the rate coefficients can be applied to field problems.

When MnO_2 is present, Cr(III) may be oxidized back to Cr(VI) and the net rate of reduction will be less than that obtained from experiments that only utilize reductants. Further, many rate experiments are conducted in stirred reactors that can abrade reactive surfaces. In soils, the rate of reaction may become surface limited as adsorbed ions and precipitates cover the reactive surfaces.

One method of obtaining the net rate of reduction is through tests on uncontaminated soils obtained from the site. These soils should be similar to those through which the contaminant plume will be migrating. Cr(VI) can be added to the soil slurry and the Cr(VI) concentrations monitored over time. The reaction vessels must exclude light to prevent photoreduction reactions and the slurry must have the same pH as the contaminant plume. A key limitation to such experiments is that they require several months to a year to complete.

Estimating Reduction from Monitoring Well Data

In principle, Cr(VI) reduction can be estimated from the decrease in the mass of Cr(VI) in the aquifer (e.g., Henderson, 1994). The key difficulty in such an approach is to estimate the mass of Cr(VI) using the aqueous concentrations. The total mass of Cr(VI) in the aquifer is the sum of the mass that is in solution, the mass that is adsorbed to the aquifer matrix, and the mass that is precipitated within the aquifer. The mass of Cr(VI) in solution is obtained by integrating the Cr(VI) concentrations over the volume of the contaminated aquifer

$$M_{aq} = \theta_v \, CV \qquad (12)$$

where V is the volume of aquifer containing a plume with a Cr(VI) concentration of C.

The mass of Cr(VI) adsorbed to the soil matrix, M_{ads}, can be computed from the adsorption isotherm. For example, if Cr(VI) follows a Langmuir isotherm, then over a volume of aquifer, V, with constant aqueous Cr(VI) concentration, C, M_{ads} can be computed as

$$M_{ads} = \rho b \left[\frac{S_{max} K_{ads} C}{1 + K_{ads} C} \right] V(1 - \theta v) \qquad (13)$$

where K_{ads} is the Langmuir adsorption constant, and S_{max} is the maximum amount of contaminant that can be adsorbed to the soil.

There is no unique amount of Cr(VI) precipitate for a given hexavalent chromium concentration. Therefore, it is impossible to estimate mass of this fraction of Cr(VI) in the subsurface using only the measured concentrations in monitoring wells. Thus, natural attenuation of Cr(VI) from mass balances using monitoring well data can only be used when it can be reasonably demonstrated the Cr(VI) precipitates cannot form within the aquifer.

Even when it is demonstrated that the formation of precipitates within the aquifer is unlikely, there are inherent problems with any monitoring system that can create uncertainties in the estimated mass of Cr(VI) during a sampling round. In the three-dimensional flow field, the highest concentrations from one sampling period may migrate between the discrete monitoring points of the next sampling round. The undetected mass is not included in the total mass estimates in the second sampling round and may be mistakenly interpreted as mass loss due to Cr(VI) reduction.

SUMMARY

Under certain conditions, toxic Cr(VI) can be reduced to the less toxic Cr(III) in soils and precipitated as an insoluble hydroxide phase. The possibility of relying on such "natural attenuation" of

Cr(VI) is attractive because of the great expense of remediating chromium-contaminated sites. Before such an option is adopted, however, it should be demonstrated that natural attenuation is likely to occur under the specific conditions at the site being investigated.

If natural attenuation is to be considered a viable option for chromium-contaminated sites, then ideally, it must be demonstrated that 1) there are natural reductants present within the aquifer, 2) the amount of Cr(VI) and other reactive constituents does not exceed the capacity of the aquifer to reduce them, 3) the time scale required to achieve the reduction of Cr(VI) to the target concentration is less than the time scale for the transport of the aqueous Cr(VI) from source area to the point of compliance, 4) the Cr(III) will remain immobile, and 5) there is no net oxidation of Cr(III) to Cr(VI). The most difficult information to obtain are the time scales for the reduction and oxidation of chromium in the soil.

Demonstrating Cr(VI) reduction in aquifer by mass balances that rely primarily on the aqueous concentrations from monitoring well networks are valid only if it is demonstrated that Cr(VI) precipitates are not forming in the aquifer. The monitoring network must be sufficiently dense that estimates of Cr(VI) are accurate.

Several soil tests are described that are useful in determining the mass of Cr(VI) and Cr(III) in the source areas and the reduction and oxidation capacities of the aquifer materials. Some simple conceptual models are presented whereby this information, combined with knowledge of the residence time of the chromium between the source and the point of compliance, can be used to determine the feasibility of natural attenuation of Cr(VI). The major limitation to this approach is the lack of information about the rate of oxidation and reduction of chromium under conditions likely to be encountered by plumes emanating from chromium sources. Without better information about these rate processes under a wider range of conditions with respect to pH, the use of the natural attenuation option for contaminated soils will continue to be a highly debated issue.

EPA CONTACT

For further information contact: Robert Puls, 405/436-8543, at RSKERL-Ada.

REFERENCES

Abbasi, S.A. and R. Soni. 1984. Teratogenic Effects of Chromium(VI) in the Environment as Evidenced by the Impact of Larvae of Amphibian *Rand tigrina*: Implications in the Environmental Management of Chromium. Int. J. Environmental Studies, 23:131–137.

Allison, J.D., D.S. Brown, and K.J. Novo-Gradac. 1990. MINTEQA2/PRODEFA2, A Geochemical Assessment Model for Environmental Systems: Version 3.0. U.S. Environmental Protection Agency, Athens, GA.

Amacher, M.C. and D.E. Baker. 1982. Redox Reactions Involving Chromium, Plutonium and Manganese in Soils. DOE/DP/04515-1. Institute for Research on Land and Water Resources, Pennsylvania State University and U.S. Department of Energy, Las Vegas, NV.

Amonette, J.E. and D. Rai. 1990. Identification of Noncrystalline (Fe,Cr)(OH)$_3$ by Infrared Spectroscopy. Clays and Clay Minerals, 38(2):129–136.

APHA. 1989. Standard Methods for the Examination of Water and Wastewater, 17th Edition. American Public Health Association, Washington, D.C. [Editor's note: 19th edition published 1995 in cooperation with Water Environmental Federation and American Water Works Association.]

Barcelona, M.J. and T.R. Holm. 1991. Oxidation-Reduction Capacities of Aquifer Solids. Environ. Sci. Technol., 25:1565–1572.

Bartlett, R.J. 1991. Chromium Cycling in Soils: Links, Gaps, and Methods. Environmental Health Perspectives, 92:17–24.

Bartlett, R.J. and J.M. Kimble. 1976. Behavior of Chromium in Soils: II. Hexavalent Forms. J. Environ. Qual., 5(4):383–386.

Bartlett, R.J. and B.R. James. 1979. Behavior of Chromium in Soils: III. Oxidation. J. Environ. Qual., 8(1):31–35.

Bartlett, R.J. and B.R. James. 1988. Mobility and Bioavailability of Chromium in Soils. In: J.O. Nriagu and E. Nieboer (eds.), Chromium in the Natural and Human Environments, Vol. 20. John Wiley & Sons, New York, pp. 267–306.

Beyersmann, D., A. Koester, B. Buttner, and P. Flessel. 1984. Model Reactions of Chromium Compounds with Mammalian and Bacterial Cells. Toxicol. Environ. Chem., 8:279–286.

Bianchi, V., A. Zantedeschi, A. Montaldi, and F. Majone. 1984. Trivalent Chromium is Neither Cytotoxic nor Mutagenic in Permealized Hamster Fibroblasts. Toxicological Letters, 23:51–59.

Bloomfield, C. and G. Pruden. 1980. The Behavior of Cr(VI) in Soil under Aerobic and Anaerobic Conditions. Environmental Pollution (Series A), 23:103–114.

Blowes, D.W. and C.J. Ptacek. 1992. Geochemical Remediation of Groundwater by Permeable Reactive Walls: Removal of Chromate by Reaction with Iron-Bearing Solids. In: Proceeding of the Subsurface Restoration Conference, June 21–24, 1992, Dallas, TX. Rice University, Houston, TX, pp. 214–216.

Bonatti, S., M. Meini, and A. Abbondandolo. 1976. Genetic Effects of Potassium Chromate in *Schizosaccharomyces pombe*. Mutat. Res., 38:147–149.

Borggaard, O.K. 1988. Phase Identification by Selective Dissolution Techniques. In: J.W. Stucki et al. (eds.), Iron in Soils and Clay Minerals. Reidel Publishing Co., pp. 83–98.

Boyko, S.L. and D.M.L. Goodgame. 1986. The Interaction of Soil Fulvic Acid and Chromium (VI) Produces Relatively Long-Lived Water Soluble Chromium(V) Species. Inorg. Chim. Acta, 123:189–191.

Calder, L.M. 1988. Chromium Contamination of Groundwater. In: J.O. Nriagu and E. Nieboer (eds.), Chromium in the Natural and Human Environments, Vol. 20. John Wiley & Sons, New York, pp. 215–230.

Chao, T.T. 1972. Selective Dissolution of Manganese Oxides from Soils and Sediments with Acidified Hydroxylamine Hydrochloride. Soil Sci. Soc. Am. Proc., 36:764–768.

Eary, L.E. and D. Rai. 1989. Kinetics of Chromate Reduction by Ferrous Ions Derived from Hematite and Biotite at 25°C. Am. J. Sci., 289:180–213.

Eary, L.E. and D. Rai. 1987. Kinetics of Chromium(III) Oxidation to Chromium(VI) by Reaction with Manganese Dioxides. Environ. Sci. Technol., 21(12):1187–1193.

Eary, L.E. and D. Rai. 1988. Chromate Removal from Aqueous Wastes by Reduction with Ferrous Iron. Environ. Sci. Technol., 22(8):972–977.

Fendorf, S.E. and R.J. Zasoski. 1992. Chromium (III) Oxidation by 13-MnO2. 1. Characterization. Environ. Sci. Technol., 26:79–85.

Gambrell, R.P. and W.H. Patrick. 1982. Manganese. In: A.L. Page et al. (eds.), Methods of Soil Analysis, Part 2. American Society of Agronomy, Madison, WI, pp. 313–322.

Goodgame, D.M.L., P.B. Hayman, and D.E. Hathway. 1984. Formation of Water Soluble Chromium(V) by the Interaction of Humic Acid and the Carcinogenic Chromium(VI). Inorg. Chim. Acta., 91:113–115.

Henderson, T. 1994. Geochemical Reduction of Hexavalent Chromium in the Trinity Sand. Ground Water, 32(3):477–486.

James, B.R. and R.J. Bartlett. 1983a. Behavior of Chromium in Soils. VI. Interactions Between Oxidation-Reduction and Organic Complexation. J. Environ. Qual., 12:173–176.

James, B.R. and R.J. Bartlett. 1983b. Behavior of Chromium in Soils: VII. Adsorption and Reduction of Hexavalent Forms. J. Environ. Qual. 12(2):177–181.

Ku, H.F.H., B.G. Katz, D.J. Sulam, and R.K. Krulikas. 1978. Scavenging of Chromium and Cadmium by Aquifer Material, South Farmingdale Massapequa Area, Long Island, New York. Ground Water, 16(2):112–118.

Lancy, L.E. 1966. Treatment of Spent Cooling Waters. U.S. Patent 3,294,960.

Mancuso, T.F. 1951. Occupational Cancer and Other Health Hazards in a Chrome Plant. A Medical Appraisal. II. Clinical and Toxicological Aspects. Ind. Med. Surg., 20:393–407.

Mancuso, T.F. and W.C. Heuper. 1951. Occupational Cancer and Other Health Hazards in a Chrome Plant. A Medical Appraisal. I. Lung Cancers in Chromate Workers. Ind. Med. Surg., 20:358–363.

Martin, C., D.R. Boone, and C.D. Palmer. 1994. Chromate-Resistant Microbes from Contaminated Soil and Their Potential for Bioaugmented Reduction of Cr(VI). In: Proc. Eighth Nat. Outdoor Action Conf. on Aquifer Restoration, Ground Water Monitoring and Geophysical Methods. National Ground Water Association, Dublin, OH, pp. 191–204.

Nelson, D.W. and L.E. Sommers. 1982. Total Carbon, Organic Carbon, and Organic Matter. In: A.L. Page et al. (eds.), Methods of Soil Analysis, Part 2, American Society of Agronomy, Madison, WI, pp. 539–580.

Nriagu, J.O. 1988a. Historical Perspectives. In: J.O. Nriagu and E. Nieboer (eds.), Chromium in the Natural and Human Environments, Vol. 20. John Wiley & Sons, New York, pp. 1–20.

Nriagu, J.O. 1988b. Production and Uses of Chromium. In: J.O. Nriagu and E. Nieboer (eds.), Chromium in the Natural and Human Environments, Vol. 20. John Wiley & Sons, New York, pp. 81–104.

Ono, B.-L. 1988. Genetic Approaches in the Study of Chromium Toxicity and Resistance in Yeast and Bacteria. In: J.O. Nriagu and E. Nieboer (eds.), Chromium in the Natural and Human Environments, Vol. 20. John Wiley & Sons, New York, pp. 351–368.

Palmer, C.D. and W. Fish. 1992. Chemically Enhanced Removal of Metals from the Subsurface. Proceeding of the Subsurface Restoration Conference, June 21–24, 1992, Dallas, TX. Rice University, Houston, TX, pp. 46–48.

Palmer, C.D. and P.R. Wittbrodt. 1990. Geochemical Characterization of the United Chrome Products Site, Final Report. In: Stage 2 Deep Aquifer Drilling Technical Report, United Chrome Products Site, Corvallis, OR, September 28, 1990, CH_2M Hill, Corvallis, OR.

Palmer, C.D. and P.R. Wittbrodt. 1991. Processes Affecting the Remediation of Chromium-Contaminated Sites. Environmental Health Perspectives, 92:25–40.

Paschin, Y.V., V.I. Kozachenko, and L.E. Sal'nikova. 1983. Differential Mutagenic Response at the HGPRT Locus in V-79 and CHO Cells after Treatment with Chromate. Mutat. Res., 122:361–365.

Rai, D., B.M. Sass, and D.A. Moore. 1987. Chromium(III) Hydrolysis Constants and Solubility of Chromium(III). Hydroxide Inorg., 26(3):345–249.

Rai, D., J.M. Zachara, L.E. Eary, C.C. Ainsworth, J.E. Amonette, C.E. Cowan, R.W. Szelmeczka, C.T. Resch, R.L. Schmidt, S.C. Smith, and D.C. Girvin. 1988. Chromium Reactions in Geologic Materials. EPRI EA-5741. Electric Power Research Institute, Palo Alto, CA, 287 pp.

Richard, F.C. and A.C.M. Bourg. 1991. Aqueous Geochemistry of Chromium: A Review. Water Research, 25(7):807–816.

Riser, J.A. and G.W. Bailey. 1992. Spectroscopic Study of Surface Redox Reactions with Manganese Oxides. Soil Sci. Soc. Am. J., 56:82–88.

Sass, B.M. and D. Rai. 1987. Solubility of Amorphous Chromium(III)-Iron(III) Hydroxide Solid Solutions. Inorg. Chem., 26(14):2228–2232.

Schott, J., R.A. Berner, and E.L. Sjoberg. 1981. Mechanism of Pyroxene and Amphibole Weathering - I. Experimental Studies with Iron-free Minerals. Geochim. et Cosmochim. Acta, 45:2123–2135.

Schroeder, D.C. and G.F. Lee. 1975. Potential Transformations of Chromium in Natural Waters. Water, Air, and Soil Pollution, 4:355–365.

Stollenwerk, K.G. and D.B. Grove. 1985. Reduction of Hexavalent Chromium in Water Samples Acidified for Preservation. J. Environ. Qual., 14(3):396–399.

Swayambunathan, V., Y.X. Liao, and D. Meisel. 1989. Stages in the Evolution of Colloidal Chromium(III) Oxide. Langmuir, 5(6):1423–1427.

Thomas, G.W. 1982. Exchangeable Cations. In: A.L. Page et al. (eds.), Methods of Soil Analysis, Part 2. American Society of Agronomy, Madison, WI, pp. 159–165.

U.S. Environmental Protection Agency (EPA). 1979. Chemical Oxygen Demand, EPA Method 410.4. In: Methods for Chemical Analysis of Water and Wastes, 2nd ed., EPA/600/4-74/020. [Editor's note: the third edition was published in 1983 with J.F. Kopp and B.D. McKee as authors; NTIS PB84-128677.)

van Weerelt, M., W.C. Pfeiffer, and M. Fiszman. 1984. Uptake and Release of 51Cr(VI) and 51Cr(III) by Barnacles (*Balanus sp.*). Mar. Environ. Res., 11:201–211.

Walkley, A. and L.A. Black. 1934. An Examination of the Degtjareff Method for Determining Soil Organic Matter and a Proposed Modification of the Chromic Acid Titration Method. Soil Science, 37:29–38.

Waterhouse, J.A.H. 1975. Cancer among Chromium Platers. Br. J. Cancer 32:262.

White, A.F. and M.F. Hochella. 1989. Electron Transfer Mechanisms Associated with the Surface Oxidation and Dissolution of Magnetite and Ilmenite. In: Proc. 6th International Symposium on Water-Rock Interaction, pp. 765–768.

White, A.F. and A. Yee. 1985. Aqueous Oxidation-Reduction Kinetics Associated with Coupled Electron-Cation Transfer from Iron Containing Silicates at 25°C. Geochim. et Cosmochim. Acta, 49:1263–1275.

Wittbrodt, P.R. and C.D. Palmer. 1992. Limitations to Pump-and-Treat Remediation of a Chromium Contaminated Site. Paper presented at Symp. on Aquifer Restoration: Pump-and-Treat and the Alternatives. National Ground Water Association National Convention, Las Vegas, NV, Sept. 30 – Oct. 2, 1992.

Wittbrodt, P.R. and C.D. Palmer. 1995. Reduction of Cr(VI) in the Presence of Excess Soil Fulvic Acid. Environ. Sci. Technol., 29:255–263.

Yassi, A. and E. Nieboer. 1988. Carcinogenicity of Chromium Compounds. In: J.O. Nriagu and E. Nieboer (eds.), Chromium in the Natural and Human Environments, Vol. 20. John Wiley & Sons, New York, pp. 443–496.

Chapter 5

Dense Nonaqueous Phase Liquids[1]

Scott G. Huling and **James W. Weaver**, U.S. EPA, Robert S. Kerr Environmental Research Laboratory, Ada, OK

INTRODUCTION

Dense nonaqueous phase liquids (DNAPLs) are present at numerous hazardous waste sites and are suspected to exist at many more. Due to the numerous variables influencing DNAPL transport and fate in the subsurface, and consequently, the ensuing complexity, *DNAPLs are largely undetected and yet are likely to be a significant limiting factor in site remediation.* This issue paper is a literature evaluation focusing on DNAPLs and provides an overview from a conceptual fate and transport point of view of DNAPL phase distribution, monitoring, site characterization, remediation, and modeling.

A nonaqueous phase liquid (NAPL) is a term used to describe the physical and chemical differences between a hydrocarbon liquid and water which result in a physical interface between a mixture of the two liquids. The interface is a physical dividing surface between the bulk phases of the two liquids, but compounds found in the NAPL are not prevented from solubilizing into the ground water. Immiscibility is typically determined based on the visual observation of a physical interface in a water-hydrocarbon mixture. There are numerous methods, however, which are used to quantify the physical and chemical properties of hydrocarbon liquids (Lyman et al., 1982).

Nonaqueous phase liquids have typically been divided into two general categories, dense and light. These terms describe the specific gravity, or the weight of the nonaqueous phase liquid relative to water. Correspondingly, the dense nonaqueous phase liquids have a specific gravity greater than water, and the light nonaqueous phase liquids (LNAPL) have a specific gravity less than water.

Several of the most common compounds associated with DNAPLs found at Superfund sites are included in Table 5-1. These compounds are a partial list of a larger list identified by a national screening of the most prevalent compounds found at Superfund sites (U.S. EPA, 1990). The general chemical categories are halogenated/nonhalogenated semi-volatiles and halogenated volatiles. These compounds are typically found in the following wastes and waste-producing processes: solvents, wood preserving wastes (creosote, pentachlorophenol), coal tars, and pesticides. The most frequently cited group of these contaminants to date are the chlorinated solvents.

DNAPL TRANSPORT AND FATE—CONCEPTUAL APPROACH

Fate and transport of DNAPLs in the subsurface will be presented from a conceptual point of view. Figures have been selected for various spill scenarios which illustrate the general behavior of DNAPL in the subsurface. Following the conceptual approach, detailed information will be presented explaining the specific mechanisms, processes, and variables which influence DNAPL fate and transport. This includes DNAPL characteristics, subsurface media characteristics, and saturation dependent parameters.

Unsaturated Zone

Figure 5-1 indicates the general scenario of a release of DNAPL into the soil which subsequently migrates vertically under both the forces of gravity and soil capillarity. Soil capillarity is also re-

---

[1] EPA/540/4-91/002.

Table 5-1. Most Prevalent Chemical Compounds at U.S. Superfund Sites (U.S. EPA, 1990) with a Specific Gravity Greater Than One

Compound	Density[a]	Dynamic[b] Viscosity	Kinematic[c] Viscosity	Water[d] Solub.		Henry's Law Constant[e]		Vapor[f] Pressure	
Halogenated Semi-Volatiles									
1,4-Dichlorobenzene	1.2475	1.2580	1.008	8.0	E+01	1.58	E-03	6	E-01
1,2-Dichlorobenzene	1.3060	1.3020	0.997	1.0	E+02	1.88	E-03	9.6	E-01
Aroclor 1242	1.3850			4.5	E-01	3.4	E-04	4.06	E-04
Aroclor 1260	1.4400			2.7	E-03	3.4	E-04	4.05	E-05
Aroclor 1254	1.5380			1.2	E-02	2.8	E-04	7.71	E-05
Chlordane	1.6	1.1040	0.69	5.6	E-02	2.2	E-04	1	E-05
Dieldrin	1.7500			1.86	E-01	9.7	E-06	1.78	E-07
2,3,4,6-Tetrachlorophenol	1.8390			1.0	E+03				
Pentachlorophenol	1.9780			1.4	E+01	2.8	E-06	1.1	E-04
Halogenated Volatiles									
Chlorobenzene	1.1060	0.7560	0.683	4.9	E+02	3.46	E-03	8.8	E+00
1,2-Dichloropropane	1.1580	0.8400	0.72	2.7	E+03	3.6	E-03	3.95	E+01
1,1-Dichloroethane	1.1750	0.3770	0.321	5.5	E+03	5.45	E-04	1.82	E+02
1,1-Dichloroethylene	1.2140	0.3300	0.27	4.0	E+02	1.49	E-03	5	E+02
1,2-Dichloroethane	1.2530	0.8400	0.67	8.69	E+03	1.1	E-03	6.37	E+01
Trans-1,2-Dichloroethylene	1.2570	0.4040	0.321	6.3	E+03	5.32	E-03	2.65	E+02
Cis-1,2-Dichloroethylene	1.2480	0.4670	0.364	3.5	E+03	7.5	E-03	2	E+02
1,1,1-Trichloroethane	1.3250	0.8580	0.647	9.5	E+02	4.08	E-03	1	E+02
Methylene Chloride	1.3250	0.4300	0.324	1.32	E+04	2.57	E-03	3.5	E+02
1,1,2-Trichloroethane	1.4436	0.1190	0.824	4.5	E+03	1.17	E-03	1.88	E+01
Trichloroethylene	1.4620	0.5700	0.390	1.0	E+03	8.92	E-03	5.87	E+01
Chloroform	1.4850	0.5630	0.379	8.22	E+03	3.75	E-03	1.6	E+02
Carbon Tetrachloride	1.5947	0.9650	0.605	8.0	E+02	2.0	E-02	9.13	E+01
1,1,2,2-Tetrachloroethane	1.6	1.7700	1.10	2.9	E+03	5.0	E-04	4.9	E+00
Tetrachloroethylene	1.6250	0.8900	0.54	1.5	E+02	2.27	E-02	1.4	E+01
Ethylene Dibromide	2.1720	1.6760	0.79	3.4	E+03	3.18	E-04	1.1	E+01

Nonhalogenated Semi-Volatiles

Compound	g/cc[a]	cp[b]	cs[c]	mg/L[d]	mm Hg[f]	atm-m³/mol[e]
2-Methyl Napthalene	1.0058			2.54E+01	5.06E-02	6.80E-02
o-Cresol	1.0273			3.1E+04	4.7E-05	2.45E-01
p-Cresol	1.0347			2.4E+04	3.5E-04	1.08E-01
2,4-Dimethylphenol	1.0360		20	6.2E+03	2.5E-06	9.8E-02
m-Cresol	1.0380	21.0	3.87	2.35E+04	3.8E-05	1.53E-01
Phenol	1.0576			8.4E+04	7.8E-07	5.293E-01
Naphthalene	1.1620			3.1E+01	1.27E-03	2.336E-01
Benzo(a)Anthracene	1.1740			1.4E-02	4.5E-06	1.16E-09
Fluorene	1.2030			1.9E+00	7.65E-05	6.67E-04
Acenaphthene	1.2250			3.88E+00	1.2E-03	2.31E-02
Anthracene	1.2500			7.5E-02	3.38E-05	1.08E-05
Dibenz(a,h)Anthracene	1.2520			2.5E-03	7.33E-08	1E-10
Fluoranthene	1.2520			2.65E-01	6.5E-06	6.02E-06
Pyrene	1.2710			1.48E-01	1.2E-05	6.67E-06
Chrysene	1.2740			6.0E-03	1.05E-06	6.3E-09
2,4-Dinitrophenol	1.6800			6.0E+03	6.45E-10	1.49E-05

Miscellaneous

Compound	g/cc[a]	cp[b]
Coal Tar	1.028[g]	18.98[g]
Creosote	1.05	1.08[h]

[a] g/cc
[b] centipoise (cp), water has a dynamic viscosity of 1 cp at 20°C.
[c] centistokes (cs)
[d] mg/L
[e] atm-m³/mol
[f] mm Hg
[g] 45°F (70)
[h] 15.5°C, varies with creosote mix (U.S. EPA, 1988)

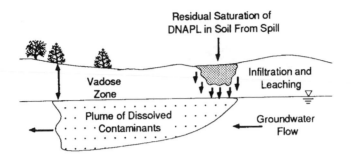

Figure 5-1. The entire volume of DNAPL is exhausted by residual saturation in the vadose zone prior to DNAPL reaching the water table. Soluble phase compounds may be leached from the DNAPL residual saturation and contaminate the ground water.

sponsible for the lateral migration of DNAPL. A point is reached at which the DNAPL no longer holds together as a continuous phase, but rather is present as isolated residual globules. The fraction of the hydrocarbon that is retained by capillary forces in the porous media is referred to as *residual saturation*. In this spill scenario, the residual saturation in the unsaturated zone exhausted the volume of DNAPL, preventing it from reaching the water table. This figure also shows the subsequent leaching (solubilization) of the DNAPL residual saturation by water percolating through the unsaturated zone (vadose zone). The leachate reaching the saturated zone results in ground-water contamination by the soluble phase components of the hydrocarbon. Additionally, the residual saturation at or near the water table is also subjected to leaching from the rise and fall of the water table (seasonal, sea level, etc.).

Increasing information is drawing attention to the importance of the possibility that gaseous-phase vapors from NAPL in the unsaturated zone are responsible for contaminating the ground water and soil (Hinchee and Reisinger, 1987; Schwille, 1988). It is reported that the greater "relative vapor density" of gaseous vapors to air will be affected by gravity and will tend to sink. In subsurface systems where lateral spreading is not restricted, spreading of the vapors may occur as indicated in Figure 5-2. The result is that a greater amount of soils and ground water will be exposed to the DNAPL vapors and may result in further contamination. The extent of contamination will depend largely on the partitioning of the DNAPL vapor phase between the aqueous and solid phases.

DNAPL Phase Distribution—Four Phase System

It is apparent from Figures 5-1 and 5-2 that the DNAPL may be present in the subsurface in various physical states or what is referred to as phases. As illustrated in Figure 5-3, there are four possible phases: gaseous, solid, water, and immiscible hydrocarbon (DNAPL) in the unsaturated zone. Contaminants associated with the release of DNAPL can, therefore, occur in four phases described as follows:

1. Air phase—contaminants may be present as vapors;
2. Solid phase—contaminants may adsorb or partition onto the soil or aquifer material;
3. Water phase—contaminants may dissolve into the water according to their solubility; and
4. Immiscible phase—contaminants may be present as dense nonaqueous phase liquids.

The four phase system is the most complex scenario because there are four phases and the contaminant can partition between any one or all four of these phases, as illustrated in Figure 5-4. For example, TCE introduced into the subsurface as a DNAPL may partition onto the soil phase, volatilize into the soil gas, and solubilize into the water phase resulting in contamination in all four phases. TCE can also partition between the water and soil, water and air, and between the soil and air. There are six pathways of phase distribution in the unsaturated zone. The distribution of a contaminant between these phases can be represented by empirical relationships referred to as partition coefficients. The partition coefficients, or the distribution of the DNAPL between the four phases, is highly site-spe-

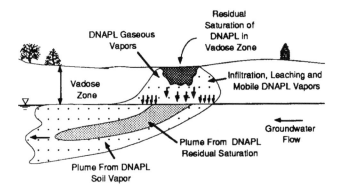

Figure 5-2. Migration of DNAPL vapors from the spill area and subsequent contamination of the soil and ground water.

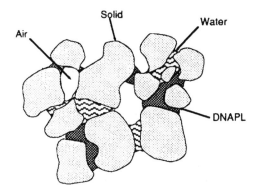

Figure 5-3. A DNAPL contaminated unsaturated zone has four physical states or phases (air, solid, water, immiscible). The contaminant may be present in any one, or all four phases.

cific and highly dependent on the characteristics of both the soil/aquifer matrix and the DNAPL. Therefore, the distribution between phases may change with time and/or location at the same site and during different stages of site remediation.

The concept of phase distribution is critical in decision-making. Understanding the phase distribution of a DNAPL introduced into the subsurface provides significant insight in determining which tools are viable options with respect to site characterization and remediation.

DNAPL represented by residual saturation in the four phase diagram is largely immobile under the usual subsurface pressure conditions and can migrate further only: 1) in water according to its solubility; or 2) in the gas phase of the unsaturated zone (Schwille, 1988). DNAPL components adsorbed onto the soil are also considered immobile. The mobile phases are, therefore, the soluble and volatile components of the DNAPL in the water and air, respectively.

The pore space in the unsaturated zone may be filled with one or all three fluid phases (gaseous, aqueous, immiscible). The presence of DNAPL as a continuous immiscible phase has the potential to be mobile. The mobility of DNAPL in the subsurface must be evaluated on a case by case basis. The maximum number of potentially mobile fluid phases is three. Simultaneous flow of the three phases (air, water, and immiscible) is considerably more complicated than two-phase flow (Schwille et al., 1984). The mobility of three phase flow in a four-phase system is complex, poorly understood, and is beyond the scope of this DNAPL overview. The relative mobility of the two phases, water and DNAPL, in a three-phase system is presented below in the section entitled "Relative Permeability."

Generally, rock aquifers contain a myriad of cracks (fractures) of various lengths, widths, and apertures (Mackay and Cherry, 1989). Fractured rock systems have been described as rock blocks bounded by discrete discontinuities comprised of fractures, joints, and shear zones which may be open, mineral-

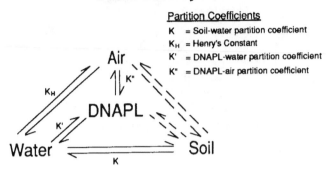

Figure 5-4. Distribution of DNAPL between the four phases found in the vadose zone.

filled, deformed, or any combination thereof (Schmelling and Ross, Chapter 10). The unsaturated zone overlying these fractured rock systems also contains the myriad of preferential pathways. DNAPL introduced into such formations (Figure 5-5) follow complex pathways due to the heterogeneous distribution of the cracks, conduits, and fractures, i.e., preferential pathways. Transport of DNAPL may follow nonDarcian flow in the open fractures and/or Darcian flow in the porous media filled fractures. Relatively small volumes of NAPL may move deep, quickly into the rock because the retention capacity offered by the dead-end fractures and the immobile fragments and globules in the larger fractures is so small (Mackay and Cherry, 1989). Currently, the capability to collect the detailed information for a complete description of a contaminated fractured rock system is regarded as neither technically possible nor economically feasible (Schmelling and Ross, Chapter 10).

Low permeability stratigraphic units such as high clay content formations may also contain a heterogeneous distribution of preferential pathways. As illustrated in Figure 5-6, DNAPL transport in these preferential pathways is correspondingly complex. Typically, it is assumed that high clay content formations are impervious to DNAPL. However, as DNAPL spreads out on low permeable formations it tends to seek out zones of higher permeability. As a result, preferential pathways allow the DNAPL to migrate further into the low permeable formation, or through it to underlying stratigraphic units. It is apparent from Figures 5-5 and 5-6 that the complexity of DNAPL transport may be significant prior to reaching the water table.

Saturated Zone

The second general scenario is one in which the volume of DNAPL is sufficient to overcome the fraction depleted by the residual saturation in the vadose zone, as illustrated in Figure 5-7. Consequently, the DNAPL reaches the water table and contaminates the ground water directly. The specific gravity of DNAPL is greater than water, therefore, the DNAPL migrates into the saturated zone. In this scenario, DNAPL continues the vertical migration through the saturated zone until the volume is eventually exhausted by the residual saturation process or until it is intercepted by a low permeable formation where it begins to migrate laterally.

DNAPL Phase Distribution—Three Phase System

Due to the lack of the gaseous phase, the saturated zone containing DNAPL is considered a three-phase system consisting of the solid, water, and immiscible hydrocarbon (Figure 5-8). Contaminant distribution in the three-phase system is less complex than the four-phase system. Again, this is highly dependent on the characteristics of both the aquifer matrix and the DNAPL. Figure 5-9 indicates the three phases and the transfer of the mass of contaminant between the phases. In this scenario, there are only three pathways of phase distribution in the saturated zone.

Note that when the DNAPL is represented by residual saturation in the three-phase system, the mobile phase of the contaminant is the water soluble components of the DNAPL and the immobile

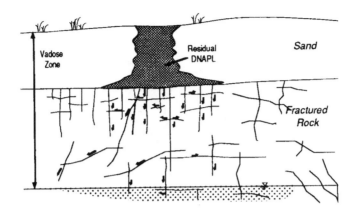

Figure 5-5. DNAPL spilled into fractured rock systems may follow a complex distribution of the preferential pathways.

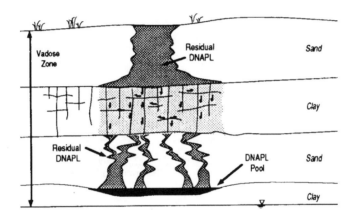

Figure 5-6. DNAPL spilled into a low permeable formation may follow a complex distribution of preferential pathways. The volume of DNAPL is exhausted in the vadose zone prior to reaching the water table.

phases are the residual saturation and the adsorbed components of the DNAPL associated with the aquifer material. The main mobilization mechanism of the residual saturation is removal of soluble phase components into the ground water. When the DNAPL is present as a continuous immiscible phase, it too is considered one of the mobile phases of the contaminant. While the continuous phase DNAPL has the potential to be mobile, immobile continuous phase DNAPL may also exist in the subsurface. Although the saturated zone is considered a three-phase system, gaseous vapors from DNAPL in the unsaturated zone do have the potential to affect ground-water quality, as was indicated earlier in Figure 5-2.

Assuming the residual saturation in the saturated zone does not deplete the entire volume of the DNAPL, the DNAPL will continue migrating vertically until it encounters a zone or stratigraphic unit of lower permeability. Upon reaching the zone of lower permeability, the DNAPL will begin to migrate laterally. The hydraulic conductivity in the vertical direction is typically less than in the horizontal direction. It is not uncommon to find vertical conductivity that is one-fifth or one-tenth the horizontal value (Bouwer, 1978). It is expected that DNAPL spilled into the subsurface will have a significant potential to migrate laterally. If the lower permeable boundary is "bowl shaped", the DNAPL will pond as a reservoir (refer to Figure 5-10). As illustrated in Figure 5-11, it is not uncommon to observe a perched DNAPL reservoir where a discontinuous impermeable layer; i.e., silt or clay lens, intercepts the vertical migration of DNAPL. When a sufficient volume of DNAPL has been released and multiple discontinuous impermeable layers exist, the DNAPL may be present in several perched reser-

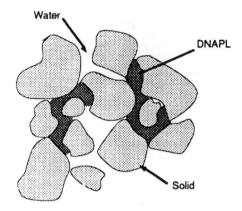

Figure 5-7. The volume of DNAPL is sufficient to overcome the residual saturation in the vadose zone and consequently penetrates the water table.

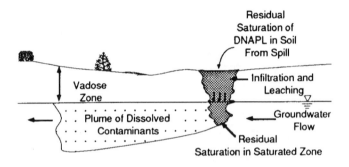

Figure 5-8. A DNAPL contaminated saturated zone has three phases (solid, water, immiscible). The contaminant may be present in any one, or all three phases.

voirs as well as a deep reservoir (refer to Figure 5-12). Lateral migration continues until either the residual saturation depletes the DNAPL or an impermeable depression immobilizes the DNAPL in a reservoir type scenario. Soluble-phase components of the DNAPL will partition into the ground water from both the residual saturation or DNAPL pools. The migration of DNAPL vertically through the aquifer results in the release of soluble-phase components of the DNAPL across the entire thickness of the aquifer. Note, that ground water becomes contaminated as it flows through, and around, the DNAPL contaminated zone.

As indicated earlier, DNAPL will migrate laterally upon reaching a stratigraphic unit of lower permeability. Transport of DNAPL will therefore be largely dependent on the gradient of the stratigraphy. Occasionally, the directional gradient of an impermeable stratigraphic unit may be different than the direction of ground-water flow as illustrated in Figure 5-13a. This may result in the migration of the continuous phase DNAPL in a direction different from the ground-water flow. Nonhorizontal stratigraphic units with varying hydraulic conductivity may also convey DNAPL in a different direction than ground-water flow, and at different rates (refer to Figure 5-13b). Determination of the direction of impermeable stratigraphic units will therefore provide useful information concerning the direction of DNAPL transport.

Similar to the unsaturated zone, the saturated zone also contains a complex distribution of preferential pathways from cracks, fractures, joints, etc. DNAPL introduced into such formations correspondingly follow the complex network of pathways through an otherwise relatively impermeable rock material. Other pathways which may behave as vertical conduits for DNAPL include root holes, stratigraphic windows, disposal wells, unsealed geotechnical boreholes, improperly sealed hydro-

Three Phase System

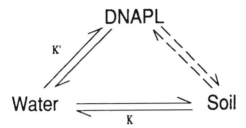

K' = DNAPL-water partition coefficient

K = Soil-water partition coefficient

Figure 5-9. Distribution of DNAPL between the three phases found in the saturated zone.

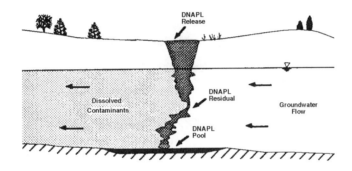

Figure 5-10. Migration of DNAPL through the vadose zone to an impermeable boundary.

geological investigation sampling holes and monitoring wells, and old uncased/unsealed water supply wells. Transport of the DNAPL may migrate very rapidly in these open conduits or follow Darcian flow in the surrounding porous media or porous media filled fractures. A relatively small volume of DNAPL can move deep into a fractured system due to the low retentive capacity of the fractured system. Consequently, fractured clay or rock stratigraphic units, which are often considered lower DNAPL boundary conditions, may have preferential pathways leading to lower formations, as depicted in Figure 5-14. Careful inspection of soil cores at one Superfund site indicated that DNAPL flow mainly occurred through preferential pathways and was not uniformly distributed throughout the soil mass (Connor et al., 1989). Due to the complex distribution of preferential pathways, characterization of the volume distribution of the DNAPL is difficult.

IMPORTANT DNAPL TRANSPORT AND FATE PARAMETERS

There are several characteristics associated with both the subsurface media and the DNAPL which largely determine the fate and transport of the DNAPL. A brief discussion of these parameters is included to help identify the specific details of DNAPL transport mechanisms. Several of the distinctive DNAPL phenomena observed on the field-scale relates back to phenomena at the pore-scale. Therefore, it is important to understand the principles from the pore-scale level to develop an understanding of field-scale observations, which is the scale at which much of the Superfund work occurs. A more complete and comprehensive review of these parameters is available (Bear, 1972; Mercer and Cohen, 1990; Villaume, 1985).

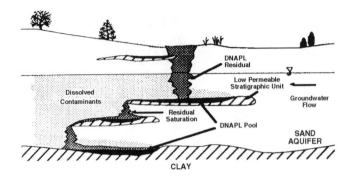

Figure 5-11. Perched DNAPL reservoir.

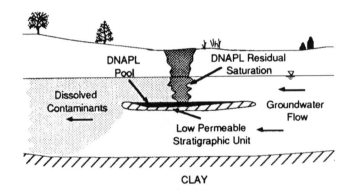

Figure 5-12. Perched and deep DNAPL reservoirs.

DNAPL Characteristics

Density

Fluid density is defined as the mass of fluid per unit volume, i.e., g/cm^3. Density of an immiscible hydrocarbon fluid is the parameter which delineates LNAPLs from DNAPLs. The property varies not only with molecular weight but also molecular interaction and structure. In general, the density varies with temperature and pressure (Bear, 1972). Equivalent methods of expressing density are specific weight and specific gravity. The specific weight is defined as the weight of fluid per unit volume, i.e., lb/ft^3. The specific gravity (S.G.) or the relative density of a fluid is defined as the ratio of the weight of a given volume of substance at a specified temperature to the weight of the same volume of water at a given temperature (Lyman et al., 1982). The S.G. is a relative indicator which ultimately determines whether the fluid will float (S.G.<1.0) on, or penetrate into (S.G.>1.0) the water table. Table 5-1 contains a list of compounds with a density greater than one that are considered DNAPLs. Note, however, that while the specific gravity of pentachlorophenol and the nonhalogenated semi-volatiles is greater than 1.00, these compounds are a solid at room temperature and would not be expected to be found as an immiscible phase liquid at wood preserving sites but are commonly found as contaminants. Pentachlorophenol is commonly used as a wood preservant and is typically dissolved (4–7%) in No. 2 or 3 fuel oil.

Viscosity

The viscosity of a fluid is a measure of its resistance to flow. Molecular cohesion is the main cause of viscosity. As the temperature increases in a liquid, the cohesive forces decrease and the absolute

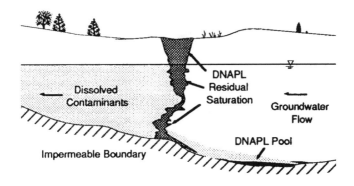

Figure 5-13a. Stratigraphic gradient different from ground water gradient results in a different direction of flow of the ground water and continuous phase DNAPL.

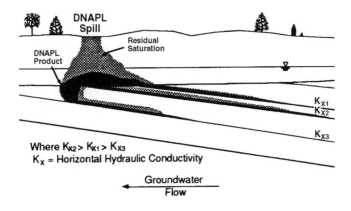

Figure 5-13b. Nonhorizontal stratigraphic units with variable hydraulic conductivity may convey DNAPL in a different direction than the ground water flow direction.

viscosity decreases. The lower the viscosity, the more readily a fluid will penetrate a porous media. The hydraulic conductivity of porous media is a function of both the density and viscosity of the fluid as indicated in equation [1]. It is apparent from this equation that fluids with either a viscosity less than water or fluids with a density greater than water have the potential to be more mobile in the subsurface, than water.

$$K = \frac{k\rho g}{\mu}$$

(1)

where, K = hydraulic conductivity
k = intrinsic permeability
ρ = fluid mass density
g = gravity
μ = dynamic (absolute) viscosity

Results from laboratory experiments indicated that several chlorinated hydrocarbons which have low viscosity (methylene chloride, perchloroethylene, 1,1,1-TCA, TCE) will infiltrate into soil notably faster than will water (Schwille, 1988). The relative value of NAPL viscosity and density, to water, indicates how fast it will flow in porous media (100% saturated) with respect to water. For example, several low viscosity chlorinated hydrocarbons (TCE, tetrachloroethylene, 1,1,1-TCA, methylene chloride, chloroform, carbon tetrachloride, refer to Table 5-1) will flow 1.5–3.0 times as

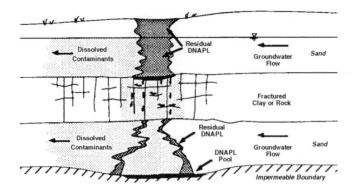

Figure 5-14. DNAPL transport in fracture and porous media stratigraphic units.

fast as water and higher viscosity compounds including light heating oil, diesel fuel, jet fuel, and crude oil (i.e., LNAPLs) will flow 2–10 times slower than water (Schwille, 1981). Both coal tar and creosote typically have a specific gravity greater than one and a viscosity greater than water. It is interesting to note that the viscosity of NAPL may change with time (Mercer and Cohen, 1990). As fresh crude oils lose the lighter volatile components from evaporation, the oils become more viscous as the heavier components compose a larger fraction of the oily mixture, resulting in an increase in viscosity.

Solubility

When an organic chemical is in physical contact with water, the organic chemical will partition into the aqueous phase. The equilibrium concentration of the organic chemical in the aqueous phase is referred to as its solubility. Table 5-1 presents the solubility of several of the most commonly found DNAPLs at EPA Superfund sites. The solubility of organic compounds varies considerably from the infinitely miscible compounds, including alcohols (ethanol, methanol) to extremely low solubility compounds such as polynuclear aromatic compounds.

Numerous variables influence the solubility of organic compounds. The pH may affect the solubility of some organic compounds. Organic acids may be expected to increase in solubility with increasing pH, while organic bases may act in the opposite way (Lyman et al., 1982). For example, pentachlorophenol is an acid which is ionized at higher pHs. In the ionized form, pentachlorophenol would be more soluble in water (U.S. EPA, 1988). Solubility in water is a function of the temperature, but the strength and direction of this function varies. The presence of dissolved salts or minerals in water leads to moderate decreases in solubility (Lyman et al., 1982). In a mixed solvent system, consisting of water and one or more water-miscible compounds, as the fraction of the cosolvent in the mixture increases, the solubility of the organic chemical increases exponentially (Fu and Luthy, 1986). In general, the greater the molecular weight and structural complexity of the organic compound, the lower the solubility.

Organic compounds are only rarely found in ground water at concentrations approaching their solubility limits, even when organic liquid phases are known or suspected to be present. The observed concentrations are usually more than a factor of 10 lower than the solubility presumably due to diffusional limitations of dissolution and the dilution of the dissolved organic contaminants by dispersion (Wilson and Conrad, 1984). This has also been attributed to: reduced solubility due to the presence of other soluble compounds, the heterogeneous distribution of DNAPL in the subsurface, and dilution from monitoring wells with long intake lengths (Feenstra, 1990). Detection of DNAPL components in the subsurface below the solubility should clearly not be interpreted as a negative indicator for the presence of DNAPL.

In a DNAPL spill scenario where the DNAPL or its vapors are in contact with the ground water, the concentration of the soluble phase components may range from non-detectable up to the solubility of the compound. The rate of dissolution has been expressed as a function of the properties of the DNAPL components (solubility), ground-water flow conditions, differential between the actual and solubility concentration, and the contact area between the DNAPL and the ground water (Feenstra, 1990). The contact area is expected to be heterogeneous and difficult to quantify. Additionally, as the time of contact increases between the DNAPL and the water, the concentration in the aqueous phase increases.

Vapor Pressure

The vapor pressure is that characteristic of the organic chemical which determines how readily vapors volatilize or evaporate from the pure phase liquid. Specifically, the partial pressure exerted at the surface by these free molecules is known as the vapor pressure (Lindeburg, 1986). Molecular activity in a liquid tends to free some surface molecules and this tendency towards vaporization is mainly dependent on temperature. The vapor pressure of DNAPLs can actually be greater than the vapor pressure of volatile organic compounds. For example, at 20°C, the ratio of the vapor pressures of TCE and benzene is 1.4 (Baehr, 1987).

Volatility

The volatility of a compound is a measure of the transfer of the compound from the aqueous phase to the gaseous phase. The transfer process from the water to the atmosphere is dependent on the chemical and physical properties of the compound, the presence of other compounds, and the physical properties (velocity, turbulence, depth) of the water body and atmosphere above it. The factors that control volatilization are the solubility, molecular weight, vapor pressure, and the nature of the air-water interface through which it must pass (Lyman et al., 1982). The Henry's constant is a valuable parameter which can be used to help evaluate the propensity of an organic compound to volatilize from the water. The Henry's law constant is defined as the vapor pressure divided by the aqueous solubility. Therefore, the greater the Henry's law constant, the greater the tendency to volatilize from the aqueous phase; refer to Table 5-1.

Interfacial Tension

The unique behavior of DNAPLs in porous media is largely attributed to the interfacial tension which exists between DNAPL and water, and between DNAPL and air. These interfacial tensions result in distinct interfaces between these fluids at the pore-scale. When two immiscible liquids are in contact, there is an interfacial energy which exists between the fluids, resulting in a physical interface. The interfacial energy arises from the difference between the inward attraction of the molecules in the interior of each phase and those at the surface of contact (Bear, 1972). The greater the interfacial tension between two immiscible liquids, the less likely emulsions will form; emulsions will be more stable if formed, and the better the phase separation after mixing. The magnitude of the interfacial tension is less than the larger of the surface tension values for the pure liquids, because the mutual attraction of unlike molecules at the interface reduces the large imbalance of forces (Lyman et al., 1982). Interfacial tension decreases with increasing temperature, and may be affected by pH, surfactants, and gases in solution (Mercer and Cohen, 1990). When this force is encountered between a liquid and a gaseous phase, the same force is called the surface tension (Wilson et al., 1990).

The displacement of water by DNAPL and the displacement of DNAPL by water in porous media often involves a phenomenon referred to as immiscible fingering. The lower the interfacial tension between immiscible fluids, the greater the instability of the water:DNAPL interface and thus the greater the immiscible fingering (Kueper and Frind, 1988). The distribution of the fingering effects in porous media has been reported to be a function of the density, viscosity, surface tension (Kueper and Frind, 1988) and the displacement velocity (Glass et al., 1989) of the fluids involved as well as the porous media heterogeneity (Kueper et al., 1989).

Wettability

Wettability refers to the relative affinity of the soil for the various fluids—water, air, and the organic phase. On a solid surface, exposed to two different fluids, the wettability can be inferred from the contact angle (Wilson et al., 1990), also referred to as the wetting angle; refer to Figure 5-15. In general, if the wetting angle is less than 90 degrees, the fluid is said to be the wetting fluid. In this scenario, water will preferentially occupy the smaller pores and will be found on solid surfaces (Hall et al., 1984). When the wetting angle is near 90 degrees, neither fluid is preferentially attracted to the solid surfaces. If the wetting angle is greater than 90 degrees, the DNAPL is said to be the wetting fluid. The wetting angle is an indicator used to determine whether the porous material will be preferentially wetted by either the hydrocarbon or the aqueous phase (Villaume, 1985). Wettability, therefore, describes the preferential spreading of one fluid over solid surfaces in a two-fluid system. The wetting angle, which is a measure of wettability, is a solid-liquid interaction and can actually be defined in terms of interfacial tensions (Villaume, 1985). Several methods have been developed to measure the wetting angle (Mercer and Cohen, 1990; Villaume, 1985). In most natural systems, water is the wetting fluid, and the immiscible fluid is the nonwetting fluid. Coal tar may be the exception (i.e., contact angle greater than 90 degrees), which is mainly attributed to the presence of surfactants (Villaume et al., 1983). The wetting fluid will tend to coat the surface of grains and occupy smaller spaces (i.e., pore throats) in porous media, the nonwetting fluid will tend to be restricted to the largest openings (Schwille, 1988).

The wetting angle depends on the character of the solid surface on which the test is conducted. The test is conducted on flat plates composed of minerals which are believed representative of the media, or on glass. Contact angle measurements for crude oil indicate that the wetting angles vary widely depending on the mineral surface (Treiber et al., 1972). Soil and aquifer material are not composed of homogeneous mineral composition nor flat surfaces. The measured wetting angle can only be viewed as a qualitative indicator of wetting behavior.

The reader is recommended to refer to Lyman et al. (1982) for review of the basic principles and for various techniques to measure the following DNAPL parameters: density, viscosity, interfacial tension, solubility, vapor pressure, and volatility.

Subsurface Media Characteristics

Capillary Force/Pressure

Capillary pressure is important in DNAPL transport because it largely determines the magnitude of the residual saturation that is left behind after a spill incident. The greater the capillary pressure, the greater the potential for residual saturation. In general, the capillary force increases in the following order: sand, silt, clay. Correspondingly, the residual saturation increases in the same order. Capillary pressure is a measure of the tendency of a porous medium to suck in the wetting fluid phase or to repel the nonwetting phase (Bear, 1972). Capillary forces are closely related to the wettability of the porous media. The preferential attraction of the wetting fluid to the solid surfaces cause that fluid to be drawn into the porous media. Capillary forces are due to both adhesion forces (the attractive force of liquid for the solids on the walls of the channels through which it moves) and cohesion forces (the attraction forces between the molecules of the liquid) (Mackay and Cherry, 1989). The capillary pressure depends on the geometry of the void space, the nature of solids and liquids, the degree of saturation (Bear, 1972) and in general, increases with a decrease in the wetting angle and in pore size, and with an increase in the interfacial tension (Villaume, 1985). All pores have some value of capillary pressure. Before a nonwetting fluid can enter porous media, the capillary pressure of the largest pores (smallest capillary pressure) must be exceeded. This minimum capillary pressure is called the entry pressure.

In the unsaturated zone, pore space may be occupied by water, air (vapors), or immiscible hydrocarbon. In this scenario, capillary pressure retains the water (wetting phase) mainly in the smaller pores where the capillary pressure is greatest. This restricts the migration of the DNAPL (nonwetting phase) through the larger pores unoccupied by water. Typically, DNAPL does not displace the pore water from the smaller pores. It is interesting to note that the migration of DNAPL through fine material (high capillary pressure) will be impeded upon reaching coarser material (low capillary pressure).

The capillary fringe will obstruct the entry of the DNAPL into the saturated zone. When a sufficient volume of DNAPL has been released and the "DNAPL pressure head" exceeds the water capillary pressure at the capillary fringe (entry pressure), the DNAPL will penetrate the water table. This is why DNAPL is sometimes observed to temporarily flatten out on top of the water table. Similarly,

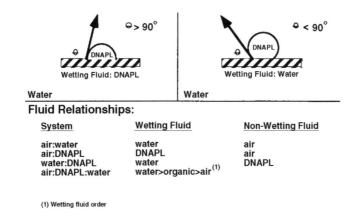

Figure 5-15. Wetting angle and typical wetting fluid relationships.

laboratory experiments have been conducted in which DNAPL (tetrachloroethylene) infiltrating through porous media was found to flow laterally and cascade off lenses too fine to penetrate (Kueper et al., 1989), (refer to Figure 5-12). This was attributed to the inability of the DNAPL to overcome the high capillary pressure associated with the lenses. Logically when "DNAPL pressure head" exceeds the capillary pressure, the DNAPL will penetrate into the smaller pores. These laboratory experiments are important because they illustrate that small differences in the capillary characteristics of porous media can induce significant lateral flow of nonwetting fluids.

A comprehensive investigation of capillary trapping and multiphase flow of organic liquids in unconsolidated porous media revealed many intricacies of this process in the vadose and saturated zone (Wilson et al., 1990). An important note is that while capillary pressure is rarely measured at hazardous waste sites, the soil texture (sand, silt, clay) is usually recorded during drilling operations and soil surveys. This information, along with soil core analyses will help to delineate the stratigraphy and the volume distribution of NAPL.

Pore Size Distribution/Initial Moisture Content

In natural porous media, the geometry of the pore space is extremely irregular and complex (Bear, 1972). The heterogeneity of the subsurface environment, i.e., the variability of the pore size distribution, directly affects the distribution of the capillary pressures along the interfaces between the aqueous and immiscible phases (Sitar et al., 1987). In saturated column experiments, it was observed that NAPL preferentially traveled through strings of macropores, almost completely by-passing the water-filled micropores (Wilson et al., 1990). In the same study, a heterogeneous distribution of coarse and fine porous material was simulated. Most of the incoming organic liquid preferentially traveled through the coarse lens material.

In short-term column drainage experiments, results indicated that the particle grain size is of primary importance in controlling the residual saturation of a gasoline hydrocarbon (Hoag and Marley, 1989). Fine and coarse sands (dry) were found to have 55% and 14% residual saturation, respectively. The finer the sand, the greater the residual saturation. During these experiments, the residual saturation was reduced 20–30% in a medium sand and 60% in a fine sand when the sands were initially wet. Soil pore water held tightly by capillary forces in the small pores will limit the NAPL to the larger pores, and thus, result in lower residual saturation. In a similar laboratory (unsaturated) column study, the smaller the grain size used in the experiment, the greater the residual saturation of the NAPL (Wilson and Conrad, 1984). The residual saturation in the saturated column experiments was found to be greater than the unsaturated columns and was independent of the particle size distribution.

These observations follow traditional capillary force theory. Residual saturation resulting from a DNAPL spill in the unsaturated zone is highly dependent on the antecedent moisture content in the porous media. When the moisture content is low, the strong capillary forces in the smaller pores will tenaciously draw in and hold the DNAPL. When the moisture content is high, the capillary forces in the smaller pores will retain the soil pore water, and DNAPL residual saturation will mainly occur in the larger pores. Therefore, greater residual saturation can be expected in dryer soils. Correspondingly, NAPL will migrate further in a wetter soil and displacement of NAPL from small pores is expected to be more difficult than from large pores.

Stratigraphic Gradient

DNAPL migrating vertically will likely encounter a zone or stratigraphic unit of lower vertical permeability. A reduction in the vertical permeability of the porous media will induce lateral flow of the DNAPL. The gradient of the lower permeable stratigraphic unit will largely determine the direction in which the DNAPL will flow. This is applicable to both the saturated and unsaturated zones. As depicted in Figures 5-13a and 5-13b, the lateral direction of DNAPL flow may be in a different direction than ground-water flow.

Ground-Water Flow Velocity

The ground-water flow velocity is a dynamic stress parameter which tends to mobilize the hydrocarbon (Ng et al., 1978). As the ground-water velocity increases, the dynamic pressure and viscous forces increase. Mobilization of DNAPL occurs when the viscous forces of the ground water acting on the DNAPL, exceed the porous media capillary forces retaining the DNAPL.

Saturation Dependent Functions

Residual Saturation

Residual saturation is defined as the volume of hydrocarbon trapped in the pores relative to the total volume of pores (Morrow, 1979) and therefore is measured as such (Wilson and Conrad, 1984). Residual saturation has also been described as the saturation at which NAPL becomes discontinuous and is immobilized by capillary forces (Mercer and Cohen, 1990). The values of residual saturation vary from as low as 0.75–1.25% for light oil in highly permeable media to as much as 20% for heavy oil (Sitar et al., 1987). Residual saturation values have also been reported to range from 10% to 50% of the total pore space (Ng et al., 1978; Wilson and Conrad, 1984). Other researchers reported that residual saturation values appear to be relatively insensitive to fluid properties and very sensitive to soil properties (and heterogeneities) (Wilson et al., 1990). Laboratory studies conducted to predict the residual saturation in soils with similar texture and grain size distribution yielded significantly different values. It was concluded that minor amounts of clay or silt in a soil may play a significant role in the observed values.

In the unsaturated zone during low moisture conditions, the DNAPL residual saturation will wet the grains in a pendular state (a ring of liquid wrapped around the contact point of a pair of adjacent grains). During high moisture conditions, the wetting fluid, which is typically water, will preferentially occupy the pendular area of adjacent grains and the hydrocarbon will occupy other available pore space, possibly as isolated droplets. In the saturated zone, the DNAPL residual saturation will be present as isolated drops in the open pores (Schwille, 1988). Furthermore, results of laboratory experimentation indicated that residual saturation increased with decreasing hydraulic conductivity in both the saturated and unsaturated zones and that the residual saturation is greatest in the saturated zone. Laboratory experiments indicated that vadose zone residual saturation was roughly one third of the residual saturation in the saturated zone (Wilson et al., 1990). The increase in residual saturation in the saturated zone is due to the following: [1] the fluid density ratio (DNAPL:air versus DNAPL: water above and below the water table, respectively) favors greater drainage in the vadose zone; [2] as the nonwetting fluid in most saturated media, NAPL is trapped in the larger pores; and, [3] as the wetting fluid in the vadose zone, NAPL tends to spread into adjacent pores and leave a lower residual content behind, a process that is inhibited in the saturated zone (Mercer and Cohen, 1990). Thus, the capacity for retention of DNAPLs in the unsaturated zone is less than the saturated zone.

Relative Permeability

Relative permeability is defined as the ratio of the permeability of a fluid at a given saturation to its permeability at 100% saturation. Thus it can have a value between 0 and 1 (Villaume, 1985). Figure 5-16 illustrates a relative permeability graph for a two fluid phase system showing the relationship between the observed permeability of each fluid for various saturations to that of the observed permeability if the sample were 100% saturated with that fluid (Williams and Wilder, 1971). The three regions of this graph are explained as follows (Villaume, 1985): Region I has a high saturation of DNAPL and is considered a continuous phase while the water is a discontinuous phase; therefore, water permeability is low. Assuming the DNAPL is the nonwetting fluid, water would fill the smaller capillaries and flow through small irregular pores. In Region II, both water and DNAPL are continuous phases although not necessarily in the same pores. Both water and NAPL flow simultaneously. However, as saturation of either phase increases, the relative permeability of the other phase correspondingly decreases. Region III exhibits a high saturation of water while the DNAPL phase is mainly discontinuous. Water flow dominates this region and there is little or no flow of DNAPL.

Both fluids flow through only a part of the pore space and thus only a part of the cross section under consideration is available for flow of each fluid. Therefore, the discharge of each fluid must be lower, corresponding to its proportion of the cross sectional area (Schwille, 1984).

Figure 5-17 is another relative permeability graph which demonstrates several points. Small increases in DNAPL saturation result in a significant reduction in the relative permeability of water. However, a small increase in water saturation does not result in a significant reduction in DNAPL relative permeability. This figure identifies two points, S_{O1} and S_{O2} where the saturation of the DNAPL and the water are greater than 0 before there is a relative permeability for this fluid. The two fluids hinder the movement of the other to different degrees and both must reach a minimum saturation before they achieve any mobility at all (Schwille, 1988). These minimum saturations, for the water and DNAPL, are identified as irreducible and residual saturation, respectively.

SITE CHARACTERIZATION FOR DNAPL

Characterization of the subsurface environment at hazardous waste sites containing DNAPL is complex and will likely be expensive. Specific details associated with the volume and timing of the DNAPL release are usually poor or are not available and subsurface heterogeneity is responsible for the complicated and unpredictable migration pathway of subsurface DNAPL transport. As discussed previously, slight changes in vertical permeability may induce a significant horizontal component to DNAPL migration.

Site characterization typically involves a significant investment in ground-water analyses. Although analysis of ground water provides useful information on the distribution of the soluble components of the DNAPL, the presence of other phases of the DNAPL may go unrecognized. The investigation must, therefore, be more detailed to obtain information concerning the phase distribution of the DNAPL at a site. Site characterization may require analyses on all four phases (aqueous, gaseous, solid, immiscible) to yield the appropriate information (refer to Table 5-2). In brief, data collected on the various phases must be compiled, evaluated and used to help identify: where the contaminant is presently located; where it has been; in what phases it occurs; and in what direction the mobile phases may be going. A comprehensive review of site characterization for subsurface investigations is available (U.S. EPA, 1991). Development of monitoring and remediation strategies can be focused more effectively and efficiently after a clear definition of the phase distribution has been completed.

Ground Water

Ground-water analyses for organic compounds, in conjunction with ground-water flow direction data, has repeatedly been used to: delineate the extent of ground-water contamination from DNAPL; determine the direction of plume migration; and to identify probable DNAPL source area(s). While this approach has been used successfully to characterize the distribution of contaminants in the subsurface, there are limitations. For example, since DNAPL and ground water may flow in different

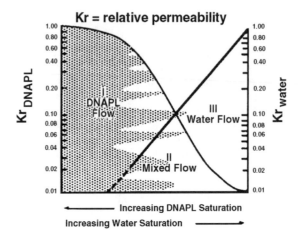

Figure 5-16. Relative permeability graph.

directions, as indicated in Figures 5-13a and 5-13b, ground-water analyses may not necessarily identify the direction of DNAPL migration.

Ground-water analyses may be useful to identify probable DNAPL source areas, but estimating the volume of DNAPL in the subsurface is limited using this approach. Soluble phase components of DNAPL are rarely found in excess of 10% of the solubility even when organic liquids are known or suspected to be present. The concentration of soluble DNAPL components in the ground water is not only a function of the amount of DNAPL present, but also the chemical and physical characteristics of the DNAPL, the contact area and time between the ground water and DNAPL and numerous transport and fate parameters (retardation, biodegradation, dispersion, etc.). One technique has been developed using chemical ratios in the ground water as a means of source identification and contaminant fate prediction (Hinchee and Reisinger, 1987).

Soil/Aquifer Material

Exploratory Borings

Physical and chemical analyses of soil and aquifer material (drill cuttings, cores) from exploratory borings will provide useful information in the delineation of the horizontal and vertical mass distribution of DNAPL. While simple visual examination for physical presence or absence of contamination might seem like a worthwhile technique, it can be deceiving and does nothing to sort out the various liquid phases and their relationships to each other (Villaume, 1985). A quantitative approach is necessary to determine DNAPL distribution.

Drill cuttings or core material brought to the surface from exploratory borings can be screened initially to help delineate the depth at which volatile components from the various phases of the hydrocarbon exist. The organic vapor analyzer and the HNU are small portable instruments that can detect certain volatile compounds in the air. These methods are used to initially screen subsurface materials for volatile components of DNAPL. Identification of individual compounds and their concentrations may be confirmed by other, more precise, analyses.

Analysis of the soil or aquifer material by more accurate means, such as gas chromatography or high pressure liquid chromatography, will take longer but will provide more specific information on a larger group of organic compounds, i.e., volatile/nonvolatile, and on specific compounds. This information is necessary to help fix the horizontal and vertical mass distribution of the contaminant and to help delineate the phase distribution. These analyses do not distinguish between soluble, sorbed or free-phase hydrocarbon, however; a low relative concentration indicates that the contaminant may mainly be present in the gaseous or aqueous phases; and a high relative concentration indicates the presence of sorbed contaminant or free phase liquid either as continuous-phase or residual saturation. A more rigorous set of analyses is required to distinguish between the various phases.

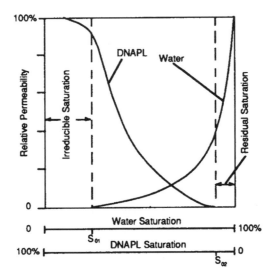

Figure 5-17. The relative permeability curve for water and a DNAPL in a porous medium as a function of the pore space saturation.

Table 5-2. Phase Distribution of DNAPL in the Subsurface

Matrix	Phase
1. ground water	aqueous—soluble components of DNAPL
2. soil/aquifer material	solid—adsorbed components of DNAPL on solid phase material
3. DNAPL	immiscible—continuous phase (mobile), residual saturation (immobile)
4. soil gas	gaseous—volatile components

Additional tests to identify the presence of NAPL in soil or aquifer core samples are currently undeveloped and research in this area is warranted. Squeezing and immiscible displacement techniques have been used to obtain the pore water from cores (Patterson et al., 1978). Other methods of phase separation involving vacuum or centrifugation may also be developed for this use. A paint filter test was proposed in one Superfund DNAPL field investigation where aquifer cores were placed in a filter/funnel apparatus, water was added, and the filtrate was examined for separate phases. These core analysis techniques have potential to provide valuable field data to characterize NAPL distribution.

Cone Penetrometer

The cone penetrometer (ASTM D3441-86; U.S. FHWA, 1977) has been used for some time to supply data on the engineering properties of soils. Recently, the application of this technology has made the leap to the hazardous waste arena. The resistance of the formation is measured by the cone penetrometer as it is driven vertically into the subsurface. The resistance is interpreted as a measure of pore pressure, and thus provides information on the relative stratigraphic nature of the subsurface. Petroleum and chlorinated hydrocarbon plumes can be detected most effectively when the cone penetrometer is used in conjunction with in-situ sensing technologies (Seitz, 1990). Features of the cone penetrometer include: a continuous reading of the stratigraphy/permeability; in-situ measurement; immediate results are available; time requirements are minimal, vertical accuracy of stratigraphic composition is high; ground-water samples can be collected in-situ: and the cost is relatively low.

Data from the cone penetrometer can be used to delineate probable pathways of DNAPL transport. This is accomplished by identifying permeability profiles in the subsurface. A zone of low permeability underlying a more permeable stratigraphic unit will likely impede vertical transport of the DNAPL. Where such a scenario is found, a collection of DNAPL is probable and further steps can be implemented to more accurately and economically investigate and confirm such an occurrence. This general approach has successfully been implemented at one Superfund site (Connor et al., 1989).

DNAPL

Well Level Measurements

In an effort to delineate the horizontal and vertical extent of the DNAPL at a spill site, it is important to determine the elevation of DNAPL in the subsurface. Monitoring DNAPL elevation over time will indicate the mobility of the DNAPL. There are several methods that can be used to determine the presence of DNAPL in a monitoring well. One method relies on the difference in electrical conductivity between the DNAPL and water. A conductivity or resistivity sensor is lowered into the well and a profile is measured. The interface of the DNAPL is accurately determined when the difference in conductivity is detected between the two fluids. This instrument may also be used to delineate LNAPL. A transparent, bottom-loading bailer can also be used to measure the thickness of (and to sample) DNAPL in a well (Mercer and Cohen, 1990). The transparent bailer is raised to the surface and the thickness of the DNAPL is made by visual measurement.

Several laboratory and field studies have been performed which investigate the anomaly between the actual and measured LNAPL levels in ground-water wells (Hall et al., 1984; Hampton and Miller, 1988; Kemblowski and Chiang, 1988, 1990). The anomaly between actual and measured NAPL thickness in the subsurface is also applicable to DNAPL, but for different reasons. The location of the screening interval is the key to understanding both scenarios. First, if the well screen interval is situated entirely in the DNAPL layer, and the hydrostatic head (water) in the well is reduced by pumping or bailing, then to maintain hydrostatic equilibrium, the DNAPL will rise in the well (Mercer and Cohen, 1990; Schmidtke et al., 1990; Villaume, 1985) (refer to Figure 5-18). Secondly, if the well screen extends into the barrier layer, the DNAPL measured thickness will exceed that in the formation by the length of the well below the barrier surface (Mercer and Cohen, 1990) (refer to Figure 5-19). Both of these scenarios will result in a greater DNAPL thickness in the well and thus a false indication (overestimate) of the actual DNAPL thickness will result. One of the main purposes of the monitoring well in a DNAPL investigation is to provide information on the thickness of the DNAPL in the aquifer. Therefore, construction of the well screen should intercept the ground water:DNAPL interface and the lower end of the screen should be placed as close as possible to the impermeable stratigraphic unit.

DNAPL Sampling

Sampling of DNAPL from a well is necessary to perform chemical and physical analyses on the sample. Two of the most common methods used to retrieve a DNAPL sample from a monitoring well are the peristaltic pump and the bailer. A peristaltic pump can be used to collect a sample if the DNAPL is not beyond the effective reach of the pump, which is typically less than 25 feet. The best method to sample DNAPL is to use a double check valve bailer. The key to sample collection is controlled, slow lowering (and raising) of the bailer to the bottom of the well (U.S. EPA, 1986). The dense phase should be collected prior to purging activities.

Soil-Gas Surveys

A soil-gas survey refers to the analysis of the soil air phase as a means to delineate underground contamination from volatile organic chemicals, and several techniques have been developed (Marrin and Kerfoot, 1988; Thompson and Marrin, 1987). This investigative tool is mainly used as a preliminary screening procedure to delineate the areal extent of volatile organic compounds in the soil and ground water. This method is quick, less expensive than drilling wells and can provide greater plume resolution (Marrin and Thompson, 1987).

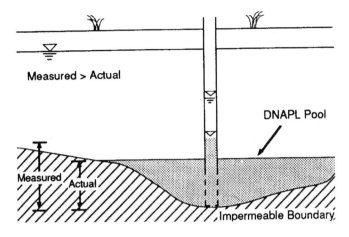

Figure 5-18. A well screened only in the DNAPL in conjunction with lower hydrostatic head (i.e., water) in the well may result in an overestimation of DNAPL thickness.

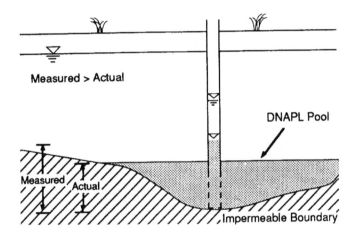

Figure 5-19. A well screened into an impermeable boundary may result in an overestimation of the DNAPL thickness.

Data from a soil-gas survey is a valuable aid in the development of a more detailed subsurface investigation where ground water monitoring wells and exploratory borings are strategically located for further site characterization. There are limitations to soil-gas surveys (Kerfoot, 1988; Thompson and Marrin, 1987) and data interpretation must be performed carefully (Marrin, 1988; Silka, 1988). Soil-gas investigations have mainly been conducted to identify the location of the organic contaminants in ground water. At the time of this publication, the scientific literature did not contain information specifically applicable to the delineation of DNAPL from soil-gas survey data. However, it is surmisable that soil-gas surveys can be used to help delineate DNAPL residual saturation in the unsaturated zone or the location of perched DNAPL reservoirs.

Miscellaneous

The vertical migration of DNAPL in the saturated zone will eventually be challenged by a low permeability stratigraphic unit. According to the principles of capillary pressure, the lower permeability unit will exhibit a greater capillary pressure. Displacement of water by DNAPL requires that the hydrostatic force from the mounding DNAPL exceed the capillary force of the low permeability unit. The Hobson formula is used to compute the critical height calculation to overcome the capillary pressure under different pore size conditions (Villaume et al., 1983).

In an effort to minimize further DNAPL contamination as a result of drilling investigations, precautionary steps should be taken. Penetration of DNAPL reservoirs in the subsurface during drilling activities offers a conduit for the DNAPL to migrate vertically into previously uncontaminated areas. It is very easy to unknowingly drill through a DNAPL pool and the bed it sits on, causing the pool to drain down the hole into a deeper pan of the aquifer or into a different aquifer (Mackay and Cherry, 1989). Special attention to grouting and sealing details during and after drilling operations will help prevent cross-contamination.

Precautionary efforts should also be considered when a DNAPL reservoir is encountered during drilling operations. The recommended approach is to cease drilling operations and install a well screen over the DNAPL zone and cease further drilling activities in the well. If it is necessary to drill deeper, construction of an adjacent well is recommended. Alternatively, if it is not necessary to screen off that interval, it is recommended to carefully seal off the DNAPL zone prior to drilling deeper.

Well construction material compatibility with DNAPL should be investigated to minimize downhole material failure. A construction material compatibility review and possible testing will prevent the costly failure of well construction material. The manufacturers of well construction material are likely to have the most extensive compatibility data and information available.

REMEDIATION

Remediation of DNAPL mainly involves physical removal by either pumping or trench-drainline systems. Removal of DNAPL early in the remediation process will eliminate the main source of contaminants. This step will substantially improve the overall recovery efficiency of the various DNAPL phases including the long term pump-and-treat remediation efforts for soluble components. Remediation technologies such as vacuum extraction, biodegradation, ground-water pumping, and soil flushing are mainly directed at the immobile DNAPL and the various phases in which its components occur. Physical barriers can be used in an effort to minimize further migration of the DNAPL.

Clean-up of DNAPL can involve sizable expenditures: they are difficult to extract and the technology for their removal is just evolving (Schmidtke et al., 1987). Historically, field recovery efforts usually proceed with a poor understanding of the volume distribution of the DNAPL. This reflects the difficulties involved in adequate site characterization, poor documentation of the release, and the complexity associated with the DNAPL transport in the subsurface.

Pumping Systems

Pumping represents an important measure to stop the mobile DNAPL from migrating as a separate phase by creating a hydraulic containment and by removal of DNAPL (Schmidtke et al., 1990). Very simply, DNAPL recovery is highly dependent on whether the DNAPL can be located in the subsurface. The best recovery scenario is one in which the DNAPL is continuous and has collected as a reservoir in a shallow, impermeable subsurface depression. Once the DNAPL has been located and recovery wells are properly installed, pumping of pure phase DNAPL is a possible option but depends largely on site specific conditions which include, but are not limited to: DNAPL thickness, viscosity, and permeability.

Many DNAPL reservoirs in the subsurface are of limited volume and areal extent. Therefore, it can be expected that both the level of DNAPL (saturated thickness) in the well will decline from the prepumping position and the percentage of DNAPL in the DNAPL:water mixture will decrease rather rapidly. Correspondingly, DNAPL recovery efficiency decreases. Field results indicate that recovery wells screened only in the DNAPL layer will maintain maximum DNAPL:water ratios (Feenstra, 1990). Well diameter was not found to influence long-term DNAPL recovery; however, large diameter wells allow high volume pumping for short durations; and small diameter wells result in lower DNAPL:water mixtures and greater drawdown.

An enhanced DNAPL recovery scheme may be used to improve recovery efficiency. An additional well is constructed with a screen interval in the ground-water zone located vertically upward from the DNAPL screen intake. Ground water is withdrawn from the upper screen, which results in an upwelling of the DNAPL (Villaume et al., 1983); refer to Figure 5-20. The upwelling of the DNAPL, coal tar in this case, improved the rate (twofold) at which the coal tar was recovered, result-

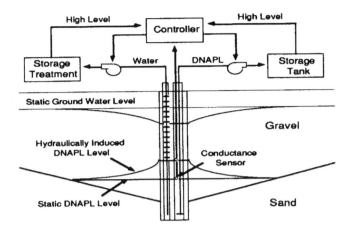

Figure 5-20. A DNAPL recovery system where deliberate upwelling of the static coal-tar surface is used to increase the flow of product into the recovery wells.

ing in a more efficient operation. The ground-water withdrawal rate must be carefully determined; too much will result in the coal tar rising excessively and being either mixed (emulsions) with or suppressed by the higher water velocity above; too low will not cause upwelling. An estimate of this upwelling can be calculated using the simplified Ghyben-Herzberg Principle under ideal conditions (Bouwer, 1978). Laboratory studies indicated that dimethyl phthalate (1.19 g/cc) recovery rate was doubled or tripled over the conventional, non-upconing, recovery scheme (Wisniewski et al., 1985). A similar application of this technique was used to increase the level of DNAPL (solvents) in a sandstone bedrock formation (Ferry and Dougherty, 1986). Other enhanced DNAPL recovery techniques were implemented utilizing both water flooding and wellbore vacuum. Essentially, this minimized drawdown, allowing a maximum pumping rate of the DNAPL:water mixture. Both techniques offered significant advantages in terms of the rate and potential degree of DNAPL removal (Connor et al., 1989).

The highly corrosive nature of some DNAPLs may increase maintenance problems associated with the recovery system. A design consideration during any DNAPL recovery program should include a material compatibility review to minimize downhole failures. This is applicable to the well construction material and the various appurtenances of the recovery system. Manufacturers of the construction material would most likely have the best compatibility information available.

While most scientists agree that the residual saturation of immiscible hydrocarbon droplets in porous media is immobile, researchers have investigated the mobility of residual saturation in porous media for enhanced oil recovery and for NAPL remediation at spill sites. Specifically, this includes a complex interplay between four forces (viscous, gravity, capillary, buoyancy). These forces are dependent on both the chemical and physical characteristics of the DNAPL and porous media. The mobilization of residual saturation mainly hinges on either increasing the ground water velocity which increases the viscous forces between the residual saturation and the ground water, or decreasing the interfacial tension between the residual saturation and the ground water which decreases the capillary forces.

The capillary number is an empirical relationship which measures the ratio between the controlling dynamic stresses (absolute viscosity and ground water velocity) and static stresses (interfacial tension) of the residual saturation (Ng et al., 1978). The former are the viscous stresses and the dynamic pressure in the water which tend to move the oil. The latter are the capillary stresses in the curved water/oil interfaces which tend to hold the oil in place. As the capillary number is increased, the mobility of the residual saturation increases. In a laboratory column study, the capillary number had to be increased two orders of magnitude from when motion was initiated to complete displacement of the hydrocarbon in a sandstone core (Wilson and Conrad, 1984). In a glass bead packed column, only one order of magnitude increase was required. However, a higher capillary number was required to initiate mobility. The difference in mobility between the two columns was attributed to the pore geometry, i.e., size, shape.

There are limitations to residual saturation mobilization. The ground water gradient (dh/dl) necessary to obtain the critical capillary number to initiate blob mobilization would be 0.24. To obtain complete NAPL removal would require a gradient of 18 (Bouchard, 1989). Ground water gradients of this magnitude are unrealistic. Another estimate of the gradient necessary to mobilize carbon tetrachloride in a fine gravel and medium sand was 0.09 and 9.0 respectively (Wilson and Conrad, 1984). The former gradient is steep but not unreasonable and the latter gradient is very steep and impractical to achieve in the field. The same researchers concluded from more recent, comprehensive studies, that the earlier predictions were optimistic, and that the gradient necessary to mobilize residual organic liquid is clearly impractical (Wilson et al., 1990). Another limitation is that along with residual saturation mobilization, the NAPL blobs disperse into smaller blobs and that the blob distribution was dependent on the resulting capillary number (Chatzis et al., 1984). Recovery of the NAPL residual saturation by pumping ground water may be more feasible where the porous media is coarse and capillary forces are low, i.e., coarse sands and gravel. However, even in this scenario, it is expected that the radius of residual saturation mobilization would be narrow.

It is held in petroleum engineering theory that the only practical means of raising the capillary number dramatically is by lowering the interfacial tension (Ng et al., 1978) and that this can be achieved by using surfactants (Wilson et al., 1990). Surfactants reduce the interfacial tension between two liquids, and therefore, are injected into the subsurface for enhanced recovery of immiscible hydrocarbons. In laboratory experiments, surfactant flushing solutions produced dramatic gains in flushing even after substantial water flushing had taken place (Tuck et al., 1988). Unfortunately, surfactants can be quite expensive and cost prohibitive in NAPL recovery operations. Surfactants are usually polymeric in nature and a surfactant residue may be left behind in the porous media which may not be environmentally acceptable. Additionally, surfactants may be alkaline and thus affect the pH of the subsurface environment. It has been suggested that such a surfactant may inhibit bacterial metabolism and thus preclude subsequent use of biological technologies at the site. Significant research in this area is currently underway which may uncover information improving the economics and feasibility of this promising technology.

In summary, practical considerations and recommendations concerning the mobilization and recovery of residual saturation include the following: greater effectiveness in very coarse porous media, i.e., coarse sands and gravel; recovery wells should be installed close to the source to minimize flow path distance; a large volume of water will require treatment disposal at the surface, compounds with high interfacial tension or viscosity will be difficult to mobilize; and implementation of linear one-dimensional sweeps through the zones of residual saturation (Wilson and Conrad, 1984) and surfactants will optimize recovery.

Pumping the soluble components (aqueous phase) of DNAPL from the immiscible (continuous and residual saturation), solid (sorbed), and gaseous phases has been perhaps one of the most effective means to date to both recover DNAPL from the subsurface and to prevent plume migration. Recovery of soluble components quite often has been the only remediation means available. This is largely attributed to the inability to locate DNAPL pools and due to low, DNAPL yielding formations. The basic principles and theory of pump-and-treat technology and the successes and failures have been summarized in other publications (Keely, 1989; Mercer et al., 1990) and are beyond the scope of this publication.

Pumping solubilized DNAPL components from fractured rock aquifers historically has been plagued with a poor recovery efficiency. Although the rock matrix has a relatively small intergranular porosity, it is commonly large enough to allow dissolved contaminants from the fractures to enter the matrix by diffusion and be stored there by adsorption (Mackay and Cherry, 1989). The release of these components is expected to be a slow diffusion dominated process. This is because little or no water flushes through dead-end fracture segments or through the porous, impervious rock matrix. Therefore, clean-up potential is estimated to be less than that expected for sand and gravel aquifers.

Trench Systems

Trench systems have also been used successfully to recover DNAPL and are used when the reservoir is located near the ground surface. Trench systems are also effective when the DNAPL is of limited thickness. Recovery lines are placed horizontally on top of the impermeable stratigraphic unit. DNAPL flows into the collection trenches and seeps into the recovery lines. The lines usually drain to a collection sump where the DNAPL is pumped to the surface. Similar to the pumping system, an enhanced DNAPL recovery scheme may be implemented using drain lines to improve recovery efficiency. This "dual drain line system" (Sale and Kuhn, 1988) utilizes a drain line located in the ground water vertically upward from the DNAPL line. Ground water is withdrawn from the upper screen which results in an upwelling of the DNAPL which is collected in the lower line; refer to Figure 5-21. This increases the hydrostatic head of the DNAPL. Excessive pumping of either single or dual drain line systems may result in the ground water "pinching off" the flow of DNAPL to the drain line. An advantage of the dual drain system is that the oil:water separation requirements at the surface are reduced.

Vacuum Extraction

Soil vacuum extraction (SVE) is a remediation technology which involves applying a vacuum to unsaturated subsurface strata to induce air flow. Figure 5-22 illustrates that the volatile contaminants present in the contaminated strata will evaporate and the vapors are recovered at the surface and treated. Common methods of treatment include granular activated carbon, catalytic oxidation, and direct combustion. SVE can effectively remove DNAPL present as residual saturation or its soluble phase components in the unsaturated zone. In general, vacuum extraction is expected to be more applicable for the chlorinated solvents (PCE, TCE, DCE) than the polycyclic aromatic compounds (wood preserving wastes, coal tars, etc.). When DNAPL is present in perched pools (Figure 5-12) it is more effective to remove the continuous phase DNAPL prior to the implementation of SVE. The same strategy is applicable in the saturated zone where DNAPL removal by SVE is attempted concomitantly with lowering the water table. Upon lowering the water table, SVE can be used to remove the remnant volatile wastes not previously recovered. Often, the precise location of the DNAPL is unknown; therefore, SVE can be used to remediate the general areas where the presence of DNAPL is suspected. Removal of DNAPL by SVE is not expected to be as rapid as direct removal of the pure phase compound. One advantage of SVE however, is that the precise location of the DNAPL need not be known.

Important parameters influencing the efficacy of SVE concern both the DNAPL and porous media. Porous media specific parameters include: soil permeability, porosity, organic carbon, moisture, structure, and particle size distribution. DNAPL specific parameters include: vapor pressure, Henry's constant, solubility, adsorption equilibrium, density, and viscosity (Hutzler et al., 1989). These parameters and their relationships must be evaluated on a site specific basis when considering the feasibility of vacuum extraction and a practical approach to the design, construction, and operation of venting systems (Johnson et al., 1990). Additionally, soil gas surveys which delineate vapor concentration as a function of depth are critical in locating the contaminant source and designing an SVE system.

Historically, SVE has been used to remove volatile compounds from the soil. Recently it has been observed that SVE enhances the biodegradation of volatile and semivolatile organic compounds in the subsurface. While SVE removes volatile components from the subsurface, it also aids in supplying oxygen to biological degradation processes in the unsaturated zone. Prior to soil venting, it was believed that biodegradation in the unsaturated zone was limited due to inadequate concentrations of oxygen (Hinchee et al., 1991). In a field study where soil venting was used to recover jet fuel, it was observed that approximately 15% of the contaminant removal was from the result of microbial degradation. Enhanced aerobic biodegradation during SVE increases the cost effectiveness of the technology due to the reduction in the required aboveground treatment.

Vacuum extraction is one form of pump-and-treat which occurs in the saturated zone where the fluid is a gas mixture. Therefore, many of the same limitations to ground water pump-and-treat are also applicable to vacuum extraction. While the application of vacuum extraction is conceptually simple, its success depends on understanding complex subsurface chemical, physical, and biological processes which provide insight into factors limiting its performance (DiGiulio and Cho, 1990).

Biodegradation

The potential for biodegradation of immiscible hydrocarbon is highly limited for several reasons. First, pure phase hydrocarbon liquid is a highly hostile environment to the survival of most micro-

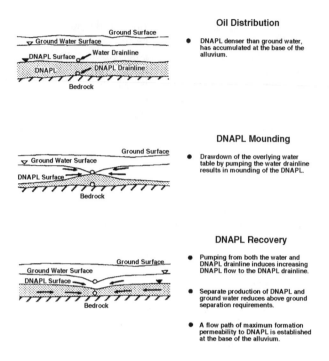

Figure 5-21. Trench recovery system of DNAPL utilizing the dual drainline concept.

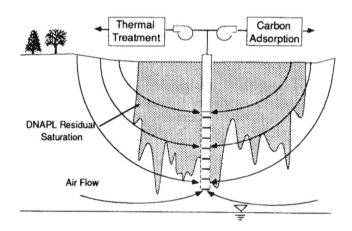

Figure 5-22. Vacuum extraction of DNAPL volatile components in the unsaturated zone. As shown here, vapors are treated by thermal combustion or carbon adsorption and the air is discharged to the atmosphere.

organisms. Secondly, the basic requirements for microbiological proliferation (nutrients, electron acceptor, pH, moisture, osmotic potential, etc.) are difficult if not impossible to deliver or maintain in the DNAPL. A major limitation to aerobic bioremediation of high concentrations of hydrocarbon is the inability to deliver sufficient oxygen. A feasible remediation approach at sites where immiscible hydrocarbon is present is a phased technology approach. Initial efforts should focus on pure phase hydrocarbon recovery to minimize further migration and to decrease the volume of NAPL requiring remediation. Following NAPL recovery, other technologies could be phased into the remediation effort. Bioremediation may be one such technology that could be utilized to further reduce the mass of contaminants at the site. NAPL recovery preceding bioremediation will improve bioremediation feasibility by reducing the toxicity, time, resources, and labor.

Similar to other remediation technologies, a comprehensive feasibility study evaluating the potential effectiveness of bioremediation is critical and must be evaluated on a site specific basis. A number of reviews of biodegradation of surface soils, ground water, and subsoils of wood preserving wastes, i.e., PAHs are available (Lee et al., 1988; Mississippi Forest Products Laboratory, 1989; Sims, 1990; U.S. EPA, 1988, 1989). A comprehensive review of microbial decomposition of chlorinated aromatic compounds is also available (Rochkind et al., 1986).

Soil Flushing

Soil flushing utilizing surfactants is a technology that was developed years ago as a method to enhance oil recovery in the petroleum industry. This technology is new to the hazardous waste arena and available information has mainly been generated from laboratory studies. Surfactant soil flushing can proceed on two distinctly different mechanistic levels: enhanced dissolution of adsorbed and dissolved phase contaminants, and displacement of free-phase nonaqueous contaminants. These two mechanisms may occur simultaneously during soil flushing (Sale et al., 1989).

Surfactants, alkalis, and polymers are chemicals used to modify the pore-level physical forces responsible for immobilizing DNAPL. In brief, surfactants and alkalis reduce the surface tension between the DNAPL and water which increases the mobility. Polymers are added to increase the viscosity of the flushing fluid to minimize the fingering effects and to maintain hydraulic control and improve flushing efficiency. Based on successful laboratory optimization studies where an alkali-polymer-surfactant mixture was used, field studies were conducted on DNAPL (creosote) which resulted in recovery of 94% of the original DNAPL (Sale et al., 1989). Laboratory research has also been conducted which indicated that aqueous surfactants resulted in orders of magnitude greater removal efficiency of adsorbed and dissolved phase contaminants than water flushing (U.S. EPA, 1985a).

Depth to contamination, DNAPL distribution, permeability, heterogeneities, soil/water incompatibility, permeability reduction, and chemical retention are important factors when considering soil flushing (Sale et al., 1989). Prior to this technology being cost effective in the field, surfactant recycling will be necessary to optimize surfactant use (U.S. EPA, 1985a). Soil flushing is complex from a physical and chemical point of view; is relatively untested in the field; and will likely be challenged regulatorily. Considerable research currently being conducted in this area may result in the increased use of this technology to improve DNAPL recovery in the future.

Thermal methods of soil flushing involve injecting hot water or steam in an effort to mobilize the NAPL. The elevated temperature increases volatilization and solubilization and decreases viscosity and density. A cold-water cap is used to prevent volatilization. The mobile phases of the DNAPL are then recovered using a secondary approach, i.e., pumping, vacuum extraction etc. This approach (Contained Recovery of Oily Wastes) to enhance recovery of DNAPL is currently under EPA's Superfund Innovative Technology Evaluation Program and a pilot-scale demonstration is forthcoming (Johnson and Guffey, 1989). A limitation in the use of thermal methods is that the DNAPL may be converted to LNAPL due to density changes (Mercer and Cohen, 1990). The adverse effects from this are that the DNAPL, existing as a thin layer, becomes buoyant and mobilizes vertically resulting in a wider dispersal of the contaminant. Other limitations involve the high energy costs associated with the elevated water temperature and the heat loss in the formation (Mercer and Cohen, 1990).

Physical Barriers

Physical barriers may be used to prevent the migration of DNAPLs in the subsurface and are typically used in conjunction with other recovery means. One feature of physical barriers is the hydraulic control it offers providing the opportunity to focus remediation strategies in treatment cells. Unfortunately, physical barriers, while satisfactory in terms of ground water control and containment of dissolved-phase plumes, may contain small gaps or discontinuities which could permit escape of DNAPL (Cherry et al., 1990). Chemical compatibility between physical barriers and construction material must agree to ensure the physical integrity of the barrier. The history of the performance of these containment technologies is poorly documented and is mainly offered here for completeness of review. A more complete review of these physical barriers is available (Cantor and Knox, 1986; U.S. EPA, 1985b).

Sheet piling involves driving lengths of steel that connect together into the ground to form an impermeable barrier to lateral migration of DNAPL. Ideally, the bottom of the sheet pile should be partially driven into an impermeable layer to complete the seal. Slurry walls involve construction of a trench which is backfilled with an impermeable slurry (bentonite) mixture. Grouting is a process where an impermeable mixture is either injected into the ground or is pumped into a series of interconnected boreholes which together form an impermeable boundary. Again, the main feature of these techniques is to physically isolate the DNAPL.

In summary, site characterization and remediation options for sites containing DNAPL are limited. Field data from site characterization and remediation efforts are also limited. This is largely due to the complexity of DNAPL transport and fate in the subsurface, poorly developed techniques currently available to observe and predict DNAPL in the subsurface, and to the fact that this issue has not been widely recognized until recently. Clearly, there is a growing realization within the scientific and regulatory community that DNAPL is a significant factor in limiting site remediation. Correspondingly, current research efforts within the private, industrial, and public sectors are focusing on both the fundamentals and applications aspects of DNAPL behavior in subsurface systems. Additionally, the number of field investigations reflecting an increased awareness of DNAPLs, is growing.

DNAPL MODELING

A modeling overview report identified nineteen (numeric and analytic) multiphase flow models which are currently available (van der Heijde et al., 1988). Most of these models were developed for salt water intrusion, LNAPL transport and heat flow. Four models are qualitatively described as immiscible flow models but do not specifically indicate DNAPL. A more recent model has been developed which simulates density driven, three phase flow, that is capable of modeling DNAPL transport (Katyal et al., 1990). Presently, very little information is available on DNAPL modeling in the scientific literature.

Multiphase flow modeling involves modeling systems where more than one continuous fluid phase (NAPL, water, gaseous) is present. Modeling any subsurface system requires a conceptual understanding of the chemical, physical, and biological processes occurring at the site. Modeling of simultaneous flow of more than one fluid phase requires a conceptual understanding of the fluids and the relationship between the fluid phases. The significance of multiphase flow over single phase flow is the increased complexity of fluid flow and the additional data requirements necessary for modeling.

As presented earlier, numerous variables strongly influence DNAPL transport and fate, and consequently, the mathematical relationship of these variables is complex. Therefore, it follows that DNAPL modeling presents paramount technical challenges.

Presently, it is exceedingly difficult to obtain accurate field data which quantitatively describes DNAPL transport and fate variables within reasonable economic constraints. DNAPL transport is highly sensitive to subsurface heterogeneities (Connor et al., 1989; Kueper and Frind, 1988; Kueper et al., 1989) which compounds the complexity of modeling. Heterogeneities are, by nature, difficult to identify and quantify and models are not well equipped to accommodate the influence of heterogeneities. Additionally, relative permeability and capillary pressure functions must be quantified to identify the relationship between fluids and between the fluids and the porous media. Unfortunately, these parameters are very difficult to measure, particularly in three phase systems. Prior to an investment of time and money to model a given site, a careful evaluation of the specific objectives and the confidence of the input and anticipated output data should be performed. This will help illuminate the costs, benefits, and therefore, the relative value of modeling in the Superfund decision making process.

In summary, DNAPL modeling at Superfund sites is presently of limited use. This is mainly due to: the fact that very little information is available in the scientific literature to evaluate previous work; accurate and quantitative input data are expected to be costly; the sensitivity of DNAPL transport to subsurface heterogeneities, and, the difficulty in defining the heterogeneities in the field and reflecting those in a model. However, multiphase flow models are valuable as learning tools.

EPA CONTACTS

For further information contact Scott G. Huling, 405/436-8610; Jim Weaver 405/436-8545; or Randall R. Ross, 405/436-8611 at RSKERL-Ada.

REFERENCES

Baehr, A.L. 1987. Selective Transport of Hydrocarbons in the Unsaturated Zone Due to Aqueous and Vapor Phase Partitioning. Water Res. Res., 23(10):1926–1938.

Bear, J. 1972. Dynamics of Fluids in Porous Media. Elsevier, New York, 763 p.

Bouchard, D. 1989. Contaminant Transport in the Subsurface: Sorption Equilibrium and the Role of Non-aqueous Phase Liquids. In: D.T. Allen, Y. Cohen, and I.R. Kaplan (eds.), Intermedia Pollutant Transport and Field Measurement. Plenum, New York pp. 189–211.

Bouwer, H. 1978. Groundwater Hydrology. McGraw-Hill, New York, 480 pp.

Canter, L.W. and R.C. Knox. 1986. Ground Water Pollution Control. Lewis Publishers, Chelsea, MI, 526 pp.

Chatzis, I., M.S. Kuntamukkula, and N.R. Morrow. 1984. Blobsize Distribution as a Function of Capillary Number in Sandstones. Paper 13213, Presented at SPE Annual Tech Conference and Exhibition, Houston, TX.

Cherry, J.A., S. Feenstra, B.H. Kueper, and D.W. McWhorter. 1990. Status of In Situ Technologies for Cleanup of Aquifers Contaminated by DNAPLs Below the Water Table. In: International Specialty Conference on How Clean is Clean? Cleanup Criteria for Contaminated Soil and Groundwater. Air and Waste Management Association. pp. 1–18.

Connor, J.A., C.J. Newell, and D.K. Wilson. 1989. Assessment, Field Testing, Conceptual Design for Managing Dense Nonaqueous Phase Liquids (DNAPL) at a Superfund Site. In: Proc. Petroleum Hydrocarbons and Organic Chemicals in Ground Water Conf. National Water Well Association, Dublin, OH, pp. 519–533.

DiGiulio, D.C. and J.S. Cho. 1990. Conducting Field Tests for Evaluation of Soil Vacuum Extraction Application. In: Proc. Fourth Nat. Outdoor Action Conf. on Aquifer Restoration, Ground Water Monitoring, and Geophysical Methods. National Water Well Association, Dublin, OH, pp. 587–601.

Feenstra, S. 1990. Evaluation of Multi-Component DNAPL Sources by Monitoring of Dissolved-Phase Concentrations. In: Proc. Conf. on Subsurface Contamination by Immiscible Fluids, International Association of Hydrogeologists, Calgary, Alberta, April 18–20, 1990.

Ferry, J.P. and P.J. Dougherty. 1986. Occurrence and Recovery of a DNAPL in a Low-Yielding Bedrock Aquifer. In: Proc. NWWA/API Conf. on Petroleum Hydrocarbons and Organic Chemicals in Ground Water. National Water Well Association, Dublin, OH, pp. 722–733.

Fu, J.K. and R.G. Luthy. 1986. Effect of Organic Solvent on Sorption of Aromatic Solutes onto Soils. J. Env. Engineering, 112(2):346–366.

Glass, R.J., T.S. Steenhuis, and J.Y. Parlange. 1989. Mechanism for Finger Persistence in Homogeneous Unsaturated Porous Media: Theory and Verification. Soil Science, 148(1):60–70.

Hall, A.C., S.H. Collins, and J.C. Melrose. 1983. Stability of Aqueous Wetting Films. Society of Petroleum Engineering Journal, 23(2):249–258.

Hall, R.A., S.B. Blake, and S.C. Champlin, Jr. 1984. Determination of Hydrocarbon Thickness in Sediments Using Borehole Data. In: Proc. of the 4th Nat. Symp. on Aquifer Restoration and Ground Water Monitoring. National Water Well Association, Dublin, OH, pp. 300–304.

Hampton, D.R. and P.D.G. Miller. 1988. Laboratory Investigation of the Relationship Between Actual and Apparent Product Thickness in Sands. In: Proc. Petroleum Hydrocarbons and Organic Chemicals in Ground Water Conf. National Water Well Association, Dublin, OH, pp. 157–181.

Hinchee, R.E. and H.J. Reisinger. 1987. A Practical Application of Multiphase Transport Theory to Ground Water Contamination Problems. Ground Water Monitoring Review, 7(1):84–92.

Hinchee, R.E., D.C. Downey, and R.R. Dupont. 1991. Enhancing Biodegradation of Petroleum Hydrocarbon Through Soil Venting. Journal of Hazardous Materials, 27:315–325.

Hoag, G.E. and M.C. Marley. 1989. Gasoline Residual Saturation in Unsaturated Uniform Aquifer Materials. J. Environ. Engineering, 112(3):586–604.

Hutzler, N.J., B.E. Murphy, and J.S. Gierke. 1989. Review of Soil Vapor Extraction System Technology. Paper presented at Soil Vapor Extraction Technology Workshop, June 28–29, 1989, Edison, NJ.

Johnson, L.A. and F.D. Guffey. 1989. Contained Recovery of Oily Wastes, Annual Progress Report. Western Research Institute, Laramie, WY.

Johnson, P.C., C.C. Stanley, M.W. Kemblowski, D.L. Byers, and J.D. Colthart. 1990. A Practical Approach to the Design, Operation, and Monitoring of In Situ Soil-Venting Systems. Ground Water Monitoring Review, 10(2):159–178.

Katyal, A.K., J.J. Kaluarachchi, and J.C. Parker. 1990. MOFAT: A Two-Dimensional Finite Element Program for Multiphase Flow and Multicomponent Transport. Program Documentation, Version 2.0. Virginia Polytechnic Institute and State University, Blacksburg, VA, 58 pp.

Keely, J.F. 1989. Performance Evaluations of Pump and Treat Remediations. Superfund Ground Water Issue, EPA/540/4-89/005, 19 pp.

Kemblowski, M.W. and C.Y. Chiang. 1988. Analysis of the Measured Free Product Thickness in Dynamic Aquifers. In: Proc. Petroleum Hydrocarbons and Organic Chemicals in Ground Water Conf. National Water Well Association, Dublin, OH, pp. 183–205.

Kemblowski, M.W. and C.Y. Chiang. 1990. Hydrocarbon Thickness Fluctuations in Monitoring Wells. Ground Water, 28(2):244–252.

Kerfoot, H.B. 1988. Is Soil-Gas Analysis an Effective Means of Tracking Contaminant Plumes in Ground Water? What are the Limitations of the Technology Currently Employed? Ground Water Monitoring Review 8(2):54–57.

Kueper, B.H. and E.O. Frind. 1988. An Overview of Immiscible Fingering in Porous Media. J. Contaminant Hydrology, 2:95–110.

Kueper, B.H., W. Abbott, and G. Farquhar. 1989. Experimental Observations of Multiphase Flow in Heterogeneous Porous Media. J. Contaminant Hydrology, 5:83–95.

Lee, M.D., J.M. Thomas, R.C. Borden, P.B. Bedient, J.T. Wilson, and C.H. Ward. 1988. Biorestoration of Aquifers Contaminated with Organic Compounds. CRC Critical Reviews in Environmental Control, 18(1):29–89.

Lindeburg, M.R. 1986. Civil Engineering Reference Manual, 4th edition. Professional Publications, Belmont, CA.

Lyman, W.J., W.F. Reehl, and D.H. Rosenblatt. 1982. Handbook of Chemical Property Estimation Methods. McGraw-Hill, New York. [Editor's note: Second edition was published in 1990 by American Chemical Society]

Mackay, D.M. and J.A. Cherry. 1989. Ground-Water Contamination: Pump and Treat Remediation. Environ. Sci. Technol., 23(6):630–636.

Marrin, D.L. 1988. Soil-Gas Sampling and Misinterpretation. Ground Water Monitoring Review, 8(2):51–54.

Marrin, D. and H. Kerfoot. 1988. Soil-Gas Surveying Techniques. Environ. Sci. Technol., 22(7):740–745.

Marrin, D.L. and G.M. Thompson. 1987. Gaseous Behavior of TCE Overlying a Contaminated Aquifer. Ground Water, 25(1):21–27.

Mercer, J.W. and R.M. Cohen. 1990. A Review of Immiscible Fluids in the Subsurface: Properties, Models, Characterization and Remediation. J. Contaminant Hydrology, 6:107–163.

Mercer, J.W., D.C. Skipp, and D. Giffin. 1990. Basics of Pump-and-Treat Ground-Water Remediation Technology. EPA/600/8-90/003, 58 pp.

Mississippi Forest Products Laboratory. 1989. Proceedings of the Bioremediation of Wood Treating Waste Forum. Mississippi State University, March 14–15, 1989.

Morrow, N.R. 1979. Interplay of Capillary, Viscous and Buoyancy Forces in the Mobilization of Residual Oil. J. Canadian Petroleum, 18(3):35–46.

Ng, K.M., H.T. Davis, and L.E. Scriven. 1978. Visualization of Blob Mechanics in Flow Through Porous Media. Chemical Engineering Science, 33:1009–1017.

Patterson, R.J., S.K. Frape, L.S. Dykes, and R.A. McLeod. 1978. A Coring and Squeezing Technique for the Detailed Study of Subsurface Water Chemistry. Canadian Journal Earth Science, 15:162–169.

Rochkind, M.L., J.W. Blackburn, and G.S. Saylor. 1986. Microbial Decomposition of Chlorinated Aromatic Compounds. EPA/600/2-86/090.

Sale, T. and B. Kuhn. 1988. Recovery of Wood-Treating Oil from an Alluvial Aquifer Using Dual Drainlines. In: Proc. Petroleum Hydrocarbons and Organic Chemicals in Ground Water Conf. National Water Well Association, Dublin, OH, pp. 419–442.

Sale, T., K. Piontek, and M. Pitts. 1989. Chemically Enhanced In-Situ Soil Washing. In: Proc. Petroleum Hydrocarbons and Organic Chemicals in Ground Water Conf. National Water Well Association, Dublin, OH, 487–503.

Schmidtke, K., E. McBean, and F. Rovers. 1987. Drawdown Impacts in Dense Non-Aqueous Phase Liquids. In: Proc. NWWA Ground Water Monitoring Symposium. National Ground Water Association, Dublin, OH, pp. 39–51.

Schmidtke, K., E. McBean, and F. Rovers. 1990. Evaluation of Collection Well Parameters for DNAPL. J. Environ. Engineering, 118(2):183–195.

Schwille, F. 1981. Groundwater Pollution in Porous Media by Fluids Immiscible with Water. The Science of the Total Environment, 21:173–185.

Schwille, F. 1984. Migration of Organic Fluids Immiscible with Water in the Unsaturated Zone. In: B. Yaron, G. Dagan, and J. Goldshmid (eds.), Pollutants in Porous Media: The Unsaturated Zone Between Soil Surface and Groundwater. Springer-Verlag, New York, pp. 27–48.

Schwille, F. 1988. Dense Chlorinated Solvents in Porous and Fractured Media: Model Experiments (English Translation). Lewis Publishers, Chelsea, MI.

Seitz, W.R. 1990. In-Situ Detection of Contaminant Plumes in Ground Water. CRREL Special Report 90-27. U.S. Army Corps of Engineers, Cold Regions Research and Engineering Laboratory, Hanover, NH, 12 pp.

Silka, L. 1988. Simulation of Vapor Transport Through the Unsaturated Zone—Interpretation of Soil-Gas Surveys. Ground Water Monitoring Review, 8(2):115–123.

Sims, R. 1990. Soil Remediation Techniques at Uncontrolled Hazardous Waste Sites. Air & Waste Management Association, 40(5):704–732.

Sitar, N., J.R. Hunt, and K.S. Udell. 1987. Movement of Nonaqueous Liquids in Groundwater. In: Proc. Specialty Conf. Geotechnical Practice for Waste Disposal '87, University of Michigan, Ann Arbor, MI, pp. 205–223.

Thompson, G. and D. Marrin. 1987. Soil Gas Contaminant Investigations: A Dynamic Approach. Ground Water Monitoring Review, 7(3):88–93.

Treiber, L.E., D.L. Archer, and W.W. Owens. 1972. A Laboratory Evaluation of Wettability of Fifty Oil-Producing Reservoirs. Society of Petroleum Engineering Journal, 12(6):531–540.

Tuck, D.M., P.R. Jaffe, and D.A. Crerar. 1988. Enhancing Recovery of Immobile Residual Non-Wetting Hydrocarbons from the Unsaturated Zone Using Surfactant Solutions. In: Proc. Petroleum Hydrocarbons and Organic Chemicals in Ground Water Conf. National Water Well Association, Dublin, OH, pp. 457–478.

U.S. Environmental Protection Agency (EPA). 1985a. Treatment of Contaminated Soils with Aqueous Surfactants. EPA/600/2-85/129 (NTIS PB86-122561), 84 pp.

U.S. Environmental Protection Agency (EPA). 1985b. Handbook Remedial Action at Waste Disposal Sites. EPA/625/6-85/006 (NTIS PB87-201034).

U.S. Environmental Protection Agency (EPA). 1986. RCRA Ground Water Monitoring Technical Enforcement Guidance Document. EPA/530/SW-86/055 (OSWER-9950.1) (NTIS PB87-107751), 332 pp. (Also published in NWWA/EPA Series, National Water Well Association, Dublin, OH. Final OSWER Directive 9950.2 (NTIS PB91-140194).

U.S. Environmental Protection Agency (EPA). 1988. Characterization and Laboratory Soil Treatability Studies for Creosote and Pentachlorophenol Sludges and Contaminated Soil. EPA/600/2-88/055 (NTIS PB89-109920), 138 p.

U.S Environmental Protection Agency (EPA). 1989. Bioremediation of Contaminated Surface Soils. EPA-600/9-89/073, 23 pp.

U.S. Environmental Protection Agency (EPA). 1990. Subsurface Contamination Reference Guide. EPA/540/2-90/011.

U.S. Environmental Protection Agency (EPA). 1991. Site Characterizations for Subsurface Remediations, EPA/625/4-91/026.

U.S. Federal Highway Administration (FHWA). 1977. Guidelines for Cone Penetration Test: Performance and Design. FHWA-T5-78-209 (TS 78 No. 209).

van der Heijde, P.K.M., A.I. El-Kadi, and S.A. Williams. 1988. Ground Water Modeling: An Overview and Status Report. EPA/600/2-89/028 (NTIS PB89-224497). [Editor's note: see also Compilation of Ground Water Models by P.K.M van der Heijde and O.A. Einawawy, EPA/600/R-93-118 (NTIS PB93-209401).]

Villaume, J.F., P.C. Lowe, and D.F. Unites. 1983. Recovery of Coal Gasification Wastes: An Innovative Approach. In: Proc. Third Nat. Symp. Aquifer Restoration and Ground Water Monitoring. National Water Well Association, Worthington, OH, pp. 434–445.

Villaume, J.F. 1985. Investigations at Sites Contaminated with Dense, Non-Aqueous Phase Liquids (NAPLs). Ground Water Monitoring Review, 5(2):60–74.

Williams, D.E. and D.G. Wilder. 1971. Gasoline Pollution of a Ground-Water Reservoir—A Case History. Ground Water, 9(6):50–54.

Wilson, J.L. and S.H. Conrad. 1984. Is Physical Displacement of Residual Hydrocarbons a Realistic Possibility in Aquifer Restoration? In: Proc. NWWA/API Conf. on Petroleum Hydrocarbons and Organic Chemicals in Ground Water. National Water Well Association, Worthington, OH, pp. 274–298.

Wilson, J.L., S.H. Conrad, W.R. Mason, W. Peplinski, and E. Hagen. 1990. Laboratory Investigation of Residual Liquid Organics. EPA/600/6-90/004, 267 pp.

Wisniewski, G.M., G.P. Lennon, J.F. Villaume, and C.L. Young. 1985. Response of a Dense Fluid Under Pumping Stress. In: Proceedings of the 17th Mid-Atlantic Industrial Waste Conference, Lehigh University, pp. 226–237.

Chapter 6

Facilitated Transport[1]

Scott G. Huling, U.S. EPA, Robert S. Kerr Environmental Research Laboratory, Ada, OK

INTRODUCTION

Any process that has the potential to speed the transport of a pollutant beyond what is expected based solely on considerations of idealized Darcian flow and equilibrium sorptive interactions with an immobile solid phase has been broadly termed, "facilitated transport." Hydrodynamic dispersion, a transport mechanism which fits this description of facilitated transport, is not discussed herein.

Research and literature indicates that hydrophobic organic contaminants (HOCs) (i.e., PCBs, DDT, dioxins, polynuclear aromatic hydrocarbons (PAHs)) and heavy metals have a high affinity for mobile subsurface particles and that such an attraction may alter the mobility of the contaminant. Facilitated transport is a relatively new area of study in the field of contaminant transport. Considerable research and interest is currently focused in this area. Although incompletely understood at this point, the effects of facilitated transport at Superfund sites may range from paramount to negligible. There may be an abundance of field data currently available that identifies both the occurrence and the importance of these transport mechanisms. However, relatively little information is available in the scientific literature which attempts to correlate the occurrence of these transport mechanisms with field data.

Most Superfund sites are characterized as having the following conditions: a complex mixture of organic and inorganic wastes; highly variable chemical and physical characteristics; a broad range of chemical concentrations; and a broad spectrum of soil and hydrogeological characteristics. Therefore, several facilitated transport mechanisms may be occurring simultaneously at any site.

Idealized laboratory experiments reported in the literature have been designed to simulate specific physical and chemical conditions. These laboratory conditions have allowed researchers to control the variables which affect the behavior of contaminants in the subsurface and to identify the mechanisms which are likely to occur in the field. An understanding of the various mechanisms of facilitated transport will provide a more thorough understanding of the fate and transport of contaminants in the ground water and ultimately will provide the framework for further development of ground-water remediation technology. The following is a brief technical overview of facilitated transport prepared in support of the Regional Superfund Ground Water Forum. Chapter 7 addresses facilitated transport by organic liquids in more detail.

COSOLVENT EFFECTS

Many releases from land disposal or waste storage systems consist of a mixture of water and organic compounds. High concentrations of organic compounds or solvents in water have significant potential for facilitated transport of usually immobile HOCs. An HOC which partitions into a solvent may exhibit increased mobility, above which is typically predicted from idealized Darcian flow and adsorption/desorption kinetics, due to its intimate association with the mobile solvent. In a mixed solvent (cosolvent) system, organic solutes are subjected to a wide range of chemical and physical processes which ultimately determine how a particular solute will be distributed and transported in the subsurface.

In a mixed solvent system consisting of water and one or more water miscible organic compounds (i.e., methanol, acetone, methyl ethyl ketone, etc.), sorption of HOCs onto the solid phase does not

---

[1] EPA/540/4-89/003.

follow the same sorption behavior as seen for water without the solvent mixture. Instead, as the fraction of cosolvent in the mixture increases, the solubility of the HOC increases exponentially (Fu and Luthy, 1986a). Correspondingly, the sorption coefficient decreases logarithmically and the retardation factor decreases drastically (Fu and Luthy, 1986a,b; Nkedi-Kizza et al., 1985, 1987; Rao et al., 1985; Woodburn et al., 1986). As the sorption coefficient decreases, less HOC will be sorbed onto the solid phase and subsequently becomes more mobile. The decrease in the sorption coefficient has been shown to be a function of the increased solubility of the hydrophobic compound in the cosolvent (Rao et al., 1985). In one set of laboratory column studies, the breakthrough curves for some pesticides in a cosolvent system were equal to that of a conservative tracer, suggesting no measurable retardation of the pesticide had occurred (Nkedi-Kizza et al., 1987). This mechanism of facilitated transport is significant at cosolvent concentrations above a few percent. Therefore, the effects of this transport mechanism are expected to be greater near the source, prior to dilution. A model has been developed to quantitatively describe the sorption and transport of hydrophobic organic chemicals in an aqueous and mixed solvent system (Rao et al., 1985).

Research has shown that an organic cosolvent can also accelerate the movement of metals through a soil matrix. Based on the results of laboratory soil column experiments, ethylene glycol was shown to increase the rate of cadmium migration through three soils compared to water, while 2-propanol increased the rate of cadmium migration through two of the three soils (Sheets and Fuller, 1986). This research indicates that metal contaminants may be found deeper in soils than originally expected because of cosolvent effects.

Immiscible flow of solvents and petroleum fluids in the subsurface has been observed at numerous waste disposal sites. The presence of a mobile immiscible phase can facilitate the transport of HOCs in both the saturated and unsaturated zones. The impact of this facilitated transport mechanism has been described utilizing an analytical chemical transport model (Enfield, 1985). Using this method of analysis, it was observed that ignoring the presence of organic compounds moving either with the ground water or as a separate phase could greatly underestimate the mobility of chemicals.

COLLOIDAL PROCESSES

The transport of contaminants in ground water has typically been characterized as a mass balance of the contaminant governed by the partitioning of the contaminant between the mobile aqueous phase and the immobile solid phase. However, under certain conditions, small solid phase particles and macromolecules, which exist in some subsurface environments, are transported in the aqueous phase and have been characterized as mobile sorbent.

Colloids, defined as particles with diameters less than 10 micrometers (Stumm and Morgan, 1981), are widely recognized as mobile particles in both the unsaturated and saturated zones of the subsurface. Many hydrophobic organic contaminants, generally considered to be highly retarded due to strong interactions with immobile aquifer material, have a high affinity for the mobile colloidal material. Consequently, the association between the contaminant and colloid ultimately affects the transport of the contaminant (McCarthy, 1986). Research has found that batch adsorption experiments which are often relied upon to predict the adsorption potential of a compound may give misleading results if consideration is not given to the presence of the nonsettleable particulate phase or macromolecular phase (Gschwend and Wu, 1985). Furthermore, current solute transport models that assume partitioning between a mobile aqueous phase and a stationary organic carbon or mineral phase may significantly underestimate contaminant mobility (Bouchard et al., 1989).

The significance of dissolved colloidal material to the fate of contaminants depends on the following factors: (a) the identity and concentration of dissolved colloidal matter; (b) the nature of the interaction between the contaminants and the dissolved colloidal matter; and (c) the mobility of the colloidal matter in an aquifer (Kan and Tomson, 1988).

Ground water typically contains a few mg/L dissolved organic matter, but the dissolved organic matter may reach a few hundred mg/L in surface water and ground water near a dump site (Kan and Tomson, 1988). Consequently, the potential effects of facilitated transport are likely to be greater in waste disposal areas. The nature of the interactions between contaminants and colloidal material are diverse. Colloids typically are divided into two groups: organic and inorganic, and the contaminants which colloids interact with are typically divided into three groups: organic compounds, metals, and radionuclides. Therefore, it is apparent that there are many interactions which may occur in a complex mixture of colloids and contaminants. The various interactions between colloidal material and contaminants are further discussed below. The mobility of a diverse range of colloidal matter has been reported by one reviewer to occur in the ground water under a variety of conditions (McCarthy and Zachara, 1989). However the ability to accurately assess the mobility of colloidal material in the subsurface is difficult and at present, is incompletely understood.

Organic Colloids

Natural and anthropogenic organic colloids occurring in the subsurface can assume the role of either the sorbent in the adsorption-desorption and cation exchange mechanisms or the solvent in a solvent-cosolvent scenario. Organic colloids range in size over several orders of magnitude. There are at least three general classes of organic colloids: (a) biocolloids, such as bacteria, spores, and viruses, (b) macromolecules, such as high molecular weight polymers, humic substances, pulp fibers, proteins, and (c) nonaqueous-phase liquids, such as oil droplets or detergent micelles (McCarthy, 1986; Weber, 1972).

Organic Colloids: Interactions with Metal Contaminants

The association of metals with organic matter is a relationship that has been documented repeatedly both in the field and the laboratory. Due to the large surface area per unit mass and anionic surface functional groups associated with some organic colloidal material, metals have a significant potential to be adsorbed. Due to the association with mobile colloidal matter, the metal may become more mobile.

The complexation of metal ions with organic colloids is reported in the literature to vary considerably with a number of experimental variables. Complexation increases at higher pHs and higher humic substance concentrations and decreases at higher ionic strengths. Generally, complexation also varies with the nature of metal ion (McCarthy, 1986).

The chemical and/or physical reaction which influences the metal complexation with organic colloids is a reversible process. Parameters which influence reversibility include: pH, ionic strength, and metal and organic compound concentrations. Complexation reversibility may have important repercussions when ground water from various flow regimes mixes together in common hydrogeological units. When complexation reactions are reversed, the fate and transport mechanisms associated with the complexation may change accordingly.

Although the association between organic matter and metals has been investigated intensively, little information is available on this association with respect to transport in a porous media system. This is an area of considerable research effort at the present time.

Organic Colloids: Interactions with Organic Contaminants

Organic colloids are reported to associate with HOCs by: (a) sorbing organic contaminants; (b) behaving as a solvent to the organic contaminant; and (c) participating in ionic exchange reactions with cationic organic compounds. The association of the mobile organic colloidal matter results in the increased mobility of the contaminant through the porous media. A summary report on the role of colloids in contaminant transport processes indicates that the sorption of organic contaminants onto colloids appears to be a simple partitioning process between the water and the organic colloidal phase. This sorption process is also found to be mathematically predictable (McCarthy, 1986).

Hydrophobic organic contaminants have a high affinity for association with organic macromolecules, i.e., humic substances. Enhancement of the solubility of HOCs by the organic macromolecules can be accounted for by a partition-like interaction of the HOCs with the macromolecule (Chiou et al., 1986; Kan and Tomson, 1988). Enhanced solubility, also referred to as apparent solubility, as used in reference to colloids describes the increased contaminant concentration in an aqueous sample due to the presence of colloids. These two terms do not describe a condition where the water solubility, i.e., the physical constant, of a contaminant increases. Instead, the suspended colloids provide a mechanism whereby the chemical stays associated with the solid phase while suspended in the liquid phase.

The apparent solubility of the HOCs increases with an increase in the colloid concentration (McCarthy, 1986) and with a decrease in HOC solubility. Therefore, the greater the concentration of organic colloids, and the more hydrophobic the compound, the greater the potential mobility of the contaminant by this facilitated transport mechanism. Additional organic colloid features which have been reported to affect the apparent solubility of the HOCs include: molecular size, polarity, and molecular configuration (Chiou et al., 1986). In a laboratory column experiment where an aqueous mixture of organic macromolecules and hexachlorobenzene were introduced together, the transport of the hexachlorobenzene occurred more rapidly than in a mixture without macromolecules (Bengtsson et al., 1987). The presence of hydrophilic macromolecules may change the relative mobility of HOCs, by an order of magnitude in low organic carbon soils (Bouchard et al., 1989).

Several polar organic contaminants are characterized as cationic (positively charged). The sorption of these contaminants onto the solid phase is governed by both electrostatic and hydrophobic forces. Therefore, the retention of these contaminants not only depends on its physical and chemical characteristics and the colloid organic carbon content, but also on the cation exchange capacity of the colloid.

Surfactants

Aggregates of surfactant molecules or micelles may be classified as organic colloids or organic microdroplets that may interact with both metal and organic contaminants and increase the mobility of these contaminants. At critical concentration levels, surfactants form discrete structures called micelles. Micelles are distinctly different from the bulk aqueous phase, and in most instances, serve as efficient media for the partitioning of hydrophobic pollutants (Piwoni, undated). The micelle then can strongly influence the transportation of the contaminants (McDowell-Boyer et al., 1986). The existence of such micelles in leachates has yet to be demonstrated (Piwoni, undated).

Presently, there is little information in the literature which correlates the facilitated transport of organic contaminants by organic colloids with field data. However, the literature does contain several publications of laboratory studies which demonstrate facilitated transport processes involving colloids (Bengtsson et al., 1987; Chiou et al., 1986; Kan and Tomson, 1988; West, 1984).

In conjunction with the numerous interactions which may occur between colloids and contaminants is the high degree of variability and uncertainty of the chemical, physical, and biological subsurface environment. Consequently, estimating the effects of facilitated transport the field is often difficult. However, the concept of facilitated transport of trace organic compounds helps rationalize the occurrence of hydrophobic contaminants 30 meters below waste disposal sites in Ohio (Bengtsson et al., 1987), a distance much greater than predicted by conventional sorption theory.

Inorganic Colloids

Inorganic colloids include clay, metal oxides, and inorganic precipitates in the sub-micrometer size range (McCarthy, 1986). These colloids occur both naturally and from anthropogenic sources. Anthropogenic formation of ferrous phosphate colloids was reported to occur when sewage-derived phosphate combined with the ferrous iron that was released from aquifer solids (Gschwend and Reynolds, 1987). These colloids were detected in the ground water downgradient from the disposal site indicating that the colloids were mobile in the aquifer system.

Although most Superfund sites do not contain radioactive wastes, radionuclide research of inorganic colloids is useful to identify facilitated transport mechanisms. The transport of clay particles has been reported to vary with the ionic strength of the aqueous environment. Laboratory column experiments indicate that clay particles passing through porous media are increasingly retained as the salinity of the solution is increased. Additionally, saline aqueous solutions are less likely to adsorb cesium from solution and, once adsorbed, are less likely to desorb into saline water (Eichholz et al., 1982). These studies show that kaolinite colloids pass readily through various soil media and readily adsorb cationic radionuclides, indicating that facilitated transport may potentially occur at high level radioactive waste repositories.

Little information is currently available concerning the association between inorganic colloids and organic contaminants. Due to both the existing data base concerning organic contaminant sorption to typical subsurface mineral surfaces (McCarthy, 1986) and to inorganic colloidal transport, the scientific framework suggests facilitated transport is a viable transport mechanism. Further research is necessary to elucidate specific mechanisms and the importance of this particular colloid-contaminant association.

PRACTICAL CONSIDERATIONS

The potential role of facilitated transport should be considered while assessing the areal and vertical extent of contaminants in the ground water, particularly if the following pertain: the contaminant is known to associate strongly with organic or inorganic surfaces (e.g., hydrophobic organic compounds, metals); the ground water contains a relatively high concentration of dissolved organic carbon, total dissolved solids, or total suspended solids; the aquifer is relatively porous or fractured, and flow rates are relatively high; or aqueous chemistry undergoes natural or contaminant associated alterations that could mobilize colloidal particles (McCarthy, 1986). Facilitated transport has the potential to disperse contaminants which are usually relatively immobile thereby increasing problems associated with contaminant migration control. On the other hand, low sorption of contaminants in the saturated zone material is desirable from the standpoint of ground-water remediation in that solute removal by pumping to the surface is facilitated (Bouchard et al., 1989).

There are several areas related to field work which must be given special consideration to determine whether facilitated transport may be playing an important role in contaminant transport. These areas are as follows (McCarthy, 1986):

Drilling Methods

Drilling operations, by nature, disrupt the subsurface environment. Drilling may redistribute material and create fine particles as a result of the associated abrasive activities. In addition, many drilling techniques involve the injection of foreign materials into the borehole such as drilling muds, water, and compressed air. The particles introduced into the system may become associated with the contaminants entering the well screen area. Depending on numerous factors surrounding the particle-contaminant association and sampling technique, the contaminant may be undetected in the ground water. Augering is the least disruptive technique available for shallow holes in unconsolidated material. In deeper holes or harder materials casing drive techniques may be required. However, there will be occasions when the more traditional drilling methods are necessary. Careful evaluation of the impacts of the drilling technique and materials is essential to evaluate contaminant transport in the well area.

Well Construction

Materials used in the construction of recovery or monitoring wells may have an impact on the subsurface chemical environment. Sampling artifacts may arise through contact of various well materials with the water that is drawn into the well and sampled. In particular, the sand pack may act as a source of fine particles. As previously discussed, these particles may result in the contaminant being undetected. If the sand (filter) pack is constructed with very fine material, it may function as a filter medium effectively removing larger colloids that may have contaminants adsorbed to their surface.

Well Development

One purpose of well development is to remove drilling muds and fine particles introduced or created during the course of well construction. This process involves dislodging and transporting the particles from the system. Although the objective is to remove the artificially placed particles, this activity may introduce naturally occurring particulate material into the well area. However, every type of drilling operation alters the characteristics of formation materials in the vicinity of the borehole. Therefore, well development is generally recommended to eliminate the particulate matter potentially available to interfere with contaminant transport to the well.

Well Purging

The well is a conduit for the surface atmosphere to artificially contact the ground water. Ground water in the area of the well is in contact not only with the atmosphere, but with the construction material of the well. Additionally, the ground water in the well becomes stagnant and unrepresentative of actual ground-water quality. For these reasons, it is standard practice in ground-water sampling to purge a predetermined volume of water from the well before taking the sample. The purpose is to draw in fresh and presumably representative formation water to be sampled. Excessive rapid pumping, however, may create a dramatically different ground-water gradient and flow pattern from the natural state and affect the distribution of suspended particles in the sampled water. Recently, field methods were implemented during a ground-water investigation to distinguish whether colloidal particles were introduced during sampling operations or if the colloids were truly suspended and moving with the ground water in-situ (Gschwend et al., 1990). This was performed by using very low pumping rates to purge the well in conjunction with a dissolved oxygen sample handling technique to prevent the atmospheric exposure of ground-water samples. These steps yielded ground-water colloid suspensions which the researchers believed were representative of ground-water quality.

Sample Handling

Perhaps the single most important aspect of groundwater sampling that has paramount effects on the detection of contaminants resulting from facilitated transport is filtering the ground-water sample. Essentially, filtering the sample (usually with a 0.45 micron filter) removes some of the colloid and macromolecule material which may be responsible for contaminant transport. Therefore, when the filtered sample is analyzed, there is reduced probability that the contaminant will be detected in the ground water. Further discussion on the repercussion of filtering ground-water samples can be found in Chapters 18 through 20.

EPA CONTACTS

For further information, contact: Scott G. Huling, 405/436-8610; Candida West, 405/436-8542; Robert Puls, 405/436-8543, RSKERL-Ada.

REFERENCES

Bengtsson, G., C.G. Enfield, and R. Lindqvist. 1987. Macromolecules Facilitate Transport of Trace Organics. Sci. of the Total Environment, 67:159–169. [Editor's note: see also Enfield et al. (1989).]

Bouchard, D.C., C.G. Enfield, and M.D. Piwoni. 1989. Transport Processes Involving Organic Chemicals. In: Reactions and Movement of Organic Chemicals in Soils. Soil Science Society of America, Madison, WI, Chapter 16.

Chiou, C.T., R.L. Malcom, T.I. Brinton, and D.E. Kile. 1986. Water Solubility Enhancement of Some Organic Pollutants and Particles by Dissolved Humic and Fulvic Acids. Environ. Sci. Technol., 20(5):502–508.

Eichholz, G.G., B.G. Wahlig, G.F. Powell, and T.F. Craft. 1982. Subsurface Migration of Radioactive Waste Materials by Particulate Transport. Nuclear Technology, 58(September):511–519.

Enfield, C.G. 1985. Chemical Transport Facilitated by Multiphase Flow Systems. Water Sci. and Tech., 17(9):1–12.

Enfield, C.G., G. Bengtsson, and R. Lindqvist. 1989. Influence of Macromolecules on Chemical Transport. Environ. Sci. Technol., 23(10):1278–1286. [Not cited in text].

Fu, J.K. and R.G. Luthy. 1986a. Aromatic Compound Solubility in Solvent/Water Mixtures. J. Environ. Engineering, 112(2):328–345.

Fu, J.K. and R.G. Luthy. 1986b. Effect of Organic Solvent on Sorption of Aromatic Solutes onto Soils. J. Environ. Engineering, 112(2):346–366.

Gschwend, P.M. and M.D. Reynolds. 1987. Monodisperse Ferrous Phosphate Colloids in an Anoxic Ground-water Plume, J. Contaminant Hydrology, 1:309–327.

Gschwend, P.M. and S.C. Wu. 1985. On the Constancy of Sediment-Water Partition Coefficients of Hydrophobic Organic Pollutants. Environ. Sci. Technol., 19(1):90–96.

Gschwend, P.M., D.A. Backus, and J.K. MacFarlane. 1990. Mobilization of Colloids in Groundwater Due to Infiltration of Water at a Coal Ash Disposal Site. J. Contaminant Hydrology 6:307–320.

Kan, A.T. and M.B. Tomson. 1988. Factors Affecting the Movement of Organic Compounds in Soil-Facilitated Transport by Macromolecules and Micelles. Final Report. National Center for Ground Water Research.

McCarthy, J.F. 1986. Summary Report of Transport of Contaminants in the Subsurface: The Role of Organic and Inorganic Colloidal Particles. International Series of Interactive Seminars, October 6–9, 1986.

McCarthy, J.F. and J.M. Zachara. 1989. Subsurface Transport of Contaminants. Environ. Sci. Technol., 23(5):496–502.

McDowell-Boyer, L.M., J.R. Hunt, and N. Sitar. 1986. Particle Transport through Porous Media. Water Resources Research, 22(13):1901–1921.

Nkedi-Kizza, P., P.S.C. Rao, and A.G. Hornsby. 1985. Influence of Organic Cosolvents on Sorption of Hydrophobic Organic Chemicals by Soils. Environ. Sci. Technol., 19(10):975–979.

Nkedi-Kizza, P., P.S.C. Rao, and A.G. Hornsby. 1987. Influence of Organic Cosolvents on Leaching of Hydrophobic Organic Chemicals through Soils. Environ. Sci. Technol., 21(11):1107–1111.

Piwoni, M. Undated. Facilitated Transport: An Overview. Internal Report, U.S. EPA R.S. Kerr, Environmental Research Laboratory, Ada, OK.

Rao, P.S.C., A.G. Hornsby, D.P. Kilcrease, and P. Nkedi-Kizza. 1985. Sorption and Transport of Hydrophobic Organic Chemicals in Aqueous and Mixed Solvent Systems: Model Development and Preliminary Evaluation. J. Environ. Qual., 14(3):376–383.

Sheets, P.J. and W.H. Fuller. 1986. Transport of Cadmium by Organic Solvents through Soil. Soil Sci. Soc. Am. J., 50:24–28.

Stumm, W. and J.J. Morgan. 1981. Aquatic Chemistry. Wiley-Interscience, New York, 780 pp.

Weber, W.J.. Jr., 1972. Physicochemical Processes for Water Quality Control. Wiley-Interscience, New York, 640 pp.

West, C.C. 1984. Dissolved Organic Carbon Facilitated Transport of Neutral Organic Compounds in Subsurface Systems. Ph.D. Thesis. Rice University, Houston, TX.

Woodburn, K.B., P.S.C. Rao, M. Fukui, and P.N. Kizza. 1986. Solvophobic Approach for Predicting Sorption of Hydrophobic Organic Chemicals on Synthetic Sorbents and Soils. J. Contaminant Hydrology, 1:227–241.

Chapter 7

Complex Mixtures and Ground Water Quality[1]

M.L. Brusseau, Department of Soil and Water Science, University of Arizona, Tucson, AZ

INTRODUCTION

The occurrence of organic chemicals in soil and ground water has become an issue of great interest and import. Concomitantly, research on the transport and fate of organic contaminants in subsurface environments has expanded greatly in recent years. Much of this research has been focused on dissolved constituents in aqueous systems. However, the behavior of "complex mixtures" is beginning to receive increased attention. By complex mixture we mean any system other than the simple system of water containing a single solute. Examples of pertinent problems involving complex mixtures include the transport of oxygenated gasoline in the subsurface, the dissolution of diesel fuel and coal tar, and the use of chemical agents such as surfactants or solvents to enhance the removal of contaminants by pump-and-treat remediation. A discussion of these few selected examples will serve to highlight some of the issues associated with complex mixtures, with a focus on potential ground water contamination and remediation.

COMPLEX MIXTURES AND SUBSURFACE CONTAMINATION

Miscible Organic Liquids and Alternative Fuels

Concern about air pollution and the dependency on foreign sources of oil has led to major programs promoting the use of alternative fuels in the U.S.A. Currently, oxygenates, either neat or as additives, appear to be the principal alternative fuel candidates (Haggin, 1989). Of the oxygenates, methanol and ethanol are the primary miscible compounds in use (Hanson, 1991). The advent of alternative fuels has fomented increased interest in the transport and fate of miscible organic liquids in the subsurface. It has also increased interest in the effects of these liquids on the transport and fate of other contaminants.

1. Transport and Fate of Miscible Organic Liquids in the Subsurface

The sorption of miscible organic liquids by soil is generally extremely low. Little sorption is expected for compounds such as methanol and ethanol because of their polarity and large (infinite) aqueous solubility. The minimal sorption of alcohols has been widely demonstrated in the chromatography literature. Limited data for soil systems has also shown negligible sorption of alcohols (cf., Garrett et al., 1986; Wood et al., 1990). Hence, these compounds will be minimally retarded and will travel through the subsurface at essentially the velocity of water. This large mobility can be a useful characteristic. For example, alcohols may be useful as an "early warning" sign of the impending arrival of a contaminant plume emanating from a fuel spill. In regard to the use of alcohols for in-situ soil washing, the greater mobility means that an injected pulse of alcohol may be able to overtake a plume of a retarded solute.

Alcohols such as methanol have been reported to be biodegradable under both aerobic and anaerobic conditions (cf., Colby et al., 1979; Lettinga et al., 1981; Novak et al., 1985). However, the concentrations of alcohol at which biodegradation occurred were less than 1%. Large concentrations (>10%) of alcohol are generally considered to be toxic to most microorganisms and therefore not biodegradable.

---

[1] EPA/600/S-93/004.

2. Effect of Miscible Organic Liquids on the Subsurface Environment

The addition of a miscible organic liquid, such as methanol, to water results in a reduction of surface tension. For example, surface tension is reduced by approximately one-half in systems containing 5% acetone (Paluch and Rybska, 1991) or 50% methanol (Wells, 1981). Very large reductions in interfacial (liquid-liquid) tension are required to mobilize immiscible liquids trapped in porous media (Puig et al., 1982). Using the surface tension data as a guide, cosolvents will probably not produce such large reductions in interfacial tension. Thus, the presence of a cosolvent is not expected to produce emulsions or to mobilize residuals of immiscible liquids.

The presence of organic liquids has been shown to cause shrinking of clay materials and of soils consisting of large portions of clay. For example, clay materials have been demonstrated to shrink (in relation to status in aqueous system) with the addition of acetone or ethanol (Green et al., 1983; Brown and Thomas, 1987; Chen et al., 1987). This shrinkage can result in an increase in hydraulic conductivity (Brown and Thomas, 1987). Thus, it is possible that the presence of large concentrations of cosolvent could cause shrinking and cracking of subsurface domains containing large fractions of clay. This perturbation may alter the hydraulic conductivity and, thereby, affect fluid flow and solute transport.

The presence of organic liquids can also affect the properties of naturally occurring organic components of the soil. It is well known in polymer science that organic liquids can cause organic polymers to swell. The degree of swelling is dependent upon the properties of the solvent (polarity) and of the polymer (type, structure). The addition of an organic liquid has been shown to cause natural organic materials to swell (Freeman and Cheung, 1981; Lyon and Rhodes, 1991). One potential effect of the swelling of organic matter associated with the subsurface solid phase is a reduction in permeability due to blockage of pores. Given the relatively small content of organic matter associated with most subsurface materials, this effect will probably not lead to a measurable reduction in permeability in most cases. Another potential effect is the dissolution of components (e.g., humic or fulvic acids) from the solid-phase organic matter. A great deal of research has been reported describing the effect of dissolved organic matter on the solubility, sorption, and transport of organic and inorganic compounds. There is a possibility that large concentrations of cosolvents could extract organic material from the soil, and that this dissolved organic matter could affect the transport of contaminants. This effect will probably be of importance for limited conditions, i.e., for systems with high organic-carbon content soils and highly hydrophobic compounds.

Another potential effect of the swelling of organic matter is the enhanced release of organic compounds (contaminants) residing in the matrix of organic matter. It is generally accepted that the organic fraction of soil is the predominant sorbent for low polarity organic compounds. It is likely that sorbed organic compounds reside in internal as well as external domains of the organic matter. It is quite possible that high concentrations of cosolvents could enhance the release of organic contaminants retained within the organic phase. The swelling of the organic matrix with the addition of a cosolvent allows greater diffusive mass transfer and thus enhances the release of sorbed compounds (Freeman and Cheung, 1981; Brusseau et al., 1991a). This concept is used in analytical chemistry in terms of solvent extraction of contaminated soils. This is discussed in more detail in the following section.

As previously mentioned, large concentrations (>10%) of alcohol are generally considered to be toxic to most microorganisms. Hence, it is possible that a release of a fuel containing large concentrations of alcohol could deleteriously affect the subsurface biota. The potential effect of large concentrations of alcohols on microbial communities in the subsurface appears to have received minimal attention.

3. Effect of Miscible Organic Liquids on the Transport and Fate of Organic Contaminants in the Subsurface

The influence of an organic liquid (cosolvent) on the solution phase activity of organic compounds is dependent upon the nature of the solute and of the solvent-cosolvent system. For many of the systems of environmental interest, water is the solvent, the cosolvent is less polar than water, and the solutes are of relatively low polarity. For this case, the addition of a cosolvent tends to increase the amount of solute that can reside in solution under equilibrium conditions. A simple relationship describing the influence of cosolvent on the solubility of a solute in the mixed-solvent system is the log-linear cosolvency model (Yalkowsky et al., 1972)

$$\log S_m = \log S_w + \sigma f_c \qquad (1)$$

where S is the solubility in water (w) and mixed-solvent (m), σ represents the cosolvency power of the cosolvent expressed as the slope of the solubilization profile (i.e., log solubility versus f_c), and f_c is the volume fraction of organic cosolvent.

Given that the sorption of low-polarity organic compounds by soils, sediments, and aquifer materials ("soil") is considered to be driven primarily by an entropic, solute-solvent interaction process, it is expected that the presence of a cosolvent should significantly affect sorption. A log-linear cosolvency model, relating the equilibrium sorption constant (K_p) to the volume fraction of cosolvent, for sorption of organic solutes from binary mixed solvents has been presented in the chromatography and soil science literature (Dolan et al., 1979; Rao et al., 1985). This equation is:

$$\log K_{p,m} = \log K_{p,w} - \alpha\sigma f_c \qquad (2)$$

where $K_{p,m}$ and $K_{p,w}$ are the equilibrium sorption constants (mL g^{-1}) for the mixed-solvent and aqueous systems, respectively, and   is an empirical constant that represents any deviation of the sorption-f_c functionality from that observed for solubilization. The latter term is generally considered to represent solvent-sorbent interactions.

The decrease in K_p caused by addition of a cosolvent results in a reduction in retardation (i.e., retardation factor, R, = 1 + (ρ/θ)K_p where ρ and θ are soil bulk density and volumetric water content, respectively). The cosolvency effect has been demonstrated by experiment to cause a decrease in the sorption and retardation of many organic solutes (cf., Nkedi-Kizza et al., 1985; 1987; 1989; Fu and Luthy, 1986; Wood et al., 1990; Brusseau et al., 1991a). An example of this effect is shown in Figure 7-1, where log K_p values obtained for sorption of anthracene by a sandy soil are plotted versus volume fraction of methanol (Figure 7-1A). The effect of methanol on the transport of anthracene in a column packed with the sandy soil is shown in Figure 7-1B.

The discussion of the cosolvency effect presented above was focused on low-polarity organic compounds. A number of environmentally important compounds, however, are ionizable acids or bases (e.g., phenols, amines). The impact of organic cosolvents on the sorption of ionizable organic solutes has received very little attention to date. The decreases in sorption of ionizable solutes, present in the neutral form, obtained with increasing fraction of cosolvent were similar to those observed for nonionizable solutes (Fu and Luthy, 1986; Lee et al., 1991), as might be expected. In these cases, however, the system pH was fixed. The impact of cosolvents on sorption of ionizable solutes in systems where pH is not controlled is of great interest, considering the effect organic cosolvents can have on the pH of the system and on the pK_a of the solute. The pK_a of an ionizable solute changes with the composition of the solvent because of the so-called medium effect, which results from differences in solvent-solvent and solute-solvent interactions (cf., Bates, 1969). The pK_a value of an organic acid will increase with increasing fraction of cosolvent (cf., Parsons and Rochester, 1975; Rubino and Berryhill, 1986), while that of an organic base will decrease (cf., Gowland and Schmid, 1969). Observe that for both cases, the shift in pK_a promotes formation of the neutral species. This shift in speciation could significantly affect the nature and magnitude of sorption.

To illustrate the impact of cosolvent on transport of ionizable solutes, breakthrough curves obtained for pentafluorobenzoate in water and methanol systems are compared in Figure 7-2. Note that no sorption is observed for the aqueous system and that the retardation factor is, therefore, 1. No sorption of pentafluorobenzoate is expected since it is in the anionic form under the experimental conditions. The fact that sorption is essentially nonexistent for many organic acids under conditions typical to the subsurface (pK_a<<pH; net negative surfaces) has fomented the use of these organic acids as groundwater tracers. In contrast, R is greater than 1 for the methanol system. This change in R would negate the use of pentafluorobenzoate as a tracer to delineate the velocity of fluid flow. The increase in retardation with addition of an organic cosolvent has also been observed for other acids such as dicamba, 2,4-dichlorophenoxyacetic acid, and chlorophenols (Hassett et al., 1981; Brusseau, 1990; Lee et al., 1993). This phenomenon may be important at waste-disposal sites, where ionogenic chemicals may coexist with organic solvents.

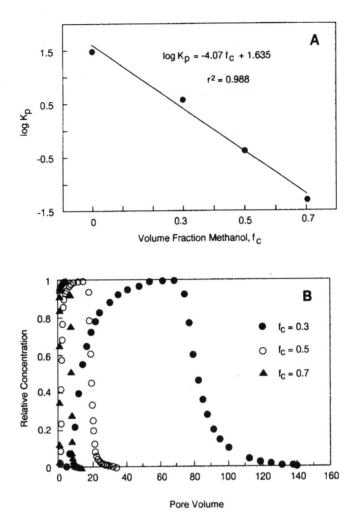

Figure 7-1. The influence of methanol on the sorption and transport of anthracene in a Eustis sand; A) the log-linear relationship between the equilibrium sorption constant (K_p) and volume fraction of cosolvent (f_c). B) The influence of cosolvent on the retardation and transport of anthracene. Data from Brusseau et al., 1991a.

In comparison to the amount of research devoted to the effect of cosolvents on solubility and equilibrium sorption of organic contaminants, there has been little work reported on the impact of cosolvents on nonequilibrium sorption of organic solutes. A decrease in the asymmetry of break-through curves with increasing volume fraction of cosolvent was reported by Nkedi-Kizza et al., (1987), who were investigating the transport of two herbicides (diuron and atrazine) in columns packed with a sandy soil. Breakthrough-curve asymmetry, which was attributed by the authors to nonequilibrium sorption, decreased with increasing cosolvent content suggesting that the rate of sorption is greater in the presence of a cosolvent. The sorption of dioxins by soils from water/methanol mixtures was observed to be more rapid at higher methanol contents (Walters and Guiseppi-Elie, 1988). The desorption rate constant (k_2) has been observed to increase with increasing fraction of cosolvent (Nkedi-Kizza et al., 1989; Shorten and Elzerman, 1990; Brusseau et al., 1991a; Lee et al., 1991).

A quantitative investigation of the impact of organic cosolvents on nonequilibrium sorption of organic solutes was presented by Brusseau et al. (1991a). They presented a model that predicts a log-linear relationship between k_2 and f_c:

$$\log k_{2,m} = \log k_{2,w} + \phi \, f_c \tag{3}$$

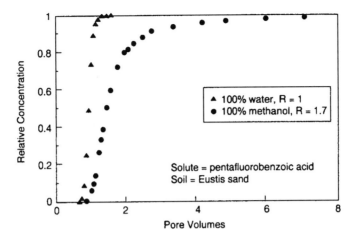

Figure 7-2. The effect of methanol on the transport of an organic acid (pentafluorobenzoate) in a sandy soil; data from Brusseau, 1990.

where $k_{2,m}$ and $k_{2,w}$ are the reverse sorption-rate constants for the mixed-solvent and aqueous systems, respectively; $\phi = a\alpha\sigma$; and a is the slope of the linear relationship between log $k_{2,w}$ and log $K_{p,w}$. The validity of this model was substantiated using experimental data. Examples of their results are presented in Figure 7-3. The mechanism responsible for the cosolvency effect on sorption kinetics was postulated to involve changes in conformation of the organic carbon associated with the sorbent. These conformational changes were induced by the changes in solvent polarity that resulted from the addition of a cosolvent.

The concentrations of cosolvent required to produce substantial enhancement in solubility and reduction in sorption are relatively large (% level) for many solutes of interest. Thus, it has been difficult to envision scenarios wherein cosolvency could be important. The use of oxygenated and alternative fuels, however, has presented cases where cosolvency could be very important. For example, the presence of the cosolvent in alternative fuels (e.g., 50% methanol, 50% gasoline) could enhance the transport of the gasoline constituents contained in the fuel, thus increasing the potential for ground water contamination resulting from a spill. In any case, the effect would probably be limited to the region near the spill (i.e., the near-field domain).

Immiscible Liquids: Multi-Component Systems, Dissolution Kinetics, and Transport of Cosolutes

The disposition of immiscible organic liquids in the subsurface is of interest to environmental scientists, hydrologists, environmental/civil engineers, and petroleum engineers. The vast majority of research performed by these groups has focused on the movement, entrapment, and displacement of the liquid (cf., Marle, 1981; Schwille, 1988). This reflects concerns associated with petroleum-reservoir engineering as well as remediation of solvent- and petroleum-contaminated sites. Other aspects that have begun to receive attention are the dissolution of residual immiscible phases, including the partitioning behavior of multi-component liquids and the rate of mass transfer to the aqueous phase, and the effect of immiscible liquids on the transport of co-solutes.

1. Transport, Entrapment, and Dissolution of Immiscible Organic Liquids in the Subsurface

The movement, entrapment, and mobilization of immiscible organic liquids in porous media has been the focus of a tremendous research effort (see, for example, Chapter 5). Entire volumes have been published on this subject and there is no need to reproduce this material. Instead, the dissolution of immiscible organic liquids, a topic that has received less attention, will be briefly discussed.

Mass transfer of a constituent between two liquids can be represented by (Cussler, 1984):

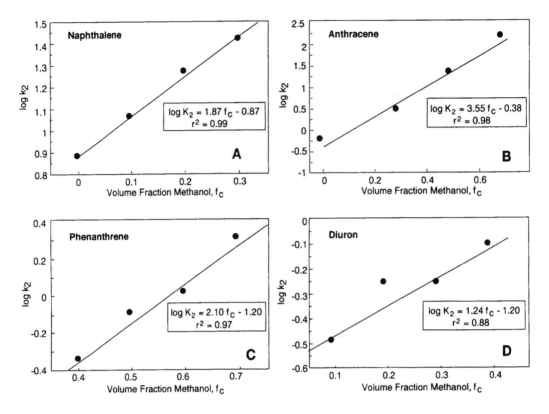

Figure 7-3. The effect of methanol on the reverse sorption rate coefficient (k_2); figure adapted from Brusseau et al., 1991a.

$$\partial C_r / \partial t = k_r (K_r C_m - C_r) \tag{4}$$

where C_r and C_m are the concentrations of the solute in the residual and aqueous phases, respectively; K_r is the liquid-liquid partition coefficient; k_r is the mass-transfer constant (1/T); and t is time (T). The appropriate driving force for mass transfer is the difference between the actual solute concentration in the residual phase and that attained at equilibrium ($K_r C_m$) (Cussler, 1984). Equation 4 is based on a macroscopic approach and the mass transfer term is a global parameter. Microscopic approaches where mass transfer across individual interfaces is explicitly simulated have also been developed. This latter approach, however, is constrained by the difficulty of specifying the nature and magnitude of the interfaces present in the system.

Consideration of the kinetics of dissolution of residual phases of immiscible organic liquids is a departure from the majority of models developed for multi-phase systems, which are based on instantaneous attainment of equilibrium between residual and water phases. The results of several laboratory experiments have suggested that mass transfer between immiscible liquid and water is relatively rapid (cf., van der Waarden et al., 1971; Fried et al., 1979; Schwille, 1988; Miller et al., 1990). Other investigations, however, have shown that liquid-liquid transfer can be significantly rate-limited, especially under conditions that may be found in the field (cf., Hunt et al., 1988; Powers et al., 1991; Brusseau, 1992a). Thus, the use of the equilibrium assumption for mass transfer in the development of mathematical models is still open to question. Much additional research is needed in this area to identify the conditions under which dissolution will be rate limited and the local equilibrium assumption is not valid. Liquid-liquid mass transfer in heterogeneous porous media is of special concern.

2. Partitioning of Multi-Component Liquids

While some of the most widely studied immiscible liquids are composed of a single component (e.g., trichloroethene), many others (e.g., gasoline, diesel fuel, coal tar) are multi-component liquids.

Knowledge of the partitioning behavior of multicomponent liquids is essential to the prediction of their impact on groundwater quality. The partitioning of components into water is controlled by the aqueous solubility of the component and the composition of the liquid. A simple approach to estimating partitioning involves an assumption of ideal behavior in both aqueous and organic phases and the application of Raoult's law:

$$C_i^w = X_i^o \, S_i^w \tag{5}$$

where C_i^w is aqueous concentration (mol/L) of component i, S_i^w is aqueous solubility (mol/L) of component i, and X_i^o is mole fraction of component i in the organic liquid. The liquid-liquid partition coefficient, K_i, is given by:

$$K_i = C_i^o / X_i^o \, S_i^w \tag{6}$$

where C_i^o is concentration (mol/L) of i in the organic liquid and where C_i^o/X_i^o is equivalent to the inverse of the molar volume of the organic liquid. The Raoult's law-based approach has been used successfully to predict aqueous-phase concentrations of compounds (or partition coefficients) for gasoline (Cline et al., 1991), diesel fuel (Lee et al., 1992a), and coal-tar (Lee et al., 1992b) systems (see Figure 7-4). One result of this and other work (Banerjee, 1984; Picel et al., 1988; Vadas et al., 1991) is that it appears that many multi-component liquids can be approximated as ideal mixtures.

3. Effect of Immiscible Liquids on Solute Transport

The impact of immiscible liquids present as a separate phase on the sorption and transport of organic solutes was evaluated by Brusseau (1990). An analysis of experimental data obtained from systems where an immiscible liquid (e.g., toluene) was the mobile phase showed that the retardation of organic solutes (e.g., benzene) was near unity and much lower than that which would be obtained with water as the solvent. This enhanced transport by mobile immiscible liquids is to be expected based upon the relative solubilities of low-polarity organic solutes in organic liquids and water.

The opposite effect is observed, however, when the immiscible liquid is present as a fixed residual phase. The residual phase serves as a sink for organic solutes, resulting in enhanced retention and retardation. For example, the presence of a residual phase of aviation gas was observed to increase retention of petroleum constituents (e.g., toluene) in columns packed with an aquifer material (Bouchard et al., 1989). The presence of residual petroleum or PCB oils was shown to increase the sorption of pentachlorophenol, toluene, and 2-chlorobiphenyl (Boyd and Sun, 1990). A large increase in retardation of naphthalene was observed when a residual phase of tetrachloroethene was emplaced in a column packed with aquifer material (Brusseau, 1990). A mathematical model describing the effect of immobile immiscible organic phases on the transport of solutes was presented by Brusseau (1992a). The model was used to predict the transport of toluene in a column packed with an aquifer material contaminated with a residual of aviation gas (data reported by Bouchard et al., 1989). The simulated prediction produced with the model provided a good description of the data (see Figure 7-5). Based on these investigations, it appears possible that residual phases of immiscible organic liquids can serve as long-term sinks and sources for organic solutes.

When multiple contaminants are present in solution, a primary question to be addressed is the occurrence of antagonistic or synergistic interactions among the solutes, and between the solutes and the solid and aqueous phases. The presence of a cosolute at high concentrations can affect the behavior of organic compounds in several ways, resulting in the following three phenomena: (1) competitive sorption; (2) cooperative sorption; and (3) cosolvency. The first and third phenomenon reduce sorption and thus enhance the transport of solutes, whereas cooperative sorption has the opposite effect. A potential source of these multi-contaminant solutions is the dissolution of immiscible liquids into water residing in or entering the subsurface. The relatively slow movement of water in the subsurface creates the possibility of relatively high solute concentrations (e.g., near $X_i^o S_i^w$ limit) in the vicinity of the immiscible liquid phases.

Competitive sorption, where sorption of a solute is reduced by the presence of a cosolute, has been investigated by several researchers and their results have generally shown no competition for nonionic, low-polarity organic solutes such as naphthalene and chlorinated benzenes (cf., Karickhoff

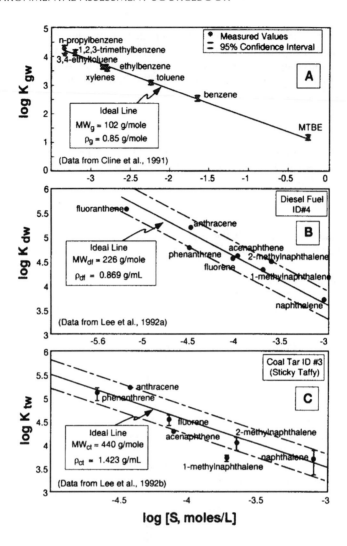

Figure 7-4. Comparison of data obtained from multi-component partitioning experiments to ideal behavior predicted by use of Raoult's law. A) Gasoline system, data from Cline et al., 1991; B) Diesel Fuel system, data from Lee et al., 1992a; C) Coal Tar system, data from Lee et al., 1992b. S is aqueous solubility of the compound, K_{tw}, K_{dw}, and K_{gw} are the equilibrium partition coefficients of the compounds for distribution between the organic and aqueous phases.

et al., 1979; Chiou et al., 1983). Indeed, noncompetition is considered a defining characteristic of the sorption of nonionic, low-polarity organic solutes by a "partitioning" mechanism (Chiou et al., 1983). However, some researchers have reported relatively small decreases in sorption resulting from competition (MacIntyre and deFur, 1985; Abdul and Gibson, 1986; McGinley et al., 1989). The vast majority of studies on sorption in multi-solute systems have used sorbents with relatively high organic-carbon contents (i.e., greater than 0.1%). Conversely, few studies have been reported for systems comprised of sorbents containing small organic-carbon contents, which are representative of many sand aquifers. The sorption of trichloroethene and p-xylene from single and binary solute solutions by two organic carbon-poor aquifer materials was examined by Lee et al. (1988). They observed no difference in sorption between the single and binary systems. The sorption of trichloroethene by a sandy aquifer material in single and ternary solute systems was observed by Brusseau and Rao (1991) to be essentially identical.

Cooperative sorption, where sorption of nonionic, low-polarity organic solutes is enhanced by the presence of other nonionic, low-polarity organic solutes, has been studied by few researchers.

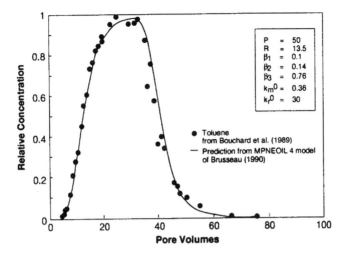

Figure 7-5. The effect of a residual phase of immiscible organic liquid on the transport of toluene in an aquifer material; figure adapted from Brusseau 1990, 1992a.

Brusseau (1991) investigated the effect of a nonionic, low-polarity cosolute (tetrachloroethene) on the sorption of three nonionic, low-polarity organic chemicals (naphthalene, p-xylene, 1,4-dichlorobenzene) by two aquifer materials with small organic-carbon contents (<0.03 %). In all cases, the sorption of the primary solute was enhanced by the presence of high concentrations of tetrachloroethene. Equilibrium sorption constants measured in binary-solute systems were 1.5 to 3 times larger than those measured for the single-solute systems. Hence, tetrachloroethene had a synergistic (i.e., cooperative), rather than an antagonistic (i.e., competitive), effect on the sorption of the primary solutes. The enhanced sorption was postulated to result from sorbed tetrachloroethene increasing the effective organic carbon content of the sorbent. Enhanced sorption was observed by Onken and Traina (1991) in recently reported experiments that used synthetic organo-clay complexes. They examined the sorption of pyrene by $CaCO_3$ treated with humic acid to obtain an organic carbon content of 0.003%. The sorption of pyrene in a binary solution with anthracene as the cosolute was greater than that measured with no anthracene. The potential for competitive or cooperative interactions associated with large concentrations of solute dissolving from immiscible liquids requires further study, especially for systems consisting of solids with small organic-carbon contents.

Competitive and cooperative sorption results primarily from solute-sorbent interactions. In contrast, cosolvency, where the cosolute is considered a cosolvent, results from solute-solvent interactions. Interest in cosolvency is focused on the impact of the cosolvent on the physicochemical properties of water and the resultant effects on solute behavior in the mixed-solvent system. The vast majority of research on cosolvency has involved miscible liquids, as discussed above. It might be expected that the cosolvency effect of immiscible liquids present at concentrations below phase separation will generally follow the behavior of miscible cosolvents, with two major differences. First, the immiscible liquids are generally of lesser polarity than are the miscible solvents. By this measure, the immiscible cosolvent should have a greater effect on the solubility and sorption of a low-polarity organic solute. However, the lower polarity of the immiscible cosolvent also limits the amount of cosolvent that can reside in the aqueous phase. Thus, the volume fraction of many immiscible cosolvents may be limited to less than 1%. These small volume fractions may not be sufficient to induce a significant cosolvency effect.

The cosolvency of water-immiscible liquids was investigated by Pinal et al. (1990) and Rao et al. (1990). They found that, while the impact of immiscible cosolvents on solubility and sorption of hydrophobic organic solutes depended upon the polarity of the cosolvent, the general trends were similar to those observed for miscible cosolvents. However, for some immiscible liquids, the presence of a miscible cosolvent was required to enhance the solubility of the immiscible liquid to levels such that the immiscible cosolvent had an appreciable cosolvency effect. Much more research is needed on the potential cosolvency effect of solutes dissolving from immiscible liquids.

COMPLEX MIXTURES AND REMEDIATION OF
CONTAMINATED SOIL AND GROUND WATER

"Pump-and-treat" is one of the most commonly used techniques for attempting to remediate contaminated ground water. In fact, approximately 68% of Superfund Records of Decision list pump-and-treat as the primary remediation technique (Travis and Doty, 1990). Confidence in and popularity of pump-and-treat is beginning to wane as its effectiveness has proven to be questionable. In a recent analysis of 19 active or completed pump-and-treat operations, it was concluded that, although ground-water extraction is an effective method for containing plumes, it is not practicable to rely solely on pump-and-treat to achieve health-based cleanup objectives (Haley et al., 1991). It was recommended that methods to enhance extraction effectiveness and efficiency be considered. In order to design enhanced removal techniques, the factors responsible for poor performance of pump-and-treat must be understood.

Two phenomena relating to poor performance of pump-and-treat systems have been observed at many sites. The first is the so-called "tailing" phenomenon, wherein the rate of reduction in contaminant concentration in water declines greatly after a relatively short phase of rapid reduction. This behavior results in an asymptotic concentration-time profile and greatly delayed cleanup times. The second phenomenon has been popularly termed "rebound" and is characterized by an increase in contaminant concentration after cessation of pumping. Both of these phenomena greatly reduce the efficacy of pump-and-treat remediation systems.

Factors Influencing the Efficacy of Pump-and-Treat Remediation

The tailing and rebound phenomena discussed above are indicative of nonideal contaminant transport. The fact that transport nonideality can have a significant impact on the effectiveness of pump-and-treat remediation is just beginning to be acknowledged (cf., Hall, 1988; Brusseau and Rao, 1989; Keely, 1989; Mackay and Cherry, 1989). Of primary concern for this technique is the removal efficiency associated with a given pumping regime or, in other words, the amount of time and water required to flush the aquifer to a specified contaminant concentration level. The concentration/time function is sensitive to nonideal transport. In general, most nonideality factors will increase the time and the volume of water required to effect remediation.

Some of the major factors that can cause nonideal transport are briefly discussed.

1. *Flow in heterogeneous porous media*: Aquifers are heterogeneous in nature; hydraulic conductivity and sorption capacity are generally the two most significant properties. The hydrodynamics of fluid flow in heterogeneous systems causes nonideal solute transport. For example, the existence of low-conductivity media (e.g., silt/clay lenses) within a sandy aquifer creates domains through which advective flow and transport are minimal in comparison to the surrounding sand. Contaminant associated with the silt/clay lenses, or the "nonadvective" domain, is released to flowing groundwater primarily by pore-water diffusion. Increasing the flow rate can increase the state of disequilibrium between the advective and nonadvective domains and result in delayed removal (i.e., "tailing"). The effects of variable velocity fields caused by hydraulic conductivity heterogeneity can also be caused by sorption capacity variability.
2. *Sorption/desorption kinetics*: Recent research has revealed that adsorption/desorption of organic solutes by aquifer materials can be significantly rate limited (Lee et al., 1988; Ball and Roberts, 1991; Brusseau and Reid, 1991; Brusseau et al., 1991b). The rate-limiting mechanism apparently involves constrained diffusion within the sorbent matrix (Ball and Roberts, 1991; Brusseau et al., 1991c). The validity of the local equilibrium assumption is dependent, in part, upon the hydrodynamic residence time of the contaminant in the system, which is a function of, among other factors, pore-water velocity. Increasing the velocity, as is done in pump-and-treat, can cause or enhance nonequilibrium conditions as a result of reduced residence time. Nonequilibrium will produce aqueous-phase concentration values lower than those obtained under ideal, equilibrium conditions. Thus, tailing will occur and removal by flushing will take longer.

3. *Immiscible liquid dissolution kinetics*: In many cases, residual phases of immiscible organic liquids may exist in portions of the contaminated subsurface. It has been shown that very large pore-water velocities (i.e., hydraulic gradients) are required to displace residual saturation (Wilson and Conrad, 1984; Willhite, 1986; Hunt et al., 1988). Hence, the primary means of removal will be dissolution into water and volatilization into the soil atmosphere. The immiscible liquid, therefore, serves as a long-term source of contaminant. As discussed above, the dissolution of immiscible liquid into water may be rate limited and, in such cases, would be dependent upon pore water velocity. Increased velocity would enhance nonequilibrium conditions and, thus, result in tailing and delayed removal.

4. *Contaminant aging*: Recent research has shown that contaminants that have been in contact with porous media for long times are much more resistant to desorption, extraction, and degradation. For example, contaminated soil samples taken from field sites exhibit solid:aqueous distribution ratios that are much larger than those measured or estimated based on spiking the porous media with the same contaminant (e.g., adding contaminant to uncontaminated sample) (Steinberg et al., 1987; Pignatello et al., 1990; Smith et al., 1990; Scribner et al. 1992). In addition, the desorption rate coefficients determined for previously contaminated media collected from the field have been shown to be much smaller than the values obtained for spiked samples (Steinberg et al., 1987). These field-based observations are supported by laboratory experiments that show desorption rate coefficients to decrease with increasing time of contact prior to desorption (Karickhoff, 1980; McCall and Agin, 1985; Coates and Elzerman, 1986; Brusseau et al., 1991c). These phenomena are significant not only because of the delayed removal they can cause, but also because the aged contaminants appear to be highly resistant to degradative processes (cf., Steinberg et al., 1987; Scribner et al., 1992). Thus, these aged contaminant residues may be resistant to remediation, except perhaps by use of an enhancement technique.

5. *Other Factors*: Other factors, such as nonuniform flowpaths and stagnation zones, can contribute to observed nonideal phenomena such as tailing during a pump-and-treat remediation. The effects of these factors are, however, much more a function of well-field dynamics than contaminant-media interactions and, as such, would not be affected by chemical enhancements.

It is apparent from the above discussion that several factors influencing contaminant transport can have deleterious effects on the efficacy of pump-and-treat remediation. These effects can create conditions where the expected, desirable result of large decreases in remediation time is not obtained when pumping is initiated or increased. These factors must be considered when designing pump-and-treat remediation systems.

Unfortunately, there has been very little quantitative analysis of the impact of nonideal transport on aquifer flushing. An example taken from one of the few such analyses is presented in Figure 7-6 (adapted from Brusseau, 1993). The data presented in the figure were obtained from a pilot-scale aquifer flushing system wherein a two-well injection-withdrawal couplet was used to evaluate the effect of injecting clean water into a contaminated aquifer (Whiffen and Bahr, 1984). These, as well as other data were used by Brusseau (1992b) to evaluate the ability of a multifactor nonideality model to predict field-scale solute transport. The data were subsequently used to quantitatively evaluate the effect of porous-media heterogeneity and nonequilibrium sorption on the effectiveness of pump-and-treat (Brusseau, 1993). The predicted removal curve for the case of uniform aquifer properties and instantaneous sorption/desorption is shown in Figure 7-6. It is evident that the prediction greatly underestimates the volume of water required to remove the contaminant. The predicted simulation obtained for the case of variable hydraulic conductivity and rate-limited sorption/ desorption matches the field data extremely well (see Figure 7-6). A comparison of this prediction to the one obtained for ideal conditions clearly illustrates the effect that nonideal transport factors can have on aquifer flushing.

The predicted removal of contaminant for the case of spatially variable hydraulic conductivity and instantaneous sorption/ desorption is also shown in Figure 7-6. While this prediction does not match the early field observations, at large pore volumes the simulated curve approaches the curve obtained by including the combined effects of variable conductivity and rate-limited sorption/desorption. This suggests that, while both factors contribute to nonideal transport, spatially variable conductivity may be the more important factor constraining the efficacy of aquifer flushing in this system. The knowl-

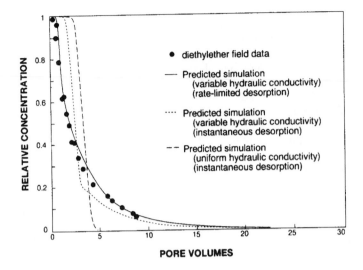

Figure 7-6. The effect of nonideal transport on removal of organic contaminants from aquifers by flushing. Field data from Whiffen and Bahr, 1984; model used for simulations from Brusseau et al., 1989. Figure adapted from Brusseau, 1993.

edge of which factor or factors is the major cause of nonideal transport is essential in the design of an effective method for enhancing the efficiency of a pump-and-treat operation.

Chemical Enhancement of Pump-and-Treat Remediation

Several chemical-based techniques for enhancing contaminant removal in the subsurface are under investigation (e.g., addition of surfactants, cosolvents, complexing agents), and each has advantages and disadvantages. A detailed discussion of chemical enhancement techniques was presented by Palmer and Fish (1992). However, several aspects relating to the impact of nonideal transport phenomena on the efficacy of chemical enhancement were not discussed.

Surfactants are currently the focus of the research effort on chemical enhancements and, based on preliminary laboratory data, appear to have promise for enhancing pump-and-treat remediation in some situations. The use of dissolved organic matter (DOM) and of cosolvents is also being investigated, albeit at a smaller scale. Miscible cosolvents, such as methanol, reduce the net polarity of the mixed solvent when added to water and thereby increase the quantity of a nonionic organic compound that can dissolve in the mixed solvent. This increase, in turn, results in a smaller equilibrium sorption constant and less attendant retardation. Thus, the addition of a cosolvent can reduce the volume of water required to flush a contaminant from porous media by altering the equilibrium phase distribution. A similar result is obtained with surfactants and DOM, although by different mechanisms. Hence, surfactants, DOM, and cosolvents act to increase the aqueous-phase concentration of organic compounds, the so-called "solubilization" effect. This effect is of special interest for the removal of residual phases of immiscible liquids. The other major method of removing trapped residual phases, mobilization, will not be considered in the present discussion.

A comparison of the relative degree to which aqueous-phase concentration of contaminant is enhanced by the various additives favors the surfactants. However, a comparison of this type can be very misleading without considering such factors as potential interactions between the additive and the porous media. It is well known, for example, that surfactant molecules (cf., Ducreux et al., 1990; Kan and Tomson, 1990; Jafvert and Heath, 1991) and DOM (cf., Dunnivant et al., 1992; Moore et al., 1992) can sorb to surfaces of solids, thereby reducing the concentration of additive available for dissolving the contaminant. In addition, surfactants and DOM may precipitate under certain conditions. In contrast, most subsurface solids have a low affinity for miscible solvents such as methanol. Thus, it is possible that, whereas the "active" mass of a surfactant or DOM may be significantly less than the total mass injected into the subsurface, that of a solvent may be essentially the same.

Table 7-1. Enhanced Solubilization Data Collected from the Literature

Additive	Compound	Sorption of Additive#
SDS	TCE (Shiau et al., 1992)	R = variable (Jafvert and Heath, 1991)
SDS	Naphthalene (Gannon et al., 1989)	R = variable (Jafvert and Heath, 1991)
SDS	Pyrene (Jafvert, 1991)	R = variable (Jafvert and Heath, 1991)
Triton	TCE (West, 1992)	R = 2,10 (Kan and Tomson, 1990)
Triton	Naphthalene (Edwards et al., 1991)	R = 2,10 (Kan and Tomson, 1990)
Triton	Pyrene (Edwards et al., 1991)	R = 2,10 (Kan and Tomson, 1990)
Ethanol	TCE (Morris et al., 1988)	R = 1 (Wood et al., 1990)
Ethanol	Naphthalene (Morris et al., 1988)	R = 1 (Wood et al., 1990)
Ethanol	Pyrene (Morris et al., 1988)	R = 1 (Wood et al., 1990)
Humic Acid	TCE (Garbarini and Lion, 1986)	R = 2 (Dunnivant et al., 1992)
Humic Acid	Naphthalene (McCarthy and Jiminez, 1985)	R = 2 (Dunnivant et al., 1992)
Humic Acid	Pyrene (Gauthier et al., 1987)	R = 2 (Dunnivant et al., 1992)

SDS = sodium dodecyl sulfate; TCE = trichloroethene; Triton = triton X-100; Humic Acid = Aldrich humic acid; #Retardation factor, R, of an additive in a hypothetical soil was estimated from data reported in the references cited in this column.

A comparison of the impact of several potential chemical additives on the apparent solubility of selected organic compounds was developed by collecting and synthesizing data reported in the literature (see Table 7-1). The effect of sorption and precipitation of the additives was taken into account. The results of the analyses are presented in Figure 7-7A to C. For all three solutes, the nonionic surfactant (Triton), with low assumed sorption, produced the greatest enhancement. The cosolvent (ethanol) produced the lowest degree of enhancement for all three solutes. The solubilization effect of ethanol increases dramatically at cosolvent concentrations above those used in these analyses. It is readily apparent that the relative enhancement effect will vary by solute, and by other factors such as the nature of the sorbent. The comparison of the effectiveness of various additives under a range of conditions is a topic requiring more research.

The primary criterion upon which chemical enhancement additives are judged is their solubilization potential. The impact of interactions between the additive and the solid phase on this enhancement is an important factor to consider, as discussed above. However, there are several other factors that should also be considered when selecting an enhancement agent. In this regard, cosolvents have several benefits that surfactants and DOM do not.

First, the addition of a cosolvent increases the magnitude of the desorption rate coefficient (not to be confused with an increase in the rate of desorption), thereby reducing the time required to attain equilibrium. This reduction in the degree of nonequilibrium would result in reduced tailing during pumping. This, in turn, would decrease the volume of water and the time required to remove the contaminant by flushing. As previously discussed, rate-limited desorption may impose a significant constraint on the efficacy of pump-and-treat remediation. If so, the ability of a cosolvent to reduce the degree of nonequilibrium would be a major attribute. There is no reason to expect surfactants or DOM to increase desorption rate coefficients.

Second, cosolvents may be able to "extract" the highly retained, aged contaminants that have been observed in field studies (see discussion above). There is no reason to suppose that surfactants or DOM could act in an "extractive" manner. Conversely, there is good reason to suppose that cosolvents could enhance the release of aged contaminants, based on the results of solvent extraction techniques used in the analysis of contaminated soils (cf., Sawhney et al., 1988) and on the results of experiments that evaluated the effect of cosolvents on the desorption of organic compounds (Freeman and Cheung, 1981; Nkedi-Kizza et al., 1989; Brusseau et al., 1991a).

Third, cosolvents may be able to access contaminant that is residing in low hydraulic-conductivity domains such as clay lenses. During a pump-and-treat remediation, as discussed above, contaminant in these domains is probably removed primarily through diffusion. The clay particles provide a large surface area with which a surfactant or DOM may interact and thereby reduce its availability for enhancing contaminant removal. In addition, the sorption of the surfactant or DOM can enhance the retention of the organic solutes by providing an increase in stationary organic carbon. Surfactant

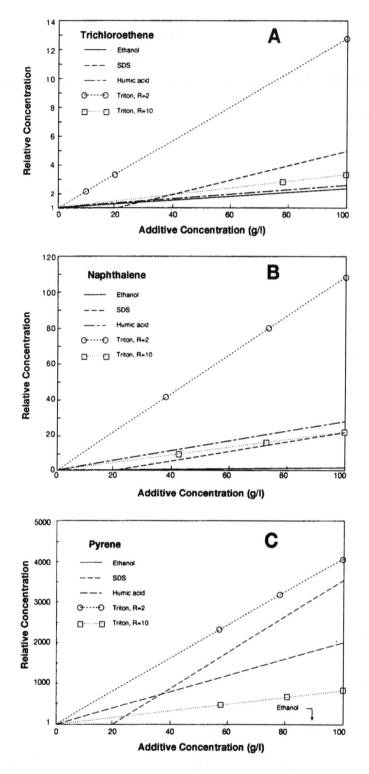

Figure 7-7. The effect of several additives on the aqueous-phase concentration of (A) trichloroethene, (B) naphthalene, and (C) pyrene.

micelles and larger DOM particles may possibly be excluded from the smaller pore-size domains, which would limit accessibility. Cosolvents such as methanol do not sorb significantly to solid surfaces and, because of their small size, would not be excluded from any pore domains in which contaminants would be found. In addition, as discussed above, cosolvents have been found to cause cracking of clayey materials. This cracking results in larger permeabilities, which could enhance the rate of contaminant removal from the lenses. Thus, in comparison to surfactants and DOM, cosolvents may have a much greater potential for enhancing the release of contaminants trapped in fine-grained media.

Fourth, cosolvents have the potential for being used in an integrated, chemical-biological remediation technique. For example, methanol is the initial intermediate in the oxidation of methane by methanotrophic bacteria. The addition of methanol to the ground water environment at low concentrations may stimulate useful cometabolic transformations, causing the destruction of otherwise refractory contaminants such as trichloroethene. Under (locally) anaerobic conditions, cosolvent addition may also drive reductive dehalogenation, particularly of compounds such as tetrachloroethene (cf., DiStefano et al., 1991; Gibson and Sewell, 1992). It is possible to envision situations where addition of cosolvents such as methanol or ethanol may initiate transformations that result directly or indirectly in degradation to nontoxic products. The negative effects of high concentrations of cosolvent on the subsurface microbial community may initially preclude the development of biodegradative activity. However, such activity could occur following dilution of the cosolvent during transport.

Considering the preceding discussion, cosolvents may have specific properties that make them useful for enhanced pump-and-treat. However, given these same properties, it is likely that the use of cosolvents will be limited to smaller scale problems. The clean-up of near-field contamination problems is probably where cosolvents can be put to best use.

CONCLUSION

Experience has shown that many soil and ground-water contamination problems involve complex mixtures of chemicals. As discussed in this chapter, these mixtures may affect contaminant behavior through a variety of mechanisms. Because many of these mechanisms are not well understood, approaches for dealing with complex mixtures in the subsurface often involve direct application or untested extrapolation of knowledge derived from relatively simple aqueous systems. Not surprisingly, the results are frequently less than satisfactory.

The primary purpose of this chapter is to identify and discuss, in a generic sense, some of the important processes which must be considered when dealing with complex mixtures in the subsurface, and to illustrate how these may impact ground-water quality. From the discussion, it is apparent that complex mixtures may play a role in ground-water reclamation as well as degradation of ground-water quality. Equally apparent, however, is the need for improved scientific understanding of the processes associated with the transport of complex mixtures and of the influence that chemical mixtures have on the behavior of specific contaminants.

REFERENCES

Abdul, A.S. and T.L. Gibson. 1986. Equilibrium batch experiments with six polycyclic aromatic hydrocarbons and two aquifer materials. Hazard. Waste Hazard. Mater., 3:125.

Ball, W.P. and P.V. Roberts. 1991. Long-term sorption of halogenated organic chemicals by aquifer materials-Part 2. intraparticle diffusion. Environ. Sci. Technol., 25:1237.

Banerjee, S. 1984. Solubility of organic mixtures in water. Environ. Sci. Technol., 18:587.

Bates, R.G. 1969. Medium effects and pH in nonaqueous solvents. In: Coetzee, J.F. and C.D. Ritchie, (eds.), Solute-Solvent Interactions. Marcel Dekker, New York, Chapter 2.

Bouchard, D.C., C.G. Enfield, and M.D. Piwoni. 1989. Transport processes involving organic chemicals. In: Reactions and Movement of Organic Chemicals in Soils. Soil Science Society of America, Madison, WI, pp. 349–371.

Boyd, S.A. and S. Sun. 1990. Residual petroleum and polychlorinatedbiphenyl oils as sorptive phases for organic contaminants in soils. Environ. Sci. Technol., 24:142.

Brown, K.W. and J.C. Thomas. 1987. A mechanism by which organic liquids increase the hydraulic conductivity of compacted clay materials. Soil Sci. Soc. Am. J., 51:1452.

Brusseau, M.L. 1990. Mass transfer processes and field-scale transport of organic solutes. In: G. Moltyaner, (ed.), Transport and Mass Exchange Processes in Sand and Gravel Aquifers: Field and Modelling Studies. Atom. Energy Canada, Chalk River, Ontario, Canada, pp. 816–840.

Brusseau, M.L. 1991. Cooperative sorption of organic chemicals in systems composed of low organic carbon aquifer materials. Environ. Sci. Technol., 25:1747.

Brusseau, M.L. 1992a. Rate-limited mass transfer and transport of organic solutes in porous media that contain immobile immiscible organic liquid. Water Resour. Res., 28:33.

Brusseau, M.L. 1992b. Transport of rate-limited sorbing solutes in heterogeneous porous media: Application of a one-dimensional multifactor nonideality model to field data. Water Resour. Res., 28:2485.

Brusseau, M.L. 1993. The effect of porous-media heterogeneity and rate-limiting desorption on pump-and-treat remediation. In: Proc. Nat. Meeting American Chemical Society, Div. of Environ. Chem., 33(1):65–68.

Brusseau, M.L. and P.S.C. Rao. 1989. Sorption nonideality during organic contaminant transport in porous media. CRC Critical Reviews in Environ. Control, 19:33.

Brusseau, M.L. and P.S.C. Rao. 1991. Influence of sorbate structure on nonequilibrium sorption of organic compounds. Environ. Sci. Technol., 25:1501.

Brusseau, M.L. and M.L. Reid. 1991. Nonequilibrium sorption of organic chemicals by low organic carbon aquifer materials. Chemosphere, 22:341.

Brusseau, M.L., R.E. Jessup, and P.S.C. Rao. 1989. Modeling the transport of solutes influenced by multi-process nonequilibrium. Water Resour. Res., 25:1971.

Brusseau, M.L., A.L. Wood, and P.S.C. Rao. 1991a. The influence of organic cosolvents on the sorption kinetics of hydrophobic organic chemicals. Environ. Sci. Technol., 25:903.

Brusseau, M.L., T. Larsen, and T.H. Christensen. 1991b. Rate limited sorption and nonequilibrium transport of organic chemicals in low organic carbon aquifer materials. Water Resour. Res., 27:1137.

Brusseau, M.L., R.E. Jessup, and P.S.C. Rao. 1991c. Nonequilibrium sorption of organic chemicals: Elucidation of rate-limiting processes. Environ. Sci. Technol., 25:134.

Chen, S., P.F. Low, J.H. Cushman, and C.B. Roth. 1987. Organic compound effects on swelling and flocculation of upton montmorillonite. Soil Sci. Soc. Am. J., 51:1444.

Chiou, C.T., P.E. Porter, and D.W. Schmedding. 1983. Partition equilibria of nonionic organic compounds between soil organic matter and water. Environ. Sci. Technol., 17:227.

Cline, P.V., J.J. Delfino, and P.S.C. Rao. 1991. Partitioning of aromatic constituents into water from gasoline and other complex solvent mixtures. Environ. Sci. Technol., 25:914.

Coates, J.T. and A.W. Elzerman. 1986. Desorption kinetics for selected PCB congeners from river sediments. J. Contam. Hydrol., 1:191.

Colby, J., H. Dalton, and R. Whittenburg. 1979. Biological and biochemical aspects of microbial growth on C_1 compounds. Ann. Rev. Microbiol., 33:481.

Cussler, E.L. 1984. Diffusion: Mass Transfer in Fluid Systems. Cambridge University Press, New York.

DiStefano, T.D., J.M. Gosset, and S.H. Zinder. 1991. Reductive dechlorination of high concentrations of tetrachloroethene to ethene by an anaerobic enrichment culture in the absence of methanogenesis. App. Environ. Micro., 57:2287.

Dolan, J.W., J.R. Gant, and L.R. Snyder. 1979. Gradient elution in high-performance liquid chromatography. J. Chromat., 165:31.

Ducreux, J., C. Bocard, P. Muntzer, O. Razakarisoa, and L. Zilliox. 1990. Mobility of soluble and non-soluble hydrocarbons in contaminated aquifer. Water Sci. Technol., 22:27.

Dunnivant, F.M., P.M. Jardine, D.L. Taylor, and J.F. McCarthy. 1992. Transport of naturally occurring dissolved organic carbon in laboratory columns containing aquifer material. Soil Sci. Soc. Am. J., 56:437.

Edwards, D.A., R.G. Luthy, and Z. Liu. 1991. Solubilization of polycyclic aromatic hydrocarbons in micellar nonionic surfactant solutions. Environ. Sci. Technol., 25:127.

Freeman, D.H. and L.W. Cheung. 1981. A gel-partition model for organic desorption from a pond sediment. Science, 214:790.

Fried, J.J., P. Muntzer, and L. Zilliox. 1979. Ground-water pollution by transfer of oil hydrocarbons. Ground Water, 17:586.

Fu, J. and R.G. Luthy. 1986. Effect of organic solvent on sorption of aromatic solutes onto soils. J. Environ. Engineering, 112:346.

Gannon, O.K., P. Bibring, K. Raney, J.A. Ward, and D.J. Wilson. 1989. Soil cleanup by in-situ surfactant flushing. III. Laboratory results. Separ. Sci. Technol., 24:1073.

Garbarini, D.R. and L.W. Lion. 1986. Influence of the nature of soil organics on the sorption of toluene and trichloroethylene. Environ. Sci. Technol., 20:1263.

Garrett, P., M. Moreau, and J.D. Lowry. 1986. MTBE as a ground water contaminant, In: Proc. Petroleum Hydrocarbons and Organic Chemicals in Ground Water Conf. National Water Well Association, Dublin, OH, pp. 227–238.

Gauthier, T.D., W.R. Seitz, and C.L. Grant. 1987. Effects of structural and compositional variations in dissolved humic material on pyrene K_{oc} values. Environ. Sci. Technol., 21:243.

Gibson, S.A. and G.W. Sewell. 1992. Simulation of reductive dechlorination of tetrachloroethene in anaerobic aquifer microcosms by addition of short-chain organic acids or alcohols. App. Environ. Microbiol., 58:1392.

Gowland, J.A. and G.H. Schmid. 1969. Two linear correlations of pK_a vs. solvent composition. Canad. J. Chem., 47:2953–2958.

Green, W.J., G.F. Lee, R.A. Jones, and T. Palit. 1983. Interaction of clay soils with water and organic solvents: Implications for the disposal of hazardous wastes. Environ. Sci. Technol., 17:278.

Haggin, J. 1989. Alternative fuels to petroleum gain increased attention. Chem. Engin. News, 67:25.

Haley, J.L., B. Hanson, C. Enfield, and J. Glass. 1991. Evaluating the effectiveness of groundwater extraction systems. Ground Water Monitoring Review, 11:119.

Hall, C.W. 1988. Practical limits to pump-and-treat technology for aquifer remediation. Hazard. Mater. Tech. Center Report 7.

Hanson, D. 1991. Air pollution cleanup: Pact set for reformulating gasolines. Chem. Engin. News, 69:4.

Hassett, J.J., W.L. Banwart, S.G. Wood, and J.C. Means. 1981. Sorption of naphthol: Implications concerning the limits of hydrophobic sorption. Soil Sci. Soc. Am. J., 45:38.

Hunt, J.R., N. Sitar, and K.S. Udell. 1988. Nonaqueous phase liquid transport and cleanup 1. Analysis of mechanisms. Water Resour. Res., 24:1247.

Jafvert, C.T. 1991. Sediment- and saturated-soil-associated reactions involving an anionic surfactant (dodecylsulfate). 2. Partition of PAH compounds among phases. Environ. Sci. Technol., 25:1039.

Jafvert, C.T. and J.K. Heath. 1991. Sediment- and saturated-soil associated reactions involving an anionic surfactant (dodecylsulfate). 1. Precipitation and micelle formation. Environ. Sci. Technol., 25:1031.

Kan, A.T. and M.B. Tomson. 1990. Groundwater transport of hydrophobic organic compounds in the presence of dissolved organic matter. Environ. Toxic. Chem., 9:253.

Karickhoff, S.W. 1980. Sorption kinetics of hydrophobic pollutants in natural sediments. In: R.A. Baker (ed.), Contaminants and Sediments. Ann Arbor Science, Ann Arbor, MI, pp. 193–205.

Karickhoff, S.W., D.S. Brown, and T.A. Scott. 1979. Sorption of hydrophobic pollutants on natural sediments. Water Res., 13:241.

Keely, J.F. 1989. Performance Evaluations of Pump and Treat Remediations. Superfund Ground Water Issue, EPA/540/4-89/005, 19 pp.

Lee, L.S., P.S.C. Rao, M.L. Brusseau, and R.A. Ogwada. 1988. Nonequilibrium sorption of organic contaminants during flow through columns of aquifer materials. Environ. Toxicol. Chem., 7:779.

Lee, L.S., P.S.C. Rao, and M.L. Brusseau. 1991. Nonequilibrium sorption and transport of neutral and ionized chlorophenols. Environ. Sci. Technol., 25:722.

Lee, L.S., M. Hagwell, J.J. Delfino, and P.S.C. Rao. 1992a. Partitioning of polycyclic aromatic hydrocarbons from diesel fuel into water. Environ. Sci. Technol., 26:2104.

Lee, L.S., P.S.C. Rao, and I. Okuda. 1992b. Equilibrium partitioning of polycyclic aromatic hydrocarbons from coal tar into water. Environ. Sci. Technol., 26:2110.

Lee, L.S., C.A. Bellin, R. Pinal, and P.S.C. Rao. 1993. Cosolvent effects on sorption of organic acids by soils from mixed-solvents. Environ. Sci. Technol., 27:165–171.

Lettinga, G., W. deZeeuw, and E. Ouborg. 1981. Anaerobic treatment of wastes containing methanol and higher alcohols. Water Res., 15:171.

Lyon, W.G. and D.E. Rhodes. 1991. The swelling properties of soil organic matter and their relation to sorption of non-ionic organic compounds. EPA/600/2-91/033.

Macintyre, W.G. and P.O. deFur. 1985. The effect of hydrocarbon mixtures on adsorption of substituted naphthalenes by clay and sediment from water. Chemosphere, 14:103.

Mackay, D.M. and J.A. Cherry. 1989. Groundwater contamination: Pump-and-treat remediation. Environ. Sci. Technol., 23:630.

Marle, C.M. 1981. Multiphase Flow in Porous Media. Gulf Publ. Co., Paris.

McCall, P.J. and G.L. Agin. 1985. Desorption kinetics of picloram as affected by residence time in soil. Environ. Toxicol. Chem., 4:37.

McCarthy, J.F. and B.D. Jiminez. 1985. Interactions between polycyclic aromatic hydrocarbons and dissolved humic material: Binding and dissociation. Environ. Sci. Technol., 19:1072.

McGinley, P.M., L.E. Katz, and W.J. Weber. 1989. Abstract, Amer. Chem. Soc., Div. of Environ. Chem., 29:146.

Miller, C.T., M.M. Poirier-McNeill, and A.S. Mayer. 1990. Dissolution of trapped nonaqueous phase liquids: Mass transfer characteristics. Water Resour. Res., 26:2783.

Moore, T.R., W. de Souza, and J.F. Koprivnjak. 1992. Controls on the sorption of dissolved organic carbon by soils. Soil Science, 154:120.

Morris, K.R., R. Abramowitz, R. Pinal, P. Davis, and S.H. Yalkowsky. 1988. Solubility of aromatic pollutants in mixed solvents. Chemosphere, 17:285.

Nkedi-Kizza, P., P.S.C. Rao, and A.G. Hornsby. 1985. The influence of organic cosolvents on sorption of hydrophobic organic chemicals by soils. Environ. Sci. Technol., 19:975.

Nkedi-Kizza, P., P.S.C. Rao, and A.G. Hornsby. 1987. The influence of organic cosolvents on leaching of hydrophobic organic chemicals through soils. Environ. Sci. Technol., 21:1107.

Nkedi-Kizza, P., M.L. Brusseau, P.S.C. Rao, and A.G. Hornsby. 1989. Nonequilibrium sorption during displacement of hydrophobic organic contaminants and ^{45}Ca through soil columns with aqueous and mixed solvents. Environ. Sci. Technol., 23:814.

Novak, J.T., C.D. Goldsmith, R.E. Benoit, and J.H. O'Brien. 1985. Biodegradation of methanol and tertiary butyl alcohol in subsurface systems. In: Degradation, Retention, and Dispersion of Pollutants in Ground Water. Inter. Assoc. Water Pollution Control Research, Great Britain, pp. 71–85.

Onken, B.M. and S.J. Traina. 1991. Agronomy Abstracts. American Society of Agronomy, Madison, WI.

Palmer, C.D. and W. Fish. 1992. Chemical enhancements to pump-and-treat remediation. Ground Water Issue Paper, EPA/540/S-92/001. (See Chapter 5, EPA Environmental Engineering Sourcebook.)

Paluch, M. and J. Rybska. 1991. Influence of some organic substances on the surface potential and on the surface tension at the water/air interface. J. Coll. Inter. Sci., 145:219.

Parsons, G.H. and C.H. Rochester. 1975. Acid ionization constants of 4-substituted phenols in methanol+water mixtures. J. Chem. Soc., Trans. Faraday Soc. I, 71(5):1058–1068.

Picel, K.C., V.C. Stamoudis, and M.S. Simmons. 1988. Distribution coefficients for chemical components of a coal-oil/water system. Water. Res., 22:1189.

Pignatello, J.J., C.R. Frink, P.A. Marin, and E.X. Droste. 1990. Field-observed ethylene dibromide in an aquifer after two decades. J. Contam. Hydrol., 5:195.

Pinal R., P.S.C. Rao, L.S. Lee, P.V. Cline, and S.H. Yalkowsky. 1990. Cosolvency of partially miscible organic solvents on the solubility of hydrophobic organic chemicals. Environ. Sci. Technol., 24:639.

Powers, S.E., C.O. Loureiro, L.M. Abriola, and W.J. Weber. 1991. Theoretical study of the significance of nonequilibrium dissolution of nonaqueous phase liquids in subsurface systems. Water Resour. Res., 27:463.

Puig, J.E., L.E. Scriven, H.T. Davis, and W.G. Miller. 1982. Fluid microstructures and enhanced oil recovery. In: D. Wasan and A. Payatakes (eds.), Interfacial Phenomena in Enhanced Oil Recovery. American Institute of Chemical Engineering, New York, NY, pp. 1–27.

Rao, P.S.C., A.G. Hornsby, D.P. Kilcrease, and P. Nkedi-Kizza. 1985. Sorption and transport of hydrophobic organic chemicals in aqueous and mixed solvent systems: Model development and preliminary evaluation. J. Environ. Qual., 14:376.

Rao, P.S.C., L.S. Lee, and R. Pinal. 1990. Cosolvency and sorption of hydrophobic organic chemicals. Environ. Sci. Technol., 24:647.

Rubino, J.T. and W.S. Berryhill. 1986. Effects of solvent polarity on the acid dissociation constants of benzoic acids. J. Pharm. Sci., 75(2):182–186.

Sawhney, B.L., J.J. Pignatello, and S.M. Steinberg. 1988. Determination of 1,2-dibromoethane (EDB) in field soils: implications for volatile organic compounds. J. Environ. Qual., 17:149.

Schwille, F. 1988. Dense Chlorinated Solvents in Porous and Fractured Media. Lewis Publishers, Chelsea, MI.

Scribner, S.L., T.R. Benzing, S. Sun, and S.A. Boyd. 1992. Desorption and bioavailability of aged simazine residues in soil from a continuous corn field. J. Environ. Qual., 21:1115.

Shiau, B.J., D.A. Sabatini, A. Gupta, and J.H. Harwell. 1992. Enhanced solubilization and mobilization of subsurface DNAPL contamination using edible surfactants. In: Proc. Int. Conf. on Subsurface Restoration. National Center Groundwater Research, Houston, TX, pp. 266–268.

Shorten, C.V. and A.W. Elzerman. 1990. Methods for the determination of PAH desorption kinetics in coal fines and coal contaminated sediments. Chemosphere, 20:137.

Smith, J.A., C.T. Chiou, J.A. Kammer, and D.E. Kile. 1990. Effect of soil moisture on the sorption of trichloroethene vapor to vadose zone soil at Picatinny arsenal, New Jersey. Environ. Sci. Technol., 24:676.

Steinberg, S.M., J.J. Pignatello, and B.L. Sawhney. 1987. Persistence of 1,2-dibromoethane in soils: Entrapment in intraparticle micropores. Environ. Sci. Technol., 21:1201.

Travis, C.C. and C.B. Doty. 1990. Can contaminated aquifers at Superfund sites be remediated? Environ. Sci. Technol., 24:1464.

Vadas, G.G., W.G. Macintyre, and D.R. Burris. 1991. Aqueous solubility of liquid hydrocarbon mixtures containing dissolved solid components. Environ. Toxic. Chem., 10:633.

van der Waarden, M., A.L.A.M. Bridie, and W.M. Groenewoud. 1971. Transport of mineral oil components to groundwater 1. Model experiments on the transfer of hydrocarbons from a residual oil zone to trickling water. Water Res., 5:213.

Waiters, R.W. and A. Guiseppi-Elie. 1988. Sorption of 2,3,7,8-Tetrachlorodibenzo-p-dioxin to soils from water/methanol mixtures. Environ. Sci. Technol., 22:819.

Wells, M.J.M. 1981. Ph.D. Thesis, Auburn University, Auburn, AL.

West, C.C. 1992. Surfactant-enhanced solubilization of tetrachloroethylene and degradation products in pump and treat remediation. In: D.A. Sabatini and R.C. Knox (eds.), Transport and Remediation of Subsurface Contaminants. American Chemical Society, Washington, D.C., Chapter 12.

Whiffen, R.B. and J.M. Bahr. 1984. Assessment of Purge Well Effectiveness for Aquifer Decontamination. In: Proc. of the Fourth Nat. Symp. on Aquifer Restoration and Groundwater Monitoring. National Water Well Association, Dublin, OH, pp. 75–81.

Willhite, G.P. 1986. Waterflooding. Society of Petroleum Engineers, Richardson, TX.

Wilson, J.L. and S.H. Conrad. 1984. Is physical displacement of residual hydrocarbons a realistic possibility in aquifer restoration? In: Proc. Petroleum Hydrocarbons and Organic Chemicals in Ground Water Conf. National Water Well Association, Dublin, OH, pp. 274–298.

Wood, A.L., D.C. Bouchard, M.L. Brusseau, and P.S.C. Rao. 1990. Cosolvent effects on sorption and mobility of organic contaminants in soils. Chemosphere, 21:575.

Yalkowsky, S.H., G.L. Flynn, and G.L. Amidon. 1972. Solubilities of nonelectrolytes in polar solvents. J. Pharm. Sci., 61:983.

DISCLAIMER

The information in this document has been funded in part by the U.S. Environmental Protection Agency under Cooperative Agreement No. CR-818757. This document has been subjected to the Agency's peer review and has been approved for publication as an EPA document.

QUALITY ASSURANCE STATEMENT

This project did not involve physical measurements and, as such, did not require a QA plan.

Chapter 8

Reductive Dehalogenation of Organic Contaminants in Soils and Ground Water[1]

Judith L. Sims, Water Research Laboratory, Utah State University, Logan, UT
Joseph M. Suflita, University of Oklahoma, Norman, OK
Hugh H. Russell, U.S. Army Corps of Engineers, Tulsa, OK

INTRODUCTION

Processes which influence the behavior of contaminants in the subsurface must be considered both in evaluating the potential for movement as well as in designing remediation activities at hazardous waste sites. Such factors not only tend to regulate the mobility of contaminants, but also their form and stability. Reductive dehalogenation is a process which may prove to be of paramount importance in dealing with a particularly persistent class of contaminants often found in soil and ground water at Superfund sites. This chapter summarizes concepts associated with reductive dehalogenation and describes applications and limitations to its use as a remediation technology.

Large scale production of synthetic halogenated organic compounds, which are often resistant to both biotic and abiotic degradation, has occurred only in the last few decades (Hutzinger and Verkamp, 1981). However, naturally occurring halogenated organic compounds have existed in marine systems for perhaps millions of years. These compounds, including aliphatic and aromatic compounds containing chlorine, bromine, or iodine, are produced by macroalgae and invertebrates. The presence of these natural compounds, at potentially high concentrations, may have resulted in populations of bacteria that are effective dehalogenators (King, 1988). Microorganisms exposed to halogenated compounds in soil and ground water may also have developed enzymatic capabilities similar to those in marine environments. Enzyme systems that have evolved to degrade nonchlorinated compounds may also be specific enough to degrade those that are chlorinated (Tiedje and Stevens, 1987).

Many halogenated organic compounds are not very soluble and tend to be highly lipophilic, therefore having the potential to bioaccumulate in some food chains. These chemical properties, along with their toxicity and resistance to degradation, present the potential for adverse health effects and ecosystem perturbations upon exposure (Rochkind et al., 1986).

Recent research findings indicate that anaerobic processes that remove halogens from these compounds produce dehalogenated compounds that are generally less toxic, less likely to bioaccumulate, and more susceptible to further microbial attack, especially by aerobic microorganisms utilizing oxidative biodegradative processes. Both aromatic and nonaromatic organic compounds are subject to these dehalogenation processes. Technological application of these processes for remediation of contaminated soils and ground waters is a relatively new concept.

Recent research also has shown that anaerobic dehalogenation reactions specifically involving reductive processes can effectively degrade a wide variety of halogenated contaminants in soil and ground water (Vogel et al., 1987; Kuhn and Suflita, 1989a). Organic compounds generally represent reduced forms of carbon, making degradation by oxidation energetically favorable. However, halogenated organic compounds are relatively oxidized by the presence of halogen substituents, which are highly electronegative and thus more susceptible to reduction. A compound with more halogen substituents is therefore more oxidized and more susceptible to reduction. Thus, with increased halogenation, reduction becomes more likely than does oxidation (Vogel et al., 1987).

An organic compound is considered to be reduced if a reaction leads to an increase in its hydrogen content or a decrease in its oxygen content; however, many reduction reactions (e.g., the vicinal reduction process) do not involve changes in the hydrogen or oxygen content of a compound. Oxidation

---

[1] EPA/540/4-90/054.

and reduction reactions are more precisely defined in terms of electron transfers. An organic chemical is said to be reduced if it undergoes a net gain of electrons as the result of a chemical reaction (electron acceptor), and is said to be oxidized if it undergoes a net loss of electrons (electron donor). Under environmental conditions, oxygen commonly acts as the electron acceptor when present. When oxygen is not present (anoxic conditions), microorganisms can use organic chemicals or inorganic anions as alternate electron acceptors under metabolic conditions referred to as fermentative, denitrifying, sulfate-reducing or methanogenic.

Generally, organic compounds present at a contaminated site represent potential electron donors to support microbial metabolism. However, halogenated compounds can act as electron acceptors, and thus become reduced in the reductive dehalogenation process. Specifically, dehalogenation by reduction is the replacement of a halogen such as chloride, bromide, fluoride, or iodide on an organic molecule by a hydrogen atom. *Vicinal reduction* occurs when two halogens are released while two electrons are incorporated into the compound.

An organic chemical would be expected to be reduced if the electrode potential of the specific soil or ground-water system, in which the chemical is present, is less than that of the organic chemical (Dragun, 1988). The electrode potential is described by the oxidation-reduction (redox) status of the system, referring to potential for the transfer of electrons to a reducible material. The electron (e^-) participates in chemical reactions in soil and ground water similar to the hydrogen ion (H^+) in that electrons are donated from a reduced compound to an oxidized. Redox potential (Eh) is usually reported in volts and is measured using a reference electrode in combination with a metallic electrode, such as platinum, which is sensitive and reversible to oxidation reduction conditions.

The redox potential of a soil system is complex. The oxidation state of each soil constituent, such as organic compounds, humus, iron, manganese, and sulfur, contributes to the measured redox potential. The contribution of each constituent in a system varies with such factors as soil water content, oxygen activity, and pH. Well-oxidized soils have redox potentials of 0.4 to 0.8 V, while extremely reduced soils may have potentials of -0.1 to -0.5 V (Dragun, 1988).

The potential for anaerobic biological processes to reductively dehalogenate organic compounds may be important in the bioremediation of soils and aquifers contaminated with these compounds. These environments often become anaerobic due to depletion of oxygen by the microbial degradation of more easily degradable organic matter. When compounds can be degraded under anaerobic conditions, the cost associated with the maintenance of an aerobic environment by providing air, ozone, or hydrogen peroxide would be eliminated (Suflita et al., 1988).

While anaerobic biological mediated reductive dehalogenation mechanisms were demonstrated as early as 1953 (Allan, 1955), the utilization of this process as a remedial alternative to reduce the overall mass of halogenated organic compounds from soil and ground water is a new concept and still subject to field demonstrations.

For this reason research is currently underway to better define the basic mechanisms of reductive dehalogenation reactions. Such approaches may include: (1) stimulation of desirable metabolic sequences in soil and ground water through the intentional introduction of suitable electron donor and acceptor combinations (Suflita et al., 1988); (2) addition of adequate nutrients to meet the nutritional requirements of dehalogenating microorganisms (Palmer et al., 1989); (3) use of engineered microorganisms with optimum dehalogenating activity (Palmer et al., 1989); and (4) addition of cell-free enzymes capable of catalyzing reductive dehalogenation reactions (DeWeerd and Suflita, 1990).

DEHALOGENATION MECHANISMS

Anaerobic reductive dehalogenation is only one of the mechanisms available to remove halogens from organic compounds. Other anaerobic dehalogenation processes are identified in Figure 8-1 (Kuhn and Suflita, 1989a). The reactions are classified according to the type of compound undergoing dehalogenation, i.e., aromatic or nonaromatic.

Dehalogenation of Aromatic Compounds

Two mechanisms of dehalogenation for aromatic compounds under anaerobic conditions have been observed: reduction and hydrolysis. Reductive mechanisms are recognized as the predominant pathway for removal of halogens from homocyclic aromatic rings under anaerobic conditions, while

ANAEROBIC DEHALOGENATION MECHANISMS

Aromatic Compounds

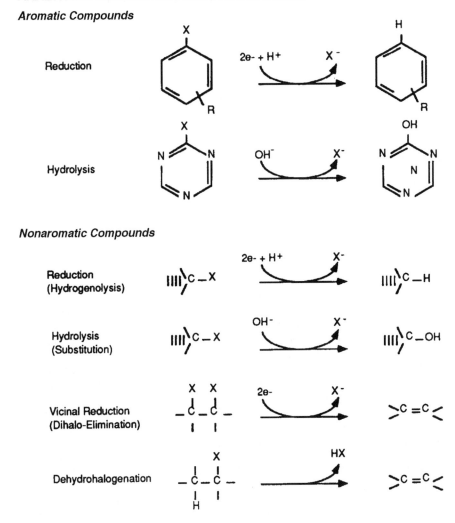

Figure 8-1. Examples of anaerobic dehalogenation mechanisms for aromatic and nonaromatic pesticides (Kuhn and Suflita, 1989a).

hydrolytic dehalogenation (including both chemically and enzymatically mediated reactions) is the preferred mechanism for heterocyclic aromatic compounds (Suflita et al., 1982; Kuhn and Suflita, 1989a). However, Adrian and Suflita (1989) have recently demonstrated reductive debromination of the herbicide bromacil under methanogenic conditions. This is the first report of reductive dehalogenation of a heterocyclic aromatic compound.

Reductive Dehalogenation of Aromatic Compounds

Many classes of halogenated aromatic compounds have been shown to be degraded by reductive dehalogenation processes (Table 8-1). Evidence for the involvement of microorganisms in aryl or aromatic reductive dehalogenation reactions include: (1) the specificity of the reductive reaction; (2) characteristic lag periods required before significant dehalogenation is observed; (3) the absence of activity in autoclaved controls; and (4) the isolation of aryl dehalogenating bacteria.

Reductive dehalogenation is rare in well-aerated environments. Methanogenic conditions, in which the typical redox potential is -0.3 V, the preferred electron acceptor is carbon dioxide, and the product

Table 8-1. Classes of Halogenated Aromatic Compounds Demonstrated to be Susceptible to Degradation by Reductive Dehalogenation Processes (Kuhn and Suflita 1989a)

Class of Halogenated Aromatic Compounds	Examples of Specific Compounds
Carboxylated Benzenes	Amiben
	Dicamba
	2,3,6-trichlorobenzoate
Oxygen-Substituted Benzenes	Pentachlorophenol
	Chlorinated phenoxyacetates (e.g., 2,4-D,2,4,5-T
	Halogenated diphenyl ether herbicides
	(e.g., chloronitrofen)
Nitrogen-Substituted Benzenes	3,4-Dihalogenated aromatic compounds (diuron,
	DCPU, linuron, DCIPC, propanil)
	Pentachloronitrobenzene
Cyano-Substituted Benzenes	2,4,5,6-tetachloroisophthalonitrile (TPN)
Methylene-Substituted Benzenes	Benthiocarb
Chlorinated Benzenes	Hexachlorobenzene
Polychlorinated Biphenyls	Aroclors (commercial PCB products)

is methane (Dragun, 1988), appear to be optimal for this type of biotransformation. Genthner et al. (1989) have recently investigated dehalogenation of monochlorophenols and monochlorobenzoates under four anaerobic enrichment conditions: methanogenic, nitrate-reducing, sulfate-reducing, and bromoethane sulfonic acid (BESA)-amended. BESA is a potent inhibitor of methanogenesis and was used to promote reductive dechlorination as a terminal electron process.

Aquatic sediments used as inocula were collected from a salinity gradient that included both freshwater and estuarine environments and varying degrees of exposure to industrial effluents. Degradation was observed least often in enrichments with nitrate or sulfate, and most often when amended with 1 mM BESA. In contrast to 1 mM BESA, 10 mM BESA prevented or delayed the degradation of several of the chloroaromatic compounds, suggesting inhibition of methanogenesis or inhibition of reductive dechlorination by BESA. Other sulfur oxyanions also have been shown to inhibit anaerobic dehalogenation reactions where sulfate is present as an inorganic contaminant (DeWeerd et al., 1986; Gibson and Suflita, 1986; Suflita et al., 1988; Kuhn and Suflita, 1989b). Additional research is being conducted in environments where sulfate occurs naturally. King (1988) showed that sulfate-reducing bacteria did not participate in dehalogenation of 2,4-dibromophenol (DBP), a naturally occurring halogenated organic compound in some marine sediments, but did appear to degrade phenol, a metabolic product of DBP dehalogenation.

The reductive dehalogenation of chlorinated compounds, as shown in Table 8-1, is characterized by their specificity for compounds within a particular chemical class; for example benzoates, phenols, or phenoxyacetates (Suflita et al., 1982; Gibson and Suflita, 1986; Suflita and Miller, 1985; Kuhn and Suflita, 1989a). Recently, however, research has shown that cross-acclimation between compound classes can occur. Struijs and Rogers (1989) demonstrated the reductive dehalogenation of dichloroanilines by anaerobic microorganisms in pond sediments acclimated to dehalogenate dichlorophenols. Since both hydroxyl and amino groups have a tendency to donate electrons, the authors hypothesized that organisms that were capable of dechlorinating dichlorophenols, which have been shown to be relatively nonpersistent in the environment, could possibly dechlorinate the more persistent dichloroanilines. The monochloroanilines produced by dechlorination of the dichloroanilines were stable under anaerobic conditions, but have been shown previously to be readily degraded under aerobic conditions (Zeyer and Kearney, 1982; Zeyer et al., 1985).

The specificity of dehalogenation also is dependent on the position of halogens on the aromatic ring within a class of compounds. For example, chlorinated benzoates are generally more readily dehalogenated at the meta position, followed by the ortho and para positions (Suflita et al., 1982; Genthner et al., 1989). Hydroxy, alkoxy, and nitrogen-substituted aromatic compounds generally are dehalogenated faster at *ortho* and *para* halogens (Kuhn and Suflita, 1989a,b); however, Genthner et al. (1989) recently have shown that the order of degradability of monochlorophenols was *meta* > *ortho* > *para*.

Mikesell and Boyd (1986) have shown that three groups of acclimated microorganisms can act in concert to completely dehalogenate pentachlorophenol (PCP) to form phenol, a substrate that was labile under the methanogenic conditions of their experiments. Each type of microorganism, acclimated to one of three monochlorophenol isomers, transformed PCP by removal of halogens from the same relative ring position at which they dehalogenated the monochlorophenol substrates. The 2-chlorophenol adapted cells dehalogenated PCP at the two *ortho* positions as well as from the *para* position. Similarly, 4-chlorophenol adapted cells cleaved the *para* chlorine of PCP in addition to the two *ortho* substituents. In contrast, the 3-chlorophenol adapted cells exclusively dehalogenated the *meta* position.

Other studies of PCP degradation have shown accumulation of tri- and tetrachlorophenol intermediates, which indicates that higher halogenated phenols tend to be more readily dehalogenated than their lesser halogenated congeners. Similarly, dehalogenation of chlorinated anilines shows shorter lag periods and faster dehalogenation rates with multi-halogenated compounds compared to di- and monohalogenated anilines. Dehalogenation of aromatic amines occurs predominately at the *ortho* and *para* positions as has been demonstrated with the dechlorination of anilines (Kuhn and Suflita, 1989b), though removal of *meta* halogens from this group of compounds has also been demonstrated.

Reductive dehalogenation may require the induction of enzymes responsible for dehalogenation. DeWeerd and Suflita (1990) have demonstrated reductive dehalogenation of 3-chlorobenzoate using cell-free extracts of an anaerobic bacterium. The extracts exhibited the same substrate specificity as whole cells. Rapid dehalogenation activity was found only in extracts of cells cultured in the presence of the halogenated molecule, indicating that the enzymes responsible required induction. Dehalogenation was inhibited by sulfite, thiosulfate, and sulfide. Dehalogenation activity was associated with the membrane fraction and required a low potential electron donor. These results suggest that a specific enzyme is made by the cells for dehalogenation of selected halogenated substrates. Research into the use of enzymes as a potential amendment to enhance bioremediation should be encouraged.

Further evidence that reductive dehalogenation may depend upon the induction of enzymes has been presented by Linkfield et al. (1989). Acclimation periods prior to detectable dehalogenation of halogenated benzoates in anaerobic lake sediments ranged from 3 weeks to 6 months. These periods were reproducible over time and among sampling sites and characteristic of the specific benzoate compound tested. The lengthy acclimation period appeared to represent an induction phase in which little or no aryl dehalogenation was observed. This was followed by an exponential increase in activity typical of an enrichment response. Extremely low activities during the early days of acclimation, coupled with the fact that dehalogenation yields no carbon to support microbial growth, suggests that slow continuous growth from time of the first exposure of the chemical was not responsible for the acclimation period. The characteristic acclimation period for each chemical also argues against nutritional deficiency, inhibitory environmental conditions, or predation by protozoa or other microbial grazers as the cause of the acclimation period. The reproducibility of the findings with time and space and among replicates argues against genetic changes as the explanation.

The removal of chloride or bromide from an aromatic molecule proceeds more easily when the ring also is substituted with electron destabilizing groups, such as carboxy, hydroxy, or cyano groups (Kuhn and Suflita, 1989a). Other chemical groups attached to the aromatic ring by nitrogen or oxygen bonds may have the same effect on the reductive dehalogenation reaction. However, recent research has shown that even highly chlorinated, poorly water soluble aromatic hydrocarbons that do not contain polar functional groups can also undergo reductive dehalogenation. Hexachlorobenzene (HCB) has generally been considered recalcitrant to microbial attack, particularly in the absence of oxygen (Bouwer and McCarty, 1984; Kuhn et al., 1985); however, HCB was shown to degrade to tri- and dichlorobenzenes by Fathepure et al. (1988). Brown et al. (1987) performed standard thermochemical calculations of free-energy changes associated with the oxidation of organic compounds (in this case, glucose) coupled with the reduction of chlorobenzene compounds. The reactions involving HCB and monochlorobenzene offered more energy to anaerobic bacteria than the reduction of compounds available naturally in anaerobic environments, such as sulfate and carbon dioxide (Table 8-2). Also, more energy could be obtained from the dehalogenation of hexachlorobenzene to benzene than the dehalogenation of monochlorobenzene, indicating that dehalogenation reactions are more likely

Table 8-2. Standard Free-Energy Changes for the Oxidation of Glucose to CO_2 and H_2O Using Various Oxidants (Brown et al., 1987)

Oxidant	Reduced Product	ΔG (kcal/mol)
Molecular Oxygen (O_2)	Water (H_2O)	-676.10
Hexachlorobenzene (C_6Cl_6)	Benzene (C_6H_6)	-410.16
Monochlorobenzene (C_6H_5Cl)	Benzene (C_6H_6)	-369.50
Sulfate (SO_4^{2-})	Reduced Sulfur	-131.78
Carbon Dioxide (CO_2)	Methane (CH_4)	-95.63

to occur with aromatic compounds containing many chloro groups since they are more highly oxidized and more electronegative than those containing fewer chloro groups.

Polychlorinated biphenyls (PCBs), commonly thought to be resistant to biodegradative processes, have also been shown to be susceptible to degradation by reductive dehalogenation (Brown et al., 1987; Quensen et al., 1988). Brown et al. (1987) suggest that dehalogenated products formed were less toxic than the original PCB congeners and may possibly be more susceptible to oxidative biodegradation by aerobic bacteria.

Hydrolytic Dehalogenation of Aromatic Compounds

Hydrolytic dehalogenation represents a substitution reaction in which a hydroxyl group replaces a halogen on an organic molecule (Figure 8-1). In general, the anaerobic hydrolytic removal of halogen substituents from homocyclic aromatic compounds is rare (Kuhn and Suflita, 1989a), but has been observed under aerobic conditions. Also, the enzymes involved have been shown to be active in reduced media, and some were inhibited by oxygen (Marks et al., 1984; Thiele et al., 1988). This transformation has been observed in anaerobic soil for a single herbicide, flamprop-methyl; however, no anaerobic bacteria were isolated with the ability to catalyze this type of dehalogenation. A hydrolytic defluorination product of the herbicide was identified in anaerobic soil incubation studies (Roberts and Standen, 1978).

Heterocyclic chloroaromatic compounds, such as chlorinated triazine herbicides, tend to react more readily with hydroxy, amino, or sulfhydryl groups than their homocyclic chemical counterparts. Hydrolytic dehalogenation is, therefore, the preferred mechanism for removing halogens from heterocyclic aromatic compounds under anaerobic conditions (Adrian and Suflita, 1989).

The hydrolysis of triazine herbicides to form dehalogenated and less phytotoxic products has been known for many years (Paris and Lewis, 1973). However, there has been controversy over the involvement of microorganisms in this process. Reactions with reactive soil surfaces, such as clays and organic matter, appear to be significant with regard to the rate of hydrolysis (Kuhn and Suflita, 1989a). Dechlorination of s-triazines has been shown to be catalyzed by microorganisms. This was demonstrated by Cook and Huetter (1984, 1986). The organisms studied were aerobic, but biotransformation of the herbicides did not require molecular O_2 and was functional under anaerobic conditions.

Dehalogenation of Nonaromatic Compounds

Dehalogenation of nonaromatic compounds, particularly halogenated aliphatic chemicals, is generally better understood than aryl dehalogenation reactions. The reductive processes of hydrolysis and dehydrohalogenation have been identified as anaerobic dehalogenation mechanisms (Figure 8-1).

In general, biologically mediated anaerobic dehalogenation of nonaromatic compounds tends to be faster than dehalogenation of aromatic compounds, does not require long adaptation times, and does not exhibit a high degree of substrate specificity. Some of these reactions also are not too sensitive to the presence of oxygen and have been observed in aerobic incubation systems. The greater variety of reaction mechanisms potentially available to metabolize nonaromatic halogenated compounds in general results in rendering these compounds more susceptible to biodegradation than the haloaromatic compounds (Vogel et al., 1987; Kuhn and Suflita, 1989a).

Dehalogenation has been demonstrated with many bacterial species representing diverse genera. Mesophilic and thermophilic methanogenic bacteria as well as some thermophilic clostridial species may catalyze dehalogenation of some aliphatic compounds. For example, metabolism of hexa-chlorocyclohexanes by thermophilic clostridia was reported by Sethunathan (1973). Dehalogenation reactions are also sometimes heat resistant, suggesting that some reactions may not be enzymatically mediated, and therefore not dependent on intact microorganisms or microbial consortia. The dehalog-enation of nonaromatic compounds can be catalyzed by transition metal complexes with or without the involvement of enzymes (Kuhn and Suflita, 1989a).

Reductive and Vicinal Dehalogenation of Nonaromatic Compounds

If a nonaromatic carbon atom in a synthetic molecule is highly halogenated, dehalogenation is more easily accomplished by reductive, vicinal reductive or elimination reactions (Vogel et al., 1987). Compounds that have been demonstrated to be degraded by reduction or vicinal reduction mechanisms are listed in Table 8-3.

Reductive and vicinal dehalogenation reactions are dependent on the redox potential of the elec-tron donor and acceptor. To be thermodynamically feasible, the E_h of the electron accepting reactant (dehalogenation) must be higher than that of the electron donating reactant. This requirement can limit the number of available electron donors for dehalogenation of some compounds (Castro et al., 1985; Vogel et al., 1987; Kuhn and Suflita, 1989a). For example, free ferrous iron (Fe(II)) has a redox potential of +0.77 V; but most of the halogenated alkanes and alkenes with lower redox poten-tials will not react with this transition metal. However, when Fe(II) is in a complexed form, such as a porphyrin or as ferredoxin, the redox potential is dramatically lowered, and the reaction is possible (Kuhn and Suflita, 1989a). As examples, Fe(II)deuteroporphin IX and cytochrome P-450 have re-dox potentials of 0.00 V and -0.17 V, respectively.

Active transition metal complexes, which include complexes of iron (Fe), cobalt (Co), nickel (Ni), and perhaps chromium (Cr) and zinc (Zn), have redox potentials less than zero and can be as low as -0.8 V for the cobalt complexed vitamin $B_{1}2$. The low redox potentials of these electron donors allow for their reduction to be coupled with dehalogenation of many nonaromatic com-pounds having redox potentials which range from 0 to 1.2 V (Vogel et al., 1987).

Highly halogenated aliphatic compounds have higher reduction potentials than their lesser ha-logenated analogues; therefore, more energy is released by their dehalogenation, indicating a greater driving force for these reactions. In general, reductive dehalogenation of tetra- and tri-halogenated carbon atoms is easier than di- or monohalogenated congeners (Vogel et al., 1987).

In natural environments, Fe(II) porphyrins (e.g., cytochromes), Co complexes (e.g., vitamin $B_{1}2$), and Ni complexes (e.g., F430) are likely to be dominant in the reductive dehalogenation process. Dead cells can release these stable transition metal complexes which are then more available for participa-tion in the dehalogenation process. Such complexes are also active in living cells, as was demonstrated with *Pseudomonas putida* by Castro et al. (1985). *Pseudomonas putida* contains Fe(II)porphyrin bound to the cytochrome P-450 complex, but movement of halogenated compounds across the bacterial mem-brane and diffusion to the active iron center can limit the rate of dehalogenation.

Another potential reductant available for dehalogenation of haloaliphatic compounds in natural environments is the flavin/flavoprotein complex, which has been shown to mediate many of the known reductive reactions of xenobiotic compounds in laboratory studies (Esaac and Matsumura, 1980). To date, no studies have clearly demonstrated the environmental significance of this reduc-tant. Relative to other dehalogenation reaction mechanisms, dehalogenation by vicinal reduction appears to be more tolerant of oxidized conditions and may even be independent of transition metals or metallo-organic complexes (Kuhn and Suflita, 1989a).

Dehydrohalogenation of Nonaromatic Compounds

Dehydrohalogenation is an elimination reaction in which two groups are lost from adjacent carbon atoms so that a double bond is formed, resulting in the release of a halogen and a proton (HX) and the formation of an alkene (Figure 8-1). The rate of dehalogenation is higher when additional chloride ions are bonded to the carbon atom that loses its chloride ion substituent (Vogel et al., 1987). Bromine atoms rather than chlorine atoms are generally more readily eliminated by the reaction. Elimination reactions can proceed spontaneously (1,1,1-trichloroethane; 1,2-dibromoethane) or can be catalyzed

Table 8-3. Classes of Halogenated Nonaromatic Compounds Demonstrated to be Susceptible to Degradation by Reductive Dehalogenation Processes (Kuhn and Suflita, 1989a)

Class of Halogenated Nonaromatic Compound	Examples of Specific Compounds
Aliphatic Compounds	Tetrachloromethane (carbon tetrachloride)
	Trichloromethane (chloroform)
	Dichloromethane (methylene chloride)
	Chloromethane (methyl chloride)
	Bromomethane (methyl bromide)
	Trichloronitromethane (chloropicrin)
	Hexachloroethane
	Tetrachloroethene (perchloroethylene)
	1,1,1-Trichloroethane
	Trichloroethene (trichloroethylene)
	1,2-Dichloroethane (ethylene dichloride, EDC)
	1,2-dibromoethane (ethylene dibromide, EDB)
	1,2-dibromo-3-chloropropane (DBCP)
	1,1,1-trichloro-2,2-bis (p-chlorophenyl)ethane
(DDT) (aliphatic portion)	
Alicyclic Compounds	Toxaphene
	Mirex
	Heptachlor
Hexahalocyclohexanes	Lindane and its isomers

by microbial enzymes such as the dechlorinase enzyme which is responsible for the conversion of DDT to DDE—a dechlorination reaction involving the aliphatic portion of the DDT molecule (Kuhn and Suflita, 1989a).

Hydrolytic Dehalogenation

Hydrolysis, a substitution reaction in which one substituent on a molecule is replaced by another, has been demonstrated with many aliphatic compounds. Hydrolysis is favored for carbon atoms with only one or two halogens; however, hydrolytic dehalogenation has been shown with higher chlorinated compounds, such as 1,1,1-trichloroethane. This transformation can be chemically or biologically catalyzed by methanogenic mixed cultures and by a number of aerobic bacterial isolates. Bromine loss tends to be favored compared to the corresponding chlorinated compounds (Kuhn and Suflita, 1989a).

APPLICATIONS AND LIMITATIONS OF REDUCTIVE DEHALOGENATION OF ORGANIC HALOGENATED POLLUTANTS

The degradation of trichloroethylene (TCE), as shown in Figure 8-2, may be used to illustrate the potential effectiveness of the reductive dehalogenation process to remove common pollutants from the environment, as well as to present some of the cautions that should be observed (Dragun, 1988). TCE is an industrial solvent used extensively for degreasing metal as well as in dry-cleaning operations, organic synthesis, refrigerants, and fumigants. Most septic tank cleaning fluids contain TCE (Craun, 1984).

Also illustrated in Figure 8-2 are possible degradative pathways of tetrachloroethylene (PCE) and 1,1,1-trichloroethane (1,1,1-TCA). PCE is a solvent widely used in dry cleaning and degreasing operations; 1,1,1-TCA is used extensively as an industrial cleaner and degreaser of metals, spot remover, adhesive, and vapor pressure depressant (Craun, 1984). These compounds have relatively high water solubility (e.g., 1000 mg/L for TCE) and are highly mobile in soils and aquifer materials and often are found in ground waters. Since they are suspected carcinogens (Infante and Tsongas, 1982), they represent a threat to human health.

The degradative pathway for TCE (Dragun, 1988) can be described as follows:

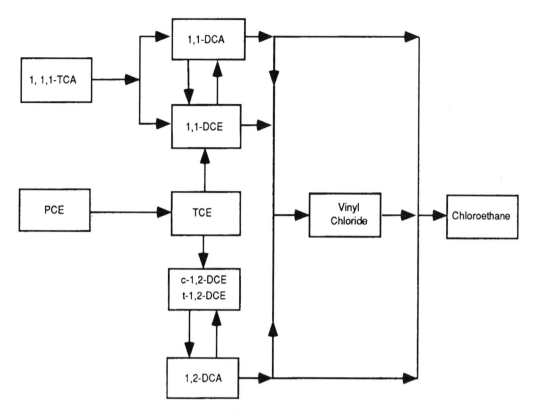

Figure 8-2. Transformation pathways for various chlorinated volatile hydrocarbons in soil systems (Dragun, 1988).

1. TCE can undergo reductive dehalogenation, i.e., the removal of one chloride atom (CI) and the addition of one hydrogen (H) atom. Three possible reaction products can be formed: 1,1-dichloroethylene (1,1-DCE), cis-1,2-dichloroethylene (c-1,2-DCE), and/or trans-1,2-dichloroethylene (t-1.2-DCE).
2. 1,1-DCE can undergo reductive dehalogenation to form vinyl chloride, or its carbon-carbon double bond can be reduced to form 1,1-dichloroethane (1,1-DCA).
3. The two dichloroethylene compounds, c-1,2-DCE and t-1,2-DCE can undergo reductive dehalogenation to form vinyl chloride. Their carbon-carbon double bonds can be reduced to form 1,2-dichloroethane (1,2-DCA).
4. 1,1 -DCA and 1,2-DCA can undergo dehydrohalogenation to form vinyl chloride. These two chemicals can also undergo reductive dehalogenation to form chloroethane.

The degradation pathway of a single compound, TCE, can lead to the production of six chlorinated volatile hydrocarbons. The degradation of PCE can lead to the production of seven chlorinated volatile hydrocarbons, while the degradation of 1,1,1-TCA can lead to the production of four chlorinated hydrocarbons. Two of the metabolic products formed, vinyl chloride and 1,1-DCA, have been classified as a carcinogen and a probable carcinogen, respectively (Vogel et al., 1987). The dichloroethylene products, c-1,2-DCE and t-1,2-DCE, and vinyl chloride are also regulated under the 1986 Safe Drinking Water Amendments (Freedman and Gossett, 1989). Vinyl chloride is the most persistent of the compounds under anaerobic conditions, but can be rapidly degraded under aerobic conditions (Hartsmans et al., 1985; Fogel et al., 1986).

Management of a bioremediation system to accomplish treatment of these compounds in a manner to protect human health and the environment should incorporate considerations of detoxification as well as disappearance of the parent compounds. Disappearance is not synonymous, however, with mineralization to inorganic salts, carbon dioxide, and water. Partial degradation of organic substrates can result in the production of metabolic products that generate their own environmental and health consequences. Such contaminants may be of more toxicological concern than the parent compounds (Suflita et al., 1985).

Fathepure and Boyd (1988) recently suggested that in situ dechlorination of PCE to TCE could be enhanced by stimulating methanogenesis. They found that reductive dechlorination of PCE occurred only during methanogenesis, and no dechlorination was seen when methane production ceased. There was a clear dependence of the extent of PCE dechlorination on the amount of methanogenic substrate (methanol) consumed. Methanogenic bacteria are present in a diversity of environmental habitats, including those where chloroethylenes are commonly found as contaminants (e.g., soils, ground waters, and aquifers near landfills).

A bioremediation system for chlorinated ethylenes and ethanes could consist of maintenance of an anaerobic environment, followed by aeration to complete the degradation process after anaerobic degradative processes have reduced the parent compounds to acceptable levels. Recent research, however, by Freedman and Gossett (1989) has shown that PCE and TCE can be degraded to ethylene, a nonchlorinated environmentally acceptable biotransformation product, under anaerobic methanogenic conditions if an adequate supply of electron donors was provided to a mixed anaerobic enrichment culture. Methanol was the most effective electron donor, although hydrogen, formate, acetate, and glucose also served.

Ethylene is sparingly soluble in water and has not been associated with any long-term toxicological problems (Autian, 1980). It is also a naturally occurring plant hormone. Since complete conversion of VC to ethylene was not observed in the study, the authors suggested that further research is required to determine the concentration of electron donors required to complete the conversion.

A major operational cost of this method of enhanced anaerobic bioremediation will be the supply of electron donors. Alternatively, means to channel more of the donors into the reductive dechlorination process and less into methane production should be investigated.

As proposed by Fathepure et al. (1988), a similar potential for the use of an anaerobic environment followed by an aerobic environment, for mineralization and detoxification of halogenated organic pollutants, is illustrated by the degradation of hexachlorobenzene (HCB) (Figure 8-3). HCB is a fungicide used as a seed coating for cereal crops. Two pathways of dechlorination were proposed: (1) a major pathway in which 1,3,5-trichlorobenzene (1,3,5-TCB) is formed via pentachlorobenzene and 1,2,3,5-tetrachlorobenzene (1,2,3,5-TTCB); and (2) a minor pathway in which dichlorobenzenes are formed via 1,2,4,5-TTCB and 1,2,4-TCB.

The authors presented explanations for the existence of two pathways. One is that there were two populations, each using a different pathway. The other is that the products reflect the distribution of reactive ring intermediates in which a chlorine, between two other chlorines, was lost most readily and dechlorination ceased when there are no adjacent chlorines as with 1,3,5-TCB.

Reductive dechlorination appeared to occur in a stepwise fashion until lower chlorinated compounds accumulated. Most of the added HCB accumulated as 1,3,5-TCB, which remained unchanged. Although metabolic products identified in this study were not further utilized by the anaerobic sludge populations used to elucidate the metabolic pathways, it is likely that they would be degraded by aerobic organisms (Reineke and Knackmuss, 1984; deBont et al., 1986; Schraa et al., 1986; Spain and Nishino, 1987) or by facultative anaerobes possessing dechlorinating activity (Tsuchiya and Yamaha, 1984).

The U.S. Environmental Protection Agency is presently sponsoring research to develop engineered microorganisms capable of anaerobic reductive dehalogenation of organic halogenated compounds (Palmer et al., 1989). *Desulfomonile tiedjei* (DeWeerd et al., 1990), formerly known as DCB-1, is the first obligate anaerobe known to accomplish reductive dehalogenation. Results using this organism indicated that no plasmid genes responsible for dehalogenating activity could be detected. Therefore, in order to clone the gene or genes responsible for the activity, a genomic library of the bacterial chromosome is being constructed to isolate the dehalogenase gene. The isolation of the gene would be greatly facilitated by the isolation and characterization of the requisite dehalogenase.

SUMMARY

Bioremediation of soils and ground waters contaminated with organic pollutants involves management of the contaminated system to control and enhance biodegradation of the pollutants present

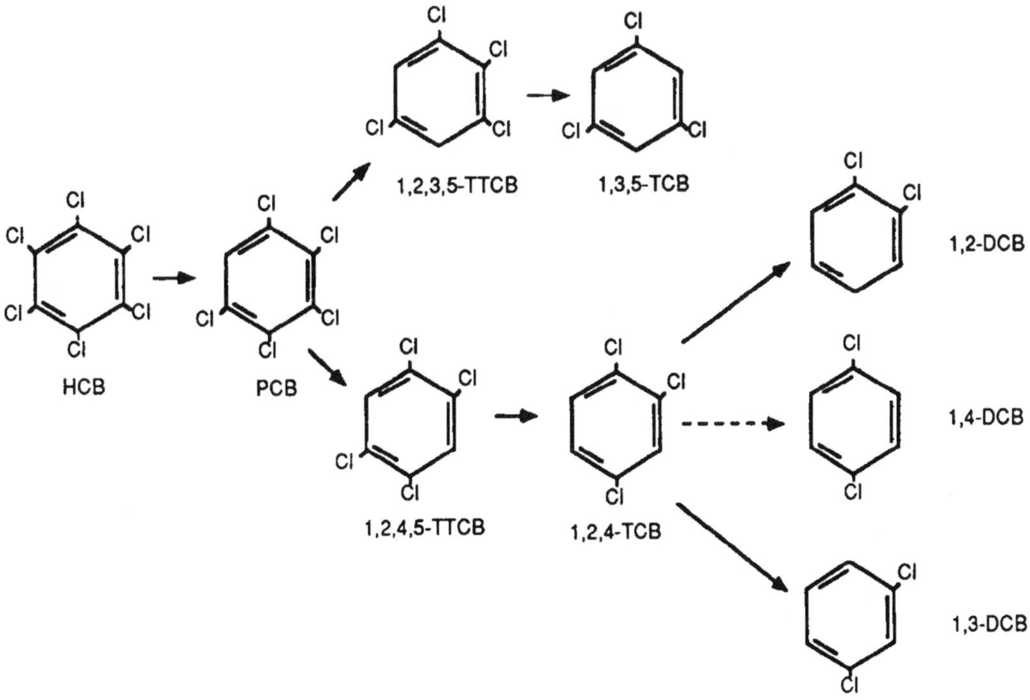

Figure 8-3. Proposed pathway for HCB dechlorination by an anaerobic microbial community (Fathepure et al., 1988).

(Sims et al., 1989; Thomas and Ward, 1989). Reductive dehalogenation appears to be a potentially powerful process for achieving bioremediation of a site contaminated with organic halogenated pollutants, if mechanisms and pathways of degradation are known and can be managed to achieve removal of the compounds of interest as well as potentially toxic metabolic degradation products.

EPA CONTACT

For further information contact: Guy Sewell, 405/436-8566, at RSKERL-Ada.

REFERENCES

Adrian, N.R. and J.M. Suflita. 1989. Reductive dehalogenation of a nitrogen heterocyclic herbicide in anoxic aquifer slurries. Appl. Environ. Microbiol. 56:292–294.

Allan, J. 1955. Loss of biological efficiency of cattle-dipping wash containing benzene hexachloride. Nature (London) 175:1131–1132.

Autian, J. 1980. Plastics. In: J. Doull, C.D. Klaassen, and M.O. Amdur (eds.), Casarett and Doull's Toxicology. Macmillan, New York, NY, pp. 531–556.

Bouwer, E.J. and P.L. McCarty. 1984. Utilization rates of trace halogenated organic compounds in acetate-grown biofilms. Biotechnol. Bioeng. 27:1564–1571.

Brown, J.F., Jr., R.E. Wagner, H. Feng, D.L. Bedard, M.J. Brennan, J.C. Carnahan, and R.J. May. 1987. Environmental dechlorination of PCBs. Environ. Toxicol. Chem. 6:579–593.

Castro, C.E., R.S. Wade, and N.O. Belser. 1985. Biodehalogenation: Reactions of cytochrome P-450 with polyhalomethanes. Biochemistry 24:204–210.

Cook, A.M. and R. Huetter. 1984. Deethylsimazine: Bacterial dechlorination, deamination, and complete degradation. J. Agric. Food Chem. 32:581–585.

Cook, A.M. and R. Huetter. 1986. Ring dechlorination of deethylsimazine by hydrolases from *Rhodococcus corallinus*. FEMS Microbiol Letters 34:335–338.

Craun, G.F. 1984. Health Aspects of Groundwater Pollution. In: G. Bitton and C. Gerba (eds.). Groundwater Pollution Microbiology. John Wiley & Sons, New York, NY, pp. 135–179.

deBont, J.A.M., M.J.A.W. Vorage, S. Hartmans, and W.J.J. van den Tweel. 1986. Microbial degradation of 1,3-dichlorobenzene. Appl. Environ. Microbiol. 52:677–680.

DeWeerd, K.A. and J.M. Suflita. 1990. Anaerobic aryl dehalogenation of halobenzolates by cell extracts of "Desulfomonile tiedjei". Appl. Environ. Microbiol. 56(10):2999–3005.

DeWeerd, K.A., J.M. Suflita, T. Linkfield, J.M. Tiedje, and P.H. Pritchard. 1986. The relationship between reductive dechlorination and other aryl substituent removal reactions catalyzed by anaerobes. FEMS Microbiol. Ecol. 38:331–340.

DeWeerd, K.A., L. Mandelco, R.S. Tanner, C.R. Woese, and J.M. Suflita. 1990. Desulfomonile tiedjei gen. nov. and sp. nov., a novel anaerobic, dehalogenating sulfate-reducing bacterium. Arch. Microbiol. 154:23–30.

Dragun, J. 1988. The Soil Chemistry of Hazardous Materials. Hazardous Materials Control Research Institute, Silver Spring, MD.

Esaac, E.G. and F. Matsumura. 1980. Metabolism of insecticides by reductive systems. Pharmac. Ther. 9:1–26.

Fathepure, B.Z. and S.A. Boyd. 1988. Dependence of tetrachloroethylene dechlorination on methanogenic substrate consumption by Methanosarcina sp. strain DCM. Appl. Environ. Microbiol. 54:2976–2980.

Fathepure, B.Z., J.M. Tiedje, and S.A. Boyd. 1988. Reductive dechlorination of hexachlorobenzene to tri- and dichlorobenzenes in anaerobic sewage sludge. Appl. Environ. Microbiol. 54:327–330.

Fogel, M.M., A.R. Taddeo, and S. Fogel. 1986. Biodegradation of chlorinated ethenes by a methane-utilizing mixed culture. Appl. Environ. Microbiol. 51:720–724.

Freedman, D.L. and J.M. Gossett. 1989. Biological reductive dechlorination of tetrachloroethylene and trichloroethylene to ethylene under methanogenic conditions. Appl. Environ. Microbiol. 55:2144–2151.

Genthner, B.R.S., W.A. Price, II, and H.P. Pritchard. 1989. Anaerobic degradation of chloroaromatic compounds in aquatic sediments under a variety of enrichment conditions. Appl. Environ. Microbiol. 55:1466–1471.

Gibson, S.A. and J.M. Suflita. 1986. Extrapolation of biodegradation results to groundwater aquifers: Reductive dehalogenation of aromatic compounds. Appl. Environ. Microbiol. 52:681–688.

Hartsmans, S., J.A.M. de Bont, J. Tramper, and K.Ch.M.A. Luyben. 1985. Bacterial degradation of vinyl chloride. Biotechnol. Letters 7:383–388.

Hutzinger, O. and W. Verkamp. 1981. Xenobiotic chemicals with pollution potential. In: T. Leisinger, A.M. Cook, R. Hutter, and J. Nuesch (eds.), Microbial Degradation of Xenobiotic and Recalcitrant Compounds. Academic Press, London, pp. 3–46.

Infante, P.F. and T.A. Tsongas. 1982. Mutagenic and oncogenic effects of chloromethanes, chloroethanes, and halogenated analogs of vinyl chloride. Environ. Sci. Res. 25:301–327.

King, G.M. 1988. Dehalogenation in marine sediments containing natural sources of halophenols. Appl. Environ. Microbiol. 54:3079–3085.

Kuhn, E.P., P.J. Colberg, J.L. Schnoor, O. Wanner, A.J.B. Zehnder, and R.P. Schwarzenbach. 1985. Microbial transformation of substituted benzenes during infiltration of river water to ground water:laboratory column studies. Environ. Sci. Technol. 19:981–968.

Kuhn, E.P. and J.M. Suflita. 1989a. Dehalogenation of pesticides by anaerobic microorganisms in soils and groundwater—a review. In: B.L. Sawhney and K. Brown (eds.), Reactions and Movement of Organic Chemicals in Soils. Soil Science Society of America, Madison, WI, pp. 111–180.

Kuhn, E.P. and J.M. Suflita. 1989b. The sequential reductive dehalogenation of chloroanilines by microorganisms from a methanogenic aquifer. Environ. Sci. Technol. 23:848–852.

Linkfield, T.G., J.M. Suflita, and J.M. Tiedje. 1989. Characterization of the acclimation period prior to the anaerobic biodegradation of haloaromatic compounds. Appl. Environ. Microbiol. 55:2773–2778.

Marks, T.S., A.R.W. Smith, and A.V. Quirk. 1984. Degradation of 4-chlorobenzoic acid by an Arthrobacter sp. Appl. Environ. Microbiol 48:1020–1025.

Mikesell, M.D. and S.A. Boyd. 1986. Complete reductive dechlorination and mineralization of pentachlorophenol by anaerobic microorganisms. Appl. Environ. Microbiol. 52:861–865.

Palmer, D.T., T.G. Linkfield, J.B. Robinson, B.R.S. Genthner, and G.E. Pierce. 1989. Determination and Enhancement of Anaerobic Dehalogenation: Degradation of Chlorinated Organics in Aqueous Systems. EPA/600/S2-88/054.

Paris, D.F. and D.L. Lewis. 1973. Chemical and microbial degradation of ten selected pesticides in aquatic systems. Residue Rev. 45:95–124.

Quensen, J.F., III, J.M. Tiedje, and S.A. Boyd. 1988. Reductive dechlorination of polychlorinated biphenyls by anaerobic microorganisms from sediments. Science 242:752–754.

Reineke, W. and H.J. Knackmuss. 1984. Microbial metabolism of haloaromatics: isolation and properties of a chlorobenzene-degrading bacterium. Appl. Environ. Microbiol. 47:395–402.

Roberts, T.R. and M.E. Standen. 1978. Degradation of the herbicide flamprop-methyl in soil under anaerobic conditions. Pestic. Biochem. Physiol. 9:322–333.

Rochkind, M.L., J.W. Blackbum, and G.S. Sayler. 1986. Microbial Decomposition of Chlorinated Aromatic Compounds. EPA/600/2-86/090.

Schraa, G., M.L. Boone, M.M. Jetten, A.R.W. van Neerven, P.J. Colberg, and A.J.B. Zehnder. 1986. Degradation of 1,4-dichlorobenzene by *Alcaligenes* sp. strain A175. Appl. Environ. Microbiol. 52:1374–1381.

Sethunathan, N. 1973. Microbial degradation of insecticides in flooded soil and in anaerobic cultures. Residue Rev. 47:143–165.

Sims, J.L., R.C. Sims, and J.E. Matthews. 1989. Bioremediation of Contaminated Soils. EPA/600/9-89/073 (NTIS PB90-164047).

Spain, J.C. and S.F. Nishino. 1987. Degradation of 1,4-dichlorobenzene by *Pseudomonas* sp. Appl. Environ. Microbiol 53:1010–1019.

Struijs, J. and J.E. Rogers. 1989. Reductive dehalogenation of dichloroanilines by anaerobic microorganisms in fresh and dichlorophenol-acclimated pond sediment. Appl. Environ. Microbiol. 55:2527–2531.

Suflita, J.M., A. Horowitz, D.R. Shelton, and J.M. Tiedje. 1982. Dehalogenation: A novel pathway for anaerobic biodegradation of haloaromatic compounds. Science 218:1115–1117.

Suflita, J.M. and G.D. Miller. 1985. Microbial metabolism of chlorophenolic compounds in groundwater aquifers. Environ. Toxicol. Chem. 4:751–758.

Suflita, J.M., S.A. Gibson, and R.E. Beeman. 1988. Anaerobic biotransformation of pollutant chemicals in aquifers. J. Ind. Microbiol. 3:179–194.

Thomas, J.M. and C.H. Ward. 1989. In situ biorestoration of organic contaminants in the subsurface. Environ. Sci. Technol. 23:760–766.

Thiele, J., R. Muller, and F. Lingens. 1988. Enzymatic dehalogenation of chlorinated nitroaromatic compounds. Appl. Environ. Microbiol. 54:1199–1202.

Tiedje, J.M. and T.O. Stevens. 1987. The ecology of an anaerobic dechlorinating consortium. In: G.S. Omenn (ed.), Environmental Biotechnology: Reducing Risks from Environmental Chemicals through Biotechnology. Plenum Press, New York, NY, pp. 3–14.

Tsuchiya, T. and T. Yamaha. 1984. Reductive dechlorination of 1,2,4-trichlorobenzene by *Staphylococcus epidermis* isolated from intestinal contents of rats. Agric. Biol. Chem. 48:1545–1550.

Vogel, T.M., C.S. Criddle, and P.L. McCarty. 1987. Transformations of halogenated aliphatic compounds. Environ. Sci. Technol. 21:722–736.

Zeyer, J. and P.C. Kearney. 1982. Microbial degradation of para-chloroaniline as sole carbon and nitrogen source. Pestic. Biochem. Physiol. 17:215–223.

Zeyer, J., A. Wasserfallen, and K.N. Timmis. 1985. Microbial mineralization of ring-substituted anilines through an ortho-cleavage pathway. Appl. Environ. Microbiol. 50:447–453.

Chapter 9

Fundamentals of Ground-Water Modeling[1]

Jacob Bear, Technion - Israel Institute of Technology
Milovan S. Beljin, University of Cincinnati, Cincinnati, OH
Randall R. Ross, U.S. EPA, Robert S. Kerr Environmental Research Laboratory, Ada, OK

INTRODUCTION

Ground-water flow and contaminant transport modeling has been used at many hazardous waste sites with varying degrees of success. Models may be used throughout all phases of the site investigation and remediation processes. The ability to reliably predict the rate and direction of ground-water flow and contaminant transport is critical in planning and implementing ground-water remediations. This chapter presents an overview of the essential components of ground-water flow and contaminant transport modeling in saturated porous media. While fractured rocks and fractured porous rocks may behave like porous media with respect to many flow and contaminant transport phenomena, they require a separate discussion and are not included in this chapter (see Chapter 10). Similarly, the special features of flow and contaminant transport in the unsaturated zone are also not included. This chapter was prepared for an audience with some technical background and a basic working knowledge of ground-water flow and contaminant transport processes. A suggested format for ground-water modeling reports and a selected bibliography are included as Appendices A and B, respectively.

MODELING AS A MANAGEMENT TOOL

The management of any system means making decisions aimed at achieving the system's goals, without violating specified technical and nontechnical constraints imposed on it. In a ground-water system, management decisions may be related to rates and location of pumping and artificial recharge, changes in water quality, location and rates of pumping in pump-and-treat operations, etc. Management's objective function should be to evaluate the time and cost necessary to achieve remediation goals. Management decisions are aimed at minimizing this cost while maximizing the benefits to be derived from operating the system.

The value of management's objective function (e.g., minimize cost and maximize effectiveness of remediation) usually depends on both the values of the decision variables (e.g., areal and temporal distributions of pumpage) and on the response of the aquifer system to the implementation of these decisions. Constraints are expressed in terms of future values of state variables of the considered ground-water system, such as water table elevations and concentrations of specific contaminants in the water. Typical constraints may be that the concentration of a certain contaminant should not exceed a specified value, or that the water level at a certain location should not drop below specified levels. Only by comparing predicted values with specified constraints can decision makers conclude whether or not a specific constraint has been violated.

An essential part of a good decision-making process is that the response of a system to the implementation of contemplated decisions must be known *before* they are implemented.

In the management of a ground-water system in which decisions must be made with respect to both water quality and water quantity, a tool is needed to provide the decision maker with information about the future response of the system to the effects of management decisions. Depending on the nature of the management problem, decision variables, objective functions, and constraints, the

---

[1] EPA/540/S-92/005.

response may take the form of future spatial distributions of contaminant concentrations, water levels, etc. This tool is the *model.*

Examples of potential model applications include:

- design and/or evaluation of pump-and-treat systems
- design and/or evaluation of hydraulic containment systems
- evaluation of physical containment systems (e.g., slurry walls)
- analysis of "no action" alternatives
- evaluation of past migration patterns of contaminants
- assessment of attenuation/transformation processes
- evaluation of the impact of nonaqueous phase liquids (NAPL) on remediation activities (dissolution studies)

WHAT IS A GROUND-WATER MODEL?

A model may be defined as a simplified version of a real-world system (here, a ground-water system) that approximately simulates the relevant excitation-response relations of the real-world system. Since real-world systems are very complex, there is a need for simplification in making planning and management decisions. The simplification is introduced as a set of assumptions which expresses the nature of the system and those features of its behavior that are relevant to the problem under investigation. These assumptions will relate, among other factors, to the geometry of the investigated domain, the way various heterogeneities will be smoothed out, the nature of the porous medium (e.g., its homogeneity, isotropy), the properties of the fluid (or fluids) involved, and the type of flow regime under investigation. Because a model is a simplified version of a real-world system, no model is unique to a given ground-water system. Different sets of simplifying assumptions will result in different models, each approximating the investigated ground-water system in a different way. The first step in the modeling process is the construction of a *conceptual model* consisting of a set of assumptions that *verbally* describes the system's composition, the transport processes that take place in it, the mechanisms that govern them, and the relevant medium properties. This is envisioned or approximated by the modeler for the purpose of constructing a model intended to provide information for a specific problem.

Content of a Conceptual Model

The assumptions that constitute a conceptual model should relate to such items as:

- the geometry of the boundaries of the investigated aquifer domain;
- the kind of solid matrix comprising the aquifer (with reference to its homogeneity, isotropy, etc.);
- the mode of flow in the aquifer (e.g., one-dimensional, two-dimensional horizontal, or three-dimensional);
- the flow regime (laminar or nonlaminar);
- the properties of the water (with reference to its homogeneity, compressibility, effect of dissolved solids and/or temperature on density and viscosity, etc.);
- the presence of assumed sharp fluid-fluid boundaries, such as a phreatic surface;
- the relevant state variables and the area, or volume, over which the averages of such variables are taken;
- sources and sinks of water and of relevant contaminants, within the domain and on its boundaries (with reference to their approximation as point sinks and sources, or distributed sources);
- initial conditions within the considered domain; and
- the conditions on the boundaries of the considered domain that express the interactions with its surrounding environment.

Selecting the appropriate conceptual model for a given problem is one of the most important steps in the modeling process. Oversimplification may lead to a model that lacks the required information, while undersimplification may result in a costly model, or in the lack of data required for *model calibration* and *parameter estimation,* or both. It is, therefore, important that all features relevant to a considered problem be included in the conceptual model and that irrelevant ones be excluded.

The selection of an appropriate conceptual model and the degree of simplification in any particular case depends on:

- the objectives of the management problem;
- the available resources;
- the available field data;
- the legal and regulatory framework applying to the situation.

The objectives dictate which features of the investigated problem should be represented in the model, and to what degree of accuracy. In some cases averaged water levels taken over large areas may be satisfactory, while in others, water levels at specified points may be necessary. Natural recharge may be introduced as monthly, seasonal or annual averages. Pumping may be assumed to be uniformly distributed over large areas, or it may be represented as point sinks. Obviously, a more detailed model is more costly and requires more skilled manpower, more sophisticated codes and larger computers. It is important to select the appropriate degree of simplification in each case.

Selection of the appropriate conceptual model for a given problem is not necessarily a conclusive activity at the initial stage of the investigations. Instead, modeling should be considered as a continuous activity in which assumptions are reexamined, added, deleted and modified as the investigations continue. It is important to emphasize that the availability of field data required for model calibration and parameter estimation dictates the type of conceptual model to be selected and the degree of approximation involved.

The next step in the modeling process is to express the (verbal) conceptual model in the form of a *mathematical model.* The solution of the mathematical model yields the required predictions of the real-world system's behavior in response to various sources and/or sinks.

Most models express nothing but a balance of the considered extensive quantity (e.g., mass of water or mass of solute). In the *continuum approach,* the balance equations are written "at a point within the domain," and should be interpreted to mean "per unit area or volume, as the case may be, in the vicinity of the point." Under such conditions, the balance takes the form of a partial differential equation. Each term in that equation expresses a quantity added per unit area or per unit volume, and per unit time. Often, a number of extensive quantities of interest are transposed simultaneously; for example, mass of a number of fluid phases with each phase containing more than one relevant species. The mathematical model will then contain a balance equation for each extensive quantity.

Content of a Mathematical Model

The complete statement of a mathematical model consists of the following items:

- a definition of the geometry of the considered domain and its boundaries;
- an equation (or equations) that expresses the balance of the considered extensive quantity (or quantities);
- flux equations that relate the flux(es) of the considered extensive quantity(ies) to the relevant state variables of the problem;
- constitutive equations that define the behavior of the fluids and solids involved;
- an equation (or equations) that expresses initial conditions that describe the known state of the considered system at some initial time; and
- an equation (or equations) that defines boundary conditions that describe the interaction of the considered domain with its environment.

All the equations must be expressed in terms of the dependent variables selected for the problem. The selection of the appropriate variables to be used in a particular case depends on the available data. The number of equations included in the model must be equal to the number of dependent variables. The boundary conditions should be such that they enable a unique, stable solution.

The most general boundary condition for any extensive quantity states that the difference in the normal component of the total flux of that quantity, on both sides of the boundary, is equal to the strength of the source of that quantity. If a source does not exist, the statement reduces to an equality of the normal component of the total flux on both sides of the boundary. In such equalities, the information related to the external side must be known (Bear and Verruijt, 1987). It is obtained from field measurements or on the basis of past experience.

The mathematical model contains the same information as the conceptual one, but expressed as a set of equations which are amenable to analytical and numerical solutions. Many mathematical models have been proposed and published by researchers and practitioners (see Appendix B). They cover most cases of flow and contaminant transport in aquifers encountered by hydrologists and water resource managers. Nevertheless, it is important to understand the procedure of model development.

The following section introduces three fundamental assumptions, or items, in conceptual models that are always made when modeling ground-water flow and contaminant transport and fate.

The Porous Medium as a Continuum

A *porous medium* is a continuum that replaces the real, complex system of solids and voids, filled with one or more fluids, that comprise the aquifer. Inability to model and solve problems of water flow and contaminant transport within the void space is due to the lack of detailed data on its configuration. Even if problems could be described and solved at the *microscopic* level, measurements cannot be taken at that level (i.e., at a point within the void space), in order to validate the model. To circumvent this difficulty, the porous medium domain is visualized as a continuum with fluid or solid matrix variables defined at *every* point. Not only is the porous medium domain as a whole visualized as a continuum, but each of the phases and components within it is also visualized as a continuum, with all continua overlapping each other within the domain.

The passage from the microscopic description of transport phenomena to a macroscopic one is achieved by introducing the concept of a *representative elementary volume* (REV) of the porous medium domain. The main characteristic of an REV is that the averages of fluid and solid properties taken over it are independent of its size. To conform to this definition, the REV should be much larger than the microscopic scale of heterogeneity associated with the presence of solid and void spaces, and much smaller than the size of the considered domain. With this concept of an REV in mind, a porous medium domain can be defined as a portion of space occupied by a number of phases: a solid phase (i.e., the solid matrix), and one or more fluid phases, for which an REV can be found.

Thus, a macroscopic value at a point within a porous medium domain is interpreted as the average of that variable taken over the REV centered at that point. By averaging a variable over all points within a porous medium domain, a continuous field of that variable is obtained.

By representing the actual porous medium as a continuum, the need to know the detailed microscopic configuration of the void space is circumvented. However, at the macroscopic level, the complex geometry of the void-solid interface is replaced by various solid matrix coefficients, such as porosity, permeability and dispersivity. Thus, a coefficient that appears in a macroscopic model represents the relevant effect of the microscopic void-space configuration.

In practice, all models describing ground-water flow and contaminant transport are written at the continuum, or macroscopic level. They are obtained by averaging the corresponding microscopic models over the REV. This means that one must start by understanding phenomena that occur at the microscopic level, (e.g., on the boundary between adjacent phases) before deriving the macroscopic model. For most models of practical interest, this has already been done and published.

Horizontal Two-Dimensional Modeling

A second fundamental approximation often employed in dealing with regional problems of flow and contaminant transport is that ground-water flow is essentially horizontal. The term "regional" is used here to indicate a relatively large aquifer domain. Typically, the horizontal dimension may be from tens to hundreds of kilometers with a thickness of tens to hundreds of meters.

In principle, ground-water flow and contaminant transport in a porous medium domain are three-dimensional. However, when considering regional problems, one should note that because of the ratio of aquifer thickness to horizontal length, the flow in the aquifer is practically horizontal. This observation also remains valid when small changes exist in the thickness of a confined aquifer, or in the saturated thickness of an unconfined aquifer. On the basis of this observation, the assumption that ground-water flow is essentially horizontal is often made and included in the conceptual model. This leads to an aquifer flow model written in horizontal two dimensions only. Formally, the two-dimensional horizontal flow model is obtained by integrating the corresponding three-dimensional variable over the aquifer's thickness. This procedure is known as the *hydraulic approach*. The two-dimensional horizontal flow model is written in terms of variables which are averaged over the vertical thickness of the aquifer and thus are a function of the horizontal coordinates only.

In the process of transforming a three-dimensional problem into a two-dimensional one, new aquifer transport and storage coefficients (e.g., aquifer transmissivity and storativity) appear. In addition to the advantage of having to solve a two-dimensional rather than a three-dimensional mathematical model, fewer field observations may be required for the determination of these coefficients.

Whenever justified on the basis of the geometry (i.e., thickness versus horizontal length) and the flow pattern, the assumption of essentially horizontal flow greatly simplifies the mathematical analysis of the flow in an aquifer. The error introduced by this assumption is small in most cases of practical interest.

The assumption of horizontal flow fails in regions where the flow has a large vertical component (e.g., in the vicinity of springs, rivers or partially penetrating wells). However, even in these cases, at some distance from the source or sink, the assumption of horizontal flow is valid again. As a general rule, one may assume horizontal flow at distances larger than 1.5 to 2 times the thickness of the aquifer in that vicinity (Bear, 1979). At smaller distances the flow is three-dimensional and should be treated as such.

The assumption of horizontal flow is also applicable to leaky aquifers. When the hydraulic conductivity of the aquifer is much larger than that of the semipermeable layer, and the aquifer thickness is much larger than the thickness of the aquitard, it follows from the law of refraction of streamlines ("tangent law") that the flow in the aquifer is essentially horizontal, while it is practically vertical in the aquitards (de Marsily, 1986).

When considering contaminant transport in aquifers, the model user must be cautious in attempting to utilize a two-dimensional model, because in most cases the hydraulic approach is not justified. The contaminant may be transported through only a small fraction of the aquifer's thickness. In addition, velocities in different strata may vary appreciably in heterogeneous aquifers, resulting in a marked difference in the rates of advance and spreading of a contaminant.

Momentum Balance

The third concept relates to the fluid's momentum balance. In the continuum approach, subject to certain simplifying assumptions included in the conceptual model, the momentum balance equation reduces to the linear motion equation known as *Darcy's law*. This equation is used as a flux equation for fluid flow in a porous medium domain. With certain modifications, it is also applicable to multi-phase flows (e.g., air-water flow in the unsaturated zone).

MAJOR BALANCE EQUATIONS

The following examples of major balance equations constitute the core of models that describe flow and contaminant transport in porous medium domains. A number of simplifying assumptions must be stated before any of these equations can be written. Although these assumptions are not listed here, they must be included in the conceptual model of the respective cases.

Mass balance for 3-D saturated flow in a porous medium domain:

$$\text{So } \frac{\partial \varphi}{\partial t} = \nabla \bullet (K \bullet \nabla \varphi) \tag{1}$$

where S_o = specific storativity of porous medium
        φ = piezometric head
        K = hydraulic conductivity tensor

The specific storativity, S_o, is defined as the volume of water added to storage in a unit volume of porous medium, per unit rise of piezometric head. Hence, the left side of Equation 1 expresses the volume of water added to storage in the porous medium domain per unit volume of porous medium per unit time. The divergence of a flux vector, $\mathbf{q}$, written mathematically as $\nabla \bullet \mathbf{q}$, expresses the excess of outflow over inflow per unit volume of porous medium, per unit time. The flux $\mathbf{q}$ is expressed by Darcy's law,

$$\mathbf{q} = - K \bullet \nabla \varphi$$

Note that in Equation 1, the operators ∇ (scalar) (to be read as "gradient of the scalar"), and $\nabla \bullet$ (vector) (to be read as the "divergence of the vector"), are in the three-dimensional space. The variable to be solved is $\varphi (x,y,z,t)$.

Thus, Equation 1 states that the excess of inflow over outflow of water in a unit volume of porous medium, per unit time, at a point, is equal to the rate at which water volume is being stored, where storage is due to fluid and solid matrix compressibilities.

Mass balance for 2-D saturated flow in a confined aquifer:

$$S\frac{\partial \varphi}{\partial t} = \nabla \bullet (T \bullet \nabla\varphi) - P(x,y,t) + R(x,y,t) \tag{2}$$

where S = aquifer storativity
       φ = piezometric head
       T   = aquifer transmissivity tensor
       $P(x,y,t)$ = rate of pumping (per unit area of aquifer)
       $R(x,y,t)$ = rate of recharge (per unit area of aquifer)

The storativity, S, is defined as the volume of water added to storage in a unit area of aquifer, per unit rise of piezometric head. Hence, the left side of equation (2) expresses the volume of water added to storage in the aquifer, per unit area per unit time. The divergence of a flux vector, $(= -T \bullet \nabla\varphi)$, expresses the excess of outflow over inflow per unit area, per unit time. Note that here, the two operators are in the two-dimensional horizontal coordinates, and the variable to be solved is $\varphi(x,y,t)$.

Thus, Equation 2 states that the excess of inflow over outflow of water in a unit area of an aquifer, per unit time, at a point, is equal to the rate at which water volume is being stored, where storage is due to fluid and solid matrix compressibilities.

Mass balance for a solute in 3-D saturated flow:

The left side of Equation 3 expresses the mass of the conservative solute added to storage per unit volume of porous medium per unit time (e.g., it does not adsorb, decay or interact with the solid matrix).

$$\frac{\partial \phi c}{\partial t} = -\nabla \bullet (cq + \phi J^* + \phi J) + \Gamma \tag{3}$$

where c = concentration of considered solute
       ϕ = porosity of porous medium
       q = specific discharge of water (= volume of water passing through a unit area of porous medium per unit time)
       J^* = dispersive flux of solute (per unit area of fluid)
       J = diffusive flux of solute (per unit area of fluid)
       Γ = strength of solute source (added quantity per unit volume of porous medium per unit time)

The first term on the right side of Equation 3 (to be read as "minus divergence of the total flux of the solute"), expresses the excess of the solute's inflow over outflow, per unit volume of porous medium, per unit time. This total flux is made up of an advective flux with the fluid, a dispersive flux and a diffusive flux. The second term on the right side of Equation 3 expresses the added mass by various sources.

The dispersive and diffusive fluxes appearing in Equation 3 must be expressed in terms of the concentration, c, which serves as the variable to be solved in this equation. For example,

$$\mathbf{J} = -D* \bullet \nabla c, \quad \mathbf{J}* = -\mathbf{D} \bullet \nabla c,$$

where   D = coefficient of dispersion
D^* = coefficient of molecular diffusion in a porous medium

MODEL COEFFICIENTS AND THEIR ESTIMATION

In passing from the microscopic level of describing transport to the macroscopic level, various coefficients of transport and storage are introduced. The permeability of a porous medium, aquifer transmissivity, aquifer storativity, and porous medium dispersivity, may serve as examples of such coefficients. Permeability and dispersivity are examples of coefficients that express the macroscopic effects of microscopic configuration of the solid-fluid interfaces of a porous medium. They are introduced in the passage from the microscopic level of description to the macroscopic, continuum, level. The coefficients of aquifer storativity and transmissivity are introduced by the further averaging of the three-dimensional macroscopic model over the thickness of an aquifer in order to obtain a two-dimensional model. All these coefficients are coefficients of the models, and therefore, in spite of the similarity in their names in different models, their interpretation and actual values may differ from one model to the next.

This point can be illustrated by the following example. To obtain the drawdown in a pumping well and in its vicinity, one employs a conceptual model that assumes radially converging flow to an infinitesimally small well in a homogeneous, isotropic aquifer of constant thickness and of infinite areal extent. The same model is used to obtain the aquifer's storativity and transmissivity by conducting an aquifer pumping test and solving the model's equation for these coefficients. It is common practice to refer to these coefficients as the aquifer's coefficients and not as coefficients of the aquifer's model. However, it is important to realize that the coefficients thus derived actually correspond to that particular model. These coefficients should not be employed in a model that describes the flow in a finite heterogeneous aquifer with variable thickness and with nonradial flow in the vicinity of the well. Sometimes, however, there is no choice because this is the only information available. Then, the information must be used, keeping in mind that when coefficients are derived by employing one model in another model for a given domain, the magnitude of the error will depend on the differences between the two models. In principle, in order to employ a particular model, the values of the coefficients appearing in it should be determined using some parameter identification technique for that particular model.

Obviously, no model can be employed in any specified domain unless the numerical values of all the coefficients appearing in it are known. Estimates of natural recharge and a *priori* location and type of boundaries may be included in the list of model coefficients and parameters to be identified. The activity of identifying these model coefficients is often referred to as the *identification problem*.

In principle, the only way to obtain the values of the coefficients for a considered model is to start by investigating the real-world aquifer system to find a period (or periods) in the past for which information is available on (i) initial conditions of the system; (ii) excitations of the system, as in the form of pumping and artificial recharge (quality and quantity), natural recharge introduction of contaminants, or changes in boundary conditions, and (iii) observations of the response of the system, as in the form of temporal and spatial distributions of water levels and solute concentrations. If such a period (or periods) can be found, one can (i) impose the known initial conditions on the model, (ii) excite the model by the known excitations of the real system, and (iii) derive the response of the model to these excitations. Obviously, in order to derive the model's response, one has to assume some trial values for the coefficients and compare the response observed in the real system with that predicted by the model. The sought values of the coefficients are those that will make the two sets of values of state variables identical. However, because the model is only an approximation of the real system, one should never expect these two sets of values to be identical. Instead, the "best fit" between them must be sought according to some criterion. Various techniques exist for determining the "best" or "optimal" values of these coefficients (i.e., values that will make the predicted values and the measured ones sufficiently close to each other). Obviously, the values of the coefficients eventually accepted as "best" for the model depend on the criteria selected for "goodness of fit" between the observed and predicted values of the relevant state variables. These, in turn, depend on the objective of the modeling.

Some techniques use the basic trial-and-error method described above, while others employ more sophisticated optimization methods. In some methods, *a priori* estimates of the coefficients, as well as information about lower and upper bounds, are introduced. In addition to the question of selecting the appropriate criteria, there remains the question of the conditions under which the identification problem, also called the inverse problem, will result in a unique solution.

As stressed above, no model can be used for predicting the behavior of a system unless the numerical values of its parameters have been determined by some identification procedure. This requires that data be obtained by field measurements. However, even without such data, certain important questions about the suitability of the model can be studied. Sensitivity analysis enables the modeler to investigate whether a certain percentage change in a parameter has any real significance; that is, whether it is a dominant parameter or not. The major point to be established from a sensitivity analysis is the relative sensitivity of the model predictions to changes in the values of the model parameters within the estimated range of such changes.

A successful model application requires appropriate site characterization and expert insight into the modeling process. Figure 9-1 illustrates a simple diagram of a model application process. Each phase of the process may consist of various steps; often, results from one step are used as feedback in previous steps, resulting in an iterative procedure (van der Heijde et al., 1988).

METHODS OF SOLUTION

Once a well-posed model for a given problem has been constructed, including the numerical values of all the coefficients that appear in the model, it must be solved for any given set of excitations (i.e., initial and boundary conditions, sources and sinks). The preferable method of solution is the analytical one, as once such a solution is derived, it can be used for a variety of cases (e.g., different values of coefficients, different pumping rates, etc). However, for most cases of practical interest, this method of solution is not possible due to the irregularity of the domain's shape, the heterogeneity of the domain with respect to various coefficients, and various nonlinearities. Instead, numerical models are employed.

Although a numerical model is derived from the mathematical model, a numerical model of a given problem need not necessarily be considered as the numerical method of solution, but as a model of the problem in its own right. By adding assumptions to the conceptual model of the given problem (e.g., assumptions related to time and space discretization) a new conceptual model is obtained which, in turn, leads to the numerical model of the given problem. Such a model represents a different approximate version of the real system.

Even those who consider a numerical model as a model in its own right very often verify it by comparing the model results with those obtained by an analytical solution of the corresponding mathematical model (for relatively simple cases for which such solutions can be derived). One of the main reasons for such a verification is the need to eliminate errors resulting from the numerical approximations alone. Until the early 1970s, physical (e.g., sand box) and analog (e.g., electrical) laboratory models were used as practical tools for solving the mathematical models that described ground-water flow problems. With the introduction of computers and their application in the solution of numerical models, physical and analog models have become cumbersome as tools for simulating ground-water regimes. However, laboratory experiments in soil columns are still needed when new phenomena are being investigated and to validate new models (i.e., to examine whether certain assumptions that underlie the model are valid).

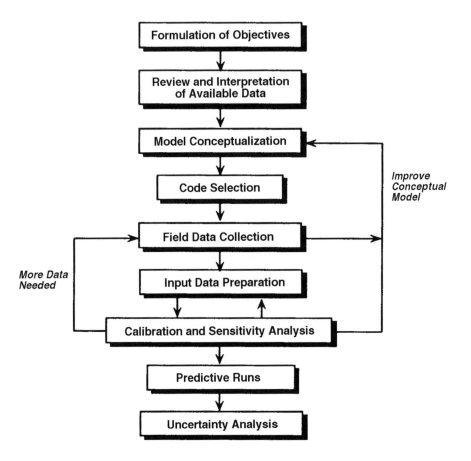

Figure 9-1. Model application process.

ANALYTICAL MODELS

During the early phase of a ground-water contamination study, analytical models offer an inexpensive way to evaluate the physical characteristics of a ground-water system. Such models enable investigators to conduct a rapid preliminary analysis of ground-water contamination and to perform sensitivity analysis. A number of simplifying assumptions regarding the ground-water system are necessary to obtain an analytical solution. Although these assumptions do not necessarily dictate that analytical models cannot be used in "real-life" situations they do require sound professional judgment and experience in their application to field situations. Nonetheless, it is also true that in many field situations few data are available; hence, complex numerical models are often of limited use. When sufficient data have been collected, however, numerical models may be used for predictive evaluation and decision assessment. This can be done during the later phase of the study. Analytical models should be viewed as a useful complement to numerical models.

For more information on analytical solutions, the reader is referred to Bear (1979), van Genuchten and Alves (1982), and Walton (1989).

NUMERICAL MODELS

Once the conceptual model is translated into a mathematical model in the form of governing equations, with associated boundary and initial conditions, a solution can be obtained by transforming it into a numerical model and writing a computer program (code) for solving it using a digital computer.

Depending on the numerical technique(s) employed in solving the mathematical model, there exist several types of numerical models:

- finite-difference models
- finite-element models
- boundary-element models
- particle tracking models
  —method-of-characteristics models
  —random walk models, and
- integrated finite-difference models.

The main features of the various numerical models are:

1. The solution is sought for the numerical values of state variables only at specified points in the space and time domains defined for the problem (rather than their continuous variations in these domains).
2. The partial differential equations that represent balances of the considered extensive quantities are replaced by a set of algebraic equations (written in terms of the sought, discrete values of the state variables at the discrete points in space and time).
3. The solution is obtained for a specified set of numerical values of the various model coefficients (rather than as general relationships in terms of these coefficients).
4. Because of the large number of equations that must be solved simultaneously, a computer program is prepared.

In recent years, codes have been developed for almost all classes of problems encountered in the management of ground water. Some codes are very comprehensive and can handle a variety of specific problems as special cases, while others are tailor-made for particular problems. Many of them are available in the public domain, or for a nominal fee. More recently, many codes have been developed or adapted for microcomputers.

UNCERTAINTY

Much uncertainty is associated with the modeling of a given problem. Among them, uncertainties exist in

- the transport mechanisms;
- the various sink/source phenomena for the considered extensive quantity;
- the values of model coefficients, and their spatial (and sometimes temporal) variation;
- initial conditions;
- the location of domain boundaries and the conditions prevailing on them;
- the meaning of measured data employed in model calibration; and
- the ability of the model to cope with a problem in which the solid matrix heterogeneity spans a range of scales, sometimes orders of magnitude apart.

The degree of uncertainty is increased in most cases by the lack of sufficient data for parameter estimation and model validation. Errors in observed data used for parameter identification also contribute to uncertainty in the estimated values of model parameters.

Various methods for introducing uncertainty into the models and the modeling process have been proposed. For example, one approach is to employ Monte Carlo methods in which the various possibilities are represented in a large number of simulated realizations. Another approach is to construct stochastic models in which the various coefficients are represented as probability distributions rather than deterministic values.

Often the question is raised as to whether, in view of all these uncertainties which always exist in any real-world problem, models should still be regarded as reliable tools for providing predictions of real-world behavior—*there is no alternative!* However, the kind of answers models should be expected to provide and the very objectives of employing models, should be broadened beyond the simple requirement that they provide the predicted response of the system to the planned excitations. Stochastic models provide probabilistic predictions rather than deterministic ones. Management must then make use of such predictions in the decision-making process. Methodologies for evaluating uncertainties will have to be developed; especially methods for evaluating the worth of data in reducing uncertainty. It then becomes a management decision whether or not to invest more in data acquisition.

In view of the uncertainty involved in modeling, models should be used for additional roles, beyond predicting or estimating the deterministic or probabilistic responses to planned excitations. Such roles include:

- predicting trends and direction of changes;
- providing information on the sensitivity of the system to variations in various parameters, so that more resources can be allocated to reduce their uncertainty;
- deepening our understanding of the system and of the phenomena of interest that take place within it; and
- improving the design of observation networks.

Many researchers are currently engaged in developing methods that incorporate the element of uncertainty in both the forecasting and the inverse models (Freeze et al., 1989; Gelhar, 1986; Yeh, 1986; Neuman et al., 1987; and others).

MODEL MISUSE

As stated above, the most crucial step in ground-water modeling is the development of the conceptual model. If the conceptual model is wrong (i.e., does not represent the relevant flow and contaminant transport phenomena), the rest of the modeling efforts—translating the conceptual model into mathematical and numerical models, and solving for cases of interest—are a waste of time and money. However, mistakes and misuses may occur during any phase of the modeling process (Mercer, 1991).

Following is a list of the more common misuses and mistakes related to modeling. They may be divided into four categories (Mercer and Faust, 1981):

1. Improper conceptualization of the considered problem:

   - improper delineation of the model's domain;
   - wrong selection of model geometry: a 2-D horizontal model, or a 3-D model;
   - improper selection of boundary conditions;
   - wrong assumptions related to homogeneity and isotropy of aquifer material;
   - wrong assumptions related to the significant processes, especially in cases of contaminant transport. These may include the type of sink/source phenomena, chemical and biological transformations, fluid-solid interactions, etc.; and
   - selecting a model that involves coefficients that vary in space, but for which there are insufficient data for model calibration and parameter estimation.

2. Selection of an inappropriate code for solving the model:

   - selecting a code much more powerful/versatile than necessary for the considered problem;
   - selection of a code that has not been verified and tested.

3. Improper model application:

   - selection of improper values for model parameters and other input data;
   - misrepresentation of aquitards in a multi-layer system; mistakes related to the selection of grid size and time steps;
   - making predictions with a model that has been calibrated under different conditions;
   - making mistakes in model calibration (history matching); and
   - improper selection of computational parameters (closure criterion, etc.).

4. Misinterpretation of model results:

- wrong hydrological interpretation of model results;
- mass balance is not achieved.

SOURCES OF INFORMATION

In selecting a code, its applicability to a given problem and its efficiency in solving the problem are important criteria. In evaluating a code's applicability to a problem and its efficiency, a good description of these characteristics should be accessible. For a large number of ground-water models, such information is available from the International Ground Water Modeling Center (IGWMC, Institute for Ground-Water Research and Education, Colorado School of Mines, Golden, Colorado 80401), which operates a clearinghouse service for information and software pertinent to ground-water modeling. Information databases have been developed to efficiently organize, update and access information on ground-water models for mainframe and microcomputers. The model annotation databases have been developed and maintained over the years with major support from U.S. EPA's Robert S. Kerr Environmental Research Laboratory (RSKERL), Ada, Oklahoma.

The Center for Subsurface Modeling Support (CSMoS), located at the RSKERL (P.O. Box 1198, Ada, OK 74820), provides ground-water and vadose zone modeling software and services to public agencies and private companies throughout the nation. CSMoS primarily manages and supports ground-water models and databases resulting from research at RSKERL. CSMoS integrates the expertise of individuals in all aspects of the environmental field in an effort to apply models to better understand and resolve subsurface problems. CSMoS is supported internally by RSKERL scientists and engineers, and externally by the IGWMC, National Center for Ground Water Research and numerous ground-water modeling consultants from academia and the private consulting community.

The National Ground Water Information Center (NGWIC, 6375 Riverside Drive, Dublin, Ohio 43017) is an information-gathering and dissemination business that performs customized literature searches on various ground-water-related topics, and locates and retrieves copies of available documents. The center maintains its own on-line databases.

EPA CONTACTS

For further information, contact David Burden, 405/436-8606; Randall Ross, 405/435-8611; or Joe Williams, 405/435-8608, at RSKERL-Ada.

APPENDIX A: SUGGESTED FORMAT FOR A GROUND-WATER MODELING REPORT

Following is a suggested standardized format for a report that involves modeling and analyses of model results. The emphasis is on the modeling efforts and related activities. It is not an attempt to propose a structure for a project report. The Ground Water Modeling Section (D-18.21.10) of the American Society for Testing and Materials (ASTM) Subcommittee on Ground Water and Vadose Zone Investigations is in the process of developing standards on ground-water modeling. Additionally, specific information regarding the content of ground-water modeling studies is addressed by Anderson and Woessner (1992, Chapter 9).

INTRODUCTION

The introduction may start with a description of the problem that led to the investigations. The description will include the domain in which the phenomena of interest take place, and what decisions are contemplated in connection with these phenomena. The description should also include information about the geography, topography, geology, hydrology, climate, soils, and other relevant features (of the domain and the considered transport phenomena). Sources of information should be given. The description of the problem should lead to the kind of information that is required by management/decision maker, which the investigations described in the report are supposed to provide. This section should continue to outline the methodology used for obtaining the required information. In most cases, a model of the problem domain and the transport (i.e., flow and contaminant) phenomena will be the tool for providing management with the required information. On the premise that this section concludes that such a model is needed, the objective of the report is to describe the construction of the model, the model runs, and the results leading to the required information.

PREVIOUS STUDIES

This section should contain a description of earlier relevant studies in the area, whether on the same problem or in connection with other problems. The objective of this section is to examine the data and conclusions in these investigations, as far as they relate to the current study.

THE CONCEPTUAL MODEL

Because the previous section concluded that a model is required, the objective of this section is to construct the conceptual model of the problem, including the problem domain and the transport phenomena taking place within it. The content of a conceptual model has been outlined in the text. However, the importance of the conceptual model cannot be overemphasized. It is possible that the existing data will indicate more than one alternative model, if the available data (or lack of it) so dictates.

THE MATHEMATICAL MODEL

The conceptual model should be translated into a complete, well-posed mathematical one. At this stage, the various terms that appear in the mathematical model should be analyzed, with the objective of deleting nondominant effects. Further simplifying assumptions may be added to the original conceptual model at this stage.

If more than one conceptual model has been visualized, a corresponding mathematical model should be presented for each. This section should conclude with a list of coefficients and parameters that appear in the model. The modeler should then indicate for which coefficients values, or at least initial ones, are available (including the actual numerical value and the source of information), and for which coefficients the required information is missing. In addition, the kind of field work or exploration required to obtain that information should be reported. If possible, an estimate should be given for the missing values, their possible range, etc. At this stage, it is important to conduct and report a sensitivity analysis in order to indicate the significance of the missing information, bearing in mind the kind of information that the model is expected to provide.

SELECTION OF NUMERICAL MODEL AND CODE

The selected numerical model and the reasons for preferring it over other models (public domain or proprietary) should be presented. Some of the questions that should be answered are: Was the code used as is, or was it modified for the purpose of the project? What were the modifications? If so stated in the contract the modified code may have to be included in the appendix to the report. The full details of the code (name, version, manual, author, etc.) should be supplied. This section may include a description of the hardware used in running the code, as well as any other software (pre- and post processors). More information about model selection can be found in Simmons and Cole (1985), Beljin and van der Heijde (1991).

MODEL CALIBRATION

Every model must be calibrated before it can be used as a tool for predicting the behavior of a considered system. During the calibration phase, the initial estimates of model coefficients may be modified. The sensitivity analysis may be postponed until a numerical model and a code for its solution have been selected.

In this section objectives of the calibration or history matching, the adjusted parameters/coefficients, the criterion of the calibration (e.g., minimizing the difference between observed and predicted water levels), the available data, the model calibration runs, etc., should be described.

The conclusions should be the modified set of parameters and coefficients to be used in the model.

MODEL RUNS

Justification and reasoning for the various runs.

MODEL RESULTS

This section includes all tables and graphic output. Ranges and uncertainties in model results should be indicated. Results of sensitivity analysis and the significance of various factors should also be discussed.

CONCLUSIONS

The information required by the decision maker should be clearly outlined.

APPENDICES

Tables and graphs, figures, and maps not presented in the body of the report, along with a list of symbols, references, codes, etc., should be included.

APPENDIX B: SELECTED BIBLIOGRAPHY

(References cited in the main text and Appendix A are indicated by an "*")

Anderson, M.P. 1979. Using Models to Simulate the Movement of Contaminants through Ground Water Flow Systems. Critical Reviews in Environmental Control, 9(2):97–156.

Anderson, M.P. 1984. Movement of Contaminants in Groundwater: Groundwater Transport—Advection and Dispersion. In: Groundwater Contamination. National Academy Press, Washington, D.C.

*Anderson, M.P. and W.W. Woessner. 1992. Applied Groundwater Modeling. Academic Press, San Diego, CA.

Appel, C.A. and T.E. Reilly. 1988. Selected Reports That Include Computer Programs Produced by the U.S. Geological Survey for Simulation of Ground-Water Flow and Quality. U.S. Geological Survey Water Resources Investigations Report WRI 87-4271.

Bear, J. 1972. Dynamics or Fluids in Porous Media. Elsevier, New York, NY.

*Bear, J. 1979. Hydraulics of Groundwater. McGraw-Hill, New York, NY.

*Bear, J. and A. Verruijt. 1987. Modeling Groundwater Flow and Pollution. Kluwer Academic Publishers, Hingham, MA.

Bear, J. and Y. Bachmat. 1990. Introduction to Modeling of Transport Phenomena in Porous Media. Kluwer Academic Publishers, Hingham, MA.

Beck, M.B. 1985. Water Quality Management: A Review of the Development and Application of Mathematical Models. IIASA 11, Springer-Verlag, Berlin, West Germany.

Beljin, M.S. and P.K.M. van der Heijde. 1989. Testing Verification, and Validation of Two-Dimensional Solute Transport Models. In: G. Jousma et al. (eds.), Groundwater Contamination: Use of Models in Decision-Making. Kluwer Academic Publishers, Hingham, MA.

*Beljin, M.S. and P.K.M. van der Heijde. 1991. Selection of Groundwater Models for WHPA Delineation. In: Proc. the AWWA Computer Conference, Houston, TX.

Boonstra, J. and N.A. De Ridder. 1981. Numerical Modelling of Groundwater Basins. International Institute for Land Reclamation and Improvement, Wageningen, The Netherlands.

Boutwell, S.H., S.M. Brown, B.R. Roberts, and D.F. Atwood. 1985. Modeling Remedial Actions of Uncontrolled Hazardous Waste Sites. EPA 540/2-85/001 (NTIS PB85-211357).

*de Marsily, G. 1986. Quantitative Hydrogeology. Academic Press, Orlando, FL.

Domenico, P.A. 1972. Concepts and Models in Groundwater Hydrology. McGraw-Hill, New York, NY.

*Freeze, R.A., G. DeMarsily, L. Smith, and J. Massmann. 1989. Some Uncertainties About Uncertainty. In: B.E. Buxton (ed.), Proceedings of the Conference Geostatistical, Sensitivity, and Uncertainty Methods for Ground-Water Flow and Radionuclide Transport Modeling. CONF-870971. Battelle Press, Columbus, Ohio.

Gelhar, L.W., A.L. Gutjahr, and R.L. Naff. 1979. Stochastic Analysis of Macrodispersion in Aquifers. Water Resources Research, 15(6):1387–1397.

Gelhar, L.W. 1984. Stochastic Analysis of Flow in Heterogeneous Porous Media. In: J. Bear and M.Y. Corapcioglu (eds.), Fundamentals of Transport Phenomena in Porous Media. Marinus Nijhoff Publishers, Dordrecht, The Netherlands.

*Gelhar, L.W. 1986. Stochastic Subsurface Hydrology from Theory to Applications. Water Resources Research, 22(9):135S–145S.

Gorelick, S.M. 1983. A Review of Distributed Parameter Groundwater Management Modeling Methods. Water Resources Research, 19(2):305–319.

Grove, D.B. and K.G. Stollenwerk. 1987. Chemical Reactions Simulated by Ground-Water Quality Models. Water Resources Bulletin, 23(4):601–615.

Herrling, B. and A. Heckele. 1986. Coupling of Finite Element and Optimization Methods for the Management of Groundwater Systems. Advances in Water Resources, 9(4):190–195.

Hunt, B. 1983. Mathematical Analysis of Groundwater Resources. Butterworths Publishers, Stoneham, MA.

Huyakorn, P.S. and G.F. Pinder. 1983. Computational Methods in Subsurface Flow. Academic Press, New York, NY.

Huyakorn, P.S., B.H. Lester, and C.R. Faust. 1983. Finite Element Techniques for Modeling Ground Water Flow in Fractured Aquifers. Water Resources Research, 19(4):1019–1035.

Istok, J. 1989. Groundwater Modeling by the Finite-Element Method. AGU Water Resources Monograph 13. American Geophysical Union, Washington, D.C.

Javandel, I., C. Doughty, and C.F. Tsang. 1984. Groundwater Transport: Handbook of Mathematical Models. AGU Water Resources Monograph 10. American Geophysical Union, Washington, D.C.

Keely, J.F. 1987. The Use of Models in Managing Ground-Water Protection Programs. EPA/600/8-87/003 (NITS PB87-166203).

Kinzelbach, W. 1986. Groundwater Modeling: An Introduction with Sample Programs in BASIC. Elsevier, Amsterdam, The Netherlands.

Konikow, L.F. and J.D. Bredehoeft. 1978. Computer Model of Two-Dimensional Solute Transport and Dispersion in Ground Water. U.S. Geological Survey Techniques of Water-Resources Investigations, Book 7, Chap. C2, 90 pp.

Ligget, J.A. and P.L-F. Liu. 1983. The Boundary Integral Equation Method for Porous Media Flow. Allen and Unwin, Winchester, MA.

*Mercer, J.W. 1991. Common Mistakes in Model Applications. In: Proc. ASCE Symposium on Ground Water. American Society of Civil Engineers, New York, NY.

*Mercer, J.W. and C.R. Faust. 1981. Ground-Water Modeling. National Water Well Association (NWWA), Worthington, Ohio.

Mercer, J.W., S.D. Thomas, and B. Ross. 1982. Parameters and Variables Appearing in Repository Siting Models. Report NUREG/CR-3066, U.S. Regulatory Commission Washington, D.C.

Moore, J.E. 1979. Contribution of Ground-water Modeling to Planning. J. Hydrology, 43:121–128.

Narasimhan, T.N. and P.A. Witherspoon. 1976. An Integrated Finite-Difference Method for Analyzers Fluid Flow in Porous Media. Water Resources Research, 12(1):57–64.

Narasimhan, T.N. 1982. Numerical Modeling in Hydrogeology. In: T.N. Narasimhan (ed.), Recent Trends in Hydrogeology. Special Paper 189. Geological Society of America, Boulder, CO, pp. 273–296.

National Research Council (NRC). 1990. Ground Water Models: Scientific and Regulatory Application. National Academy Press, Washington, D.C.

*Neuman, S.P., C.L. Winter, and C.M. Newman. 1987. Stochastic Theory of Field-Scale Fickian Dispersion in Anisotropic Porous Media. Water Resources Research, v. 23(3):453–466.

Pickens, J.F. and G.E. Grisak. 1981. Modeling of Scale-Dependent Dispersion in Hydrologic Systems. Water Resources Research, 17(6):1701–1711.

Pinder, G.F. and J.D. Bredehoeft. 1968. Application of the Digital Computer for Aquifer Evaluation. Water Resources Research, 4(5):1069–1093.

Pinder, G.F. and W.G. Gray. 1977. Finite Element Simulation in Surface and Subsurface Hydrology. Academic Press, New York, NY, 295 pp.

Pinder, G.F. and L. Abriola. 1986. On the Simulation of Nonaqueous Phase Organic Compounds in the Subsurface. Water Resources Research, 22(9):1092–1192.

Prickett, T.A. 1975. Modeling Techniques for Groundwater Evaluation. In: Ven Te Chow (ed.), Advances in Hydroscience, Vol. 10.

Prickett, T.A. and C.G. Lonnquist. 1982. A Random-Walk Solute Transport Model for Selected Groundwater Quality Evaluations. Bull. No. 65. Illinois State Water Survey, Urbana, IL, 105 pp.

Remson, I., G.M. Hornberger, and F.J. Molz. 1971. Numerical Methods in Subsurface Hydrology. John Wiley & Sons, New York, NY.

Rushton, K.R. and S.C. Redshaw. 1979. Seepage and Groundwater Flow: Numerical Analysis by Analog and Digital Methods. John Wiley & Sons, Chichester, U.K.

Schmelling, S.G. and R.R. Ross. 1989. Contaminant Transport in Fractured Media: Models for Decision Makers. Superfund Ground Water Issue Paper, EPA/540/4-89/004. [See Chapter 10.]

*Simmons, C.S. and C.R. Cole. 1985. Guidelines for Selecting Codes for Ground-Water Transport Modeling of Low-Level Waste Burial Sites, 2 Vols. PNL-4980. Battelle Pacific Northwest Labs, Richland, WA.

Strack, O.D.L. 1989. Groundwater Mechanics. Prentice Hall, Englewood Cliffs, NJ.

Trescott, P.C., G.F. Pinder, and S.P. Larson. 1976. Finite-Difference Model for Aquifer Simulation in Two-Dimensions with Results of Numerical Experiments. U.S. Geological Survey Techniques of Water Resources Investigation, Book 7, Chap. C1, 116 pp.

U.S. Office of Technology Assessment (OTA). 1982. Use of Models for Water Resources Management, Planning, and Policy. OTA, Washington, D.C.

van der Heijde, P.K.M. et al. 1985. Groundwater Management: The Use of Numerical Models, 2nd edition. Water Resources Monograph no. 5. American Geophysical Union, Washington, D.C.

van der Heijde, P.K.M. and M.S. Beljin. 1988. Model Assessment for Delineating Wellhead Protection Areas. EPA/440/6-88-002 (NTIS PB88-231485).

*van der Heijde, P.K.M., A.I. El-Kadi, and S.A. Williams. 1988. Groundwater Modeling: An Overview and Status Report. EPA/600/2-89/028 (NTIS PB89-224497).

*van Genuchten, M.Th. and W.J. Alves. 1982. Analytical Solutions of the One-Dimensional Convective-Dispersive Solute Transport Equation. U.S. Dept. of Agriculture Tech. Bull. No. 1661.

Walton, W. 1985. Practical Aspects of Ground Water Modeling. Lewis Publishers, Chelsea, MI.

*Walton, W. 1989. Analytical Ground Water Modeling. Lewis Publishers, Chelsea, MI.

Wang, H.F. and M.P. Anderson. 1982. Introduction to Groundwater Modeling. W.H. Freeman, San Francisco, CA.

*Yeh, W.W-G. 1986. Review of Parameter Identification Procedures in Groundwater Hydrology: The Inverse Problem. Water Resources Research, 22(2):95–108.

Chapter 10

Contaminant Transport in Fractured Media: Models for Decision Makers[1]

Stephen G. Schmelling and **Randall R. Ross**, U.S. EPA, Robert S. Kerr Environmental Research Laboratory, Ada, OK

SUMMARY

The ability to reliably predict the rate and direction of ground-water flow and contaminant transport in fractured rock systems would be of great value in planning and implementing the remediation of contaminated aquifers. This chapter summarizes the current status of modeling ground-water flow and contaminant transport in fractured rock systems.

Mathematical models have a potentially useful role to play in arriving at a decision on the remedial action to be taken at a contaminated site. Where there is a need for a quantitative estimate of the threat to public health resulting from a particular course of action, of the estimated cost and time of clean-up for a particular remediation strategy, or of the results of other actions to be taken at a contaminated site, mathematical models have a greater potential to provide the needed information than any other approach to the problem. For contaminated sites in fractured rock, however, this potential has yet to be realized.

The development of predictive models for ground-water flow and contaminant transport in fractured rock systems is an active area of research, but field-validated models that are directly applicable to the remediation of contaminated sites are not yet available. Nonetheless, when used with appropriate site characterization data, the available models can be helpful in developing a qualitative understanding of the behavior of the fractured rock system and the interactions of contaminants with the system.

Selection of a suitable model requires the model user to have a specific objective in mind. For example, is the purpose of the modeling effort to determine the location of additional monitoring wells, to design optimal well placement for hydraulic control during site remediation, to interpret existing data, or to determine sources or predict the fate of a pollutant? No single model will serve all purposes. The choice of model will depend on the system conditions, the decision to be made, and the extent and availability of site characterization data.

Before ground-water models can be applied to any system fractured or not, it is necessary to have extensive data about that system. Data are needed to (1) select or develop an appropriate model based on the processes acting on the system; (2) define boundaries in space and time of the domain in which these processes are acting; (3) determine the state of the system at some point in time from which predictions, either forward or backward in time, can be made; and (4) estimate the effects of future stresses or inputs to the system (Konikow and Mercer, 1988). Modeling and data collection are complementary activities, neither being a substitute for the other. Not only are data necessary for successful modeling, but modeling results may be used to guide data collection efforts.

Because of the heterogeneous and anisotropic nature of fractures in the subsurface, the data requirements for modeling the movement of water and contaminants in fractured media are somewhat different than the requirements for modeling more homogeneous unconsolidated porous media. The development of techniques to characterize the hydrogeologic properties of fractured rock systems has proceeded in parallel with the development of models. These techniques are often more complex and more difficult to interpret than analogous techniques used in the unconsolidated media.

---

[1] EPA/540/4-89/004.

There are at least four categories of models to describe flow and transport in fractured rock systems. (1) Models developed for use in unconsolidated porous media have been successfully applied to certain fractured rock systems. These models consider the fractured rock system as an equivalent porous medium (EPM). EPM models are more likely to accurately predict ground-water flux than to correctly predict solute transport (Endo et al., 1984). (2) A second category of fractured rock models explicitly considers discrete fractures. The extensive data required by discrete fracture models for fracture system characterization limit their use to sites with a relatively small number of well defined fractures. (3) A third category of models represents the fractured system by a set of matrix blocks of well defined geometry. Such models are largely research tools that are useful for enhancing our conceptual understanding of pollutant transport in fractured rock. (4) A fourth category of models uses a stochastic approach to describe the fracture distribution. At the present time these are research models. It is important to note again that the choice of an appropriate model depends on the conditions present at the site, and on the decision to be reached by using the model.

Before discussing models in more detail, Section II provides some basic information on ground-water flow and contaminant transport in fractured rock systems. Section III briefly discusses methods of characterizing contaminated fractured rock sites. Site characterization and modeling are complementary activities and each is essential to the other. The last part of the chapter discusses the conceptual basis of ground-water models and gives some specific examples of the types of models that are publicly available.

FRACTURED ROCK SYSTEMS

Development of the theory of flow through porous media began with experimental work by Henri Darcy, published in 1857. The study of fluid flow through fractured rock was first developed in the petroleum industry. These studies resulted from observations that oil and gas production could be significantly increased by fracturing the producing formations near the well bore (Duguid and Lee, 1977). Gale (1982) notes that the first comprehensive experiments on flow through artificial fractures were conducted in the early 1950s. During the past decades, the amount of research on flow and transport in unconsolidated porous media has greatly exceeded that devoted to fractured media. This is due in part to the complexity of fractured rock systems and the lack of economic incentives.

Most fractured rock systems consist of rock blocks bounded by discrete discontinuities comprised of fractures, joints, and shear zones, usually occurring in sets with similar geometries (Witherspoon et al., 1987). Fractures may be open, mineral-filled, deformed, or any combination thereof (Nelson, 1985).

Open fractures may provide conduits for the movement of ground water and contaminants through an otherwise relatively impermeable rock mass. Mineral-filled fractures are filled either partially or completely by secondary cementing materials such as quartz or carbonate minerals, thereby reducing or eliminating fracture porosity and permeability. Deformed fractures may be in filled with permeability-reducing gouge, a finely abraded material produced by the cataclasis of grains in contact across a fault plane during displacement of the rock masses. Other deformed fracture features include slickensides, which are striated surfaces formed by frictional sliding along a fault plane. Slickensides reduce permeability perpendicular to the fracture plane, but the mismatch of fracture surfaces may increase permeability along the fracture plane. Very little displacement is necessary to produce gouge or slickensides. The deposition of a thin layer of low permeability material, fracture skin, may prevent the free exchange of fluids between the rock matrix and fracture (Moench, 1984).

Major factors affecting ground-water flow through fractured rock include fracture density, orientation, effective aperture width, and the nature of the rock matrix. Fracture density (number of fractures per unit volume of rock) and orientation are important determinants of the degree of interconnection of fracture sets, which is a critical feature contributing to the hydraulic conductivity of a fractured rock system (Witherspoon et al., 1987). Only interconnected fractures provide pathways for ground-water flow and contaminant transport. Fractures oriented parallel to the hydraulic gradient are more likely to provide effective pathways than fractures oriented perpendicular to the hydraulic gradient. Fractured rock systems simulate equivalent porous media when the fracture apertures are constant, the fracture orientations are randomly distributed and the fracture spacing is small relative to the scale of the system (Long et al., 1982).

The cross-sectional area of a fracture will have an important effect on flow through the fracture. Fracture-flux is proportional to the cube of the fracture aperture (distance between rock blocks). The relationship between flux and aperture appears to be true for fractures with apertures greater than 10 microns (Witherspoon et al., 1987). Fracture apertures, and therefore flow through fractures, are highly stress-dependent, and generally decrease with depth (Gale, 1982).

The nature of the rock matrix plays an important role in the movement of water and contaminants through fractured rock systems. Metamorphic and igneous rocks generally have very low primary porosity and permeability. Fractures may account for most of the permeability in such systems and the movement of water and contaminants into and out of the rock matrix may be minimal. Sedimentary rocks generally have higher primary porosity and varying permeability. Coarse-grained materials such as sandstone have relatively high primary porosity and significant matrix permeability. Fine-grained materials such as shale have high primary porosity and low permeability. Fractures may enhance the permeability of all types of materials. High porosity allows significant storage of water and contaminants in the rock matrix. Authigenic clays formed during the weathering of certain rock-forming minerals may significantly reduce the porosity and permeability of the fractures and rock matrix. Rates of contaminant migration into and out of the rock matrix will depend on the permeability of the matrix, the presence of low permeability fracture skins, and the matrix diffusion coefficient of the contaminant.

A complete description of a contaminated fractured rock system would include data on the dimensions of the system, the length, aperture width, location, and orientation of each fracture, the hydraulic head throughout the system, the porosity and permeability of the rock matrix, the sources of water and contaminants, the nature and concentrations of the contaminants throughout the system, and the chemical interactions between the contaminants and rock matrix. Presently, collection of such detailed information is neither technically possible, nor economically feasible on the scale of most contaminated sites. However, most ground-water models, especially those describing contaminant transport, require this type of information as input. In general, the more detailed the site characterization, the greater the probability of success in modeling the site. The accuracy of flow and transport modeling in fractured rock systems is highly dependent on the accuracy and extent of site characterization data.

HYDROGEOLOGIC CHARACTERIZATION METHODS

Hydrogeologic characterization methods are usually most successful when used in conjunction with one another. These methods may include coring, aquifer tests, tracer tests, surface and borehole geophysical techniques, borehole flowmeters, and other tools. Important information may be gathered before, during, and after drilling operations.

Coring

Core material obtained during drilling operations can yield information on the density, location, and orientation of fractures, and provide samples for physical and chemical testing. Information concerning fracture roughness and mineral precipitation on fracture surfaces can also be obtained from core samples. Information collected during air hammer drilling operations with open hole completions includes the location of major water bearing fractures, changes in hydraulic head with depth, and changes in the ground-water geochemistry. In certain instances, cores may be taken diagonally to intercept near vertical fractures and determine fracture azimuth. A major drawback of coring is the relatively high cost. However, the information obtained from coring operations often makes this characterization technique cost-effective.

Aquifer Tests

Aquifer tests, including constant rate pumping tests and slug tests, can provide hydraulic conductivity and anisotropy information for fractured formations. These tests also allow the estimation of average fracture apertures of a medium. The same tests that are commonly used for unconsolidated porous media can be used for fractured media. The test results, however, will generally be more difficult to interpret. Barker and Black (1983) note that transmissivity values will always be overestimated by applying standard type curve analysis to fissured aquifers. Other more complex tests, such as cross-hole packer tests, are particularly applicable to fractured media.

Hsieh and Neuman (1985) and et al. (1985) describe a method of determining the three-dimensional hydraulic conductivity tensor. The method consists of injecting fluid into, or withdrawing fluid out of, selected intervals isolated by inflatable packers and monitoring the transient response in isolated intervals of neighboring wells.

This method is applicable to situations where the principal directions of the hydraulic conductivity tensor are not necessarily vertical and horizontal. A minimum of six cross-hole tests is required to determine the six independent components of the hydraulic conductivity tensor. In practice, scatter in the data is likely to be such that more than six cross-hole tests will be required. Hsieh et al. conclude that failure to fit data to an ellipsoidal representation indicates that the rock cannot be represented by an equivalent, continuous, uniform, anisotropic medium on the scale of the test. Depending on the application to be made, the test may be repeated on a larger scale, or the data may be interpreted in terms of discrete fractures of the system.

Aquifer tests can provide information on aquifer anisotropy, heterogeneity and boundary conditions, but do not provide information on the range of fracture apertures or surface roughness. One of the major drawbacks associated with long-term aquifer testing is storage and treatment of the large volume of water discharged during the test.

Tracer Tests

Tracer tests can provide information on effective porosity, dispersion and matrix diffusion, generally unobtainable from other hydrogeologic methods. Tracer tests can either be conducted under natural gradient or forced gradient conditions. The primary disadvantages of tracer tests include the time, expense, number of necessary sampling points, and difficulties associated with data interpretation. However, the important information provided by tracer tests is difficult to obtain by any other means. Davis et al. (1985) provide a good introduction to the use of tracers in ground-water investigations.

Geophysical Tools

Both surface and borehole geophysical methods can be used to characterize fractured rock systems. Application of surface geophysical methods such as ground-penetrating radar, magnetometer surveys, and seismic and remote sensing techniques should be evaluated before a drilling program is initiated. These techniques may provide insight to potential monitoring well locations by revealing the orientation of major fracture systems. However, the correlation of major surface geophysical features with contaminant transport processes in fractured media has yet to be thoroughly characterized.

Borehole walls are usually less susceptible to fractures induced during drilling operations than cores. Borehole geophysical techniques can usually provide a more reliable estimate of fracture density than cores. However, as indicated by Nelson (1985) in a review of down-hole techniques, responses used to detect fractures on well logs are nonunique and require detailed knowledge of the tool and the various rock property effects, which could cause fracture-like responses. Borehole geophysical methods include acoustic, electrical resistivity, caliper, gamma and other high energy borehole logging techniques. The acoustic televiewer presents a continuous image of the acoustic response of the borehole face, and can detect fracture apertures as small as one millimeter. This oriented tool also allows the determination of fracture orientations. Caliper logs are best suited for determining relative fracture intensity in continuous, competent rock. Advances in electronic miniaturization have led to the development of down-hole cameras, capable of providing in-situ viewing of fractures in the subsurface.

Borehole Flowmeters

Flowmeters have been used for many years in industry. However, only recently has instrumentation been developed capable of accurately measuring very low flow rates. Borehole flowmeters measure the incremental discharge along screened or open hole portions of wells during small-scale pumping tests. The three major types of flowmeters currently being developed include impeller, heat-pulse, and electromagnetic. Heat-pulse and electromagnetic flowmeters have no moving parts that may deteriorate over time; they also have greater sensitivity than impeller flowmeters (Young and Waldrop, 1989). The greater sensitivity may allow the detection of the vertical movement of water within the borehole under nonpumping conditions. Under pumping conditions, fracture zones contributing ground water to a borehole may be identified. Currently only prototype heat-pulse and electromagnetic flowmeters have been developed. However, commercial models should be available in the near future.

Other Characterization Methods

Fracture traces, fault planes and other lineaments are often identifiable on aerial photographs, but must be field verified to distinguish anthropogenic features such as fences and buried pipelines from geologic features. The orientation of all fractures identified from aerial photographs and field observations (e.g., outcrops and excavations) should be measured and plotted on rose diagrams to identify major fracture trends. Such trends are usually related to the geologic (tectonic) history of a site. A basic understanding of a site's tectonic history and subsequent fracture orientations should allow a better understanding of potential contaminant pathways.

Graphical geochemical techniques commonly used in porous media may provide valuable information at fractured rock sites. Hem (1985) and Lloyd and Heathcote (1985) provide overviews of methods used to identify the sources and extent of mixing of ground waters.

MODELS

Geometric Concepts

A model is a simplified representation of a physical system. The focus of this chapter is on mathematical models which may be appropriately described as "a mathematical description of the processes active in a ground-water system, coded in a programming language, together with a quantification of the ground-water system it simulates in the form of boundary conditions and parameters" (van der Heijde et al., 1988). Preceding and underlying the mathematical model is a largely qualitative description of the structure of the system under study and the physical, chemical, and biological processes to be included in the model. This qualitative description is called a conceptual model. Several different conceptual models have been used to describe flow and transport in fractured media.

The most common conceptual picture of flow and contaminant transport in a fractured porous medium is that the advective flow of water and transport of pollutants is largely, or entirely, through the fractures. Water and contaminants may diffuse into and out of the porous rock matrix. This diffusion can act to spread out the contaminant plume in space and time, and to retard it. In situations where transient water flow is involved, water may also be stored in, and released from, the rock matrix. To the extent that there is sufficient primary porosity in the matrix to allow advective flow and transport, as might be the case for a sandstone, this basic conceptual picture will be in error as will any model that is based on it. If the rock matrix has very low porosity, such as would be the case for granite, then the role of the rock matrix can often be neglected.

Several different approaches, or concepts, have been used to model flow and transport in fractured media. Models can be roughly classified as equivalent porous media models, discrete fracture models, geometrically based models, and stochastic fracture distribution models (van der Heijde et al., 1988). One could also develop models that overlap these categories.

The EPM approach is to treat the fractured rock system as if it were an unconsolidated porous medium. This approach is most likely to be successful when the spacing of the fractures is small compared to the scale of the system being studied, and the fractures are interconnected. Good results in modeling groundwater flow have been obtained when these conditions were met (Pankow et al., 1986). The validity of using the EPM approach to model pollutant transport in a fractured system is less well established.

A modification of this approach is to model the system as if it were composed of two overlapping continua with different porosities and permeabilities. Low porosity and high permeability are associated with the fractures and high porosity and low permeability are associated with the rock matrix. The model allows for transfer of contaminants between the fractures and the rock matrix. This multiple interacting continua (MINC) approach (Preuss and Narasimhan, 1985) requires that the fractures be closely spaced relative to the size of the system and that the fractures be frequently interconnected.

In the discrete fracture approach, the fracture geometry is explicitly included (e.g., Grisak and Pickens, 1980; Sudicky and Frind, 1982). Fractures are most often represented as channels with parallel sides, and the individual fractures are combined into fracture networks. The simplest network has a set of parallel fractures in what is basically a one-dimensional problem. A more complex network has two sets of parallel fractures oriented at some angle to each other in a two-dimensional array (Smith and Schwartz, 1984). Another increase in complexity, and one step closer to reality, is to allow the fractures to have varying lengths, locations, and orientations relative to one another (Long and Billaux, 1987). These models can have either two- or three-dimensional fracture arrays. Some of the discrete fracture models only account for solute transport by advection, and others include both advection and dispersion. Essentially all of the discrete fracture models are research models. One obvious problem in the practical application of discrete fracture models is that it is almost impossible to define the fracture system at a site in fine enough detail to apply the model. The best possibility for this approach seems to be through some sort of statistical modeling of the fracture system to duplicate the measured hydrology at the site. Most of the work on complex discrete fracture networks has been done in connection with the disposal of nuclear waste in crystalline rocks and has not included diffusion into the rock matrix.

Another approach to modeling flow in fractured media is to represent the fractured system by a set of porous matrix blocks of well defined geometry. The most common examples are parallel prismatic blocks (e.g., cubes) or spheres arranged in a regular array. The spaces between the blocks are the fracture channels. The blocks are assumed to be porous so that solutes can diffuse into and out of the matrix. This approach combines dual porosity with the discrete fracture approach. While no real aquifer has such a well defined geometry, the model can provide insight into the important factors in solute transport in fractured porous media. A recent review article by van Genuchten and Dalton (1986) provides an excellent summary of work using this approach.

Real rock fractures may have rough surfaces that are not parallel to each other, and the fracture may be partially blocked by translocated or precipitated filling material. Research models have been developed that attempt to account for these effects. A recent paper by Tsang and Tsang (1987) describes a fracture system with flow through a series of tortuous intersecting channels.

None of the above conceptual pictures is "best" in an absolute sense. Rather, each may be appropriate for a particular situation. Models that are conceptually simpler have the advantage of being easier to implement as a rule, but they may also oversimplify the situation and miss important phenomena that are taking place. More complex models have the potential to provide a more detailed description of what is happening at the site being modeled, but they are also likely to be more difficult to implement and may require data that cannot be collected with currently available techniques.

Pankow, et al. (1986) compared two contaminated fractured rock sites which differed in regard to fracture aperture, fracture spacing, matrix porosity, and matrix diffusion coefficient. They concluded that the EPM approach would work well in describing contaminant transport for the system with small interfracture spacing and high enough matrix porosity and diffusion coefficient to rapidly establish matrix/fracture equilibrium. They also concluded that the EPM approach would not be appropriate for the other system where matrix/fracture equilibrium was not rapidly established. Pankow's paper presents an excellent summary of attempts to model contamination at real fractured rock sites.

Model Interactions and Processes

A complete model for flow and transport of contaminants in a fractured rock system would need to include all of the interactions and processes that one has in a model for flow and transport in unconsolidated porous media. For any given situation, some of these interactions and processes will be important, and some can be neglected. The existing models that describe flow and transport in fractured systems are as a rule less complete than models for unconsolidated porous media. The appropriateness of a model for a particular circumstance will obviously depend on how well the assumptions and processes built into the model match the conditions of the system to which the model is being applied.

Flow Conditions

Models assume that ground-water flow is laminar. It is apparent from observations of flow issuing from fractured systems that this assumption is not always valid. However, at the present time, the assumption of laminar flow is not a major limitation on the use of models to describe flow and transport in fractured systems.

Virtually all the models describing flow and transport in fractured formations assume that the flow of water and the advective transport of contaminants is only through the fractures. In many models, water and contaminants diffuse in and out of the rock matrix in a direction perpendicular to the direction of flow in the fracture, but there is no flow or advective transport of contaminants through the matrix. There are some situations where this assumption will not hold, and it will not be appropriate to make it.

The discussion in this chapter is largely concerned with models that describe flow and transport in the saturated zone. Flow through fractures in the unsaturated zone can be exceedingly complex and is more difficult to model than it is in the saturated zone. For example, the distribution of water between the fractures and the matrix in fractured porous rock depends on the water content. As the water content decreases, a greater and greater proportion of the water is found in the matrix. Likewise, other parameters controlling flow are also dependent on the water content. While flow and transport through unsaturated fractured rock will be important at some sites, the prospects for modeling these phenomena at the present time are less good than they are in saturated fractured rock. Good summaries of modeling in unsaturated fractured crystalline rock have recently been published by Dykysien (1987) and Evans and Nicholson (1987).

Diffusion and Dispersion

As a rule, the models assume that the concentration of the contaminant is constant across the narrow dimension of the fracture. Mechanical dispersion consists of longitudinal dispersion only. The geometry of the fracture system is a major determinant of variation in the flow velocity and consequently of the mechanical dispersion.

Molecular diffusion within the fracture is usually considered to be unimportant relative to mechanical dispersion. However, as mentioned above, diffusion is the main process by which contaminants are assumed to move within the rock matrix. Diffusion in and out of the rock matrix will be significantly affected by the nature of the surface of the fracture. A thin layer of low permeability, or "fracture skin," can impede the interchange of water and contaminants between the fracture and the matrix (Moench, 1984). Experimental work on the diffusion of contaminants through the rock matrix and between the matrix and the fracture is very limited, and more research is needed in this area.

Adsorption and Desorption

Models for solute transport generally account for adsorption and desorption of contaminants on the surface of the fractures and within the rock matrix. To date, all modeling of adsorption and desorption assumes that the processes are described by linear isotherms and ignores sorption kinetics. Some models account separately for sorption processes in the fractures and within the rock matrix. In porous rocks, the available surface area within the matrix is likely to be so much greater than that in the fractures that sorption within the matrix will probably be more important than sorption in the fractures, assuming that the contaminants have time to diffuse into the matrix.

None of the available models appear to explicitly account for ion-exchange processes. While many of the organic chemicals of concern are not ionized in solution, other contaminants such as heavy metals could be, depending on the pH of the system. Little experimental or theoretical work has been done in this area: more work is needed.

Radioactive Decay

Much of the work on modeling flow and transport in fractured systems has been motivated by concerns about the disposal of radioactive waste. Consequently, there are a number of models that account for the radioactive decay of single radionuclides and radionuclide chains.

Chemical Reactions and Biological Processes

Very little work has been done that deals specifically with chemical reactions and biological processes in fractures. None of the models account for these processes. This is an important topic, and more work needs to be done on it.

Multiphase Flow

Models for flow and transport in fractured systems appear to be limited to single-phase flow. That is, they can simulate the flow of water alone, or the transport of contaminants that are dissolved in water. The models cannot simulate the flow of a system of water and an immiscible phase such as an oily waste, nor the transport of a contaminant dissolved in an immiscible phase. At the present time neither the capability of modeling multiphase flow in homogeneous media, nor the capability of modeling solute transport in fractured systems is advanced enough to implement a practical code for modeling multiphase flow in fractured systems (Streile and Simmons, 1986). Schwille (1988) has studied the qualitative behavior of dense nonaqueous liquids in laboratory models. His book contains a number of interesting photographs. This is another area where more research is needed.

AVAILABLE MODELS

This section describes types of models that are available to describe flow and transport in fractured rock systems. Specific models will not be mentioned by name because the information is likely to become outdated in a short period of time. A good starting place for obtaining information on publicly available models is the International Ground Water Modeling Center (IGWMC), located at Colorado School of Mines, Golden, CO 80401. They can provide a list of available models and information on specific models on the list.

Freeze and Cherry (1979) describe the development and use of a mathematical ground-water model as "a four-step process, involving (1) examination of the physical problem, (2) replacement of the physical problem by an equivalent mathematical problem, (3) solution of the mathematical problem with accepted techniques of mathematics, and (4) interpretation of the mathematical results in terms of the physical problem." Successful modeling of a ground-water contamination problem, whether in fractured rock or not, requires that all four of these steps be carried out correctly. While step (3), solution of the mathematical problem, could conceivably be carried out by a person who knew almost nothing about ground water, successful completion of the other three steps requires a thorough knowledge of hydrogeology in general, along with specific knowledge of the hydrogeology of the site to which the model is to be applied.

Fractured systems present several difficulties which hinder the replacement of the physical problem by an equivalent mathematical problem—step (2). One difficulty is that the spatial distribution of the fractures and the way in which they control the flow is usually not known, nor is it even knowable in a practical sense. A second difficulty is that even if this information were available, including it in the mathematical problem would make the mathematical problem so complex that a solution could not be found. As a result, all mathematical models include certain assumptions about, and simplifications of, the actual physical problem. For example, the model may assume that the fractures are of uniform width with parallel sides, and/or that they form a regular geometric pattern. Comparable assumptions are also made about other physical, chemical, and biological processes. Consequently, the mathematical model provides only an approximate description of the physical system under study. The model can still be very useful, but anyone using a mathematical model should be fully aware of these assumptions and simplifications and their effect on the appropriateness of the model for the problem of interest.

Mathematical models that describe ground-water systems are usually written in terms of partial differential equations. If the equations are simple enough, the solution to the equations can be expressed in a closed mathematical form (e.g., a formula). This type of solution is called an analytical solution. More generally, the equations in the model are too complex to find an analytical solution, and a numerical method must be used to solve the problem. Models for fractured systems include those with analytical solutions as well as those with numerical solutions.

For either type of solution, the product available to the model user is a computer code in a high level language such as FORTRAN. The hardware requirements to run the code will vary from a personal computer (PC) to a main-frame type of computer. As expected, the more complex models usually have greater hardware requirements.

Models with Analytical Solutions

Models for which analytical solutions have been obtained are basically one dimensional. An example of this type of solution is a model describing solute transport in a single fracture or a set of parallel fractures. Processes that are included in the model include diffusion in and out of the rock matrix along a direction perpendicular to the plane of the fracture, adsorption on the fracture face and in the rock matrix, and radioactive decay. The solution to this problem has been published in the open literature (Sudicky and Frind, 1982) and is simple enough that the computer code can run on a personal computer.

To arrive at an analytical solution for this problem, the parallel fracture model assumes that the fracture or set of fractures has a uniform aperture and is in a homogeneous rock matrix, and that the fractures in a set of parallel fractures are uniformly spaced. To use this model, one must have an estimate or measurement of the following parameters: the flow velocity in the fracture, the longitudinal dispersivity in the fracture, the fracture aperture or width, the fracture spacing for a set of fractures, the matrix porosity, the matrix tortuosity, the diffusion coefficient of the solute in water, the fracture retardation factor or partition coefficient, the matrix retardation factor or partition coefficient, and the half-life if the solute is a radioactive species.

This model obviously describes a highly idealized situation and would not be a suitable predictive tool for dealing with a real contamination problem. However, it could have some use in building an understanding of the system and the interactions of the pollutants within the system. It is easy to vary the effect of the fracture apertures, fracture spacing, matrix porosity, and so forth, and see the effect that each of these parameters has on the rate at which pollutants move through the system. Used with the proper degree of professional judgement, the results of the model could provide guidance in making a decision. One possible application would be in comparing solute transport in two fractured systems from which cores had been collected to provide information on the parameters that are included in the model.

Analytical solutions have also been published in the open literature for dual-porosity, or "two-region" models of one dimensional flow through systems composed of porous blocks with well-defined geometry (van Genuchten and Dalton, 1986). Those geometries for which solutions are available include close-packed spheres, hollow cylindrical macropores, close packed solid cylinders, and rectangular blocks. Data and hardware requirements for running these codes are similar to those for the parallel crack model.

Models with Numerical Solutions

Models for which only numerical solutions are available are often referred to as numerical models. Codes for these models are likely to require more input data and greater computer power than those for analytical models. The reward for this extra work is that one can investigate more complicated problems using numerical models than one can using only analytical models.

One example of a numerical model for fractured rock systems is a two-dimensional model that can simulate both groundwater flow and contaminant transport in a fractured aquifer. The step up from a one-dimensional system to a two-dimensional system allows one to model a more complex situation, but it also requires a more complex set of differential equations and a more complex code. The model uses a dual porosity approach and allows for some specific fracture geometries. Processes that are included in the model include advective dispersive transport in the fractures, diffusion in the matrix blocks, sorption in the fractures and in the matrix, and radionuclide decay chains.

This two-dimensional code requires data on the system dimensions, the transmissivity, the storage coefficient, and the fracture aperture and spacing if it is to be used to predict ground-water flow. The input data requirements for predicting solute transport include all of those listed for the one dimensional analytical model described above plus values for the solute concentrations at the system boundaries.

While codes like this have utility for understanding system behavior, they should not be used as predictive tools. Like all ground-water models, they will be most useful when applied by a person with the necessary training and experience—typically, a professional hydrogeologist. To quote a recent report (van der Heijde et al., 1988), "The application of computer simulation models to field problems is a qualitative procedure, a combination of science and art."

There are a number of numerical models that have been written to model flow and transport through systems of randomly oriented fractures and compare the results with experimental data. The results of this work have been of use in understanding the nature of flow and transport in fractured media, but this type of modeling is a research effort at this time.

SUMMARY REMARKS

The development of models to enhance understanding of and to predict contaminant transport in fractured rock systems continues to be an active area of research. Reliable, field-validated models that can be used to predict the results of clean-up scenarios at contaminated sites are not yet available. The models that are available help in developing an understanding of the behavior of the fractured rock system.

The application of mathematical models to contamination in fractured rock systems is hampered by difficulties in at least two major areas. The first problem is site characterization—the collection of the necessary data to adequately describe the geologic and hydrologic properties of the system. Mathematical modeling is not a substitute for collecting data. In fact, data collection is an essential part of modeling the behavior of a site. Collecting the data required by existing models is difficult and expensive, and in many cases not possible with present techniques. More research is needed to find better ways to measure the properties of fractured rock systems. Conversely, there may be value in developing models that require data that can be collected.

The second problem is model validation—comparing the results of modeling to results obtained in the field. Validation of models is necessary if decision makers are to have confidence in them and be able to use them in planning and carrying out remedial work. Research is being done to validate models of contaminant transport in fractured rock systems, but more work is needed. One problem with model validation studies is the shortage of data sets for sites with a variety of geological and hydrogeological characteristics. This is where cooperation and coordination between those in the research community and those charged with remediating contaminated sites could prove mutually beneficial.

EPA CONTACTS

For further information contact Stephen G. Schmelling, 405/436-8540; or Randall R. Ross, 405/436-8611, at RSKERL-Ada.

REFERENCES

Barker, J.A. and J.H. Black. 1983. Slug Tests in Fissured Aquifers. Water Resour. Res. 19:1558–1564.
Davis, S.N., Campbell, D.J., Bently, H.W., and T.J. Flynn. 1985. Ground-water Tracers. National Water Well Association, Worthington, Ohio, 200 pp.
Duguid, J.O. and P.C.Y. Lee. 1977. Flow in Fractured Porous Media. Water Resour. Res. 13:558–566.
Dykysien, R.C. 1987. Transport of Solutes through Unsaturated Fractured Media. Water Res. 12:1531–1539.
Endo, H.K., J.C.S. Long, C.R. Wilson, and P.A. Witherspoon. 1984. A Model for Investigating Transport in Fracture Networks. Water Resour. Res. 20:1390–1400.

Evans, D. and T. Nicholson (eds.). 1987. Flow and Transport Through Unsaturated Fractured Rock. AGU Monograph 42. American Geophysical Union, Washington, DC.

Freeze, R.A. and J.A. Cherry. 1979. Groundwater. Prentice Hall, Englewood Cliffs, NJ.

Gale, J.E. 1982. Assessing the Permeability Characteristics of Fractured Rock. In: T.N. Narasimhan (ed.), Recent Trends in Hydrogeology. Geological Society of America Special Paper 189, pp. 163–181.

Grisak, G.E. and J.F. Pickens. 1980. Solute Transport Through Fractured Media. Water Resour. Res. 16:719–730.

Hem, J.D. 1985. Study and Interpretation of the Chemical Characteristics of Natural Water, 3rd edition. U.S. Geological Survey Water-Supply Paper 2254, 263 pp.

Hsieh, P.A. and S.P. Neuman. 1985. Field Determination of the Three-Dimensional Hydraulic Conductivity Tensor of Anisotropic Media, 1. Theory. Water Resour. Res. 21:1655–1665.

Hsieh, P.A., S.P. Neuman, G.K. Stiles, and E.S. Simpson. 1985. Field Determination of the Three-Dimensional Hydraulic Conductivity Tensor of Anisotropic Media, 2. Methodology and Application to Fractured Rocks. Water Resour. Res. 21:1667–1676.

Konikow, L.F. and J.W. Mercer. 1988. Groundwater Flow and Transport Modeling. J. Hydrology 100:379–409.

Lloyd, J.W. and J.A. Heathcote. 1985. Natural Inorganic Hydrochemistry in Relation to Groundwater. Clarendon Press, Oxford, 296 pp.

Long, J.C.S. and D.M. Billaux. 1987. From Field Data to Fracture Network Modeling. Water Resour. Res. 23:1201–1216.

Long, J.C.S., J.S. Remer, C.R. Wilson, and P.A. Witherspoon. 1982. Porous Media Equivalents for Networks of Discontinuous Fractures. Water Resour. Res. 18:645–658.

Moench, A.F. 1984. Double-Porosity Models for a Fissured Groundwater Reservoir with Fracture Skin. Water Resour. Res. 20:831–846.

Nelson, R.A. 1985. Geologic Analysis of Naturally Fractured Reservoirs. Contributions in Petroleum Geology and Engineering, v. 1, Gulf Publishing Company, Houston, Texas, 320 pp.

Pankow, J.F., R.L. Johnson, J.P. Hewetson, and J.A. Cherry. 1986. An Evaluation of Contaminant Migration Patterns at Two Waste Disposal Sites on Fractured Porous Media in Terms of the Equivalent Porous Medium (EPM) Model. J. Contaminant Hydrology 1:65–76.

Preuss, K. and T.N. Narasimhan. 1985. A Practical Method for Modeling Fluid and Heat Flow in Fractured Porous Media. Soc. of Pet. Engr. J. 25:14–26.

Schwille, F. 1988. Dense Chlorinated Solvents in Porous and Fractured Media (translated by J. Pankow). Lewis Publishers, Chelsea, MI.

Smith, L. and F.W. Schwartz. 1984. An Analysis of the Influence of Fracture Geometry on Mass Transport in Fractured Media. Water Resour. Res. 20:1241–1252.

Streile, G.P. and C.S. Simmons. 1986. Subsurface Flow and Transport of Organic Chemicals: An Assessment of Current Modeling Capability and Priority for Future Research Directions (1987–1995). PNL-6043. Pacific Northwest Laboratory, Richland, WA.

Sudicky, E.A. and E.O. Frind. 1982. Contaminant Transport in Fractured Porous Media: Analytical Solutions for a System of Parallel Fractures. Water Resour. Res. 18:1634–1642.

Tsang, Y.W. and C.F. Tsang. 1987. Channel Model of Flow Through Fractured Media. Water Resour. Res. 23:467–479.

van der Heijde, P.K.M., A.I. El-Kadi, and S.A. Williams. 1988. Groundwater Modeling: An Overview and Status Report. EPA/600/2-89/028 (NTIS PB89-224497), 259 pp.

van Genuchten, M.T. and F.N. Dalton. 1986. Models for Simulating Salt Movement in Aggregated Field Soils. Geoderma 38:165–183.

Witherspoon, P.A., J.C.S. Long, E.L. Majer, and L.R. Myer. 1987. A New Seismic-Hydraulic Approach to Modeling Flow in Fractured Rocks. In: Proc. NWWA/IGWMC Conference on Solving Ground-Water Problems with Models. National Water Well Association, Dublin, OH.

Young, S.C. and W.R. Waldrop. 1989. An Electromagnetic Borehole Flowmeter for Measuring Hydraulic Conductivity Variability. In: Proc. Conf. New Field Techniques for Quantifying the Physical and Chemical Properties of Heterogeneous Aquifers. National Water Well Association, Dublin, OH, pp. 463–475.

PART II

Site Characterization
and
Monitoring

Chapter 11

Technology Preselection Data Requirements[1]

Jim Rawe and Robert Hartley, Science Applications International Corporation (SAIC), Cincinnati, OH

INTRODUCTION

This chapter provides a listing of soil, water, and contaminant data elements needed to evaluate the potential applicability of technologies for treating contaminated soils and water. With this base set of data in hand, experts familiar with the applicability of treatment technologies can better focus the advice and assistance they give to those involved at Superfund sites. The data compiled should permit preselection of applicable treatment methods and the direct elimination of others.

This chapter emphasizes the site physical and chemical soil and water characteristics for which observations and measurements should be compiled. However, several other kinds of information may be equally helpful in assessing the potential success of a treatment technology, including the activity history of the site, how and where wastes were disposed, topographic and hydrologic detail, and site stratigraphy. Gathering and analyzing the information called for in this chapter prior to extensive field investigations (i.e., the Remedial Investigation and Feasibility Study—RI/FS) will facilitate streamlining and targeting of the sampling and analytical objectives of the overall program.

Additional information on site data requirements for the selection of specific treatment technologies may be found in several Environmental Protection Agency publications (Galer, 1988; U.S. EPA, 1987a, 1987b, 1988, 1989a). These documents form much of the basis for this chapter.

BACKGROUND INFORMATION

The background information collected during the Site Screening Investigation and Preliminary Assessment identifies the probable types and locations of contaminants present. Study of the chemicals used or stored at the site and the disposal methods used during the period(s) of operation is essential. When chemical-use records are unavailable for an industrial site, knowledge of the Standard Industrial Classification may indicate the probability of the presence of metals, inorganics, pesticides, dioxins/furans, or other organics. Information on what classes and concentrations of chemicals contaminate the site, where they are distributed, and in what media they appear is essential in beginning the preselection of treatment technologies (Galer, 1988, p. 7).

The contaminant distribution, types, and concentrations will affect the choice of treatment technology. Other considerations in the selection of treatment options include the proximity of residential areas and the location of buildings and other structures. These aspects should be determined early in the investigation process. Much of the determination of the range and diversity of contamination, as well as likely contaminant sources, may be observational, rather than measurement-based.

BASIC MEASUREMENT DATA REQUIREMENTS

The discussion of data requirements is divided into two sections, soil and water. For each of the two media, the vertical and horizontal contaminant profiles should be defined as much as possible. Information on the overall range and diversity of contamination across the site is critical to treatment technology selection. This generally means that samples will be taken and their physical and chemi-

---

[1] EPA/540/S-92/009.

cal characteristics determined. The following subsections present the characteristics and rationale for collection of preselection data for each of the two media. Other documents present similar data requirements, especially for soils (Breckenridge et al., 1991).

The minimum set of soil measurement data elements usually necessary for soil treatment technology preselection is presented in Table 11-1. Table 11-2 presents the basic set of data necessary for contaminated water treatment technology preselection. It is common for the two media at one site to be contaminated with the same substances, thus many of the required data elements are similar. The information contained in Table 11-1 and Table 11-2 is based on professional judgement.

The ratings in Table 11-1 and Table 11-2 are related to measured values of the parameters. The values are described as "higher" and "lower" in defining their tendency toward preselecting a technology group. In general, these descriptors are related to the tendency of the parameter to enhance or to inhibit particular processes. Where no symbol is shown for a characteristic in Table 11-1 and Table 11-2, the effect on the associated technology is considered inconsequential.

Each characteristic is judged, or rated, as to its effect in preselecting each of the treatment technology groups which represent various treatment processes. A rating applies generally to a technology, but it does not ensure that the rating will be applicable to each specific technology within a technology group. Examples of specific treatments within the technology around are as follows:

- Physical
Soil washing	Vapor extraction
Soil flushing	Carbon adsorption
Steam extraction	Filtration
Air stripping	Gravity separation
Solvent extraction	

- Chemical
Oxidation	Reduction
Hydrolysis	Precipitation
Polymerization	

- Thermal
Incineration	Pyrolysis
Plasma Arc	Thermal desorption

- Biological
Aerobic	Anaerobic
Slurry reactor	Land treatment

- Solidification/Stabilization
Cement-based	Vitrification
Fly ash/lime	Asphalt
Kiln dust	

SOIL

Site soil conditions are frequently process-limiting. Process-limiting characteristics such as pH or moisture content (Breckenridge et al., 1991) may sometimes be adjusted. In other cases, a treatment technology may be eliminated based upon the soil classification (e.g., particle-size distribution) or other soil characteristics.

Soils are inherently variable in their physical and chemical characteristics. Frequently the variability is much greater vertically than horizontally, resulting from the variability in the sedimentation processes that originally formed the soils. The soil variability, in turn, will result in variability in the distribution of water and contaminants and in the ease with which they can be transported within, and removed from, the soil at a particular site.

Many data elements are relatively easy to obtain, and in some cases, more than one test method exists: Breckenridge et al., 1991; Page et al., 1982; NIOSH, 1984; Kopp and McKee, 1983; ASTM,

Table 11-1. Soil Characteristics that Assist in Treatment Technology Preselection (see also Table 15-4)

Characteristic	Treatment Technology Group				
	Physical	Chemical	Biological	Thermal	S/S
Particle size	■	▼	▼	■	■
Bulk density	▼			■	
Particle density	■				
Permeability	■		■		
Moisture content	▼		■	●	●
pH and Eh		▼	▼	▼	
Humic content	●	●	●	▼	●
Total organic carbon (TOC)		▼	■	■	▼
Biochemical oxygen demand (BOD)			■		
Chemical oxygen demand (COD)		■	■		
Oil and grease	▼	●			●
Organic contaminants					
Halogenated volatiles	▼	▼	●	■	●
Halogenated semivolatiles	▼	▼	●	■	●
Nonhalogenated volatiles	▼	▼	▼	■	●
Nonhalogenated semivolatiles	▼	▼	▼	■	●
PCBs	▼	▼	▼	■	●
Pesticides	▼	▼	▼	■	●
Dioxins/Furans	▼	▼	▼	■	●
Organic cyanides	▼	▼	▼	■	●
Organic corrosives	▼	▼	▼	●	●
Light Nonaqueous-Phase Liquid	▼		▼	■	●
Dense Nonaqueous-Phase Liquid	▼		▼	▼	●
Heating value (Btu content)				■	
Inorganic contaminants					
Volatile metals		▼		●	
Nonvolatile metals	■	▼	●	●	■
Asbestos				●	■
Radioactive materials	▼	▼	●	●	▼
Inorganic cyanides		▼		▼	▼
Inorganic corrosives		▼		●	▼
Reactive contaminants					
Oxidizers		▼			
Reducers		▼			

■ = higher values support preselection of technology group.
● = lower values support preselection of technology group.
▼ = Effect is variable among options within a technology group.
Where no symbol is shown, the effect of that characteristic is considered inconsequential.

annual; U.S. EPA, 1986, 1987c. Field procedures, usually visual inspection and/or operation of simple hand-held devices (e.g., auger), are performed by trained geologists or soils engineers to determine the classification, moisture content, and permeability of soils across a site. Due to the fact that zones of gross contamination may be directly observed, field reports describing soil variability may lessen the need for large numbers of samples and measurements in describing site characteristics. Common field information-gathering often includes descriptions of natural soil exposures, weathering that may have taken place, trench cross-sections, and subsurface cores. Such an effort can sometimes identify probable areas of past disposal through observation of soil type differences, subsidence, overfill, etc.

While field investigations are important, they cannot eliminate the need for or lessen the importance of soil sampling and measurements sufficient to define those characteristics that are essential to the selection and design of soil treatment technologies.

Table 11-2. Water Characteristics that Assist in Treatment Technology Preselection

Characteristic	Treatment Technology Group			
	Physical	Chemical	Biological	Thermal
pH, Eh		▼	▼	▼
Total organic carbon (TOC)		▼	■	■
Biochemical oxygen demand (BOD)			■	
Chemical oxygen demand (COD)		■	■	
Oil and grease	▼	●		
Suspended solids	▼	▼	▼	
Nitrogen and phosphorus			▼	
Organic Contaminants				
Halogenated volatiles	▼	▼	●	■
Halogenated semivolatiles	▼	▼	●	■
Nonhalogenated volatiles	▼	▼	▼	■
Nonhalogenated semivolatiles	▼	▼	▼	■
PCBs	▼	▼	▼	■
Pesticides	▼	▼	▼	■
Dioxins/Furans	▼	▼	●	■
Organic cyanides	▼	▼	▼	■
Organic corrosives	▼	▼	▼	●
Light Nonaqueous-Phase Liquid	▼		▼	■
Dense Nonaqueous-Phase Liquid	▼		▼	▼
Inorganic Contaminants				
Asbestos				●
Radioactive materials	▼	▼	●	●
Metals (Drinking Water Stds.)	▼	■	●	●

■ = higher values support preselection of technology group.
● = lower values support preselection of technology group.
▼ = Effect is variable among options within a technology group.
Where no symbol is shown, the effect of that characteristic is considered inconsequential.

Soil *particle-size distribution* is an important factor in many soil treatment technologies. In general, sands and fine gravels are easiest to deal with. Soil washing may not be effective where the soil is composed of large percentages of silt and clay because of the difficult of separating fine particles from each other and from wash fluids (U.S. EPA, 1990a, p. 1). Fine particles also can result in high particulate loading in flue gases due to turbulence in rotary kilns. Heterogeneities in soil and waste composition may produce nonuniform feed streams for incineration that result in inconsistent removal rates (U.S. EPA, 1987a, 1989b). Fine particles may delay setting and curing times and can surround larger particles causing weakened bonds in solidification/stabilization processes. Clays may cause poor performance of the thermal desorption technology due to caking (Rawe and Saylor, 1991, p. 2). High silt and clay content can cause soil malleability and low permeability during steam extraction, thus lowering the efficiency of the process (Cook, 1991, p. 2). Bioremediation processes, such as in slurry reactors, are generally facilitated by finer particles that increase the contact area between the waste and microorganisms (U.S. EPA, 1989b; Michaels, 1991, p. 1).

In situ technologies dependent on the subsurface flowability of fluids, such as soil flushing, steam extraction, vacuum extraction, and in situ biodegradation, will be negatively influenced by the impeding effects of clay layers (Rawe and Saylor, 1991, p. 2; U.S. EPA, 1990b, p. 4). Undesirable channeling may be created in alternating layers of clay and sand, resulting in inconsistent treatment (Galer, 1988, p. 79). Larger particles, such as coarse gravel or cobbles, are undesirable for vitrification and chemical extraction processes and also may not be suitable for the stabilization/solidification technology (Galer, 1988, p. 93).

The *bulk density* of soil is the weight of the soil per unit volume including water and voids. It is used in converting weight to volume in materials handling calculations (Cullinane et al., 1986, p. 3-

3). Soil bulk density and particle size distribution are interrelated in determining if proper mixing and heat transfer will occur in fluidized bed reactors (Galer, 1988, p. 39).

Particle density is the specific gravity of a soil particle. Differences in particle density are important in heavy mineral/metal separation processes (heavy media separation). Particle density is also important in soil washing and in determining the settling velocity of suspended soil particles in flocculation and sedimentation processes (U.S. EPA, 1990a, p. 1).

Soil *permeability* is one of the controlling factors in the effectiveness of in situ treatment technologies. The ability of soil-flushing fluids (e.g., water, steam, solvents, etc.) to contact and remove contaminants can be reduced by low soil permeability or by variations in the permeability of different soil layers (Cook, 1991, p. 2; Cullinane et al., 1986, p. 4-9). Low permeability also hinders the movement of air and vapors through the soil matrix, lessening the volatilization of VOCs in vapor extraction (Michaels, 1991, p. 2). Similarly, nutrient solutions, used to accelerate in situ bioremediation, may not be able to penetrate low-permeability soils in a reasonable time (U.S. EPA, 1987a). Low permeability may also limit the effectiveness of in situ vitrification by slowing vapor releases (Galer, 1988, p. 59).

Soil *moisture* may hinder the movement of air through the soil in vacuum extraction systems (U.S. EPA, 1989a, p. 90; Michaels, 1991, p. 1). High soil moisture may cause excavation and material transport problems (U.S. EPA, 1990c, p. 2) and may negatively impact material feed in many processes (Galer, 1988; Rawe and Saylor, 1991, p. 2; Cullinane et al., 1986, p. 4; PEI Associates, 1991). Moisture affects the application of vitrification and other thermal treatments by increasing energy requirements, thereby increasing costs. On the other hand, increased soil moisture favors in situ biological treatment (Chambers et al., 1990, p. 40).

Many treatment technologies are affected by the *pH* of the waste being treated. For example, low pH can interfere with chemical oxidation and reduction processes. The solubility and speciation of inorganic contaminants are affected by pH. Ion exchange and flocculation processes, applied after various liquid extraction processes, may be negatively influenced by pH (U.S. EPA, 1987a, p. 5; Cook, 1991). Microbial diversity and activity in bioremediation processes can be reduced by extreme pH ranges. High pH in soil normally improves the feasibility of applying chemical extraction and alkaline dehalogenation processes (Galer, 1988, p. 67).

Eh is the oxidation-reduction (redox) potential of the material being considered. For oxidation to occur in soil systems, the Eh of the solid phase must be greater than that of the organic chemical contaminant (Chambers et al., 1990, p. 19). Maintaining anaerobiosis, and thus a low Eh, in the liquid phase, enhances decomposition of certain halogenated organic compounds (Kobayashi and Rittman, 1982).

Humic content (humus) is the decomposing part of the naturally occurring organic content of the soil. The effects of high humic content upon treatment technologies are usually negative. It can inhibit soil-vapor extraction, steam extraction, soil washing, and soil flushing due to strong adsorption of the contaminant by the organic material (Galer, 1988, p. 76; Michaels, 1991, p. 2). Reaction times for chemical dehalogenation processes can be increased by the presence of large amounts of humic materials. High organic content may also exert an excessive oxygen demand, adversely affecting bioremediation and chemical oxidation (U.S. EPA, 1990d, p. 2; Groeber, 1991, p. 1).

Total organic carbon (TOC) provides an indication of the total organic material present. It is often used as an indicator (but not a measure) of the amount of waste available for biodegradation (Galer, 1988, p. 109). TOC includes the carbon both from naturally-occurring organic material and organic chemical contaminants. Ordinarily, not all of the organic carbon is contaminating, but all of it may compete in redox reactions, leading to the need for larger amounts of chemical reduction/oxidation reagents than would be required by the organic chemical contaminants alone (Galer, 1988, p. 97).

Biochemical oxygen demand (BOD) provides an estimate of the biological treatability of the soil contaminants by measuring the oxygen consumption of the organic material which is readily biodegraded (U.S. EPA, 1989a, p. 89). *Chemical oxygen demand* (COD) is a measure of the oxygen equivalent of organic content in a sample that can be oxidized by a strong chemical oxidant. Sometimes COD and BOD can be correlated, and COD can give another indication of biological treatability or treatability by chemical oxidation (Galer, 1988, p. 97). COD is also useful in assessing the applicability of wet air oxidation (Galer, 1988, p. 51).

Oil and grease, when present in a soil, will coat the soil particles. The coating tends to weaken the bond between soil and cement in cement-based solidification (U.S. EPA, 1989a). Similarly, oil and grease can also interfere with reactant-to-waste contact in chemical reduction/oxidation reactions thus reducing the efficiency of those reactions (Galer, 1988, p. 97).

Identification of the site *organic and inorganic contaminants* is the most important information necessary for technology prescreening. At this stage, it may not be necessary to identify specific contaminants, but the presence or absence of the groups shown in Table 11-1 should be known. These groups have been presented in the other Engineering Bulletins in order to describe the effectiveness of the particular treatment technology under consideration (see the companion to this volume, EPA Environmental Engineering Sourcebook).

The soil may be contaminated with organic chemicals that are not miscible with water. Often, they will be lighter than water and float on top of the water table. These are called light nonaqueous-phase liquids (LNAPLs). Those heavier than water are called dense nonaqueous-phase liquids (DNAPLs). Most of these liquids can be physically separated from water within the soil, especially if they are not adsorbed to soil particles.

Volatile, semivolatile, and other organics may be adsorbed in the soil matrix. Volatiles may be in the form of vapors in the pores of nonsaturated soil, and may be amenable to soil-vapor extraction. Fuel value, or Btu content, of the contaminated soil is directly related to the organic chemical content. High Btu content favors thermal treatment, or perhaps recovery for fuel use.

High halogen concentrations, as in chlorinated organics, lead to the formation of corrosive acids in incineration systems. Volatile metals produce emissions that are difficult to remove, and nonvolatile metals remain in the ash (U.S. EPA, 1989b).

Metals may be found sometimes in the elemental form, but more often they are found as salts mixed in the soil. Radioactive materials are not ordinarily found at waste disposal sites. However, where they are found, treatment options are probably limited to volume reduction, and permanent containment is required. Asbestos fibers require special care to prevent their escape during handling and disposal; permanent containment must be provided. Radioactive materials and asbestos require special handling techniques to maintain worker safety.

Often, specific technologies may be ruled out, or the list of potential technologies may be immediately narrowed, on the basis of the presence or absence of one or more of the chemical groups. The relative amounts of each may tend to favor certain technologies. For example, significant amounts of dioxin/furans, regardless of the concentrations of other organics, will ordinarily lead to preselection of thermal treatment as an alternative.

Data available from the preliminary assessment, the site inspection and the National Priorities List (NPL) activities may provide most of the contaminant information needed at the technology prescreening stage. If the data are not sufficient, waste samples may be scanned for selected priority pollutants or contaminants from the CERCLA Hazardous Substances List. During the ensuing RI/FS scoping phase, these data are evaluated to identify additional data which must be gathered during the site characterization. Guidance is available on the RI/FS process and on field methods, sampling procedures, and data quality objectives (Breckenridge et al., 1991; U.S. EPA, 1987b, 1987c, 1988) and therefore is not discussed in this chapter.

WATER

It is common for ground water and surface water drainage to be contaminated with the same substances found in soils derived from previous activities. At Superfund sites, many of the required data elements are similar, e.g., pH, TOC, BOD, COD, oil and grease, and contaminant identification and quantification. Frequently, many of the water data elements will be available from existing analytical data. Some initial data requirements may even be precluded by the collection of existing regional or local information on surface and ground-water conditions. When data are not available, knowledge of the site conditions and its history may contribute to arriving at a list of contaminants and cost-effective analytical methods.

As with soils, the *pH* of ground-water and surface water is important in determining the applicability of many treatment processes. Often, the pH must be adjusted before or during a treatment process. Low pH can interfere with chemical redox processes. Extreme pH levels can limit microbial diversity and hamper the application of both in situ and above-ground applications of biological treatment (Galer, 1988, p. 97). Contaminant solubility and toxicity may be affected by changes in pH. The species of metals and inorganics present are influenced by the pH of the water, as are the type of phenolic, and nitrogen-containing compounds present. Processes such as carbon adsorption, ion exchange, and flocculation may be impacted by pH changes (U.S. EPA, 1987a, p. 5).

Eh helps to define, with pH, the state of oxidation-reduction equilibria in ground water or aqueous waste streams. The Eh must be below approximately 0.35 volts for significant reductive chlorination to take place, but exact requirements depend on the individual compounds being reduced. As noted earlier in the soils section, maintaining anaerobiosis (low Eh) enhances decomposition of certain halogenated compounds (Kobayashi and Rittman, 1982).

BOD, COD, and TOC measurements in contaminated water, as in soils, provide indications of the biodegradable, chemically oxidizable, or combustible fractions of the organic contamination, respectively. These measurements are not interchangeable, although correlations may sometimes be made in order to convert the more precise TOC and/or COD measurements to estimates of BOD. Interpretation of these data should be made by an expert in the technologies being considered.

Oil and grease may be present in water to the extent that they are the primary site contaminants. In that case, oil-water separation may be called for as the principal treatment. Even in lower concentrations, oil and grease may still require pretreatment to prevent clogging of ion exchange resins, activated carbon systems, or other treatment system components (U.S. EPA, 1989a, p. 91).

Suspended solids can cause resin binding in ion exchange systems and clogging of reverse osmosis membranes, filtration systems and carbon adsorption units. Suspended solids above 5 percent indicate that analysis of total and soluble metals should be made (U.S. EPA, 1987a, p. 14).

Standard analytical methods are used to identify the specific *organic and inorganic contaminants.* Properties of organic chemical contaminants important in treatment processes include solubility in water, specific gravity, boiling point, and vapor pressure. For the identified contaminants, these properties can generally be found in standard references Budavari (1989) or in EPA/RREL's Treatability Database (U.S. EPA, 1993).

Insoluble organic contaminants may be present as nonaqueous phase liquids (NAPLs). DNAPLs will tend to sink to the bottom of surface water and ground water aquifers (see Chapter 5). LNAPLs will float on top of surface water and ground water. In addition, LNAPLs may adhere to the soil through the capillary fringe and may be found on top of water in temporary or perched aquifers in the vadose zone.

As noted previously, volatile organics may be in the form of vapors in the pores of nonsaturated soil, or they may be dissolved in water. Even low-solubility organics may be present at low concentrations dissolved in water. Some organics (e.g., certain halogenated compounds, pesticides, and dioxins/furans in water) resist biological treatment, while others may be amenable to several technologies.

Dissolved metals may be found at toxic levels or levels exceeding drinking water standards. Often they will require chemical treatment. The speciation of metals may be important in determining the solubility, toxicity, and reactivity of metal compounds.

STATUS OF DATA REQUIREMENTS

The data requirements presented in Tables 11-1 and 11-2 are based on currently available information. Preselection of new and evolving technologies, or of currently used technologies that have been modified, may require the collection of additional data. New analytical methods may be devised to replace or supplement existing methods. Such improvements in analytical technology also could require additional data to be collected. This bulletin may be updated if major changes occur in data requirements for preselection of treatment technology alternatives.

EPA CONTACT

Specific questions regarding technology preselection data requirements may be directed to:

Eugene Harris
U.S. Environmental Protection Agency
Office of Research and Development, Risk Reduction Engineering Laboratory
26 West Martin Luther King Drive
Cincinnati, Ohio 45268
(513) 569-7862

ACKNOWLEDGMENTS

This engineering bulletin was prepared for the U.S. Environmental Protection Agency, Office of Research and Development (ORD), Risk Reduction Engineering Laboratory (RREL), Cincinnati, Ohio, by Science Applications International Corporation (SAIC) under EPA Contract No. 68-C8-0062. Mr. Eugene Harris served as the EPA Technical Project Monitor. Mr. Gary Baker was SAIC's Work Assignment Manager. Mr. Jim Rawe (SAIC) and Mr. Robert Hartley (SAIC) were the authors of the bulletin.

The following other Agency and contractor personnel have contributed their time and comments by participating in the expert review meetings and/or peer reviewing the document: Mr. Eric Saylor, SAIC.

REFERENCES

(References marked with an "*" are included in the companion to this volume titled EPA Environmental Engineering Sourcebook)

American Society for Testing and Materials (ASTM). Annual Books of ASTM Standards. ASTM, Philadelphia PA. [See in particular Vols. 4.08 and 4.09 (Soil and Rock; Vols. 11.01 and 11.02 (Water); 11.04 (Environmental Assessment; Hazardous Substances and Oil Spill Response; Waste Management) and 11.05 (Biological Effects and Environmental Fate.]

Breckenridge, R.P., J.R. Williams, and J.F. Keck. 1991. Characterizing Soils for Hazardous Waste Site Assessments. Ground Water Issue, EPA/540/4-91/003. [See Chapter 14.]

Budavari, S. (ed.). 1989. The Merck Index, 11th Edition. Merck & Company, Rathway, NJ.

Chambers, L.D. et al. [7 authors] 1990. Handbook of In Situ Treatment of Hazardous Waste Contaminated Soils. EPA/540/2-90/002 (NTIS PB90-155607), 157 pp.

Cook, K. 1991. In-Situ Steam Extraction Treatment. Engineering Bulletin EPA/ 540/2-91/005.*

Cullinane, M.J., L.W. Jones, and P.G. Malone. 1986. Handbook for Stabilization/Solidification of Hazardous Wastes. EPA/540/2-86/001 (NTIS PB87-116745), 170 pp.

Galer. 1988. Technology Screening Guide for Treatment of CERCLA Soils and Sludges. EPA/540/2-88/004 (NTIS PB89-132674), 136 pp.

Groeber, M.M. 1991. Chemical Oxidation Treatment. Engineering Bulletin EPA/540/2-91/025.*

Koboyashi, H. and B.E. Rittman. 1982. Microbial Removal of Hazardous Organic Compounds. Environ. Sci. Technol., 16:170A–183A.

Kopp, J.F. and G.D. McKee. 1983. Methods for Chemical Analysis of Water and Wastes, 3rd edition. EPA/600/4-74/020 (NTIS PB84-128677). [Supersedes report with the same title dated 1979.]

Michaels, P. 1991. In-Situ Soil Vapor Extraction Treatment. Engineering Bulletin EPA/540/2-91/006.*

NIOSH. 1984. Manual of Analytical Methods, Third Edition.

Page, A.L., R.H. Miller, and D.R. Keeney (eds.). 1982. Methods of Soil Analysis. Part 2. Chemical and Microbiological Properties, 2nd ed. ASA Monograph 9, American Society of Agronomy, Madison, WI.

PEI Associates. 1991. Issues Affecting the Applicability and Success of Remedial/Removal Incineration Projects. Superfund Engineering Issue EPA/540/2-91/004.*

Rawe, J. and E. Saylor. 1991. Thermal Desorption Treatment. Engineering Bulletin EPA/540/2-91/008.*

U.S. Environmental Protection Agency (EPA). 1986. Test Methods for Evaluating Solid Waste, 3rd edition. EPA/530/SW-846 (NTIS PB88-239223); First update, 3rd edition. EPA/530/SW-846.3-1 (NTIS PB89-148076). [Current edition and updates available on a subscription basis from U.S. Government Printing Office, Stock #955-001-00000-1.]

U.S. Environmental Protection Agency (EPA). 1987a. A Compendium of Technologies Used in the Treatment of Hazardous Wastes. EPA/625/8-87/014. (NTIS PB89-184626), 195 pp.

U.S. Environmental Protection Agency (EPA). 1987b. A Compendium of Superfund Field Operations Methods. EPA/540/P-87/001 (NTIS PB88-181557), 644 pp.

U.S. Environmental Protection Agency (EPA). 1987c. Data Quality Objective for Remedial Response Activities, Example Scenario: RI/FS Activities at a Site with Contaminated Soils and Ground Water. EPA/540/G-87/004, OSWER Directive 9355.0-7B.

U.S. Environmental Protection Agency (EPA). 1988. Guidance for Conducting Remedial Investigations and Feasibility Studies Under CERCLA. EPA/540/G-89/004.

U.S. Environmental Protection Agency (EPA). 1989a. Guide for Conducting Treatability Studies Under CERCLA—Interim Final. EPA/540/2-89/058 (NTIS PB90-249772), 118 pp.

U.S. Environmental Protection Agency (EPA). 1989b. Summary of Treatment Technology Effectiveness for Contaminated Soil. EPA/540/2-89/053.

U.S. Environmental Protection Agency (EPA). 1990a. Soil Washing Treatment. Engineering Bulletin EPA/540/2-90/017.*

U.S. Environmental Protection Agency (EPA). 1990b. Slurry Biodegradation. Engineering Bulletin EPA/540/290/016.*

U.S. Environmental Protection Agency (EPA). 1990c. Mobile/Transportable Incineration Treatment. Engineering Bulletin EPA/540/2-90/014.*

U.S. Environmental Protection Agency (EPA). 1990d. Chemical Dehalogenation Treatment: APEG Treatment. Engineering Bulletin EPA/540/2-90/015.*

U.S. Environmental Protection Agency (EPA). 1993. RREL Treatability Data Base, Version 5.0. EPA/C-93/003a. [Computer disk available from Risk Reduction Engineering Laboratory, Cincinnati, OH.]

Chapter 12

Accuracy of Depth to Water Measurements[1]

Jerry T. Thornhill, Retired, U.S. EPA, Robert S. Kerr Environmental Research Laboratory, Ada, OK

INTRODUCTION

Accuracy of depth to water measurements is an issue identified by the Forum as a concern of Superfund decision-makers as they attempt to determine directions of ground-water flow, areas of recharge or discharge, the hydraulic characteristics of aquifers, or the effects of man-made stresses on the ground-water system.

Perhaps the most extensive investigation into methods for measuring water levels in wells has been conducted by the U.S. Geological Survey. The USGS, in conjunction with 32 other federal agencies put together a "National Handbook of Recommended Methods for Water-Data Acquisition," (USGS, 1977) which includes an entire section on water-level measurements. The following discussion is based on that document.

The graduated steel tape (wetted-tape method) the electrical measuring line, and the air line are the most common tools for manually measuring water level in nonflowing wells. Chapter 14, Appendix A provides additional guidance on methods for measuring water levels during aquifer tests.

GRADUATED STEEL TAPE

The graduated steel tape method is considered to be the most accurate for measuring the water level in nonflowing wells. Steel surveying tapes in lengths of 100, 200, 300, 500, and 1,000 feet are commonly used. The tapes, up to 500-foot lengths, are mounted on hand-cranked reels; the 1,000-foot tapes usually required a motor-driven tape drive. A slender weight, usually made of lead, is attached to the ring at the end of the tape to ensure plumbness and to permit some feel for obstructions. The choice of a suitable weight, i.e., lead, stainless steel, etc. is dictated by the water-quality parameters of interest in a specific study. Lead weights are used so that if the weight should fall off the tape in a well that has a pump, the soft lead would be less likely to damage the pump. The weight is attached in such a way that if it becomes lodged in the well, the tape can still be pulled free.

The lower few feet of the graduated tape is chalked by pulling a piece of blue carpenter's chalk across the tape. When the chalk becomes wet, a line of color change between the dry and wet chalk denotes the length of tape immersed in water. The tape footage is read at the measuring point, and at the water mark on the tape. The difference between these two readings is the depth to water below the measuring point.

Submergence of the weight and tape may temporarily cause a water-level rise in wells or piezometers having very small diameters. This effect can be significant if the well is in materials of very low hydraulic conductivity. Under dry surface conditions, it may be desirable to pull the chalked part of the tape rapidly to the surface before the wetted part of the tape dries, and read the water mark before rewinding the tape onto the reel. This is accomplished by pulling the tape from the well by hand, being careful not to allow it to become kinked. In cold regions rapid withdrawal of the tape from the well is necessary before the wet part freezes and becomes difficult to read.

Garber and Koopman (1968, p. 3-6) describe corrections for effects of thermal expansion of tapes and of stretch due to the suspended weight of the tape and plumb weight. Errors resulting from these effects can become significant at high temperatures and for measured depths in excess of 1,000 feet.

---

[1] EPA/540-4-89/002.

As a standard of good practice, the observer should make two measurements. If two measurements of static water level made within a few minutes do not agree within about 0.01 or 0.02 foot (generally regarded as the practical limit of precision) in observation wells having a depth to water of less than two hundred feet, continue to measure until the reason for the lack of agreement is determined or until the results are shown to be reliable. Where water is dripping into the hole or covering its wall, it may be impossible to get a good water mark on the chalked tape.

Unless the well is equipped with an access pipe that is placed to eliminate the possibility of lowering the tape into the pump impellers, the graduated-tape method should not be used to measure pumping levels in wells.

After each well measurement, the portion of the tape that was wetted should be disinfected to avoid contamination of other walls.

A simple and reliable method for measuring the depth to water in observation holes between 1-1/2 and 6 inches in diameter is a steel tape with a popper. The popper is a metal cylinder 1 to 1-1/2 inches in diameter and 2 to 3 inches long with a concave undersurface, and is fastened to the end of a steel tape. The popper is raised a few inches and then dropped to hit the water surface, where it makes a distinct "pop." By adjusting the length of the tape, the point at which the popper just hits the surface is rapidly determined (Bureau of Reclamation, 1981).

ELECTRICAL METHODS

Many types of electrical instruments have been devised for measuring water levels; most operate on the principle that a circuit is completed when two electrodes are immersed in water. Some instruments consist of a single conductor that is lowered into the well where the metal well casing is used as the second conductor. More commonly, a two-conductor cable and special probe are used. Various forms of electrolytic cells using two electrodes of dissimilar metals have been used, but current is more commonly supplied by batteries.

Ordinarily, two-conductor electric tapes are 500-feet long and are mounted on a hand-cranked reel that contains space for the batteries and some device for signaling when the circuit is closed. Electrodes are generally contained in a weighted probe that keeps the tape taut while providing some shielding of the electrodes against false indications as the probe is being lowered into the hole. The electric tapes generally are marked at 5-foot intervals with clamped-on metal bands.

Before lowering the probe in the well, the circuitry can be checked by dipping the probe in water and observing the indicator. The probe should be lowered slowly into the well until contact with the water surface is indicated. The electric tape is marked at the measuring point and partly withdrawn; the distance from the mark to the nearest tape band is measured and added to (or subtracted from) the band reading to obtain the depth to water. It is good practice to take a second or third check reading before withdrawing the electric tape from the well.

The tape should not rub across the top of the casing because the metal bands can become displaced; consequently, placement of the bands should be checked frequently with a steel tape.

Electric tapes are more cumbersome and inconvenient to use than the wetted-tape method, and they normally give less accurate results. In some situations, however, they are superior. Where water is dripping into the hole or covering its walls, it may be impossible to get a good water mark on the chalked tape. In wells that are being pumped, particularly with large discharge pumps, the splashing of the water surface makes consistent results by the wetted-tape method impossible. Where a series of measurements are needed in quick succession, such as in aquifer tests, electric tapes have the advantage of not having to be removed from the well for each reading. Electric tapes are also safer to use in pumping wells because the water is sensed as soon as the probe reaches the water surface and there is less danger of lowering the tape into the pump impellers.

Independent electric tape measurements of static water levels using the same tape should agree within ± 0.04 feet for depths of less than about 200 feet. At greater depths, independent measurements may not be this close. For a depth of about 500 feet, the maximum difference of independent measurements using the same tape should be within ± 0.1 foot.

It is especially important to check the electric line length by measuring with a steel tape after the line has been used for a long time or after it has been pulled hard in attempting to free the line. Some electric lines, especially the single line wire, are subject to considerable permanent stretch. In addition, because the probe is larger in diameter than the wire, the probe can become lodged in a well.

Some operators attach the probe by twisting the wires together by hand and using only enough electrical tape to support the weight of the probe. In this manner, the point of probe attachment is the weakest point of the entire line. Should the probe become "hung in the hole," the line may be pulled and breakage will occur at the probe attachment point, allowing the line to be withdrawn.

AIR LINE METHODS

The air line method is especially useful in pumped wells where water turbulence may preclude using more precise methods. A small diameter air-type tube of known length is installed from the surface to a depth below the lowest water level expected. Compressed air (compressor, bottled air, or tire pump) is used to purge the water from the tube. The pressure, in pounds per square inch (psi), needed to purge the water from the air line multiplied by 2.31 (feet of water or one psi) equals the length in feet of submerged airline. The depth to water below the center of the pressure gage can be easily calculated by subtracting the length of air line below the water surface from the total length of the air line (assuming the air line is essentially straight). Accuracy depends on the precision to which the pressure can be read.

The air line and any connections to it must be airtight throughout its entire length. If the line is broken or leaky, large errors may occur. A long-term increase in air line pressure may indicate a gradual clogging of the air line. A relatively sudden decrease in air line pressure may indicate a leak or break in the air line. Air line pressures that never go above a constant low value may indicate that the water level has dropped below the outlet orifice of the air line. To minimize the effect of turbulence, the lower end of the air line should be at least five feet above or below the pump intake.

FREQUENCY OF MEASUREMENTS

The frequency for measuring water levels in wells depends on the nature of the aquifer under investigation, and on the problems that are to be solved. Thus, the frequency of measurement should be adjusted to the circumstances; i.e., water-level measurements at a given location should be made at approximately the same time of day whenever possible.

At the beginning of an investigation, when details of the ground-water system are not yet known, water levels are commonly made at regular intervals; for example, 10 times a month for water-table conditions and 5 times a month for artesian conditions at key observation sites (Brown et al., 1983).

The reader is referred to the references for detailed handling on the subject of frequency of measurement in various applications.

EPA CONTACT

For further information contact: Steven Acree, 405/436-8609, RSKERL-Ada.

REFERENCES

Brown, R.H., A.A. Konoplyantsev, J. Ineson, and V.S. Kovalensky. 1983. Ground-Water Studies: An International Guide for Research and Practice. Studies and Reports in Hydrology No. 7. UNESCO, Paris.

Bureau of Reclamation. 1981. Ground Water Manual—A Water Resources Technical Publication, 2nd ed. U.S. Department of the Interior, Bureau of Reclamation, Denver, CO, 480 pp.

Garber, M.S. and F.C. Koopman. 1968. Methods of Measuring Water Levels in Deep Wells. U.S. Geological Survey Techniques of Water-Resource Investigations TWRI 8-A1, 23 pp.

U.S. Geological Survey. 1977. National Handbook of Recommended Methods for Water-Data Acquisition. USGS Office of Water Data Coordination, Reston, VA.

Chapter 13

Suggested Operating Procedures for Aquifer Pumping Tests[1]

Paul S. Osborne, U.S. EPA, Region VIII, Denver, CO

INTRODUCTION

In recent years, there has been an increased interest in ground-water resources throughout the United States. This interest has resulted from a combination of an increase in ground-water development for public and domestic use; an increase in mining, agricultural, and industrial activities which might impact ground-water quality; and an increase in studies of already contaminated aquifers. Decision-making agencies involved in these ground-water activities require studies of the aquifers to develop reliable information on the hydrologic properties and behavior of aquifers and aquitards.

A very important aspect of ground-water remediation is the capability to determine accurate estimates of aquifer hydraulic characteristics. This chapter was developed to provide an overview of all the elements of an aquifer test to assist Remedial Project Managers and On Site Coordinators in the initial design of such tests or in the review of tests performed by other groups.

The most reliable type of aquifer test usually conducted is a pumping test. In addition, some site studies involve the use of short term slug tests to obtain estimates of hydraulic conductivity, usually for a specific zone or very limited portion of the aquifer. It should be emphasized that slug tests provide very limited information on the hydraulic properties of the aquifer and often produce estimates which are only accurate within an order of magnitude. Many experts believe that slug tests are much too heavily relied upon in site characterization and contamination studies. This group of professionals recommends use of slug testing during the initial site studies to assist in developing a site conceptual model and in pumping test design.

This chapter is intended as a primer, describing the process for the design and performance of an "aquifer test" (how to obtain reliable data from a pumping test) to obtain accurate estimates of aquifer parameters. It is intended for use by those professionals involved in characterizing sites which require corrective action as well as those which are proposed for ground-water development, agricultural development, industrial development, or disposal activities. The goal of the document is to provide the reader with a complete picture of all of the elements of aquifer (pumping) test design and performance and an understanding of how those elements can affect the quality of the final data.

The determination of accurate estimates of aquifer hydraulic characteristics is dependent on the availability of reliable data from an aquifer test. This chapter outlines the planning, equipment, and test procedures for designing and conducting an accurate aquifer test. The design and operation of a slug test is not included in this chapter, although slug tests are often run prior to the design and implementation of an aquifer test. The slug test information can be very useful in developing the aquifer test design (see ASTM Methods D4050 and D4104). If an accurate conceptual model of the site is developed and the proper equipment, wells, and procedures are selected during the design phase, the resulting data should be reliable. The aquifer estimates obtained from analyzing the data will, of course, depend on the method of analysis.

This chapter is not intended to be an overview of aquifer test analysis. The analysis and evaluation of pumping test data is adequately covered by numerous texts on the subject (Dawson and Istok, 1991; Kruseman and de Ridder, 1991; Lohman, 1972; Walton, 1962; and Ferris et al., 1962). It should be emphasized, however, that information on the methods for analyzing test data should be

---

[1] EPA/540/S-93/503.

reviewed in detail during the planning phase. This is especially important for determining the number, location, and construction details for all wells involved in the test.

A simple "pump" (specific capacity) test involves the pumping of a single well with no associated observation wells. The purpose of a pump test is to obtain information on well yield, observed drawdown, pump efficiency, and calculated specific capacity. The information is used mainly for developing the final design of the pump facility and water delivery system. The pump test usually has a duration of 2 to 12 hours with periodic water level and discharge measurements. The pump is generally allowed to run at maximum capacity with little or no attempt to maintain constant discharge. Discharge variations are often as high as 50 percent. Short-term pump tests with poor control of discharge are not suitable for estimating parameters needed for adequate aquifer characterization. If the pump test is, however, run in such a way that the discharge rate varies less than 5 percent and water levels are measured frequently, the test data can also be used to obtain some reliable estimates of aquifer performance. It should be emphasized that an estimate of aquifer transmissivity obtained in this manner will not be as accurate as that obtained using an aquifer test including observation wells.

By controlling the discharge variation and pumping for a sufficient duration, it is possible to obtain reliable estimates of transmissivity using water level data obtained during the pump test. However, this method does not provide information on boundaries, storativity, leaky aquifers, and other information needed to adequately characterize the hydrology of an aquifer. For the purpose of this chapter, an aquifer test is defined as a controlled field experiment using a discharging (control) well and at least one observation well.

The aquifer test is accomplished by applying a known stress to an aquifer of known or assumed dimensions and observing the water level response over time. Hydraulic characteristics which can be estimated, if the test is designed and implemented properly, include the coefficient of storage, specific yield, transmissivity, vertical and horizontal permeability, and confining layer leakage. Depending on the location of observation wells, it may be possible to determine the location of aquifer boundaries. If measurements are made on nearby springs, it may also be possible to determine the impact of pumping on surface-water features.

TEST DESIGN

Adequate attention to the planning and design phase of the aquifer pumping test will assure that the effort and expense of conducting a test will produce useful results. Individuals involved in designing an aquifer test should review the relevant ASTM Standards relating to: 1) appropriate field procedures for determining aquifer hydraulic properties (D4050 and D4106); 2) selection of aquifer test method (D4043); and 3) design and installation of ground-water monitoring wells (D5092). The relevant portions of these standards should be incorporated into the design.

All available information regarding the aquifer and the site should be collected and reviewed at the commencement of the test design phase. This information will provide the basis for development of a conceptual model of the site and for selecting the final design. It is important that the geometry of the site, location and depth of observation wells and piezometers, and the pumping period agree with the mathematical model to be used in the analysis of the data. A test should be designed for the most important parameters to be determined, and other parameters may have to be deemphasized.

Aquifer Data Needs

The initial element of the test design, formulating a conceptual model of the site, involves the collection and analysis of existing data regarding the aquifer and related geologic and hydrologic units. All available information on the aquifer itself, such as saturated thickness, locations of aquifer boundaries, locations of springs, information on all on-site and all nearby wells (construction, well logs, pumping schedules, etc.), estimates of regional transmissivities, and other pertinent data, should be collected. Detailed information relating to the geology and hydrology is needed to formulate the conceptual model and to determine which mathematical model should be utilized to estimate the most important parameters. It is also important to review various methods for the analyses and evaluation of pumping test data (Ferris et al., 1962; Kruseman and de Ridder, 1991; and Walton, 1962 and 1970). Information relating to the various analytical methods and associated data needs will assist the hydrologist in reviewing the existing data, identifying gaps in information, and formulating a program for filling any gaps that exist.

The conceptual model of the site should be prepared after carrying out a detailed site visit and an evaluation of the assembled information. The review of available records should include files available from the U.S. Geological Survey, appropriate state agencies, and information from local drillers with experience in the area. Formulation of a conceptual model should include a brief analysis of how the local hydrology/geology fits into the regional hydrogeologic setting.

Aquifer Location

The depth to, thickness of, areal extent of, and lithology of the aquifer to be tested should be delineated, if possible.

Aquifer Boundaries

Nearby aquifer discontinuities caused by changes in lithology or by incised streams and lakes should be mapped. All known and suspected boundaries should be mapped such that observation wells can be placed (chosen) where they will provide the best opportunity to measure the aquifer's response to the pumping and the boundary effects during the pumping test.

Hydraulic Properties

Estimates of all pertinent hydraulic properties of the aquifers and pertinent geologic units must be made by any means feasible. Estimates of transmissivity and the storage coefficient should be made, and if leaky confining beds are detected, leakage coefficients should be estimated. The estimation of transmissivity and the storage coefficient should be carried out by making a close examination of existing well logs and core data in the area or by gathering information from nearby aquifer tests, slug tests, or drill stem tests conducted on the aquifer(s) in question. It may also be feasible to run a slug test on the wells near the site to get preliminary values. (See ASTM Methods D4044 and D4104). It should be noted that some investigators have found that slug tests often produce results which are as much as an order of magnitude low. Although some investigators have reported results which are two orders of magnitude high because the sand pack dominated the test. Such tests will, however, provide a starting point for the design. If no core analyses are available, the well log review should form a basis for utilizing an available table which correlates the type of aquifer material with the hydraulic conductivity. If detailed sample results from drill holes are available and they have grain size analyses, there are empirical formulas for estimation of transmissivity. Estimation of storage coefficient is more difficult, but can be based on the expected porosity of the material or the expected confinement of the aquifer. It is recommended that a range of values be chosen to provide a worst case and best case scenario (Freeze and Cherry, 1979). Trial calculations of well drawdown using these estimated values should be made to finalize the design, location, and operation of test and observation wells (Ferris et al., 1962; Campbell and Lehr, 1973; and Stallman, 1971).

If local perched aquifers are of a significant size and location to impact the pump test, this impact should be estimated if possible. The final test design should include adequate monitoring of any perched aquifers and leaky confining beds. This might involve the placing of piezometers into and/or above the leaky confining zone or into the perched aquifer.

Evaluation of Existing Well Information

Because the drilling of new production wells and observation wells expressly for an aquifer test can be expensive, it is advisable to use existing wells for conducting an aquifer test when possible. However, many existing wells are not suitable for aquifer testing. They may be unsuitably constructed (such as a well which is not completed in the same aquifer zone as the pumping well) or may be inappropriately located. It is also important to note that well logs and well completion data for existing facilities are not always reliable. Existing data should be verified whenever possible. The design of each well, whether existing or to be drilled, must be carefully considered to determine if it will meet the needs of the proposed test plan and analytical methods. Special attention must be paid to well location, the depth and interval of the well screen or perforation, and the present condition of existing perforations.

After the process of developing the site model and determining which analytical methods should be used, it is possible to move to the final design stage. The final stage of the design involves development of the key elements of the aquifer test: 1) number and location of observation wells; 2) design of observation wells; 3) approximate duration of the test; and 4) discharge rate.

Design of Pumping Facility

There are seven principal elements to be considered during the pumping facility design phase: 1) well construction; 2) the well development procedure; 3) well access for water level measurements; 4) a reliable power source; 5) the type of pump; 6) the discharge-control and measurement equipment; and 7) the method of water disposal. These elements are discussed in the following sections.

Well Construction

The diameter, depth and position of all intervals open to the aquifer in the pumping well should be known, as should total depth. The diameter must be large enough to accommodate a test pump and allow for water level measurements. All openings to the aquifer(s) must be known *and only those openings located in the aquifer to be tested should be open to the well during the testing.* If the pumping well has to be drilled, the type, size, and number of perforations should be established using data from existing well logs and from the information obtained during the drilling of the new well itself. The screen or perforated interval should be designed to have sufficient open area to minimize well losses caused by fluid entry into the well (Campbell and Lehr, 1973; and Driscoll, 1986).

A well into an unconsolidated aquifer should be completed with a filter pack in the annular space between the well screen and the aquifer material. To design an adequate filter pack, it is essential that the grain size makeup of the aquifer be defined. This is generally done by running a sieve analysis of the major lithologic units making up the aquifer. The sizing of the filter pack will depend on the grain size distribution of the aquifer material. The well screen size would be established by the sizing of the chosen filter pack (Driscoll, 1986). The filter pack should extend at least one (1) foot above the top of the well screen. A seal of bentonite pellets should be placed on top of the filter pack. A minimum of three (3) feet of pellets should be used. An annulus seal of cement and/or bentonite grout should be placed on top of the bentonite pellets. The well casing should be protected at the surface with a concrete pad around the well to isolate the wellbore from surface runoff (ASTM Practice D5092; Aller et al., 1989; Barcelona et al., 1983).

Well Development

Information on how the pumping well was constructed and developed should be collected during the review of existing site information. It may be necessary to interview the driller. If the well has not been adequately developed, the data collected from the well may not be representative of the aquifer. For instance, the efficiency of the well may be reduced, thereby causing increased drawdown in the pumping well. When a well is pumped, there are two components of drawdown: 1) the head losses in the aquifer: and 2) the head losses associated with entry into the well. A well which is poorly constructed or has a plugged well screen will have a high head loss associated with entry into the well. These losses will affect the accuracy of the estimates of aquifer hydraulic parameters made using data from that well. If the well is suspected to have been poorly developed, or nothing is known, it is advisable to run a step drawdown test on the well to determine the extent of the problem. The step drawdown test entails conducting three or more steps of increasing discharge, producing drawdown curves such as shown in Figure 13-1. The data provided by the step drawdown test (multiple discharge test) can be analyzed using various techniques (Rorabough, 1953; and Driscoll, 1986) to obtain an estimate of well entry losses. If a determination is made that plugging results in significant losses, the well should be redeveloped prior to the pumping test using a surge block and/or a pump

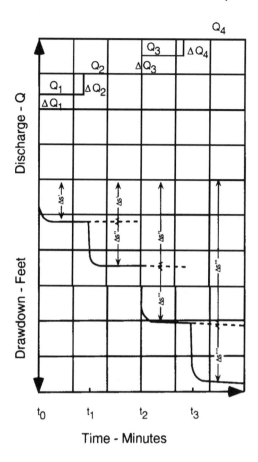

Figure 13-1. Variation of discharge and drawdown in multiple discharge tests (step drawdown tests).

until the well discharge is clear: i.e., the development results in the well achieving acceptable turbidity unit limits (Driscoll, 1986). In many cases, running a step drawdown test to determine well efficiency after the well has been surged is needed to assess the results of the development process. The results of the post development test should be compared with the step-drawdown test run prior to development. This analysis will provide a means of verifying the success of the well development.

Water Level Measurement Access

It must be possible to measure depth to the water level in the pumping well before, during, and after pumping. The quickest and generally the most accurate means of measuring the water levels in the pumped well during an aquifer test is to use an electric sounder or pressure transducer system. The transducer system may be expensive and may be difficult to install in an existing well. It may be possible to run a 1/4 inch copper line into the well as an air line. If the control well is newly constructed, the continuous copper line should be strapped to the pump column as it is being installed. If it is correctly installed, an air line can be used with somewhat less accuracy than an electric sounder or steel tape. An air line with a bubbler and either a transducer or precision pressure gage should be adequate for running an aquifer test.

With adequate temperature compensation, a surface mounted pressure transducer is as precise as one that is submerged. Steel tapes cannot always be used quickly enough in a pumping well, except in wells with a small depth to water (less than 100 feet) where the pump test crew has a fair amount of experience and the well is modified for access of the steel tape. Such modification often involves hanging a 3/4 inch pipe in the well as access for the steel tape. The pipe should be capped at the bottom with numerous 1/16 to 1/8 inch holes drilled in the pipe and cap (especially needed for wells subject to cascading water or surging). This will dampen water-level surging caused by the pump and will eliminate the problems caused by cascading water. In general, the use of a steel tape is usually confined to the later stages of the pump test where rapid changes in water levels are not occurring.

In cases where the pump is isolated by a packer to allow production from a particular zone, a transducer system should be used to monitor pumping hydraulic heads. It is important, however, to calibrate the transducers before and after the test. In addition, reference checks with an electric sounder or steel tape should be made before, during, and after the test. The ASTM Standard Test Method for determining subsurface liquid levels in a borehole or monitoring well (D4750) should be reviewed as part of the design process.

Reliable Power Source

Having power continuously available to the pump, for the duration of the test, is crucial to the success of the test. If power is interrupted during the test, it may be necessary to terminate the test and allow for sufficient recovery so that prepumping water-level trends can be extrapolated. At that point, a new test would be run. If, however, brief interruptions in power occur late in the test, the effect of the interruption can be eliminated by pumping at a calculated higher rate for some period so that the average rate remains unchanged. The increased rate must be calculated such that the final portion of the test compensates for the pumpage that would have occurred during the interruption of pumping.

Pump Selection

A reliable pump is a necessity during an aquifer test. The pump should be operated continuously during the test. Should a pump fail during the pumping period of the test, the time, effort, and expense of conducting the test could be wasted. Electrically powered pumps produce the most constant discharge and are often recommended for use during an aquifer test. However, in irrigation areas, line loads can fluctuate greatly, causing variations in the pumping rate of electric motors. Furthermore, electric motors are nearly constant-load devices, so that as the lift increases (water level declines), the pumping rate decreases. This is a particular problem for inefficient wells or low transmissivity aquifers.

The discharge of engine-powered (usually gasoline or diesel) pumps may vary greatly over a 24 hour period, requiring more frequent monitoring of the discharge rate during the test. For example, under extreme conditions a diesel-powered turbine pump may have more than a 10 percent change in discharge as a result of the daily variation in temperature. The change in air temperature affects the combustion ratio of the engine, resulting in a variation in engine revolutions per minute (rpm). The greater the daily temperature range, the greater the range in engine rpm. Variations in barometric pressure may also affect the engine operation and resulting rpm. Running the engine at full throttle will reduce operational flexibility for adjusting engine rpm and the resulting discharge. In areas where outside temperatures are extreme, such as the desert or a very cold region, it may be advisable to undertake measures to prevent the engine from overheating or freezing.

In order to obtain good data during the period of recovery at the end of pumping, it is necessary to have a check valve installed at the base of the pump column pipe in the discharging well. This will prevent the back flow of water from the column pipe into the well when the pumping portion of the test is terminated and the recovery begins. Any back flow into the well will interfere with or totally mask the water level recovery of the aquifer and this would make any aquifer analysis based on recovery data useless or, at best, questionable (Schafer, 1978).

Discharge-Control and Measurement Equipment

The well bore and discharge lines should be accessible for installing discharge control and monitoring equipment. When considering an existing well for the test well to be pumped (control well), the well must either already be equipped with discharge measuring and regulating equipment, or the well must have been constructed such that the necessary equipment can be added.

Control of the pumping rate during the test requires an accurate means for measuring the discharge of the pump and a convenient means of adjusting the rate to keep it as nearly constant as possible. Common methods of measuring well discharge include the use of an orifice plate and manometer, an inline flow meter, an inline calibrated pitot tube, a calibrated weir or flume, or, for low discharge rates, observing the length of time taken for the discharging water to fill a container of known volume (e.g., 5 gallon bucket; 55 gallon drum).

In addition to the potentially large variation in discharge associated with the pump motor or engine, the discharge rate is also related to the drop in water level near the pumping well during the aquifer test. As the pumping lift increases, the rate of discharge at a given level of power (such as engine rpm) will decrease. The pump should not be operated at its maximum rate. As a general rule, the pumping unit, including the engine, should be designed so that the maximum pumping rate is at least 20 percent more than the estimated long term sustainable yield of the aquifer. The long term yield of the aquifer should be determined by collecting data on pumping rates in nearby wells. If possible, a short term test of one to two hours should be run when the pump is installed. This test data should be compared to the historic data as part of the estimation process.

The pumping rate can be controlled by placing valves on the discharge line and/or by placing controls on the pump power source. A valve installed in the discharge line to create back pressure provides effective control of the discharge rate while conducting an aquifer test, especially when using an electric powered pump. A rheostatic control on the electric pump will also allow accurate control of the discharge rate. When an engine-powered pump is being utilized, installation of a micrometer throttle adjustment device to accurately control engine rpm is recommended in addition to a valve in the line.

Water Disposal

Discharging water immediately adjacent to the pumping well can cause problems with the aquifer test, especially in tests of permeable unconfined alluvial aquifers. The water becomes a source of recharge which will affect the results of the test. *It is essential that the volumes of produced water, the storage needs, the disposal alternatives, and the treatment needs be assessed early in the planning process.* The produced water from the test well must be transported away from the control well and observation wells so it cannot return to the aquifer during the test. This may necessitate the laying of a temporary pipeline (sprinkler irrigation line is often used) to convey the discharge water a sufficient distance from the test site. In some cases, it may be necessary to have on-site storage, such as steel storage tanks or lined ponds. This is especially critical when testing contaminated zones where water treatment capacity is not available. The test designer should carefully review applicable requirements of the RCRA hazardous waste program, the underground injection control program, and the surface water discharge program prior to making decisions about this phase of the design. It may be necessary to obtain permits for on-site storage and final disposal of the contaminated fluids. Final disposal could involve treatment and reinjection into the source aquifer or appropriate treatment and discharge.

Design of Observation Well(s)

Verification of Well Response

As part of the process of selecting the location of the observation wells needed for the chosen aquifer test design, existing wells should be tested for their suitability as observation wells. The existing information regarding well construction should be reviewed as a screening mechanism for identifying suitable candidates. The wells that are identified as potential observation wells should be field tested to verify that they are suitable for monitoring aquifer response. The perforations or well screens of abandoned wells tend to become restricted by the buildup of iron compounds, carbonate compounds, sulfate compounds or bacterial growth as a result of not pumping the well. Consequently, the response test is one of the most important pre-pumping examinations to be made if such wells are to be used for observation (Stallman, 1971; and Black and Kip, 1977). The reaction of all wells to changing water levels should be tested by injecting or removing a known volume of water into each well and measuring the subsequent change of water level. Any wells which appear to have poor response should be either redeveloped, replaced, or dropped from consideration in favor of another available well selected.

Total Depth

In general, observation wells should penetrate the tested aquifer to the same stratigraphic horizon as the well screen or perforated interval of the pumping well. This will require close evaluation of logs to adjust for dipping formations. This assumes the observation well is to be used for monitoring response in the same aquifer from which the discharging well is pumping. Actual screen design will depend on aquifer geometry and site specific lithology. If the aquifer test is designed to detect hydraulic connection between aquifers, one observation well should be screened in the strata for which hydraulic inter-connection is suspected. Depending on how much information is needed, additional wells screened in other strata may be needed (Bredehoeft et al., 1983; Walton, 1970; Dawson and Istok, 1991; and Hamlin, 1983).

Well Diameter

In general, observation well casing should have a diameter just large enough to allow for accurate, rapid water level measurements. A two-inch well casing is usually adequate for use as an observation well in shallow aquifers which are less than 100 feet in depth. They are, however, often difficult to develop. A four- to six-inch diameter well will withstand a more vigorous development process, and should have better aquifer response when properly developed. Additionally, a four or six inch diameter well may be required if a water-depth recorder is planned, depending on the type of recording equipment to be used. The difficulties in drilling a straight hole usually dictate that a well over 200 feet deep be at least four inches in diameter.

Well Construction

Ideally, the observation well(s) should have five to twenty feet of perforated casing or well screen near the bottom of the well. The final well screened interval(s) will depend on the nature of geologic conditions at the site and the types of parameters to be estimated. Any openings which allow water to enter the well from aquifers which are not to be tested should be sealed or closed off for the duration of the test. Ideally, the annular space between the casing and the hole wall should be gravel packed adjacent to the perforated interval to be tested. The use of a filter pack in wells with more than one screened interval will, however, create a problem. There is no reliable method for sealing the annular space of any unwanted filter packed interval even though the screen can be isolated. The size of the filter material should be based on the grain size distribution of the zone to be screened (preferably based on a sieve analysis of the material). The screen size should be determined based on the filter pack design (Driscoll, 1986). The space above the gravel should be sealed with a sufficient amount of bentonite or other grout to isolate the gravel pack from vertical flow from above. If the bentonite does not extend to the surface, it will be necessary to put a cement seal on top of the bentonite prior to back filling the remaining annular space. A concrete pad should be placed around the well to prevent surface fluids from entering the annular material.

After installation is finished, the observation well should be developed by surging with a block, and/or submersible pump (Campbell and Lehr, 1973; and Driscoll, 1986) for a sufficient period (usually several hours) to meet a pre-determined level of turbidity.

Radial Distance and Location Relative to the Pumped Well

If only *one* observation well is to be used, it is usually located 50 to 300 feet from the pumped well. However, each test situation should be evaluated individually, because certain hydraulic conditions may exist which warrant the use of a closer or more distant observation well. If the test design requires multiple observation wells, the wells are often placed in a straight line or along rays that are perpendicular from the pumping well. In the case of multiple boundaries or leaky aquifers, the observation wells need

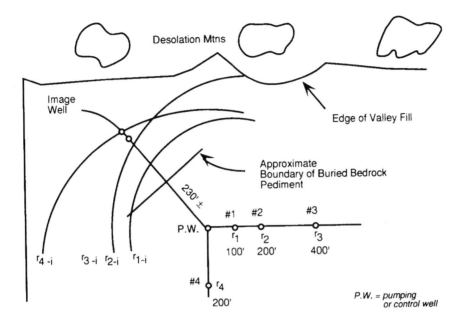

Figure 13-2. Observation well/pumping well location to determine buried impermeable boundary.

to be located in a manner which will identify the location and effect of the boundaries. If the location of the boundary is suspected before the test, it is desirable to locate most of the wells along a line parallel to the boundary and running through the pumping well, as shown in Figure 13-2. If aquifer anisotropy is expected, the observation wells should be located in a pattern based on the suspected or known anisotropic conditions at the site (Bentall et al., 1963; Ferris et al., 1962; Walton, 1962 and 1970; and Dawson and Istok, 1991). If the principal directions of anisotropy are known, drawdown data from two wells located on different rays from the pumping well will be sufficient. If the principal directions of anisotropy are not known, at least three wells on different rays are needed.

FIELD PROCEDURES

Well thought out field procedures and accurate monitoring equipment are the key to a successful aquifer test. The following three sections provide an overview of the methods and equipment for establishing a pre-test baseline condition and running the test itself.

Necessary Equipment for Data Collection

During an aquifer test, equipment is needed to measure/record water levels, well discharges, and the time since the beginning of the test, and to record accumulated data. Appendix A contains a detailed description of the types of equipment commonly used during an aquifer test. Appendix B is an example form for recording test data.

Establish Baseline Trend

Collecting data on pre-test water levels is essential if the analysis of the test data is to be completely successful. The baseline data provides a basis for correcting the test data to account for on-going regional water level changes. Although the wells on-site are the main target for baseline measurements, it is important to measure key wells adjacent to the site and to account for off-site pumping which may affect the test results.

Baseline Water Levels

Prior to beginning the test, it will be necessary to establish a baseline trend in the water levels in the pumping and all observation wells. As a general rule, the period of observation before the start of the test (t_0), should be at least one week. Baseline measurements must be made for a period which is sufficient to establish the pre-pumping water level trends on site (see Figure 13-3). The baseline data must be sufficient to explain any differences between individual observation wells. As shown in Figure 13-3, the water levels in on-site wells were declining prior to the test. The drawdown during the test must be corrected to account for the pre-pumping trend.

Nearby Pumping Activities

During the baseline measurements, the on-off times should be recorded for any nearby wells in use. The well discharge rates should be noted as should any observed changes in the proposed on-site control well and observation wells. Baseline water level measurements should be made in all off-site wells within the anticipated area of influence. As shown in Figure 13-3, the baseline period should be sufficient to establish the pretest pumping trends and to explain any differences in trends between individual off-site wells.

Significant effects due to nearby pumping wells can often be removed from the test data if the on-off times of the wells are monitored before and during the test. Interference effects may not, however, always be observable. In any case, changes associated with nearby pumping wells will make analysis more difficult. If possible, the cooperation of nearby well owners should be obtained to either cease pumping prior to and during the test period or to control the discharge of these wells during the baseline and test period. The underlying principle is to minimize changes in regional effects during the baseline, test and recovery periods.

Barometric Pressure Changes

During the baseline trend observation period, it is desirable to monitor and record the barometric pressure to a sensitivity of plus or minus 0.01 inches of mercury. The monitoring should continue throughout the test and for at least one day to a week after the completion of the recovery measurement period. These data, when combined with the water level trends measured during the baseline period, can be used to correct for the effects of barometric changes that may occur during the test (Clark, 1967).

Local Activities Which May Affect Test

Changes in depth to water level, observed during the test, may be due to several variables such as recharge, barometric response, or "noise" resulting from operation of nearby wells, or loading of the aquifer by trains or other surface disturbances (King, 1982). It is important to identify all major activities (especially cyclic activities) which may impact the test data. Enough measurements have to be made to fully characterize the pre-pumping trends of these activities. This may necessitate the installation of recording equipment. A summary of this information should be noted in the comments section of the pumping test data forms.

Test Procedures

Initial Water Level Measurements

Immediately before pumping is to begin, static water levels in all test wells should be recorded. Measurements of drawdown in the pumping well can be simplified by taping a calibrated steel tape to the electric sounder wire. The zero point of the tape may be taped at the point representing static water level. This will enable the drawdown to be measured directly rather than by depth to water.

Map of Aquifer Test Site

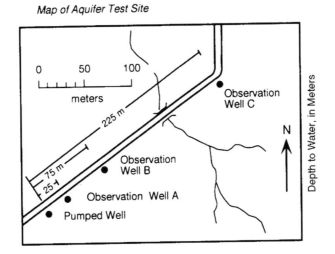

Change of Water Level in Well B

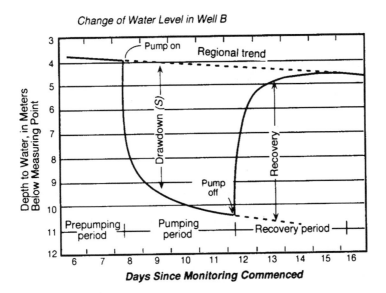

Figure 13-3. Example test site showing baseline, pumping test and recovery water level measurements in one of the wells.

Measuring Water Levels During Test

If drawdown is expected in the observation well(s) soon after testing begins and continuous water level recorders are not installed, an observer should be stationed at each observation well to record water levels during the first two to three hours of testing. Subsequently, a single observer is usually able to record water levels in all wells because simultaneous measurements are unnecessary. If there are numerous observation wells, a pressure transducer/data-logging system should be considered to reduce manpower needs.

Time Frame for Measuring Water Levels

Table 13-1 shows the recommended maximum time intervals for recording water levels in the pumped well. Note: the times provided in Table 13-1 are only the maximum recommended time intervals—more frequent measurements may be taken if test conditions warrant. For instance, it is

Table 13-1. Maximum Recommended Time Intervals for Aquifer Test Water Level Measurements[*]

0 to 3 minutes	every 30 seconds
3 to 15 minutes	every minute
15 to 60 minutes	every 5 minutes
60 to 120 minutes	every 10 minutes
120 min. to 10 hours	every 30 minutes
10 hours to 48 hours	every 4 hours
48 hours to shut down	every 24 hours

[*] Dr. John Harshbarger, personal communication, 1968.

recommended that water level measurements be taken at least every 30 seconds for the first several minutes of the test (see ASTM Method D4050). Figure 13-4 is a hypothetical logarithmic plot of drawdown versus time for an observation well. This plot illustrates the need for the frequency of measurements given in Table 13-1. As shown on the plot, frequent measurements during early times are needed to define the drawdown curve. The data used in Figure 13-4 was collected with a down-hole pressure transducer and electronic data recording equipment. Thus, water levels could be collected about every 6 seconds initially and less frequently as the test progresses. As time since pumping started increases, the logarithmic scale dictates that less frequent measurements are needed to adequately define the curve.

Measurements in the observation well(s) should occur often enough and soon enough after testing begins to avoid missing the initial drawdown values. Actual timing will depend on the aquifer and well conditions which vary from test area to test area. Estimates for timing should be made during the planning stages of aquifer testing using estimated aquifer parameters based on the conceptual model of the site.

Monitoring Discharge Rate

During the initial hour of the aquifer test, well discharge in the pumping well should be monitored and recorded as frequently as practical. Ideally, the pretest discharge will equal zero. If it does not, the discharge should be measured for the first time within a minute or two after the pump is started.

It is important when starting a test to bring the discharge up to the chosen rate as quickly as possible. How frequently the discharge needs to be measured and adjusted for a test depends on the pump, well, aquifer, and power characteristics. Output from electrically driven equipment requires less frequent adjustments than from all other pumping equipment. Engine-driven pumps generally require adjustments several times a day because of variation that occurs in the motor performance due to a number of factors, including air temperature effects. At a minimum, the discharge should be checked four times per day: 1) early morning (2 AM); 2) mid-morning (10 AM); 3) mid-afternoon (3 PM); and 4) early evening (8 PM). *The discharge should never be allowed to vary more than plus or minus 5 percent* (Ferris, J.G., personal communication, 1/19/68). The lower the discharge rate, the more important it is to hold the variation to less than 5 percent. The variation of discharge rate has a large effect on permeability estimates calculated using data collected during a test. The importance of controlling the discharge rate can be demonstrated using a sensitivity analysis of pumping test data. An analysis of this type indicates that a 10 percent variation in discharge can result in a 100 percent variation in the estimate of aquifer transmissivity. Thus, short-term pumping tests with poor control of discharge are not suitable for estimating parameters needed for adequate site characterization. If, however, the pumping test is run in such a way that the discharge rate varies less than 5 percent and water levels are measured frequently, the short-term pumping test data can be used to obtain some reliable estimates of aquifer performance.

It should be emphasized, however, that some random, short-term variations in discharge may be acceptable, if the average discharge does not vary by more than plus or minus 5 percent. A systematic or monotonic change in discharge (usually, a decrease in discharge with increasing time) is, however, unacceptable.

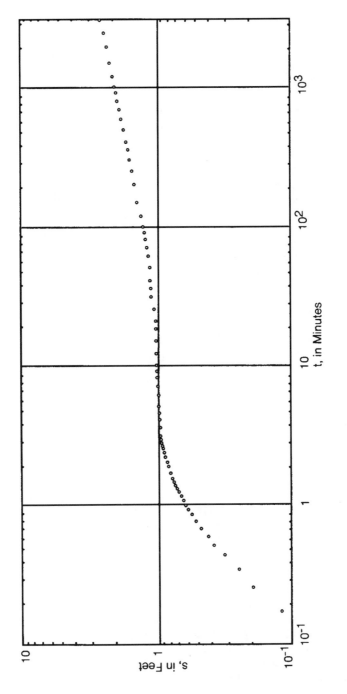

Figure 13-4. Logarithmic plot of s vs. t for observation well.

Water Level Recovery

Recovery measurements should be made in the same manner as the drawdown measurements. After pumping is terminated, recovery measurements should be taken at the same frequency as the drawdown measurements listed above in Table 13-1.

Length of Test

The amount of time the aquifer should be pumped depends on the objectives of the test, the type of aquifer, location of suspected boundaries, the degree of accuracy needed to establish the storage coefficient and transmissivity, and the rate of pumping. The test should continue until the data are adequate to define the shape of the type curve sufficiently so that the parameters required are defined. This may require pumping for a significant period after the rate of water level change becomes small (so called water level "stabilization"). This is especially the case when the locations of boundaries or the effects of delayed drainage are of interest. Their influence may occur a few hours after pumping starts (see Figure 13-3), or it may be days or weeks. Some aquifer tests may never achieve equilibrium, or exhibit boundary effects.

Although it is not necessary for the pumping to continue until equilibrium is approached, it is recommended that pumping be continued for as long as possible and at least for 24 hours. Recovery measurements should be made for a similar period or until the projected pre-pumping water level trend has been attained. The costs of running the pump a few extra hours are low compared with the total costs of the test, and the improvement in additional information gained could be the difference between a conclusive and an inconclusive aquifer test.

Water Disposal

As discussed previously, the water being pumped must be disposed of legally within applicable local, state, and federal rules and regulations. This is especially true if the ground water is contaminated or is of poor quality compared to that at the point of disposal. During the pumping test, the individuals carrying out the test should carry out water quality monitoring as required by the test plan and any necessary disposal permits. This monitoring should include periodic checks to assure that the water disposal procedures are following the test design and are not recharging the aquifer in a manner that would adversely affect the test results. The field notes for the test should document when and how monitoring was performed.

Recordkeeping

All data should be recorded on the forms prepared prior to testing (See Appendix B). An accurate recording of the time, water level, and discharge measurements and comments during the test will prove valuable and necessary during the data analyses stage following the test.

Plotting Data

During the test, a plot of drawdown versus time on semi-log paper should always be prepared and updated as new data are collected for each observation well. A plot of the data prepared during the actual test is essential for monitoring the status and effectiveness of the test. The plot of drawdown versus time will reveal the effects of boundaries or other hydraulic features if they are encountered during the test, and will indicate when enough data for a solution have been recorded. A semi-log or log-log mass plot of water level data from all observation wells should be prepared as time allows. Such a plot can be used to show when aquifer conditions are beginning to affect individual wells. More importantly, it enables the observer to identify erroneous data. This is especially important if transducers are being used for data collection. The utilization of a portable PC with a graphics package is an option for use in carrying out additional field manipulation of the data. It should not, however, be a substitute for a manual plot of the data.

Precautions

(a) Care should be taken for all observers to use the same measuring point on the top of the well casing for each well. If it is necessary to change the measuring point during the test, the time at which the point was changed should be noted and the new measuring point described in detail including the elevation of the new point.

(b) *Regardless* of the prescribed time interval, the actual time of measurement should be recorded for all measurements. It is recognized that the measurements will not be taken at the exact time intervals suggested.

(c) If measurements in observation well(s) are taken by several individuals during the early stages of testing, care should be taken to synchronize stop watches to assure that the time since pumping started is standardized.

(d) It is important to remember to start all stop watches at the time pumping is started (or stopped if performing a recovery test).

(e) Comments can be valuable in analyzing the data. It is important to note any problems, or situations which may alter the test data or the accuracy with which the observer is working.

(f) If several sounders are to be used, they should be compared before the start of the test to assure that constant readings can be made. If the sounder in use is changed, the change should be noted and the new sounder identified in the notes.

PUMPING TEST DATA REDUCTION AND PRESENTATION

All forms required for recording the test data should be prepared prior to the start of the test and should be attached to a clip board for ease of use in the field. It is an option to have a portable PC located on-site with appropriate spreadsheets and graphics package to allow for easier manipulation of the data during the test. The hard copy of the forms should be maintained for the files.

Tabular Data

All raw data in tabular form should be submitted along with the analysis and computations. The data should clearly indicate the well location(s), and date of test and type of test. All data corrections, for pre-pumping trends, barometric pressure fluctuations and other corrections should be given individually and clearly labeled. All graphs used for corrections should be referenced on the specific table. These graphs should be attached to the data package.

Graphs

All graphs or plots should be drafted carefully so that the individual points which reflect the measured data can be retrieved. Semi-logarithmic and logarithmic data plots (see Figures 13-5 and 13-6) should be on paper scaled appropriately for the anticipated length of the test and the anticipated drawdown. All X-Y coordinates shall be carefully labeled on each plot. All plots must include the well location, date of test, and an explanation of any points plotted or symbols used.

ANALYSIS OF TEST RESULTS

Data analysis involves using the raw field data to calculate estimated values of hydraulic properties. If the design and field-observation phases of the aquifer test are conducted successfully, data analyses should be routine and successful. The method(s) of analysis utilized will depend, of course, on particular aquifer conditions in the area (known or assumed) and the parameters to be estimated.

Calculations

All calculations and data analyses must accompany the final report. All calculations should clearly show the data used for input, the equations used and the results achieved. Any assumptions made as

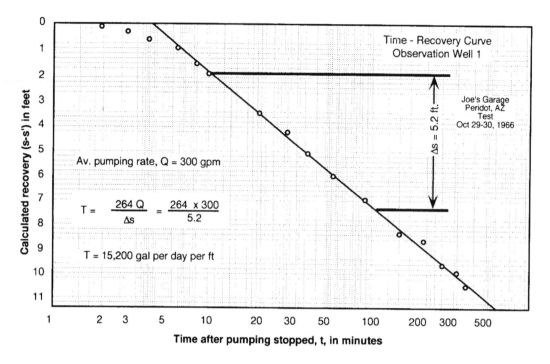

Figure 13-5. Time recovery curve for observation well—October 30, 1966.

part of the analysis should be noted in the calculation section. This is especially important if the data were corrected to account for barometric pressure changes, off-site pumping changes, or other activities which have affected the test. The calculations should reference the appropriate tables and graphs used for a particular calculation.

Aquifer Test Results

The results of an aquifer pumping and recovery test should be submitted in narrative format. The narrative report should include the raw data in tabular form, the plots of the data, the complete calculations and a summary of the results of the test. The assumptions made in utilizing a particular method of analysis should also be included.

SUMMARY—EXAMPLE FACILITY DESIGN

As a means of focusing the discussions presented in the preceding sections, the following example of an aquifer pumping test is described. The facility layout is shown in Figure 13-7. The site is located near a normally dry river channel which is subject to flood flows. The site was constructed for the purpose of carrying out experiments relating to artificial recharge of a shallow alluvial aquifer. The proposed methods of recharge involved use of a pit and a well.

The aquifer at the site is comprised of unconsolidated basin fill material, mainly silty sand and gravel with some clay lenses. The depth to water is generally greater than 50 feet and the river is a source of recharge when it flows. There are extensive gravel lenses above the water table which outcrop at the base of the river channel. These lenses occur beneath the site.

Figure 13-7 shows the locations of the various monitoring wells relative to the recharge facilities and the river. The well locations were selected to facilitate both characterization of the site and subsequent evaluation of the various recharge tests. The recharge well (used as the pumping well during the site aquifer tests) and the eight inch observation wells were completed to a depth of 150 feet in the upper water bearing unit of a basin fill aquifer. The depth to water in the area was about 75 feet. The recharge and observation wells were screened from about 80 feet to 140 feet. The 1-3/4 inch access tubes were 80–100 feet deep with a five-foot well screen on the bottom of each tube.

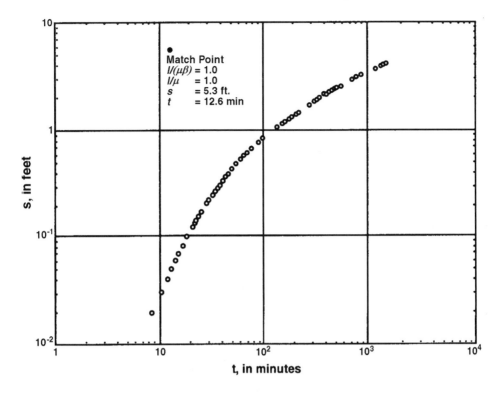

Figure 13-6. Logarithmic plot of s vs. t for Observation Well 23S/25E-17Q$_2$ at Pixley, CA.

The eight-inch observation wells were placed in a line parallel to the river to assess both the effect of flood flows on the aquifer and the hydraulic characteristics of the recharge site itself. The 1-3/4 inch access tubes were positioned for monitoring ground-water movement near the top of the water table in response to aquifer recharge and discharge (pumping) tests. The two inch piezometers at varying depths were constructed to evaluate shallow ground-water movement in response to recharge.

Figure 13-8 is a plan view of the recharge facility showing the pumping/recharge well and the water distribution system. The pumping well was equipped with a downhole turbine pump powered by a methane driven, cylinder engine. As indicated on Figure 13-8, the pump discharge was measured using a Parshall flume (see Figure 13-9). The water from pumping tests was discharged off-site via the concrete box and distribution line. To prevent interference with test results from nearby recharge of the pumping test water, a temporary pipeline was constructed from irrigation pipe. This temporary line ran from the end of the river drain line to a point 1200 feet down stream, out of the estimated area of influence. The ground water was not contaminated. Thus, special water quality monitoring was not required.

The pumping tests for site characterization involved the following monitoring procedure:

1. The eight-inch observation well closest to the recharge well (Well A) was equipped with a Stevens water stage recorder with an electric clock geared for a 4-hour chart cycle;
2. The other two eight-inch observation wells (Wells B and C) were equipped with Stevens water stage recorders with an electric clock geared for a 12-hour chart cycle;
3. The pumping well was equipped with a stilling well composed of a 3/4-inch pipe strapped to the pump column. The stilling well was drilled with 1/4-inch holes through the length. The stilling well was used for assessing the well for water level measurements with a 150-foot steel tape. The steel tape was marked in 0.01 ft. increments for the first 100 feet and in 0.1 ft. increments for the remaining 50 feet;
4. The 1-3/4 inch access wells were monitored at least once a day with a neutron moisture logger to assess changes in saturation as the water level declined in response to the test. This information was used to verify the water level declines in the regular monitoring wells and to

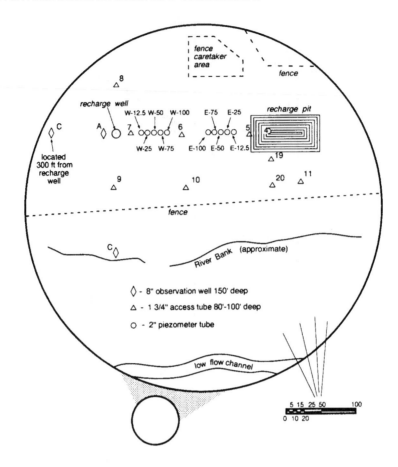

Figure 13-7. Recharge facility well layout.

aid in assessing the delayed drainage effects which were to be estimated using the water level response data from the eight-inch observation wells;

5. A continuous recording barograph was located in a standard construction, USDA weather station shed located between access Wells 9 and 10; and

6. The pump engine was equipped with an rpm gage to monitor pump performance and a micrometer adjustment on the throttle.

A step drawdown test and several short-term pumping tests were run at the site prior to running the principal aquifer characterization test. The step drawdown test was used as a means of selecting the final pumping test design. The short term tests were used to obtain an initial picture of aquifer response.

The results of the step drawdown test run on the recharge well after development indicated that the well was suitable for use as a test well. The results of the step test were also used to estimate well efficiency at different rates. Table 13-2 gives the efficiencies for three (3) discharge rates. As indicated, the well efficiency was greater than 90% for a rate of about 200 gpm. Based on these data, the design rate for the long-term test was set at about 200 gpm (actual average was 204 gpm).

Because the initial short-term tests indicated that delayed drainage was an issue at the site, the main test was designed to run for a continuous period of at least 20 days. The actual scheduling of the test was established to try to avoid flow in the river as a result of a major precipitation event during the background, pumping, and recovery periods. The chosen test period was in the fall after the end of the irrigation season, which also minimized off-site pumping that might affect the results. It should be noted that two short-term tests were planned to follow the main pumping test during the winter rainy season when flow in the river was possible. This was done to allow the impacts of an uncon-

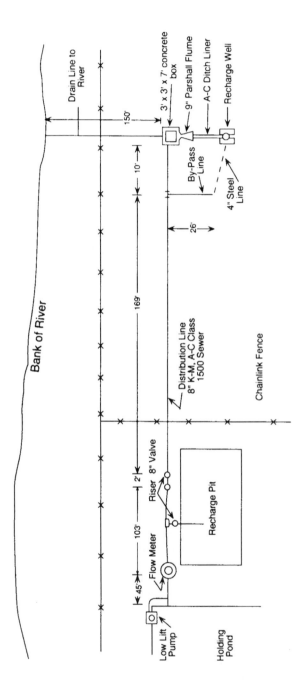

Figure 13-8. Water distribution and drainage facilities at the artificial recharge site.

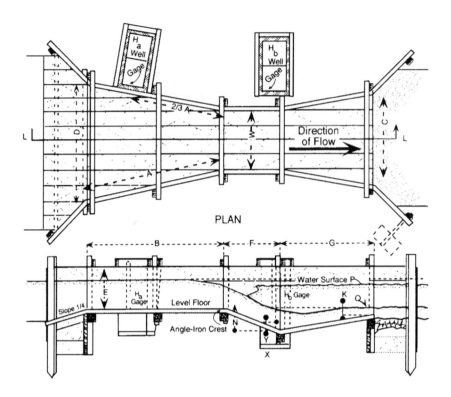

Figure 13-9. Parshall flume dimensions.

Table 13-2. Well Efficiency of R#1 after 200 Minutes of Pumping

Discharge (gpm)	Theoretical Drawdown (ft)	Actual Drawdown (ft)	Well Efficiency (percent)
189	7.00	7.51	92
326	11.88	14.71	81
474	17.27	25.41	68

trolled recharge event on the system to be assessed. The main pumping test would provide a basis for comparison.

The discharging well was measured on a time schedule per the criteria in Table 13-1, except that measurements for the initial 10 minute period were taken every 30 seconds. The observation wells were observed manually on the same schedule for the initial 30 minute period and then the recorders were utilized. Discharge measurements were monitored at least every 5 minutes for the first 30 minutes and then were monitored with water levels for the first 12 hours. Discharge measurements were monitored at least four times daily until the end of the test. The access tubes were monitored twice daily to assess changes in saturation near the water table.

The results from the long term pumping test are shown on Figure 13-10 as a semi-log data mass plot (drawdown versus log time) of the data for the three (3) observation wells. The large initial water level decline for Observation Well A is due to its close proximity to the pumping well (15 feet). The rise in water level at the end of the test was caused by a slight decrease in discharge rate.

Values of T and S were obtained by the nonequilibrium method. The plots of drawdown as a function of log time did not give a good overlay on the nonequilibrium type curve for early times. For later times, it was possible to obtain a good match. The match points obtained for the three observation wells are listed in Table 13-3. The values of T and S are also shown in Table 13-3. As indicated, the estimates of T and S were in close agreement.

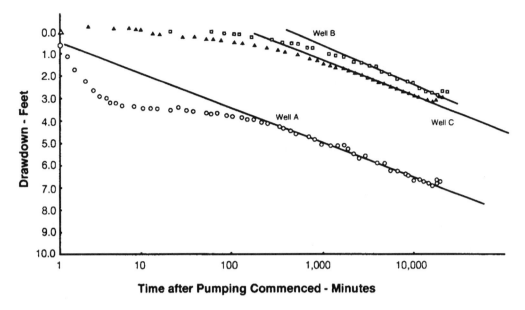

Figure 13-10. Drawdown vs. log of time in observation wells A, B, and C during pumping of R#1.

Table 13-3. Values of T and S Obtained by Nonequilibrium Equation for Discharge Conditions

Location	w(u)	l/u	s (ft)	t (min)	r (ft)	T (gpd/ft)	S
Well A	110	10^5	0.62	14900	14.7	37,600	0.01
Well B	1	10	0.62	1780	280.0	37,600	0.03
Well C	1	10	0.58	530	175.4	40,200	0.03

The estimates for storativity were also in reasonable agreement. It is important to note that the test results showed delayed drainage to be a significant factor at this site. The initial estimates of storativity using data from the early part of the test were about 1×10^{-5} rather than 3×10^{-2} estimated after 20 days of pumping. This effect was expected because of the heterogeneous nature of the basin fill. As a means of comparison, water balance studies on a large well field located 15 miles away (completed in the same material) were reviewed. These studies provided an estimate of storage coefficient (based on 10 years of pumpage) of about 0.15. Thus, it was concluded that the aquifer at the site was under water table conditions, but significant delayed drainage effects were present.

The results of the pumping tests at the site were used to characterize the site and design several long-term recharge experiments. This included monitoring design for evaluation of the effect of river flows on the regional aquifer.

APPENDIX A. EQUIPMENT FOR DATA COLLECTION

a. Water Levels

Water level measurements can be made with electric sounders, air line and pressure gages, calibrated steel tapes, or pressure transducers (Garber and Koopman, 1968; Bentall et al., 1963; Chapter 13).

(1) Electric Sounders

    (a) An electric sounder is recommended for measuring water levels in the pumping well because it will allow for rapid, multiple water level readings, especially important during the early stages of aquifer pumping and recovery tests.

(b) A dedicated sounder should be assigned to each observation well throughout the duration of the test. This is particularly important in ground-water quality studies to prevent cross contamination.

(c) Each sounder should be calibrated prior to the commencement of testing to assure accurate readings during the test.

(2) Air Lines and Pressure Gages

(a) Air lines are only recommended when electric sounders or steel tapes cannot be used to obtain water level measurements. Their usefulness is limited by the accuracy of the gage used and by difficulties in eliminating leakage from the air line. A gage capable of being read to 0.01 psi will be needed to obtain the necessary level of accuracy for determining water level change. A continuous copper or plastic line of known length should be strapped to the column pipe when the pump is installed. This will minimize the potential for leaks.

(b) When air lines are used, the same precision pressure gage should be used on all wells.

(c) Each pressure gage should be calibrated immediately prior to and after the test to assure accurate readings.

(d) The air line and pressure gage assembly should also be calibrated prior to the test by obtaining static water level by another method, if possible.

(3) Calibrated Steel Tapes

(a) Steel tapes marked to .01 ft. are preferred unless rapid water level drawdown or buildup is anticipated. If rapid drawdown, cascading water, or high frequency oscillation are anticipated, electric sounders, float actuated recorders or pressure transducers are preferred.

(b) Steel tapes are not recommended for use in the pumping well because of fluctuating water levels caused by the pump action, possible cascading water and the necessity for obtaining rapid water level measurements during the early portions of the aquifer pumping and recovery tests. If tapes are used, and the water level fluctuates, the well must be equipped with a means of dampening fluctuating water levels. Additional manpower will be needed during the initial stages of the test.

(4) Pressure Transducers

Pressure transducers are often used in situations where access to the well is restricted, such as a well where packers are being used to isolate a certain zone. They may also be applicable in large-scale tests using a computerized data collection system. Such a system will significantly reduce the manpower needed during the initial stages of a multiple well test. The most common installation uses down hole transducers with recording of the results taking place on the surface

(a) Transducers should be calibrated prior to installation, and should be capable of accurately detecting changes of less than .005 psi. Transducer systems which will accurately record water level changes of .001 feet are available. The resolution of transducers, however, depends on the full scale range. Where large drawdowns are expected, such resolution is not possible.

(b) After installation, the transducers and recording equipment should be calibrated by comparing pressure readings to actual water level measurements taken with a steel tape. Periodic measurements of the water level should be made during the test to verify that the transducers are functioning properly.

(c) The effect of barometric changes on the transducers should be determined prior to and during the test. This will require continuous monitoring of the barometric pressure at the site as well as periodic comparisons of water level and transducer readings (Clark, 1967).

b. Discharge Measurement

The equipment commonly used for measuring discharge in the pumping well includes orifice plates, in-line water meters, Parshall flumes and recorders, V-notch weirs, or, for low discharge rates, a container of known volume, and a stop watch (Driscoll, 1986). The choice of method will depend upon a combination of factors, including i) accuracy needed, ii) planned discharge rate, iii) facility layout, and iv) point of discharge. If, for instance, it is necessary to discharge the water a half mile from the pump, a flume or weir will probably not be used, because the distance between the point of discharge control and the point of discharge would make logistics too difficult. An in-line flow meter or a pitot tube would be the most likely calibrated devices (Bureau of Reclamation, 1981; King, 1982; Berg, 1982; and Leupold and Stevens, 1991).

(1) Orifice Plate

(a) Orifice plates with manometers (see Figure 13-11) are an inexpensive and accurate means of obtaining discharge measurements during testing. The thin plate orifice is the best choice for the typical pump test. An orifice plate has an opening smaller than that of the discharge pipe. A manometer is installed into and onto the end of the discharge pipe. The diameter of the plate opening must be small enough to ensure that the discharge pipe behind the plate is full at the chosen rate of discharge. The reading shown on the manometer represents the difference between the upstream and downstream heads.

(b) Assuming the devices are manufactured accurately and are installed correctly, an orifice plate will provide an accuracy of between two and five percent. The orifice tube must be horizontal and full at all times to achieve the design accuracy.

(c) The accuracy should be established prior to testing by pumping into a container of known volume over a given time. This should be repeated for several rates.

(2) In-line Flow Meter

(a) In-line flow meters can give accurate readings of the flow if they are installed and calibrated properly. The meter must be located sufficiently far from valves, bends in the pipe, couplings, etc., to minimize turbulence which will affect the accuracy of the meter. *The meter must be installed so that it is completely submerged during operation.*

(b) Use of a meter is an easy way to monitor the discharge rate by recording the volume of flow through the meter using a totalizer or other means at one minute intervals and subtracting the two readings. Some meters register instantaneous rate of flow and total flow volume.

(c) The meter should be calibrated after installation (prior to the test) to ensure its accuracy.

(3) Flumes and Weirs

(a) There are numerous accurate flumes and weirs on the market. The choice depends mainly on the approximate discharge anticipated, the location of the discharge point and the nature of the facility. The cost of installation will preclude use at many non-permanent facilities.

(b) The weir (see Figure 13-12) or flume should be located close to the pump. There should be a permanent recorder on the device as well as means of making manual measurements (e.g., staff gage).

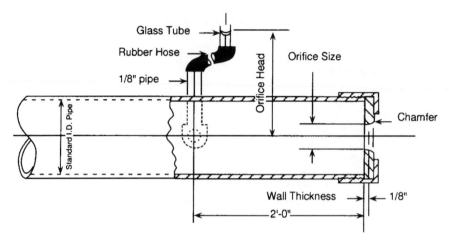

Figure 13-11. Diagram of orifice meter.

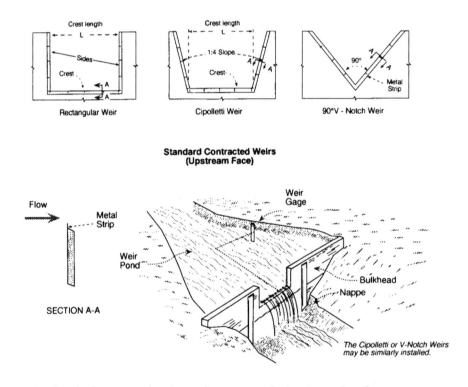

Figure 13-12. Standard contracted weirs, and temporary discharging at free flow.

(c) The discharge canal should have a sufficient length of unobstructed upstream channel so as not to affect the accuracy of the chosen weir or flume.

(4) Pitot Tube

(a) The pitot tube is a velocity meter which is installed in the discharge pipe to establish the velocity profile in the pipe. Commercially available devices consist of a combined piezometer and a total head meter.

(b) The tube must be installed at a point such that the upstream section is free of valves, tees, elbows, etc., for a minimum distance equal to 15 to 20 times the pipe diameter to minimize turbulence at the location of the tube.

(c) Since the pitot tube becomes inaccurate at low velocities, the diameter of the pipe should be small enough to maintain reasonably high velocities.

(5) Container of Known Volume and Stop Watch

(a) The use of a container of known volume and a stop watch is a simple way to measure the discharge rate of a low volume discharging well.
(b) By recording the length of time taken for the discharging water to fill a container of known volume, the discharge rate can be calculated.
(c) This method can be used only where it is possible to precisely measure the time interval required for a known volume to be collected. If rates are sufficiently high so that water "sloshes" in the container, or they prohibit development of a relatively smooth surface on the water in the container, this method is likely to be inaccurate. Restricting use of this method to flows of less than 10 gpm is probably a conservative rule of thumb.

c. Discharge Regulation

(1) The size of the discharge line and the gate valve should be such that the valve will be from one-half to three-fourths open when pumping at the desired rate (during the initial phase of the test) with a full pipe.
(2) The valve should be placed a minimum of five (5) pipe diameters downstream from an in-line flow meter, to ensure that the pipe is full and flow is not disturbed by excessive turbulence. In the case of some meters, such as a pitot tube, an in-line manometer, or an orifice plate, the valve would need to be upstream. (In this case the pipe downstream of the valve must be sized to be full at all times.)

d. Time

(1) A stop watch is recommended for use during an aquifer pumping and recovery test. Time should be recorded to the nearest second while drawdown is rapid, and to the nearest minute as the time period between measurements is increased beyond 15 minutes.
(2) If more than one stop watch is to be used during the testing, then all watches should be synchronized to assure that there is no error caused by the imprecise measurements of elapsed time.
(3) Accuracy of time is critical during the early stage of a pump or aquifer test and it is crucial to have all stop watches reflect the exact time. Later in the test the time recorded to the nearest minute becomes less critical.
(4) A master clock should be kept on site for tests longer than one day. This will provide a backup in case of stop watch problems.

APPENDIX B. RECORDING FORMS

It is very important that each well data form stand alone. The data forms must contain all information which may have a bearing on the analysis of the data. See the suggested format for pumping test data recording sheets located at the end of this appendix. The form should allow for the following data to be recorded on the data sheet for each well:

(a) date
(b) temperature
(c) discharge rate
(d) weather
(e) well location
(f) well number
(g) owner of the well

(h) type of test (drawdown or recovery)
(i) description of measuring point
(j) elevation of measuring point
(k) type of measuring equipment
(l) radial distance from center of pumped well to the center of the observation well
(m) static depth to water
(n) person recording the data
(o) page number of total pages

In addition to the above information to be recorded on each page, the forms should have columns for recording of the following data:

(a) the elapsed time since pumping started, shown as the value (t)
(b) the elapsed time since pumping stopped, shown as (t')
(c) the depth in feet to the water level
(d) drawdown or recovery of the water level in feet
(e) the time since pumping started, divided by the time since pumping stopped, shown as (t/t')
(f) the discharge rate in gallons per minute
(g) a column for comments to note any problems encountered, weather changes (i.e., barometric changes, precipitation), natural disasters, or other pertinent data.

AQUIFER TEST FIELD DATA SHEET

Page____ of____

_____ Pumped Well No._____   Date _____

_____ Observation Well No._____   Weather _____

Owner   _____   Location _____

Observers: _____

Measuring Point is _____ which is _____   feet above/below surface.

Static Water Level _____ feet below land surface.

Distance to pumped well _____ feet.   Type of Test _____

Discharge rate of pumped well _____ gpm (gallons per minute).

Total number of observation wells _____ .

Water Measurement Technique_____ .

Recorded by _____ .   Temperature during test_____ .

Clock Time	Elapsed Time Since Pump Started or Stopped (min)	Depth to Water Below Land (feet)	Drawdown or Recovery (feet)	Discharge or Recharge (GPM)	t/t'	Comments

AQUIFER TEST FIELD DATA SHEET

Continuation Sheet

Distance to pumped well _____   Bearing _____   Page _____ of _____

_____ Pumped Well No. _____   Date _____
_____ Observation Well No. _____   Recorded by _____

Clock Time	Elapsed Time Since Pump Started or Stopped (min)	Depth to Water Below Land (feet)	Drawdown or Recovery (feet)	Discharge or Recharge (GPM)	t/t'	Comments

EPA CONTACTS

For further information, contact: Steven Acree, RSKERL-Ada, 405/436-8609; or Paul Osborne, EPA Region VIII, 303/293-1418.

ACKNOWLEDGMENTS

This chapter would not have been possible without the critical assistance of a number of persons, especially Helen Simonson who had to read my often cryptic handwriting.

The following individuals reviewed the document and provided numerous technical and editorial comments:

Dr. L.G. Wilson, Department of Hydrology and Water Resources University of Arizona, Tucson, Arizona;

John McLean, US Geological Survey, Regional Hydrologist's Office, Denver, Colorado;

Dr. Fred G. Baker, Baker Consultants, Inc., Golden, Colorado;

Jerry Thornhill, US EPA, Robert S. Kerr Environmental Research Laboratory, Ada, Oklahoma;

Marc Herman, US EPA Region VIII, Denver, Colorado;

Alan Peckham, US EPA, NEIC, Denver, Colorado;

Darcy Campbell, US EPA Region VIII, Denver, Colorado;

Mike Wireman, US EPA Region VIII, Denver, Colorado;

Steve Acree, US EPA, Robert S. Kerr Environmental Research Laboratory, Ada, Oklahoma;

Dean McKinnis, US EPA Region VIII, Denver, Colorado.

GLOSSARY

Aquifer: A unit of geologic material that contains sufficient saturated permeable material to conduct ground water and to yield economically significant quantities of ground water to wells and springs. The term was originally defined by Meinzer (1923, p. 30) as any water-bearing formation. Syn: water horizon; ground-water reservoir; nappe; aquifer.

Aquifer Test: A test involving the withdrawal of measured quantities of water from, or addition of water to, a well and the measurement of resulting changes in head in the aquifer both during and after the period of discharge or addition.

Aquitard: A confining bed that retards but does not prevent the flow of water to or from an adjacent aquifer; a leaky confining bed. It does not readily yield water to wells or springs, but may serve as a confining bed storage unit for ground water. Cf: aquifuge; aquiclude.

Capillary Fringe: The lower subdivision of the zone of aeration, immediately above the water table in which the interstices contain water under pressure less than that of the atmosphere, being continuous with the water below the water table but held above it by surface tension. Its upper boundary with the intermediate belt is indistinct, but is sometimes defined arbitrarily as the level at which 50 percent of the interstices are filled with water. Syn: zone of capillarity; capillary-moisture zone.

Confined Aquifer: An aquifer bounded above and below by impermeable beds or beds of distinctly lower permeability than that of the aquifer itself; an aquifer containing confined ground water. Syn: artesian aquifer.

Confining Bed: A confining bed is a unit of distinctly less permeable geologic material stratigraphically adjacent to an aquifer. "Aquitard" is a commonly used synonym. Confining beds can have a wide range of hydraulic conductivities and a confining bed of one area may have a hydraulic conductivity greater than an aquifer of another area.

Drawdown: The vertical distance between the static water level and the surface of the cone of depression at a given location and point of time.

Effective Porosity: Effective porosity refers to the amount of interconnected pore space and fracture openings available for the transmission of fluids, expressed as the volume of interconnected pores and openings to the volume of rock.

Ground Water: Subsurface water that occurs beneath the water table in soils and geologic formations that are fully saturated.

Hydraulic Conductivity: Hydraulic conductivity, K, replaces the term "coefficient of permeability" and is a volume of water that will move in unit time under a unit hydraulic gradient through a unit area measured at right angles to the direction of flow. Hydraulic conductivity is a function of the properties of the medium and the fluid viscosity and specific gravity; intrinsic permeability times specific gravity divided by viscosity. Dimensions are L/T with common units being centimeters per second or feet/day.

Hydraulic Gradient: Hydraulic gradient is the change in head per unit of distance in the direction of maximum rate of decrease in head.

Hydraulic Head: Hydraulic head is the sum of two components: the elevation of the point of measurement and the pressure head.

Intrinsic Permeability: Intrinsic permeability, k, is a property of the porous medium and has dimensions of L^2. It is a measure of the resistance to fluid flow through a given porous medium. It is, however, often used incorrectly to mean the same thing as hydraulic conductivity.

Porosity: Porosity of a rock or soil expresses its property of containing interstices or voids and is the ratio of the volume of interstices to the total volume, expressed as a decimal or percentage. Total porosity is comprised of primary and secondary openings. Primary porosity is controlled by shape, sorting and packing arrangements of grains and is independent of grain size. Secondary porosity is that void space created sometime after the initial formation of the porous medium due to secondary solution phenomena and fracture formation.

Potentiometric Surface: Potentiometric surface is an imaginary surface representing the static head of ground water and defined by the level to which water will rise in a well under static conditions. The water table is a particular potentiometric surface for an unconfined aquifer representing zero atmospheric gage pressure.

Recharge Zone: A recharge zone is the area in which water is absorbed and added to the saturated soil or geologic formation, either directly into a formation, or indirectly by way of another formation.

Residual Drawdown: The difference between the original static water level and the depth to water at a given instant during the recovery period.

Saturated Zone: The saturated zone is that part of the water-bearing material in which all voids are filled with water. Fluid pressure is always greater than or equal to atmospheric, and the hydraulic conductivity does not vary with pressure head.

Specific Capacity: The rate of discharge of a water well per unit of drawdown, commonly expressed in gpm/ft. It varies with duration of discharge.

Specific Storage: Specific storage, S, is defined as the volume of water that a unit volume of aquifer releases from storage because of expansion of the water and compression of the matrix or medium under a unit decline in average hydraulic head within the unit volume. For an unconfined aquifer, for all practical purposes, it has the same value as specific yield. The dimensions are L^1. It is a property of both the medium and the fluid.

Specific Yield: Specific yield is the fraction of drainable water yielded by gravity drainage when the water table declines. It is the ratio of the volume of water yielded by gravity to the volume of rock. Specific yield is equal to total porosity minus specific retention. Dimensionless.

Storage Coefficient: The storage coefficient, S, or storativity, is defined as the volume of water an aquifer releases from or takes into storage per unit surface area of aquifer per unit change in hydraulic head. It is dimensionless.

Transmissivity: Transmissivity, T, is defined as the rate of flow of water through a vertical strip of aquifer one unit wide extending the full saturated thickness of the aquifer under a unit hydraulic gradient. It is equal to hydraulic conductivity times aquifer saturated thickness. Dimensions are L^2/t.

Unconfined Ground Water: Unconfined ground water is water in an aquifer that has a water table. Also, it is aquifer water found at or near atmospheric pressure.

Unsaturated Zone: The unsaturated zone (also referred to as the vadose zone) is the soil or rock material between the land surface and water table. It includes the capillary fringe. Characteristically this zone contains liquid water under less than atmospheric pressure, with water vapor and other gases generally at atmospheric pressure.

Water Table: The water table is an imaginary surface in an unconfined water body at which the water pressure is atmospheric. It is essentially the top of the saturated zone.

Well Efficiency: The well efficiency is the theoretical drawdown divided by the measured drawdown. The theoretical drawdown is estimated by using pumping test data from several observation wells to construct a distance drawdown graph to estimate drawdown in the pumping well if there were no losses.

CITED ASTM STANDARDS

(All the standards listed below are in Volume 4.08 of the ASTM Annual Book of Standards except for D5092, which is in Volume 4.09; ASTM's new address, as of October 1995 is 100 Barr Harbor Drive, West Conshohocken, PA 19428-29590)

D4043. Standard Guide for Selection of Aquifer Test Method in Determining of Hydraulic Properties by Well Techniques.

D4044. Standard Test Method for (Field Procedures) Instantaneous Change in Head (Slug Tests) for Determining Hydraulic Properties of Aquifers.

D4050. Standard Test Method (Field Procedure) for Withdrawal and Injection Well Tests for Determining Hydraulic Properties of Aquifer Systems.

D4104. Standard Test Method (Analytical Procedure) for Determining Transmissivity of Nonleaky Confined Aquifers by Overdamped Well Response to Instantaneous Change in Head (Slug Test).

D4106. Standard Test Method (Analytical Procedure) for Determining Transmissivity and Storage Coefficient of Nonleaky Confined Aquifers by the Modified Theis Nonequilibrium Method.

D4750. Standard Test Method for Determining Subsurface Liquid Levels in a Borehole or Monitoring Well (Observation Well).

D5092. Standard Practice for Design and Installation of Ground Water Monitoring Wells in Aquifers.

REFERENCES

Aller, L. et al. 1989. Handbook of Suggested Practices for the Design and Installation of Ground Water Monitoring Wells. EPA 600/4-89/034, 388 pp.

Anderson, K.E. 1971. Water Well Handbook. Missouri Water Well and Pump Contractors Association.

Barcelona, M.J., J.P. Gibb, and R.A. Miller. 1983. A Guide to the Selection of Materials for Monitoring Well Construction and Ground Water Sampling. ISWS Contract Report 327. Illinois State Water Survey, Urbana, IL, 28 pp.

Bentall, R. et al. 1963. Shortcuts and Special Problems in Aquifer Tests. U.S. Geological Survey Water Supply Paper 1545-C, 117 pp.

Berg, E.L. 1982. Handbook for Sampling and Sample Preservation of Water and Wastewater, 2nd edition. EPA/600/4-82/029 (NTIS PB83-124503), 414 pp.

Black, J.H. and K.L. Kip. 1977. Observation Well Response Time and Its Effect Upon Aquifer Test Results. J. Hydrology 34:297–306.

Bredehoeft, J.D. et al. 1983. Regional Flow in the Dakota Aquifer: Study of the Role of Confining Layers. U.S. Geological Survey Water Supply Paper 2237.

Bureau of Reclamation. 1981. Ground Water Manual—A Water Resources Technical Publication, 2nd ed. U.S. Department of the Interior, Bureau of Reclamation, Denver, CO, 480 pp.

Campbell, M.D. and J.H. Lehr. 1973. Water Well Technology. McGraw-Hill, New York, NY, 681 pp.

Clark, W.E. 1967. Computing the Barometric Efficiency of a Well. J. Hydraulic Division ASCE 93(HY4):93–98.

Dawson, K.J. and J.D. Istok. 1991. Aquifer Testing: Design and Analysis of Pumping and Slug Tests. Lewis Publishers, Chelsea, MI, 344 pp.

Driscoll, F.G. 1986. Ground Water and Wells, 2nd Edition. Johnson Division, St. Paul, MN, 1089 pp.

Ferris, J.G., D.B. Knowles, R.H. Brown, and R.W. Stallman. 1962. Theory of Aquifer Test. U.S. Geological Survey Water Supply Paper 1536-E.

Freeze, R.A. and J.A. Cherry. 1979. Groundwater. Prentice-Hall, Englewood Cliffs, NJ, 604 pp.

Garber, M.S. and F.C. Koopman. 1968. Methods of Measuring Water Levels in Deep Wells. U.S. Geological Survey Techniques of Water-Resource Investigations TWRI 8-A1, 23 pp.

Glover, R.E. 1966. Ground Water Movement. U.S. Bureau of Reclamation Engineering Monograph No. 31.

Hamlin, S.N. 1983. Injection of Treated Wastewater for Ground Water Recharge in the Palo Alto Baylands, CA: Hydraulic and Chemical Intervention. U.S. Geological Survey Water Resources Investigation 82-4121.

Kruseman, G.P. and N.A. de Ridder. 1991. Analysis and Evaluation of Pumping Test Data, 2nd Edition. International Institute for Land Reclamation and Improvement, Wageningen, The Netherlands, 377 pp.

King, H.W. 1982. Handbook of Hydraulics. McGraw-Hill, New York, NY.

Leupold and Stevens. 1991. Stevens Water Resources Data Book, 5th ed. Beaverton, WA.

Lohman, S.W. 1972. Ground Water Hydraulics. U.S. Geological Survey Professional Paper 708.

Meinzer, O.E. 1923. The Occurrence of Ground Water in the United States. U.S. Geological Survey Water Supply Paper 489, 321 pp.

Osborne, P.S. 1969. Analysis of Well Losses Pertaining to Artificial Recharge. M.S. Thesis, University of Arizona.

Rorabough, M.I. 1953. Graphical and Theoretical Analysis of Step Drawdown Test of Artesian Wells. Proc. American Society Civil Engineers, Vol. 79.

Schafer, D.C. 1978. Casing Storage Can Effect Pumping Test Data. The Johnson Drillers Journal, pp. 1–5.

Stallman, R.W. 1971. Aquifer-Test Design. Observation and Data Analysis. U.S. Geological Survey Techniques of Water Resources Investigations, Book 3, Chapter B1, 26 pp. (Reprinted 1983.)

Walton, W.C. 1962. Selected Analytical Methods for Well and Aquifer Evaluations. Illinois State Water Survey Bulletin 49, Urbana, IL, 81 pp.

Walton, W.C. 1970. Ground Water Resource Evaluation. McGraw-Hill, New York, NY, 664 pp.

Chapter 14

Characterizing Soils for Hazardous Waste Site Assessments[1]

R.P. Breckenridge, Idaho National Engineering Laboratory, Environmental Assessment and Technology Group, Idaho Falls, ID
J.R. Williams, U.S. EPA, R.S. Kerr Environmental Research Laboratory, Ada, OK
J.F. Keck, Idaho National Engineering Laboratory, Environmental Science and Technology Group, Idaho Falls, ID

INTRODUCTION

Site investigation and remediation under the Superfund program is performed using the CERCLA remedial investigation/feasibility study (RI/FS) process. The goal of the RI/FS process is to reach a Record of Decision (ROD) in a timely manner. Soil characterization provides data types required for decision-making in three distinct RI/FS tasks:

1.   Determination of the nature and extent of soil contamination.
2.   Risk assessment, and determination of risk-based soil clean-up levels.
3.   Determination of the potential effectiveness of soil remediation alternatives.

Identification of data types required for the first task, determination of the nature and extent of contamination, is relatively straightforward. The nature of contamination is related to the types of operations conducted at the site. Existing records, if available, and interviews with personnel familiar with the site history are good sources of information to help determine the types of contaminants potentially present. This information may be used to shorten the list of target analytes from the several hundred contaminants of concern in the 40 CFR Part 264 list (Date 7-1-89). Numerous guidance documents are available for planning all aspects of the subsequent sampling effort (U.S. EPA, 1987a,b, 1988a,b, and Jenkins et al., 1988).

The extent of contamination is also related to the types of operations conducted at the site. Existing records, if available, and interviews with personnel familiar with the site history are also good sources of information to help determine the extent of contamination potentially present. The extent of contamination is dependent on the nature of the contaminant source(s) and the extent of contaminant migration from the source(s). Migration routes may include air, via volatilization and fugitive dust emissions, overland flow; direct discharge; leachate migration to ground water and surface run-off and erosion. Preparation of a preliminary site conceptual model is therefore an important step in planning and directing the sampling effort. The conceptual model should identify the most likely locations of contaminants in soil and the pathways through which they move.

The data type requirements for tasks 2 and 3 are frequently less well understood. Tasks 2 and 3 require knowledge of both the nature and extent of contamination, the environmental fate and transport of the contaminants, and an appreciation of the need for quality data to select a viable remedial treatment technique.

Contaminant fate and transport estimation is usually performed by computer modeling. Site-specific information about the soils in which contamination occurs, migrates, and interacts with, is required as input to a model. The accuracy of the model output is no better than the accuracy of the input information.

---

[1]   EPA/540/4-91/003.

The purpose of this chapter is to provide guidance to Remedial Project Managers (RPM) and On-Scene Coordinators (OSC) concerning soil characterization data types required for decision-making in the CERCLA RI/FS process related to risk assessment and remedial alternative evaluation for contaminated soils. Many of the problems that arise are due to a lack of understanding the data types required for tasks 2 and 3 above. This chapter describes the soil characterization data types required to conduct model based risk assessment for task 2 and the selection of remedial design for task 3. The information presented in this chapter is a compilation of current information from the literature and from experience combined to meet the purpose of this chapter.

Characterization of a hazardous waste site should be done using an integrated investigative approach to determine quickly and cost effectively the potential health effects and appropriate response measures at a site. An integrated approach involves consideration of the different types and sources of contaminants, their fate as they are transported through and are partitioned, and their impact on different parts of the environment.

CONCERNS

This chapter addresses two concerns related to soil characterization for CERCLA remedial response. The first concern is the applicability of traditional soil classification methods to CERCLA soil characterization. The second is the identification of soil characterization data types required for CERCLA risk assessment and analysis of remedial alternatives. These concerns are related, in that the Data Quality Objective (DQO) process addresses both. The DQO process was developed, in part, to assist CERCLA decision-makers in identifying the data types, data quality, and data quantity required to support decisions that must be made during the RI/FS process. *Data Quality Objectives for Remedial Response Activities: Development Process* (U.S. EPA, 1987a) is a guidebook on developing DQOs. This process as it relates to CERCLA soil characterization is discussed in the Data Quality Objective section of this chapter.

Data types required for soil characterization must be determined early in the RI/FS process, using the DQO process. Often, the first soil data types related to risk assessment and remedial alternative selection available during a CERCLA site investigation are soil textural descriptions from the borehole logs prepared by a geologist during investigations of the nature and extent of contamination. These boreholes might include installation of ground-water monitoring wells, or soil boreholes. Typically, borehole logs contain soil lithology and textural descriptions, based on visual analysis of drill cuttings.

Preliminary site data are potentially valuable, and can provide modelers and engineers with data to begin preparation of the conceptual model and perform scoping calculations. Soil texture affects movement of air and water in soil, infiltration rate, porosity, water holding capacity, and other parameters. Changes in lithology identify heterogeneities in the subsurface (i.e., low permeability layers, etc.). Soil textural classification is therefore important to contaminant fate and transport modeling, and to screening and analysis of remedial alternatives. However, unless collected properly, soil textural descriptions are of limited value for the following reasons:

1.   There are several different systems for classification of soil particles with respect to size. To address this problem it is important to identify which system has been or will be used to classify a soil so that data can be properly compared. Figure 14-1 can be used to compare the different systems (Gee and Bauder, 1986). *Keys to Soil Taxonomy* (Soil Survey Staff, 1994) provides details to one of the more useful systems that should be consulted prior to classifying a site's soils.

2.   The accuracy of the field classification is dependent on the skill of the observer. To overcome this concern RPMs and OSCs should collect soil textural data that are quantitative rather than qualitative. Soil texture can be determined from a soil sample by sieve analysis or hydrometer. These data types are superior to qualitative description based on visual analysis and are more likely to meet DQOs.

3.   Even if the field person accurately classifies a soil (e.g., as a silty sand or a sandy loam), textural descriptions do not afford accurate estimations of actual physical properties required for modeling and remedial alternative evaluation, such as hydraulic conductivity. For example, the hydraulic conductivity of silty-sand can range from 10^{-5} to 10^{-1} cm/sec (four orders of magnitude).

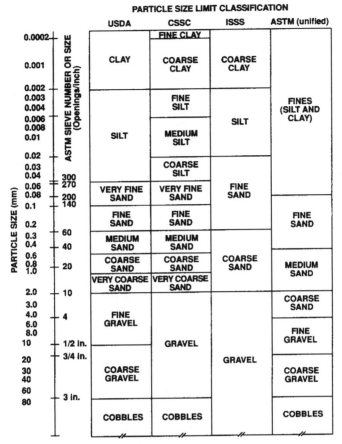

Figure 14-1. Particle-size limits according to several current classification schemes. (Gee and Bauder, 1986).

These ranges of values may be used for bounding calculations, or to assist in preparation of the preliminary conceptual model. These data may therefore meet DQOs for initial screening of remedial alternatives, for example, but will likely not meet DQOs for detailed analysis of alternatives.

DATA QUALITY OBJECTIVES

EPA has developed the Data Quality Objective (DQO) process to guide CERCLA site characterization. The relationship between CERCLA RI/FS activities and the DQO process is shown in Figure 14-2 (U.S. EPA, 1988c, 1987a). The DQO process occurs in three stages:

- *Stage 1. Identify Decision Types.* In this stage the types of decisions that must be made during the RI/FS are identified.

  The types of decisions vary throughout the RI/FS process, but in general they become increasingly quantitative as the process proceeds. During this stage it is important to identify and involve the data users (e.g., modelers, engineers, and scientists), evaluate available data, develop a conceptual site model, and specify objectives and decisions.

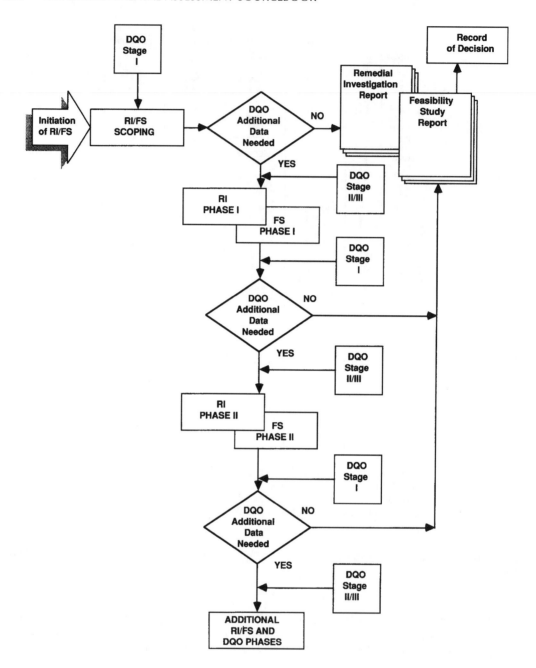

Figure 14-2. Phased RI/FS approach and the DQO process (U.S. EPA, 1987a).

- *Stage 2. Identify Data Uses/Needs.* In this stage data uses are defined. This includes identification of the required data types, data quality and data quantity required to make decisions on how to:
  — Perform risk assessment
  — Perform contaminant fate and transport modeling
  — Identify and screen remedial alternatives

- *Stage 3. Design Data Collection Program.* After Stage 1 and 2 activities have been defined and reviewed, a data collection program addressing the data types, data quantity (number of samples) and data quality required to make these decisions needs to be developed as part of a sampling and analysis plan.

Although this chapter focuses on data types required for decision-making in the CERCLA RI/FS process related to soil contamination, references are provided to address data quantity quality issues.

Data Types

The OSC or RPM must determine which soil parameters are needed to make various RI/FS decisions. The types of decisions to be made therefore drive selection of data types. Data types required for RI/FS activities including risk assessment, contaminant fate and transport modeling, and remedial alternative selection are discussed in Soil Characteristics Data Types Required for Modeling section, and the Soil Characterization Data Type Required for Remedial Alternative Selection section.

Data Quality

The RPM or OSC must decide "How good does the data need to be in order for me to make a given decision?" EPA has assigned quality levels to different RI/FS activities as a guideline. Data Quality Objectives for Remedial Response Activities (U.S. EPA, 1987a) offers guidance on this subject and contains many useful references.

Data Quantity

The RPM or OSC must decide "How many samples do I need to determine the mean and standard deviation of a given parameter at a given site?," or "How does a given parameter vary spatially across the site?" Decisions of this type must be addressed by statistical design of the sampling effort. The *Soil Sampling Quality Assurance User's Guide* (Barth et al., 1989) and *Data Quality Objectives for Remedial Response Activities* (U.S. EPA, 1987a) offer guidance on this subject and contain many useful references.

IMPORTANT SOIL CHARACTERISTICS IN SITE EVALUATION

Tables 14-1 and 14-2 identify methods for collecting and determining data types for soil characteristics either in the field, laboratory, or by calculation. Soil characteristics in Table 14-1 are considered the primary indicators that are needed to complete Phase I of the RI/FS process. This is a short, but concise list of soil data types that are needed to make CERCLA decisions and should be planned for and collected early in the sampling effort. These primary data types should allow for the initial screening of remedial treatment alternatives and preliminary modeling of the site for risk assessment. Many of these characteristics can be obtained relatively inexpensively during periods of early field work when the necessary drilling and sampling equipment are already on site. Investigators should plan to collect data for all the soil characteristics at the same locations and times soil boring is done to install monitoring wells. Geophysical logging of the well should also be considered as a cost effective method for collecting lithologic information prior to casing the well. Data quality and quantity must also be considered before beginning collection of the appropriate data types.

The soil characteristics in Table 14-2 are considered ancillary only because they are needed in the later stages and tasks of the DQO process and the RI/FS process. If the site budget allows, collection of these data types during early periods of field work will improve the database available to make decisions on remedial treatment selection and model-based risk assessments. Advanced planning and knowledge of the need for the ancillary soil characteristics should be factored into early site work to reduce overall costs and the time required to reach a ROD. A small additional investment to collect ancillary data during early site visits is almost always more cost effective than having to send crews back to the field to conduct additional soil sampling.

Further detailed descriptions of the soil characteristics in Tables 14-1 and 14-2 can be found in *Fundamentals of Soil Physics* and *Applications of Soil Physics* (Hillel, 1980a; see also Hillel, 1980b) and in a series of articles by Dragun (1988a,b,c). These references provide excellent discussions of these characteristics and their influence on water movement in soils as well as contaminant fate and transport.

Table 14-1. Measurement Methods for Primary Soil Characteristics Needed to Support CERCLA Decision-Making Process

| Soil Characteristic[a] | Measurement Technique/Method (w/Reference) | | Calculation or Lookup Method |
	Field	Laboratory	
Bulk density	Neutron probe (ASTM D2922), Gamma radiation (Blake and Hartge, 1986; Blake, 1965).	Coring or excavation for lab analysis (Blake and Hartge, 1986).	Not applicable.
Soil pH	Measured in field in same manner as in laboratory.	Using a glass electrode in an aqueous slurry (Thompson et al., 1989). Analytical Method—Method 9045, U.S. EPA (1986).	Not applicable.
Texture	Collect composite sample for each soil type. No field methods are available, except through considerable experience of "feeling" the soil for an estimation of % sand, silt, and clay.	ASTM D422. Sieve analysis better at hazardous waste sites because organics can effect hydrometer analysis.	Not applicable.
Depth to ground water	Ground-water monitoring wells or piezometers using EPA approved methods (Barcelona et al., 1985).	Not applicable.	Not applicable.
Horizons or stratigraphy	Soil pits dug with backhoe are best. If safety and cost are a concern, soil bores can be collected with either a thin wall sample driver or Veihmeyer tube (Brown et al., 1990).	Not applicable.	May be possible to obtain information from SCS soil survey for the site.
Hydraulic conductivity (saturated)	Auger-hole and piezometer methods (Amoozegar and Warrick, 1986) and Guelph permeameter (Reynolds and Elrick, 1985; 1986).	Constant head and falling head methods (Amoozegar and Warrick, 1986).	Although there are tables available that list the values for the saturated hydraulic conductivity, it should be understood that the values are given for specific soil textures that may not be the same as those on the site.

Water retention (soil water characteristic curves)	Field methods require a considerable amount of time, effort, and equipment. For a good discussion of these methods refer to Bruce and Luxmoore (1986).	Obtained through wetting or drainage of core samples through a series of known pressure heads from low to high or high to low, respectively (Klute, 1986).	Some lookup and estimation methods are available; however, due to high spatial variability in this characteristic they are not generally recommended unless their use is justified.
Air permeability and water content relationships	None.	Several methods have been used; however, all use disturbed soil samples. For field applications the structure of soils is very important. For more information refer to Corey (1986).	Estimation methods for air permeability exist that closely resemble the estimation methods for unsaturated hydraulic conductivity. Example models, those developed by Brooks and Corey (1964) and van Genuchten (1980).
Porosity (pore volume)		Gas pycnometer (Danielson and Sutherland, 1986).	Calculated from particle and bulk densities (Danielson and Sutherland, 1986).
Climate	Precipitation measured using either Sacramento gauge for accumulated value or weighing gauge or tipping bucket gauge for continuous measurement (Finkelstein et al., 1983; Kite, 1979). Soil temperature measured using thermocouple.	Not applicable.	Data are provided in the Climatic Atlas of the United States or are available from the National Climatic Data Center, Asheville, NC, Telephone (704) 259-0682.

[a] Soil characteristics are discussed in general except where specific cases relate to different waste types (i.e., metals, hydrophobic organics or polar organics).

Table 14-2. Measurement Methods for Ancillary Soil Parameters Needed to Support CERCLA Decision-Making Process

| Soil Characteristic[a] | Measurement Technique/Method (w/Reference) | | |
	Field	Laboratory	Calculation or Lookup Method
Organic carbon	Not applicable.	High temperature combustion (either wet or dry) and oxidation techniques (Powell et al., 1989) (Powell, 1990). (Rhoades, 1982).	Not applicable.
Cation Exchange Capacity (CEC)	See Rhoades for field methods.	Not applicable.	Estimated using standard equations and graphs (Israelsen et al., 1980) field data for slope, field length, and cover type required as input. Soils data can be obtained from the local Soil Conservation Service (SCS) office.
Erodibility			
Water erosion: Universal Soil Loss Equation (USLE) or Revised USLE (RUSLE)	Measurement/survey of slope (in ft rise/ft run or %), length of field, vegetative cover.	Not applicable.	A modified universal soil loss equation (USLE) (Williams, 1975) presented in Mills et al. (1985), and U.S. EPA (1988d) source for equations.
Wind erosion	Air monitoring for mass of containment. Field length along prevailing wind direction.	Not applicable.	The SCS wind loss equation (Israelsen et al., 1980) must be adjusted (reduced) to account for suspended particles of diameter 10 m. See Cowherd et al. (1985), for a rapid evaluation (24 hr) of particle emission for a Superfund site. See also U.S. EPA (1985).
Vegetative cover	Visual observation and documented using map. USDA can aid in identification of unknown vegetation.	Not applicable.	
Soil structure	Classified into 10 standard kinds—see local SCS office for assistance (Soil Survey Staff, 1994) or Taylor and Ashcroft (1972), p. 310.	Not applicable.	See local soil survey for the site.

Soil characteristic	Field method	Laboratory method	Comment
Organic carbon partition coefficient (K_{oc})	In situ tracer tests (Freeze and Cherry, 1979).	ASTM E1195	Calculated from K_{ow}, water solubility (Mills et al., 1985; Sims et al., 1986).
Redox couple ratios of waste/soil system	Platinum electrode used on lysimeter sample (ASTM D1498).	Same as field.	Can be calculated from concentrations of redox pairs or O_2 (Stumm and Morgan, 1981).
Linear soil/water partition coefficient	*In situ* tracer tests (Freeze and Cherry, 1979).	Batch experiment (Ash et al., 1973); column tests (van Genuchten and Wierenga, 1986).	Mills et al., 1985.
Soil oxygen content (aeration)	O_2 by membrane electrode O_2 diffusion rate by Pt microelectrode (Phene, 1986). O_2 by field GC (Smith, 1983).	Same as field.	Calculated from pE (Stumm and Morgan, 1981) or from O_2 and soil-gas diffusion rate.
Soil temperature (as it affects volatilization)	Thermometry (Taylor and Jackson, 1986).	Same as field.	
Clay mineralogy	Parent material analysis.	X-ray diffraction (Whittig and Allardice, 1986).	Brown and Associates (1983).
Unsaturated hydraulic conductivity	Unsteady drainage-flux (or instantaneous profile) method and simplified unsteady drainage flux method (Green et al., 1986). The instantaneous profile method was initially developed as a laboratory method (Watson, 1966); however, it was adapted to the field (Hillel et al., 1972). Constant-head borehole infiltration (Amoozegar and Warrick, 1986).	Not usually done; results very difficult to obtain.	A number of estimation methods exists, each with their own set of assumptions and requirements. Reviews have been presented by Mualem (1986), and van Genuchten et al. (1992).
Moisture content	Two types of techniques—indirect and direct. Direct methods, (i.e., gravimetric sampling), considered the most accurate, with no calibration required. However, methods are destructive to field systems. Methods involve collecting samples, weighing, drying and re-weighing to determine field moisture. Indirect methods rely on calibration (Gardner, 1986).		
Soil biota	No standard method exists (see model or remedial technology for input or remedial evaluation procedures).	No standard methods exists; can use agar plate count using MOSA method 99-3.	

a Soil characteristics are discussed in general except where specific cases relate to different waste types (i.e., metals, hydrophobic organics or polar organics).

SOIL CHARACTERISTICS DATA TYPES REQUIRED FOR MODELING

The information presented here is not intended as a review of all data types required for all models, instead it presents a sampling of the more appropriate models used in risk assessment and remedial design.

Uses of Vadose Zone Models for CERCLA Remedial Response Activities

Models are used in the CERCLA RI/FS process to estimate contaminant fate and transport. These estimates of contaminant behavior in the environment are subsequently used for:

- *Risk assessment.* Risk assessment includes contaminant release assessment, exposure assessment, and determining risk-based clean-up levels. Each of these activities requires estimation of the rates and extents of contaminant movement in the vadose zone, and of transformation and degradation processes.
- *Effectiveness assessment of remedial alternatives.* This task may also require determination of the rates and extents of contaminant movement in the vadose zone, and of rates and extents of transformation and degradation processes. Technology-specific data requirements are cited in the Soil Characterization Data Type Required for Remedial Alternative Selection section.

The types, quantities, and quality of site characterization data required for modeling should be carefully considered during RI/FS scoping. Several currently available vadose zone fate and transport models are listed in Table 14-3. Soil characterization data types required for each model are included in the table. Model documentation should be consulted for specific questions concerning uses and applications.

The Superfund Exposure Assessment Manual discusses various vadose zone models (U.S. EPA, 1988d). This document should be consulted to select codes that are EPA-approved.

Data Types Required for Modeling

Soil characterization data types required for modeling are included in Tables 14-1 and 14-2. Most of the models are one- or two-dimensional solutions to the advection-dispersion equation, applied to unsaturated flow. Each is different in the extent to which transformation and degradation processes may be simulated; various contaminant release scenarios are accommodated; heterogeneous soils and other site-specific characteristics are accounted for. Each, therefore, has different data type input requirements.

All models require physicochemical data for the contaminants of concern. These data are available in the literature, and from EPA databases (U.S. EPA, 1988c,d). The amount of physicochemical data required is generally related to the complexity of the model. The models that account for biodegradation of organics, vapor phase diffusion and other processes require more input data than the relatively simpler transport models.

Data Quality and Quantity Required for Modeling

DQOs for the modeling task should be defined during RI/FS scoping. The output of any computer model is only as valid as the quality of the input data and code itself. Variance may result from the data collection methodology or analytical process, or as a result of spatial variability in the soil characteristic being measured.

In general, the physical and chemical properties of soils vary spatially. This variation rarely follows well defined trends; rather it exhibits a stochastic (i.e., random) character. However, the stochastic character of many soil properties tends to follow classic statistical distributions. For example, properties such as bulk density and effective porosity of soils tend to be normally distributed (Campbell, 1985). Saturated hydraulic conductivity, in contrast, is often found to follow a log-normal distribu-

Table 14-3. Soil Characteristics Required for Vadose Zone Models

Properties and Parameters	Help (A,B)	Sesoil (C,D)	Creams (E,F)	PRZM (G,H,I)	Vadoft (H,J)	Minteq (J)	Fowl™ (K)	Ritz (L)	Vip (M)	Chemflo (N)
						Model Name [Reference(s)]				
Soil bulk density	■	●	●	●	●	■	●	●	●	●
Soil pH	▶	●	■	▶	▶	●	●	▶	▶	▶
Soil texture	●	■	■	●	●	■	■	●	▶	▶
Depth to ground water	■	■	●	■	●	●	■	■	●	■
Horizons (soil layering)	●	●	●	●	●	■	■	■	■	■
Saturated hydraulic conductivity	●	●	●	●	●	■	●	■	■	■
Water retention	●	●	●	●	●	■	●	●	●	●
Air permeability	▶	●	▶	●	●	■	▶	▶	▶	●
Climate (precipitation)	●	●	●	●	●	▶	●	■	●	▶
Soil porosity	●	●	●	●	■	▶	■	●	●	●
Soil organic content	▶	●	●	●	●	■	■	●	●	■
Cation Exchange Capacity (CEC)	▶	●	▶	▶	●	●	▶	●	●	■
					▶	●		▶	▶	▶
Degradation parameters	●	●	●	●	●	▶	▶	●	●	●
Soil grain size distribution	▶	■	■	■	■	▶	▶	▶	▶	▶
Soil redox potential	▶	■	■	▶	▶	●	▶	▶	▶	■
Soil/water partition coefficients	▶	●	●	●	●	●	●	●	●	●
Soil oxygen content	●	■	▶	▶	▶	■	▶	▶	●	▶
Soil temperature	■	●	■	●	●	●	■	●	●	▶
Soil mineralogy	▶	●	▶	▶	▶	■	▶	▶	▶	■
Unsaturated hydraulic conductivity	●	●	●	●	●	■	●	▶	▶	●

Table 14-3. Continued

Properties and Parameters	Model Name [Reference(s)]									
	Help (A,B)	Sesoil (C,D)	Creams (E,F)	PRZM (G,H,I)	Vadoft (H,I)	Minteq (J)	Fowl™ (K)	Ritz (L)	Vip (M)	Chemflo (N)
Saturated soil moisture content	●	●	●	●	●	■	●	●	●	●
Microorganism population	▼	■	▼	▼	▼	▼	▼	▼	■	▼
Soil respiration	▼	■	▼	▼	▼	▼	▼	▼	■	▼
Evaporation	●	●	●	●	■	▼	▼	●	●	●
Air/water contaminant densities	■	■	■	■	▼	■	●	●	●	■
Air/water contaminant viscosities	■	■	■	■	■	▼	■	■	■	■

● Required; ▼ Not required; ■ Used indirectly[a]

References: A. Schroeder, et al., 1984a; B. Schroeder, et al., 1984b; C. Bonazountas and Wagner, 1984; D. Chen et al., 1987; E. Leonard and Ferreira, 1984; F. Devaurs and Springer, 1988; G. Carsel et al., 1984; J.D. Dean et al., 1989a; I. Dean et al., 1989b; J. Brown and Allison, 1987; K. Hostetler et al., 1988; L. Nofziger and Williams, 1988; M. Stevens et al., 1989; N. Nofziger et al., 1989.

[a] Used in their estimation of other required characteristics or the interpretation of the models, but not directly entered as input to models.

tion. Characterization of a site, therefore, should be performed in such a manner as to permit the determination of the statistical characteristics (i.e., mean and variance) and their spatial correlations.

Significant advances have been made in understanding and describing the spatial variability of soil properties (Neilsen and Bouma, 1985). Geostatistical methods and techniques (Clark, 1982; Davis, 1986) are available for statistically characterizing soil properties important to contaminant migration. Information gained from a geostatistical analysis of data can be used for three major purposes:

- Determining the heterogeneity and complexity of the site;
- Guiding the data collection and interpretation effort and thus identifying areas where additional sampling may be needed (to reduce uncertainty by estimating error); and
- Providing data for a stochastic model of fluid flow and contaminant migration.

One of the geostatistical tools useful to help in the interpolation or mapping of a site is referred to as kriging (Davis, 1986). General kriging computer codes are presently available. Application of this type of tool, however, requires an adequate sample size. As a rule of thumb, 50 or more data points are needed to construct the semivariogram required for use in kriging. The benefit of using kriging in site characterization is that it allows one to take point measurements and estimate soil characteristics at any point within the domain of interest, such as grid points, for a computer model. Geostatistical packages are available from the U.S. EPA, Geo-EAS and GEOPACK (Englund and Sparks, 1991 and Yates and Yates, 1990).

The use of stochastic models in hydrogeology has increased significantly in recent years. Two stochastic approaches that have been widely used are the first order uncertainty method (Dettinger and Wilson, 1981) and Monte Carlo methods (Clifton et al., 1985; Sagar et al., 1986; Eslinger and Sagar, 1988). Andersson and Shapiro (1983) have compared these two approaches for the case of steady-state unsaturated flow. The Monte Carlo methods are more general and easier to implement than the first order uncertainty methods. However, the Monte Carlo method is more computationally intensive, particularly for multidimensional problems.

Application of stochastic models to hazardous waste sites has two main advantages. First, this approach provides a rigorous way to assess the uncertainty associated with the spatial variability of soil properties. Second, the approach produces model predictions in terms of the likelihood of outcomes, i.e., probability of exceeding water quality standards. The use of models at hazardous waste sites leads to a thoughtful and objective treatment of compliance issues and concerns.

In order to obtain accurate results with models, quality data types must be used. The issue of quality and confidence in data can be partially addressed by obtaining as representative data as possible. Good quality assurance and quality control plans must be in place for not only the acquisition of samples, but also for the application of the models (van der Heijde et al., 1989).

Specific soil characteristics vary both laterally and vertically in an undisturbed soil profile. Different soil characteristics have different variances. As an example, the sample size required to have 95 percent probability of detecting a change of 20 percent in the mean bulk density at a specific site was 6; however, for saturated hydraulic conductivity the sample size would need to be 502 (Jury, 1986). A good understanding of site soil characteristics can help the investigators understand these variations. This is especially true for most hazardous waste sites because the soils have often been disturbed, which may cause even greater variability.

An important aspect of site characterization data and models is that the modeling process is dynamic, i.e., as an increasing number of "simplifying" assumptions are needed, the complexity of the models must increase to adequately simulate the additional processes that must be included. Such simplifying assumptions might include an isotropic homogeneous medium or the presence of only one mobile phase (Weaver et al., 1989). In order to decrease the number of assumptions required, there is usually a need to increase the number of site-specific soil characteristic data types in a model (see Table 14-2); thus providing greater confidence in the values produced. For complex sites, an iterative process of initial data collection and evaluation leading to more data collection and evaluation until an acceptable level of confidence in the evaluation can be reached can be used.

Table 14-3 identifies selected unsaturated zone models and their soil characteristic needs. For specific questions regarding use and application of the model, the reader should refer to the associated manuals. Some of these models are also reviewed by Donigian and Rao (1986) and van der Heijde et al. (1988).

SOIL CHARACTERISTICS DATA TYPES REQUIRED FOR REMEDIAL ALTERNATIVE SELECTION

Remedial Alternative Selection Procedure

The CERCLA process involves the identification, screening and analysis of remedial alternatives at uncontrolled hazardous waste sites (U.S. EPA, 1988c). During screening and analysis, decision values for process-limiting characteristics for a given remedial alternative are compared to site-specific values of those characteristics. If site-specific values are outside the range required for effective use of a particular alternative, that alternative is less likely to be selected. Site soil conditions are critical process-limiting characteristics.

Process-Limiting Characteristics

Process-limiting characteristics are site- and waste-specific data types that are critical to the effectiveness and ability to implement remedial processes. Often, process-limiting characteristics are descriptors of rate-limiting steps in the overall remedial process. In some cases, limitations imposed by process-limiting characteristics can be overcome by adjustment of soil characteristics such as pH, soil moisture content, temperature and others. In other cases, the level of effort required to overcome these limitations will preclude use of a remedial process.

Decision values for process limiting characteristics are increasingly available in the literature, and may be calculated for processes where design equations are known. Process limiting characteristics are identified and decision values are given for several vadose zone remedial alternatives in Table 14-4. For waste/site characterization, process-limiting characteristics may be broadly grouped in four categories:

1.   Mass transport characteristics
2.   Soil reaction characteristics
3.   Contaminant properties
4.   Engineering characteristics

Thorough soil characterization is required to determine site specific values for process-limiting characteristics. Most remedial alternatives will have process-limiting characteristics in more than one category.

Mass Transport Characteristics

Mass transport is the bulk flow, or advection of fluids through soil. Mass transport characteristics are used to calculate potential rates of movement of liquids or gases through soil and include:

    Soil texture
    Unsaturated hydraulic conductivity
    Dispersivity
    Moisture content vs. soil moisture tension
    Bulk density
    Porosity
    Permeability
    Infiltration rate, stratigraphy and others.

Mass transport processes are often process-limiting for both *in situ* and extract-and-treat vadose zone remedial alternatives (Table 14-4). *In situ* alternatives frequently use a gas or liquid mobile phase to move reactants or nutrients through contaminated soil. Alternatively, extract-and-treat processes such as soil vapor extraction (SVE) or soil flushing use a gas or liquid mobile phase to move contaminants to a surface treatment site. For either type of process to be effective, mass transport rates must be large enough to clean up a site within a reasonable time.

Table 14-4. Soil Characterization Characteristics Required for Remedial Technology Evaluation, (Chambers et al., 1990; Galer, 1988; U.S. EPA, 1988e; 1989; 1991; Sims, 1990; Towers et al., 1988)

Technology	Process Limiting Characteristics	Site Data Required
Pretreatment/materials handling	Large particles interfere	Particle size distribution
	Clayey soils or hardpan difficult to handle	
	Wet soils difficult to handle	Soil moisture content
Soil vapor extraction	Applicable only to volatile organics w/significant vapor pressure >1 mm Hg	Contaminants present
	Low soil permeability inhibits air movement	Soil permeability
	Soil hydraulic conductivity >1E-8 cm/sec required	Hydraulic conductivity
	Depth to ground water >20 ft recommended	Depth to ground water
	High moisture content inhibits air movement	Soil moisture content
	High organic matter content inhibits contaminant removal	Organic matter content
In situ enhanced bioremediation	Applicable only to specific organics	Contaminants present
	Hydraulic conductivity >1E-4 cm/sec preferred to transport nutrients	Hydraulic conductivity
	Stratification should be minimal	Soil stratigraphy
	Lower permeability layers difficult to remediate	Soil stratigraphy
	Temperature 15–45°C required	Soil temperature
	Moisture content 40–80% of that at -1/3 bars tension preferred	Soil moisture characteristic curves
	pH 4.5–8.5 required	Soil pH
	Presence of microbes required	Plate count
	Minimum 10% air-filled porosity required for aeration	Porosity and soil moisture content

Table 14-4. Continued

Technology	Process Limiting Characteristics	Site Data Required
Thermal treatment	Applicable only to organics	Contaminants present
	Soil moisture content affects handling and heating requirements	Soil moisture content
	Particle size affects feeding and residuals	Particle size distribution
	pH <5 and >11 causes corrosion	pH
Solidification/stabilization	Not equally effective for all contaminants	Contaminants present
	Fine particles < No. 200 mesh may interfere	Particle size distribution
	Oil and grease >10% may interfere	Oil and grease
Chemical extraction (slurry reactors)	Not equally effective for all contaminants	Contaminants present
	Particle size <0.25 in.	Particle size distribution
	pH <10	pH
Soil washing	Not equally effective for all contaminants	Contaminants present
	Silt and clay difficult to remove from wash fluid	Particle size distribution
Soil flushing	Not equally effective for all contaminants	Contaminants present
	Required number of pore volumes	Infiltration rate and porosity
Glycolate dechlorination	Not equally effective for all contaminants	Contaminants present
	Moisture content <20%	Moisture content
	Low organic matter content required	Organic carbon
Chemical oxidation/reduction (slurry reactor)	Not equally effective for all contaminants	Contaminants present
	Oxidizable organics interfere	Organic carbon
	pH <2 interferes	pH
In situ vitrification	Maximum moisture content of 25% by weight	Moisture content
	Particle size <4 inches	Particle size distribution
	Requires soil hydraulic conductivity <1E-5 cm/sec	Hydraulic conductivity

Soil Reaction Characteristics

Soil reaction characteristics describe contaminant-soil interactions. Soil reactions include bio- and physicochemical reactions that occur between the contaminants and the site soil. Rates of reactions such as biodegradation, hydrolysis, sorption/desorption, precipitation/dissolution, redox reactions, acid-base reactions, and others are process-limiting characteristics for many remedial alternatives (Table 14-4). Soil reaction characteristics include:

K_d, specific to the site soils and contaminants
Cation exchange capacity (CEC)
Eh
pH
Soil biota
Soil nutrient content
Contaminant abiotic/biological degradation rates
Soil mineralogy
Contaminant properties, described below, and others.

Soil reaction characteristics determine the effectiveness of many remedial alternatives. For example, the ability of a soil to attenuate metals (typically described by K_d) may determine the effectiveness of an alternative that relies on capping and natural attenuation to immobilize contaminants.

Soil Contaminant Properties

Contaminant properties are critical to contaminant-soil interactions, contaminant mobility, and to the ability of treatment technologies to remove, destroy or immobilize contaminants. Important contaminant properties include:

Water solubility
Dielectric constant
Diffusion coefficient
K_{oc}
K_d
Molecular weight
Vapor pressure
Density
Aqueous solution chemistry, and others.

Soil contaminant properties will determine the effectiveness of many treatment techniques. For example, the aqueous solution chemistry of metal contaminants often dictates the potential effectiveness of stabilization/solidification alternatives.

Soil Engineering Characteristics and Properties

Engineering characteristics and properties of the soil relate both to implementability and effectiveness of the remedial action. Examples include the ability of the treatment method to remove, destroy or immobilize contaminants, the costs and difficulties in installing slurry walls and other containment options at depths greater than 60 feet; the ability of the site to withstand vehicle traffic (trafficability); costs and difficulties in deep excavation of contaminated soil; the ability of soil to be worked for implementation of *in situ* treatment technologies (tilth); and others. Knowledge of site-specific engineering characteristics and properties is therefore required for analysis of effectiveness and implementability of remedial alternatives. Engineering characteristics and properties include, but are not limited to:

Trafficability
Erodability
Tilth
Depth to ground water
Thickness of saturated zone
Depth and total volume of contaminated soil
Bearing capacity, and others.

SUMMARY AND CONCLUSIONS

The goal of the CERCLA RI/FS process is to reach a ROD in a timely manner. Soil characterization is critical to this goal. Soil characterization provides data for RI/FS tasks including determination of the nature and extent of contamination, risk assessment, and selection of remedial techniques.

This chapter is intended to inform investigators of the data types required for RI/FS tasks so that data may be collected as quickly, efficiently, and cost effectively as possible. This knowledge should improve the consistency of site evaluations, improve the ability of OSCs and RPMs to communicate data needs to site contractors, and aid in the overall goal of reaching a ROD in a timely manner.

EPA CONTACTS

For further information contact: Ken Brown, EPA Technical Support Center for Monitoring and Site Characterization, Las Vegas, NV, 702/798-2270; Robert Breckenridge at 208/526-0757.

ACKNOWLEDGMENTS

This chapter was prepared through support from EMSL-LV and RSKERL, under the direction of R.P. Breckenridge, with the support of the Superfund Technical Support Project. EMSL-Las Vegas and RSKERL-Ada convened a technical committee of experts to examine the issue and provide technical guidance based on current scientific information. Members of the committee were Joe R. Williams, RSKERL-Ada; Robert G. Baca, Robert P. Breckenridge, Alan B. Crockett, and John F. Keck from the Idaho National Engineering Laboratory, Idaho Falls, ID; Gretchen L. Rupp, PE, University of Nevada-Las Vegas; and Ken Brown; EMSL-LV.

This document was compiled by the authors and edited by the members of the committee and a group of peer reviewers.

CITED ASTM STANDARDS

(ASTM's new address, as of October 1995 is 100 Barr Harbor Drive, West Conshohocken, PA 19428-29590)

D422. Test Method for Particle-Size Analysis of Soils (Vol. 4.08).

D1498. Practice for Oxidation-Reduction Potential of Water (Vol. 11.01).

D2487. Test Method for Classification of Soils for Engineering Purposes (Vol. 4.08).

D2922. Test Method for Density of Soil and Soil Aggregate in Place by Nuclear Methods (Shallow Depth) (Vol. 4.08).

E1195. Test Method for Determining a Sorption Constant (K_{oc}) for an Organic Chemical in Soil and Sediments (Vol. 11.02).

REFERENCES

Amoozegar, A. and A.W. Warrick. 1986. Hydraulic Conductivity of Saturated Soils. In: A. Klute (ed.), Methods of Soil Analysis Part 1: Physical and Mineralogical Methods, 2nd edition. American Society of Agronomy, Madison, WI.

Andersson, J. and A.M. Shapiro. 1983. Stochastic Analysis of One-Dimensional Steady-State Unsaturated Flow: A Comparison of Monte Carlo and Perturbation Methods. Water Resources Research, 19(1):121–133.

Ash, S.G., R. Brown, and D.H. Everett. 1973. A High-Precision Apparatus for the Determination of Adsorption at the Interface Between a Solid and a Solution. J. Chem. Thermodynamics 5:239–246.

Barcelona, M.J., J.P. Gibb, J.A. Helfrich, and E.E. Garske. 1985. Practical Guide for Ground-Water Sampling. EPA/600/2-85/104 (NTIS PB86-137304).

Barth, D.S., B.J. Mason, T.H. Starks, and K.W. Brown. 1989. Soil Sampling Quality Assurance User's Guide. EPA 60018-89/046, (NTIS PB89-189864).

Blake G.R. 1965. Bulk Density. In: C.A. Black (ed.), Methods of Soil Analysis. Part 1. American Society of Agronomy, Madison, WI.

Blake, G.R. and K.H. Hartge. 1986. Bulk density. In: A. Klute (ed.), Methods of Soil Analysis Part 1: Physical and Mineralogical Methods, 2nd edition. American Society of Agronomy, Madison, WI.

Bonazountas, M. and J.M. Wagner. 1984. SESOIL: A Seasonal Soil Compartment Model. Contract No. 68-01-6271. Draft Report from Arthur D. Little, Inc. U.S. EPA Office of Toxic Substances, Washington, DC.

Brady, N.C. 1974. The Nature and Properties of Soils. MacMillan, New York, NY. [Not cited in text.]

Brooks, R.H. and A.T. Corey. 1964. Hydraulic Properties of Porous Media. Hydrology Paper No. 3. Colorado State University, Fort Collins, CO, 27 pp.

Brown, D.S. and J.D. Allison. 1987. MINTEQA1, an Equilibrium Metal Speciation Model: A User's Manual. EPA/600/3-87/012 (NTIS PB88-144167), 103 pp.

Brown, K.W. and Associates. 1983. Hazardous Waste Land Treatment. EPA SW-874 (PB89-179014).

Brown, K.W., R.P. Breckenridge, and R.C. Rope. 1990. U.S. Fish and Wildlife Service Contaminant Monitoring Operations Manual: Appendix J, Soil Sampling Reference Field Methods. EGG-EST-9222. EG&G Idaho, Idaho Falls, ID.

Bruce, R.R. and R.J. Luxmoore. 1986. Water Retention: Field Methods. In: A. Klute (ed.), Methods of Soil Analysis Part 1: Physical and Mineralogical Methods, 2nd edition. American Society of Agronomy, Madison, WI.

Campbell, G.S. 1985. Soil Physics with Basic. Elsevier, New York, NY.

Carsel, R.F., C.N. Smith, L.A. Mulkey, J.D. Dean, and P. Jowise. 1984. Users Manual for the Pesticide Root Zone Model (PRZM): Release 1. EPA/600/3-84/109 (NTIS PB85-158913).

Chambers, L.D. et al. [7 authors] 1990. Handbook of In Situ Treatment of Hazardous Waste Contaminated Soils. EPA/540/2-90/002 (NTIS PB90-155607), 157 pp.

Chen, J., S. Wollman, and J. Liu. 1987. User's Guide to SESOIL. Execution in GEMS. GSC-TR8747. Prepared by General Sciences Corporation. U.S. EPA Office of Pesticides and Toxic Substances, Washington, DC.

Clark, I. 1982. Practical Geostatistics. Applied Science Publishers, London, England.

Clifton, P.M., R.G. Baca, and R.C. Arnett. 1985. Stochastic Analysis of Groundwater Traveltimes for Long-Term Repository Performance Assessment. In: Proc. of the Materials Research Society Symposium-Scientific Basis for Nuclear Waste Management, Boston. MA.

Corey, A.T. 1986. Air Permeability. In: A. Klute (ed.), Methods of Soil Analysis Part 1: Physical and Mineralogical Methods, 2nd edition. American Society of Agronomy, Madison, WI.

Cowherd, C., G.E. Mulseki, P.J. Englehart, and D.A. Gillette, 1985. Rapid assessment of exposure to particulate emissions from surface contamination sites. NTIS PB85-192219. Midwest Research Institute, Kansas City, MO.

Danielson, R.E. and P.L. Sutherland. 1986. Porosity. In: A. Klute (ed.), Methods of Soil Analysis Part 1: Physical and Mineralogical Methods, 2nd edition. American Society of Agronomy, Madison, WI.

Davis, J.C. 1986. Statistics and Data Analysis in Geology, Second Edition. John Wiley & Sons, New York, NY.

Dean, J.D., P.S. Huyakorn, A.S. Donigian, Jr., K.A. Voos, R.W. Schanz, and R.F. Carsel. 1989. Risk of Unsaturated/Saturated Transport and Transformation of Chemical Concentrations (RUSTIC): Volume I. Theory and Code Verification. EPA/600/3-89/048a. U.S. EPA Environmental Research Laboratory, Athens, GA.

Dettinger, M.D. and J.L. Wilson. 1981. First Order Analysis of Uncertainty in Numerical Models of Groundwater Flow, Part 1, Mathematical Development. Water Resources Research, 16(1):149–161.

Devaurs, M. and E. Springer. 1988. Representing Soil Moisture in Experimental Trench Cover Designs for Waste Burial with the CREAMS Model. Hazardous Waste and Hazardous Material, 5(4):295–312.

Donigian, A.S., Jr. and P.S.C. Rao. 1986. Overview of Terrestrial Processes and Modeling. In: S.C. Hern and S.M. Melancon (eds.), Vadose Zone Modeling of Organic Pollutants. Lewis Publishers, Chelsea, MI.

Dragun, J. 1988a. The Fate of Hazardous Materials in Soil (What Every Geologist and Hydrogeologist Should Know), Part 1. Hazardous Materials Control, 1(2):30–78.

Dragun, J. 1988b. The Fate of Hazardous Materials in Soil (What Every Geologist and Hydrogeologist Should Know), Part 2. Hazardous Materials Control, 1(3):40–65.

Dragun, J. 1988c. The Fate of Hazardous Materials in Soil (What Every Geologist and Hydrogeologist Should Know), Part 3. Hazardous Materials Control, 1(5):24–43.

Englund, E. and A. Sparks. 1991. GEO-EAS 1.2.1 User's Guide. EPA/600/8-91/008. U.S. EPA Environmental Monitoring Systems Laboratory, Las Vegas, NV.

Eslinger, P.W. and B. Sagar. 1988. EPASTAT: A Computer Model for Estimating Releases at the Accessible Environment Boundary of a High-Level Nuclear Waste Repository Mathematical Model and Numerical Model. SD-BWI-TA-022. Rockwell Hanford Operations, Richland, WA.

Finkelstein, F.L., D.A. Mazzarella, T.A. Lockhart, W.J. King, and J.H. White, 1983. Quality Assurance Handbook for Air Pollution Measurement Systems. IV: Meteorological Measurements. EPA-600/4-82-060, Washington, DC.

Freeze, R.A. and J.A. Cherry. 1979. Groundwater. Prentice Hall, Englewood Cliffs, NJ.

Galer. 1988. Technology Screening Guide for Treatment of CERCLA Soils and Sludges. EPA/540/2-88/004 (NTIS PB89-132674), 136 pp.

Gardner, W.H. 1986. Water Content. In: A. Klute (ed.), Methods of Soil Analysis Part 1: Physical and Mineralogical Methods, 2nd edition. American Society of Agronomy, Madison, WI.

Gee, G.W. and J.W. Bauder. 1986. Particle-Size Analysis. In: A. Klute (ed.), Methods of Soil Analysis Part 1: Physical and Mineralogical Methods, 2nd edition. American Society of Agronomy, Madison, WI.

Green, R.E., L.R. Ahuja, and S.K. Chong. 1986. Hydraulic Conductivity, Diffusivity, and Sorptivity of Unsaturated Soils: Field Methods. In: A. Klute (ed.), Methods of Soil Analysis Part 1: Physical and Mineralogical Methods, 2nd edition. American Society of Agronomy, Madison, WI.

Hillel, D. 1980a. Fundamentals of Soil Physics. Academic Press, New York, NY.

Hillel, D., 1980b. Applications of Soil Physics. Academic Press, New York, NY.

Hillel, D., V.D. Krentos, and Y. Stylianou. 1972. Procedure and Test of an Internal Drainage Method for Measuring Soil Hydraulic Characteristics In Situ. Soil Science 114:395–400.

Hostetler C.J., R.L. Erikson, and D. Ral. 1988. The Fossil Fuel Combustion Waste Leaching (FOWL,) Code: Version 1. User's Manual. EPRI EA-57420CCM. Electric Power Research Institute, Palo Alto, CA.

Israelsen, C.E., C.G. Clyde, J.E. Fletcher, E.K. Israelsen, F.W. Haws, P.E. Packer, and E.E. Farmer, 1980. Erosion Control During Highway Construction. Manual on Principles and Practices. Transportation Research Board, National Research Council, Washington, DC.

Jenkins, R.A., W.H. Griest, R.L. Moody, M.V. Buchanan, M.P. Maskarinec, F.F. Dyer, and C.-H. Ho. 1988. Technology Assessment of Field Portable Instrumentation for Use at Rocky Mountain Arsenal. ORNL/TM-10542. Oak Ridge National Laboratory, Oak Ridge, TN.

Jury, W.A.. 1986. Spatial Variability of Soil Properties. In: S.C. Hern and S.M. Melancon (eds.), Vadose Zone Modeling of Organic Pollutants. Lewis Publishers, Chelsea, MI.

Kite, J.W. 1979. Guideline for the Design, Installation, and Operation of a Meteorological System. Radian Corporation, Austin, TX.

Klute, A. 1986. Water Retention: Laboratory Methods. In: A. Klute (ed.), Methods of Soil Analysis Part 1: Physical and Mineralogical Methods, 2nd edition. American Society of Agronomy, Madison, WI.

Leonard, R.A. and V.A. Ferreira. 1984. CREAMS2 - The Nutrient and Pesticide Models. In: Proceedings of the Natural Resources Modeling Symposium, U.S. Department of Agriculture.

McKeague, J.A. (ed.). 1978. Manual on Soil Sampling and Methods of Analysis, 2nd edition. Canadian Society Soil Science, Ottawa, Ontario.

Mills, W.B., D.B. Procella, M.J. Ungs, S.A. Gherini, K.V. Summers, L. Mok, G.L. Rupp, G.L. Bowie, and D.A. Haith, 1985. Water Quality Assessment: A Screening Procedure for Toxic and Conventional Pollutants in Surface and Ground Water. EPA/600/6-85-002a&b,

Mualem, Y. 1986. Hydraulic Conductivity of Unsaturated Soils: Prediction and Formulas. In: A. Klute (ed.), Methods of Soil Analysis Part 1: Physical and Mineralogical Methods, 2nd edition. American Society of Agronomy, Madison, WI.

Neilson, D.R. and J. Bouma (eds.). 1985. Soil Spatial Variability. Center for Agricultural Publishing and Documentation, Wageningen, The Netherlands.

Nofziger, D.L. and J.R. Williams. 1988. Interactive Simulation of the Fate of Hazardous Chemicals During Land Treatment of Oily Wastes: RITZ User's Guide. EPA/600/8-88/001 (NTIS PB88-195540)

Nofziger, D.L., K. Rajender, S.K. Nayudu, and P.Y. Su. 1989. CHEMFLOW: A One-Dimensional Water and Chemical Movement in Unsaturated Soils: User's Manual. EPA/600/8-89/076 (NTIS PB90-126020), 115 pp.

Phene, C.J. 1986. Oxygen electrode measurement. In: A. Klute (ed.), Methods of Soil Analysis Part 1: Physical and Mineralogical Methods, 2nd edition. American Society of Agronomy, Madison, WI.

Powell, R.M., Bledsoe, B.E., Johnson, R.L., and G.P. Curtis. 1989. Interlaboratory Methods Comparison for the Total Organic Carbon Analysis of Aquifer Materials. Environ. Sci. Technol., 23:1246–1249.

Powell, R.M. 1990. Total Organic Carbon Determinations in Natural and Contaminated Aquifer Materials, Relevance and Measurement. In: Proc. Fourth Nat. Outdoor Action Conference on Aquifer Restoration, Ground Water Monitoring and Geophysical Methods. National Water Well Association, Dublin, OH.

Reynolds, W.D. and D.E. Elrick. 1985. In Situ Measurement of Field-Saturated Hydraulic Conductivity, Sorptivity and the (alpha)-Parameter using the Guelph Permeameter. Soil Science, 140(4):292–302.

Reynolds, W.D. and D.E. Elrick. 1986. A Method for Simultaneous In Situ Measurement in the Vadose Zone of Field Saturated Hydraulic Conductivity, Sorptivity, and the Conductivity-Pressure Head Relationship. Ground Water Monitoring Review, 6(1):84–95.

Rhoades, J.D. 1982. Cation Exchange Capacity. In: A.L. Page, R.H. Miller, and D.R. Keeney (eds.), Methods of Soil Analysis, Part 2, Chemical and Microbiological Properties, 2nd edition. American Society of Agronomy, Madison, WI.

Roco, M.C., J. Khadilkar, and J. Zhang. 1989. Probabilistic Approach for Transport of Contaminants Through Porous Media. International Journal for Numerical Methods in Fluids, 9:1431–1451. [Not cited in text.]

Sagar, B., P.W. Eslinger, and R.G. Baca. 1986. Probabilistic Modeling of Radionuclide Release at the Waste Package Subsystems Boundary of a Repository in Basalt. Nuclear Technology, 75:338–349.

Schroeder, P.R, J.M. Morgan, T.M. Walski, and A.C. Gibson. 1984a. Hydrologic Evaluation of Landfill Performance (HELP) Model, Vol. I: User's Guide for Version 1. EPA/530/SW-84/009 (NTIS PB85-100840).

Schroeder, P.R, A.C. Gibson, and M.D. Smolen. 1984b. Hydrologic Evaluation of Landfill Performance (HELP) Model, Vol. II: Documentation of Version 1. EPA/530/SW-84/010 (NTIS PB85-100832).

Sims, R.C. 1990. Soil Remediation Techniques at Uncontrolled Hazardous Waste Sites: A Critical Review. J. Air and Waste Management Association, 40(5):704–732.

Sims, R.C., D. Sorenson, J. Sims, J. McLean, R. Mahmood, R. Dupont, J. Jurinak, and K. Wagner. 1986. Contaminated Surface Soils In-Place Treatment Techniques. Pollution Technology Review No. 132. Noyes Publications, Park Ridge, NJ.

Sims, J.L., R.C. Sims, and J.E. Matthews. 1989. Bioremediation of Contaminated Surface Soils. EPA/600/9-89/073. [Not cited in text.]

Smith, K.A. 1983. Gas Chromatographic Analysis of the Soil Atmosphere. In: K.A. Smith (ed.), Soil Analysis: Instrumental Techniques and Related Procedures. Marcel Dekker, New York, NY.

Soil Conservation Service (SCS), USDA, 1951. Soil Survey Manual. U.S. Department of Agriculture Handbook 18, p. 228, U.S. Government Printing Office, Washington, DC.

Soil Survey Staff. 1975. Soil Taxonomy: A Basic System of Soil Classification for Making and Interpreting Soil Surveys. U.S. Dept. of Agric. Agricultural Handbook No. 436, 754 pp. [See Soil Survey Staff (1994) for latest revisions.]

Soil Survey Staff. 1993. Examination and Description of Soils. In: Soil Survey Manual (new edition). U.S. Dept. of Agric. Agricultural Handbook No. 18. Soil Conservation Service, Washington, DC, Chapter 3. [Note that this supersedes the 1951 Handbook by the same title, and the 1962 supplement. U.S. Government Printing Office Stock No. 001-000-04611-0.]

Soil Survey Staff. 1994. Keys to Soil Taxonomy, 6th ed. U.S. Government Printing Office, Washington, DC, Stock No. 001-000-04612-8. [Updated every 2 years.]

Stevens, D.K., W.J. Grenney, Z. Yan, and R.C. Sims. 1989. Sensitive Parameter Evaluation for a Vadose Zone Fate and Transport Model. EPA/600/2-89/039 (NTIS PB89-213987/AS). [VIP.]

Stumm, W. and J.J. Morgan. 1981. Aquatic Chemistry, 2nd edition. Wiley-Interscience, New York, NY.

Taylor, S.A. and G.L. Ashcroft. 1972. Physical Edaphology. The Physics of Irrigated and Nonirrigated Soils. W.H. Freeman, San Francisco, CA.

Taylor, S.A. and R.D. Jackson. 1986. Temperature. In: A. Klute (ed.), Methods of Soil Analysis Part 1: Physical and Mineralogical Methods, 2nd edition. American Society of Agronomy, Madison, WI.

Thompson, C.M. et al. 1989. Techniques to Develop Data for Hydrogeochemical Models. EPRI EN-6637. Electric Power Research Institute, Palo Alto, CA, 371 pp.

Towers, D.S., M.J. Dent, and D.G. Van Arnam. 1988. Evaluation of In Situ Technologies for VHOs Contaminated Soil. In: Proc. 6th Nat. Conf. on Hazardous Wastes and Hazardous Materials. Hazardous Materials Control Research Institute, Silver Spring, MD.

U.S. Environmental Protection Agency (EPA). 1985. Compilation of Air Pollutant Emission Factors. Volume 1. Stationary Point and Area Sources, Fourth Edition. Office of Research and Development. Research Triangle Park, NC.

U.S. Environmental Protection Agency (EPA). 1986. Test Methods for Evaluating Solid Waste, 3rd edition. EPA/530/SW-846 (NTIS PB88-239223); First update, 3rd edition. EPA/530/SW-846.3-1 (NTIS PB89-148076). [Current edition and updates available on a subscription basis from U.S. Government Printing Office, Stock #955-001-00000-1.]

U.S. Environmental Protection Agency (EPA). 1987a. Data Quality Objectives for Remedial Response Activities, EPA/540/G-87/003 (NTIS PB88-131370).

U.S. Environmental Protection Agency (EPA). 1987b. A Compendium of Superfund Field Operations Methods. EPA/540/P-87/001 (NTIS PB88-181557), 644 pp.

U.S. Environmental Protection Agency (EPA). 1988a. Field Screening Methods for Hazardous Waste Site Investigations: Proceedings from the First International Symposium. EPA/600/D-89/189 (NITS PB90-132572).

U.S. Environmental Protection Agency (EPA). 1988b. Field Screening Methods Catalog. User's Guide. EPA/540/2-88/005.

U.S. Environmental Protection Agency (EPA). 1988c. Guidance on Remedial Actions for Contaminated Ground Water at Superfund Sites. EPA/540/G-88/003 OSWER Directive 9283.1-2 (NTIS PB89-184618), 180 pp.

U.S. Environmental Protection Agency (EPA). 1988d. Superfund Exposure Assessment Manual. EPA-540-1-88-001. OSWER Directive 9285.5-1.

U.S. Environmental Protection Agency (EPA). 1988e. Cleanup of Releases from Petroleum USTs: Selected Technologies. EPA/530/UST-88/001.

U.S. Environmental Protection Agency (EPA). 1989. Bioremediation of Hazardous Waste Sites Workshop: Speaker Slide Copies and Supporting Information. CERI-89-11. U.S. Environmental Protection Agency, Office of Research and Development, Washington, DC 20460.

U.S. Environmental Protection Agency (EPA). 1991. Site Characterizations for Subsurface Remediations, EPA/625/4-91/026.

van der Heijde, P.K.M., A.I. El-Kadi, and S.A. Williams. 1988. Ground Water Modeling: An Overview and Status Report. EPA/600/2-89/028 (NTIS PB89-224497). [Editor's note: see also Compilation of Ground Water Models by P.K.M van der Heijde and O.A. Einawawy, EPA/600/R-93-118 (NTIS PB93-209401).]

van der Heijde, P.K.M., W.I.M. Elderhorst, R.A. Miller, and M.J. Trehan. 1989. The Establishment of a Groundwater Research Data Center for Validation of Subsurface Flow and Transport Models. EPA/600/2-89/040.

van Genuchten, M.Th., F.J. Leis, and L.J. Lund (eds.). 1992. Indirect Methods for Estimating the Hydraulic Properties of Unsaturated Soils. U.S. Department of Agriculture Salinity Laboratory, Riverside, CA, 718 pp.

van Genuchten, M.Th. 1980. A Closed-Form Equation for Predicting the Hydraulic Conductivity of Unsaturated Soils. Soil Sci. Soc. Am. J. 44:892–898.

van Genuchten, M. and P.J. Wierenga. 1986. Solute Dispersion Coefficients and Retardation Factors. In: A. Klute (ed.), Methods of Soil Analysis Part 1: Physical and Mineralogical Methods, 2nd edition. American Society of Agronomy, Madison, WI.

Watson, K.K. 1966. An Instantaneous Profile Method for Determining the Hydraulic Conductivity of Unsaturated Porous Media. Water Resources Research 2:709–715.

Weaver, J., C.G. Enfield, S. Yates, D. Kreamer, and D. White. 1989. Predicting Subsurface Contaminant Transport and Transformation: Considerations for Model Selection and Field Validation. EPA/600/2-89/045.

Whittig, L.D. and W.R. Allardice. 1986. X-Ray Diffraction Techniques. In: A. Klute (ed.), Methods of Soil Analysis Part 1: Physical and Mineralogical Methods, 2nd edition. American Society of Agronomy, Madison, WI.

Williams, J.R. 1975. Sediment-Yield Prediction with the Universal Soil Loss Equation Using Runoff Energy Factor. In: Present and Prospective Technology for Predicting Sediment Yields and Sources. ARS-S-40. U.S. Department of Agriculture.

Yates, S.R. and M.V. Yates. 1990. Geostatistics for Waste Management: A User's Guide for the GEOPACK (Version 1.0) Geostatistical Software System. EPA/600/8-90/004.

Yong, R.N. and B.P. Warkentin. 1966. Introduction to Soil Behavior. Macmillan, New York, NY.

Chapter 15

Soil Sampling and Analysis for Volatile Organic Compounds[1]

T.E. Lewis, Southern Forest Experiment Station, Forest Health Monitoring Program, Research Triangle Park, NC
A.B. Crockett, Idaho National Engineering Laboratory, Environmental Assessment and Technology Group, Idaho Falls, ID
R.L. Siegrist, Colorado School of Mines, Golden, CO
K. Zarrabi, University of Nevada, Las Vegas, NV

PURPOSE AND SCOPE

Concerns over data quality have raised many questions related to sampling soils for volatile organic compounds (VOCs). This chapter was prepared in response to some of these questions and concerns expressed by Remedial Project Managers (RPMs) and On-Scene Coordinators (OSCs). The following questions are frequently asked:

1. Is there a specific device suggested for sampling soils for VOCs?
2. Are there significant losses of VOCs when transferring a soil sample from a sampling device (e.g., split spoon) into the sample container?
3. What is the best method for getting the sample from the split spoon (or other device) into the sample container?
4. Are there smaller devices such as subcore samplers available for collecting aliquots from the larger core and efficiently transferring the sample into the sample container?
5. Are certain containers better than others for shipping and storing soil samples for VOC analysis?
6. Are there any reliable preservation procedures for reducing VOC losses from soil samples and for extending holding times?

This chapter is intended to familiarize RPMs, OSCs, and field personnel with the current state of the science and the current thinking concerning sampling soils for VOC analysis. Guidance is provided for selecting the most effective sampling device for collecting samples from soil matrices. The techniques for sample collection, sample handling, containerizing, shipment, and storage described in this chapter reduce VOC losses and generally provide more representative samples for volatile organic analyses (VOA) than techniques in current use. For a discussion on the proper use of sampling equipment the reader should refer to other sources (Acker, 1974; Ford et al., 1984; U.S. EPA, 1986a).

Soil, as referred to in this chapter, encompasses the mass (surface and subsurface) of unconsolidated mantle of weathered rock and loose material lying above solid rock. Further, a distinction must be made as to what fraction of the unconsolidated material is soil and what fraction is not. The soil component here is defined as all mineral and naturally occurring organic material that is 2 mm or less in size. This is the size normally used to differentiate between soils (consisting of sands, silts, and clays) and gravels.

Although numerous sampling situations may be encountered, this chapter focuses on three broad categories of sites that might be sampled for VOCs:

[1] EPA/540/4-91/001.

1. Open test pit or trench
2. Surface soils (< 5 ft in depth)
3. Subsurface soils (> 5 R in depth)

BACKGROUND

VOCs are the class of compounds most commonly encountered at Superfund and other hazardous waste sites (McCoy, 1985; Plumb and Pitchford, 1985; Plumb, 1987; Ameth et al., 1988). Table 15-1 ranks the compounds most commonly encountered at Superfund sites. Many VOCs are considered hazardous because they are mutagenic, carcinogenic, or teratogenic, and they are commonly the controlling contaminants in site restoration projects. Decisions regarding the extent of contamination and the degree of cleanup have far-reaching effects; therefore, it is essential that they be based on accurate measurements of the VOC concentrations present. VOCs, however, present sampling, sample handling, and analytical difficulties, especially when encountered in soils and other solid matrices.

Methods used for sampling soils for volatile organic analysis (VOA) vary widely within and between EPA Regions, and the recovery of VOCs from soils has been highly variable. The source of variation in analyte recovery may be associated with any single step in the process or all steps, including sample collection, transfer from the sampling device to the sample container, sample shipment, sample preparation for analysis and sample analysis. The strength of the sampling chain is only as strong as its weakest link; soil sampling and transfer to the container are often the weakest links.

Sample collection and handling activities have large sources of random and systematic errors compared to the analysis itself (Barcelona, 1989). Negative bias (i.e., measured value less than true value) is perhaps the most significant and most difficult to delineate and control. This error is caused primarily by loss through volatilization during soil sample collection, storage, and handling.

There are currently no standard procedures for sampling soils for VOC analyses. Several types of samplers are available for collecting intact (undisturbed) samples and bulk (disturbed) samples. The selection of a particular device is site-specific. Samples are usually removed from the sampler and are placed in glass jars or vials that are then sealed with Teflon-lined caps. Practical experience and recent field and laboratory research, however, suggest that procedures such as these may lead to significant VOC losses (losses that would affect the utility of the data). Hanisch and McDevitt (1984) reported that any headspace present in the sample container will lead to desorption of VOCs from the soil particles into the headspace and will cause loss of VOCs upon opening of the container. Siegrist and Jennsen (1990) found that 81% of the VOCs were lost from samples containerized in glass jars sealed with Teflon-lined caps compared to samples immersed in methanol in jars.

FACTORS AFFECTING VOC RETENTION AND CONCENTRATION IN SOIL SYSTEMS

Volatile organic compounds in soil may coexist in three phases: gaseous, liquid (dissolved), and solid (sorbed). [Note: "Sorbed" is used throughout this chapter to encompass physical and chemical adsorption and phase partitioning.] The sampling, identification, and quantitation of VOCs in soil matrices are complicated because VOC molecules can coexist in these three phases. The interactions between these phases are illustrated in Figure 15-1. The phase distribution is controlled by VOC physicochemical properties (e.g., solubility, Henry's constant), soil properties, and environmental variables (e.g., soil temperature, water content, organic carbon content).

The factors that affect the concentration and retention of VOCs in soils can be divided into five categories: VOC chemical properties, soil chemical properties, soil physical properties, environmental factors, and biological factors. A brief summary of VOC, soil, and environmental factors is presented in Table 15-2 which provides an overview of the factors that interact to control VOCs in the soil environment at the time a sample is collected. The cited references provide a more detailed discussion. The chemical and physical properties of selected VOCs are further described in Table 15-3. Note that many of these properties have been determined in the laboratory under conditions (e.g., temperature, pressure) that may differ from those encountered in the field. Devitt et al. (1987) offers a more exhaustive list.

Table 15-1. Ranking of Ground Water Contaminants Based on Frequency of Detection at 358 Hazardous Waste Disposal Sites

Contaminant	Detection Frequency
Trichloroethene (V)	51.3
Tetrachloroethene (V)	36.0
1,2-trans Dichloroethene (V)	29.1
Chloroform (V)	28.4
1,1-Dichloroethene (V)	25.2
Methylene chloride (V)	19.2
1,1,1-Trichloroethane (V)	18.9
1,1-Dichloroethane (V)	17.9
1,2-Dichloroethane (V)	14.2
Phenol (A)	13.6
Acetone (V)	12.4
Toluene (V)	11.6
bis-(2-Ethylhexyl) phthalate (B)	11.5
Benzene (V)	11.2
Vinyl chloride	8.7

V = volatile, A = acid extractable, B = base/neutral

Source: Plumb and Pitchford (1985).

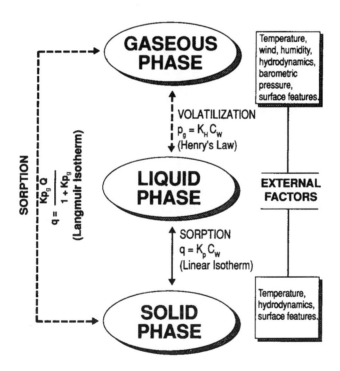

Figure 15-1. Equilibrium relationships for phase partitioning of VOCs in soil systems. See Table 16-2 for definitions of abbreviations.

Many VOCs exhibit extreme mobilities, particularly in the vapor phase, where their gas diffusion coefficients can be four times greater than their liquid diffusion coefficients. The vapor phase migration is influenced by the moisture content of the soil which alters the air-filled to water-filled pore volume ratio. The retention of VOCs by soil is largely controlled by reactions with the solid phase. This retention is especially true for the finer particles of silts and clays. The fine-grained particles

Table 15-2. Factors Affecting VOC Concentrations in Soils

Factor	Common Abbr.	Units	Effects on VOC Concentrations in Soil	References
VOC Chemical Properties				
Solubility	C_w	mg/L	Affects fate and transport in water, affects water/air partit., influences organic carbon partit.	Roy and Griffin (1985)
Henry's constant	K_H	(atm-m³)/mole	Constant of proportionality between the water and gas phase concentrations; temperature and pressure dependent.	Shen and Sewell (1982) Spencer et al. (1988)
Vapor pressure	v.p.	mm Hg	Affects rate of loss from soil.	Shen and Sewell (1982)
Organic carbon part. coeff.	K_{oc}	mg VOC/g C	Adsorption coefficient normalized for soil organic content.	Farmer et al. (1980)
Octanol/water part. coeff.	K_{ow}	mg/VOC/mg octanol	Equilibrium constant for distribution of VOC between water and an organic (octanol) phase. Gives estimate of VOC partitioning into organic fraction of soil.	Voice and Weber (1983)
Boiling point	b.p.	°C	Affects co-evaporation of VOC and water from soil surface.	Voice and Weber (1983)
Soil/water distribution coefficient	K_d	[1]	Equilibrium constant for distribution of contaminant between solid and liquid phases.	Voice and Weber (1983)
Soil Chemical Properties				
Cation exchange capacity	CEC	meq/100 g	Estimates the number of negatively charged sites on soil particles where charged VOC may sorb; pH dependent.	
Ion concentration (activity)	pH	-log[H⁺]	Influences a number of soil processes that involve non-neutral organic partitioning; affects CEC and solubility of some VOCs.	
Total organic carbon content	TOC	mg C/g soil	An important partitioning medium for non-polar, hydrophobic (high K_{oc}) VOCs; sorption of VOCs in this medium may be highly irreversible.	Chiou et al. (1988) Farmer et al. (1980)

Soil Physical Properties

Property	Symbol	Units	Description	Reference
Particle size or texture	A	% sand, silt, clay	Affects infiltration, penetration, retention, sorption, and mobility of VOCs. Influences hydraulics as well as surface-area-to-volume ratio (s.a. $\propto K_d$).(1971)	Richardson and Epstein
Specific surface area	s.a.	m^2/g	Affects adsorption of VOCs from vapor phase; affects soil porosity and other textural properties.	Karickhoff et al. (1979)
Bulk density	ρ_b	g/cm^3	Used in estimating mobility and retention of VOCs in soils; will influence soil sampling device selection.	Spencer et al. (1988)
Porosity	n	%	Void volume to total volume ratio. Affects volume, concentration, retention, and migration of VOCs in soil voids.	Farmer et al. (1980) Shen and Sewell (1982)
Percent moisture	Θ	% (w/w)	Affects hydraulic conductivity of soil and sorption of VOCs. Determines the dissolution and mobility of VOCs in soil.	Farmer et al. (1980) Chiou and Shoup (1985)
Water potential	pF	m	Relates to the rate, mobility, and concentration of VOCs in water or liquid chemicals.	
Hydraulic conductivity	K	m/d	Affects viscous flow of VOCs in soil water, depending on degree of saturation, gradients, and other physical factors.	

Environmental Factors

Property	Symbol	Units	Description	Reference
Relative humidity	R.H.	%	Could affect the movement, diffusion, and concentration of VOCs; interrelated factors; could be site specific and dependent upon soil surface–air interface differentials.	Chiou and Shoup (1985)
Temperature	T	°C		
Barometric pressure		mm Hg		
Wind speed		knots	Relevant to speed, movement, and concentration of VOCs exposed, removed, or diffusing from soil surface.	
Ground cover		%	Intensity, nature, and kind, and distribution of cover could affect movement, diffusion rates, and concentration of VOCs	

Table 15-3. Chemical Properties of Selected Volatile Organic Compounds[1]

Compound	m.w. (g/mole)	Solubilities (mg/L @ 20°C)	Vapor Pressure log K_{oc}^a	log K_{ow}^b	K_H^{cl}	(mm @ 20°C)
Acetone	58	Miscible		-0.22	-0.24	270 (@ 30°)
Benzene	78	1780	1.91	2.11	0.22	76
Bromodichloromethane	164	7500	2.18	2.10		50
Bromoform	253	3190 (@ 30°)				6 (@ 25°)
Bromomethane	95	900	1.34	1.19	1.50	1250
2-Butanone	72	270000	1.56	0.26		76
Carbon disulfide	76	2300	1.80			260
Carbon tetrachloride	154	800	2.04	2.64	0.94	90
Chlorobenzene	113	500	2.18	2.84	0.16	9
Chloroethane	65	5740	1.40	1.54	0.61	1000
2-Chloroethylvinyl ether	107					
Chloroform	120	8000	1.46	1.97	0.12	160
Chloromethane	51	8348	0.78	0.91	1.62	3800
Dibromochloromethane	208	3300	2.45	2.24		15 (@ 10.5°)
1,2-Dichlorobenzene	147	100	2.62	3.38		1
1,3-Dichlorobenzene	147	123 (@ 25°)		3.38		
1,4-Dichlorobenzene	147	49 (@ 22°)		3.39		1
1,1-Dichloroethane	99	5500	1.66	1.79	0.18	180
1,2-Dichloroethane	99	8690	1.34	1.48	0.04	61
1,1-Dichloroethene	97	400				500
trans-1,2-Dichloroethene	97	600	1.56	2.06		200 (@ 14°)
1,2-Dichloropropane	113	2700		1.99		42
cis-1,3-Dichloropropene	110	2700				34 (@ 25°)
trans-1,3-Dichloropropene	111	2800				43 (@ 25°)
Ethylbenzene	106	152	2.60	3.15		7
2-Hexanone	100	3500		1.38		2
Methylene chloride	85	20000	1.40	1.25		349
Methylisobutylketone	100	17000	1.34	1.46	0.002	6
Perchloroethylene	166	150	2.60	2.60	0.85	14

Compound	Molecular weight	Water solubility	Koc[a]	Kow[b]	Henry's constant[c]	Vapor pressure
Styrene	104	300	2.61	2.95		5
1,1,2,2-Tetrachloroethane	168	2900	2.07	2.60		5
Tetrachloroethene	166	150	2.78	3.40		18 (@ 25°)
Toluene	92	515	2.18	2.69	0.27	22
1,1,1-Trichloroethane	133	4400	2.19	2.50	1.46	100
1,1,2-Trichloroethane	133	4500	2.14	2.07		19
Trichloroethylene	132	700	2.09	2.29	0.37	60
Trichlorofluoromethane	137	1100 (@ 25°)	2.68			687
Vinyl acetate	86	25000	1.59	0.73		115 (@ 25°)
Vinyl chloride	63	1100 (@ 25°)	2.60	1.38	97.0	2660 (@ 25°)
Total xylenes	106	198	2.46		9400.0	

[1] From Verschueren, 1983; Jury, 1984.
[a] Organic carbon partitioning coefficient.
[b] Octanol/water partitioning coefficient.
[c] Henry's gas law constant (dimensionless) @ 20°C.

(<2 mm) have a large surface-to-volume ratio, a large number of reactive sites, and high sorption capacities (Richardson and Epstein, 1971; Boucher and Lee, 1972; Lotse et al., 1968). Some investigators attribute the greater sorption of VOCs onto fine-grained particles to the greater organic carbon content of smaller particles (Karickhoff et al., 1979).

Soil-moisture content affects the relative contributions of mineral and organic soil fractions to the retention of VOCs (Smith et al., 1990). Mineral clay surfaces largely control sorption when soil moisture is extremely low (<1%), and organic carbon partitioning is favored when moisture content is higher (Chiou and Shoup, 1985).

Biological factors affecting VOC retention in soil systems can be divided into microbiological and macrobiological factors. On the microbiological level, the indigenous microbial populations present in soil systems can alter VOC concentrations. Although plants and animals metabolize a diversity of chemicals, the activities of the higher organisms are often minor compared to the transformations affected by heterotrophic bacteria and fungi residing in the same habitat. The interactions between environmental factors, such as dissolved oxygen, oxidation-reduction potential (Eh), temperature, pH, availability of other compounds, salinity, particulate matter, and competing organisms, often control biodegradation. The physical and chemical characteristics of the VOC, such as solubility, volatility, hydrophobicity, and K_{ow}, also influence the ability of the compound to biodegrade. Table 15-4 illustrates some examples of the microbiological alterations of some commonly encountered soil VOCs. In general, the halogenated alkanes and alkenes are metabolized by soil microbes under anaerobic conditions (Kobayashi and Rittman, 1982; Bouwer, 1984), whereas the halogenated aromatics are metabolized under aerobic conditions. To avoid biodegradation and oxidation of VOCs in soils, scientists at the U.S. EPA Robert S. Kerr Environmental Research Laboratory in Ada, OK, extrude the sample in a glove box filled with nitrogen gas.

On a macro scale, biological factors can influence the migration of VOCs in the saturated, vadose, and surface zones (Table 15-5). Biofilms may accumulate in the saturated zone and may biodegrade and bioaccumulate VOCs from the ground water. The biofilm, depending on its thickness, may impede ground-water flow. Plant roots have a complex microflora associated with them known as mycorrhizae. The mycorrhizae may enhance VOC retention in the soil by biodegradation or bioaccumulation. The root channels may act as conduits for increasing the migration of VOCs through the soil. Similarly, animal burrows and holes may serve as paths of least resistance for the movement of VOCs through soil. These holes may range from capillary-size openings, created by worms and nematodes, to large-diameter tunnels excavated by burrowing animals. These openings may increase the depth to which surface spills penetrate the soil. A surface covering consisting of assorted vegetation is a significant barrier to volatilization of VOCs into the atmosphere. Some ground-water and vadose-zone models (e.g., RUSTIC) include subroutines to account for a vegetative cover (Dean et al., 1989).

SOIL SAMPLING AND ANALYSIS DESIGN

Prior to any sampling effort, the RPM or OSC must establish the intended purpose of the remedial investigation/feasibility study (RI/FS). The goals of collecting samples for VOA may include source identification, spill delineation, fate and transport, risk assessment, enforcement, remediation, or post-remediation confirmation. The intended purpose of the sampling effort drives the selection of the appropriate sampling approach and the devices to be used in the investigation.

The phase partitioning of the VOC can also influence which sampling device should be employed. Computer models generally are used only at the final stages of a RI/FS. However, modeling techniques can be used throughout the RI/FS process to assist in sampling device selection by estimating the phase partitioning of VOCs. The RPM is the primary data user for a RI/FS led by a federal agency. As such, the RPM must select the sampling methodology to be employed at the site. Figure 15-2 illustrates the sequence of events used to plan a VOC sampling and analysis activity.

The domains of interest also must be determined. The target domains may include surface (two dimensions) or subsurface (three dimensions) environments hot spots, a concentration greater or less than an action limit or the area above a leaking underground storage tank. Statistics that may be generated from the target domain data must be considered before a sample and analysis design is developed. Possible statistics of interest may include average analyte concentration and the variance about the mean (statistics that compare whether the observed level is significantly above or below an

Table 15-4. Microbiological Factors Affecting VOCs in Soil Systems

Organism(s)	Compound(s)	Conditions	Remarks/metabolite(s)
Various soil microbes	Pentachlorophenol	Aerobic	tetra-, tri-, di-, and m-Chlorophenol (Kobayashi and Rittman, 1982)
	1,2,3- and 1,2,4-Trichlorobenzene	Aerobic	2,6-; 2,3-Dichlorobenzene; 2,4- and 2,5-dichlorobenzene; CO_2 (Kobayashi and Rittman, 1982)
Various soil bacteria	Trichloroethane, trichloromethane, methylchloride, chloroethane, dichloroethane, vinylidiene chloride, trichloroethene, tetrachloroethene, methylene chloride, dibromo-chloromethane, bromochloromethane	Anaerobic	Reductive dehalogenation under anoxic conditions (i.e., <0.35 V) (Kobayashi and Rittman, 1982)
Various soil microbes	Tetrachloroethene	Anaerobic	Reductive dehalogenation to trichloroethene, dichloroethene, and vinyl chloride, and finally CO_2 (Vogel and McCarty, 1985)
Various soil microbes	^{13}C-labeled trichloroethene	Anaerobic	Dehalogenation to 1,2-dichloroethene and not 1,1-dichloroethene (Kleopfer et al., 1985)
Various soil bacteria	Trichloroethene	Aerobic	Mineralized to CO_2 in the presence of a mixture of natural gas and air
Actinomycetes	Chlorinated and nonchlorinated aromatics	Aerobic	Various particle breakdown products mineralized by other microorganisms (Lechevalier and Lechevalier, 1976)
Fungi	DDT	Aerobic	Complete mineralization in 10–14 days (Johnson, 1976)
Pseudomonas sp. Acinetobacter sp. Micrococcus sp.	Aromatics	Aerobic	Organisms were capable of sustaining growth in these compounds with 100% biodegradation (Jamison et al., 1975)
Acetate-grown biofilm	Chlorinated aliphatics	Aerobic Methanogenic	No biodegradation observed (Bouwer, 1984) Nearly 100% biodegradation observed (Bouwer, 1984)
	Chlorinated and nonchlorinated aromatics	Aerobic Methanogenic	Nearly 100% biodegradation (Bouwer, 1984) No biodegradation observed (Bouwer, 1984)
Blue-green algae (cyanobacteria)	Oil wastes	Aerobic	Biodegradation of automobile oil wastes, crankcase oil, etc. (Cameron, 1963)

Table 15-5. Macrobiological Factors Affecting VOCs in Soil Systems

Factor	Zone	Effects
Biofilms	Saturated	Biodegradation, bioaccumulation, formation of metabolites that are more or less toxic than parent compound, thick biofilm may retard saturated flow
Plant roots	Capillary fringe to vadose	Mycorrhizal fungi may biodegrade or bioaccumulate VOC, root channels may serve as conduits for VOC migration
Animal burrows holes	Vadose	May act as entry point for and downward migration of surface spills and serve as conduit for upward VOC migration
Vegetative cover	Soil surface	Serve as barrier to volatilization from soil surface and retard infiltration of surface spills

action level) as well as temporal and spatial trends. Data must be of sufficiently high quality to meet the goals of the sampling activity. The level of data quality is defined by the data quality objectives (DQOs). In RI/FS activities, sites are so different and information on overall measurement error (sampling plus analytical error) is so limited that it is not practical to set universal or generic precision, accuracy, representativeness, completeness, and comparability (PARCC) goals. The reader is referred to a user's guide on quality assurance in soil sampling (Barth et al., 1989) and a guidance document for the development of data quality objectives for remedial response activities (U.S. EPA, 1987).

DQOs are qualitative and quantitative statements of the level of uncertainty a decision maker is willing to accept in making decisions on the basis of environmental data. It is important to realize that if the error associated with the sample collection or preparation step is large, then the best laboratory quality assurance program will be inadequate (van Ee et al., 1990). The greatest emphasis should be placed on the phase that contributes the largest component of error. For the analysis of soils for VOCs, the greatest sources of error are the sample collection and handling phases.

The minimum confidence level (CL) required to make a decision from the data is defined by the DQOs. The minimum CL depends on the precision and accuracy in sampling and analysis and on the relative analyte concentration. Relative error may be reduced by increasing either the number or the mass of the samples to be analyzed. For instance, although 5-g aliquots collected in the field might exhibit unacceptable errors, 100-g samples will yield smaller errors and might therefore meet study or project requirements. Compositing soil samples in methanol in the field also can reduce variance by attenuating short-range spatial variability.

Field sampling personnel should coordinate with laboratory analysts to ensure that samples of a size appropriate to the analytical method are collected. For example, if the laboratory procedure for preparing aliquots calls for removing a 5-g aliquot from a 125-mL wide-mouth jar, as per SW-846, Method 8240 (U.S. EPA 1986b), then collecting a larger sample in the field will not reduce total measurement error, because additional errors will be contributed from opening the container in the laboratory and from subsequent homogenization. Aliquoting of a 5-g sample in the field into a 40-mL VOA vial that can be directly attached to the laboratory purge-and-trap unit significantly reduces loss of VOCs from the sample (U.S. EPA, 1991a). Significant losses of VOCs were observed when samples were homogenized as per Method 8240 specifications. Smaller losses were observed for smaller aliquots (1 to 5 g) placed in 40-mL VOA vials that had modified caps that allowed direct attachment to the purge-and-trap device. The procedure of collecting an aliquot in the field eliminates the need for sample preparation and eliminates subsequent VOC loss in the laboratory.

Field-screening procedures are gaining recognition as an effective means of locating sampling locations and obtaining real-time data. The benefits of soil field-screening procedures are: (1) near real-time data to guide sampling activities, (2) concentration of Contract Laboratory Program (CLP) sample collection in critical areas, (3) reduced need for a second visit to the site, and (4) reduced analytical load on the laboratory. Limitations of field-screening procedures are: (1) a priori knowledge of VOCs present at the site is needed to accurately identify the compounds, (2) methodologies and instruments are in their infancy and procedures for their use are not well documented and (3) a

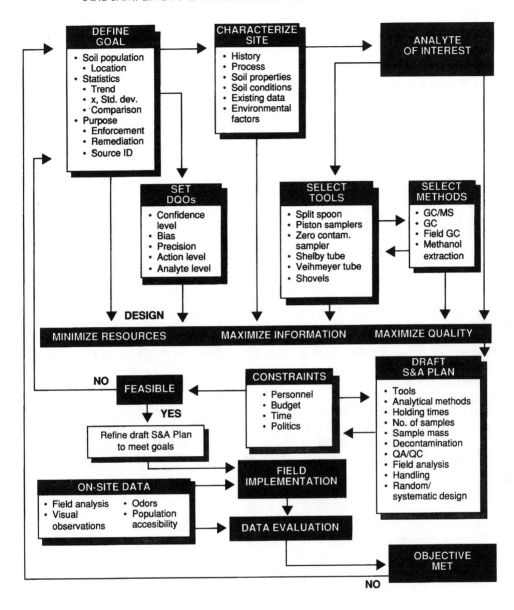

Figure 15-2. Flowchart for planning and implementation of a soil sampling and analysis activity.

more stringent level of quality assurance and quality control (QA/QC) must be employed to ensure accurate and precise measurements. The potential benefits and limitations associated with soil-screening procedures must be carefully weighed and compared to the DQOs.

Certain sampling and analytical methods have inherent limitations on the type of QA/QC that is applicable. For example, splitting soil samples in the field would not be appropriate for VOA due to excessive analyte loss. The higher the minimum CL needed to make a decision, the more rigorous the QA/QC protocols must be. As VOC concentrations in the soil sample approach the action or detection limit, the quantity and frequency of QA/QC samples must be increased, or the number of samples must be increased, to ensure that the data quality obtained is appropriate to satisfy project objectives.

One critical element in VOC analysis is the appropriate use of trip blanks. If a sample consists of a silty clay loam, a trip blank of washed sand may not be realistic, for such a blank would not retain VOC cross contaminants in the same way as the sample. The trip blank soil matrix should have a sorptive capacity similar to the actual sample. In addition, high concentration and low-concentration samples should be shipped in separate coolers.

DEVICE SELECTION CRITERIA

The selection of a sampling device and sampling procedures requires the consideration of many factors including the number of samples to be collected, available funds, soil characteristics, site limitations, ability to sample the target domain, whether or not screening procedures are to be used, the size of sample needed, and the required precision and accuracy as given in the DQOs. The number of samples to be collected can greatly affect sampling costs and the time required to complete a site characterization. If many subsurface samples are needed, it may be possible to use soil-gas sampling coupled with on-site analysis as an integrated screening technique to reduce the area of interest and thus the number of samples needed. Such a sampling approach may be applicable for cases of near-surface contamination.

Ultimately, the sampling, sample handling, containerizing, and transport of the soil sample should minimize losses of volatiles and should avoid contamination of the sample. Soil sampling equipment should be readily decontaminated in the field if it is to be reused on the job site. Decontamination of sampling equipment may require the use of decontamination pads that have impervious liners, wash and rinse troughs, and careful handling of large equipment. Whenever possible, a liner should be used inside the sampling device to reduce potential cross contamination and carryover. Decontamination procedures take time, require extra equipment, and ultimately increase site characterization costs. Ease and cost of decontamination are thus important factors to be considered in device selection.

Several soil-screening procedures are in use that include headspace analysis of soils using organic vapor analyzers: water (or NaCl-saturated water) extraction of soil, followed by static headspace analysis using an organic vapor analyzer (OVA) or gas chromatograph (GC); colorimetric test kits; methanol extraction followed by headspace analysis or direct injection into a GC; and soil-gas sampling (U.S. EPA, 1988). Field measurements may not provide absolute values but often may be a superior means of obtaining relative values. These procedures are gaining acceptance.

Site Characteristics

The remoteness of a site and the physical setting may restrict access and, therefore, affect equipment selection. Such factors as vegetation, steep slopes, rugged or rocky terrain, overhead power lines or other overhead restrictions, and lack of roads can contribute to access problems.

The presence of underground utilities, pipes, electrical lines, tanks and leach fields can also affect selection of sampling equipment. If the location or absence of these hazards cannot be established, it is desirable to conduct a nonintrusive survey of the area and select a sampling approach that minimizes hazards. For example, hand tools and a backhoe are more practical under such circumstances than a large, hollow-stem auger. The selection of a sampling device may be influenced by other contaminants of interest such as pesticides, metals, semivolatile organic compounds, radionuclides, and explosives. Where the site history indicates that the matrix is other than soil, special consideration should be given to device selection. Concrete, reinforcement bars, scrap metal, and lumber will affect sampling device selection. Under some circumstances, it may not be practical to collect deep soil samples. The presence of ordnance, drums, concrete, voids, pyrophoric materials, and high-hazard radioactive materials may preclude some sampling and may require development of alternate sampling designs, or even reconsideration of project objectives.

Soil Characteristics

The characteristics of the soil material being sampled have a marked effect upon the selection of a sampling device. An investigator must evaluate soil characteristics, the type of VOC, and the depth at which a sample is to be collected before selection of a proper sampling device. Specific characteristics that must be considered are:

1. Is the soil compacted, rocky, or rubble filled? If the answer is yes, then either hollow stem augers or pit sampling must be used.
2. Is the soil fine grained? If yes, use split spoons, Shelby tubes, liners, or hollow stem augers.
3. Are there flowing sands or water saturated soils? If yes, use samplers such as piston samplers that can retain these materials.

SOIL-GAS MEASUREMENTS

Soil-gas measurements can serve a variety of screening purposes in soil sampling and analysis programs, from initial site reconnaissance to remedial monitoring efforts. Soil-gas measurements should be used for screening purposes only, and not for definitive determination of soil-bound VOCs. Field analysis is usually by hand-held detectors, portable GC or GC/MS, infrared detectors, ion mobility spectrometers (IMS), industrial hygiene detector tubes, and, recently, fiber optic sensors.

At some sites, soil-gas sampling may be the only means of acquiring data on the presence or absence of VOCs in the soil. For example, when the size and density of rocks and cobbles at a site prevent insertion and withdrawal of the coring device and prevent sampling with shovels and trowels, unacceptable losses of VOCs would occur. Soil-gas measurements, which can be made on site or with collected soil samples, can be used to identify volatile contaminants and to determine relative magnitudes of concentration. Smith et al. (1990) have shown a disparity in soil-gas VOC concentrations and the concentration of VOCs found on the solid phase.

Soil-gas measurements have several applications. These include in situ soil-gas surveying, measurement of headspace concentrations above containerized soil samples, and scanning of soil contained in cores collected from different depths. These applications are summarized in Table 15-6. Currently, no standard protocols exist for soil-gas analysis; many investigators have devised their own techniques, which have varying degrees of efficacy. Independently, the American Society for Testing and Materials (ASTM) and EPA EMSL-LV are preparing guidance documents for soil-gas measurement. These documents should be available late in 1991.[2]

The required precision and accuracy of site characterization, as defined in the DQOs, affect the selection of a sampling device. Where maximum precision and accuracy are required, sampling devices that collect an intact core should be used, particularly for more volatile VOCs in nonretentive matrices. Augers and other devices that collect highly disturbed samples and expose the samples to the atmosphere can be used if lower precision and accuracy can be tolerated. Collection of a larger number of samples to characterize a given area, however, can compensate for a less precise sampling approach. The closer the expected contaminant level is to the action or detection limit, the more efficient the sampling device should be for obtaining an accurate measurement.

SOIL SAMPLING DEVICES

Table 15-7 lists selection criteria for different types of commercially available soil sampling devices based on soil type, moisture status, and power requirements. The sampling device needed to achieve a certain sampling and analysis goal can be located in Table 15-7 and the supplier of such a device can be identified in Table 15-8. Table 15-8 is a partial list of commercially available soil sampling devices that are currently in use for sampling soils for VOC analysis. The list is by no means exhaustive and inclusion in the list should not be construed as an endorsement for their use.

Commonly, soil samples are obtained from the near surface using shovels, scoops, trowels, and spatulas. These devices can be used to extract soil samples from trenches and pits excavated by backhoes. A precleaned shovel or scoop can be used to expose fresh soil from the face of the test pit. A thin-walled tube or small-diameter, hand-held corer can be used to collect soil from the exposed face. Bulk samplers such as shovels and trowels cause considerable disturbance of the soil and expose the sample to the atmosphere, enhancing loss of VOCs. Siegrist and Jenssen (1990) have

---

[2]   Editor's Note: ASTM D5314 (Guide for Soil Gas Monitoring in the Vadose Zone) was approved in 1992 and provides information on the advantages and disadvantages of different soil gas sampling techniques. However, ASTM standard methods for specific techniques have yet to be developed as of late 1995.

Table 15-6. Applications of Soil-Gas Measurement Techniques in Soil Sampling for VOCs

Application	Uses	Methods	Benefits/limitations
Soil vapor surveying	Identify sources and extent of contamination. Distinguish between soil and ground water contamination. Detect VOCs under asphalt, concrete, etc.	Active sampling from soil probes into canisters, glass bulbs, gas sampling bags. Passive sampling onto buried adsorptive substrates. Followed by GC or other analysis.	BENEFITS: Rapid, inexpensive screening of large areas, avoid sampling uncontaminated areas. LIMITATIONS: False positives and negatives, miss detecting localized surface spills, disequilibrium between adsorbed and vapor phase VOC concentrations.
Soil headspace measurements	Screen large numbers of soil samples	Measure headspace above containerized soil sample. Containers range from plastic sandwich bags to VOA vials. Use GC, vapor detectors, IMS, etc.	BENEFITS: More representative of adsorbed solid phase concentration. LIMITATIONS: Losses of vapor phase component during sampling and sample transfer.
Screening soil cores	Soil cores scanned to locate depth where highest VOC levels are located.	Collect core sample (e.g., unlined split spoon) and scan for vapors near core surface using portable vapor monitor.	BENEFITS: Locate and collect soil from hot spot in core for worst case. LIMITATIONS: False negatives and positives, environmental conditions can influence readings (e.g., wind speed and direction, temperature, humidity).

Table 15-7. Criteria for Selecting Soil Sampling Equipment[a]

Type of Sampler	Obtains Core Samples	Most Suitable Soil Types	Operation in Stony Soils	Suitable Soil Moisture Conditions	Relative Sample Size	Labor Requirements (# of Persons)	Manual or Power Operation
A. Mechanical Sample Recovery							
1 Hand-held power augers	No	Coh/coh'less	Unfavorable	Intermediate	Large	2+	Power
2 Solid stem flight augers	No	Coh/coh'less	Favorable	Wet to dry	Large	2+	Power
3 Hollow-stem augers	Yes	Coh/coh'less	Fav/unfav	Wet to dry	Large	2+	Power
4 Bucket augers	No	Coh/coh'less	Favorable	Wet to dry	Large	2+	Power
5 Backhoes	No	Coh/coh'less	Favorable	Wet to dry	Large	2+	Power
B Samplers							
1 Screw-type augers	No	Coh	Unfavorable	Intermediate	Small	Single	Manual
2 Barrel augers							
a Post-hole augers	No	Coh	Unfavorable	Wet	Large	Single	Manual
b Dutch augers	No	Coh	Unfavorable	Wet	Large	Single	Manual
c Regular barrel augers	No	Coh	Unfavorable	Intermediate	Large	Single	Manual
d Sand augers	No	Coh'less	Unfavorable	Intermediate	Large	Single	Manual
e Mud augers	No	Coh	Unfavorable	Wet	Large	Single	Manual
3 Tube-type samplers							
a Soil samplers	Yes	Coh	Unfavorable	Wet to dry	Small	Single	Manual
b Veihmeyer tubes	Yes	Coh	Unfavorable	Intermediate	Large	Single	Manual
c Shelby tubes	Yes	Coh	Unfavorable	Intermediate	Large	2+*	Both
d Ring-lined samplers	Yes	Coh'less	Favorable	Wet to intermediate	Large	2+*	Both
e Continuous samplers	Yes	Coh	Unfavorable	Wet to dry	Large	2+	Power
f Piston samplers	Yes	Coh	Unfavorable	Wet	Large	2+*	Both
g Zero-contamination samplers	Yes	Coh	Unfavorable	Wet to intermediate	Small	2+*	Both
h Split spoon samplers	Yes	Coh	Unfavorable	Intermediate	Large	2+*	Both
4 Bulk samplers	No	Coh	Favorable	Wet to dry	Large	Single	Manual

[a] Adapted from U.S. EPA, 1986a.

* All hand-operated versions of samplers, except for continuous samplers, can be worked by one person.

Coh = cohesive.

Table 15-8. Examples of Commercially Available Soil Sampling Devices

| Manufacturers | Sampling Devices | Specifications | | Features |
		Length (inches) I.D. (inches) Sampler Material	Liners	
Associated Design & Manufacturing Co. 814 North Henry Street Alexandria, VA 22314 703-549-5999	Purge and Trap Soil Sampler	3 0.5 Stainless steel		Will rapidly sample soils for screening by "Low Level" Purge and Trap methods.
Acker Drill Co. P.O. Box 830 Scranton, PA 717-586-2061	Heavy Duty "Lynac" Split Tube Sampler	18 & 24 1-1/2 to 4-1/2 Steel	Brass, stainless	Split tube allows for easy sample removal.
	Dennison Core Barrel	24 & 60 1-7/8 to 6-5/16	Brass	Will remove undisturbed sample from cohesive soils.
AMS Harrison at Oregon Trail American Falls, ID 83211	Core Soil Sampler	2 to 12 1-1/2 to 3 Alloy, stainless	Stainless, plastic aluminum, bronze Teflon	Good in all types of soils.
	Dual Purpose Soil Recovery Probe	12, 18 & 24 3/4 and 1 4130 Alloy, stainless	Butyrate, Teflon stainless	Adapts to AMS "up & down" hammer attachment. Use with or without liners.
	Soil Recovery Auger	8 to 12 2 & 3 Stainless	Plastic, stainless Teflon, aluminum	Adaptable to AMS extension and cross-handles.

Company	Product	Dimensions / Material	Liner	Comments
Concord, Inc. 2800 7th Ave. N. Fargo, ND 58102 701-280-1260	Speedy Soil Sampler	48 & 72 3/16 to 3-1/2 Stainless	Acetate	Automated system allows retrieval of 24 in soil sample in 12 sec.
	Zero Contamination Unit Hand-Held Sampler			
CME Central Mine Equip. Co. 6200 North Broadway St. Louis, MO 63147 800-325-8827	Continuous Sampler	60 2-1/2 to 5-3/8 Steel, stainless	Butyrate	May not be suitable in stony soils. Adapts to CMS auger.
	Bearing Head Continuous Sample Tube System	60 2-1/2 Steel, stainless	Butyrate	Versatile system. Adapts to all brands of augers.
Diedrich Drilling Equip. P.O. Box 1670 Laporte, IN 46350 800-348-8809	Heavy Duty Split Tube Sampler	18 & 24 2, 2-1/2, 3 Steel	Brass, plastic stainless, Teflon	Full line of accessories are available.
	Continuous Sampler	60 3, 3-1/2	Brass, plastic stainless, Teflon	Switch-out device easily done.
Geoprobe Systems 607 Barney St. Salina, KS 913-825-1842	Probe Drive Soil Sampler	11-1/4 0.96 Alloy steel		Remains completely sealed while pushed to depth in soil.
Giddings Machine Co. P.O. Drawer 2024 Fort Collins, CO 80522 303-485-5586	Coring Tubes	48 & 60 7/8 to 2-3/8 4130 Molychrome	Butyrate	A series of optional 5/8 in. slots permit observation of the sample.

Table 15-8. Continued

Manufacturers	Sampling Devices	Specifications			Liners	Features
		Length (inches)	I.D. (inches)	Sampler Material		
JMC Clements and Associates R.R. 1 Box 186 Newton, IA 50208 800-247-6630	Environmentalist's Sub-Soil Probe	36 & 48	0.9	Nickel plated	PETG plastic, stainless	Adapts to drop-hammer to penetrate the hardest of soils.
	Zero Contamination Tubes	12, 18 & 24	0.9	Nickel plated	PETG plastic, stainless	Adapts to power probe.
Mobile Drilling Co. 3807 Madison Ave. Indianapolis, IN 46227 800-428-4475	"Lynac" Split Barrel Sampler	18 & 24	1-1/2		Brass, plastic	Adapts to Mobile wireline sampling system.
Soiltest, Inc. 66 Albrecht Drive Lake Bluff, IL 800-323-1242	Zero Contamination Sampler	12, 18 & 24	0.9	Chrome plated	Stainless, acetate	Hand sampler good for chemical residue studies.
	Thin Wall Tube Sampler (Shelby)	30	2-1/2, 3, 3-1/2	Steel		Will take undisturbed samples in cohesive soils and clays.
	Split Tube Sampler	24	1-1/2 to 3	Steel	Brass	Forced into soil by jacking, hydraulic pressure or driving. Very popular type of sampler.

Manufacturer	Product				Description
Sprague & Henwood, Inc. Scranton, PA 18501 800-344-8506	Veihmeyer Soil Sampler Tube	48 & 72 3/4 Steel			Adapts to drop hammer for sampling in all sorts of soils.
	S & H Split Barrel Sampler	18 & 24 2 to 3-1/2	Brass, plastic		A general all-purpose sampling device designed for driving into material to be sampled.

Note: This list is not exhaustive. Inclusion in this list should not be construed as endorsement for use.

Table 15-9. Soil Samplers for VOC Analysis

Recommended	Not Recommended
Split spoon w/liners	Solid flight liners
Shelby tube (thin wall tubes)	Drilling mud auger
Hollow-stem augers	Air drilling auger
Veihmeyer or King tubes	Cable tool
w/liners	Hand augers
Piston samplers[a]	Barrel augers
Zero contamination samplers[a]	Scoop samplers
Probe-drive samplers	Excavating tools, e.g., shovels, backhoes

[a] May sustain VOC losses if not used with care.

shown that sampling procedures that cause the least amount of disturbance provide the greatest VOC recoveries. Therefore, sampling devices that obtain undisturbed soil samples using either hand-held or mechanical devices are recommended. Sampling devices that collect undisturbed samples include split-spoon samplers, ring samplers, continuous samplers, zero-contamination samplers, and Shelby tubes. These sampling devices can be used to collect surface soil samples or they can be used in conjunction with hollow-stem augers to collect subsurface samples. The soil sampling devices discussed above are summarized in Table 15-9. Devices where the soil samples can be easily and quickly removed and containerized with the least amount of disturbance and exposure to the atmosphere are highly recommended. U.S. EPA (1986a) gives a more detailed discussion on the proper use of drill rigs and sampling devices.

Liners are available for many of the devices listed in Table 15-9. Liners make soil removal from the coring device much easier and quicker. Liners reduce cross contamination between samples and the need for decontamination of the sampling device. The liner can run the entire length of the core or can be precut into sections of desired length.

When sampling for VOCs, it is critical to avoid interactions between the sample and the liner and between the sample and the sampler. Such interactions may include either adsorption of VOCs from the sample or release of VOCs to the sample. Gillman and O'Hannesin (1990) studied the sorption of six monoaromatic hydrocarbons in ground water samples by seven materials. The hydrocarbons included benzene, toluene, ethylbenzene, and o-, m-, and p-xylene. The materials examined were stainless steel, rigid PVC, flexible PVC, PTFE Teflon, polyvinylidene fluoride, fiberglass, and polyethylene. Stainless steel showed no significant sorption during an 8-week period. All polymer materials sorbed all compounds to some extent. The order of sorption was as follows: rigid PVC < fiberglass < polyvinylidene fluoride < PTFE < polyethylene < flexible PVC. Stainless steel or brass liners should be used since they exhibit the least adsorption of VOCs. Other materials such as PVC or acetate may be used, provided that contact time between the soil and the liner material is kept to a minimum. Stainless steel and brass liners have been sealed with plastic caps or paraffin before shipment to the laboratory for sectioning and analysis. VOC loss can result from permeation through the plastic or paraffin and volatilization through leaks in the seal. Acetate liners are available, but samples should not be held in these liners for any extended period, due to adsorption onto and permeation through the material. Alternatively, the soil can be extruded from the liner, and a portion can be placed into a wide-mouth glass jar. Smaller aliquots can be taken from the center of the precut liner using subcoring devices and the soil plug extruded into VOA vials.

TRANSFER OF SOIL SAMPLES FROM DEVICE TO CONTAINER

The sample transfer step is perhaps the most critical and least understood step in the sampling and analysis procedure. The key point in sample transfer, whether in the field or in the laboratory, is to minimize disturbance and the amount of time the sample is exposed to the atmosphere. It is more important to transfer the sample rapidly to the container than to accurately weigh the aliquot which is transferred, or to spend considerable time reducing headspace. Therefore, a combination of a device for obtaining the appropriate mass of sample and placement of the aliquot into a container

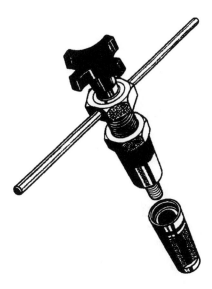

Figure 15-3. Small-diameter hand-held subcoring device made by Associated Design & Manufacturing Company (Alexandria, VA).

that can be directly connected to the analytical device in the laboratory is recommended. Several designs are available for obtaining a 5-g aliquot (or other size). Most subcoring devices consist of a plunger/barrel design with an open end. The device shown in Figure 15-3 was constructed by Associated Design & Manufacturing Company (Alexandria, VA). Other designs include syringes with the tips removed, and cork borers (Table 15-8). The device is inserted into the sample and an aliquot is withdrawn. The aliquot, which is of a known volume and approximate weight, can then be extruded into a tared 40-mL VOA vial. Routinely, the vial is then sealed with a Teflon-lined septum cap. Teflon, however, may be permeable to VOCs. Aluminum-lined caps are available to reduce losses due to permeation. At the laboratory, the vial must be opened and the contents of the vial must be transferred to a sparger tube. The transfer procedure will result in significant losses of VOCs from the headspace in the vial. The modified purge-and-trap cap shown in Figure 15-4 eliminates the loss of VOCs due to container opening and sample transfer. The soil is extruded from the subcorer into a tared 40-mL VOA vial and the modified cap is attached in the field. In the laboratory, the vial is attached directly to a purge-and-trap device without ever being opened to the ambient air.

Use of subcoring devices should produce analytical results of increased accuracy. In order to test this hypothesis, an experiment was conducted in which a bulk soil sample was spiked with 800 µg/ kg of different VOCs (Maskarinec, 1990). Three aliquots were withdrawn by scooping, and three aliquots were withdrawn by using the subcorer approach. The results are presented in Table 15-10. Although neither method produced quantitative recovery, the subcorer approach produced results that were generally five times higher than the standard approach, whereby the contents of a 125-mL wide-mouth jar are poured into an aluminum tray and homogenized with a stainless steel spatula. A 5-g sample is then placed in the sparger tube (U.S. EPA, 1986b, Method 8240). Several compounds presented problems with both approaches: styrene polymerizes, bromoform purges poorly, and 1,1,2,2-tetrachloroethane degrades quickly.

In another study (U.S. EPA, 1991a), a large quantity of well characterized soil was spiked with 33 VOCs and was homogenized. From the homogenized material, a 5-g aliquot of soil was placed in a 40-mL VOA vial and sealed with a modified purge-and-trap cap (Figure 15-4). The remaining soil was placed in 125-mL wide-mouth jars. The samples were shipped via air carrier and were analyzed by GC/MS with heated purge-and-trap. The 40-mL VOA vials were connected directly to a Tekmar purge-and-trap unit without exposure to the atmosphere. The wide-mouth jars were processed as per SW-846 Method 8240 specifications (U.S. EPA,. 1986b). Table 15-11 compares the results of the GC/MS analyses using the two pretreatment techniques. The modified method (40-mL VOA vial with a modified cap) yielded consistently higher VOC concentrations than the traditional Method 8240 procedure (U.S. EPA, 1986b).

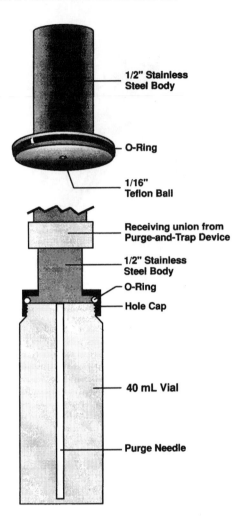

Figure 15-4. Modified purge-and-trap 40-mL VOA vial cap for containerizing samples in the field. Vial is attached directly to a purge-and-trap system without exposure of sample to the atmosphere.

The standard methods for VOC analysis, SW-846, Method 8240 and Test Method 624 (U.S. EPA, 1986b; U.S. EPA, 1982), call for the containerizing of soil samples in 40-mL VOA vials or 125-mL wide-mouth jars with minimal headspace. As previously described, wide-mouth jars may not be the most appropriate containers due to sample aliquoting requirements. Although wide-mouth jars may be equally as effective as 40-mL VOA vials in maintaining the VOC content of soil samples, the sample preparation procedure that is required with jar-held samples causes significant (>80%) loss of highly volatile VOCs (Siegrist and Jennsen, 1990). However, if samples are collected in such containers, it is important to ensure sample integrity, preferably by using amber glass jars (for photo-sensitive compounds) with solid phenolic resin caps and foam-backed Teflon liners. Aluminum-lined caps are not available for the wide-mouth jars. Soil should be wiped from the threads of the jar to ensure a tight seal.

The methanol-immersion procedure calls for the transfer of the sample into a glass jar containing a known volume of chromatographic-grade methanol (usually 100 mL) or in a 1:1 weight-to-volume ratio of soil to methanol. This has the effect of preserving the volatile components of the sample at the time the sample is placed in the container. Furthermore, surrogate compounds can be added at this time in order to identify possible changes in the sample during transport and storage. The addition of methanol to the sample raises the detection limits from 5 to 10 μg/kg to 100 to 500 μg/kg, because of the attendant dilution. However, the resulting data have been shown to be more representative of the original VOC content of the soil (Siegrist and Jennsen, 1990; Siegrist, 1991). In a

Table 15-10. Laboratory Comparison of Standard Method and Subcorer Method

Compound	Standard Method[a]	Subcorer Method[b]	Standard Method % of Recovery of Spike	Subcorer % of Recovery of Spike
Chloromethane	50	1225	6	153
Bromomethane	31	536	4	67
Chloroethane	78	946	10	118
1,1-Dichloroethene	82	655	10	82
1,1-Dichloroethane	171	739	21	92
Chloroform	158	534	20	67
Carbontetrachloride	125	658	16	82
1,2-Dichloropropane	147	766	18	96
Trichloroethene	120	512	15	64
Benzene	170	636	21	80
1,1,2-Trichloroethane	78	477	10	60
Bromoform	30	170	4	21
1,1,2,2-Tetrachloroethane	46	271	6	34
Toluene	129	656	16	82
Chlorobenzene	57	298	7	37
Ethylbenzene	68	332	8	42
Styrene	30	191	4	24

[a] mg/kg (n=3)

[b] mg/kg (n=3)

Note: Standard method of sample transfer consists of scooping and subcorer method uses device shown in Figure 15-3. Soil samples were spiked with 800 mg/kg of each VOC.

comparison of transfer techniques, Siegrist and Jennsen (1990) demonstrated that minimum losses were obtained by using an undisturbed sample followed by immediate immersion into methanol. The results for six VOCs are shown in Figure 15-5. At high VOC spike levels (mg/kg) the investigators found that headspace within the bottle caused a decrease in the concentration of VOCs in the sample. At lower spike levels, however, headspace did not seem to be a major contributor to VOC losses (Maskarinec, 1990). In another study (U.S. EPA, 1991a), it was found that a 5-g sample collected from a soil core and placed in a 40-mL VOA vial provided consistently higher VOC levels than a sample taken from the same core, placed in a 125-mL wide-mouth jar, and later poured out, homogenized, and a 5-g aliquot taken from the bulk material as per Method 8240 specifications.

SOIL SAMPLING SCENARIOS

The following recommendations for soil sampling and sample handling are presented for the three general sampling scenarios described earlier.

1. Open Test Pit or Trench

Samples are often collected from exposed test pits or trenches where remediation efforts are in progress. Sites may also be encountered where large-diameter coring devices cannot be employed. In such instances, crude sampling devices, such as trowels, spoons, shovels, spades, scoops, hand augers, or bucket augers must be used to excavate the soil.

The exposed face of an excavated test pit is scraped to uncover fresh material. Samples are collected from the scraped face by using a small-diameter, hand-held corer (Figure 15-3). If the nominal 5-g sample is to be collected, the appropriate volume (3 to 4 mL) is extruded into a tared 40-mL VOA vial and sealed with a modified purge-and-trap cap (Figure 15-4). The vial is chilled to 0° to

Table 15-11. Comparison of VOC Concentrations in Spiked Soil Analyzed by Method 8240 and Modified Method 8240

| VOC | Concentration (µg/kg) | | Difference |
	Method 8240[a]	Modified Method 8240[b]	
Bromomethane	9	44	35[c]
Vinyl chloride	3	32	29[c]
Chloroethane	6	36	30[c]
Methylene chloride	69	100	31[c]
Carbon disulfide	32	82	50[c]
1,1-Dichloroethene	12	35	23[c]
1,1-Dichloroethane	34	83	49[c]
1,2-Dichloroethene	36	66	30[c]
Chloroform	56	96	40[c]
1,1,1-Trichloroethane	26	80	54[c]
Carbon tetrachloride	18	61	43[c]
Vinyl acetate	18	26	8
1,2-Dichloroethane	101	159	58[c]
cis-1,3-Dichloropropene	136	189	53[d]
Trichloroethene	48	87	39[c]
Benzene	56	114	58[d]
Bromodichloromethane	111	166	55[d]
Dibromochloromethane	121	159	38
1,1,2-Trichloroethane	142	193	51
trans-1,3-Dichloropropene	154	203	49
Bromoform	116	140	24
Tetrachloroethene	62	124	62[c]
1,1,2,2-Tetrachloroethane	137	162	25
Toluene	85	161	76[d]
Chlorobenzene	91	132	41[c]
Ethylbenzene	85	135	50[c]
Styrene	86	114	28[d]
Total xylenes	57	85	28[c]
KETONES			
Acetone	336	497	161[d]
2-Butanone	290	365	75
2-Hexanone	200	215	15
4-Methyl-2-pentanone	264	288	24

[a] Method 8240 using 125-mL wide-mouth jar mixing subsampling in laboratory purge/trap analysis.
[b] Method 8240 using 40-mL vial. 5-g sampled in the field, shipped to laboratory purge/trap analysis.
[c] Difference significantly greater than 0, with P-value <0.01.
[d] Difference significantly greater than 0, with P-value between 0.01 and 0.05.
Note: Spike concentration was 300 µg/kg.

4°C and sent to the laboratory where the entire contents of the vial are purged without opening the vial (U.S. EPA 1991b). Though this method minimizes losses of VOCs, the small sample size may exhibit greater short-range spatial variability than larger samples.

Alternatively, a small-diameter, hand-held soil corer (Figure 15-3) can be used to collect a larger volume of soil. The soil is extruded to fill a 40-mL VOA vial with a Teflon-lined septum cap (minimal headspace), chilled, and sent to the laboratory. The major weakness with this method is that VOCs are lost in the laboratory during sample homogenization, preparation of aliquots from a subsample, and the transfer to the extraction or sparging device.

If large coarse fragments or highly compacted soils are encountered, the use of a hand-held corer may not be possible. In this case crude sampling devices are used to rapidly collect and fill (minimal

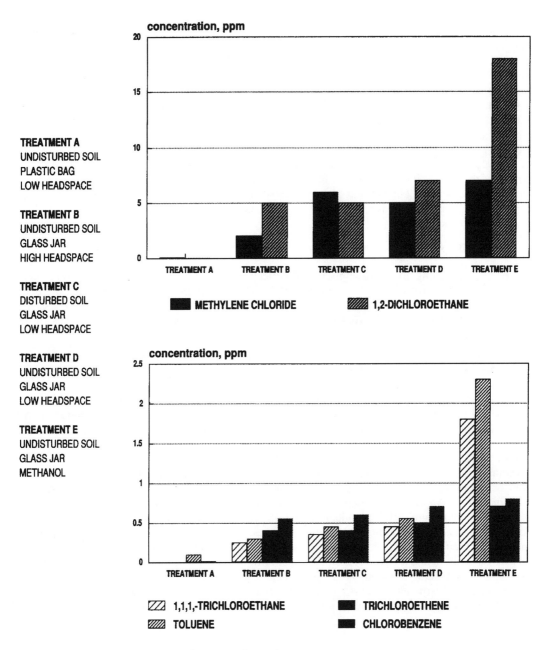

Figure 15-5. VOC recovery as a function of sample treatment.

headspace) a 125- or 250-mL wide-mouth glass jar. The threads are wiped clean and the jar is sealed with a foam-backed Teflon-lined cap. The jar is chilled immediately to 0° to 4°C for shipment to the laboratory. Losses of VOCs are considerably greater with this method due to disruption of the matrix and losses in the laboratory during sample preparation. Methanol immersion may be more suitable for these matrices.

2. Surface Soils (< 5 ft deep)

The preferred soil sampling procedures reduce VOC losses by minimizing sample disturbance during collection and transfer to a container. The collection of soil cores with direct extrusion into a container accomplishes this goal. A larger-diameter coring device (e.g., split-spoon sampler, Shelby tube, zero-contamination sampler) is used to collect an intact sample from the surface soil or from an augered hole. Many of these samplers can be used with liners, an insert that greatly reduces the time required to remove the soil and obtain a subsample. For subsamples collected from split spoons or extruded large diameter cores, the section to be subsampled is scraped and laterally subcored, or the extruded soil is cut or broken to expose fresh material at the depth or zone of interest, then longitudinally subcored. For large-diameter cores that are collected in precut liners, the liner sections are separated with a stainless steel spatula, and a small-diameter hand-held corer is used to collect a subsample from the center of the liner section. The uppermost portion of the core should not be sampled, because it is more likely to be cross contaminated. The small diameter corer (Figure 15-3) is pushed into the soil, the outside of the corer is wiped clean, and the required core volume (typically about 3 to 4 mL or 5 g) is extruded directly into a tared 40-mL glass VOA vial and sealed with a modified purge-and-trap cap (Figure 15-4). The vial threads and lip must be free of soil to ensure an airtight seal.

3. Subsurface Soils (> 5 ft deep)

The same sampling principles apply for the collection of deeper soil samples. Collection of soil cores with direct extrusion into a container greatly reduces the loss of VOCs. Tube-type samplers such as split-spoon, Shelby tubes, and zero-contamination samplers are used inside a hollow-stem auger to obtain an intact sample from greater depths. The coring device is retrieved and a subsample is obtained in a similar manner as that described for surface soils.

METHANOL IMMERSION PROCEDURE

Soil collected by protocols outlined above can be placed in a tared wide-mouth glass-jar containing pesticide-grade methanol (1:1 weight-to-volume ratio of soil to methanol). The immersion of relatively large soil samples into methanol has the advantage of extracting a much larger sample that is probably less prone to short-range spatial variability. This is of particular advantage with coarse-grained soils, materials from which it is hard to obtain a 1- to 5-g subsample for analysis.

Multiple small-diameter corers can be immersed in a single methanol-filled jar to produce a composite sample. Compositing becomes practical because VOCs are soluble in methanol, thus reducing losses. Appropriately collected composite samples can produce more representative data than a comparable number of individual samples. Short-range spatial variability is greatly reduced. Another advantage is the ability to reanalyze samples. The main disadvantages of using methanol include the requirements for handling and shipping the methanol and the detection limit that is raised by a factor of about 10 to 20. For the methanol-immersion procedure, jars filled with methanol and shipped to the laboratory are classified as a hazardous material, flammable liquid and must be labeled as per Department of Transportation specifications (49 CFR, 1982). If these disadvantages are unacceptable, then the modified purge-and-trap procedure may be applicable.

FIELD STORAGE

Material containing VOCs should be kept away from the sample and the sample container. Hand lotion, labeling tape, adhesives, and ink from waterproof pens contain VOCs that are often analytes of interest in the sample. Samples and storage containers should be kept away from vehicle and generator exhaust and other sources of VOCs. Any source of VOCs may cause contamination that may compromise the resulting data.

Once samples are removed from the sampling device and placed in the appropriate storage container, the containers should be placed in the dark at reduced temperatures (0° to 4°C). Excessively cold temperatures (<-10°C) should be avoided; studies have shown greater losses of analytes due to reduced pressures in the container, sublimation of water, and concomitant release of water-soluble VOCs into the headspace. Upon opening the container, the vacuum is quickly replaced with ambient air, thus purging out VOCs from the headspace (Maskarinec et al., 1988). Extremely cold temperatures can also loosen the seal on the container cap. Caps should be retightened after 15 minutes at reduced temperatures. Samples should be kept in ice chests while en route to the shipment facility or laboratory. At temperatures above freezing, bacterial action can have a significant impact on the observed soil VOC concentration. Numerous preservation techniques are being evaluated at the University of Nevada Environmental Research Center in Las Vegas and at Oak Ridge National Laboratory.

SHIPPING

Given the short holding times required for VOC analysis under Method 8240 (10 days from sample collection to analysis), samples are usually shipped via air carrier to the analytical laboratory. Samples should be well packed and padded to prevent breakage. Temperatures in cargo holds can increase to more than 50°C during transit, therefore, the need for adequate cold storage is critical. Styrofoam coolers are commercially available to accommodate 40-mL and 125-mL glass containers. Sufficient quantities of Blue Ice™ or Freeze-Gel™ packs should be placed in the container to ensure that samples are cooled for the duration of the shipment. A maximum-minimum thermometer (non-mercury) should be shipped with the samples. If sample containers are not adequately sealed, VOC losses can occur. These losses may be exacerbated by the reduced atmospheric pressures encountered in the cargo holds of air carriers. Figure 15-6 illustrates the changes in temperature and pressure in the cargo hold of various air carrier's aircraft. Three major air carriers have been monitored and have shown similar fluctuations in temperature and pressure (Lewis and Parolini, 1991). Lewis et al. (1990) noted decreases in VOC concentrations in soil samples that were shipped compared to samples that were analyzed in the field. If the container is of questionable or unknown integrity, it should either be evaluated prior to use or a previously characterized container should be used.

As discussed previously, samples that are immersed in methanol have special shipping requirements. These samples must be shipped as "Flammable Liquids" under Department of Transportation (DOT) requirements. A secondary container is required for shipment of any item classified as a flammable liquid.

PRESERVATION

Improvements in operational factors such as sampling device efficiency, sample transfer, containerizing, shipping, storage, laboratory sample preparation, and analysis will reduce VOC losses from soils. Two principal matrix-specific factors that can contribute to the loss of VOC in soils are biodegradation and volatilization. An effective preservation technique should act on these matrix-specific factors to reduce losses of VOCs.

The required preservation technique for soil samples is storage at 0° to 4°C in the dark. This technique retards biodegradation processes mediated by soil microorganisms. Some microorganisms, however, such as fungi, are biologically active even at 4°C. Wolf et al. (1989) investigated several methods (i.e., chemical and irradiation) for sterilizing soil and concluded that mercuric chloride is one of the most effective preservatives that causes minimal changes to the chemical and physical properties of the soil. Stuart et al. (1990) utilized mercuric chloride as an antimicrobial preservative to stabilize ground-water samples contaminated with gasoline. Other researchers (U.S. EPA 1991a) have used mercuric chloride to retard biodegradation of VOCs in soil samples. The soils were spiked with 150 µg/kg of Target Compound List (TCL) VOCs and were preserved with 2.5 mg of mercuric chloride per 5 g of soil. The results indicated that the amount of mercuric chloride needed to reduce biodegradation was directly related to the soil's organic carbon content. In addition, the levels of mercuric chloride added to samples did not interfere with sample handling or analysis. Currently, research is underway to quantitate the required mercuric chloride concentration as a function of soil organic content.

The loss of VOCs through volatilization is reduced by optimizing sample handling procedures. When samples require laboratory pretreatment, severe losses of VOCs (up to 100%) have been observed. In order to minimize volatilization losses, several preservatives have been examined (U.S. EPA 1991a), including solid adsorbents, anhydrous salts, and water/methanol extraction mixtures. The most efficient preservatives for reducing volatilization of VOCs from soils have been two solid adsorbents, Molecular Sieve - 5A™ (aluminum silicate desiccant) and Florasil™ (magnesium sili-

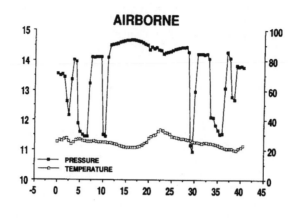

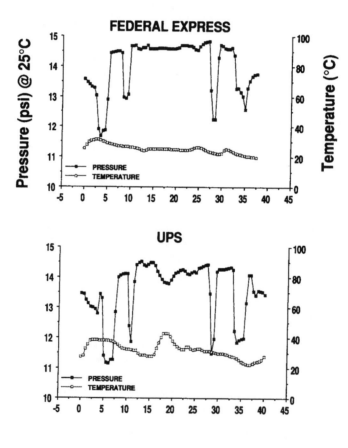

Elapsed Time (hr)

Figure 15-6. Temperature and pressure fluctuations recorded in the cargo hold of various air carriers. Recording device was shipped from Las Vegas, NV, to Pearl River, NY, and returned.

cate desiccant). The addition of 0.2 mg per 5 g of soil greatly increased the recovery of VOCs from spiked samples. The mechanism is believed to involve the displacement of water from adsorption sites on the soil particle and binding of VOCs to these freed sites. Currently, research is in progress with soils obtained from actual contaminated sites.

LABORATORY PROCEDURES

Sample Storage

Most regulatory procedures specify storage of samples for VOA at 4°C in the dark. Sample coolers should be opened under chain-of-custody conditions, and the temperature inside the cooler should be verified and noted. Samples should be transferred to controlled-temperature (4°C) refrigerators until analysis. In many cases, insufficient cooling is provided during transport. In these cases, data quality may be compromised.

Sample Preparation

The two most commonly used methods that satisfy regulatory requirements for the analysis of soil samples for VOCs are direct purge-and-trap and methanol extraction. Each procedure has benefits and limitations with respect to sample preparation prior to VOC analysis of soils.

The modified purge-and-trap procedure has the following characteristics:

- Homogenization of contents of wide-mouth jar will cause significant VOC losses. The collection of a 5-g aliquot in the field and placement into a tared vial sealed with a modified purge-and-trap cap is recommended.
- Surrogate addition should be made to the soil in the field, if possible.
- May be more susceptible to short-range spatial variability.
- Samples should be brought to ambient temperature before purging.
- May be more suitable for low-level samples.

The methanol-immersion procedure has the following characteristics:

- The key is to minimize the time samples are exposed to the atmosphere prior to immersion into methanol.
- Minimum detection limits can be raised by a factor of 10 to 20.
- The best option for sample archival because VOCs are highly soluble in methanol.
- Large-mass samples can be extracted in the field in a 1:1 ratio and the methanol extract shipped to the laboratory for analysis.
- Can collect composite samples.

The analytical methods that can be used for the analysis of soils for VOCs are summarized in Table 15-12. An analytical method should be selected that is compatible with the recommended sample collection and containerizing procedure discussed earlier.

CONCLUSIONS AND RECOMMENDATIONS

Current research on sampling soils for VOC analyses answers many of the questions asked by RPMs and OSCs who conduct site characterization and restoration.

1. There is no specific method or process that can be recommended for sampling soils for VOA. A wide variety of sampling devices are currently used for collecting soil samples for VOA. Sampling device selection is site-specific, and no single device can be recommended for use at all sites. Several different samplers, which cover a broad range of sampling conditions and circumstances, are recommended for obtaining representative samples for VOC analysis (Table 15-7). Procedures may vary for different VOCs. Experiments have shown that a procedure that collects an undisturbed, intact sample with a device that allows direct transfer to a sample container (e.g., split-spoon, Shelby tube, or zero-contamination sampler) is superior to a more disruptive procedure that uses a crude bulk sampler (e.g., shovel, trowel, scoop, or spade) for maintaining the integrity of VOCs in a soil sample. Large-diameter tube-type sampling devices are recommended for collection of near surface samples. The same types of devices can be used in conjunction with hollow-stem augers for collecting subsurface samples.

Table 15-12. Methods for VOC Analysis of Soil

Method Extraction/Analysis	Sample Size (g)	Sample Preparation Procedure	Sensitivity (mg/kg)	Data Quality Objective	Program	Comments
5030/8240 /8010 /8015 /8020 /8030 /8260	5	Purge-and-trap	5–10	Litigation	RCRA[a]	Sample transfer to purge-and-trap is critical.
5380/8240 /8010 /8015 /8020 /8030 /8260	5–100	Methanol extraction	500–1000	Litigation	RCRA	Sensitivity loss but sample transfer facilitated.
5031/8240 /8010 /8015 /8020 /8030 /8260	5	Field purge	5–10	Semi-quantitative	RCRA	Sample can only be analyzed once, transfer and shipping facilitated.
3810/8240 /8010 /8015 /8020 /8030 /8260	10	Heat to 90°C in water bath and analyze headspace	1000	Screening for purgeable organics	RCRA	Can be performed in the field.
3820	10	Hexadecane extraction followed by GC/FID	500–1000	Screening prior to GC or GC/MS analysis	RCRA	FID responses vary with type of VOC.
624	5	Purge-and-trap	5–10	Litigation	CLP[b]	Similar to method 5030/8240 in U.S. EPA (1986b).

[a] U.S. EPA, 1986b; [b] U.S. EPA, 1982.

2. Transfer of the sample from the sampling device to the container is a critical step in the process. Losses of as much as 80% have been observed during this step. The faster the soil can be removed from the sampling device and transferred into an airtight sample container, the smaller the VOC loss. Liners make the removal and subsampling of soil from the collection device more efficient.

3. The best method for transferring a sample from a large diameter coring device (or exposed test pit) into a sample container is by collecting the appropriate size aliquot (for laboratory analysis) with a small-diameter, hand-held corer and extruding the subsample into a 40-mL VOA vial, then sealing the vial with a modified purge-and-trap cap. Alternatively, contents of the large-diameter coring device can be sectioned and immersed in methanol.

4. Small-diameter, hand-held corers can be used for collecting samples from a freshly exposed face of a trench or test pit, or for obtaining a subsample from a large-diameter coring device. The use of a small-diameter, hand-held corer is recommended for obtaining subsamples from liner-held soil. Collection of a sample of the appropriate size for a particular analytical procedure is optimal. The required size of aliquot can be extruded into a 40-mL VOA vial and sealed with a modified purge-and-trap cap. The possibility exists of compositing several small-diameter core samples by immersing them in a single jar containing methanol.

5. Sample containers vary in terms of air-tightness. Data are available to indicate that there is a decrease in pressure and an increase in temperature in the cargo holds of certain air carriers. This is the worst possible set of conditions for maintaining VOCs in containerized soil samples. Intact seals on storage containers and adequate cooling is thus critical for maintaining VOCs in soil samples. Shipping and holding-time studies have shown that vials and jars may be equally suited for containing VOCs in soil samples, the laboratory pretreatment step needed to obtain an aliquot from a jar-held sample causes significant losses of VOCs. Commercially available shipping packages with built-in cooling materials (e.g., Freeze Gel Packs® or Blue Ice®) are available. Whenever possible, an integrated sampling approach should be employed to obtain the most representative samples possible. Soil-gas surveying coupled with on-site soil sampling and analyses followed by the Resource Conservation and Recovery Act (RCRA) or CLP laboratory analyses may provide valuable information on the partitioning of VOCs at a site.

6. The current preservation technique for soil samples is storage at 4°C in the dark. Biological activity may continue at this temperature. The addition of mercuric chloride to the soil may reduce biodegradation of VOCs. The amount of mercuric chloride to be added, however, is a function of the organic carbon content in the soil. The most promising preservatives for reducing losses of VOCs through volatilization are solid adsorbents such as Molecular Sieve - 5A™ and Florasil™.

EPA CONTACTS

For further information contact: Ken Brown, EPA Technical Support Center for Monitoring and Site Characterization, Las Vegas, NV, 702/798-2270.

ACKNOWLEDGMENTS

A group of scientists actively engaged in method development research on soil sampling and analysis for VOCs gathered at the Environmental Monitoring Systems Laboratory in Las Vegas to examine this issue. Members of the committee were R.E. Cameron (LESC), A.B. Crockett (EG&G), C.L. Gerlach (LESC), T.E. Lewis (LESC), M.P. Maskarinec (ORNL) B.J. Mason (ERC), C.L. Mayer (LESC) C. Ramsey (NEIC), S.R. Schroedl (LESC), R.L. Siegrist (ORNL), C.G. Urchin (Rutgers University), L.G. Wilson (University of Arizona), and K. Zarrabi (ERC). This chapter was prepared by The Committee for EMSL-LV's Monitoring and Site Characterization Technical Support Center, under the direction of T.E. Lewis, with the support of the Superfund Technical Support Project.

REFERENCES CITED

49 CFR, 1982. Code of Federal Regulations, 49, Parts 100 to 177, October 1, 1982, 231 pp.

Acker, W.L. 1974. Basic Procedures for Soil Sampling and Core Drilling. Acker Drill Co., Inc., Scranton, PA, 246 pp.

Arneth, J.-D., G. Milde, H. Kerndorff, and R. Schleyer. 1988. Waste deposit influences on groundwater quality as a tool for waste type and site selection for final storage quality. In: P. Baccini (ed.), The Landfill: Reactor and Final Storage, Swiss Workshop on Land Disposal of Solid Wastes, Gerzensee, March 14–17, pp. 399–415.

Barcelona, M.J. 1989. Overview of the Sampling Process. In: Keith, L.H. (ed.), Principles of Environmental Sampling. American Chemical Society, Washington, D.C., pp. 3–23.

Barth, D.S., B.J. Mason, T.H. Starks, and K.W. Brown. 1989. Soil Sampling Quality Assurance User's Guide, 2nd ed. EPA 600/8-89/046 (NTIS PB89-189864), 225+ pp.

Boucher, F.R. and G.F. Lee. 1972. Adsorption of Lindane and Dieldrin pesticides on unconsolidated aquifer sands. Environ. Sci. Technol. 6:538–543.

Bouwer, E.J. 1984. Biotransformation of organic micropollutants in the subsurface. In: Proc. Petroleum Hydrocarbons and Organic Chemicals in Ground Water Conf. National Well Water Association, Dublin, OH.

Cameron, R.E. 1963. Algae of southern Arizona-Part 1. Introduction to blue-green algae. Rev. Alg. N.S. 6(4):282–318.

Chiou, C.T. and T.D. Shoup. 1985. Soil sorption of organic vapors and effects of humidity on sorptive mechanism and capacity. Environ. Sci. Technol. 19(12):1196–1200.

Chiou, C.T., D.E. Kile, and R.L. Malcolm. 1988. Sorption of vapors of some organic liquids on soil humic acid and its relation to partitioning of organic compounds in soil organic matter. Environ. Sci. Technol. 22(3):298–303.

Dean, J.D., P.S. Huyakorn, A.S. Donigan, Jr., K.A. Voos, R.W. Schanz, Y.J. Meeks, and R.F. Carsel. 1989. Risk of Unsaturated/Saturated Transport and Transformation of Chemical Concentrations (RUSTIC) - Volume 1: Theory and Code Verification. EPA/600/3-89/048a, Environmental Research Laboratory, U.S. EPA, Athens, GA, 203 pp.

Devitt, D.A., R.B. Evans, W.A. Jury, T.H. Starks, and B. Eklund. 1987. Soil Gas Sensing for Detection and Mapping of Volatile Organics. EPA/600/8-87/036 (NTIS PB87-228516).

Farmer, W.J., M.-S. Yang, J. Letey, and W.S. Spencer. 1980. Land Disposal of Hexachlorobenzene Wastes: Controlling Vapor Movement in Soils. EPA-600/2-80-119.

Ford, P.J., P.J. Turina, and D.E. Seely. 1984. Characterization of Hazardous Waste Sites—A Methods Manual, Vol. II: Available Sampling Methods, 2nd edition. EPA/600/4-84/076 (NTIS PB85-521596).

Gillman, R.W. and S.F. O'Hannesin. 1990. Sorption of aromatic hydrocarbons by materials used in construction of ground-water sampling wells. In: D.M. Nielsen and A.I. Johnson (eds.), Ground Water and Vadose Zone Monitoring, ASTM STP 1053 American Society for Testing and Materials, Philadelphia, PA, pp. 108–122.

Hanisch, R.C. and M.A. McDevitt. 1984. Protocols for Sampling and Analysis of Surface Impoundments and Land Treatment Disposal Sites for VOCs. Technical Note. EPA-EMB 68-02-3850, Work Assignment 11.

Jamison, V.W., R.L. Raymond, and J.O. Hudson. 1975. Biodegradation of high-octane gasoline. In: Proceedings of the Third International Biodegradation Symposium. Applied Science Publishers Ltd., London.

Johnson, R.E. 1976. Degradation of DDT by Fungi. Residue Review 61:1–28.

Jury, W.A. 1984. A User's Manual for the Environmental Fate Screening Model Programs BAM and BCM. Dept. Soil and Environ. Sci., Univ. of California, Riverside, CA. Submitted to the California Department of Health Services.

Karickhoff, S.W., D.S. Brown, and T.A. Scott. 1979. Sorption of hydrophobic pollutants on natural sediments. Water Res. 13:241–248.

Kleopfer, R.D. et al. 1985. Anaerobic degradation of trichloroethylene in soil. Environ. Sci. Technol. 19:277–284.

Kobayashi, H. and B.E. Rittman. 1982. Microbial removal of hazardous organic compounds. Environ. Sci. Technol. 16(3):170A–183A.

Lechevalier, H.A. and M.P. Lechevalier. 1976. Actinomycetes found in sewage treatment plants of the activated sludge type. In: Actinomycetes: The Boundry Microorganisms, Toppen Co., Ltd., Tokyo, Japan.

Lewis, T.E. and J.R. Parolini. 1991. Temperature and pressure fluctuations in air shipped samples: Implications on sample integrity. Analyst (in preparation). [Editor's note: a complete citation could not be obtained; this paper had not appeared in the Analyst as of fall, 1995.]

Lewis, T.E., B.A. Deason, C.L. Gerlach, and D.W. Bottrell. 1990. Performance evaluation materials for the analysis of volatile organic compounds in soil: A preliminary assessment. J. Env. Sci. Health A25(5):505–531.

Lotse, E.G., D.A. Graetz, G. Chesters, G.B. Lee, and L.W. Newland. 1968. Lindane adsorption by lake sediments. Environ. Sci. Technol. 2:353–357.

Maskarinec, M.P. 1990. Personal Communication.

Maskarinec, M.P., L.H. Johnson, and S.K. Holladay. 1988. Preanalytical holding times. Paper presented at the Quality Assurance in Environmental Measurements Meeting, U.S. Army Toxic and Hazardous Materials Agency, Baltimore, MD, May 25–26, 1988.

McCoy, D.E. 1985. "301" studies provide insight into future of CERCLA. The Hazardous Waste Consultant 3/2:18–24.

Plumb, R.H., Jr. 1987. A practical alternative to the RCRA organic indicator parameters. In: T. Bursztynsky (ed.), Proceedings of Hazmacon 87, Santa Clara, CA, April 21–23, pp. 135–150.

Plumb, R.H., Jr. and A.M. Pitchford. 1985. Volatile organic scans: Implications for ground water monitoring. In: Proc. Petroleum Hydrocarbons and Organic Chemicals in Ground Water Conf. National Water Well Association, Dublin, OH.

Richardson, E.M. and E. Epstein. 1971. Retention of three insecticides on different size soil particles suspended in water. Soil Sci. Soc. Am. Proc. 35:884–887.

Roy, W.R. and R.A. Griffin. 1985. Mobility of organic solvents in water-saturated soil materials. Environ. Geol. Wat. Sci. 7(4):241–247.

Shen, T.T. and G.H. Sewell. 1982. Air pollution problems of uncontrolled hazardous waste sites. In: Proc. Nat. Conf. Management of Uncontrolled Hazardous Waste Sites. Hazardous Materials Control Research Institute, Silver Spring, MD, pp. 76–80.

Siegrist, R.L. 1991. Volatile organic compounds in soils: The nature and validity of the measurement process. J. Haz. Mat. 29:3–15.

Siegrist, R.L. and P.D. Jenssen. 1990. Evaluation of sampling method effects on volatile organic compound measurements in contaminated soils. Environ. Sci. Technol. 24:1387–1392.

Smith, J.A., C.T. Chiou, J.A. Kammer, and D.E. Kile. 1990. Effect of soil moisture on the sorption of trichloroethene vapor to vadose-zone soil at Picatinny Arsenal, New Jersey. Environ. Sci. Technol. 24:676–683.

Spencer, W.F. and M.M. Cliath. 1970. Desorption of Lindane from Soil as Related to Vapor Density. Soil Sci. Soc. Am. Proc. 34:574–579. [Not cited in text.]

Spencer, W.F., M.M. Cliath, W.A. Jury, and L-Z. Zhang. 1988. Volatilization of organic chemicals from soil as related to their Henry's law constants. J. Environ. Qual. 17(3):504–509.

Stuart, J.D., V.D. Roe, W.M. Nash, and G.A. Robbins. 1990. Manual headspace method to analyze for gasoline contamination of ground water by capillary column gas chromatography. Personal Communication.

U.S. EPA. 1982. Test Method 624 (Purgeables). Methods for Organic Chemical Analysis of Municipal and Industrial Wastes, EPA-600/4-82-057, U.S. EPA Environmental Support Laboratory, Cincinnati, OH.

U.S. EPA. 1986a. Permit Guidance Manual on Unsaturated Zone Monitoring for Hazardous Waste Land Treatment Units, EPA/530/-SW-86-040, pp. 11–62.

U.S. EPA. 1986b. Test Methods for Evaluating Solid Waste (SW-846), Method 8240, Off. Solid Waste and Emergency Response (3rd Edition).

U.S. EPA. 1987. Data Quality Objectives for Remedial Response Activities: Development Process. EPA/540/G-87/003, Office of Solid Waste and Emergency Response, Washington, D.C.

U.S. EPA. 1988. Field Screening Method Catalog User's Guide. EPA/540/2-88/005, Office of Emergency and Remedial Response, Washington, D.C.

U.S. EPA. 1991a. Investigation of Sample and Sample Handling Techniques for the Measurement of Volatile Organic Compounds in Soil. University of Nevada, Las Vegas, submitted to U.S. EPA, Environmental Monitoring Systems Laboratory, Las Vegas, NV (in preparation).

U.S. EPA. 1991b. Manual for Sampling Soils for Volatile Organic Compounds. Environmental Monitoring Systems Laboratory, Las Vegas, NV, 26 pp. (in preparation).

van Ee, J.J., L.J. Blume, and T.H. Starks. 1990. A Rationale for the Assessment of Errors in the Sampling of Soils. EPA/600/4-90/013, Office of Research and Development, Environmental Monitoring Systems Laboratory, Las Vegas, NV, 57 pp.

Verschueren, K. 1983. Handbook of Environmental Data on Organic Chemicals, 2nd edition. Van Nostrand Reinhold Company, New York, NY.

Vogel, T.M. and P.L. McCarty. 1985. Biotransformation of tetrachloroethylene to trichloroethylene, dichloroethylene, vinyl chloride, and carbon dioxide under methanogenic conditions. Appl. Environ. Microbiol. 49:1080–1084.

Voice, T.C. and W.J. Weber, Jr. 1983. Sorption of hydrophobic compounds by sediments, soils, and suspended solids - I. Theory and background. Water Res. 17(10):1433–1441.

Wolf, D.C., T.H. Dao, H.D. Scott, and T.L. Lavy. 1989. Influence of sterilization methods on selected soil microbiological, physical, and chemical properties. J. Environ. Qual. 18:39–44.

Chapter 16

Potential Sources of Error in Ground-Water Sampling at Hazardous Waste Sites[1]

K.F. Pohlmann and **A.J. Alduino**, Desert Research Institute, Las Vegas, NV

INTRODUCTION

Acquisition of ground-water samples that accurately represent in situ physical, chemical, and biological conditions is critical to all phases of Superfund site investigations. Nonrepresentative data collected during the remedial investigation (RI) may interfere with the characterization of site hydrogeology, contaminant distribution, and the determination of whether ground water is providing a pathway for migration of waste constituents away from the site. The feasibility study (FS) phase of the investigation depends on representative data to adequately define the optimal remediation technologies for the site. Finally, accurate data are required during the remediation phase to determine whether remedial actions are functioning effectively.

Sample error is defined here as the deviation from in situ values of hydrochemical parameters and constituents caused by the conduct of ground-water sampling investigations. Errors in ground-water quality data reduce the ability of samples to accurately represent in situ ground water conditions resulting in increased variability of analytical results and weakened confidence in ground-water data. As a consequence, the objectives of the site investigation may be jeopardized. To ensure representative data, it is necessary to identify, evaluate, and reduce potential sources of error for every aspect of the sampling program. Errors that are most difficult to identify may be the most critical to sampling programs because important conclusions may be unknowingly based on erroneous or inadequate data.

PURPOSE AND SCOPE

This chapter is intended to familiarize Remedial Project Managers (RPMs), On-Scene Coordinators (OSCs), and field personnel with the sources of error inherent to ground-water sampling, and the relative impact of these errors on sample representativeness. Elements of typical sampling protocol will be discussed in relation to how these sources of error can be identified and minimized. Where possible, the error associated with a particular method or material will be quantified and the elements ranked as to their potential for adversely impacting sample representativeness. Some of the elements of sampling protocol to be addressed include monitoring well drilling, design, construction, and purging, sample collection methods and devices, sample filtration, equipment decontamination, sample transport and storage, and analytical methods.

Each Superfund site has unique geologic, hydrologic, biologic and chemical conditions that may influence the type and magnitude of potential sample errors. This chapter provides an overview of sample error; types of error potentially important at each site must be evaluated on an individual basis. Furthermore, while this chapter will remain static, the conduct of site investigations will be in a constant state of flux as new technology is developed and as the understanding of contaminant transport and fate and the sampling process is improved. As a result, sources of sampling error described herein may be resolved through the application of new technology and methods while new sources of error are likely to be identified.

---

[1] EPA/540/S-92/019.

MONITORING WELL DESIGN

The design of ground-water monitoring installations must be consistent with geologic, hydrologic, and hydrochemical conditions to obtain representative ground-water samples. Important aspects of monitoring well design include length of well intake interval, design of the filter pack and screen, design and installation of borehole seals, and well location.

Intake Length

The length and location of well intakes have important effects on the degree with which samples represent ground-water conditions. Long well intakes (long screens) are open to a large vertical interval and therefore are more likely to provide samples that are a composite of the ground water adjacent to the entire intake. Conversely, short intakes (short screens) may be open to a single strata or zone of contamination and are more likely to provide samples that represent specific depth intervals. Wells that are screened over more than one depth interval (multi-screened wells), regardless of their screen lengths, may impact ground-water conditions and samples in much the same way as long-screened wells.

Long-screened wells have been suggested as being more cost effective in detection monitoring than several short-screened wells because they sample greater vertical sections of aquifers (Giddings, 1986). However, pumping-induced vertical flow in wells with long screens can impact ground-water flow and contaminant concentrations near the well (Kaleris, 1989). In addition, when ground-water contamination is vertically stratified, composite samples collected from a long-screened well represent some sort of average of concentrations adjacent to the screen, and provide little information about the concentrations in individual strata. In particular, in cases where contaminants may be of low concentration and restricted to thin zones, long-screened wells may lead to dilution of the contaminants to the point where they may be difficult to detect (Cohen and Rabold, 1987). Likewise, long-screen wells intersecting contaminants of differing densities may allow density-driven mixing within the well bore and subsequent dilution of contaminant concentrations (Robin and Gillham, 1987). The use of inflatable packers to isolate specific zones within a long screen may not be an effective solution because ground water may flow vertically through the filter pack from other zones in response to the reduced hydraulic head in the packed-off zone during sampling.

Vertical head gradients in aquifers near long-screened wells may lead to error in two ways: (1) if contaminants are moving through a zone with low hydraulic head, cleaner water moving from zones of higher head may dilute the contaminants, leading to detection of artificially low concentrations, and, (2) if higher concentrations of contaminants are moving through a zone of high hydraulic head, cross-contamination between water-bearing zones may occur via the well bore (McIlvride and Rector, 1988). These workers describe a case history in which two aquifer zones were identified at a site, with only the top zone contaminated with VOCs. Wells screened only in the contaminated zone resulted in detection of VOCs in the few hundred μg/L range while samples collected from long-screened wells open to both intervals showed no VOC contamination. A numerical flow model of a long-screened well developed by Reilly et al. (1989) demonstrated that very low head gradients can lead to substantial cross-flow within long-screened wells. At sites where delineation of vertical hydraulic and concentration gradients is important, errors can be reduced by utilizing a system of nested short-screened wells that can more accurately characterize the contaminant distribution.

Multilevel sampling devices provide an alternative monitoring technique in situations where vertical head gradients are important or where contamination is vertically stratified. These devices can be installed in such a way that individual zones can be sampled separately without vertical movement of ground water or contaminants between zones. Using a multilevel device, Smith et al. (1987) detected a zone containing nitrate concentrations over 10 mg/L that had been previously undetected by observation wells with two-foot screens. The samples from the multilevel sampler also detected large vertical gradients in electrical conductivity (EC) and chloride that were not detected with the monitoring wells.

Residential and municipal water-supply wells that are often used during early phases of RI programs are generally constructed with long screens, therefore concentrations of contaminants in samples collected from these wells may not represent ambient ground-water concentrations. When defining human receptors this may not be an issue because the overall quality of ground water extracted from water-supply wells may not reflect the quality of water in individual strata. In these cases, dilution may reduce concentrations of contaminants to within health-based standards. However, gross errors may be introduced into the analysis if these concentrations are used for detailed delineation of the geometry and concentrations of contaminant plumes or detection of contaminants at very low concentrations.

To mitigate hazards, waste management options at Superfund sites may include remediation of contaminated ground water by pumping and treatment. Long-screen wells are often the most effective for extraction of ground water because they are hydraulically more efficient than wells with short screens. However, because accurate ground-water contaminant concentrations cannot be determined from these wells it may be necessary to install separate wells for monitoring the progress of ground-water extraction and treatment.

Filter Pack and Well Intake

Suspended solids that originate from drilling activities or are mobilized from the formation during development, purging, or sampling may disrupt hydrochemical equilibrium during sample collection and shipment. A properly designed combination of filter pack and well intake provides an efficient hydraulic connection to a water-bearing zone and minimizes the suspended solids content of sampled water. However, to be most effective, filter pack and well intake design must be based on the sediments encountered in each borehole. Inadequate well performance resulting from application of a generic well design may lead to incomplete well development and high suspended solids content in samples. Descriptions of the methods of filter pack and intake design can be found in Driscoll (1986) and Aller et al. (1989).

Artificial filter packs should be composed of a chemically-inert material so as to reduce the potential for chemical alteration of ground water near the well. Clean silica (quartz) sand is generally recommended and widely used because it is nonreactive under most ground-water conditions. Other types of materials may induce chemical changes. For example, filter pack materials containing calcium carbonate, either as a primary component or as a contaminant, may raise the pH of water that it contacts and lead to precipitation of dissolved constituents (Aller et al., 1989).

The use of a tremie pipe to install filter pack materials minimizes the potential for introducing sample error to this phase of well construction. Dropping filter pack materials directly into an uncased borehole may lead to cross-contamination by mobilizing sediments or ground water between depth intervals. Furthermore, installation of filter pack materials by methods which introduce water to the borehole may modify hydrochemistry to an unknown extent or add contaminants to the sampling zone. Water-based methods may also lead to cross-contamination within the borehole.

Borehole Seals

Borehole seals, generally composed of expandable bentonite or cement grout, are well-known as potential sources of sampling error. The expandable bentonite clay used in many seals has high ion exchange capacity which may alter major ion composition of water (Gillham et al., 1983) or concentrations of contaminants that form complexes with these ions (Herzog et al., 1991). The effects of these reactions are seldom revealed by measurement of field parameters and normally-conducted analyses, but in cases of extreme sodium bentonite contamination may be seen as abnormally high sodium concentrations.

Cement grout can also significantly influence ground-water chemistry, particularly if the grout doesn't set properly. Contamination by grout seals, which generally results from its calcium carbonate content and high alkalinity, may be identified by elevated calcium concentrations, pH (generally over 10 pH units), EC, and alkalinity (Barcelona and Helfrich, 1986). These workers found that cement contamination of several wells persisted for over 18 months after well completion and was not reduced by ten redevelopment efforts. Barcelona et al. (1988a) indicate that solution chemistry and the distribution of chemical species can be impacted by cement contamination although these impacts have not been quantified to date. In low-permeability sediments, the impacts of grout materials may be much greater due to insufficient flushing of the installation by moving ground water.

Contamination from borehole seals can be minimized by separating the seals from sampling zones by fine-grained transition sand, estimating the volume of seal material required before installation to more easily detect bridging problems during emplacement, and by allowing sufficient time for the seals to set. In addition, cement grout can be isolated from sampling zones by installation of a bentonite seal. Error can also be reduced by installing boreholes seals with a tremie pipe. Dropping seal materials directly into an uncased borehole may lead to cross-contamination by mobilizing sediments or ground water between depth intervals, or may contaminate sampling zones if the seal materials are dropped past the sampling zone depth. Furthermore, installation of seal materials by methods which introduce water to the borehole may modify hydrochemistry to an unknown extent or introduce contaminants to the sampling zone. Water-based methods may also lead to cross-contamination within the borehole.

Well Location

The location of monitoring wells with respect to ground-water contaminant plumes is important to the accurate depiction of contaminant movement and concentration distribution, especially in areas where concentration gradients are large. A discussion of optimum well placement is beyond the scope of this document, but aspects of this topic can be found in the works of Keith et al. (1983), Meyer and Brill (1988), Scheibe and Lettenmaier (1989), Spruill and Candela (1990), and Andricevic and Foufoula-Georgiou (1991). These investigators discuss various aspects of monitoring well network design and how monitoring well coverage of the area under investigation relates to accurate quantification of spatial variation in hydrochemical parameters. Generally implied within network design is the reduction in error associated with delineating spatial variation. Sampling from wells whose locations were determined without adequate consideration of network design and geologic, hydraulic, and hydrochemical conditions may lead to significant errors in data interpretation and conclusions. For example, resolution of concentration distribution may be reduced in areas where wells spacing intervals are too large for the scale of the investigation.

To summarize the topic of monitoring well design, collection of accurate ground-water quality data in three dimensions is strongly dependent on the design of the ground-water monitoring system, including both individual wells and well networks. Significant errors can be introduced into sampling data, and the resultant conclusions, if well intakes and filter packs are not designed for ambient conditions, or are placed at inappropriate depths or over excessive vertical intervals, or if borehole seals are improperly installed. Furthermore, the design of monitoring well networks may introduce error by inadequately representing spatial variation through inadequate coverage of the site. Although the magnitude of these errors is heavily dependent on the geologic, hydraulic, and hydrochemical conditions present at a particular site, order of magnitude effects are easily within the realm of possibility.

DRILLING METHODS

Long-term or permanent disturbance of hydrogeologic and hydrochemical conditions may result from the drilling method used for monitoring well installation, possibly leading to significant error during subsequent ground-water sampling. Drilling methods may disturb sediments, allow vertical movement of ground water and/or contaminants, introduce materials foreign to the subsurface, and clog void spaces. The extent to which conditions are altered depends on the drilling method utilized and the nature of the geologic materials (Gillham et al., 1983). In addition, the properties of the contaminants at the site will influence their sensitivity to the impacts of drilling.

Monitoring wells are commonly constructed by auger, rotary, drill-through casing, and cable-tool methods. Auger drilling methods utilize hollow- or solid-stem auger flights and are generally restricted to use in unconsolidated materials. Rotary techniques are classified based on the composition of the drilling fluid (water, air, and various additives), the mode of circulation (direct or reverse), and the type of bit (e.g., roller cone, drag, or button) and are adaptable to most geologic conditions. The drill-through casing method utilizes rotary or percussion drilling techniques but uses a casing driver to advance temporary casing in conjunction with the advancing borehole. In cable-tool drilling, the borehole is advanced by alternately raising and lowering a heavy string of drilling tools suspended from a cable. Temporary casing can also be advanced as drilling progresses.

Some drilling methods may alter the hydrogeologic environment by smearing cuttings (particularly fine sediments) vertically along the borehole wall. This action may form a mudcake that can reduce the hydraulic efficiency of the borehole wall and modify ground-water flow into the completed well (McIlvride and Weiss, 1988). Smearing may also transport sediments between zones and alter the vertical distribution of contaminants adsorbed onto these sediments. In addition, methods that mix sediments horizontally near the well bore may affect the transport of contaminants near the completed well (Morin et al., 1988).

Vertical movement of ground water may occur during drilling, primarily in situations where the borehole remains uncased during drilling operations. Ground water can be transported vertically by circulating drilling fluid or by hydraulic head differences between zones. In situations where contaminated ground water is vertically stratified, vertical ground-water movement may cause cross-contamination within the well-bore and adjacent formation (Gillham et al., 1983). Movement of ground water and contaminants between zones may also disrupt hydrochemical equilibrium near the well.

Drilling activities can alter hydrochemistry as a result of contact with introduced materials foreign to the subsurface environment. For example, lubricants or hydraulic fluids may enter the borehole directly by falling from the drilling rig or may enter indirectly via drilling fluids. In the latter case, contaminants may originate in mud pumps, air compressors, or down-hole drilling equipment. Soils or other material from the drilling site may also enter the open borehole or may adhere to drilling equipment as it is prepared for use. However, the material most commonly introduced to boreholes is drilling fluid, which is used to remove cuttings, stabilize the borehole wall, and provide cooling, lubrication, and cleaning of the bit and drill pipe (Driscoll, 1986). Drilling fluids commonly are composed of water or air alone or in combination with clay (usually bentonite) and/or polymeric additives.

Water from water-based drilling fluids that migrates away from the borehole and mixes with ambient ground water may alter hydrochemical conditions (Aller et al., 1989). For example, introduction of a different water type may add contaminants or disrupt hydrochemical equilibrium and cause precipitation of dissolved constituents. During sampling, some of these precipitates may be redissolved by ground water flowing toward the well causing nonrepresentative samples.

The bentonite additives used in many drilling fluids have a high capacity for ion exchange and may alter hydrochemistry of ground-water samples if not completely removed from the borehole and surrounding formation (Gillham et al., 1983). Ion exchange reactions that alter major ion composition may also affect the concentrations of contaminants that form complexes with these ions (Herzog et al., 1991). Organic polymeric additives can introduce organic carbon into ground water and provide a substrate for microbial activity leading to errors in water quality observations for long periods. Barcelona (1984) reported that total organic carbon (TOC) levels in wells drilled with fluids containing organic additives remained over three times higher than background levels for two years. In that study, TOC levels could not be reduced to less than two times background levels, even after substantial pumping.

The presence of drilling fluids in the formation surrounding well installations, even after well development, was shown by Brobst and Buszka (1986). That study, which used chemical oxygen demand (COD) as an indicator of the presence of drilling fluid, tested three additives of water-based drilling fluids: guar fluid, guar fluid with a breakdown additive, and bentonite. Brobst and Buszka (1986) reported that, using standard well purging and sampling methods, COD levels were elevated for 50 days in a well drilled with the guar-and-additive fluid, 140 days in a well drilled with bentonite, and 320 days in a well drilled with the guar fluid alone. More intense well purging reduced the COD levels, but not to background values.

Contaminants present in drilling fluid may also mix with ground water and bias sampling results. Mud pumps used with water-based drilling fluids can add trace quantities of lubricants to the fluid and deposit them in the wellbore and surrounding formation. Air compressors used to develop and maintain pressure of air-based drilling fluids may have similar impacts. Filtration units in air-based systems are designed to prevent this occurrence; however, if feasible, the air stream should be sampled during drilling to determine the effectiveness of the filter. Filtration is generally not possible for water-based systems so if ground-water samples are to be collected for compounds related to these lubricants it may be necessary to sample the drilling fluid before it enters the borehole.

An outline of potential impacts of drilling methods on ground-water sample quality is shown in Table 16-1, which was compiled from the work of Scalf et al. (1981), Gillham et al. (1983), Keely and Boateng (1987), Aller et al. (1989), and Herzog et al. (1991).

Table 16-1. Potential Impacts of Drilling Methods on Ground-Water Sample Quality

Method	Potential Impacts
Auger	Drilling fluids generally not used but water or other materials added if heaving sands are encountered may alter hydrochemistry
	Smearing of fine sediments along borehole wall
	Vertical movement of ground water and/or contaminants within borehole
	Lateral mixing of sediments near well bore
Rotary	Drilling fluids are required and may cause cross contamination, vertical smearing of sediments, alteration of hydrochemistry, and introduction of contaminants
	Smearing of fine sediments along borehole wall
	Vertical movement of ground water and/or contaminants within borehole
Drive-Through-Casing	Drilling fluids required but advancing casing reduces potential for drilling fluid loss, cross-contamination, and vertical smearing of sediments, ground water, and contaminants.
Cable Tool	Advancing casing reduces potential for cross-contamination, and vertical smearing of sediments, ground water, and contaminants.

WELL DEVELOPMENT

Ground-water monitoring wells are developed to restore the sampling zone to conditions present prior to drilling so that sampled ground water can flow unimpeded and unaltered into the well. Materials associated with the drilling process, including borehole wall mudcake, smeared and compacted sediments, and drilling and other fluids, all must be removed from the sampling zone to the extent possible. This can be accomplished in monitoring wells by several methods including surging with a surge block mechanism, surging and pumping with compressed air, pumping and overpumping with a pump, jetting with air or water, backwashing with water, and bailing. All of these methods have the potential (to varying degrees) to influence the quality of ground-water samples; the extent depends on the nature of their action and the condition of the sampling zone after drilling.

Development should be considered complete when representative samples can be collected and can continue to be collected indefinitely. Unfortunately, under most ground-water sampling circumstances determining when samples are representative of in situ conditions is not possible, so some related criteria are often chosen. Ideally, these criteria should include (1) the production of clear water during development, and (2) the removal of a volume of water at least equal to the amount lost to the formation during drilling and well installation (Kraemer et al., 1991). In addition, certain conditions may require that development be continued after the well has been allowed to recover from the first round of development efforts. This condition may exist if the first round of samples exhibit turbidity.

Incomplete or ineffective well development may allow drilling and other introduced fluids to remain in the sampling zone or may not remove all mudcake or smeared sediments from the borehole wall. The presence of these materials may introduce error by disrupting hydrochemical equilibrium or by introducing contaminants to the well or sampling zone. In addition, these materials can reduce the hydraulic conductivity of the filter pack and formation and modify ground-water flow near the well before and during sampling.

Development methods that utilize air pressure can entrap air in the filter pack and formation, disrupt hydrochemical equilibrium through oxidation, or introduce contaminants from the air stream to the formation and filter pack. These effects may be reduced if precautions are taken to eliminate air contact with the well intake. The addition of water during development may modify hydrochemistry to an unknown extent or may introduce contaminants to the sampling zone, even if all the water is removed during development. In light of these potential problems, jetting methods that inject air or water directly above the well intake are not recommended (Keely and Boateng, 1987). Likewise, other methods that introduce air or water to the well (surging and pumping with compressed air, and backwashing, for example) also may not be suitable for monitoring well development (Aller et al., 1989).

Development of wells at very high rates may displace filter pack and formation materials and reduce the effectiveness of the filter pack, particularly if the method involves excessive surging (Keely and Boateng, 1987). On the other hand, development at low rates (as is generally attained with sampling pumps) may not provide enough agitation to meet development objectives (Kraemer et al., 1991). In many monitoring well situations, using surge-block methods to loosen material and either pumping or bailing to remove the material has been found to be an effective development technique (Aller et al., 1989).

In low-yield wells, surging methods may result in excessive mobilization of fine-grained materials. For example, in a study conducted in fine-grained glacial tills, Paul et al. (1988) found that auger-drilled wells developed by surge-block methods produced samples with up to 100 times greater turbidity than samples from similar wells developed by bailer. In addition, the turbidity of samples from the surged wells did not significantly decrease after a second round of sampling while samples from the bailed wells showed a four-fold decrease (Paul et al., 1988). Because these wells were drilled in low permeability sediments without added fluids, the action of drawing down the water level within the well by bailing may have been sufficient to provide adequate development. On the other hand, bailing or pumping techniques alone may not be effective in wells constructed by drilling methods that introduce fluids or cause significant disturbance of sediments because the development force is dissipated by the filter pack.

The potential impacts of monitoring well development on ground-water sample quality are outlined in Table 16-2 which is based on the work of Keely and Boateng (1987), Paul et al. (1988), Aller et al. (1989), and Kraemer et al. (1991).

MATERIALS

Transfer of ground water from the subsurface sampling zone to a sample container at ground surface often involves contact of the sample with a variety of materials comprising the well, sampling device, tubing, and container. Some of these materials have the potential to bias chemical concentrations in samples as a result of sorption, leaching, and chemical attack, and biological activity (Barcelona et al., 1983). As a result, the materials selected for ground-water sampling must be appropriate for the hydrochemical conditions at the site and the constituents being sampled. Other factors that may influence the choice of materials, including costs verses benefits, availability, strength, and ease of handling, can be found in Aller et al. (1989).

Materials commonly used in the ground-water sampling train can be divided into five general categories (modified from Nielsen and Schalla, 1991):

1. fluoropolymers, which include polytetrafluoroethylene (PTFE), tetrafluoroethylene (TFE), and fluorinated ethylene propylene (FEP);
2. thermoplastics, which include polyvinyl chloride (PVC), acrylonitrile butadiene styrene (ABS), polypropylene (PP), and polyethylene (PE);
3. metals, which include stainless steel (SS), carbon steel, and galvanized steel;
4. silicones; and
5. fiberglass-reinforced, which include fiberglass-reinforced epoxy (FRE) and fiberglass-reinforced plastic (FRP);

This chapter will focus on the most commonly used materials including the rigid materials PTFE, PVC, and metals (particularly SS) and the flexible materials PE, PP, PTFE, PVC, and silicone.

Chemical and Biological Impacts

Sorption, which includes the processes of adsorption and absorption, may remove chemical constituents from samples thereby reducing the concentrations of these constituents from levels present

Table 16-2. Potential Impacts of Development Methods on Ground-Water Sample Quality

Method	Potential Impacts
Surging with surge block	Displacement of filter pack and formation materials or damage to the well intake (primarily a problem in poorly designed and constructed wells when surging is conducted improperly)
	Excessive mobilization of fine-grained materials from low-permeability formations
Surging and pumping with compressed air	Entrapment of air in filter pack and formation
	Disruption of hydrochemical equilibrium
	Introduction of contaminants
Pumping and overpumping with pump	Low-volume pumps may be incapable of sufficient surging action (primarily in high-yield wells with little or no drawdown)
Jetting with air or water	Entrapment of air in filter pack and formation
	Disruption of hydrochemical equilibrium
	Introduction of contaminants
	Excessive mobilization of fine-grained materials from low-permeability formations
Backwashing with water	Disruption of hydrochemical equilibrium
	Introduction of contaminants
Bailing	May be incapable of sufficient development action

in the ambient ground water. If compounds present in the ground water are removed entirely, false negative analytical results will be produced. Additionally, desorption of compounds previously sorbed can occur if water moving past the material contains lower concentrations of the sorbant than exists in the material. In this case, contaminants may be detected in samples that do not exist in the ground water, causing false positive analytical results. Sorption/desorption processes may be particularly important in situations where contaminant concentrations are at trace levels and change with time or where samples contact potentially sorbing materials for long periods (for example, during water level recovery in low-yield wells or in inadequately purged wells).

Leaching of chemical constituents from some types of materials may occur under the conditions present at many hazardous waste sites. Constituents of the materials, matrix, or compounds added during fabrication, storage, and shipment, may have solubilities in water high enough to be leached under natural ground-water conditions (Gillham et al., 1983). Ground water contaminated by high concentrations of organic solvents may cause significant degradation of the matrix of some polymeric materials, resulting in leaching of various compounds (Barcelona et al., 1983). As a result, false positive analytical results can be produced if the source of target constituents in ground-water samples is leaching from casing materials rather than the ambient ground water. In addition, corrosion of metal casing may introduce dissolved metals to ground-water samples and reduce the integrity of the well.

Under certain ground-water conditions, well-casing materials may impact biologic activity, and vice versa, in the vicinity of the well (Barcelona et al., 1988b) and lead to errors that are difficult to predict. For example, the presence of dissolved iron in ground water may favor the growth of iron bacteria near metallic wells and degrade the casing and screen (Driscoll, 1986). In addition, permeation of contaminants or gases through materials may be a potential source of sample bias with flexible tubing (Barker et al., 1987; Holm et al., 1988) but is unlikely with rigid materials, as demonstrated by Berens (1985) for organic compounds and rigid PVC pipe over time periods less than 100 years.

Rigid Materials

Rigid materials that contact ground-water samples are generally used in well casings and screens, sampler components, and filtration equipment.

PTFE

PTFE has been widely considered the best choice for monitoring well materials because of its apparent resistance to chemical attack and low sorption and leaching potential. However, several recent laboratory studies have shown that rigid PTFE materials actually demonstrate a significant ability to sorb hydrocarbons from solution. Sykes et al. (1986) found that PTFE materials sorbed several hydrocarbons from a solution containing concentrations of approximately 100 µg/L, but did not report quantities. Parker et al. (1990) found that rigid PTFE materials sorbed significant quantities of all tested chlorinated organics and a nitroaromatic; higher, in fact, than PVC materials. These workers found that losses of some of these compounds from test solutions (initial concentrations of each compound were approximately 2 mg/L) exceeded 10% within eight hours. Likewise, rigid PTFE materials showed significant sorption of aromatic hydrocarbons in 24 hours of exposure for benzene, and six hours for several other hydrocarbons (Gillham and O'Hannesin, 1990). After eight weeks of PTFE exposure to benzene, 75% losses from the test solution were observed.

In contrast, PTFE materials tend to show lower potential for interaction with trace metals than PVC or SS (Barcelona and Helfrich, 1986). For example, lead was the only metal of four tested (arsenic, chromium, cadmium, and lead) in a laboratory study to be actively sorbed onto PTFE materials although only 5% of the lead concentration in the test solution was removed after 24 hours of exposure (Parker et al., 1990).

PVC

Early studies of PVC materials found substantial potential for sample error from sorption and leaching effects. Many of the conclusions about sorption were based on flexible PVC, which has a much higher sorption potential than rigid PVC. Leaching of high VOC concentrations was found to be a particular problem from PVC solvents and cements used for casing joints and bailer construction. Boettner et al. (1981) found cyclohexanone, methylethylketone, and tetrahydrofuran leached into water at concentrations ranging from 10 µg/L to 10 mg/L for more than 14 days after the glue was applied to PVC pipe. In addition to these compounds, methylisobutylketone was detected in ground-water samples several months after the installation of cemented PVC casing (Sosebee et al., 1982). The results of these studies indicate that alternative methods of joining PVC casing, such as threaded joints, should be utilized to reduce sample error.

Laboratory investigations show that threaded PVC well materials sorb hydrocarbon compounds, but often at lower rates than other polymers, including PTFE. Miller (1982) found little absorption of six VOCs over a six-week period, with the exception of tetrachlorethylene which showed a 50% decline in concentration in solution. These sorption results were significantly lower than those from PE and PP casing materials. Subsequent leaching from PVC was found to be at insignificant levels for all six VOCs. Gillham and O'Hannesin (1990) found that significant sorption onto rigid PVC from a solution containing six hydrocarbons did not occur until 12 hours after exposure. The PVC results were in contrast to three other rigid polymers (PTFE, FEP, and polyvinylfluoride) that showed significant uptake of at least one of the six compounds within three hours of exposure. After eight weeks of PVC exposure to benzene, 25% losses were observed from the original solution concentration of approximately 1.2 mg/L. Similar results were reported by Parker et al. (1990) who found that PVC sorption of 10% of initial organic compound concentrations didn't occur until over 72 hours of exposure, while PTFE sorption of 10% of three of the 10 tested organics occurred within eight hours of exposure. Two dichlorobenzene isomers showed the highest sorption rates on PVC: significant losses were observed within eight hours. Sykes et al. (1986) found no significant differences between PVC, PTFE, and SS materials in their tendency to sorb six organics at concentrations of approximately 100 µg/L each.

The results of these research studies indicate that rigid PVC materials have relatively low potential for sorption and leaching of organic compounds relative to other polymers when exposed to dissolved concentrations generally found at hazardous waste sites. However, Berens (1985) demonstrated that PVC may soften and allow permeation of organic compounds if exposed to nearly undiluted solvents or swelling agents for PVC. For this reason, PVC well casing should be avoided under these conditions.

PVC materials may also react with some trace metals. Miller (1982) concluded that in a six-week exposure to test solution, PVC materials did not affect chromium concentrations but that lead concentrations declined over 75%. A subsequent experiment showed that over 75% of the initial lead concentrations were desorbed from the PVC material. Parker et al. (1990) found that rigid PVC showed no measurable sorption or leaching of arsenic or chromium but that cadmium was leached and lead sorbed. For example, sorption of lead resulted in a 10% decline in lead concentration in their test solution in four hours, while subsequent desorption resulted in a 10% increase in lead concentration after four hours.

Stainless Steel

SS casing materials are often used when conditions warrant a strong, durable, corrosion-resistant material. Of the two types available, Type 316 is somewhat less likely than type 304 to be affected by pitting and corrosion caused by organic acids, sulfuric acid, and sulfur-containing species (Barcelona et al., 1983). However, long exposure to very corrosive conditions may result in chromium and nickel contamination (Barcelona et al., 1983), or iron, manganese, and chromium contamination (U.S. EPA, 1987) of samples. A field study by Barcelona and Helfrich (1986) found that stagnant water samples from SS installations showed higher levels of ferrous iron and lower levels of dissolved sulfide than nearby PTFE and PVC wells suggesting leaching from the SS and precipitation of sulfide by the excess iron. However, these workers demonstrated that proper well-purging techniques eliminated this stagnant water from ground-water samples, providing representative ground-water samples.

Laboratory experiments conducted by Parker et al. (1990) examined the potential for sorption on type 304 and 316 SS casing materials. These workers conducted experiments with aqueous solutions of arsenic, cadmium, chromium, and lead at concentrations of 50 µg/L and 100 µg/L and found that after 10 hours, sorption on both type 304 and type 316 caused a 10% decline in arsenic concentration in the test solution. Cadmium concentrations increased 10% in five hours due to leaching from type 304, before returning to initial concentrations after 72 hours. Cadmium leaching from type 316 caused a maximum 30% increase after 20 hours, with concentrations still 20% above initial values after 72 hours. No measurable sorption of chromium occurred for type 304, but 13% losses in 13 hours were observed for type 316. Sorption of lead on type 304 materials led to 20% losses after only four hours of exposure, and approximately 10% for type 316. Parker et al. (1990) concluded from this work that determinations of the concentrations of cadmium, chromium, and lead may be impacted by long-term contact with stainless steel materials. Unfortunately, these workers did not address whether well purging would eliminate these impacts and provide representative ground-water samples.

In a study with five halogenated hydrocarbons, Reynolds et al. (1990) found type 316 SS caused losses of bromoform and hexachloroethane over a five-week period. Losses of these compounds from the test solution were insignificant until one week, after which concentrations dropped up to 70% from initial concentrations of 20 to 45 µg/L. The losses were attributed to reactions involving the metal surfaces or metal ions released from the surfaces and not to sorption (Reynolds et al., 1990). A study by Parker et al. (1990) with ten organic compounds at concentrations of approximately 2 mg/L, found that type 304 and type 316 SS casing resulted in no detectable sorption or leaching effects after six weeks.

Other Metallic Materials

Steel materials other than stainless steel may be more resistant to attack from organic solutions than polymers, but corrosion is a significant problem, particularly in high dissolved-solids, acidic environments (Barcelona et al., 1985a). Ferrous materials may adsorb dissolved chemical constituents or leach ions or corrosion products such as oxides of iron and manganese (Barcelona et al., 1988a). In addition, galvanized steel may contribute zinc and cadmium species to ground-water samples. The weathered steel surfaces, as well as the solid corrosion products themselves, increase the surface area for sorption processes and may therefore act as a source of bias for both organic and inorganic constituents (Barcelona et al., 1985a; Barcelona et al., 1983). Reynolds et al. (1990) determined that galvanized steel showed a 99% reduction in concentrations of five halogenated hydrocarbons in a five-week sampling period. Aluminum casing caused concentration reductions of 90% for four of the compounds. Although many of these aspects of steel materials have not been quantified for typical ground-water environments, they may be a significant source of sample error.

Alternate Materials

Although not as widely tested or used, FRE may represent a rigid well material with relatively low potential for sample bias. In a 72-hour laboratory study, none of the 129 priority pollutants were detected to be leached from a powdered sample of the material (Cowgill, 1988). A three-week dwell-time study of casing materials by the same investigator resulted in detection of no base/neutral or acid compounds. Gillham and O'Hannesin (1990) concluded that sorption of benzene and other aromatic hydrocarbons onto FRE was slightly greater than onto rigid PVC but less than onto PTFE.

Borosilicate glass, another little-used well material, revealed no sorption effects after a 34-day exposure to five halogenated hydrocarbons (Reynolds et al., 1990). Of the ten well materials tested in that study, only the borosilicate glass showed no sorption characteristics. The low potential for sample error indicated by that study suggests that further investigation of borosilicate glass may be warranted to determine its suitability for ground-water sampling.

Flexible Materials

Semi-rigid and flexible materials are used for transfer tubing and other flexible components of the sampling/analysis train. In general, these materials contain plasticizers for flexibility that give them a higher potential than rigid materials to sorb or leach compounds. Latex rubber tubing, flexible PVC, and low density PE were all found to sorb greater quantities than more rigid materials (Reynolds et al., 1990).

In a study of five tubing materials in solutions of four chlorinated hydrocarbons, Barcelona et al. (1985b) found that most sorption occurred in the first 20 minutes of exposure. With the exception of tetrachloroethylene, the materials ranked in order of increasing sorption PTFE, PP, PE, PVC, and silicone. PE showed the highest sorption of tetrachloroethylene. Desorption from all materials occurred rapidly with the same ranking: PTFE desorbed a maximum of 13% of the sorbed concentrations after one hour while silicone desorbed 2%. From the results of this work Barcelona et al. (1985b) estimated sorptive losses of chlorinated hydrocarbons from sampling tubing under typical flow rates. As an example, using 15 m of 1/2-inch tubing, initial concentrations of 400 µg/L for the four halocarbons, and a sample delivery rate of 100 mL/min, these workers predicted 21, 29, 48, 67, and 74% sorptive losses for PTFE, PP, PE, PVC, and silicone tubing, respectively.

Sorption tests conducted by Barker et al. (1987) found that flexible PTFE led to 17% sorptive losses of benzene and 58% losses of p-xylene after two weeks. For PE, 49% losses of benzene and 91% losses of p-xylene were observed in two weeks. As found in other studies, initial rapid losses were followed by gradual concentration declines in all compounds. Desorption of these compounds followed a similar pattern; approximately 40% of the initial benzene mass and 20% of the initial p-xylene masses desorbed. Laboratory tests conducted by Gillham and O'Hannesin (1990) showed PVC and PE tubing caused sorptive losses of over 10% within five minutes of exposure to six hydrocarbons in solution. After 24 hours, 90% losses for the PVC and 80% losses for the PE had occurred.

These studies suggest that flexible PTFE tubing has lower potential for sorption and leaching than other materials, particularly PVC and silicone. However, even PTFE tubing may have significant impacts on concentrations of organic compounds in ground-water samples, depending on duration of contact. It is clear that the sorption and leaching effects of all materials used as tubing or other flexible portions of the sampling/analysis train should be considered when designing the sampling program. Those materials that demonstrate high potential for sorption and/or leaching should be avoided if those processes could impact concentrations of the compounds of interest to the investigation.

A further source of sample bias with respect to tubing is transmission of compounds or gases through the tubing materials. In a study of PE and PTFE, Barker et al. (1987) detected 2 µg/L benzene and 15 µg/L toluene passing through PE tubing within three days and 15 pg/L and 100 µg/L, respectively, after six days. Subsequent flushing of the tubing with three tubing volumes of clean water reduced the concentrations of both compounds detectable inside the tubing but they were still detectable after twenty volumes were flushed. Under the same conditions, the compounds did not pass through the PTFE tubing in detectable concentrations. These workers suggest that this mechanism may lead to sample bias in other polymeric materials, although perhaps at rates somewhat less than those exhibited by the flexible PE tubing, and could influence conclusions about when well purging procedures or remediation activities are complete. Holm et al. (1988) studied the diffusion of gases through FEP tubing, and found that the amount of gas transferred is proportional to the tubing length and inversely proportional to the flow rate through the tube. Calculations by the authors suggest that, given initially anoxic ground water, oxygen diffusion through sampling tubing could lead to detection of DO and changes in iron speciation within tens of feet. The results of these studies clearly indicate the potential errors that transmission through flexible tubing might introduce when sampling for both organic and inorganic compounds. This source of error can be reduced by using appropriate tubing materials for the sampling conditions and by minimizing tubing lengths.

Selection of Materials

It is clear from laboratory studies of casing materials that concentrations of trace metals and hydrocarbons can be impacted by sorption and leaching from PTFE, PVC, and metallic casing materials. However, laboratory studies do not attempt to duplicate the complicated, interrelated physical, chemical, and biologic conditions present in the field that may cause materials to behave very differently in the hydrogeologic environment. It is also important to keep in mind that most of these experiments were conducted under static conditions and may not adequately represent field conditions where stagnant water is generally replaced with fresh ground water during well purging. In the field, sorption of compounds onto casing materials between sampling events may not affect subsequent ground-water samples, as long as adequate purging and sampling procedures are conducted. Desorption of previously sorbed compounds after long-term exposure may be of somewhat greater importance because continuous desorption may impact trace-level concentrations, which might have important implications to remedial investigations where concentrations are expected to eventually reach nondetectable levels. But again, proper selection and implementation of materials and purging and sampling methods will reduce the impact of these processes.

Given the above discussion and current state of research, some generalizations may be made about the applicability of casing materials to various ground-water contamination scenarios, assuming that reducing sample error is the primary criterion for selection. When monitoring for low hydrocarbon concentrations in noncorrosive ground water, SS and PVC casing may be appropriate choices. Because PTFE has been shown to introduce error into hydrocarbon determinations it may be most applicable under conditions where SS and PVC are not. As examples, SS would not be appropriate in corrosive ground water or where determination of trace metal concentrations is of primary concern and PVC wells would be inappropriate in situations where solvents in moderate to high concentrations could dissolve the PVC material. A summary of the properties of rigid PVC, PTFE, and SS materials that may introduce sample error is shown in Table 16-3.

Laboratory studies indicate that the potential for error from flexible tubing is much greater than from rigid materials. For this reason, efforts should be made to use tubing with low potential for sorption and leaching and to minimize tubing length and time of contact. It appears that sample error can be significantly reduced by substituting flexible PTFE for PVC and silicone where possible.

MONITORING WELL PURGING

Purging stagnant water from monitoring wells prior to sampling is considered essential to collection of samples representative of ambient ground water. Stagnant water may result from biological, chemical and physical processes occurring between sampling events. These processes may include

Table 16-3. Properties of Commonly-Used Well Casing Materials that May Impact Ground-Water Sample Quality

Material	Properties
Polytetrafluoroethylene (PTFE)	Moderate potential for sorption of hydrocarbons.
	Low potential for leaching of organic constituents.
	Some potential for sorption and leaching of metals, but less than with thermoplastic and metallic materials.
	Particularly resistant to chemical attack, including aggressive acids and organic solvents.
	Not subject to corrosion.
	Resistant to biological attack.
Stainless Steel (SS)	Very low potential for sorption of hydrocarbons.
	Not subject to leaching of organic constituents.
	Significant potential for sorption and leaching of metals.
	Subject to chemical attack by organic acids and sulfur-containing species.
	Subject to corrosion.
	Subject to biological attack.
Polyvinylchloride (PVC)	Potential for sorption of hydrocarbons, but may be less than with fluoropolymers.
	Leaching of organic constituents may occur through chemical degradation by organic solvents.
	Sorption and leaching of some metals.
	Subject to chemical attack by organic solvents.
	Not subject to corrosion.
	Resistant to biological attack.

biological activity, sorption/desorption reactions with materials of the well leaching from the materials of the well, degassing and volatilization, atmospheric contamination, and foreign material entering the well from ground surface.

An effective purging method must allow for flushing of the well and sampling device of stagnant water without causing undesirable physical and chemical changes in the adjacent water-bearing zone that may bias subsequent samples. Important aspects of purging include purge volume, pumping rate, depth of the purging device, and purging methods for low-yield wells. Field experiments have shown that purging has important impacts on sample chemistry, perhaps greater than other aspects of sampling protocol such as sampling device and materials (Barcelona and Helfrich, 1986).

Purge Volume

To ensure complete purging of a ground-water monitoring well, there must be established criteria to determine when the water in the well is representative of ambient ground water. Three criteria commonly advocated to determine appropriate purge volume have been described by Gibs and Imbrigiotta (1990) as: (1) a specific, predetermined number of well-bore volumes, (2) stabilization of the values of field chemical indicator parameters (such as temperature, pH, and EC), and (3) hydraulic equilibrium between water stored in the casing and water entering the casing.

The use of a specific number of well-bore volumes as the sole criterion for purge volume has been applied extensively in ground-water sampling with recommendations in regulations and the literature ranging from less than one to over 20 (Herzog et al., 1991). In addition, definitions of well-bore volume have included the volume contained within the casing, that volume plus the pore volume of the filter pack, and the volume of the entire borehole. Despite its widespread use, the well-bore volume approach does not directly address the issue of obtaining representative ground water because there is no proven relation between the number of well volumes removed and the completion of purging. The combination of details of well construction, contaminant distribution, and geologic and hydrochemical conditions result in unique conditions at every well such that the volume of water required for purging cannot be determined a priori. It is impossible to predict the magnitude of error that might be introduced by arbitrarily choosing a number of well volumes that results in incomplete purging.

Determining purge volume by measuring field parameters is also widely used. The assumptions implied in this approach are that; (1) as these parameters stabilize, stagnant water in the well has been replaced by ambient ground water, and (2) this water contains representative concentrations of the compounds of interest. However, field experiments conducted by Gibs and Imbrigiotta (1990) showed that field parameters often stabilized before the concentrations of VOCs. In almost 90% of their experiments, field parameter measurements stabilized when three well casing volumes had been purged while VOC concentrations stabilized after three well volumes in only about half of the cases. Likewise, Pearsall and Eckhardt (1987) observed in a series of field experiments that trichloroethylene concentrations continued to change after three hours of pumping at 1.2 L/min while field parameters stabilized within 30 minutes. Furthermore, measurements of individual field parameters may not reach stable values at the same purge volume suggesting that some parameters are more sensitive to purging than others. For example, Pionke and Urban (1987) found that temperature, pH, and EC values of purge water from 14 wells studied generally stabilized before dissolved oxygen and nitrate concentrations. Puls et al. (1990) found that while temperature, pH, and EC values generally stabilized in less than a single well-bore volume, other indicators such as dissolved oxygen and turbidity required up to three well-bore volumes before stabilization. Puls et al. (1990) considered reduction of turbidity to stable values using low pumping rates as critical to the collection of representative metals samples. It should be pointed out that in all of the cases mentioned above, reliance on commonly measured parameters (temperature, pH, and EC) alone would apparently have underestimated the proper purge volume. These results suggest that the choice of purge indicator parameters should be made such that the indicators are sensitive to the purging process and relate to the hydrochemical constituents of interest. This can be accomplished by evaluating the patterns of indicator parameters and ground-water constituents during well purging (a purge-volume test) to determine the appropriate purge volume.

Another implied assumption of the field parameter approach is that purging will result in the stabilization of all constituent concentrations at approximately the same purge volume. In many hydrogeologic systems this assumption may not be valid. For example, in aquifers contaminated by several VOCs, concentration trends during pumping may be very different. In an evaluation of a purge-volume test, Smith et al. (1988) found that concentrations of two compounds started relatively high and decreased with purging to below detectable levels. Two other compounds that were undetected at three casing volumes were detected at four casing volumes and their concentrations increased until stabilizing at ten casing volumes. A fifth compound remained at a constant concentration throughout the purge volume test. The authors did not report the concentrations observed or the volumes pumped, but it is clear that under these conditions the choice of purging volume could significantly impact interpretations of contaminant concentrations.

It is important to keep in mind that the distribution of contaminants in limited plumes within a ground-water system is generally in contrast to the more homogeneous distribution of natural hydrochemical conditions in space and time. Consequently, attaining stable concentrations of field parameters, or even gross chemistry, may not indicate a representative sample of the targeted aquifer volume around a monitoring well (Keely and Boateng, 1987). As a result, these workers suggest that the 'inherent variability of the concentration of contaminants in many plumes far outstrips the additional variability potentially induced by incomplete purging,' and recommend that spatial and temporal variations in contaminant concentrations be studied to determine optimum purge volumes.

Methods of determining purge volume by estimating when hydraulic equilibrium occurs between water stored in the casing and water entering the casing may be useful where conservative, nonvarying constituents are being monitored. However, determining hydraulic equilibrium by estimating the time at which water levels in the well are no longer affected by casing storage (the method of Papadopulos and Cooper, 1967) may lead to erroneous results (Gibs and Imbrigiotta, 1990). These workers compared the calculated hydraulic equilibrium volume to measurements of field parameters and VOC concentrations during several well purging experiments and found that the calculated volume consistently underestimated the volumes required to reach both stable field measurements and stable VOC concentrations. The casing storage method might provide an approximation of purge volume under conditions where conservative, nonvarying constituents are being monitored but the available evidence suggests that only sampling for the constituents of interest will provide a direct indication of when their concentrations stabilize.

Recent research reviewed by Puls et al. (1990) demonstrates that contaminants may be transported in ground water by association with colloidal-sized particles which are generally described as particles less than 10 μm in diameter. Where contaminant transport by association with colloids is an important mechanism, obtaining representative concentrations of mobile colloids becomes critical to sample representativeness. However, the acts of purging, sampling, and even placing the sampling device in the well have been demonstrated to significantly impact colloidal suspension in the sampling zones of monitoring wells (Puls et al., 1991; Kearl et al., 1992). If a significant portion of contaminants are transported in association with colloids, the results of these investigations and others suggest minimizing or eliminating purging, minimizing sampling flow rates (100 to 500 mL/min), and using dedicated sampling devices placed within the well intake may all be necessary to collect representative ground-water samples. This low-volume approach to purging and sampling was earlier proposed by Robin and Gillham (1987) when sampling for conservative, nonvarying parameters in high-yield wells. Using nonreactive tracers, these workers demonstrated that natural ground-water movement through the well intake was sufficient to prevent the formation of stagnant water with respect to conservative, nonvarying parameters, making purging large volumes unnecessary. Robin and Gillham (1987) pointed out that, under these hydraulic and hydrochemical conditions, representative samples can be collected with little or no purging using dedicated devices positioned within the well intake. In order to resolve the issue of low-volume purging, however, it appears that more research is necessary to better understand colloid movement in ground-water environments, their importance to contaminant transport, and their implications to purging and sampling techniques.

Purge Rate and Depth

It was suggested previously that the pumping rate at which purging is conducted may impact sampling results. Although few detailed studies have been conducted to directly address this issue, the results of a few specific field studies suggest the types of impacts that purging rates might have on sampling results. For example, Imbrigiotta et al. (1988) reported that purging rates of 40 L/min were found to produce VOC concentrations up to 40% higher than concentrations obtained at purging rates of 1 L/min. Likewise, purging with a high-speed submersible pump at a rate of 30 L/min was found to generally produce higher colloid concentrations and larger particle sizes than a low-speed pump at rates lower than 4 L/min (Puls et al., 1990). Despite these colloid differences, however, metals and cation concentrations did not necessarily correlate to pumping rate. Both investigators attributed the variability to the effects that different pumping rates had on the distribution of hydrochemical conditions near the well. Imbrigiotta et al. (1988) further concluded that the variability in VOC concentrations caused by purging rate was of the same magnitude as that observed in a comparison of seven types of sampling devices, suggesting that purging rate may be at least as important to the collection of representative samples as the type of device utilized. Puls et al. (1990) suggested that the colloid differences might also have resulted from entrainment of normally nonmobile suspended particulates in the wells.

Although the issue remains unresolved, it appears that employing pumping rates that allow sample collection with minimal disturbance of the sample and the hydrochemical environment in and near the well may aid in minimizing sampling error. To this end, it has been suggested that the purging rate be chosen such that the rate of ground water entering the well intake is not significantly higher than the ambient ground-water flow rate (Puls and Barcelona, 1989). Under typical hydraulic conditions, this may be possible with pumping rates between 100 and 500 mL/min.

The depth at which purging is conducted may also affect sample representativeness. At high pumping rates or in low- and medium-yield wells, purging at depths far below the air-water interface may introduce error because stagnant water from the well above the pump may be drawn into the pump inlet. Under these conditions, pumping near the air-water interface significantly reduces the time required to remove stagnant water by reducing mixing from above the pump intake (Unwin and Huis, 1983; Robin and Gillham, 1987). Keely and Boateng (1987) suggest lowering the pump during purging so as to further reduce the possibility of migration of stagnant water into the intake during sample collection. On the other hand, under high-yield conditions, placing the pump at the well intake and utilizing low pumping rates may serve to isolate the stagnant water in the well bore above the pump thereby providing representative samples with minimal purging (Barcelona et al., 1985a; Robin and Gillham, 1987). Unwin and Maltby (1988) reported that pumping at virtually any depth within a well, including the intake, may lead to contamination of samples by stagnant water from above the pump inlet although their laboratory investigation demonstrated that at a pumping rate of 1 L/min, samples collected within the well intake contained less stagnant water than samples collected above the well intake. Regardless of the depth of the pumping device, if a stagnant water zone develops near the water surface subsequent movement of the pump or placement of a sampling device through this zone may cause contamination of the device by stagnant water.

As suggested above in the discussion of purge volume, certain hydrogeologic conditions and chemical constituents may require that samples be collected with little or no purging using dedicated devices positioned within the well intake. Under these circumstances, it would also be necessary to utilize low purging and sampling rates so as to minimize disturbance of the sample and sampling environment and to prevent migration of stagnant water from the well bore down into the sampler intake.

Purging in Low-Yield Wells

Purging low-yield wells introduces conditions that by definition don't occur in medium- to high-yield wells. These conditions, which tend to have their greatest impact on constituents that are sensitive to pressure changes and/or exposure to construction materials or the atmosphere, often result from dewatering the filter pack and well intake. Dewatering may produce a large hydraulic gradient between the adjacent water-bearing zone and the filter pack as a result of the large drawdown in the well and the low hydraulic conductivity of the formation. One consequence of this condition may be the formation of a seepage face at the borehole wall causing ground water entering the borehole to flow down the borehole wall and fill the dewatered filter pack from the bottom up. Formation of a seepage face increases the surface area of the interface between the liquid phase (ground water) and vapor phase (headspace in the well) available for transfer of solutes. Another consequence of the large hydraulic gradient is the sudden pressure decline from the pressure head in the water-bearing zone to atmospheric pressure in the pumped well. The sudden release of this pressure may cause losses from solution (by degassing or volatilization) of solutes that have combined partial pressures, with that of water, greater than atmospheric. Finally, because water levels recover slowly in low-yield wells, significant changes in the chemical composition of the ground water may occur through sorption, leaching, or volatilization before sufficient volume is available for sample collection.

In a field study of purging and sampling in low-yield wells, Herzog et al. (1988) found that some VOC concentrations increased significantly from pre-purging conditions during the first two hours of water level recovery. For example, chlorobenzene concentrations increased from 25 µg/L before purging to over 125 µg/L at two hours after purging. Concentrations generally did not change significantly after two hours, although some concentrations declined. Although Herzog (1988) provided no explanation for the observed concentration trends, they were likely caused by more representative ground water entering the well and replacing the purged stagnant water. Smith et al. (1988) reported very different results in their field study of a trichloroethylene plume. Concentrations of trichloroethylene declined from 100 µg/L directly after purging to 10 µg/L 24 hours after purging. In a laboratory study, McAlary and Barker (1987) found that if the water level in a simulated well was drawn down below the intake, VOC concentrations during recovery declined 10% in five minutes and 70% in one hour. These changes were attributed to volatilization from the water as it entered and filled the well.

In summary, aspects of well purging important to collection of representative samples include purging volume, pumping rate, depth of the purging device, and time of sampling in low-yield wells. Although error is strictly dependent on individual well and site conditions, the available evidence suggests that order of magnitude errors may easily result from improper purging techniques. In low-yield wells, time of sampling is clearly an important source of error although there are too few data available to completely understand concentration trends in these situations.

Contamination concentrations during purging vary in ways that are often difficult to predict, and various compounds may even exhibit opposite trends. To estimate the appropriate purge volume, it may be necessary to conduct preliminary purge volume tests with sampling at regular intervals during purging. These tests may be useful for determining how indicator parameters and constituent concentrations respond to purging rates, purging volumes, and the distribution of contaminants around the well. In addition, for certain sensitive constituents such as trace metals under certain hydrogeologic and hydrochemical conditions, low-volume purging and sampling should be considered with dedicated sampling devices installed at the well intake.

SAMPLE COLLECTION

Sample collection involves physical removal and transport of ground water from depth (generally from a monitoring well) to ground surface and into a sample container. As such, collection methods may have great potential for alteration of the sample's chemical state. Sampling devices must be chosen and used carefully to ensure that error is minimized. Important aspects of sample collection include sampling device, collection time after purging, and sampling depth.

Chemical Impacts

Sampling devices can cause chemical changes in the sample by contact with materials of the device (sorption, desorption, or leaching) or by the physical action of the device. Although the materials of the device are a potentially significant source of sample error, that topic was discussed previously and the following discussion will address chemical changes produced only by the operation of the sampling device.

Because fluid pressure in the saturated zone is greater than atmospheric, ground-water samples brought to the surface will tend to be under higher pressure conditions than the ambient atmosphere. Exposure of these samples to the lower atmospheric pressure will cause degassing and/or loss of volatile constituents until the partial pressures of the contained volatile components reaches equilibrium with atmospheric pressure. Degassing may cause losses of oxygen (O_2), methane (CH_4), nitrogen (N_2), or carbon dioxide (CO_2), while volatilization might affect any solute that exists as a liquid, solid, or gas under in situ ground-water temperature and pressure conditions (Gillham et al., 1983). Furthermore, loss of CO_2 may raise the pH which can lead to precipitation of dissolved constituents, particularly iron (Gibb et al., 1981). Constrictions in the flow path within a device may also raise the sample pH by changing the partial pressure of CO_2 (Herzog et al., 1991).

Exposure of samples to the atmosphere, or the driving gas used in some devices, may introduce oxygen causing oxidation of iron, manganese, cadmium, or other species. Oxidation of ferrous iron to ferric iron has important implications to the speciation and concentrations of many constituents in ground-water samples (Herzog et al., 1991). Contaminants may also be added to the sample by exposing it to the atmosphere or driving gas.

Sampling Devices

Sampling devices designed for use in conventional monitoring wells can be divided into four general types: grab, positive displacement (no gas contact), suction lift, and gas contact (Pohlmann and Hess, 1988). Grab samplers include open bailers, point-source bailers, and syringe samplers. Positive displacement samplers are usually submersible pumps such as bladder pumps, gear-drive pumps, helical-rotor pumps, and piston pumps. Suction lift devices include peristaltic pumps and surface centrifugal pumps while gas contact pumps include those devices that lift water to the surface by direct gas pressure. Submersible centrifugal pumps, which operate on the principle of positive displacement at low flow rates, develop a partial vacuum at the pump impellers at higher flow rates. For this reason, high-speed submersible centrifugal pumps without variable motor speed capability should be considered as distinct from positive displacement pumps. On the other hand, submersible centrifugal pumps are now available that can be used in 5.1-cm (2-inch) diameter wells and that allow adjustment of the motor speed to produce very low flow rates. If used at low flow rates, these low-speed pumps could conceivably eliminate the application of a partial vacuum to the sample and thereby can be considered as positive displacement pumps. Discussion of the operating principles of many of ground-water sampling devices, and their potential for sample bias, can be found in Gillham et al. (1983).

Sampling devices for conventional monitoring wells can be used either portably or in a dedicated mode. Portable devices are used to collect samples in more than one well and so may cause cross-contamination between installations or sampling events if not properly decontaminated. Dedicated devices are permanently installed in a single well and are generally not removed for cleaning between sampling events. Dedicated samplers, when also used for well purging, may not have adequate flow control for effective purging in large wells (high discharge rate) and sampling (low discharge rate). Furthermore, parts of dedicated samplers may sorb contaminants during periods of contact with ground water between sampling events and then release them during sample collection. Alternatively, if inappropriate materials are used in the construction of dedicated samplers, contaminants may leach from these materials between sampling events.

To study the effects of sampling devices on sample quality, investigations have been conducted both in the laboratory and in the field. Laboratory studies can provide values of absolute sample error by testing under controlled conditions, particularly constituent concentration. However, by their very nature, laboratory experiments represent ideal conditions that can never be duplicated in the field and therefore may not include important field-related errors. On the other hand, field studies include all the physical, chemical, biological, and operating conditions present in field sampling efforts, but the true concentration of the constituents of interest are unknown. As a result, field comparison studies cannot provide values of absolute sample error, only the relative ability of individual devices to recover the constituent of interest.

Values of field chemical indicator parameters can often be the first indication of sample errors due to sampling device. Laboratory investigations of a wide range of sampling devices by Barcelona et al. (1984) revealed that pH and redox potential (Eh) were the most sensitive to sampling device. The largest errors were produced by a peristaltic pump (an increase of 0.05 pH units and a 20 mV decline in Eh). All tested devices had O_2 and CH_4 losses of 1% to 24%, although positive displacement devices and an open-top bailer resulted in the lowest losses and the highest precision in that study. A field study by Schuller et al. (1981) found that, as a result of CO_2 stripping, an air-lift pump and a nitrogen-lift pump produced pH values up to 1.0 pH unit higher than a peristaltic pump and open top bailer. Other field studies concluded that open-top and dual-valve bailers produced no more error in field parameter values than bladder pumps (Houghton and Berger, 1984). In that study, which used bladder pump values as a standard for comparison, a peristaltic pump and a high-speed submersible centrifugal pump had increases in pH of about 0.06 pH units and approximately 20% declines in dissolved oxygen (DO) concentrations. A gas-driven piston pump had an increase in DO of 8% to 36%. Temperatures increased up to 5% in samples collected with the peristaltic and piston pumps and 14% in samples collected with the high-speed submersible centrifugal pump.

Most major dissolved ions are relatively stable and not greatly affected by collection method. Schuller et al. (1981) determined that concentrations of calcium, chloride, fluoride, potassium, magnesium, and sodium collected at two field sites were not significantly affected by the choice of suction, gas-contact, or bailer device. Dissolved metals, on the other hand, are very sensitive to sample aeration and degassing during sampling. Schuller et al. (1981) found that iron and zinc concentrations in samples collected with two gas contact devices were, at most 30% of those collected with either a peristaltic pump or a bailer. Field studies of 18 wells with seven sampling devices by Houghton and Berger (1984) showed significant declines in metals concentrations for a gas contact device when compared to positive displacement pumps, grab samplers, and a peristaltic pump. Houghton and Berger (1984) also found that coprecipitation of arsenic and zinc with iron led to significant losses of these constituents in samples collected with a high-speed submersible centrifugal pump.

Sampling device impact on VOC concentrations is of particular importance because of the high sensitivity of these compounds to sample aeration and degassing and the critical need for accurate VOC data in many site investigations. Several laboratory experiments have shown that positive displacement devices (bladder, piston, and helical-rotor pumps) and conventional grab samplers (open-top and dual-valve bailers) provide the most accurate VOC concentrations (Barcelona et al. 1984; Unwin, 1984; Schalla et al., 1988; Unwin and Maltby, 1988). Although the bladder pump and bailers that Barcelona et al. (1984) tested produced less than 3% losses in VOC concentrations, these same devices produced up to 10% losses in other studies, even under carefully-controlled conditions. Suction and gas-contact devices tested in these studies, and a study of peristaltic pumps by Ho (1983), resulted in 4% to 30% losses in VOC concentrations. Of those devices that performed well, no relation was found between sampler accuracy and VOC concentration over a range of 80 to 8000 μg/L (Barcelona et al. 1984; Unwin, 1984). The devices that performed poorly, however, often revealed significant increases in error as concentration increased (Barcelona et al., 1984). From these laboratory studies it appears that certain classes of samplers, specifically suction and gas-contact, can lead to significant error in VOC concentrations as a result of volatilization from the sample during collection.

A positive relation between increased losses of VOCs from solution with increase in Henry's law constant was predicted by Pankow (1986) based on theoretical considerations of the factors leading to bubble formation in water during sampling. Physical experiments have shown a strong positive correlation between compound volatility and Henry's law constant for a peristaltic pump, some correlation for a helical-rotor pump, but no correlation for a bailer and bladder pump (Unwin and Maltby, 1988). On the other hand, Barker et al. (1987) found no clear correlation for a peristaltic pump and gas-drive sampler and Barker and Dickhout (1988) found no clear correlation for a peristaltic, bladder, or inertial-lift pump, although the range of Henry's law constants was small. These findings suggest that compound volatility may not be an important source of bias for some positive displacement and grab samplers but there may be potential for losses for samplers that impose a suction on the sample.

Many field comparisons of sampler effectiveness verify the findings of laboratory experiments, despite the increased number of variables involved in the field studies. Investigations involving a variety of field conditions by Muska et al. (1986) Pearsall and Eckhardt (1987), Imbrigiotta et al. (1988), Liikala et al. (1988), Yeskis et al. (1988), and Pohlmann et al. (1990) concluded that positive displacement devices produced the highest VOC concentrations, and therefore introduced the least error into VOC determinations. The accuracy of grab samplers was more variable: some studies showed little difference between the VOC recoveries of bailers and positive displacement pumps (Muska et al. (1986); Imbrigiotta et al. (1988); Liikala et al. (1988)), but Imbrigiotta et al. (1987), Yeskis et al. (1988), and Pohlmann et al. (1990) reported that bailer VOC concentrations were significantly lower than positive displacement pumps; 46% to 84% lower in the work of Yeskis et al. (1988). Pearsall and Eckhardt (1987) found that a bailer was as accurate as a positive displacement pump at concentrations in the range of 76 to 79 μg/L but recovered 12% to 15% lower concentrations in the range 23 to 29 μg/L.

Another grab sampler, the syringe sampler, also produced mixed results. Muska et al. (1986) concluded that syringe sampler accuracy and precision were not significantly different from those of the positive displacement pumps while Imbrigiotta et al. (1988) concluded that syringe sampler accuracy was lower than the pumps but that precision was comparable. Other samplers field-tested produced significant error: a peristaltic pump and surface centrifugal pump were found by Pearsall and Eckhardt (1987) to be less accurate, but not necessarily less precise than the other samplers tested. Imbrigiotta et al. (1988) found the same for a peristaltic pump.

In ground-water environments charged with dissolved gases, collection of accurate VOC samples can be even more problematic. VOC losses of 9% to 33% were produced by a peristaltic pump in laboratory and field studies of water containing high CO_2 (laboratory study) and CH_4 (field study) concentrations (Barker and Dickhout, 1988). Losses of 13% to 20% were produced by a bladder pump in the laboratory study, while an inertial-lift pump produced no losses. No differences between results from these two pumps were observed in the field. The CO_2 concentrations used in the laboratory investigation were higher than under environmental conditions, but this study nonetheless suggests that degassing during sample collection, even with a positive displacement pump, can lead to significant error in VOC concentrations (Barker and Dickhout, 1988).

Several "in situ" devices have been developed to alleviate some of the problems inherent to conventional monitoring wells and sampling devices. These devices generally utilize sample containers under reduced pressure to collect samples directly from the water-bearing zone, without exposure to the atmosphere or excessive agitation. In a field study, Pohlmann et al. (1990) found that two types of in situ devices delivered samples with VOC concentrations that were not significantly different from those collected by a bladder pump in a conventional monitoring well.

Although the field studies outlined above cannot provide values of absolute sample error, they do provide information on the effectiveness of various devices under actual operating conditions. The results of the laboratory studies, in conjunction with field studies, indicate that suction pumps are very likely to introduce significant error into VOC determinations. Grab samplers, especially bailers, are also likely to produce errors if not operated with great care because their successful operation is closely related to operator skill. Under certain conditions, for certain parameters, and if operated by skilled personnel, bailers can produce representative samples. However, much of the research outlined here indicates that positive displacement pumps consistently provide the lowest potential for sample error. Appropriate application of most types of positive displacement pumps can reduce sampling device contribution to error well below the levels of some other aspects of ground-water sampling protocol.

A summary of the impacts that some commonly-used sampling devices have on ground-water sample quality is shown in Table 16-4 which was compiled from the sources referenced in this section and Nielsen and Yeates (1985).

Collection Depth and Time after Purging

The length of time between well purging and sample collection may influence the representativeness of samples by exposing ground water to the effects of atmospheric diffusion, interaction with well materials, and contaminant volatilization. Smith et al. (1988) found that trichloroethane concentrations in a well declined from 170 µg/L immediately after purging to 10 µg/L 24 hours later. To ensure consistency and to reduce potential errors when sampling in high-yield wells, it is generally recommended that samples be collected immediately following completion of well bore purging. In low-yield wells, however, low water level recovery rates may require that sampling be delayed until sufficient volume is available. Determination of sample collection time in low-yield wells is more problematic and may require site-specific sampling experiments.

To reduce potential errors caused by mixing with stagnant well water during sampling, research has suggested that the sampler intake be located either within the screened interval (Giddings, 1983; Bryden et al., 1986; Robin and Gillham, 1987) or at the top of the screened interval (Unwin, 1982; Barcelona and Helfrich, 1986) so samples can be obtained soon after fresh ground water enters the well bore. However, in cases where wells are screened over a long interval, it is important to determine if contaminants are vertically stratified in the well. Pearsall and Eckhardt (1987) found that TCE concentrations of samples collected at the top of a 10-foot screened interval were 30% lower than those collected at the bottom and attributed the difference to vertical stratification of VOCs within the screened interval. Errors associated with sampler intake placement have not been quantified to date but are likely strongly controlled by conditions at each well.

The use of samplers that must pass through the zone of stagnant water that invariably remains near the water level, even in a properly-purged well, may also introduce error. For example, grab samplers, which often require repeated entry and retrieval from the well during sampling, may be contaminated by this zone of stagnant water or may mix stagnant water into the water column. Likewise, if the purging device is not used for sampling, removal of the purging device and installation of the sampling device may have a similar effect. The use of a dedicated device for both purging and sampling would significantly reduce this source of error but may introduce others.

SAMPLE FILTRATION

Ground-water samples collected for analysis of certain constituents are often filtered in the field prior to transfer to the appropriate container. Reasons for filtration include prevention of geochemical reactions that might occur with particulates during sample shipment and storage, removal of

Table 16-4. Some Impacts That the Operating Principles of Ground-Water Sampling Devices May Have on Ground-Water Sample Quality (with the exception of grab samplers, it is assumed that these devices remain in the well during the sampling process).

Operating Principle	Impacts
Gas Contact	Contact with drive gas may cause loss of dissolved gases and increase pH.
	Contact with drive gas may volatilize sensitive solutes.
	Exposure to driving gas may introduce contaminants or oxidize sensitive constituents.
Grab	Contact with atmosphere during sample recovery and transfer may cause loss of dissolved gases and increase pH.
	Contact with atmosphere during sample recovery and transfer may volatilize sensitive solutes.
	Exposure to atmosphere during sample recovery and transfer may introduce contaminants or oxidize sensitive constituents.
	May be contaminated when passing through zone of stagnant water.
Positive Displacement	Minimal if discharge rate is low.
Suction Lift	Application of suction to sample may cause loss of dissolved gases and increase pH.
	Application of suction to sample may volatilize sensitive solutes.
High-Speed Submersible Centrifugal	Suction applied at pump intake may cause loss of dissolved gases and increase pH.
	Suction applied at pump intake may cause volatilization of sensitive solutes.
	Application of excessive head to the sample may cause degassing or volatilization.
	Heat produced by pump motor may increase sample temperature.

suspended sediments so as to analyze only dissolved constituents, and removal of fine-grained sediments which might interfere with laboratory analyses. Because filtration may contribute to sample error by the method employed or by the choice to filter, it is of the utmost importance to confirm the objectives of the sampling program and the implications of filtering when choosing whether to filter and, if so, the filtration technique.

Puls and Barcelona (1989) point out that if mobile trace metal species are of interest to the investigation filtration may remove metals adsorbed onto some colloidal particles, leading to underestimates of dissolved metals concentrations and, therefore, concentrations of mobile species. Conversely, if the objective of metals analysis is to quantify total dissolved metals concentrations, colloids with sorbed metals that pass through the filter material may result in overestimates of dissolved metals concentrations (Puls and Barcelona, 1989). These workers indicate that filtration should not be used as a means of removing from the sample particulates that result from poor well construction, purging, or sampling procedures because the misapplication of filtration may introduce substantial bias to trace metal determinations. If filtration is deemed necessary, it should be conducted soon after sample collection as temperature changes, CO_2 invasion, or the presence of particulates may have adverse effects on trace metal concentrations or dissolved solids content (Unwin, 1982). Factors important to proper field filtration include filter pore size, material, and method, and holding time prior to filtration.

Filter pore size has very important implications for determinations of metal species and major ions in ground-water samples as a result of the inclusion of undissolved material. Constituents showing the greatest sensitivity to filter pore size include iron and zinc (Gibb et al., 1981), iron and aluminum (Wagemann and Brunskill, 1975), and iron, aluminum, manganese, and titanium (Kennedy et al., 1974). In all cases, larger filter pore sizes produced higher concentrations of these constituents because the larger pore-size filters allowed more particulates to pass. In fact, Kennedy et al. (1974) found that concentrations of some metal species in samples filtered through 0.45 μm filters were up to five times higher than in samples filtered through 0.10 μm filters. These results suggest that if field-filtering is deemed necessary, smaller pore size filters may reduce sample error.

Sorptive losses of trace metals during filtration can also introduce error into metals determinations. Truitt and Weber (1979) found that both cellulose acetate and polycarbonate 0.4 μm filter membranes sorbed copper and lead from solution. For example, losses of copper averaged 8.6% with cellulose acetate membranes and 1.1% with polycarbonate membranes. Gardner and Hunt (1981) found that sorption of lead onto cellulose acetate membranes resulted in losses of 20 to 44% from a synthetic solution. These losses were reduced to 5 to 24% by pre-rinsing the filter apparatus with the test solution (Gardner and Hunt, 1981). Studies by Jay (1985) found that virtually all filters require pre-rinsing to avoid sample contamination by leaching of anions from the filter material.

Although filter material and pore size have been the subject of considerable research, less effort has been directed toward understanding the effects of filtration method on dissolved constituents. Of the few studies available, Stolzenburg and Nichols (1985) investigated the effects of sampling and filtration method on concentrations of iron and arsenic. Their laboratory study showed that samples that were vacuum-filtered after a 10-minute holding time delay experienced iron losses of 20 to 90% and arsenic losses of 45% to 100% compared to in-line filtered samples. The ranges of percentages were due to the use of several types of sampling devices. Later experiments by Stolzenburg and Nichols (1986) added immediate vacuum filtering of samples. Both immediate and delayed vacuum filtration produced similar iron concentrations but these concentrations were 17% to 67% lower than concentrations produced by in-line filtration. In both the 1985 and 1986 reports, in-line filtering produced concentrations that were comparable to the source concentrations of approximately 8 mg/L iron and 0.05 mg/L arsenic suggesting that in-line filtration methods were the most effective of those tested. These experiments also suggested that filtration method may cause greater losses of certain constituents than the type of sampling device used. Unfortunately, commonly-used pressure filtration methods were not compared to in-line and vacuum filtration methods in these experiments.

Clearly, sample filtration can lead to substantial error in trace metal determinations even if procedures are carefully followed. Because of this great potential for error, filtration should not be used to correct for sedimentation problems that result from poorly designed or constructed wells or incomplete development. If filtration is deemed necessary, pre-cleaning the filters can reduce error. In addition, the limited research into filtration methods in ground-water investigations suggests that in-line methods may result in the least sample error. However, even under ideal conditions, sample filtration may lead to significant error in determinations of metals concentrations, suggesting that analysis of both filtered and nonfiltered samples should be considered.

EQUIPMENT DECONTAMINATION

Contaminants on equipment that contacts ground water and samples, including drilling equipment, well materials, sampling devices, and sample bottles may be another source of sample error. Error may be introduced by the addition of contaminants to ground water or samples (contamination) or by the conveyance of ground water and/or contaminants from one sampling installation or zone to another (cross-contamination). Cross-contamination is most often a problem when equipment, particularly sampling devices, is used portably but not properly cleaned between installations. The process of cleaning equipment before installation or after sampling is generally referred to as decontamination.

Drilling equipment can be a source of gasoline, diesel fuel, hydraulic fluid, lubricating oils and greases, and paint, all of which can be introduced into the subsurface during drilling operations. In addition, contaminated soil, scale, or water from the site may enter the borehole directly or by adhering to drilling pipe or other down-hole equipment. If these contaminants originate from other sites or boreholes, cross-contamination may result (Fetter, 1983). Steam cleaning is often recommended as a method of decontaminating the drilling rig and equipment before use and between boreholes. In addition placing down-hole drilling equipment on plastic sheeting or other appropriate material while not in use may reduce contamination from soils or other sources of contaminants at ground surface.

Well casing and screen materials may contain residues of the manufacturing process including cutting oils, cleaning solvents lubricants, and waxes (Aller et al., 1989). These residues must be removed prior to well installation to prevent contamination or other chemical impacts on samples. A procedure generally recommended is to wash the casing in a strong detergent solution followed by a tap water rinse (Barcelona et al., 1983; Curran and Tomson, 1983) although steam cleaning or a high-pressure hot water wash may be required for removal of some oils, lubricants, and solvents (Aller et al., 1989).

Equipment used portably can lead to cross-contamination by transferring water and contaminants from one installation to another. In a survey of state and federal environmental regulatory agencies, Mickham et al. (1989) found that procedures for decontamination of sampling equipment generally include a tap water rinse, acid or solvent rinse (depending on type of contamination), organic-free water rinse, and air drying. The survey also showed that equipment that does not directly contact samples is generally cleaned by detergent washes and steam cleaning. These workers found little research into the effectiveness of decontamination procedures.

Korte and Kearl (1985) suggest that high-volume pumping may sufficiently clean sampling pumps. In contrast, field experiments conducted by Matteoli and Noonan (1987) determined that 90 minutes of pumping clean water through 200 feet of PTFE tubing was required to reduce the concentrations of several organic and inorganic constituents to below detection levels. These workers found that the time required for effective decontamination was generally related to the type of constituent. Freon was still detectable after 120 minutes of pumping.

The effects of cross-contamination can be reduced or eliminated by utilizing equipment dedicated to individual monitoring wells. As discussed previously, a potential disadvantage of this approach may be interactions between the device and ground water in the well between sampling events.

The use of plastic sample bottles may be another potential source of contamination through leaching of organic and inorganic constituents from the bottle materials (Gillham et al., 1983). An experiment comparing acid-washed and water-washed plastic sample containers determined that the risk of contamination from trace elements in the bottles was greatest for cadmium, copper, and zinc (Ross, 1986). In some cases copper concentrations were 50 times higher in samples collected in bottles that were not acid-washed. Moody and Lindstrom (1977) suggested that plastic sample containers are most effectively cleaned with rinses in both hydrochloric acid and nitric acid to leach impurities from the plastics. Their study further determined that, after acid-washing, PTFE and PE containers were the least contaminating plastic or polymeric materials.

Interference of ground-water sample chemistry may result from direct introduction of foreign materials to ground water and samples or from cross-contamination. Although it appears that currently used decontamination procedures are adequate in a general way, little research has been conducted to determine the effectiveness of specific procedures for individual contaminants. Because they are not standardized, the contribution to sample error of a particular procedure must be evaluated, perhaps on a case-by-case basis.

To prevent cross-contamination when using sampling devices portably, rinsate blanks (also referred to as equipment blanks) should be collected to ensure the effectiveness of decontamination procedures. This may be accomplished by flushing or filling the device with Type II reagent-grade water and collecting a sample of the rinsate water. Analysis of rinsate blanks for the contaminants being sampled will provide an indication of the effectiveness of the cleaning method (U.S. EPA, 1986) and indicate if modifications of the procedures are required.

SAMPLE TRANSPORT AND STORAGE

Ground-water samples require proper containers, treatment, transport, and storage to ensure the chemical and physical state of the sample is preserved until analysis. Factors that could potentially lead to error include volatilization, adsorption, diffusion, precipitation, photodegradation, biodegradation, and cross-contamination (Parr et al., 1988). Methods developed, and widely accepted, to minimize these effects are summarized in U.S. EPA (1986) and Herzog et al. (1991).

To reduce the potential for bias during sample handling, appropriate chemical preservation of samples should take place immediately upon collection. Increases in pH of 0.3 to 0.4 units and declines in iron and zinc concentrations of several orders of magnitude have been observed within seven hours of sample collection (Schuller et al., 1981). These investigators also noted slight declines in the concentrations of calcium, potassium, magnesium, manganese, and sodium in unpreserved samples within 48 hours of collection. To ensure immediate preservation, it may be advisable in some cases to add chemical preservatives to bottles immediately before sample collection. If this method is utilized it is important to prevent the bottle from overflowing which might cause the loss of some of the preservative.

Plastic bottles are usually used for metals and major ions samples to avoid the sorption effects that may occur with glass. Most types of plastic bottles can be cleaned with hydrochloric acid and nitric acid rinses which effectively leach impurities from the material. PTFE and PE bottles tend to not leach impurities to samples (Moody and Lindstrom, 1977) and therefore are the easiest to clean and have the lowest potential to contaminate samples. The quantities of impurities leached in these studies are in the very low ng/cm² range generally below the levels in most site investigations. Sorption of metals onto plastic bottles although normally not a problem, is reduced by acidifying the sample and thereby keeping the metals ions in solution (Parr et al., 1988). Clearly, if adequate cleaning is carried out and preanalysis holding times are not exceeded, contamination of major ion and trace metal samples by sample bottles is unlikely.

Organic samples are usually placed in glass containers to avoid the chemical interferences that may occur with plastic bottles. The borosilicate glass used in bottles for water samples for organic analyses is easily cleaned and has very little potential for contamination of samples or sorption from samples.

Cross-contamination of VOC samples during transport and storage can be minimized if accepted procedures are carefully followed. The evidence presently available indicates that cross-contamination of VOC samples at concentrations typical of hazardous waste sites is negligible under conditions normally present during sample storage (Levine et al., 1983; Maskarinec and Moody, 1988). Levine et al. (1983) did note, however, the thickness of the PTFE lining under the VOC vial septum was critical to the prevention of cross-contamination and that contamination was evident when samples were stored near vials containing saturated aqueous solutions of VOCs. Trip blanks can be utilized to evaluate the potential for contamination of samples during shipment to the laboratory. These blanks, which consist of reagent-grade water in bottles of the same type used for sampling, can be shipped to the site and laboratory in the same shipping containers used for samples.

The length of time that a sample can be stored without degradation is related to the potential sources of error covered here. If adequate measures are taken to reduce these errors, chemical alteration of the sample during storage can be minimized. Using commonly-accepted storage methods, concentrations of VOCs have been shown to be stable after 34 days (Friedman et al., 1986) and 56 days (Maskarinec and Moody, 1988).

ANALYTICAL TECHNIQUES

To gain perspective into the relative magnitude and importance of errors introduced during groundwater sampling, it is useful to quantify the errors involved in laboratory analysis. Potential sources of error in the laboratory include glassware, reagents, laboratory preparation techniques, and analytical equipment and apparatus (Lewis, 1988). It is beyond the scope of this document to discuss how each of these aspects of laboratory operation can impact sample quality except to say that errors can be detected and controlled by the use of various quality control checks. Vitale et al., (1991) describe the blanks, duplicate samples, and spikes that ensure the identification of laboratory error. Through the use of these checks, analytical errors often can be quantified, unlike many aspects of sampling protocol where comparison to 'true' concentrations is usually impossible.

In a review of the EPA Contract Laboratory Program (CLP) database for gas chromatograph/ mass spectrometer (GC/MS) analysis of VOCs, Flotard et al. (1986) analyzed the deviations in reported concentrations from actual concentrations in blind performance evaluation samples. These deviations can be considered measures of analytical errors, with underreported concentrations considered negative error and overreported concentrations considered positive error. The Flotard et al. (1986) study found errors in reported concentrations of 22 VOCs from -46.4% for 1,1-dichloroethane to +6.5% for bromoform. The results for methylene chloride exhibited an apparent error of +36.6% but this value was attributed to laboratory contamination of samples and not analysis error. Their review indicated that 55% of the 22 evaluated VOCs resulted in reported concentrations that were more than 20% lower than actual concentrations. Interlaboratory errors from 35 laboratories were found to be from -3.9% to zero, although data from only three compounds were analyzed.

A similar review of the CU database for semi-volatile analyses conducted by Wolff et al. (1986) concluded that the greatest analytical errors were associated with phenolic compounds, whose concentrations were consistently underreported. Other classes of semi-volatiles showed no general trends. In that study, analytical errors ranged from -48% for 1,3-dichlorobenzene and 2,6-dinitrotoluene to +12% for 4-chlorophenylphenylether. The review indicated that 60% of the 33 compounds evaluated showed analytical errors in excess of -20%, slightly more than for VOC analyses. Interlaboratory errors for six compounds ranged from -51% for phenol-d_5 to -16% for p-terphenyl, considerably greater than for the volatile analyses.

The CLP database has also been evaluated for errors introduced by inorganic analytical methods (Aleckson et al., 1986). These workers found that analytical errors ranged from -26.5% to +10.0%, with most errors falling in the range -10.0% to zero. The greatest negative errors were found for selenium, silver, and thallium.

Barcelona et al. (1989) tabulated laboratory errors for inorganic constituents during an intensive time-series investigation of ground-water chemistry variation. They found that errors in determinations of major ions in external performance samples ranged from -8.1% (potassium) to +12.1% (total iron). An evaluation of eight analytical laboratories was conducted by Rice et al. (1988) as part of a uranium mill tailings ground-water quality investigation. Constituents of interest included total dissolved solids, major ions, trace metals, and radionuclides. Analysis of external performance samples during the study showed that 67% of all analyses were within the acceptable range but that 60% of the reported values were higher than the known concentrations. Iron and aluminum were among the constituents showing the highest analytical errors.

SUMMARY AND CONCLUSIONS

As shown here, many aspects of ground-water investigations may introduce error into determinations of concentrations of hydrochemical constituents. The potential errors associated with many of these aspects are summarized in Table 16-5.

Errors produced during certain aspects of sampling programs can be identified, quantified, and controlled through the use of accepted procedures in conjunction with performance evaluation samples. For example, equipment decontamination and sample transport and storage have considerable potential for introducing sample error if not conducted in a careful and consistent manner. In the case of equipment decontamination, collection and analysis of rinsate blanks from cleaned equipment can be useful for evaluating the effectiveness of decontamination procedures. Likewise, errors that may occur during sample transport can be identified by the use of trip blanks that are transported to the site and laboratory in the same shipping containers as field samples. An aspect that may require particular attention and further research is the effectiveness of decontamination of flexible tubing used for conveying samples from the sampler to sample bottle.

The potential errors associated with other aspects of sampling programs are relatively well understood and can be minimized through appropriate choice of equipment and materials. For instance, advances in sampling device design and construction have resulted in the development and widespread use of positive displacement sampling devices whose operation generally introduces little sample error. For most compounds, including VOCs, positive displacement devices allow collection of accurate and precise samples, with concentrations of VOCs typically within 10% of true concentrations. Some grab samplers, particularly bailers, may also produce representative samples but their effectiveness is highly dependent on mode of operation and the constituents of interest. Under unfavorable field conditions or when operated improperly, bailers may produce errors in VOC concentrations from -10% to -80% or more. Most other types of samplers produce errors of unpredictable magnitude but show VOC errors of at least -20% in controlled laboratory experiments. The unpredictable magnitude of errors associated with many of these devices also means that they often cannot

Table 16-5. Potential Sources of Error Associated with Elements of Ground-Water Sampling Programs at Hazardous Waste Sites

Program Element	Type of Error	Ability to Avoid Error	Methods for Error Avoidance	Ability to Detect Error	Methods for Error Detection
Well Intake Length	Long-screened and multi-screened wells may lead to cross-contamination or contamination dilution.	Easy to Moderate	Identify specific zones of interest. Use intake length appropriate to program objectives and hydrogeologic and hydrochemical conditions.	Difficult	Compare with data from short-screen wells or field-screening methods.
Well Intake Depth	Well intake may miss zone of interest.	Easy to Moderate	Identify specific zones of interest. Use intake length appropriate to program objectives and hydrogeologic and hydrochemical conditions.	Difficult	Compare with data from other wells or field-screening methods.
Well Intake Design	Presence of particulates in samples	Easy to Moderate	Design in conjunction with filter pack for hydrogeologic conditions.	Easy to Moderate	Turbid samples.
Filter Pack	Presence of particulates in samples. Reaction with filter pack materials or introduced contaminants may alter hydrochemistry. Vertical connection of naturally isolated zones if filter pack too long. Invasion of borehole seal materials if filter pack too short.	Easy to Moderate	Design in conjunction with well intake for hydrogeologic conditions. Use clean, non-reactive materials. Install with tremie pipe and measure depths and volumes during installation to ensure correct placement.	Easy to Moderate	Turbid samples. Sorption/leaching studies of materials before installation.
Borehole Seals	If improperly placed, bentonite materials may alter hydrochemistry through ion exchange. If improperly placed, cement may elevate values of ground-water pH, EC, alkalinity, calcium concentration.	Moderate	Design for hydrogeologic conditions. Isolate seals from sampling zone. Install with tremie pipe and measure depths and volumes during installation to ensure correct placement.	Moderate to Difficult	Bentonite: High sodium concentrations if sodium bentonite used and samples are highly contaminated. Cement: Sample pH over 10, and high EC, alkalinity, and calcium concentrations.

Well Location	Inadequate coverage of area of investigation.	Moderate	Careful design of monitoring well network.	Difficult	Compare with data from nearby wells or field-screening methods.
Drilling	Depends on method. Contamination by drilling or other fluids may alter hydrochemistry. Smearing and mixing of fluids and sediments at borehole wall. Cross-contamination within borehole.	Moderate	Careful consideration and application of methods that are appropriate for program objectives and hydrogeologic and hydrochemical conditions. Minimize use of water-based drilling fluids and additives. If constituents sensitive to atmospheric exposure will be sampled, minimize use of air-based drilling fluids. Determine the chemical quality of drilling fluids used. Use appropriate development methods to minimize impacts of drilling.	Moderate to Difficult	Drilling fluid contamination. Depends on composition of fluid. Compare with data from nearby wells and field-screening methods. Evaluate chemical quality of fluids used.
Well Development	Depends on method. Incomplete development may lead to turbid samples or poor hydraulic efficiency. Alteration of hydrochemistry by development action. Introduction of contaminants (including air and water).	Easy to Moderate	Careful consideration and application of methods that are appropriate for program objectives and hydrogeologic and hydrochemical conditions. Avoid adding fluids to well. If adding fluids is necessary, determine the chemical quality of the fluids used.	Moderate	Turbid samples and production of sediments during pumping may indicate incomplete development or inadequate design of filter pack and well intake. If fluids were added, evaluate chemical quality of fluids used.
Materials	Depends on material, contaminants, hydrochemical conditions, and time of contact. Sorption/desorption of chemical constituents. Leaching of constituents from materials' matrix. Biologic activity. Possible transmission through flexible materials.	Easy to Moderate	Select materials that are appropriate for program objectives and hydrogeologic and hydrochemical conditions. Use appropriate well purging techniques.	Difficult	Sorption/leaching studies of materials before installation. Detection after installation depends on material, contaminants, hydrochemical conditions, and time of contact.

Table 16-5. Continued

Program Element	Type of Error	Ability to Avoid Error	Methods for Error Avoidance	Ability to Detect Error	Methods for Error Detection
Well Purging	Incomplete removal of stagnant water (water affected by contact with atmosphere and well and sampling device materials). Disturbance of ambient hydrochemical conditions.	Easy to Moderate (Moderate to Difficult under low-yield conditions)	Choose indicator parameters that are sensitive to purging process and relate to the chemical constituents of interest. Conduct purge-volume test to determine when parameters or constituents of interest reach stable values. Determine if low flow-rate and/or low volume purging is appropriate. If not, minimize volume of stagnant water above device intake by purging near water surface or lower device during purging or before sampling. Avoid drawing water level below top of well intake.	Easy to Moderate (Moderate to Difficult under low-yield conditions)	Conduct purge-volume test to determine when parameters or constituents of interest reach stable values.
Sampling Device	Depends on operating principle of sampling device. Sorption, desorption, and leaching from materials. Degassing or volatilization from sample. Atmospheric contamination.	Easy	Select device that is appropriate for sample type, hydrochemical conditions, and program objectives.	Moderate to Difficult	Depends on sampler type. Compare with data collected with other devices.
Sample Collection Time and Depth	Mixing with stagnant water in well. As time after purging increases, water in well becomes more stagnant.	Easy	Collect samples from within or immediately above well intake. Use appropriate sampling rate. Avoid moving sampler within water column during sampling. High-yield wells: Sample immediately after purging. Low-yield wells: Determine appropriate sampling time based on response of well and purge-volume test.	Moderate to Difficult	Test different scenarios and compare results, although may be very difficult to determine which results are the most representative.

Sample Filtration	Type of filter system used and length of pre-filtration holding time determines extent of temperature changes, atmospheric contamination, degassing, and sorption onto particulates. Filter pore size may affect passage of certain constituents and suspended material. Filter material and filter pre-cleaning may affect results. Erroneous conclusions about metals concentrations may result from association of metals with colloids.	Easy to Moderate	Determine if filtration is necessary for the objectives of the program. Minimize pre-filtration holding time. Use pre-cleaned in-line filters. Some situations may warrant use of pore sizes other than 0.45μm.	Moderate	Compare analytical results of filtered and unfiltered samples. Compare analytical results of different filtration methods.
Equipment Decontamination	Cross-contamination between wells if sampling equipment is used portably. Incomplete removal residues from manufacture or contaminants from storage, transport, or use.	Easy	Use appropriate cleaning and decontamination procedures.	Easy	Collect rinsate blanks after cleaning.
Sample Preservation	Changes in hydrochemistry during sample shipment and storage.	Easy	Use appropriate physical and chemical preservation procedures.	Moderate to Difficult	Indirectly identified by evaluating how well procedures are being followed.
Sample Transport and Storage	Cross-contamination between sample bottles. Materials' effects from sample bottles. Loss of volatile constituents.	Easy	Use appropriate sample bottle type and cleaning procedure. Do not exceed sample holding times.	Easy	Transport trip blanks with samples.
Laboratory Analysis	Deviation from true concentrations.	Moderate	Use appropriate analytical methods and laboratory procedures.	Easy to Moderate	Analyze blind performance evaluation samples, blanks, and standards.

provide the precise, or repeatable, measurements usually associated with positive displacement devices. As a result, the use of positive displacement sampling devices may minimize the introduction of error into determinations of the concentrations of sensitive hydrochemical constituents. Use of other types of devices may introduce error of unpredictable magnitude.

Potential impacts of materials used in well and sampler construction have been demonstrated, but the implications of these effects in a field setting remain unclear. Laboratory comparison studies conducted under static conditions have demonstrated the potential for rigid PTFE, PVC, and metallic materials to introduce error into concentrations of some trace metals and hydrocarbon compounds. However, little work has been concluded under conditions simulating dynamic ground- or sample-water flow or, more importantly, well-purging effects. Despite these unresolved issues, materials, impacts can be minimized by choosing well materials compatible with the objectives of the sampling program and the hydrogeologic and hydrochemical conditions of the site. The proper choice of materials can reduce chemical effects on water stored in the well between sampling events and make removal of stagnant water during well purging less difficult. When monitoring for low hydrocarbon concentrations in noncorrosive ground water, SS and PVC casing may be the most appropriate choices. Because PTFE has been shown to introduce error into hydrocarbon determinations, it may be most applicable under conditions where SS and PVC are not considered appropriate. For example, SS would probably not be considered an appropriate material in corrosive ground water or where determinations of trace metal concentrations are of primary concern. Likewise, PVC probably would not be considered an appropriate material in situations where solvents in moderate to high concentrations might dissolve the PVC material.

Flexible tubing can introduce significant error through sorption of contaminants onto tubing material, leaching of constituents of the tubing material into sampled water, and possibly transmission of organic compounds and gases through tubing walls. These errors are generally greater than for rigid materials and may be particularly important during site remediation efforts when declines in ground-water concentrations may be masked by desorption of previously sorbed compounds. Laboratory research has demonstrated the potential for errors under static conditions, but further research is required to understand how sorption/desorption mechanisms can impact samples during the dynamic sampling process. These studies suggest, however, that sample error can be minimized by substituting PTFE for other types of flexible materials.

Filtration of samples for trace metals determinations may introduce sample error either by the equipment and methods utilized or by the actual decision to filter. Due to the presence of colloidal sized particles in ground water, filtration can have dramatic impacts on determinations of the concentrations of both mobile and total dissolved metals. Indiscriminate filtration of metals samples may lead to gross errors in these concentrations and result in erroneous conclusions about ground-water transport of metals. In view of this, the objectives of the sampling program must be carefully considered before samples are filtered. If it is decided to filter samples, in-line filtration with pre-cleaned, lower pore-size filters can reduce errors associated with filtration.

In contrast to most aspects of the sampling process, errors introduced during laboratory analysis may be relatively well quantified. Analysis of the CLP database has shown errors in reported concentrations of performance samples of -20% to -30% for volatile and semivolatile compounds and -10% to zero for inorganic constituents. Errors in analytical methods, as with sample transport, sample storage, and equipment decontamination, can be quantified for individual investigations by analyzing standards and blind quality evaluation samples. Although the magnitude of analytical error may be greater than the error introduced during some aspects of sample collection, analysis of quality evaluation samples leads to easier identification and quantification of analytical error.

Errors associated with other aspects of site investigations, including well drilling and construction, are more difficult to identify because true concentrations of hydrochemical constituents are unknown in field investigations. During the drilling phase of site investigations, hydrogeologic disturbances can be minimized by utilizing appropriate drilling methods. Likewise drilling-related hydrochemical disturbances can be reduced by avoiding the use of fluids that might alter ground-water chemistry through ion exchange reactions or exposure to organic polymers. Well construction and development methods appropriate to the site hydrogeologic conditions are capable of removing artifacts from the drilling process and improving the hydraulic efficiency of the well with minimal impact on subsequent samples. Proper design, installation, and isolation of cement or bentonite seals reduces the potential for chemical alterations from these materials. Any of these aspects of drilling and well construction can lead to large errors if not carefully controlled; however, the magnitude of error is directly related to site conditions and the extent to which methods have been misapplied. Careful consideration and application of methods and materials during well drilling and construction can significantly reduce sample error.

Well purging method, purging rate, and the volume purged prior to sample collection all possess great potential for introducing significant error when sampling for sensitive constituents. For example, setting the purging device far below the air-water interface and using a high purge rate may contaminate samples by allowing stagnant water to mix with sampled water. However it is possible to identify these potential sources of error and modify purging procedures to minimize the errors. Conducting a preliminary purge test may aid in identification of the depth and rate that results in the most representative samples; however, determination of when purging is complete (purge volume) may be more difficult. Although purge volume can be calculated by several indirect methods, this volume may not directly correlate with the volume of water required to provide representative samples. In particular, stabilization of the values of field chemical indicator parameters such as temperature, pH, and EC may not coincide with stabilization of other hydrochemical parameters and constituents. Due to the often complex three-dimensional distribution of many contaminants, concentrations of individual constituents may not stabilize at the same time, or may never stabilize. Despite these possibilities, the potential for sample error can be reduced by choosing indicator parameters that are sensitive to the purging process and relate to the constituents of interest.

To reduce error when sampling for constituents that may be associated with colloids, or other very sensitive constituents, it is particularly important to minimize disturbance of the samples and the sampling environment during the purging and sampling process. To this end, reducing or eliminating purging, minimizing purging and sampling flow rates, and using dedicated sampling devices placed within the well intake interval should all be considered. Because this issue remains unresolved, general recommendations are not possible and it may be necessary to conduct preliminary purge tests to determine how indicator parameters and concentrations of important constituents vary with purging rate, volume, method, and distribution of contaminants around the well. Inadequate determination of these factors may lead to order-of-magnitude, or more, errors in concentration determinations, especially in low-yield wells.

The errors most critical to sampling programs are those that are difficult or impossible to identify because important conclusions may be unknowingly based on erroneous or inadequate data. Well location and design are aspects of sampling that are very likely to produce undetected errors. Errors produced by well location are virtually impossible to identify because their magnitude is entirely specific to that particular location. The appropriate placement of a well can mean the difference between detection of a contaminant plume or missing it entirely, so the potential for error is virtually infinite. Even if a well is located in the targeted zone of contamination or plume, little can be deduced about small-scale hydrogeologic properties or contaminant distribution without a well-designed monitoring network that accounts for individual site characteristics and program objectives.

Well design, particularly the depth and interval of the well intake, can also be a large potential source of undetectable errors. To delineate the vertical distribution of contaminants at a single location, samples must be collected at specific depths, hence, wells must be screened over short intervals and adequately sealed between sampling zones. Dilution and cross-contamination resulting from long-screened wells or poor well seals may produce order-of-magnitude errors in concentrations that far outweigh errors produced in all other aspects of the sampling process. For example, dilution of samples collected from long-screened remediation wells may mask true contaminant concentrations, leading to erroneous conclusions about the effectiveness of remedial efforts.

In conclusion, it can be stated that virtually all aspects of ground-water investigations, from well location to laboratory analysis, have the potential to introduce error into the determinations of concentrations of hydrochemical constituents. General definition of the magnitude of potential errors is difficult because errors will be influenced by the complex interaction of geologic, hydraulic, and hydrochemical conditions unique to each site, as well as the design and performance of the sampling program. Potential sources of error related to site conditions must be identified during early phases of the remedial investigation (RI) and then minimized by careful design of the sampling program. Modifications to the program design may then be necessary to address issues that might arise as the RI proceeds. Methods of detecting errors that may be introduced during the performance of the sampling program must be utilized so that these errors can be identified and minimized. However, errors that are difficult or impossible to detect may provide the greatest obstacles to the collection of representative data.

EPA CONTACTS

For further information contact: Ken Brown, EPA Technical Support Center for Monitoring and Site Characterization, Las Vegas, NV, 702/798-2270; or K.F. Pohlmann at 702/895-0485.

ACKNOWLEDGMENTS

This chapter was prepared under the direction of K.F. Pohlmann of the Desert Research Institute/ Water Resources Center, with the support of the Environmental Monitoring Systems Laboratory Las Vegas (EMSL-LV) and the Superfund Technical Support Project.

REFERENCES

Aleckson, K.A., J.W. Fowler, and Y. Joyce Lee. 1986. Inorganic analytical methods performance and quality control considerations. In: C.L. Perket (ed.), Quality Control in Remedial Site Investigation: Hazardous and Industrial Solid Waste Testing, Fifth Volume. ASTM STP 925. American Society for Testing and Materials, Philadelphia, PA, pp. 112–123.

Aller, L., T.W. Bennett, G. Hackett, R.J. Petty, J.H. Lehr, H. Sedoris, D.M. Nielsen, and J.E. Denne. 1989. Handbook of Suggested Practices for the Design and Installation of Ground-Water Monitoring Wells. EPA/600/4-89/034, 221 p.

Andricevic, R. and E. Foufoula-Georgiou. 1991. A transfer function approach to sampling network design for groundwater contamination. Water Resources Research 27(10):2759–2769.

Barcelona, M.J. 1984. TOC determinations in ground water. Ground Water 22(1):18–24.

Barcelona, M.J. and J.A. Helfrich. 1986. Well construction and purging effects on groundwater samples. Environ. Sci. Technol. 20(11):1179–1184.

Barcelona, M.J., J.P. Gibb, and R.A. Miller. 1983. A Guide to the Selection of Materials for Monitoring Well Construction and Ground-Water Sampling. EPA/600/52-84/024, 78 pp. [Also published as Illinois State Water Survey Contract Report No. 327.]

Barcelona, M.J., J.A. Helfrich, E.E. Garske, and J.P. Gibb. 1984. A laboratory evaluation of ground water sampling mechanisms. Ground Water Monitoring Review 4(2):32–41.

Barcelona, M.J., J.P. Gibb, J.A. Helfrich, and E.E. Garske. 1985a. Practical Guide for Ground-Water Sampling. EPA/600/2-85/104 (NTIS PB86-137304), 94 pp. [Also published as ISWS Contract Report 374, Illinois State Water Survey, Champaign, IL.]

Barcelona, M.J., J.A. Helfrich, and E.E. Garske. 1985b. Sampling tubing effects on groundwater samples. Analytical Chemistry 57(2):460–464.

Barcelona, M.J., J.A. Helfrich, and E.E. Garske. 1988a. Verification of sampling methods and selection of materials for groundwater contamination studies. In: A.G. Collins and A.I. Johnson (eds.), Ground-Water Contamination: Field Methods. ASTM STP 963. American Society for Testing and Materials, Philadelphia, PA, pp. 221–231.

Barcelona, M.J., G.K. George, and M.R. Schock. 1988b. Comparison of Water Samples from PTFE, PVC, and SS Monitoring Wells. EPA/600/X-88/091. Environmental Monitoring Systems Laboratory, Las Vegas, NV, 37 pp.

Barcelona, M.J., H.A. Wehrmann, M.R. Schock, M.E. Sievers, and J.R. Karny. 1989. Sampling Frequency for Ground-Water Quality Monitoring. EPA/600/4-89/032, 191 pp.

Barker, J.F. and R. Dickhout. 1988. An evaluation of some systems for sampling gas-charged ground water for volatile organic analysis. Ground Water Monitoring Review 8(4):112–120.

Barker, J.F., G.C. Patrick, L. Lemon, and G.M. Travis. 1987. Some biases in sampling multilevel piezometers for volatile organics. Ground Water Monitoring Review 7(2):48–54.

Berens, A.R. 1985. Prediction of organic chemical permeation through PVC pipe. Journal of the American Water Works Association 77(1):57–64.

Boettner, E.A., G.L. Ball, Z. Hollingsworth, and R. Aquino. 1981. Organic and Organotin Compounds Leached from PVC and CPVC Pipe. U.S. Environmental Protection Agency. EPA/600/1-81/062, 102 pp.

Brobst, R.B. and P.M. Buszka. 1986. The effect of three drilling fluids on groundwater sample chemistry. Ground Water Monitoring Review 6(1):62–70.

Bryden, G.W., W.R. Mabey, and K.M. Robine. 1986. Sampling for toxic contaminants in ground water. Ground Water Monitoring Review 6(2):67–72.

Cohen, R.M. and R.R. Rabold. 1987. Numerical evaluation of monitoring well design. In: Proc. First Nat. Outdoor Action Conference. National Water Well Association, Dublin, Ohio. pp. 267–283.

Cowgill, U.M. 1988. Sampling waters: The impact of sampling variability on planning and confidence levels. In: L.H. Keith (ed.), Principles of Environmental Sampling. American Chemical Society, Washington, DC, pp. 171–189.

Curran, C.M. and M.B. Tomson. 1983. Leaching of trace organics into water from five common plastics. Ground Water Monitoring Review 3(3):68–71.

Driscoll, F.G. 1986. Ground Water and Wells, 2nd Ed. Johnson Division. St. Paul. Minnesota, 1108 pp.

Fetter, C.W. 1983. Potential sources of contamination in ground-water monitoring. Ground Water Monitoring Review 3(2):60–64.

Flotard, R.D., M.T. Homsher, J.S. Wolff, and J.M. Moore. 1986. Volatile organic analytical methods performance and quality control considerations. In: C.L. Perket (ed.), Quality Control in Remedial Site Investigation: Hazardous and Industrial Solid Waste Testing, Fifth Volume. ASTM STP 925. American Society for Testing and Materials, Philadelphia, PA, pp. 185–197.

Friedman, L.C., L.J. Schroder, and M.G. Brooks. 1986. Recovery of several volatile organic compounds from simulated water samples: Effect of transport and storage. Environ. Sci. Technol. 20(8):826–829.

Gardner, M.J. and D.T. Hunt. 1981. Adsorption of trace metals during filtration of potable water samples with particular reference to the determination of filterable lead concentrations. Analyst 106:471–474.

Gibb, J.P., R.M. Schuller, and R.A. Griffin. 1981. Procedures for the Collection of Representative Water Quality Data from Monitoring Wells. Cooperative Groundwater Report #7. Illinois Department of Energy and Natural Resources, Champaign, Illinois, 61 pp.

Gibs, J. and T.E. Imbrigiotta. 1990. Well purging criteria for sampling purgeable organic compounds. Ground Water 28(1):68–78.

Giddings, T. 1983. Bore-volume purging to improve monitoring well performance: an often mandated myth. In: Proc. Third Nat. Symp. on Aquifer Restoration and Ground Water Monitoring. National Water Well Association, Columbus, OH, pp. 253–256.

Giddings, T. 1986. Screen length selection for use in detection monitoring well networks. In: Proc. Sixth Nat, Symp. on Aquifer Restoration and Ground Water Monitoring. National Water Well Association, Dublin, OH, pp. 316–319.

Gillham, R.W., M.J.L. Robin, J.F. Barker, and J.A. Cherry. 1983. Groundwater Monitoring and Sample Bias. API Publication No. 4367. American Petroleum Institute, Washington, DC, 206 pp.

Gillham, R.W. and S.F. O'Hannesin. 1990. Sorption of aromatic hydrocarbons by materials used in construction of ground-water sampling wells. In: D. M. Nielsen and A.I. Johnson (eds.), Ground Water and Vadose Zone Monitoring. ASTM STP 1053. American Society for Testing and Materials, Philadelphia, PA, pp. 108–122.

Herzog, B.L., S.J. Chou, J.R. Valkenburg, and R.A. Griffin. 1988. Changes in volatile organic chemical concentrations after purging slowly recovering wells. Ground Water Monitoring Review 8(4):93–99.

Herzog, B., J. Pennino, and G. Nielsen. 1991. Ground-water sampling. In: D.M. Nielsen (ed.), Practical Handbook of Ground-Water Monitoring. Lewis Publishers. Chelsea, MI. pp. 449–499.

Ho, J.S. 1983. Effect of sampling variables on recovery of volatile organics in water. Journal of the American Water Works Association 12:583–586.

Holm, T.R., G.K. George, and M.J. Barcelona. 1988. Oxygen transfer through flexible tubing and its effects on ground water sampling results. Ground Water Monitoring Review 8(3):83–89.

Houghton, R.L. and M.E. Berger. 1984. Effects of well-casing composition and sampling method on apparent quality of ground water. In: Proc. Fourth Nat. Symp. Aquifer Restoration and Ground Water Monitoring. National Water Well Association, Dublin, Ohio, pp. 203–213.

Imbrigiotta, T.E., J. Gibs, J.F. Pankow, and M.E. Rosen. 1987. Field comparison of downhole and surface sampling devices for purgeable organic compounds in ground water (Abstract). In: B. J. Franks (ed.), U.S. Geological Survey Program on Toxic Waste-Ground-Water Contamination: Proceedings of the Third Technical Meeting, Pensacola, Florida. U.S. Geological Survey Open-File Report 87-109, pp. E5–E6.

Imbrigiotta, T.E., J. Gibs, T.V. Fusillo, G.R. Kish, and J.J. Hochreiter. 1988. Field evaluation of seven sampling devices for purgeable organic compounds in ground-water. In: A.G. Collins and A.I. Johnson (eds.),

Ground-Water Contamination: Field Methods. ASTM STP 963. American Society for Testing and Materials, Philadelphia, PA, pp. 258–273.

Jay, P.C. 1985. Anion contamination of environmental water samples introduced by filter media. Analytical Chemistry 57(3):780–782.

Kaleris, V. 1989. Inflow into monitoring wells with long screens. In: H.E. Kobust and W. Kinzelbach (eds.), Contaminant Transport in Groundwater. A.A. Balkema, Rotterdam, pp. 41–50.

Kearl, P.M., N.E. Korte, and T.A. Cronk. 1992. Suggested modifications to ground water sampling procedures based on observations from the colloidal boroscope. Ground Water Monitoring Review, 12(2):155–161.

Keely, J.F. and K. Boateng. 1987. Monitoring well installation, purging, and sampling techniques - part 1: conceptualizations. Ground Water 25(4):427–439.

Keith, S.J., L.G. Wilson, H.R. Fitch, and D.M. Esposito. 1983. Sources of spatial-temporal variability in ground-water quality data and methods of control. Ground Water Monitoring Review 3(2):21–32.

Kennedy, V.C., G.W. Zellweger, and B.F. Jones. 1974. Filter pore-size effects on the analysis of Al, Fe, Mn and Ti in water. Water Resources Research 10(4):785–790.

Korte, N. and P. Kearl. 1985. Procedures for the Collection and Preservation of Groundwater and Surface Water Samples and for the Installation of Monitoring Wells. GJ/TMC-08. U.S. Department of Energy, 68 pp.

Kraemer, C.A., J.A. Shultz, and J.W. Ashley. 1991. Monitoring well post-installation considerations. In: D.M. Nielsen (ed.), Practical Handbook of Ground-Water Monitoring. Lewis Publishers, Chelsea, MI, pp. 333–365.

Levine, S.P., M.A. Puskar, P.O. Dymerski, B.J. Warner, and C.S. Friedman. 1983. Cross-contamination of water samples taken for analysis of purgeable organic compounds. Environ. Sci. Technol. 17(2):125–127.

Lewis, D.L. 1988. Assessing and controlling sample contamination. In: L.H. Keith (ed.), Principles of Environmental Sampling. American Chemical Society, Washington, DC.

Liikala, T.L., D.S. Daly, and A.P. Toste. 1988. An Evaluation of the Effects of Well Construction Materials and Groundwater Sampling Equipment on Concentrations of Volatile Organic Compounds. PNL-6585 UC-11. Pacific Northwest Laboratory, Richland, WA, 25 pp.

Maskarinec, M.P. and R.L. Moody, 1988. Storage and preservation of environmental samples. In: L.H. Keith (ed.), Principles of Environmental Sampling. American Chemical Society, Washington, DC, pp. 145–155.

Matteoli, R.J. and J.M. Noonan. 1987. Decontamination of rubber hose and Teflon tubing for ground sampling. In: Proc. First Nat. Outdoor Action Conference. National Water Well Association, Dublin, OH, pp. 159–183.

McAlary, T.A. and J.F. Barker. 1987. Volatilization losses of organics during ground water sampling from low permeability materials. Ground Water Monitoring Review 7(4):63–68.

McIlvride, W.A. and R.B. Rector. 1988. Comparison of short- and long-screen monitoring wells in alluvial sediments. In: Proc. Second Nat. Outdoor Action Conference. National Water Well Association, Dublin, OH, pp. 277–287.

McIlvride, W.A. and R.B. Weiss. 1988. Drilling method effects on well performance. In: Proc. Second Nat. Outdoor Action Conference. National Water Well Association, Dublin, OH, pp. 277–287.

Meyer, P.D. and E.D. Brill, Jr. 1988. A method for locating wells in a groundwater monitoring network under conditions of uncertainty. Water Resources Research 24(8):1277–1282.

Mickham, J.T., R. Bellandi, and E.C. Tiff. 1989. Equipment contamination procedures for ground water and vadose zone monitoring programs: Status and prospects. Ground Water Monitoring Review 19(2):100–121.

Miller, G.D. 1982. Uptake and release of lead, chromium, and trace level volatile organics exposed to synthetic well casings. In: Proc. Second Nat. Symp. on Aquifer Restoration and Ground Water Monitoring. National Water Well Association, Dublin, OH, pp. 236–245.

Moody, J.R. and R.M. Lindstrom. 1977. Selection and cleaning of plastic containers for storage. Analytical Chemistry 49(14):2264–2267.

Morin, R.H., D.R. LeBlanc, and W.E. Teasdale. 1988. A statistical evaluation of formation disturbance produced by well-casing installation methods. Ground Water 26(2):207–217.

Muska, C.F., W.P. Colven, V.D. Jones, J.T. Scoglin, B.B. Looney, and V. Price, Jr. 1986. Field evaluation of ground water sampling devices for volatile organic compounds. In: Proc. Sixth Nat. Symp. on Aquifer Restoration and Ground Water Monitoring. National Water Well Association, Dublin, OH, pp. 235–246.

Nielsen, D.M. and G.L. Yeates. 1985. A comparison of sampling mechanisms available for small diameter ground water monitoring wells. Ground Water Monitoring Review 5(2):83–99.

Nielsen, D.M. and R. Schalla. 1991. Design and installation of ground-water monitoring wells. In: D.M. Nielsen (ed.), Practical Handbook of Ground-Water Monitoring. Lewis Publishers, Chelsea, MI, pp. 239–331.

Pankow, J.F. 1986. Magnitude of artifacts caused by bubbles and headspace in the determination of volatile organic compounds in chemistry. Analytical Chemistry 58:1822–1826.

Papadopulos, I.S. and H.H. Cooper, Jr. 1967. Drawdown in a well of large diameter. Water Resources Research 3:241–244.

Parker, L.V., A.D. Hewitt, and T.F. Jenkins. 1990. Influence of casing materials on trace-level chemicals in well water. Ground Water Monitoring Review 10(2):146–156.

Parr, J., M. Bollinger, O. Callaway, and K. Carlberg. 1988. Preservation techniques for organic and inorganic compounds in water samples. In: L.H. Keith (ed.), Principles of Environmental Sampling. American Chemical Society, Washington, DC, pp. 221–230.

Paul, D.G., C.D. Palmer, and D.S. Cherkauer. 1988. The effect of construction, installation, and development on the turbidity of water in monitoring wells in fine-grained glacial till. Ground Water Monitoring Review, 8(1):73–82.

Pearsall, K.A. and A.V. Eckhardt. 1987. Effects of selected sampling equipment and procedures on the concentrations of trichlorethylene and related compounds in ground water samples. Ground Water Monitoring Review 7(2):64–73.

Pionke, H.B. and J.B. Urban. 1987. Sampling the chemistry of shallow aquifer systems—a case study. Ground Water Monitoring Review 7(2):79–88.

Pohlmann, K.F. and J.W. Hess. 1988. Generalized ground water sampling device matrix. Ground Water Monitoring Review 8(4):82–84.

Pohlmann, K.F., R.P. Blegen, and J.W. Hess. 1990. Field Comparison of Ground-Water Sampling Devices for Hazardous Waste Sites: An Evaluation Using Volatile Organic Compounds. EPA/600/4-90/028, 102 pp.

Puls, R.W. and M.J. Barcelona. 1989. Ground Water Sampling for Metals Analyses. U.S. Environmental Protection Agency. Superfund Issue Paper, EPA/540/4-89/001. [See Chapter 18.]

Puls, R.W., J.H. Eychaner, and R.M. Powell. 1990. Colloidal-Facilitated Transport of Inorganic Contaminants in Ground Water: Part I. Sampling Considerations. Environmental Research Brief EPA/600/M-90/023. [See Chapter 19.]

Puls, R.W., R.M. Powell, D.A. Clark, and C.J. Paul. 1991. Facilitated Transport of Inorganic Contaminants in Ground Water: Part II. Colloidal Transport. Environmental Research Brief. EPA/600/M-91/040. [See Chapter 20.]

Reilly, T.E., O.L. Franke, and G.D. Bennett. 1989. Bias in groundwater samples caused by wellbore flow. Journal of Hydraulic Engineering 115(2):270–277.

Reynolds, G.W., J.T. Hoff, and R.W. Gillham. 1990. Sampling bias caused by materials used to monitor halocarbons in groundwater. Environ. Sci. Technol. 24(1):135–142.

Rice, G., J. Brinkman, and D. Muller. 1988. Reliability of chemical analyses of water samples—the experience of the UMTRA project. Ground Water Monitoring Review 8(3):71–75.

Robin, M.J.L. and R.W. Gillham. 1987. Field evaluation of well purging procedures. Ground Water Monitoring Review 7(4):85–93.

Ross, H.B. 1986. The importance of reducing sample contamination in routine monitoring of trace metals in atmospheric precipitation. Atmospheric Environment 20(2):401–405.

Scalf, M.R., J.F. McNabb, W.J. Dunlap, R.L. Cosby, and J. Fryberger. 1981. Manual of Ground-Water Quality Sampling Procedures. EPA/600/2-81/160 (NTIS PB82-103045). [Also published in NWWA/EPA Series, National Water Well Association, Dublin OH.]

Schalla, R., D.A. Myers, M.A. Simmons, J.M. Thomas, and A.P. Toste. 1988. The sensitivity of four monitoring well sampling systems to low concentrations of three volatile organics. Ground Water Monitoring Review 8(3):90–96.

Scheibe, T.D. and D.P. Lettenmaier. 1989. Risk-based selection of monitoring wells for assessing agricultural chemical contamination of ground water. Ground Water Monitoring Review 9(4):98–108.

Schuller, R.M., J.P. Gibb, and R.A. Griffin. 1981. Recommended sampling procedures for monitoring wells. Ground Water Monitoring Review 1(1):42–46.

Smith, R.L., R.W. Harvey, J.H. Duff, and D.R. LeBlanc. 1987. Importance of close-interval vertical sampling in delineating chemical and microbiological gradients in ground water studies. In: B. J. Franks (ed.), U.S.

Geological Survey Program on Toxic Waste-Ground-Water Contamination: Proceedings of the Third Technical Meeting, Pensacola, Florida. U.S. Geological Survey Open-File Report 87-109, pp. 33–35.

Smith, F., S. Kulkarni, L.E. Myers, and M.J. Messner. 1988. Evaluating and presenting quality assurance sampling data. In: L. H. Keith (ed.), Principles of Environmental Sampling. American Chemical Society, Washington, DC.

Sosebee, J.B., P.C. Geiszler, D.L. Winegardner, and C.R. Fisher. 1982. Contamination of groundwater samples with poly (vinyl chloride) adhesives and poly (vinyl chloride) primer from monitoring wells. In: R.A. Conway and W.P. Gulledge (eds.), Hazardous and Industrial Solid Waste Testing: Second Symposium. ASTM STP 805. American Society for Testing and Materials, Philadelphia, PA, pp. 38–50.

Spruill, T.B. and L. Candela. 1990. Two approaches to design of monitoring networks. Ground Water 28(3):430–442.

Stolzenburg, T.R. and D.G. Nichols. 1985. Preliminary Results on Chemical Changes in Groundwater Samples Due to Sampling Devices. EPRI EA-4118. Electric Power Research Institute, Palo Alto, CA, 84 pp.

Stolzenburg, T.R. and D.G. Nichols. 1986. Effects of filtration method and sampling devices on inorganic chemistry of sampled well water. In: Proc. Sixth Nat. Symp. on Aquifer Restoration and Groundwater Monitoring. National Water Well Association. Dublin, OH, pp. 216–234.

Sykes, A.L., R.A. McAllister, and J.B. Homolya. 1986. Sorption of organics by monitoring well construction materials. Ground Water Monitoring Review 6(4):44–47.

Truitt, R.E. and J.H. Weber. 1979. Trace metal ion filtration losses at pH 5 and 7. Analytical Chemistry 51(12):2057–2059.

Unwin, J.P. 1982. A Guide to Ground-Water Sampling. Stream Improvement Technical Bulletin No. 362. National Council of the Paper Industry for Air and Stream Improvement, 124 pp.

Unwin, J.P. and D. Huis. 1983. A laboratory investigation of the purging behavior of small-diameter monitoring wells. In: Proc. Third Nat. Symp. on Aquifer Restoration and Ground Water Monitoring. National Water Well Association, Columbus, OH, pp. 257–262.

Unwin, J.P. 1984. Sampling ground water for volatile organic compounds: The effects of sampling method, compound volatility and concentration. In: Proc. Fourth Nat. Symp. on Aquifer Restoration and Ground Water Monitoring. National Water Well Association, Dublin, OH, pp. 214–220.

Unwin, J.P. and V. Maltby. 1988. Investigations of techniques for purging ground-water monitoring wells and sampling ground water for volatile organic compounds. In: A.G. Collins and A.I. Johnson (eds.), Ground-Water Contamination: Field Methods. ASTM STP 963. American Society for Testing and Materials, Philadelphia, PA, pp. 240–252.

U.S. Environmental Protection Agency (EPA). 1986. RCRA Ground Water Monitoring Technical Enforcement Guidance Document. EPA/530/SW-86/055 (OSWER-9950.1) (NTIS PB87-107751), 332 pp. [Also published in NWWA/EPA Series, National Water Well Association, Dublin, OH. Final OSWER Directive 9950.2 (NTIS PB91-140194. See also U.S. EPA (1993) for latest draft guidance.]

U.S. Environmental Protection Agency (EPA). 1987. Handbook: Groundwater. EPA/625/6-87/016, 212 pp.

U.S. Environmental Protection Agency (EPA). 1993. RCRA Ground Water Monitoring: Draft Technical Guidance. EPA/530/R-93/001 (NTIS PB93-139350).

Vitale, R.J., O. Braids, and R. Schuller, 1991. Ground-water sample analysis. In: D.M. Nielsen (ed.), Practical Handbook of Ground-Water Monitoring. Lewis Publishers, Chelsea, MI, pp. 501–539.

Wagemann, R. and G.J. Brunskill. 1975. The effect of filter pore size on analytical concentrations of some trace elements in filtrates of natural water. International Journal of Environmental Analytical Chemistry 4(1):75–84.

Wolff, J.S., M.T. Homsher, R.D. Flotard, and J.G. Pearson. 1986. Semi-volatile organic analytical methods performance and quality control considerations. In: C.L. Perket (ed.), Quality Control in Remedial Site Investigation: Hazardous and Industrial Solid Waste Testing, Fifth Volume. ASTM STP 925. American Society for Testing and Materials, Philadelphia, PA, pp. 157–171.

Yeskis, D., K. Chiu, S. Meyers, J. Weiss, and T. Bloom. 1988. A field study of various sampling devices and their effects on volatile organic contaminants. In: Proc. Second Nat. Outdoor Action Conference. National Water Well Association, Dublin, OH, pp. 471–479.

Chapter 17

Survey of Laboratory Studies Relating to the Sorption/Desorption of Contaminants on Selected Well Casing Materials[1]

José L. Llopis, Geotechnical Laboratory, U.S. Army Corps of Engineers Waterways Experiment Station, Vicksburg, MS

INTRODUCTION

All aspects of a ground-water sampling program have the potential to affect the composition of a ground-water sample. The potential for the introduction of sample error exists from the time drilling commences and continues to the time water samples are analyzed in the laboratory. The high degree of accuracy (parts per billion (ppb) range) required of some chemical analysis dictates that all potential sources of error of a ground-water sampling program be identified and sources of error in such aspects be minimized. One potential source of error is the interaction of the ground-water sample with material used in well casings for monitoring wells. Well casing materials may introduce error in a sample by interacting with water while it is still in the well and altering the water composition. Proper selection of casing materials used for ground-water monitoring wells is critical in minimizing errors introduced by this interaction. This chapter is a survey of scientific studies related to a specific process which potentially affects materials used to produce monitoring well casings and screens. This chapter should not be exclusively used to select the proper well casing/screen material for a site specific situation. Other factors must be considered in the selection process, including: site specific water chemistry, substrate physical bearing properties, formation conductivity, design life of monitoring well, presence of NAPLs,[2] etc.

Selection of the proper casing material for monitoring wells has been a subject of much controversy since the publication of the U.S. EPA's Resource Conservation and Recovery Act (RCRA) Ground-Water Monitoring Technical Enforcement Guidance Document (TEGD) (U.S. EPA 1986). The TEGD suggests the use of polytetrafluoroethylene (PTFE, Teflon®) or stainless steel (SS) for sampling volatile organics in the saturated zone and further states "National Sanitation Foundation (NSF) or American Society for Testing and Materials (ASTM) approved polyvinylchloride (PVC) well casing and screens may be appropriate if only trace metals or nonvolatile organics are the contaminants anticipated."

SOURCES OF ERROR

Error can be introduced into the ground-water sample by casing materials with several processes including:

a. Chemical attack of the casing material.
b. Sorption and desorption.
c. Leaching of the casing material.
d. Microbial colonization and attack (Barcelona et al., 1985).

---

[1] EPA/540/4-91/005.
[2] See list of abbreviations at the end of the chapter.

Before proceeding further, it is necessary to define the terminology used in this report. The terms "sorbed" or "sorption" are used many times in the literature to refer to the processes of adsorption and absorption especially when the exact mechanism is not known. Adsorption is defined as the adherence of atoms, ions, or molecules of a gas or liquid called the adsorbate onto the surface of another substance, called the adsorbent; whereas, absorption is the penetration of one substance (absorbate) into the inner structure of another called the absorbent. In this report, rather than distinguishing between the processes of adsorption and absorption, the term sorbed will be used synonymously with both processes, unless otherwise noted. Desorption refers to the process of removing a sorbed material from the solid on which it is sorbed. Leaching refers to the removal or extraction of soluble components of a material (i.e., casing material) by a solvent (Sax and Lewis, 1987).

Casing material in contact with a liquid has the potential to allow either leaching and/or sorption. Factors influencing sorption of organics and metals are discussed by Jones and Miller (1988) and Massee et al. (1981), respectively. These factors include:

1. The surface area of the casing. The greater the ratio of casing material surface area to the volume of adsorbate, the greater the sorption potential.
2. Nature of the analyte (chemical form and concentration).
3. Characteristics of the solution. This includes factors such as pH, dissolved material (e.g., salinity, hardness), complexing agents, dissolved gases (especially oxygen, which may influence the oxidation state), suspended matter (competitor in the sorption process), and microorganisms (e.g., trace element take-up by algae).
4. Nature of the casing material (adsorbent). This includes factors such as the chemical and physical properties of the casing material.
5. External factors. These factors include temperature, contact time, access of light, and occurrence of agitation.

According to Barcelona et al., (1988) considerations for selecting casing material should also include the subsurface geochemistry and the nature and concentration of the contaminants of interest. They also state that strength, durability, and inertness of the casing material should be balanced with cost considerations. Ford (1979) summarized factors related to the analyte that can affect adsorption (Table 17-1).

Berens and Hopfenberg (1981) conducted an investigation to determine a correlation between diffusivity and size and shape of the penetrant molecules. Their study indicated that as the diameter of "spherical" penetrant molecules increased, the diffusivity decreased exponentially. Another finding of the study was that flattened or elongated penetrant molecules such as n-alkanes had greater diffusivities than spherical molecules of similar volume or molecular weight. This may indicate that elongated molecules can move along their long axis when diffusing through a polymer.

Reynolds and Gillham (1985) used a mathematical model to predict the absorption of organic compounds by the different polymer materials. Curves based on their model were fit to experimental data and showed reasonable agreement. This agreement supports their concept that uptake is the result of absorption. They also determined that no relationship was found between the order of absorption and readily available parameters such as aqueous solubility or octanol/water partitioning coefficient. They concluded that predicting the amount of absorption for a particular organic compound was not possible at that time.

Gillham and O'Hannesin (1990) attempted to predict the rate of uptake of benzene, toluene, ethylbenzene, and p-, m-, and o-xylene onto samples SS316, PTFE, rigid PVC, flexible PVC, polyvinylidene fluoride (PVDF), flexible PE, and FRE employing the same model as that used by Reynolds and Gillham (1985). Their results showed the diffusion model data fitted their experimental data quite well, suggesting the sorption mechanism was absorption into the polymer materials agreeing with the results of Reynolds and Gillham (1985). They also determined, that for the organic compounds used in this study, the rate of uptake increased with increasing hydrophobicity of the organic compound and varied with the physical characteristics of the polymer casing material.

TYPES OF CASING MATERIALS

A variety of materials may be used for casing and screening ground-water monitoring wells. These materials include glass and metallic and synthetic materials. Rigid glass has the least potential

Table 17-1. Factors Affecting Adsorption

1. An increasing solubility of the solute in the liquid carrier decreases its adsorbability.

2. Branched chains are usually more adsorbable than straight chains. An increasing length of the chain decreases solubility.

3. Substituent groups affect adsorbability.

Substituent Group	Nature of Influence
Hydroxyl	Generally reduces absorbability; extent of decrease depends on structure of host molecule.
Amino	Effect similar to that of hydroxyl but somewhat greater. Many amino acids are not adsorbed to any appreciable extent.
Carbonyl	Effect varies according to host molecule; glyoxylic are more adsorbable than acetic but similar increase does not occur when introduced into higher fatty acids.
Double Bonds	Variable effect as with carbonyl.
Halogens	Variable effect.
Sulfonic	Usually decreases adsorbability.
Nitro	Often increases adsorbability.
Aromatic Rings	Greatly increases adsorbability.

4. Generally, strong ionized solutions are not as adsorbable as weakly ionized ones; i.e., undissociated molecules are in general preferentially adsorbed.

5. The amount of hydrolytic adsorption depends on the ability of the hydrolysis to form an adsorbable acid or base.

6. Unless the screening action of the adsorbent pores intervene, large molecules are more sorbable than small molecules of similar chemical nature. This is attributed to more solute-adsorbent chemical bonds being formed, making desorption more difficult.

7. Molecules with low polarity are more sorbable than highly polar ones.

Source: Ford, 1979

for affecting a sample and is the material of choice for sampling organics (Pettyjohn et al., 1981). However, because the use of glass as a casing material is impractical for field applications because of its brittleness, it will not be further considered in this report. Instead, this report will focus on the metallic and synthetic materials most commonly used for monitoring well construction.

Metals

Metals are often chosen as casing materials because of their strength. Metals used for casing include SS, carbon steel, galvanized steel, cast iron, aluminum, and copper. The various metals used for well casings may react differently to different compounds. Reynolds et al. (1990) conducted a study using SS, aluminum, and galvanized steel to determine their potential to cause problems in samples collected for analysis for halogenated hydrocarbons. The metals were subjected to aqueous solutions of 1,1,1-trichloroethane (1,1,1-TCA), 1,1,2,2-tetrachloroethane (1,1,2,2,-TET), hexachloroethane (HCE), bromoform (BRO), and tetrachloroethylene (PCE) for periods up to 5 weeks. The study indicated that, of the metals used, SS was the least reactive followed by aluminum and galvanized steel. Stainless steel caused a 70 percent reduction of BRO and HCE after 5 weeks. Aluminum caused over a 90 percent reduction for all but one of the compounds while galvanized steel showed over a 99 percent reduction for all of the compounds.

Many investigations have shown that errors may be introduced into the water sample as a result of using metal casings. For instance, Marsh and Lloyd (1980) determined steel-cased wells modified the chemistry of the formation water. They state that trace element concentrations of the ground water collected from the wells were not representative of the aquifer conditions and did not recommend the use of steel casing for constructing monitoring wells. They suspected that reactions between the ground water and the steel casing raise the pH of the water which causes the release of metal ions into solution. Pettyjohn et al. (1981) found metals strongly adsorb organic compounds. For example, they claim that DDT is strongly adsorbed even by SS. Hunkin et al. (1984) maintain that steel-cased wells are known to add anomalously high iron and alloy levels as well as byproducts of bacterial growth and corrosion to a sample. Houghton and Berger (1984) discovered that samples from steel-cased wells were enriched in cadmium (Cd), chromium (Cr), copper (Cu), iron, manganese, and zinc (Zn) relative to samples obtained from plastic-cased wells.

Stainless steel is one type of metal used for casing and that appears to have a high resistance to corrosion. In fact, the U.S. EPA (1987) states that SS is the most chemically resistant of the ferrous materials. Two types of SS extensively used for groundwater monitoring are stainless steel 304 (SS304) and stainless steel 316 (SS316). These are classified as austenitic type SS and contain approximately 18 percent chromium and 8 percent nickel. The chemical composition of SS304 and SS316 is identical, with the exception being SS316 which contains 2–3% molybdenum. Brainard-Kilman (1990) indicate SS316 has improved resistance to sulfuric and saline conditions and better resistance to stress-corrosion.

The corrosion resistance of SS is due to a passive oxide layer which forms on the surface in oxidizing environments. This protective layer is only a few molecules thick. It recovers quickly even if removed by abrasion (Fletcher, 1990). However, several investigators note that SS is still susceptible to corrosion. Under corrosive conditions, SS may release iron, chromium, or nickel (Barcelona et al., 1988). Hewitt (1989a) found in a laboratory study that samples of SS316 and SS304 were susceptible to oxidation at locations near cuts and welds. When these cuts and welds are immersed in ground water, this surface oxidation provides active sites for sorption and also releases impurities and major constituents. SS may be sensitive to the chloride ion, which can cause pitting corrosion, especially over long term exposures under acidic conditions (U.S. EPA, 1987).

Parker et al. (1989) evaluated samples of SS304 and SS316 for their potential to affect aqueous solutions of 10 organic compounds. The 10 organics used in the study were RDX, trinitrobenzene (TNB), c-1,2-DCE, t-1,2-DCE, m-nitrotoluene (MNT), TCE, MCB, o-dichlorobenzene (ODCB), p-dichlorobenzene (PDCB), and m-dichlorobenzene (MDCB) at concentrations of 2 mg/L. Their study indicated the SS well casings did not affect the concentration of any of the analytes in solution.

Synthetic Materials

Synthetic materials used for casing evaluation include PTFE, PVC, polypropylene (PP), polyethylene (PE), nylon, fiberglass reinforced epoxy (FRE), and acrylonitrile butadiene styrene (ABS). The two most commonly used synthetic casing materials are PVC and PTFE. Very little information regarding the suitability of FRE as a casing material is presently available in the literature; however, a 3-week dwell-time study conducted by Cowgill (1988) indicated that FRE revealed no detectable quantities of the substances used in its manufacture. Hewitt (1989a and 1989b) determined that PTFE was the material of choice for sampling inorganic compounds, whereas Barcelona et al. (1985) recommend PTFE for most all monitoring applications.

PTFE is a man-made material composed of very long chains of linked fluorocarbon units. PTFE is considered as a thermoplastic with unique properties. It is very inert chemically and no substance has been found that will dissolve this polymer (The Merck Co. Inc., 1984). The Merck Co. Inc. (1984) reports that nothing sticks to this polymer. This antistick property may prevent grouts from adhering to PTFE casing and prevent the development of an effective seal around a PTFE casing. PTFE also has a very wide useful temperature range, -100° to +480°F; however, for most groundwater monitoring applications these extremes of temperature would rarely be encountered.

PTFE has a low modulus of elasticity making the screened portion PTFE casing prone to slot compression under the weight of the well casing above. PTFE is also very flexible and the casing sometimes has the tendency to become "crooked" or "snake" especially in deep boreholes. Special procedures are then required to install the casing. Morrison (1986) and Dablow et al. (1988) discuss different techniques used to overcome installation problems inherent to PTFE wells. PTFE also has the tendency to stretch, thus making PTFE cased wells susceptible to leaks around threaded joints.

PVC casing is an attractive alternative to PTFE and SS because it is inexpensive, durable, light-weight, has better modulus and strength properties than PTFE, and is easy to install. However, these characteristics alone do not justify its use as a monitoring well casing material. The casing material must not react significantly with the surrounding ground water, leach, sorb, or desorb any substances that might introduce error into the sample. Many studies have been conducted comparing PVC to other casing materials to determine its suitability for use in monitoring wells.

Various compounds are added to the basic PVC polymer during the manufacturing process of rigid PVC. These compounds include thermal stabilizers, lubricants, fungicides, fillers, and pigments (Boettner et al., 1981; Packham, 1971). It is presumed that the additional compounds have the potential to leach into the ground water. Tin, found in some thermal stabilizers, is one of the compounds suspected of leaching from PVC. Boettner et al., (1981) found that as much as 35 ppb dimethyltin could be leached from PVC in a 24-hour period. Other compounds used as thermal stabilizers, and potential sources of contaminants, are calcium, Zn, and antimony.

Another compound suspected of leaching from PVC casing is residual vinyl chloride monomer (RVCM). According to Jones and Miller (1988), 1-inch diameter Schedule 40 PVC pipe containing 10-ppm RVCM leaches undetectable quantities (at the 2.0-ppb sensitivity level) of vinyl chloride into stagnant water retained in the pipe. They also report that 98 percent of the PVC casing currently manufactured in North America contains less than 10-ppm RVCM and most casing contains less than 1 ppm RVCM. This implies that a 1-inch diameter pipe should leach 2.0-ppb or less RVCM. The amount of RVCM leached would also decrease as the casing diameter increased because of the lower specific surface. Specific surface (R) is defined as the ratio of the surface area of the casing material in contact with the solution, to the volume of the solution. Thus, as casing diameter increases, the specific area decreases.

The National Sanitation Foundation (NSF, 1989) has established maximum permissible levels (MPL) for many chemical substances used in the manufacturing of PVC casing (Table 17-2). These levels are for substances found in low pH extractant water following extraction procedures described by the NSF (1989). Sara (1986) recommends the use of NSF-tested and approved PVC formulations to reduce the possibility of leaching RVCM, fillers, stabilizers, and plasticizers.

Common practice was to use cleaner-primers and solvent cements to join PVC casing sections used in monitoring wells. Cements used for joining casing sections dissolve some of the polymer and "weld" the casing sections together. Past studies showed a correlation between certain organic compounds found in ground-water samples and the use of PVC solvent cement (Boettner et al., 1981; Pettyjohn et al., 1981; Sosebee et al., 1983; Curran and Tomson, 1983). Sosebee et al. (1983) found high levels of tetrahydrofuran, methylethylketone, methylisobutylketone, and cyclohexanone, the major constituents of PVC primer and adhesive, in water surrounding cemented casing joints months after installation. Sosebee et al. (1983) determined that besides contaminating the ground-water sample these contaminants have the potential to mask other compounds found in the ground water during laboratory analysis. Boettner et al., (1981) found, in an experiment in which solvent cement was used for joining PVC casing, methylethylketone, tetrahydrofuran, and cyclohexanone leaching into water supplies after more than 2 weeks of testing.

Houghton and Berger (1984) conducted a study to determine the effects of well casing composition and sampling method on water-sample quality. Three wells were drilled on 20-ft centers to a depth of 60 feet and cased with PVC, ABS, and steel. Samples collected from the wells indicated ABS-cased wells were enriched in dissolved organic carbon by 67 percent and in total organic carbon (TOC) by 44 percent relative to samples from the steel-cased well. The PVC-cased well was enriched in dissolved organic carbon and TOC by approximately 10 percent relative to the steel-cased well. The high TOC concentrations found in the ABS and PVC casings are suspected to have been derived from the cement used to connect the casing sections.

Other compounds suspected of leaching from PVC and into ground water are chloroform ($CHCl_3$) and carbon tetrachloride (CCl_4). Desrosiers and Dunnigan (1983) determined that PVC pipe did not leach $CHCl_3$ or CCl_4 into deionized, demineralized, organic-free water, or tap water in the absence of solvent cement even after a 2-week dwell time.

PVC primers and adhesives should not be used for joining PVC monitoring well casing sections. The recommended means for joining PVC casing is to use flush-joint threaded pipe casing. Foster

Table 17-2. Maximum Permissible Levels for Chemical Substances

Substances	MPL mg/L	Action levels mg/L
Antimony	0.05	
Arsenic	0.050	
Cadmium	0.005	
Copper	1.3	
Lead	0.020	
Mercury	0.002	
Phenolic Substances		0.05[b]
Tin	0.05	
Total Organic Carbon		5.0[b]
Total Trihalomethanes	0.10	
Residual Vinyl Chloride Monomer[a]	3.2	2.0[c]

[a]   In the finished product ppm (mg/kg).

[b]   This is an action level. If the level is exceeded, further review and/or testing shall be initiated to identify the specific substance(s), and acceptance or rejection shall be based on the level of specific substances in the water.

[c]   Additional samples shall be selected from inventory and tested to monitor for conformance to the MPL.

Source: NSF Standard Number 14.

(1989) provides a review of ASTM guideline F480-88A which describes in detail the standard PVC flush-joint thread.

Junk et al. (1974) passed "organic free" water through PE, PP, latex, and PVC tubings, and a plastic garden hose. They found o-creosol, naphthalene, butyloctylfumarate, and butylchloroacetate leaching from the PVC tubing. These contaminants are related to plasticizers which are added to PVC during the manufacturing process to make it more flexible. Rigid PVC well casing contains a much smaller quantity of plasticizer and should be less prone to leaching contaminants (Jones and Miller, 1988).

LEACHING AND SORPTION STUDIES

Many studies have been undertaken to determine the interaction of different casing materials with volatile organic compounds (VOCs) and trace metals. Much of the research has been aimed at determining whether PVC can be used as a substitute for more expensive materials such as PTFE, FRE, and SS. A review of the literature investigating the potential effects of assorted well casing materials on ground-water samples is presented below.

Organic Studies

Lawrence and Tosine (1976) found that PVC was effective for adsorbing polychlorinated biphenyls (PCB) from aqueous sewage solutions. They reported that the low solubility and hydrophobic nature of the PCBs makes them relatively easy to adsorb from aqueous solution. Parker et al. (1989) suggest the PVC appears to be effective only in sorbing PCBs at concentrations close to their solubility limits.

Pettyjohn et al. (1981) discuss materials used for sampling organic compounds. They provide a list of preferred materials for use in sampling organic compounds in water. Their choice in order of preference is glass, PTFE, SS, PP, polyethylene, other plastics and metals, and rubber. They do not indicate whether the materials in the list were sections of rigid or flexible tubing or what testing procedures were followed. They note that experimental data on the sorption and desorbtion potential of casing materials using varied organic compounds were not available.

Miller (1982) conducted a laboratory study in which one of the objectives was to quantify adsorption of selected organic pollutants on Schedule 40 PVC 1120, low density PE, and PP well casing materials. These materials were exposed to six organic pollutants and monitored for adsorption over a 6-week period. The VOCs used, along with their initial concentrations, were BRO (4 ppb), PCE (2 ppb), trichloroethylene (TCE) (3 ppb), trichlorofluoromethane (2 ppb), 1,1,1-TCA (2 ppb), and 1,1,2-trichloroethane (14 ppb). The results showed that PVC adsorbed only PCE. The PVC adsorbed approximately 25 to 50 percent of the PCE present. The PP and PE samples adsorbed all six of the organics in amounts ranging from 25 to 100 percent of the amount present.

Curran and Tomson (1983) compared the sorption potential of PTFE, PE, PP, rigid PVC (glued and unglued), and Tygon (flexible PVC). The procedures used in this investigation consisted of pumping 20 L of organic-free water with a 0.5-ppb naphthalene spike through each tubing at a rate of 30 mL/min. The tests showed that 80 to 100 percent of the naphthalene was recovered from the water for all materials except Tygon tubing. Tygon tubing sorbed over 50 percent of the naphthalene. PTFE showed the least contaminant leaching of the synthetic materials tested. They concluded that PVC can be used as a substitute for PTFE in monitoring wells if the casing is properly washed and rinsed with room temperature water before installation. They also conclude that PE and PP could suitably be used as well casings.

Barcelona et al. (1985) presented a ranking of the preferred rigid materials based on a review of manufacturers' literature and a poll of the scientific community. The list presented by Barcelona et al. (1985) recommended the following casing materials in order of decreasing preference: PTFE, SS316, SS304, PVC, galvanized steel, and low carbon steel. Table 17-3 presents recommended casing materials tabulated in Barcelona et al. (1985), along with specific monitoring situations.

Reynolds and Gillham (1985) conducted a laboratory study to determine the effects of five halogenated compounds on six polymer materials. The five compounds used in this study were 1,1,1-TCA, 1,1,2,2-TET, HCE, BRO, and PCE. The polymer materials studied were PVC rod, PTFE tubing, nylon plate, low density PP tubing, low density PE tubing, and latex rubber tubing. The authors evaluated nylon plate because nylon mesh is often used as a filter material around screened portions of wells. Latex rubber tubing was evaluated as a material that represented maximum absorption. The materials were tested under static conditions to simulate water standing in the borehole. Measurements were made over contact times that ran from 5 minutes to 5 weeks.

Results of the study are presented in Table 17-4. The results show that PVC absorbed four of the five compounds; however, the rate of absorption was relatively slow (periods of days to weeks). Given this slow absorption rate, they do not consider there would be significant absorption by PVC if wells were purged and sampled the same day. The one organic compound that was not absorbed significantly by the PVC during the 5-week test period was 1,1,1-TCA. The loss of BRO to PVC in this study was approximately 43 percent after 6 weeks; whereas, Miller (1982), in a similar experiment, indicated no losses from solution over the same time period.

PTFE showed absorption of four of the five compounds tested. There was no significant absorption of BRO over the 5-week test period. It is noted that approximately 50 percent of the original concentration of PCE was absorbed within an 8-hour period. The concentration of this compound may be affected even when the time between purging and sampling is short.

The other casing materials demonstrated significant absorption losses within minutes to a few hours after exposure to the organic compounds. The use of nylon, latex rubber, PP, and PE as a well casing material will cause a significant reduction in the concentration of the organic compounds even when the time between purging and sampling is short. They state that agreement between the model study and experimental results support the concept that absorption of the organic compounds by the polymers occur by sorption/dissolution of the compounds into the polymer surface followed by diffusion into the polymer matrix.

Parker and Jenkins (1986) conducted a laboratory study to determine if PVC casing was a suitable material for monitoring low levels of the explosives 2,4,6-trinitrotoluene (TNT), hexahydro-1,3,5-trinitro-1,3,5-triazine (RDX), octahydro-1,3,5,7-tetranitro 1,3,5,7-tetrazocine (HMX), and 2,4-dinitrotoluene (DNT). Samples of PVC casing were placed in glass jars containing an aqueous solution of TNT, RDX, HMX, and DNT. After 80 days, the solution was tested to determine the concentration of TNT, RDX, HMX, and DNT left in solution. After the 80 days the solutions containing RDX, HMX, and DNT showed little loss, whereas TNT showed a significant loss. PVC casing was tested under sterile and nonsterile conditions in a 25-day experiment to determine whether microbial degradation or sorption by PVC was the cause for losses of TNT, RDX, HMX, and DNT. Results indicated that the loss of TNT in the test was caused by microbial activity rather than adsorption. The

Table 17-3. Recommendations for Rigid Materials in Sampling Applications (In decreasing order of preference)

Materials	Recommendations
PTFE (Teflon®)	Recommended for most monitoring situations with detailed organic analytical needs, particularly for aggressive, organic leachate impacted hydrogeologic conditions. Virtually an ideal material for corrosive situations where inorganic contaminants are of interest.
Stainless Steel 316 (flush threaded)	Recommended for most monitoring (flush threaded) situations with detailed organic analytical needs, particularly for aggressive, organic leachate impacted by hydrogeologic conditions.
Stainless Steel 304 (flush threaded)	May be prone to slow pitting corrosion in contact with acidic high total dissolved solids aqueous solutions. Corrosion products limited mainly to Fe and possibly Cr and Ni.
PVC (flush threaded) other noncemented connections, only NSF-approved materials for casing or potable water applications.	Recommended for limited monitoring situations where inorganic contaminants are of interest and it is known that aggressive organic leachate mixtures will not be contacted. Cemented installations have caused documented interferences. The potential for interaction and interferences from PVC well casing in contact with aggressive aqueous organic mixtures is difficult to predict. PVC is not recommended for detailed organic analytical schemes.

Recommended for monitoring inorganic contaminants in corrosive, acidic inorganic situations. May release Sn or Sb compounds from the original heat stabilizers in the formulation after long exposure. |
| Low Carbon Steel, Galvanized Steel, Carbon Steel | May be superior to PVC for exposures to aggressive aqueous organic mixtures. These materials must be very carefully cleaned to remove oily manufacturing residues. Corrosion is likely in high dissolved solids acidic environment, particularly when sulfides are present. Products of corrosion are mainly Fe and Mn, except for galvanized steel which may release Zn and Cd. Weathered steel surfaces present very active sites for trace organic and inorganic chemical species. |

Source: Barcelona et al., 1985

increased microbial activity may be caused by bacteria initially present on the unsterilized PVC casing, increased surface area for colonization provided by the PVC surface, leaching of nutrients from the casing increasing the growth of bacteria, and the rate of biodegradation.

Parker and Jenkins (1986) do not consider PVC casing to significantly affect ground-water samples when monitoring for TNT, RDX, DNT, and HMX if the time between purging of the well and sampling is short. They concluded PVC is an acceptable casing material for ground-water monitoring of TNT, RDX, DNT, and HMX.

Sykes et al., (1986) performed a laboratory study to determine if there was a significant difference in the sorption potential between PVC, PTFE, and SS316 when exposed to methylene chloride (dichloromethane or DCM), 1,2-dichloroethane (1,2-DCA), trans-1,2-dichloroethylene (t-1,2-DCE), toluene, and chlorobenzene (MCB). Samples of the various well casing materials were placed in jars containing aqueous solutions of the solvents at concentrations of approximately 100 ppb. The concentration of each solvent was determined after 24 hours and again after 7 days. The study concluded that there were no statistically different chemical changes in the solutions exposed to PVC, PTFE, and SS316 casing. Thus, it could be presumed that PVC, PTFE, or SS316 are suitable casing materials for monitoring DCM, 1,2-DCA, t-1,2-DCE, toluene, and MCB when the period between well purging and sampling is less than 24 hours.

Table 17-4. Time at Which Absorption Reduced the Relative Concentration in Solution to 0.9

PVC	1,1,1-TCA	1,1,2,2-TET	BRO	HCE	PCE
	>5 weeks	-2 weeks	-3 days	-1 day	-1 day
PTFE	BRO	1,1,2,2-TET	1,1,1-TCA	HCE	PCE
	>5 weeks	-2 weeks	-1 day	-1 day	<5 minutes
Nylon	1,1,1-TCE	1,1,2,2-TET	BRO	PCE	HCE
	-6 hours	-1 hour	-30 minutes	-30 minutes	<5 minutes
PP	1,1,2,2-TET	BRO	1,1,1-TCA	HCE	PCE
	-4 hours	-1 hour	-1 hour	<5 minutes	<5 minutes
PE	1,1,2,2-TET	BRO	1,1,1-TCA	HCE	PCE
	-15 minutes	<5 minutes	<5 minutes	<5 minutes	<5 minutes
Latex Rubber	1,1,2,2-TET	1,1,1-TCA	BRO	PCE	HCE
	<5 minutes	<5 minutes	<5 minutes	<5 minutes	<5 minutes

Source: Reynolds and Gillham, 1985.

Barcelona and Helfrich (1986) conducted a field study at two landfills to determine the effects of different casing materials on sample quality. Wells were constructed upgradient and downgradient of each of the two landfill sites. The wells at Landfill 1 were constructed of PTFE, PVC, and SS304; whereas, the wells at Landfill 2 were constructed of PVC and SS.

They observed that the downgradient SS and PTFE wells at Landfill 1 showed higher levels of TOC than did the PVC wells. The upgradient wells at Landfill 1 showed no significant difference among casing material type. TOC sampling at Landfill 2 showed similar results; however, no significant differences among material types were determined either upgradient or downgradient of the landfill.

Levels of 1,1-dichloroethane (1,1-DCA) and cis-1,2-dichloroethylene (c-1,2-DCE) were significantly higher for the downgradient SS wells than for PTFE and PVC cased wells at Landfill 1. They suspect that PTFE and PVC tend to have a greater affinity for these organic compounds than does SS.

At Landfill 2 they noted greater levels of 1,1-DCA and total volatile halocarbons in the PVC wells than in the SS wells. They hypothesize that the higher levels of the organic compounds found in the water samples from the PVC cased well may be caused by the sorptive and leaching properties of PVC which tend to maintain a higher background level of organic compounds in the ground water relative to SS. They did not suspect the SS and PVC wells at Landfill 2 are intercepting ground water of different quality since the wells are approximately 4 feet apart. The authors conclude that well casing materials exert significant, though unpredictable effects on TOC and specific VOC determinations. Parker et al. (1989) suspect that a larger statistical base is needed before such conclusions can be drawn. Parker et al. (1989) also suggest the possibility that differences in well construction methods may have had an effect on the quality of these water samples.

Gossett and Hegg (1987) conducted a laboratory test to determine the effects of using a PVC bailer, a PTFE bailer, and an ISCO Model 2600 portable pump on the recovery of $CHCl_3$, benzene, and 1,2-DCA. The effect on recovery of VOCs was studied by varying the lift height and the casing material. The casing materials consisted of either PVC or SS. In their conclusion they state that either PVC or SS would be suitable for collecting VOC samples.

Parker et al. (1989) performed a laboratory study to compare the performance of PVC, SS304, SS316, and PTFE subjected to aqueous solutions of RDX, trinitrobenzene (TNB), c-1,2-DCE, t-1,2-DCE, m-nitrotoluene (MNT), TCE, MCB, o-dichlorobenzene (ODCB), p-dichlorobenzene (PDCB), and m-dichlorobenzene (MDCB) at concentrations of 2 mg/L. A biocide was added to the samples to eliminate possible losses due to biodegradation.

Prior to the experiment, they conducted a test to determine if the casing materials were capable of leaching any compounds into water. Samples of casing material were placed in vials containing well water and allowed to stand for 1 week. No evidence of materials leaching from any of the casing materials was noted.

Casing samples were placed in sample jars containing an aqueous solution of the organic compounds and sampled initially and at intervals between 1 hour and 6 weeks. Table 17-5 presents results after a 1-hour, 24-hour, and 6-week dwell time. The test results indicated that after 6 weeks PTFE had sorbed significant amounts of all the compounds with the exception of RDX and TNB. In the same time period, PVC showed significant sorption of TCE, MCB, ODCB, PDCB and MDCB. In each one of the cases where the PVC and PTFE both sorbed significant amounts of analytes, PTFE always had the greatest sorption rate. After 6 weeks, the SS samples exhibited no significant sorption of the tested compounds.

At the 24-hour mark, PTFE and PVC had experienced significant sorption of all the compounds with the exception of RDX, TNB, and MNT. For the compounds sorbed by PTFE and PVC, PTFE had the higher rate of uptake with the exception of c-1,2-DCE. SS showed no significant sorption of any of the compounds tested. It appears that PTFE cased wells will introduce a greater bias into ground-water samples than those cased with PVC if the time between sampling and purging is 24 hours.

They also conducted a desorption experiment on the samples that had sorbed organics for 6 weeks. After 3 days of testing, the PVC and PTFE samples showed desorption of analytes sorbed in the previous experiment. The desorption study showed that PTFE, in general, showed a greater loss of analytes than PVC.

Jones and Miller (1988) conducted laboratory experiments to evaluate the adsorption and leaching potential of Schedule 40 PVC (PVC-40), Schedule 80 PVC (PVC-80), ABS, SS, Teflon-PFA, Teflon-FEP, PTFE, and Kynar-PVDF. Organic compounds used in this experiment were 2,4,6-trichlorophenol (2,4,6-TCP), 4-nitrophenol, diethyl pthalate, acenaphthene, naphthalene, MDCB, 1,2,4-trichlorobenzene, and hexachlorobenzene. Samples of casing material were placed into glass vials each containing an organic compound having an approximate initial concentration of 250 ppb.

In their first experiment, the organic compounds were mixed with neutral pH ground water. The batches were sampled immediately and then at intervals of 1-, 3-, and 6-weeks. The results showed that there was no appreciable change in adsorption of the compounds after 1 week except for 2,4,6-TCP, which totally adsorbed after 3 weeks. The results also indicate that PTFE might be less likely to adsorb these compounds. Jones and Miller (1988) also point out that at the concentrations used in this study, PTFE, PVC-40, and PVC-80 exhibited very little difference in the amounts of adsorption.

In their second experiment, Jones and Miller (1988) attempted to determine the amount of the adsorbed compounds that would be released back into uncontaminated ground water after a 6-week exposure time. After a 2-week period, very little release of organic contaminants was observed. They state that only zero to trace amounts of the sorbed contaminants were desorbed into the non-contaminated ground water. Only PVC-80 and Teflon-PFA desorbed naphthalene.

They repeated their adsorption and leaching experiments using polluted ground water with a pH of 3.0. The adsorption experiment showed that, with the exception of ABS casing, the casing materials showed less adsorption at the contaminated low pH level than at the noncontaminated neutral pH level. One possible explanation is there could be stronger binding and more preferential complexing of the experimental pollutants with other pollutants in the contaminated ground water. Another, more likely explanation, is that there is a relationship between the extent of adsorption, pH, and pK, with a maximum adsorption occurring when the pH is approximately equal to pK. They explain that as the pH decreases, the hydrogen ion concentration increases and the adsorption tends to decrease, suggesting a replacement of the adsorbed compound by the more preferentially adsorbed hydrogen ions.

Jones and Miller (1988) concluded there is no clear advantage to the use of one particular well casing material over the others for the organics used in the study. Well purging procedures, sampling device selection and composition, and sample storage are probably of greater influence to sample integrity and representativeness than well casing material selection. They found the amount of adsorption generally correlates with the solubility of the chemical independent of the well casing material.

Gillham and O'Hannesin (1990) conducted a laboratory study to investigate the sorption of six monoaromatic hydrocarbons onto/into seven casing materials. The six organic compounds used were benzene, toluene, ethylbenzene, and p-, m-, and o-xylene. The seven casing materials used in the evaluation were SS316 PTFE, rigid PVC, flexible PVC, polyvinylidene fluoride (PVDF), flexible PE, and FRE. The materials were placed in vials containing an aqueous solution of all six organic materials. Concentrations of the organics in the solution ranged between 1.0 and 1.4 mg/L. Sodium azide (0.05 percent), a biocide, was added to the solution to prevent biodegradation of the organics. The solutions were sampled 14 times from 5 minutes to 8 weeks.

Table 17-5. Normalized[a] Concentration of Analytes for Four Well Casings with Time

Analyte	Treatment	1 hour	24 hours	6 weeks
RDX	PTFE	1.03	1.00	0.99
	PVC	1.01	0.98	1.00
	SS304	0.99	1.01	0.98
	SS316	1.01	1.01	1.00
TNB	PTFE	1.01	1.00	1.01
	PVC	1.01	0.98	1.02
	SS304	0.99	1.00	1.00
	SS316	1.02	1.01	1.02
c-1,2-DCE	PTFE	1.01	0.96[b]	0.79[b]
	PVC	1.00	0.95[b]	0.90
	SS304	0.97	1.00	0.98
	SS316	0.95	1.00	0.99
t-1,2-DCE	PTFE	1.00	0.88[b]	0.56[b]
	PVC	1.00	0.93[b]	0.83
	SS304	0.95[b]	1.00	1.00
	SS316	1.00	1.00	1.00
MNT	PTFE	1.03	0.99	0.90[b]
	PVC	1.02	0.98	0.94
	SS304	1.00	1.01	1.07
	SS316	1.02	1.02	0.99
TCE	PTFE	1.00	0.85[b]	0.40[b]
	PVC	1.01	0.94[b]	0.88[b]
	SS304	0.96	1.01	0.99
	SS316	1.00	1.00	1.00
MCB	PTFE	1.01	0.90[b]	0.51[b]
	PVC	1.01	0.95[b]	0.86[b]
	SS304	0.98	1.00	0.99
	SS316	0.99	1.01	0.99
ODCB	PTFE	1.01	0.88[b]	0.43[b]
	PVC	1.02	0.94[b]	0.86[b]
	SS304	0.98	1.00	1.00
	SS316	1.01	1.01	1.00
PDCB	PTFE	0.92[b]	0.77[b]	0.26[b]
	PVC	0.95	0.92[b]	0.80[b]
	SS304	0.91[b]	1.00	1.02
	SS316	0.94	1.00	1.02
MDCB	PTFE	1.00	0.78[b]	0.26[b]
	PVC	1.02	0.92[b]	0.80[b]
	SS304	0.99	1.00	1.02
	SS316	1.03	1.00	1.01

[a] The values given here are determined by dividing the mean concentration of a given analyte at a given time and for a particular well casing by the mean concentration (for the same analyte) of the control samples taken at the same time.
[b] Values significantly different from control values.
Source: Parker et al., 1989.

Results of the study are presented in Table 17-6 and indicate that SS is the most favorable casing material for sampling organics. Stainless steel showed no significant uptake after an 8-week exposure period, whereas all the polymer materials adsorbed all the organic compounds to some degree. The order of magnitude of adsorption for the various polymer materials tested was flexible PVC >

Table 17-6. Time Interval Within Which the Concentration Phase for the Compound and Casing Material Became Significantly Different from 1.0

Material	Time, hours					
	Benzene	Toluene	Ethylbenzene	m-Xylene	o-Xylene	p-Xylene
SS316	>1344					
PVC (rigid)	48–96	24–48	12–24	12–24	12–24	12–24
FRE	24–48	3–6	0.1–1.0	3–6	3–6	3–6
PVDF	24–48	3–6	1–3	1–3	0.1–1.0	1–3
PTFE	24–48	3–6	1–3	3–6	6–12	1–3
PE	0–0.1	0–0.1	0–0.1	0–0.1	0–0.1	0–0.1
PVC (flexible)	0–0.1	0–0.1	0–0.1	0–0.1	0–0.1	0–0.1

Source: Gillham and O'Hannesin, 1990.

PE > PTFE > PVDF > FRE > rigid PVC (from greatest to least sorption). Flexible tubing materials showed substantial uptake after 5 minutes of exposure. Rigid PVC showed the lowest rate of uptake of the polymer materials.

Gillham and O'Hannesin (1990) conclude all of the polymer materials tested, except flexible PVC and PE, are suitable casing materials in monitoring wells. This is based on selection of an appropriate casing diameter and an appropriate interval between purging and sampling. They state rigid PVC is the most favorable polymer material for casing in monitoring wells.

Reynolds et al. (1990) conducted laboratory tests to evaluate the effects of five halogenated hydro-carbons on several casing materials. The halogenated hydrocarbons and casing materials used in the experiment were identical to those used by Reynolds and Gillham (1985) with the addition of glass, SS316, aluminum, and galvanized sheet metal to the casing materials.

The results indicated borosilicate glass was the least likely of the 10 materials to affect the samples. The results also showed that all of the metals had the potential to sorb compounds from solution. The order of the compound sorption rate for the metals was galvanized steel > aluminum > SS (greatest to least sorption).

Results of the sorption experiments indicated rigid PVC was preferable to PTFE for sampling low concentrations of halogenated hydrocarbons. The compound sorption rates, from greatest to least sorption, are latex > low density PE > PP > nylon > PTFE > rigid PVC. The rates of compound loss, from greatest to least loss, are PCE > HCE > 1,1,1-TCA > BRO > 1,1,2,2-TET. It should be noted the inequalities shown above are not necessarily significant. For example, the rates between PTFE and rigid PVC are not significant and the same is true for nylon and PP. Their study showed flexible polymer tubing is likely to have greater sorption rates than rigid polymers which is in agreement with Barcelona et al. (1985). They also found evidence that there is a correlation between compound solubility and sorption, substantiating earlier studies. Reynolds et al. (1990) found diffusivity decreased as mean molecular diameter increased which agrees with a study performed by Berens and Hopfenberg (1982), based on polymeric diffusivity tests.

They suggest the use of PTFE in monitoring wells in areas where higher concentrations might be encountered, for instance near a solvent spill. Their study showed a polymer exposed to high concentrations of an organic compound that is a good solvent for the polymer, that the polymer will absorb large quantities of the solvent and swell. However, it is difficult to predict the swelling power of various solvents. As an example, rigid PVC can absorb over 800 percent of its weight in DCM but only 1 percent of CCl_4. Schmidt (1987), however, found no swelling or distortion of rigid PVC casing or screen when exposed to various gasolines for 6.5 months.

Taylor and Parker (1990) visually examined PVC, PTFE, SS304, and SS316 with a scanning electron microscope (SEM) to determine how they were affected by long-term exposures (1 week to 6 months) to organic compounds. Organics used in this test were PDCB, ODCB, toluene, and PCE at concentrations of 17.3, 33.5, 138, and 35.0 mg/L, respectively (approximately 25 percent of their solubilities in water).

SEM examinations showed no obvious surface structure changes for any of the materials exposed to the different concentrated organic aqueous solutions. They caution, however, that this study cannot be extended to instances where casing materials are exposed to pure organic solvents. They did not report the amount of compound sorbed by the different casing materials.

Inorganic Studies

Massee et al. (1981) studied the sorption of silver (Ag), arsenic (As), Cd, selenium (Se), and Zn from distilled water and artificial sea water by borosilicate glass, high-pressure PE, and PTFE containers. The effect of specific surface (R in cm^{-1}), i.e., the ratio of the surface area of the material in contact with the solution, to the volume of the solution, was also studied. Metals were added to the distilled and artificial sea water. The pH levels of the aqueous solutions used were 1, 2, 4, and 8.5. Water samples were tested at intervals ranging between 1 minute and 28 days. Losses of As and Se were insignificant for all the treatments. At pH levels of 1 and 2, no significant sorption from either distilled water or artificial sea water was observed for any of the containers or metals used in this study. Test results of the sorption of Ag, Cd, and Zn from distilled water and sea water are presented in Tables 17-7 and 17-8, respectively.

The results showed PTFE sorbed substantial amounts of Ag, Cd, Zn, and the amounts sorbed were dependent on the pH and salinity of the solutions. Specific surface was found to have a significant effect on the sorption of metals by PTFE. For example, at the end of 28 days the loss of Ag to PTFE with R = 5.5 cm^{-1} was almost 4 times higher than for R = 1.0 cm^{-1}.

Massee et al. (1981) concluded that sorption losses are difficult to predict because the behavior of trace elements depends on a variety of factors such as trace element concentration, material, pH, and salinity. They noted that a reduction in contact time, specific surface, and acidification may reduce sorption losses. Miller (1982) conducted a study to determine the potential of PVC, PE, and PP to sorb and release Cr(VI) and lead (Pb) when in a Cr(VI)-Pb solution and in a solution of these two metals along with the following organics; BRO, PCE, TCE, trichlorofluromethane, 1,1,1-TCA, and 1,1,2-trichloroethane. Tables 17-9 and 17-10, respectively, present the results for the Cr(VI) and Pb adsorption and leaching studies. The results showed that none of the materials tested adsorbed Cr(VI) to any significant extent when in a solution with Pb. When in a solution with Pb and 6 other organics, 25 percent of Cr(VI) was adsorbed by the 3 casing materials. No leaching of Cr(VI) was observed from any of the materials either in the metals only or metals and organics solutions. Seventy-five percent of the Pb was adsorbed by PVC when in a solution with Cr(VI) and also when in a solution of Cr(VI) and the six organics. PE and PP showed about 50 percent adsorption of Pb when in a solution with Cr(VI). The casing materials did not leach any Pb when in a solution with Cr(VI); however, when in a solution with Cr(VI) and 6 organics, the 3 casing materials leached approximately 50 percent of the Pb initially adsorbed. In his study, Miller found that PVC generally causes fewer monitoring interferences with VOCs than PE and PP and that PVC adsorbed and released organic pollutants at a slower rate relative to PE and PP.

Hewitt (1989a) examined the potential of PVC, PTFE, SS304, and SS316 to sorb and leach As, Cd, Cr, and Pb when exposed to ground water. The pH, TOC, and metal concentrations of the solution were varied and samples taken between 0.5 and 72 hours. The study showed that PTFE had the least-active surface and showed an affinity only to Pb (10 percent sorption after 72 hours). PVC and SS leached and sorbed some of the metals tested. PVC was a source for Cd and sorbed Pb (26 percent sorption after 72 hours). The SSs were the most active of the materials tested. SS304 was a source of Cd and sorbed As and Pb. SS316 was also a source of Cd and sorbed As, Cd, and Pb. The study showed results were affected by the solution variables (i.e., pH, TOC, and concentration). SS304 and SS316 showed evidence of corrosion near cuts and welds which may provide active sites for sorption and release of contaminants. Hewitt (1989a) concludes PTFE is the best material for monitoring the metals used in this study, whereas SSs are not suitable. He states that although PVC was affected by Cd and Pb it should still be considered as a useful casing material based on economics, and that when the time between purging and sampling is less than 24 hours, the effects of Cd and Pb on PVC may be of less concern.

Hewitt (1989b) conducted a study to determine the amounts of barium, Cd, Cr, Pb, Cu, As, Hg, Se, and Ag leached from PTFE, PVC, SS304, and SS316 in ground water. Table 17-11 summarizes the results of the investigation. Results indicate that PTFE was the only material tested not to leach any metals into the groundwater solution. PTFE, however, did show a trend to sorb Cu with time. PVC and SS316 showed a tendency to leach Cd; in addition, these two materials, along with SS304,

Table 17-7. Sorption Behavior of Silver, Cadmium and Zinc in Distilled Water

Material		PE				Borosilicate Glass				PTFE			
pH		4		8.5		4		8.5		4		8.5	
R(cm⁻¹)		1.4	3.4	1.0	3.4	1.0	4.2	1.0	4.2	1.4	5.5	1.0	5.5
Metal	Contract Time	Sorption (%)											
Ag	1 hour	10	15	25	36	*	4	9	21	*	*	*	10
	1 day	25	66	72	49	32	18	26	48	4	6	5	25
	28 days	96	100	59	100	82	80	72	63	15	55	22	28
Cd	1 hour	*	*	7	69	*	*	6	26	*	*	7	38
	1 day	*	*	*	47	*	*	10	32	*	*	10	48
	28 days	*	*	*	31	*	*	*	*	*	*	15	46
Zn	1 hour	*	*	*	65	*	*	23	22	*	*	3	16
	1 day	*	*	8	56	*	*	26	22	*	*	5	27
	28 days	*	*	12	56	*	*	*	*	*	*	6	20

* Denotes a loss smaller than 3 percent.
Source: Massee et al., 1981.

Table 17-8. Sorption Behavior of Silver, Cadmium and Zinc in Artificial Sea Water

Material		PE				Borosilicate Glass				PTFE			
pH		4		8.5		4		8.5		4		8.5	
R(cm⁻¹)		1.4	3.4	1.0	3.4	1.0	4.2	1.0	4.2	1.4	5.5	1.0	5.5
Metal	Contract Time	Sorption (%)											
Ag	1 hour	*	*	6	5	*	*	3	3	*	*	*	4
	1 day	*	*	24	28	4	4	6	9	*	*	6	12
	28 days	*	*	46	78	82	71	40	67	*	*	27	37
Cd	1 hour	*	*	*	*	*	*	*	*	*	*	*	*
	1 day	*	*	*	*	*	*	*	*	*	*	*	*
	28 days	*	*	*	*	14	36	*	*	*	*	*	*
Zn	1 hour	*	*	*	*	*	*	9	31	*	*	*	*
	1 day	*	*	*	*	*	*	5	26	4	*	*	*
	28 days	*	*	*	*	20	19	4	9	5	*	*	*

* Denotes a loss smaller than 3 percent.
Source: Massee et al., 1981.

sorbed Pb. PVC was also shown to leach Cr and provide sorption sites for Cu. SS316 significantly increased the concentration of Ba and Cu in the ground-water solution. SS304 consistently contributed Cr with time to the ground-water solution. None of the well casing materials contributed significant levels of As, Hg, Ag, or Se to the ground water.

Hewitt (1989b) concludes PTFE is the best casing material when testing for trace metals while SS should be avoided. He also states PVC is an appropriate second choice because its influence on metal analytes appears to be predictable and small.

Casing Material Cost Comparison

A consideration when installing monitoring wells is cost. Costs to be considered in the installation of monitoring wells are cost of construction materials, drilling costs, and expected life (replacement costs) of the casing material. Table 17-12 presents a cost comparison among five casing materials: PVC, SS304, SS316, PTFE, and FRE. The prices shown were obtained from Brainard-Kilman (1990)

Table 17-9. Trends of Chromium (VI) Exposed to Synthetic Well Casing (Compared to Controls)

Casing Material	Adsorption		Adsorption/Leaching	
	Metals Only	Metals and Organics	Metals Only	Metals and Organics
PVC	No adsorption	Slight (25%) adsorption	No leaching	No leaching
PE	No adsorption	Slight (25%) adsorption	No leaching	No leaching
PP	No adsorption	Slight (25%) adsorption	No leaching	No leaching

Source: Miller, 1982.

Table 17-10. Trends of Lead Exposed to Synthetic Well Casing (Compared to Control)

Casing Material	Adsorption		Adsorption/Leaching	
	Metals Only	Metals and Organics	Metals Only	Metals and Organics
PVC	Mostly (75%) adsorbed	Mostly (75%) adsorbed	No leaching	Mostly (75%) adsorbed
PE	Moderate (50%) adsorption (delayed)	Moderate (50%) adsorption	No leaching	Mostly (75%) adsorbed
PP	Moderate (50%) adsorption (delayed)	Slight (25%) adsorption	No leaching	Mostly (75%) adsorbed

Source: Miller, 1982.

Table 17-11. Summary of Results

	Ba	Cd	Cr	Pb	Cu
Materials that leached >1% of the EPA drinking water quality level in ground-water solutions	SS316 PVC	SS316 PVC	SS304 SS316 PVC	SS304 PVC SS316	NA*
Materials that showed the highest average overall amount of analyte leached	SS316	SS316	SS304	SS304	SS316

* Not applicable.
(Source: Hewitt, 1989b).

with the exception of the FRE casing whose price was provided by ENCO (1989). The cost estimates are for ten 10-feet sections (100 feet) of 2-inch threaded casing, 5 feet of 0.010-inch slotted screen, and a bottom plug.

The cost of materials for one PTFE well is approximately 18 times greater than one constructed with PVC (Table 17-12). At first glance, PVC, by far, is the most economical material for constructing monitoring wells. However, if drilling and material (bentonite, cement, sand, etc.) costs are considered, the percent difference in cost between PVC wells and wells constructed of SS, FRE, or PTFE is reduced.

For example, assume that the cost of installing, materials, and completing a 100-feet deep monitoring well (exclusive of casing material costs) in unconsolidated material is $5,000. When the cost of casing material is added to the drilling and materials costs, a PVC-cased well costs $5,179.50 and an SS316-cased well $6,896.00. When drilling and materials costs are considered, a PVC-cased well

Table 17-12. Casing Material Cost Comparison

Prices reflect the cost of ten 10-ft long by 2-in. diameter casing sections, a 5-ft long 0.010-in slotted screen, and a bottom plug.

Casing Material	Price
PVC[a]	$ 179.50
FRE[b]	966.00
SS304	1,205.00
SS316	1,896.00
PTFE	3,293.50

[a] Schedule 40 PVC.
[b] Low flow screen.

costs approximately 25 percent less than a SS316-cased well. However, when drilling and materials costs are not taken into account, PVC casing looks especially attractive since it is approximately 90 percent less expensive than SS316 casing. In this case, a SS316-cased well may be considered to be cost effective especially if organics are expected to be sampled. Thus, the significance of the "cost of casing materials versus ground water-casing interaction" issue is reduced.

CONCLUSIONS

All aspects of a ground-water sampling program have the potential to introduce error to a ground-water sample. Interaction between monitoring well casing materials and ground water is only one of the ways in which error may be introduced in a sampling program. Presently, there are a variety of materials available for fabricating monitoring wells. The potential for these casing materials to inter-act with ground water has been found to be affected by many factors, including pH and composition of the ground water and the casing-ground water contact time. The complex and varied nature of ground water makes it very difficult to predict the sorption and leaching potential of the various casing materials. Consequently, the selection of the proper casing material for a particular mon-itoring application is difficult. This is evidenced by the lack of agreement among researchers on which is the "best" material. The problem is compounded by the inconclusive and incomplete results of laboratory studies on the effects of rigid well casing materials with inorganic or organic dissolved species.

Many of the experiments examined the effects of time on the sorption and leaching potential of the various casing materials. The experiments were usually run under laboratory conditions in which distilled or "organic free" water was used and casing materials were subject to contaminants for periods ranging from minutes to months. These experiments, in general, indicate a trend for the materials to be more reactive with the aqueous solutions with time. Experiments showed if the time between well purging and sampling is relatively short, some of the more sorptive materials could be used without significantly affecting sample quality.

The selection of appropriate materials for monitoring well casing at a particular site must take into account the site hydrogeology and several general requirements. These general requirements for the screens and casing of wells that are used for groundwater monitoring are the following:

1. Depth to zones being monitored and total depth of well must be considered.
2. The geochemistry of the geologic materials over the entire interval in which the well is to be cased and screened must be taken into account.
3. The wells must be chemically resistant to naturally occurring waters.
4. The well materials must be chemically resistant to any contaminants that are present in any and all contaminated zones of the aquifer or aquifers being monitored.
5. The strength of the materials must be physically strong enough to withstand all compressive and tensile stresses that are expected during the construction and operation of the monitoring well over the expected lifetime.

6. Installation and completion into the borehole during construction of the monitoring well must be relatively easy.

7. The well materials must be chemically resistant to any anticipated treatments which are strongly corrosive or oxidizing.

It may be necessary to conduct site-specific, comparative performance studies to justify preference for a particular well casing or screening material over another.

EPA CONTACT

For further information contact: Ken Brown, EPA Technical Support Center for Monitoring and Site Characterization, Las Vegas, NV, 702/798-2270.

ACKNOWLEDGMENTS

This paper was prepared through support from the Environmental Monitoring Systems Laboratory-Las Vegas (EMSL-LV), under the direction of J. Lary Jack, with the support of the Superfund Technical Support Project.

REFERENCES

Barcelona, M.J. and J.A. Helfrich. 1986. Well Construction and Purging Effects on Ground-Water Samples. Environ. Sci. Technol. 20(11):1179–1184.

Barcelona, M.J., J.P. Gibb, J.A. Helfrich, and E.E. Garske. 1985. Practical Guide for Ground-Water Sampling. ISWS Contract Report 374. Illinois State Water Survey, Champaign, IL, 94 pp.

Barcelona, M.J., J.A. Helfrich, and E.E. Garske. 1988. Verification of Sampling Methods and Selection of Materials for Ground-Water Contamination Studies. In: A.G. Collins and A.I. Johnson (eds.), Ground-Water Contamination: Field Methods. ASTM STP 963. American Society for Testing and Materials, Philadelphia, PA, pp. 221–231.

Boethner, E.A., G.L. Ball, Z. Hollingsworth, and R. Aquino. 1981. Organic and Organotin Compounds Leached from PVC and CPVC Pipe. U.S. Environmental Protection Agency. EPA/600/1-81/062, 102 pp.

Berens, A.R. and H.B. Hopfenberg. 1982. Diffusion of Organic Vapors at Low Concentrations in Glassy PVC, Polystyrene, and PMMA. Journal of Membrane Science 10:283–303.

Brainard-Kilman Drill Company. 1990 Catalog. Stone Mountain, GA.

Budavari, S. (ed.). 1989. The Merck Index, 11th Edition. Merck & Company, Rathway, NJ.

Curran, C.M. and M.B. Tomson. 1983. Leaching of trace organics into water from five common plastics. Ground Water Monitoring Review 3(3):68–71.

Cowgill, U.M. 1988. The Chemical Composition of Leachate from a Two-Week Dwell-Time Study of PVC Well Casing and Three-Week Dwell-Time Study of Fiberglass Reinforced Epoxy Well Casing. In: A.G. Collins and A.I. Johnson (eds.), Ground-Water Contamination: Field Methods. ASTM STP 963. American Society for Testing and Materials, Philadelphia, PA, pp. 172–184.

Dablow, J.F., III, D. Perisco, and G.R. Walker. 1988. Design Considerations and Installation Techniques for Monitoring Wells Cased with Teflon PTFE. In: A.G. Collins and A.I. Johnson (eds.), Ground-Water Contamination: Field Methods. ASTM STP 963. American Society for Testing and Materials, Philadelphia, PA, pp. 199–205.

Desrosiers, D.G. and P.C. Dunnigan. 1983. The Diffusion of Chloroform and Carbon Tetrachloride from Rigid PVC Pipe and Rigid CPVC Pipe Into Water. Journal of Vinyl Technology 5(4):187–191.

ENCO. EMC, Price List, September, 1989, Austin, TX.

Fletcher, J.R. Stainless Steels. Engineering, November, 1990.

Ford, D.L. 1979. Current State of the Art Activated Carbon Treatment. In: Activated Carbon Treatment of Industrial Wastewaters - Selected Technical Papers. EPA-600/2-79-177.

Foster, S. 1989. Flush-Joint Threads Find a Home. Ground Water Monitoring Review 9(2):55–58.

Gillham, R.W. and S.F. O'Hannesin. 1990. Sorption of Aromatic Hydrocarbons by Materials Used in Construction of Ground-Water Sampling Wells. In: D. M. Nielsen and A.I. Johnson (eds.), Ground Water and

Vadose Zone Monitoring. ASTM STP 1053. American Society for Testing and Materials, Philadelphia, PA, pp. 108–122.

Gossett, R.E. and R.O. Hegg. 1987. Comparison of Three Sampling Devices for Measuring Volatile Organics in Groundwater. Transactions of the American Society of Agricultural Engineers 30(2):387–390.

Hewitt, A.D. 1989a. Influence of Well Casing Composition on Trace Metals in Ground Water. CRREL Special Report 89-9. U.S. Army Engineers Cold Regions Research and Engineering Laboratory, Hanover, NH.

Hewitt, A.D. 1989b. Leaching of Metal Pollutants from Four Well Casings Used for Ground-Water Monitoring. CRREL Special Report 89-32. U.S. Army Engineers Cold Regions Research and Engineering Laboratory, Hanover, NH.

Houghton, R.L. and M.E. Berger. 1984. Effects of Well-Casing Composition and Sampling Method on Apparent Quality of Ground Water. In: Proc. Fourth Nat. Symp. Aquifer Restoration and Ground Water Monitoring. National Water Well Association, Dublin, Ohio, pp. 203–213.

Hunkin, G.G., T.A. Reed, and G.N. Brand. 1984. Some Observations on Field Experiences with Monitor Wells. Ground Water Monitoring Review 4(1):43–45.

Jones, J.N. and G.D. Miller. 1988. Adsorption of Selected Organic Contaminants onto Possible Well Casing Materials. In: A.G. Collins and A.I. Johnson (eds.), Ground-Water Contamination: Field Methods. ASTM STP 963. American Society for Testing and Materials, Philadelphia, PA, pp. 185–198.

Junk, G.A., H.J. Svec, R.D. Vick, and M.J. Avery. 1974. Contamination of Water by Synthetic Polymer Tubes. Environ. Sci. Technol. 8(13):1100–1106.

Lawrence, J. and H.M. Tosine. 1976. Adsorption of Polychlorinated Biphenyls from Aqueous Solutions and Sewage. Environ. Sci. Technol. 10(4):381–383.

Marsh, J.M. and J.W. Lloyd. 1980. Details of Hydrochemical Variations in Flowing Wells. Ground Water 18(4):366–373.

Massee, R., F.J.M.J. Maessen, and J.J.M. De Goeij. 1981. Losses of Silver, Arsenic, Cadmium, Selenium, and Zinc Traces from Distilled Water and Artificial Sea-Water by Sorption on Various Container Surfaces. Analytica Chimica Acta 127:181–193.

The Merck Index 1984. Tenth Edition, Merck and Co., Inc., Rahway, NJ. [Editors Note: See Budavari (1989) for 11th edition.]

Miller, G.D. 1982. Uptake and Release of Lead, Chromium, and Trace Level Volatile Organics Exposed to Synthetic Well Casings. In: Proc. Second Nat. Conf. on Aquifer Restoration and Ground Water Monitoring, National Water Well Association, Worthington, OH, pp. 236–245.

Morrison, R.D. 1986. The New Monitoring Well. Ground Water Age, April, pp. 19–23.

National Sanitation Foundation (NSF). 1989. Standard Number 14, Plastics Piping Components and Related Materials, Ann Arbor, MI.

Packham, R.F. 1971. The Leaching of Toxic Stabilizers From Unplasticized PVC Water Pipe: Part I—A Critical Study of Laboratory Test Procedures. Water Treatment and Examination 20(2):152–164.

Parker, L.V. and T.F. Jenkins. 1986. Suitability of Polyvinyl Chloride Well Casings for Monitoring Munitions in Ground Water. Ground Water Monitoring Review 6(3):92–98.

Parker, L.V., T.F. Jenkins, and P.B. Black. 1989. Evaluation of Four Well Casing Materials for Monitoring Selected Trace Level Organics in Ground Water. CRREL Report 89-18. U.S. Army Engineers Cold Regions Research and Engineering Laboratory, Hanover, NH.

Pettyjohn, W.W., W.J. Dunlap, R. Cosby, and J.W. Keeley. 1981. Sampling Ground Water for Organic Contaminants. Ground Water 19(2):180–189.

Reynolds G.W. and R.W. Gillham. 1985. Absorption of Halogenated Organic Compounds by Polymer Materials Commonly Used in Ground Water Monitors. In: Proc. Second Canadian/American Conf. on Hydrogeology: Hazardous Waste in Ground Water: A Soluble Dilemma. National Water Well Association, Dublin, OH, pp. 125–132.

Reynolds, G.W., J.T. Hoff, and R.W. Gillham. 1990. Sampling Bias Caused by Materials Used to Monitor Halocarbons in Groundwater. Environ. Sci. Technol. 24(1):135–142

Sara, M.N. 1986. A Review of Materials Used in Monitoring and Monitoring Well Construction. In: Proc. Sixth Nat. Symp. on Aquifer Restoration and Ground Water Monitoring. National Water Well Association Dublin, OH, pp 330–339.

Sax, N.I. and R.J. Lewis, Sr. 1987. Hawley's Condensed Chemical Dictionary, Eleventh Edition. Van Nostrand Reinhold, New York, NY.

Schmidt, G.W. 1987. The Use of PVC Casing and Screen in the Presence of Gasolines on the Ground Water. Ground Water Monitoring Review 7(2):94–95.

Sosebee, J.B., Jr., P.C. Geiszler, D.L. Winegardner, and C.R. Fisher. 1983. Contamination of Groundwater Samples with Poly (Vinyl Chloride) Adhesives and Poly (Vinyl Chloride) Primer from Monitor Wells. In: R.A. Conway and W.P. Gulledge (eds.), Hazardous and Industrial Solid Waste Testing: Second Symposium. ASTM STP 805. American Society for Testing and Materials, Philadelphia, PA, pp. 38–50.

Sykes, A.L., R.A. McAllister, and J.B. Homolya. 1986. Sorption of Organics by Monitoring Well Construction Materials. Ground Water Monitoring Review 6(4):44–47.

Taylor, S. and L. Parker. 1990. Surface Changes in Well Casing Pipe Exposed to High Concentrations of Organics in Aqueous Solution. CRREL Special Report 90-7. U.S. Army Engineers Cold Regions Research and Engineering Laboratory, Hanover, NH.

U.S. Environmental Protection Agency (EPA). 1986. RCRA Ground Water Monitoring Technical Enforcement Guidance Document. EPA/530/SW-86/055 (OSWER-9950.1) (NTIS PB87-107751), 332 pp. [Also published in NWWA/EPA Series, National Water Well Association, Dublin, OH. Final OSWER Directive 9950.2 (NTIS PB91-140194. See also U.S. EPA (1993) for latest draft guidance.]

U.S. Environmental Protection Agency (EPA). 1987. Handbook: Groundwater. EPA/625/6-87/016, 212 pp.

U.S. Environmental Protection Agency (EPA). 1993. RCRA Ground Water Monitoring: Draft Technical Guidance. EPA/530/R-93/001 (NTIS PB93-139350).

ABBREVIATIONS

1,1-DCA	1,1-Dichloroethane
1,1,1-TCA	1,1,1-Trichloroethane
1,1,2,2-TET	1,2,2,2-Tetrachlorethane
1,2-DCA	1,2-Dichloroethane
2,4,6-TCP	2,4,6-Trichlorophenol
ALS	Acrylonitrile butadiene styrene
Ag	Silver
As	Arsenic
ASTM	American Society for Testing and Materials
BRO	Bromoform
c-1,2-DCE	cis-1,2-Dichloroethylene
CCl_4	Carbon tetrachloride
Cd	Cadmium
$CHCl_3$	Chloroform
Cr	Chromium
Cu	Copper
DCM	Methylene chloride (dichloromethane)
DNT	2,4-Dinitrotoluene
EMSL-LV	Environmental Monitoring Systems Laboratory-Las Vegas
FRE	Fiberglass reinforced epoxy
HCE	Hexachloroethane
Hg	Mercury
HMX	Octabydro-1,2,5,7-tetranitro 1,3,5,7-tetrazocine
m-	Meta
MCB	Chlorobenzene
MDCB	m-Dichlorobenzene
MNT	m-Nitrotoluene
MPL	Maximum permissible levels
NAPL	Nonaqueous phase liquid
NSF	National Sanitation Foundation
o-	Ortho
ODCB	o-Dichlorobenzene
p-	Para
Pb	Lead
PCB	Polychlorinated biphenyl
PCE	Tetrachloroethylene
PDCB	p-Dichlorobenzene

PE	Polyethylene
pH	Hydrogen ion concentration of the solution
pK	Log dissociation constant
PP	Polypropylene
ppb	Parts per billion (by weight)
ppm	Parts per million (by weight)
PTFE	Polytetrafluoroethylene (Teflon®)
PVC	Polyvinylchloride
RCRA	Resource Conservation and Recovery Act
RDX	Hexahydro-1,3,5,7-trinitro-1,3,5-triazine
RVCM	Residual vinyl chloride monomer
Se	Selenium
SEM	Scanning electron microscope
SS	Stainless steel
SS304	Stainless steel 304
SS316	Stainless steel 316
t-1,2-DCE	trans-1,2-Dichloroethylene
TCE	Trichloroethylene
TEGD	Technical Enforcement Guidance Document
TNB	Trinitrobenzene
TNT	2,4,6-Trinitrotoluene
TOC	Total organic carbon
U.S. EPA	U.S. Environmental Protection Agency
VOC	Volatile organic compound
Zn	Zinc

Chapter 18

Ground Water Sampling for Metals Analysis[1]

Robert W. Puls, U.S. EPA Robert S. Kerr Environmental Research Laboratory, Ada, OK
Michael J. Barcelona, Department of Civil and Environmental Engineering, University of Michigan, Ann Arbor, MI

INTRODUCTION

Inconsistency in EPA Superfund cleanup practices occurs where one EPA Region implements a remedial action based on unfiltered ground-water samples, while another Region may consider a similar site to be clean based on filtered ground-water samples. RSKERL-Ada and EMSL-Las Vegas have convened a technical committee of experts in the areas of ground-water geochemistry, inorganic chemistry, colloidal transport and ground-water sampling technology to examine this issue and provide technical guidance based on current scientific information (see Acknowledgments for committee membership).

The findings and recommendations of the committee were that use of a 0.45 micron[2] filter was not useful, appropriate or reproducible in providing information on metals mobility in ground-water systems, nor was it appropriate for determination of truly "dissolved" constituents in ground water. A dual sampling approach was recommended, with collection of both filtered and unfiltered samples. If the purpose of the sampling is to determine possible mobile contaminant species, the unfiltered samples should be given priority. This means that added emphasis is placed on appropriate well construction methods, materials and ground-water sampling procedures. For accurate estimations of truly "dissolved" species concentrations, filtration with a nominal pore size smaller than 0.45 microns was recommended. It was further concluded that filtration could not compensate for inadequate construction or sampling procedures.

BACKGROUND/SUPPORT INFORMATION

Filtration of ground-water samples for metal analyses will not provide accurate information concerning the mobility of metal contaminants. This is because some mobile species are likely to be removed by filtration before chemical analysis. Metal contaminants may move through fractured and porous media not only as dissolved species, but also as precipitated phases, polymeric species, or adsorbed to inorganic or organic particles of colloidal dimensions. Colloids are generally considered as particles with diameters less than 10 microns (Stumm and Morgan, 1981). Numerous investigators have suggested the facilitated transport of contaminants in association with mobile colloidal particles (see also Chapter 6). Kim et al. (1984) suggested that sorption to ground-water colloidal material caused the mobilization of some radionuclides in Gorleben ground waters. Saltelli et al. (1984) studied americium percolation in glauconitic sand columns and attributed the unretained fractions to migrating colloidal species.

These colloids were either homogeneous hydrous precipitates, or were formed from the adsorption of the radionuclide onto colloidal size mineral particles. Colloidal particles generated in batch experiments by Sheppard et al. (1979) were shown to adsorb significant quantities of radionuclides. Further work by Sheppard et al. (1980) concluded that the transport of radionuclides by colloidal clay particles must be considered in any contaminant transport model. Champlin and Eichholz (1968) showed that the movement of radioactive sodium and ruthenium in sand beds was associated with

---

[1] EPA/540/4-89/001.
[2] Micron = μm = 10^{-6} meter

particulate matter of micron dimensions. Gschwend and Reynolds (1987) demonstrated that submicron ferrous phosphate colloids were suspended and presumably mobile in a sand and gravel aquifer.

Studies by Yao et al. (1971) and O'Melia (1980) indicate that colloidal particles in the range 0.1 to 1.0 micron may be most mobile in a sandy, porous medium. Kovenya et al. (1972) concluded that particles in the range 0.1 to 0.5 μm were most mobile in soil column studies. As much as 200 ppb copper, lead and cadmium was found associated with colloidal material in size range 0.015–0.450 μm by Tillekeratne et al. (1986). Rapid transport of plutonium (Pu) in core column studies by Champ et al. (1982) was attributed to colloidal transport, with 48% of the Pu associated with colloids in the size range 0.003–0.050 μm and 23% in the range 0.050–0.450 μm. Reynolds (1985) using carboxylated polystyrene beads ranging from 0.10 to 0.91 μm in size, recovered 45% of the 0.91 μm size beads, and greater than 70% of 0.10 and 0.28 μm size beads in laboratory sand column effluents.

Lake and estuarine studies by Baker et al. (1986) and Means and Wijayaratne (1982) demonstrated the importance of natural colloidal material in the transport of hydrophobic contaminants. Carter and Suffet (1982) found that a significant fraction of "dissolved" DDT in surface waters was bound to colloidal humic material. Takayanagi and Wong (1984) found over 70% of the total selenium in river waters was associated with organic and inorganic colloidal particles.

Analytical methods used to determine "dissolved" metal concentrations have historically used 0.45 micron filters to separate dissolved and particulate phases. If the purpose of such determinations is an evaluation of "mobile" species in solution, significant underestimations of mobility may result, due to colloidal associations. On the other hand, if the purpose of such filtration is to determine truly dissolved aqueous species, the passage of colloidal material less than 0.45 microns in size may result in the overestimation of dissolved concentrations (Bergseth, 1983; Kim et al. 1984; Wagemann and Brunskill, 1975). Kennedy and Zellweger (1974) found errors of an order of magnitude or more in the determination of dissolved concentrations of aluminum, iron, manganese and titanium using 0.45 micron filtration. Sources of error were attributed to filter passage of fine-grained clay particles. Additionally, filtration of anoxic ground-water samples is very difficult without iron oxidation and colloid formation, causing a removal of previously dissolved species to be filtered. Filter loading and clogging of pores with fine particles may also occur, reducing the nominal size (Danielsson, 1982). Filtration should be viewed as only one approach for determining the "true" solution geochemistry of ground water, and others should be applied whenever possible.

PURPOSE OF SAMPLING

It is important to identify the purpose of ground-water sampling before decisions regarding filtration, centrifugation or other phase separation techniques are made. Is it to determine the mobility of contaminants or to determine in situ aqueous geochemistry? The following definitions are also useful for consideration of this issue:

1. Total Contaminant Load Per Unit Volume of Aquifer = Mobile + Immobile Species.
2. Mobile Species = Dissolved + Suspended Species.
3. Dissolved = Free Ions + Inorganic Complexes + Low Molecular Weight Organic Complexes.
4. Suspended = Adsorbed + Precipitated + Polymeric + High Molecular Weight Organic Complexes.

For an assessment of mobility, all mobile species must be considered, including suspended particles acting as adsorbents for contaminants. While not all suspended species may necessarily be sufficiently mobile or toxic to pose a health risk, a conservative approach is proposed at this time until more definitive data are available. Contaminant transport models which account for an additional aqueous mobile colloidal phase have been proposed by Avogadro and DeMarsily (1984) and Enfield and Bengtsson (1988).

A principal objective in a sampling effort for testing a geochemical speciation model is to obtain estimates of the free ion activities of the major and trace elements of interest. Since there are relatively few easily performed analytical procedures for making these experimental estimates, an alternative procedure is to test the analytically determined dissolved concentrations with model predictions including both free and complexed species. More and more remedial investigations are utilizing such models to make predictions about contaminant behavior based on dissolved concentrations. It is not the purpose of this report to suggest how to perform these analytical determinations, but as noted above, the use of a 0.45 micron filter as the operational definition of "dissolved" may be inappropriate. Analytical techniques such as ion selective electrodes, ion exchange and polarography may be more accurate. Research utilizing these and other techniques to correlate "dissolved" with filter size is recommended (see Chapter 23).

If one adopts the conservative approach with no filtration for contaminant mobility estimations, increased importance is placed on proper well construction, and purging and sampling procedures to eliminate or minimize sources of sampling artifacts.

SOURCES OF SAMPLING ARTIFACTS VS. "REAL" GROUNDWATER ENVIRONMENT

The disturbance of the subsurface environment as a result of well construction and sampling procedures presents serious obstacles to the interpretation of ground-water quality results. Some degree of disturbance of natural conditions is inevitable. However, the impact of improper well construction and sampling techniques can permanently bias the usefulness and integrity of wells as sampling points. Several aspects of well construction and sampling procedures must be carefully considered to avoid errors associated with the introduction of foreign particles or the alteration of ambient subsurface conditions which may affect natural dissolved or suspended materials.

Well Construction

The design, drilling, and construction of monitoring wells have been identified as particularly important steps in the collection of representative water chemistry and hydrologic data. Several references have emphasized the minimization of both the disturbance and the introduction of foreign materials (U.S. EPA, 1986; Barcelona et al., 1983, 1985) because of the potential impact on water chemistry. The RCRA Technical Enforcement Guidance Document (U.S. EPA, 1986) suggests that the well must allow for sufficient ground-water flow for sampling, minimize passage of formation materials into the well, and exhibit sufficient structural integrity to prevent collapse of the intake structure. It should be recognized, however, that the well must first provide a representative hydraulic connection to the geologic formation of interest. Without the assurance of this hydraulic integrity, the water chemistry information cannot be interpreted in relation to the dynamics of the flow system or the transport of chemical constituents.

More specific guidance is therefore necessary to maintain or restore the natural hydraulic conductivity of the formation in the vicinity of the screened portion of monitoring wells through the drilling, construction and development procedures. The literature on water well technology can be most helpful in this regard since minimal disturbances of the subsurface is a common goal in maximizing both the yield of water supply wells and the representativeness of water samples and hydraulic information from monitoring wells (Driscoll, 1986).

To ensure the long-term integrity of monitoring wells, particularly with respect to excluding foreign particles and permitting the passage of mobile (i.e., dissolved and suspended) contaminants, specific items which should be observed are:

1. If no alternative to the use of drilling muds or fluids exists, these materials must be removed from the well bore and adjacent formations by careful well development (Driscoll, 1986). This guidance also applies to the removal of the low permeability "skin" which is caused by abrasion, oxidation and invasive muds which may seal the well bore from the screened interval and bias in situ determinations of hydraulic conductivity (Faust and Mercer, 1984; Moench and Hsieh, 1985; Faust and Mercer, 1985). Pumping rates during development should be documented and care should be taken not to exceed these rates during purging or sampling since further development and well damage may aggravate suspended particulate and turbidity problems even in properly designed wells.

2. The emplacement of grouts and seals to isolate the screened interval must be carefully done. The use of tremie pipes and frequent checking of the depth of emplacement of clay or cement grouts during well construction are strongly encouraged. It is also important to take care to follow manufacturer's guidelines on the hydration of cement or expanding cement as grouts or

seals. Excess water addition and grading of cement components or materials due to free fall through standing water can permanently damage the well's integrity (Evans and Ellingson, 1988).

3. Casing and screen materials must be selected to retain their integrity in the subsurface environment (i.e., avoid iron, steel), minimize bias to water samples and ensure that screen openings are not reduced by the buildup of corrosion products or by compression (U.S. EPA, 1986; see also Chapter 18). These effects can be checked by repeat determinations of in situ hydraulic conductivity over the useful life of the well. Redevelopment and replacement of the well should be considered if deterioration or significant changes in hydraulic conductivity are observed. Erratic water level readings and sudden changes in turbidity or purging behavior of monitoring wells prior to sampling are warning signs of possible loss of material integrity.

4. Well design fundamentals with regard to the selection of a filter pack and screen size are among the most important issues in obtaining representative hydraulic and water quality information. The exclusion of fines, clays, and silts can be achieved by selecting the grain-size distribution for the filter pack by multiplying the 50-percent retained size of the finest formation sample by a factor of two (Driscoll, 1986). The filter pack material should be cleaned and washed free of fines to ensure that extraneous contaminants or particles are removed. The well screen slot openings should be chosen to retain 90% of the filter pack material after development. In natural packed wells it may be advisable to select a screen slot size which will retain at least 50% of the finest material in the screened interval. Minimizing slot screen width however, often leads to greater time and energy spent in well development. The need to document well development procedures cannot be overemphasized.

Maintenance of the hydraulic performance of monitoring wells and the connection of wells to the zones of greatest hydraulic conductivity, where contaminant transport is most probable, should take equal importance to the collection of representative water quality data.

Purging and Sampling

Water that remains in the well casing between sampling periods is unrepresentative of water in the formation opposite the screened interval. It must be removed by purging or isolated from the collected sample by a packer arrangement prior to the collection of representative water samples. Water level readings must be made carefully to avoid the disturbance of fines or precipitates which may enter or form in the well due to chemical reactions or microbial processes and accumulate on the interior walls of the well casing screen or at the bottom of the well. Similarly, it is important to purge the stagnant water at flow rates below those used in development to avoid further development, well damage or the disturbance of accumulated corrosion or reaction products in the well. The use of certain sampling devices, particularly bailers and air-lift arrangements, should be discouraged in order to avoid the entrainment of suspended materials which are not representative of mobile chemical constituents in the formation of interest.

A note of caution should be voiced to encourage repetitive sampling of monitoring wells prior to judging the representativeness of determinations of hydraulic conductivity, water level readings and water quality data. The effects of the inevitable "trauma" due to drilling, sealing and development of monitoring wells can bias observations of water chemistry until the subsurface is allowed to equilibrate sufficiently (Walker, 1983). Estimates of the time to achieve equilibration vary substantially, particularly when drilling fluids are used in highly permeable formations (Brobst, 1984; Driscoll, 1986); however, periods of weeks to several months may be necessary before even major ionic constituents of ground water equilibrate to previous levels (Barcelona et al., 1988).

RECOMMENDATIONS FOR SAMPLING

In general, the zone of interest must be isolated, the sample pumped slowly to minimize turbidity and sample collected in such manner as to eliminate O_2 and CO_2 exchange with the atmosphere. No filtration for mobile metals determination is recommended. If the unfiltered values exceed maximum contaminant level concentrations for ground-water quality, additional analyses and re-evaluation of sampling artifacts are required. It should be emphasized that extreme differences between unfiltered and 0.45 μm filtered samples does not preclude the use of unfiltered data for risk assessment decisions. Significant particulate mobility may be occurring at such a site, and additional analyses with other larger filters (e.g. >0.45 μm) may be most appropriate given the current size estimates for upper limits for mobile particles.

Isolation of Sampling Zone

Isolation of the sampling zone is necessary to minimize the purge volume as well as to minimize air contact. This is especially important since Eh/pH conditions of the formation waters are notoriously sensitive to dissolved gases content. Inflatable packers can be used to achieve isolation of the sampling zone.

Pumping for Sample Collection

It is recommended that a positive displacement pump can be used. Other types of sample collection (e.g., bailing) may cause displacement of nonmobile particles or significantly alter groundwater chemistry leading to colloid formation (e.g., vacuum pumps). Surging must be avoided, and a flow rate as close to the actual ground-water flow rate should be employed. Acknowledging that this may be impossible or impractical in some instances, a pumping flow rate based on the linear groundwater flow rate and open screen area is proposed, where

$$\text{pumping flow rate} \sim \text{linear GW flow rate} \times 2 \times \text{screen ht.} \times \text{well radius} \times 10$$

While an initial approximation, flow rates around 100 mL/min have been used to successfully sample ground waters in a quiescent mode.

Additional research is needed in this area, particularly with respect to the appropriateness of this generic equation. An inexpensive flow-through type cell set-up utilizing this approach was described by Garske and Schock (1986).

Assessment of Water Constituents While Sampling

Monitoring of the pumped ground water for dissolved oxygen, temperature, conductivity and pH aids in the interpretation or establishment of ground-water background quality. Gschwend and co-workers (personal communication) have observed that turbidity diminished dramatically after prolonged pumping, changing similarly, although possibly more slowly, than other water quality parameters (e.g., O_2, conductivity). An initial estimate proposed for time of pumping necessary to collect water from a formation is around two times the time required to get plateau values for the above parameters.

No Filtration for Mobile Fraction Determination

Those samples intended to indicate the mobile substance load should not be filtered. Steps to preserve their integrity, such as acidification, should be performed as soon as possible.

Filtration for Specific Geochemical Information

Any filtration for estimates of dissolved subsurface species loads should be performed in the field with no air contact and immediate preservation and storage. In-line pressure filtration is best with as small a filter pore size as practically possible (e.g., 0.05, 0.10 micron). Using a smaller pore size filter will require longer sample collection time, increasing the need for air exclusion from the sample (Laxen and Chandler, 1982, Holm et al., 1988). Polycarbonate membrane-type filters with uniform and sharp size cutoffs are recommended to minimize particle loading on the filter. Although membrane filters are more prone to clogging than fiber-type filters, the uniform pore size, ease of cleaning, and minimization of adsorptive losses from the sample tend to improve the precision and accuracy in the analytical data. The filter holder should be of material compatible with the metals of interest. Holders made of steel are subject to corrosion and may introduce nonformation metals to samples. Large diameter filter holders (e.g., >47 mm) are recommended to reduce clogging and pore size reduction and for ease of filter pad replacement. The use of disposable in-line filters are suggested for convenience if of sufficient quality. Prewashing of filters should be routinely performed. Work by Jay (1985) shows that virtually all filters require prewashing to avoid sample contamination.

Quality assurance and quality control becomes increasingly important when adopting the above recommendations. The use of field blanks and standards for field sampling is essential. Field blanks and standards enable quantitative correction for bias due to collection, storage and transport. Analysis of the filters themselves and their particulate load is suggested as a check on mass balance and filtration effects on solid/solution separation efficiency.

EPA CONTACTS

For further information contact: Robert Puls, RSKERL-Ada, 405/436-8543.

ACKNOWLEDGMENTS

Members of the committee that helped develop this chapter were Robert W. Puls, Bert E. Bledsoe and Don A. Clark of RSKERL; Michael J. Barcelona, Illinois State Water Survey; Phillip M. Gschwend, Massachusetts Institute of Technology; Terry F. Rees, USGS-Denver; John W. Hess, Desert Research Institute (EMSL-LV); and Nicholous T. Loux, ERL-Athens. This chapter was written by Robert W. Puls and Michael J. Barcelona and edited by all members of the committee.

REFERENCES

Avogadro, A. and G. De Marsily. 1984. The Role of Colloids in Nuclear Waste Disposal. In: Gary L. McVay (ed.), Scientific Basis for Nuclear Waste Management, pp. 495–505.

Backhus, D., P.R. Gschwend, and M.D. Reynolds. 1986. Sampling Colloids in Groundwater (Abstract). EOS 67:954.

Baker, J.E., P.D. Capel, and S.J. Eisenreich. 1986. Influence of Colloids on Sediment-Water Partition Coefficients of Polychlorobiphenyl Congeners in Natural Waters. Environ. Sci. Technol. 20(11):1136–1143.

Barcelona, M.J., J.P. Gibb, and R.A. Miller. 1983. A Guide to the Selection of Materials for Monitoring Well Construction and Ground-Water Sampling. EPA/600/52-84/024, 78 pp. [Also published as Illinois State Water Survey Contract Report No. 327.]

Barcelona, M. J., J.P. Gibb, J.A. Helfrich, and E.E. Garske. 1985. Practical Guide for Ground-Water Sampling. EPA/600/2-85/104 (NTIS PB86-137304), 94 pp. [Also published as ISWS Contract Report 374, Illinois State Water Survey, Champaign, IL.]

Barcelona, M.J., G.K. George, and M.R. Schock. 1988. Comparison of Water Samples from PTFE, PVC, and SS Monitoring Wells. EPA/600/X-88/091. Environmental Monitoring Systems Laboratory, Las Vegas, NV, 37 pp.

Bergseth, H. 1983. Effect of Filter Type and Filtrate Treatment on the Measured Content of Al and Other Ions in Groundwater. Acta Agriculture Scandinavica 33:353–359.

Brobst, R.B. 1984. Effects of Two Selected Drilling Fluids on Ground Water Sample Chemistry; Monitoring Wells, Their Place in the Water Well Industry. Educational Session, NWWA National Meeting and Exposition Las Vegas, NV.

Carter, C.W. and I.H. Suffet. 1982. Binding of DDT to Dissolved Humic Material. Environ. Sci. Technol. 16(11):735–740.

Champ, D.R., W.F. Merritt, and J.L. Young. 1982. Potential for Rapid Transport of Pu in Groundwater as Demonstrated by Core Column Studies. In: Scientific Basis for Radioactive Waste Management, Vol. 5. Elsevier, New York, NY.

Champlin, J.B.F. and G.G. Eichholz. 1968. The Movement of Radioactive Sodium and Ruthenium Through a Simulated Aquifer. Water Resour. Res. 4(1):147–158.

Danielsson, L.G. 1982. On the Use of Filters for Distinguishing Between Dissolved and Particulate Fractions in Natural Waters. Water Res. 16:179–182.

Driscoll, F.G. 1986. Ground Water and Wells, 2nd Ed. Johnson Division, St. Paul, MN, 1108 pp., pp. 497, 438–9, 722, 725–26.

Enfield, C.G. and G. Bengtsson. 1988. Macromolecular Transport of Hydrophobic Contaminants in Aqueous Environments. Ground Water 26(1):64–70.

Evans, L.G. and S.B. Ellingson. 1988. The Formation of Cement Bleed-Water and Minimizing Its Effect on Water Quality Samples. In: Proc. Ground Water Geochemistry Conference. National Water Well Association, Dublin, OH, pp. 377–389.

Faust, C.R. and J.W. Mercer. 1984. Evaluation of Slug Tests in Wells Containing a Finite Thickness Skin. Water Resour. Res. 20(4):504–506.

Faust, C.R. and J.W. Mercer. 1985. Reply. Water Resources 21(9):1462.

Garske, E.E. and M.R. Schock. 1986. An Inexpensive Flow Through Cell and Measurement System for Monitoring Selected Chemical Parameters in Ground Water. Ground Water Monitoring Review 6(3):79–84.

Gschwend, P.M. and M.D. Reynolds. 1987. Monodisperse Ferrous Phosphate Colloids in an Anoxic Groundwater Plume. J. Contaminant Hydrol. 1(1987):309–327.

Holm, T.R., G.K. George, and M.J. Barcelona. 1988. Oxygen Transfer Through Flexible Tubing and its Effects on Ground Water Sampling Results. Ground Water Monitoring Review 8(3):83–89.

Jay, P.C. 1985. Anion Contamination of Environmental Water Samples Introduced by Filter Media. Analytical Chemistry 57(3):780–782.

Kennedy, V.C. and G.W. Zellweger. 1974. Filter Pore-Size Effects on the Analysis of Al, Fe, Mn, and Ti in Water. Water Resour. Res. 10(4):785–790.

Kim, J.I., G. Buckau, F. Baumgartner, H.C. Moon, and D. Lux. 1984. Colloid Generation and the Actinide Migration in Gorbelen Groundwaters. In: G.L. McVay (ed.), Scientific Basis for Nuclear Waste Management, Vol. 7. Elsevier, New York, NY, pp. 31–40.

Kovenya, S.V., M.K. Melenikova, and A.S. Frid. 1972. Study of the Role of Mechanical Forces and Geometric Conditions in the Movement of Highly Dispersed Particles in Soil Columns. Pochvovedeniye 10:133–140.

Laxen, D.P.H. and I.M. Chandler. 1982. Comparison of Filtration Techniques for Size Distribution in Freshwaters. Analytical Chemistry 54(8):1350–1355.

Means, J.C. and R. Wijayaratne. 1982. Role of Natural Colloids in the Transport of Hydrophobic Pollutants. Science 215(19):968–970.

Moench, A.F. and P.A. Hsieh. 1985. Comment on "Evaluation of Slug Tests in Wells Containing a Finite Skin" by C.R. Faust and J.W. Mercer. Water Resour. Res. 21(9):1459–1461.

O'Melia, C.R. 1980. Aquasols: The Behavior of Small Particles in Aquatic Systems. Environ. Sci. Technol. 14(9):1052–1060.

Reynolds, M.D. Colloids in Groundwater. 1985. Master's Thesis. Mass. Inst. of Tech. Boston, MA.

Saltelli, A., A. Avogadro, and G. Bidoglio. 1984. Americium Filtration in Glauconitic Sand Columns. Nuclear Technol. 67:245–254.

Sheppard, J.C., M.J. Campbell, and J.A. Kittrick. 1979. Retention of Neptunium, Americium and Curium by Diffusible Soil Particles. Environ. Sci. Technol. 13(6):680–684.

Sheppard, J.C., M.J. Campbell, T. Cheng, and J.A. Kittrick. 1980. Retention of Radionuclides by Mobile Humic Compounds. Environ. Sci. Technol. 14(11):1349–1353.

Stumm, W. and J.J. Morgan. 1981. Aquatic Chemistry. John Wiley & Sons, New York, NY.

Takayanagi, K. and G.T.F. Wong. 1984. Organic and Colloidal Selenium in South Chesapeake Bay and Adjacent Waters. Marine Chem. 14:141–148.

Tillekeratne, S., T. Miwa, and A. Mizuike. 1986. Determination of Traces of Heavy Metals in Positively Charged Inorganic Colloids in Fresh Water. Mikrochimica Acta B:289–296.

U.S. Environmental Protection Agency (EPA). 1986. RCRA Ground Water Monitoring Technical Enforcement Guidance Document. EPA/530/SW-86/055 (OSWER-9950.1) (NTIS PB87-107751), 332 pp. [Also published in NWWA/EPA Series, National Water Well Association, Dublin, OH. Final OSWER Directive 9950.2 (NTIS PB91-140194. See also U.S. EPA (1993) for latest draft guidance.]

U.S. Environmental Protection Agency (EPA). 1993. RCRA Ground Water Monitoring: Draft Technical Guidance. EPA/530/R-93/001 (NTIS PB93-139350).

Wagemann, R. and G.J. Brunskill. 1975. The Effect of Filter Pore-Size on Analytical Concentrations of Some Trace Elements in Filtrates of Natural Water. Intern. J. Environ. Anal. Chem. 4:75–84.

Walker, S.E. 1983. Background Water Quality Monitoring: Well Installation Trauma. In: Proc. Third Nat. Symp. on Aquifer Restoration and Ground Water Monitoring. National Water Well Association, Worthington, OH, pp. 235–246.

Yao, K., M.T. Habibian, and C.R. O'Melia. 1971. Water and Waste Water Filtration: Concepts and Applications. Environ. Sci. Technol. 5(11):1105–1112.

Chapter 19

Colloidal-Facilitated Transport of Inorganic Contaminants in Ground Water: Part I. Sampling Considerations[1]

Robert W. Puls, U.S. EPA, Robert S. Kerr Environmental Research Laboratory, Ada OK
James H. Eychaner, U.S. Geological Survey, Tucson, AZ
Robert M. Powell, Man Tech Environmental Technology, Inc., Robert S. Kerr Environmental Research Laboratory, Ada, OK

INTRODUCTION

Ground-water samples that are representative of actual ground-water quality are, at best, difficult to obtain (Claassen, 1982). Disturbance of the subsurface environment is unavoidable during well construction activities. Additional disturbance during sample collection may drastically alter ground-water chemistry due to oxidation, sorption, mixing, and turbulent flow resulting in inaccurate estimations of contaminant loading and transport predictions. A common study objective is to determine what constituents are mobile in an aquifer. Many ground-water samples are filtered to exclude particles dislodged from the local well environment, because those particles are not mobile at ordinary ground-water velocities. Because geochemical models are based on the thermodynamics of dissolved constituents, small pore-diameter filters have been preferred as the best way to separate dissolved from particulate constituents.

In practice, 0.45-μm filters are commonly used to balance between the objectives of isolating dissolved constituents and permitting reasonable use in the field. Unfortunately, particle sizes do not have an express lower bound so that the right filter cannot perfectly separate particles from solutes. Particles with diameters from 0.003 to 10 μm, referred to as colloids, may form in certain environments and be mobile at ground-water velocities. Use of 0.45-μm filtration may exclude an important component of the contaminant load at some waste sites, particularly where highly toxic metals are involved (Puls and Barcelona, 1989).

Many studies have demonstrated contaminant transport by colloidal mobility (Gschwend and Reynolds, 1987; Eichholz et al., 1982; Enfield and Bengtsson, 1988; Robertson, 1984). There is increasing concern that current methods of ground-water sample collection may exclude this component of the contaminant loading in a given system. If the purpose of sampling is to estimate contaminant transport, substantial underestimations of mobility may result, because of colloidal associations. Numerous studies attest to the strong sorptive capabilities of secondary clay minerals; hydrous Fe, Al, and Mn oxides; and humic material of colloidal dimensions. Takayanagi and Wong (1984) determined that more than 70 percent of the total Se in river waters adjacent to the Chesapeake Bay was associated with organic and inorganic colloidal particles. Buddemeier and Rego (1986) found that virtually all the activity of Mn, Co, Sb, Cs, Ce, and Eu was associated with colloidal particles in ground-water samples from underground nuclear-test cavities at the Nevada Test Site. Colloidal particles generated in batch experiments by Sheppard et al. (1979) and Puls et al. (1989) were shown to retain substantial proportions of radionuclides. Further work by Sheppard et al. (1980) concluded that the transport of radionuclides by colloidal clay particles should be considered in contaminant-transport models.

Filtration is part of this concern; but other factors, such as sample exposure to atmospheres different from aquifer environments and pump-induced disturbance of the sampling zone, are also impor-

---

[1] EPA/ 600/M-90/023.

tant. Oxidation-induced precipitation and sorption processes, many of which are kinetically rapid (seconds to minutes), may cause previously dissolved species to be removed during filtration, resulting in lower metal concentrations than are actually present in the aquifer. Filter loading and clogging with fine particles may also occur, reducing the nominal pore size of the filter and introducing errors due to changing effective pore size (Danielsson, 1982).

BACKGROUND

A workshop was convened at the Robert S. Kerr Environmental Research Laboratory (RSKERL) of the U.S. Environmental Protection Agency in 1988 to examine these issues and provide technical guidance based on currently available scientific information. A Superfund Ground Water Issue Paper resulting from the workshop emphasized the importance of well construction and sampling methodology in obtaining representative water chemistry data (Puls and Barcelona, 1989). Workshop recommendations in the area of ground-water sampling are briefly summarized below:

Purging

Water that remains in the well casing between sampling periods is unrepresentative of water in the formation opposite the screened interval. It must be removed by purging or isolated from the collected sample by a packer arrangement prior to the collection of representative water samples. It is important to purge the stagnant water at flow rates below those used in development to avoid further development well damage or the disturbance of accumulated corrosion of reaction products in the well.

Isolation of Sampling Zone

Isolation of the sampling zone is necessary to minimize the purge volume as well as to minimize air contact. This is especially important since Eh/pH conditions of the formation waters are often sensitive to dissolved-gas content. Inflatable packers can be used to achieve isolation of the sampling zone.

Pumping for Sample Collection

It is recommended that a positive displacement pump be used. Other types of sample collection (e.g., bailing) may cause displacement of nonmobile particles or substantially alter ground-water chemistry leading to colloid formation (e.g., vacuum pumps). Surging must be avoided, and a flow rate close to the actual ground-water flow rate should be employed. While an initial approximation, flow rates around 100 to 500 ml/min have been used to successfully sample ground waters in a quiescent mode.

Assessment of Water Constituents During Purging and Sampling

Monitoring for dissolved oxygen, temperature, specific conductance, pH and turbidity during purging and sampling is recommended to determine baseline ground-water quality conditions prior to sampling.

Filtration

For estimates of contaminant mobility, filtration with coarse filters (≥ 2 μm) using the same procedures as above or collection of unfiltered samples is recommended. Filtration for accurate estimations of geochemistry should be performed in the field with in-line pressure filtration using a large (e.g., 142 mm) polycarbonate-type (thin with sharp pore-size cutoff) 0.1 μm filter. Air contact should be minimized and entirely excluded for some samples. Acidification of samples to < pH 2 should be performed immediately. The filter holder should be nonmetallic. Holders made of steel are subject to corrosion and may introduce nonformation metals into samples. Prewashing of filters should be routinely performed.

In an effort to test the efficacy of these recommendations, a joint study by the U.S. Environmental Protection Agency and the U.S. Geological Survey was begun in the spring of 1988. Collection of representative unfiltered samples is quite challenging in many systems because of the difficulty of excluding nonsuspended or artifact particulates. Because no sampling technique is totally passive, all contaminant-mobility estimates based on unfiltered samples are biased toward overestimation. An attempt was made to minimize this bias by carefully following the workshop recommendations.

PURPOSE AND OBJECTIVES

The specific objectives of the study were to evaluate perturbations to the ground-water geochemistry during sample collection and in particular, to identify those factors that caused significant differences in elemental concentrations or concentrations and size distributions of suspended particles in samples collected for analysis. Samples for both dissolved and suspended contaminants were collected. Filters smaller than 0.45 µm were used to sample for dissolved constituents and for comparison with the unfiltered or coarsely filtered samples. This chapter summarizes the results of the study and addresses the efficacy of the 1988 RSKERL filtration workshop recommendations on ground-water sampling for metals analyses.

STUDY SITE

The study site is located at Pinal Creek, near Globe, Arizona, about 130 km east of Phoenix and about 170 km north of Tucson. Copper has been mined since 1903 from granite porphyry adjacent to an aquifer at the site. A band of unconsolidated alluvium 300 to 800 m wide, as much as 50 m thick, and about 20 km long forms the upper, central part of the aquifer in a valley along Miami Wash and Pinal Creek (Figures 19-1 and 19-2). Most of the sediment in the alluvium ranges in size from fine sand to coarse gravel, but clay and boulder lenses also are present. Alluvial basin fill more than 100 m thick forms the remainder of the aquifer beneath and adjacent to the unconsolidated alluvium. Peterson (1962) described the geology of the area.

During 1940–1986, acidic mining waste solutions were discarded in an unlined lake formed behind waste and tailings piles. In 1986, pH at the lake surface was about 2.7 and the lake volume was about 5.5 x 106 m³. By May 1988, virtually all the lake water had been spread on inactive tailings piles to evaporate. Contamination of ground and surface waters in the area has been described by Eychaner (1989). The distribution of pH in the aquifer was used as a guide in selecting wells to sample for this study (Figure 19-1).

Water levels and chemical quality have been monitored since 1984 in several groups of observation wells (Figure 19-1). Each group consists of separate wells individually completed at different depths with 10-cm-diameter polyvinylchloride casing and a single well screen. Most of the well screens are 0.9 m long; the longest screen in a well sampled for this study is 6.1 m. Most of the wells were drilled by the hydraulic rotary method using bentonite-based drilling mud, five wells were drilled by the hollow-stem auger method. The annulus in the screened interval was packed with washed pea gravel from a nearby uncontaminated area. The gravel pack was capped with a 1-m layer of bentonite pellets. Each well was developed by jetting high-pressure air through the screen to dislodge and remove fine-grained material. Comprehensive data from the study area are available (Eychaner et al., 1989).

In the alluvium, hydraulic conductivity is on the order of 200 m/d on the basis of cross-sectional area, hydraulic gradient, and measured outflow (C.C. Neaville, hydrologist, U.S. Geological Survey written commun., 1990). For thick sections of basin fill hydraulic conductivity was estimated from aquifer tests of two wells to range from 0.1 to 0.2 m/d (Neaville, written communication, 1990).

Near the sampled wells, hydraulic conductivity was estimated on the basis of measured water-level declines and pumping rates during sampling periods using the solution of the unsteady ground-water flow equation (Lohman, 1979, eq. 44). The estimates are within an order of magnitude at best, but are useful for comparisons among the wells because of the similarities in construction. The estimates range from 10 to 150 m/d for wells in the alluvium or uppermost basin fill. Estimated

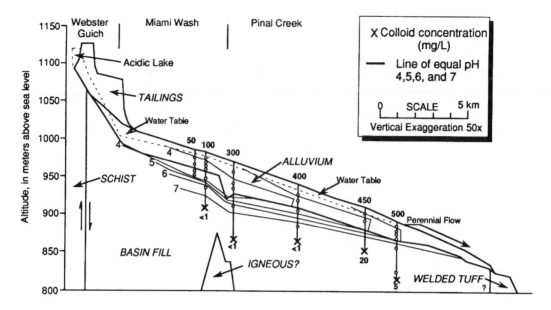

Figure 19-1. Hydrogeologic section of the aquifer.

hydraulic conductivity for well 105, deeper in the basin fill, was 0.5 m/d. On the basis of hydraulic gradients that range from 0.005 to 0.008 and assumed porosity of 0.2 or 0.3, average ground-water flow velocities near the wells range from 0.02 to 3 m/d.

INSTRUMENTATION AND METHODS

Ground water was collected during two field seasons from twelve wells selected to represent the range of pH, solute concentration, and hydraulic conductivity along Pinal Creek (Figures 19-1 and 19-2). Three different pumps were used (Table 19-1). At the lowest discharge, velocities induced at the borehole face were estimated to range from 1 to 5 times the average groundwater velocity close to each well in the alluvium. In the basin fill underlying the alluvium, even the lowest discharge resulted in velocities more than 400 times that of the ground water.

Water that remained in the well between sampling sessions was purged, as it was judged to be unrepresentative of formation water. An inflatable packer was used with the bladder and low rate submersible pumps to reduce necessary purge volumes. During purging, a Hydrolab Surveyor 11, with a flow-through cell was used to monitor temperature, specific conductance, pH, dissolved oxygen, and oxidation-reduction potential (Pt electrode). Samples were collected only after each indicator reached an acceptably stable value, generally a value that changed by less than its measurement uncertainty during one purge volume. From 3 to 24 volumes were purged before sampling, and the high flow rate submersible pump generally purged the larger volumes.

During the second field season, a Malvern Autosizer IIc was used to measure suspended particles in the diameter range from 0.003 to 3 μm. The instrument determines the size distribution of suspended particles in this size range using laser light scattering techniques together with photon correlation spectroscopy. Particle concentration estimates were based on calibration curves constructed using linear correlation ($r^2 = 0.999$) between photon counts by the instrument and known concentrations of kaolinite, a secondary clay mineral. The kaolinite used was a reference standard obtained from the Clay Minerals Repository at the University of Missouri. Kaolinite was identified by Scanning Electron Microscopy with Energy Dispersive X-Ray (SEM-EDX) on many of the filters from the sampled wells. Other particles captured on filters and identified by SEM-EDX included iron oxides, smectite, jarosite, silica, and gypsum. Although the assumption that minerals in the reference standard adequately represent the sum total of all the colloids in the aquifer is not entirely true, photon counts provide at least a relative measure of suspended particle concentrations.

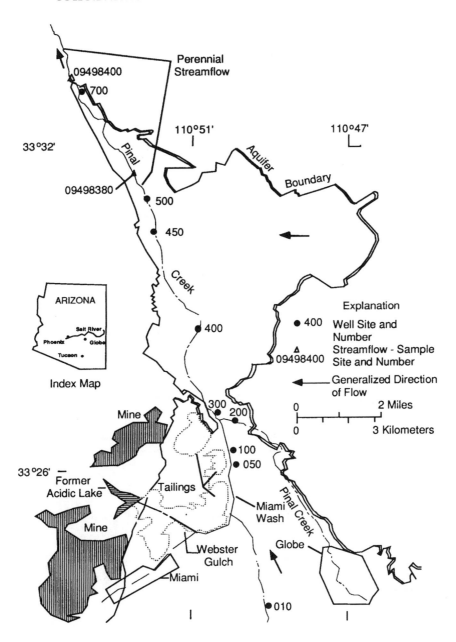

Figure 19-2. Plan-view of study site.

Colloid concentrations took longer to stabilize than other field indicators, about 50 percent longer than dissolved oxygen or redox potential, and about twice as long as specific conductance pH, or temperature. Well 107 was representative of the variation of the indicators during purging at most of the wells (Figure 19-3). Stable values of the indicators at selected wells are listed in Table 19-2.

Samples were collected both in air and under nitrogen using a field glove box. Unfiltered and filtered samples were collected, the latter using 142-mm-diameter Millipore and Nucleopore membrane filters ranging in pore size from 0.03 to 10.0 μm. Samples were acidified in the field immediately after filtering with double distilled concentrated nitric acid to pH < 2. Working in the glove box was difficult, and handling thin membrane filters with latex gloves was particularly cumbersome.

Elemental analyses were performed with inductively coupled plasma (ICP) for most elements; atomic absorption with graphite furnace (MGF) for Cd, Pb, and As; and ion chromatography (IC) for

Table 19-1. Pumps Used in Ground-Water Sampling

Brand[a]	Power Type	Diameter Supply	Discharge (mm)	(L/min)
GeoTech	bladder	compressed air	44	0.6–1.1
Keck	submersible	12 V dc	44	2.8–3.8
Grundfos	submersible	240 V ac	95	12–92

[a]   Use of brand names is for identification purposes only and does not imply endorsement by any agency of the United States Government.

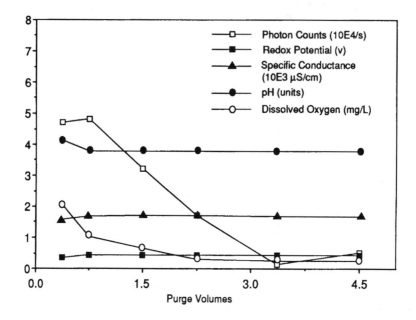

Figure 19-3. Changes in water quality indicators during purging of well 107 (Keck Pump, 3/89).

chloride and sulfate. Analytical precision on the ICP and AAGF were $\leq \pm$ 10 percent, and on the IC $\leq \pm$ 5 percent. Scanning Electron Microscopy with Energy Dispersive X-Ray (SEM-EDX) was used to identify colloidal material captured on the membrane filters.

EFFECTS OF SAMPLING VARIABLES

Pumping Rates

Differences in pumping rates were expected to cause differences in the concentrations and size distributions of colloidal particles in suspensions and differences in elemental concentrations after filtration. Ten wells were purged and sampled with as many as three different types of pumps in June 1988 and March 1989. Pumping rates ranged from 0.6 to 92 L/min, corresponding to velocities of 25 to 3900 m/d at the well screens. Samples were filtered in air through 0.4-μm filters, filtrates were analyzed for cations using ICP, and the filters were examined using SEM-EDX. Particle concentrations and size distributions were monitored in 1989 for five wells on unfiltered samples.

Cation concentrations differed by less than 10 percent between pumping rates for seven of the ten wells. These seven wells generally had low particle counts, and low filter loading was observed using SEM-EDX. Well 503, in the alluvium, was representative of the seven wells. Figure 19-4 illustrates changes in water-quality indicators in well 503, where the bladder pump was used to purge and sample, followed by use of the low-rate and high-rate submersible pumps. The well there-

Table 19-2. Ground-Water Quality Indicators for Selected Wells

Well:	104	105	107	303	403	451	503
pH (units)	3.92	6.08	3.48	4.27	5.05	4.73	5.74
Sp. Cond. (µS/cm)	3020	4300	7070	3210	3200	4060	3620
Temp. (°C)	18.0	19.0	18.4	19.0	18.8	18.9	18.9
Oxygen (mg/L)	0.39	—	0.14	0.01	0.07	0.24	0.22
Redox Pot. (v)	0.44	0.28	0.44	0.37	0.38	0.25	0.32
Colloids (mg/L)	—	0.4	0.3	—	—	20	0.1

fore was purged with the bladder pump prior to placement of the latter two pumps. Colloid concentration stabilized at 0.1 mg/L during pumping at 1.1 L/min and increased to 0.7 mg/L when discharge increased to 3.8 L/min before stabilizing again at 0.1 mg/L. When discharge increased to 30 L/min, however, colloid concentration initially increased to 4.4 mg/L before finally stabilizing at 0.2 mg/L. Particle-size distributions for the final sample with each pump are also shown in Figure 19-4. The low-discharge pumps produced monomodal distributions of the same size particles. The highest discharge produced larger and slightly more particles in a bimodal distribution because of increased turbulence. The predominant mineral identified on the filters from well 503 was gypsum, which was accompanied by some iron oxide, kaolinite, and other particles that contained Fe+Al+S. Analytical concentrations of metals did not differ significantly but did reflect the observed mineralogy.

For samples from the three wells where observed cation differences exceeded 10 percent, measured particle counts and filter loading were also significantly higher than for the other seven wells. Particle counts differed by factors of 5 to 130 between pumping rates. Cation concentrations differed by as much as 50 percent for both major and trace elements. Cation concentrations were generally highest in samples with the lowest counts (least turbid), but some anomalous behavior was observed for some elements (Table 19-3). Pump-induced entrainment of colloidal particles could decrease dissolved cation concentrations by sorption on freshly exposed surfaces of particles which had been retained on filters.

Differences in cation concentrations were especially noticeable at well 105. In March 1989, pumping at 2.8 L/min mobilized 13 times more particles and decreased Ca, Mg, Mn, and Sr concentrations by 10 to 25 percent, compared to pumping at 0.9 L/min (Table 19-3). For equal volumes of filtrate, SEM photographs showed that the proportion of the area of a 0.1 µm filter covered with particles was about 1 percent for the lower pumping rate and about 30 percent for the higher rate. In June 1988, pumping at 12 L/min decreased concentrations of Ca, Mg, Mn, Co, Ni, and Sr by 20 to 50 percent compared to pumping at 1 L/min. Well 105 is screened in the basin fill, which has the lowest ground-water flow velocity in this study. Even at the lowest pumping rate, the velocity induced at the borehole face was more than 400 times the normal ground-water velocity. Water pumped from well 105 was visibly murky at times.

Pumping well 451 at 0.8 L/min produced seven times more particles than pumping at 3.4 L/min and decreased concentrations of six cations by 10 to 50 percent. Again, the less turbid water generally had the larger concentrations, but the higher pumping rate unexpectedly produced the less turbid water. This well had the highest colloid concentrations of any well (Table 19-4). The samples collected in March 1989 were noticeably turbid, even after 2 hours of purging with the bladder pump. In fact, lower particle counts by the slightly higher rate pump may have resulted from the additional purge time, as the latter was inserted following purging and sampling with the bladder pump. Two factors may contribute to the high colloid concentrations at well 451:

- it is in relatively fine grained sediment in the alluvium, and
- it is in a part of the aquifer where pH is changing rapidly and iron oxide coatings on colloidal clay are dissolving.

For this data set, particle concentrations were not predictable from pumping rate, purge volume, flow velocity at the screen, or the ratio of velocity induced at the borehole face to local groundwater flow velocity. Measured particle concentrations appear to depend on interactions of these factors as well as geology, well construction, and water chemistry.

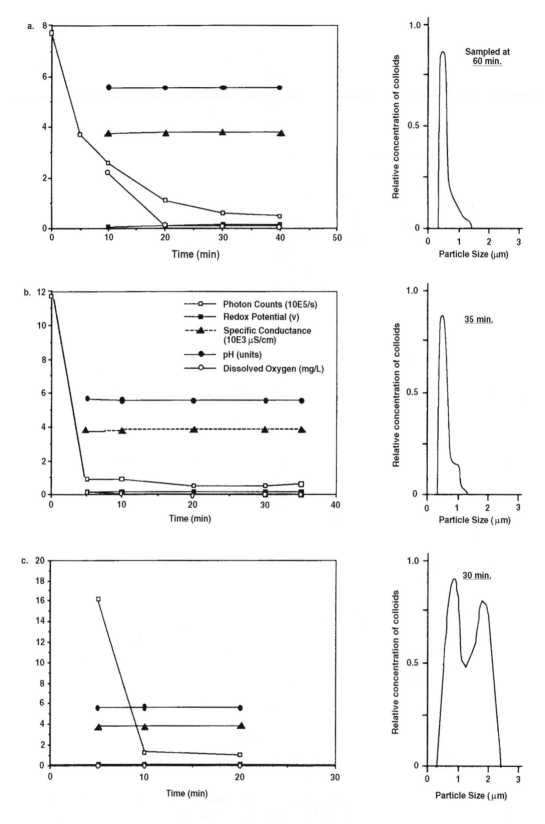

Figure 19-4. Changes in water quality indicators during purging of well 503: (a) Bladder pump; (b) Low-speed submersible pump; (c) High-speed submersible pump.

Table 19-3. Cation and Colloid Concentrations, mg/L, After Purging at Different Rates (March 1989, 0.4 μm Filter, Sampled in Air)

Well	105	105	451	451	503	503	503
Discharge (L/min)	0.9	2.8	0.8	3.4	1.1	3.8	30
Colloids	0.3	4.0	20	3.0	0.1	0.1	0.2
Ca	579	478	586	623	703	704	704
Mg	149	117	150	162	148	146	147
K	40	37	16	13	12	11	11
Fe	<.4	<.4	156	151	<.4	<.4	<.4
Mn	6.6	5.0	108	113	76	76	73
Al	<.4	<.4	6.5	10.0	<.4	<.4	<.4
Cu	<.4	<.4	6.4	12.4	<.4	<.4	<.4
Co	<.4	<.4	1.5	1.8	<.4	<.4	<.4
Ni	<.4	<.4	0.3	0.4	0.6	0.6	0.6
Sr	1.6	1.4	1.9	2.1	2.3	2.3	2.3
Zn	0.7	0.9	3.0	3.9	0.06	0.04	0.04

Table 19-4. Pumping Rate Data for Selected Wells and Pumps

Well	Date Sampled	Pump Discharge (L/min)	Intake Velocity (m/d)	Formation Velocity (m/d)	Colloid Relative Velocity[a]	Concentration (mg/L)
105	6-14-88	1.0	42	0.012	460	
		12	510		5500	
	3-7-89	0.9	38		410	0.3
		2.8	120		1300	4.0
303	6-15-88	0.7	30	1.33	2.9	
		24	1000		99	
403	6-15-88	0.8	34	2.93	1.5	
		27	1100		51	
451	3-9-89	0.8	26	0.25	5.3	20
		3.4	110		22	3.0
452	3-9-89	0.8	28	0.75	1.8	0.2
		28	980		61	10
503	6-16-88	1.0	42	1.63	3.4	
		45	1900		150	
	3-8-89	1.1	47		3.7	0.1
		3.8	160		13	0.1
		30	1300		100	0.2

[a] Ratio of induced velocity at the borehole face to average ground-water velocity in the adjacent formation.

Filtration Differences

Concentration differences among samples filtered through pore sizes ranging from 0.1 to 10 μm were generally less than 10 percent. Only wells 303 (Table 19-5) and well 503 had differences of greater than 10 percent in most elemental concentrations. The larger differences commonly were associated with use of the high-rate submersible pump, and concentrations generally increased with increasing filter-pore size.

Differences less than 10 percent generally were observed for waters that have pH less than 4, which does not favor colloid formation. The largest observed differences for well 403, for example, were for Al, Cu, Fe, and Mg, but no consistent trend of concentration with filter pore size is apparent (Table 19-6).

Table 19-5. Cation Concentrations, in mg/L, for Well 303 Using Different Filters (June 1988, 24 L/min, Sampled in Air)

Element	0.1 μm	0.4 μm	10 μm
Ca	391	424	492
Mg	91	100	20
K	4.73	5.49	9.76
Fe	171	87	211
Mn	37.7	40.8	45.5
Al	6.74	7.61	9.93
Co	0.68	0.75	0.86
Cu	15.0	16.7	19.2
Ni	0.68	0.75	0.88
Zn	2.75	3.27	4.13

Table 19-6. Cation Concentrations in mg/L, for Well 403 Using Different Filters (June 1988, 0.8 L/min, Sampled in Air)

Element	0.1 μm	0.4 μm	10 μm
Ca	533	533	554
Mg	133	113	116
K	5.58	5.47	5.65
Fe	0.45	6.63	1.22
Mn	34.6	34.9	34.7
Al	1.22	1.91	1.17
Co	0.36	0.36	0.37
Cu	1.62	2.14	1.57
Ni	0.41	0.42	0.44
Zn	0.90	0.95	1.60

Filtration differences of greater than 10 percent were also generally associated with use of the high-rate submersible pump because of the increased entrainment of particulates as observed above.

Oxidation of Samples

Oxidation of samples during sample collection, filtration, and preservation generally resulted in substantial differences in most wells between samples collected under nitrogen or in air. Work by Holm et al. (1988) showed that diffusion of atmospheric gases through pump tubing can introduce measurable concentrations of oxygen into waters initially low in dissolved oxygen. This source of possible contamination for both sets of samples was minimized by collection of samples adjacent to the wellhead. Samples collected in air were directly exposed to atmospheric gases during filtration and acidification procedures. Significant differences (> 10 percent) were observed in many of the wells. Variations in differences from well to well may have been caused by a number of different factors including:

- slightly different exposure times to air, depending on water-table depth and duration of filtration and preservation,
- dissolved-oxygen level,
- redox potential (Eh), and
- dissolved iron concentration.

Large differences in concentrations were measured for well 303, where dissolved iron concentration was greater than 200 mg/L (Table 19-7). Differences similar to those for well 303 were also ob-

Table 19-7. Cation Concentrations, in mg/L, for Samples Collected in Air and Nitrogen Under Atmosphere (mg/L, 0.40-μm Filter, < 1 L/min)

Element	Well 303		Well 503	
	Air	Nitrogen	Air	Nitrogen
Fe	177	215	0.04	0.09
Mn	37.4	44.7	68.3	68.7
Cd	0.02	0.02	0.01	0.01
Co	0.69	0.82	0.01	0.02
Cu	15.5	18.6	0.01	0.04
Ni	0.70	0.84	0.47	0.48
Zn	2.53	3.11	0.21	0.30

served in wells 51, 104, and 403. In contrast, the differences were small for well 503, where the dissolved iron concentration was less than 0.1 ma/L.

Another indication of the extent of oxidative effects on sample integrity was reflected in Eh values determined by various methods for well 51 (Figure 19-1). The field-measured Eh value using a Pt electrode was 0.43 V. A calculated Eh value, assuming equilibrium between Fe^{3+} and $Fe(OH)_3$, was 0.57 V (Stollenwerk and Eychaner, 1989). In March 1989, Fe^{2+} and Fe_{total} for well 51 were determined within one week of sample collection; Fe^{3+} was computed by difference, and Eh was calculated from the ratio of Fe^{3+} to Fe^{2+}. The calculated Eh was 0.51 V for the sample collected and analyzed in a nitrogen atmosphere and 0.76 V for the sample collected in air. Samples collected in the glove box were transported in nitrogen-pressurized containers, and the determinations were performed in laboratory glove boxes also pressurized with nitrogen.

Several possible errors are associated with all these Eh evaluation methods. Lindberg and Runnells (1984) showed that many field Eh measurements may not reflect true redox conditions in ground waters. However, in acidic waters such as these, field measurements using Pt electrodes may be valid (Nordstrom et al., 1979). Values calculated from equilibrium constants rely on the assumption that $Fe(OH)_3$ is the predominant solubility controlling phase. Stollenwerk and Eychaner (1989) used the equilibrium expression:

$$Fe^{3+} + 3H_2O \rightarrow Fe(OH)_3 + 3H^+ \qquad \log K_T = -4.891,$$

although other values have been reported for this reaction. Samples collected under nitrogen may have received some exposure to oxygen during sample collection, processing, and analysis. The Fe^{3+} values for March 1989 were small differences between two large numbers and are uncertain. Irrespective of these and other limitations in estimating Eh, the large difference observed between 0.76 V for the sample collected in air and the other Eh values for well 51 demonstrates the extent of oxidation that can occur if care is not taken to limit oxygen exposure during sample-collection activities in suboxic and anoxic environments.

CONCLUSIONS

Research at this site indicates that monitoring of water-quality indicators during well purging and sampling is important. In addition to the indicators most often monitored, turbidity also needs to be evaluated before collecting samples. In lieu of the use of a turbidimeter, purging for twice the time required for dissolved-oxygen equilibration may be a good rule of thumb.

The use of a low flow rate pump can minimize entrainment of nonmobile suspended particulates, oxygenation of formation water, and mixing of adjacent, possibly geochemically distinct, ground waters. Collection and processing of anoxic or suboxic ground water excluding atmospheric gases to the extent possible is desirable for representative and accurate water-chemistry data. The glove box used for collection of samples under nitrogen was cumbersome and difficult to use, especially in handling the thin membrane filters. If tubing of minimum length and maximum thickness were used, in-line filtration would probably mitigate the oxidation effects observed in the present study, making the use of a field glove box and accompanying nitrogen cylinders unnecessary. Although filtration differences generally were not significant at this site, trends indicate that care needs to be taken in selection of filter pore size and that samples need to be filtered in the field. Additional research is needed at sites with distinctly different hydrology, geology, and chemistry before final recommendations can be made concerning filtration. In the interim, collection of filtered and unfiltered samples for comparison purposes is suggested for at least a fraction of the samples collected. Filtered samples are needed for accurate aqueous geochemistry estimations, and unfiltered samples provide conservative estimates of contaminant mobility.

The sampling recommendations proposed by the RSKERL 1988 workshop participants were realistic and relatively easy to apply in the present study. Additional time was required for purging and sampling, but the additional care was warranted to obtain ground water chemistry data which were as representative as possible.

ACKNOWLEDGMENTS

The authors gratefully acknowledge the support of Terry F. Rees, U.S. Geological Survey, Denver, CO, for the SEM-EDX analyses; Donald Clark, Robert S. Kerr Environmental Research Laboratory Ada, OK, for the ICP and AAGF analyses; and Narong Chamkasem, NSI Technology Services Corporation, Ada, OK, for the IC analyses.

REFERENCES

Buddemeier, R.W. and J.H. Rego. 1986. Colloidal Radionuclides in Groundwater. Annual Report. Lawrence Livermore National Laboratory, Livermore, CA. UCAR 10062/85-1.

Claassen, H.C. 1982. Guidelines and Techniques for Obtaining Water Samples that Accurately Represent the Water Chemistry of an Aquifer. U.S Geological Survey Open-file Report 82-1024, 49 pp.

Danielsson, L.G. 1982. On the Use of Filters for Distinguishing Between Dissolved and Particulate Fractions in Natural Waters. Water Res. 16:179.

Eichholz, G.G., B.G. Wahlig, G.F. Powell, and T.F. Craft. 1982. Subsurface Migration of Radioactive Waste Materials by Particulate Transport. Nuclear Technology 58:511.

Enfield, C.G. and G. Bengtsson. 1988. Macromolecular Transport of Hydrophobic Contaminants in Aqueous Environments. Ground Water 26(1):64.

Eychaner, J.H. 1989. Movement of inorganic contaminants in acidic water near Globe, Arizona. In: G.E. Mallard and S.E. Ragone (eds.), U.S. Geological Survey Toxic Substances Hydrology Program—Proceedings of the Technical Meeting, Phoenix Arizona, September 26–30, 1988. U.S. Geological Survey Water Resources Investigations Report 88-4220, pp. 567–575.

Eychaner, J.H., M.R. Rehmann, and J.G. Brown. 1989. Chemical, Geologic, and Hydrologic Data from the Study of Acidic Contamination in the Miami Wash-Pinal Creek Area, Arizona, Water Years 1984–1987. U.S. Geological Survey Open-File Report 89-410, 105 pp.

Gschwend, P.M. and M.D. Reynolds. 1987. Monodisperse Ferrous Phosphate Colloids in an Anoxic Groundwater Plume. J. Contaminant Hydrol. 1:309.

Holm, T.R., G.K. George, and M.J. Barcelona. 1988. Oxygen Transfer Through Flexible Tubing and its Effects on Ground Water Sampling Results. Ground Water Monitoring Review 8(3):83.

Lindberg, R.D. and D.D. Runnells. 1984. Ground Water Redox Reactions: An Analysis of Equilibrium State Applied to Eh Measurements and Geochemical Modeling. Science 225:925–927.

Lohman, S.W. 1979. Ground-Water Hydraulics. U.S. Geological Survey Professional Paper 708, 70 pp.

Nordstrom, D.K., E.A. Jenne, and J.W. Ball. 1979. Redox Equilibria of Iron in Acid Mine Waters, In: E.A. Jenne (ed.), Chemical Modeling in Aqueous Systems. ACS Symp. Series 93. American Chemical Society, Washington, DC, pp. 51–79.

Peterson, N.P. 1962. Geology and Ore Deposits of the Globe Miami District, Arizona. U.S. Geological Survey Professional Paper 342, 151 pp.

Puls, R.W. and M.J. Barcelona. 1989. Ground Water Sampling for Metals Analyses. EPA/540/4-89/001. [See Chapter 19.]

Puls, R.W., L.L. Ames, and J.E. McGarrah. 1989. The Use of Batch Tests as a Screening Tool for Radionuclide Sorption Characterization Studies, Hanford, Washington, U.S.A. Applied Geochemistry 4:63–77.

Robertson, W.D. 1984. Contamination of an Unconfined Sand Aquifer by Waste Pulp Liquor: A Case Study. Ground Water 22(2):191.

Sheppard, J.C., M.J. Campbell, and J.A. Kittrick. 1979. Retention of Neptunium, Americium and Curium by Diffusible Soil Particles. Environ. Sci. Technol. 13(6):680–684.

Sheppard, J.C., M.J. Campbell, T. Cheng, and J.A. Kittrick. 1980. Retention of Radionuclides by Mobile Humic Compounds. Environ. Sci. Technol. 14(11):1349–1353.

Stollenwerk, K.G. and J.H. Eychaner. 1989. Solubility of Aluminum and Iron in Ground-Water Near Globe, Arizona. In: G.E. Mallard, and S.E. Ragone (eds.), U.S. Geological Survey Toxic Substances Hydrology Program—Proceedings of the Technical Meeting, Phoenix Arizona, September 26–30, 1988. U.S. Geological Survey Water Resources Investigations Report 88-4220.

Takayanagi, K. and G.T.F. Wong. 1984. Organic and Colloidal Selenium in South Chesapeake Bay and Adjacent Waters. Marina Chem 14:141–148.

DISCLAIMER

The information in this chapter has been funded wholly or in part by the United States Environmental Protection Agency. This document has been subject to the Agency's peer and administrative review and has been approved for publication as an EPA document.

Chapter 20

Colloidal-Facilitated Transport of Inorganic Contaminants in Ground Water: Part II. Colloidal Transport[1]

Robert W. Puls, U.S. EPA, Robert S. Kerr Environmental Research Laboratory, Ada, OK
Robert M. Powell, Man Tech Environmental Technology, Inc., Robert S. Kerr Environmental Research Laboratory, Ada, OK
Don A. Clark, Retired, U.S. EPA, Robert S. Kerr Environmental Research Laboratory, Ada, OK
Cynthia J. Paul, Man Tech Environmental Technology, Inc., Robert S. Kerr Environmental Research Laboratory, Ada, OK

INTRODUCTION

Understanding the transport and fate of inorganic contaminants in the subsurface environment has been complicated by recent field studies that show contaminant mobility to be greater than had been predicted. These predictions have been based on properties such as speciation, solubility, ion exchange, and sorption-desorption but have failed to account for the potential interactions between inorganic contaminants and mobile colloids. Colloids are generally considered to be particles with diameters less than 10 micrometers (Stumm and Morgan, 1981), and can include both organic and inorganic materials. In addition to having a high surface area per unit mass and volume, particles of dissolved organic carbon, clay minerals and iron oxides are also extremely reactive sorbents for radionuclides and other contaminants. Drastic changes in aqueous geochemistry can bring about supersaturated conditions in which inorganic colloidal species are formed. Decreases in pH or changes in redox potential can cause the dissolution of soil or geologic matrix cementing agents, promoting the release of particles. Decreases in the ionic strength of the aqueous phase can enhance colloidal stability and promote their transport. If mobile, these particles may increase the mobility of sorbed contaminants above that predicted by our current simple dissolved-phase transport models.

Several studies have demonstrated the presence of such colloidal material in ground water, with indications that colloidal mobility may facilitate the transport of contaminants in some systems. These studies have also provided data on the size range of mobile colloids, with evidence that particles with diameters greater than 1 μm may actually move faster than the average ground-water flow velocity in porous media due to effects such as size exclusion from smaller pore spaces. Other studies have demonstrated the strong binding and enormous sorption capacities of colloidal particles for inorganic and organic contaminants. The significance of colloidal mobility as a contaminant transport mechanism ultimately depends on the presence of sufficient quantities of reactive particles in ground water. With current techniques, our ability to differentiate between naturally suspended particles and those which are brought artificially into suspension during sample acquisition is questionable.

Inherent to this problem is the arbitrary designation of 0.45 μm as an operational cutoff point for distinguishing between particulate and dissolved species. If particles as large as 1–2 μm are mobile, present in significant quantities, and capable of transporting contaminants long distances, then sampling protocols must quantify this component of transport. Transport models must then incorporate this mechanism to provide better contaminant migration predictions.

---

[1] EPA/600/M-91/040.

Colloidal Reactivity, Mobility and Size

Numerous studies demonstrate the strong adsorptive capabilities of secondary clay minerals, hydrous iron, aluminum and manganese oxides and humic material (Sheppard et al. 1979; Takayanagi and Wong, 1984; Sandhu and Mills, 1987; Means and Wijayaratne, 1982). In studies at underground nuclear-test cavities at the Nevada Test Site, Buddemeier and Rego (1986) found that virtually all of the activity of Mn, Co, Sb, Cs, Ce and Eu was associated with colloidal particles in ground-water samples. Sandhu and Mills (1987) found over 90% of the chromium and arsenic present in a laboratory column study was associated with colloidal iron and manganese oxide. Nelson et al. (1985) determined that colloidal organic carbon was a major factor controlling the distribution of plutonium between the solid and dissolved phases.

The mobility of these reactive particles has already been demonstrated. Gschwend and Reynolds (1987) concluded that submicron ferrous phosphate particles were suspended and presumably mobile in a sand and gravel aquifer. These particles were formed from sewage-derived phosphate that combined with iron released from aquifer solids by reduction and dissolution of ferric iron. Size distribution analyses indicated a large population of 100 nm particles, and a lesser quantity in the range 600–800 nm. In complementary laboratory experiments with sand columns and carboxylated polystyrene beads ranging in size from 0.10 to 0.91 µm as model colloids, Reynolds (1985) recovered 45% of the 0.91 µm size beads, and greater than 70% of 0.10 and 0.28 µm size beads. Field studies by Nightingale and Bianchi (1977) showed that, under certain conditions, submicrometer-sized particles within the surface weathered zone were mobilized for some distance both vertically and laterally and affect ground-water turbidity. In laboratory tests, Eichholz et al. (1982) found that cationic nuclides were competitively adsorbed on suspended clay particles capable of travelling at bulk water flow velocity in porous mineral columns. Particulate matter of micrometer dimensions was shown to be responsible for the transport of radioactive sodium and ruthenium in sand beds by Champlin and Eichholz (1968). As much as 200 µg/L copper, lead, and cadmium were found to be associated with colloidal material in the size range 0.015–0.450 µm by Tillekeratne et al. (1986). Rapid transport of plutonium in core column studies by Champ et al. (1982) was attributed to colloidal transport, with 48% of the plutonium associated with particles in the size range 0.003–0.050 µm and 23% in the range 0.050–0.450 µm.

Harvey et al. (1989) showed that, in a shallow sand and gravel aquifer, 1.35 µm latex particles traveled faster than the 0.23 µm size particles. This phenomenon was due to size exclusion effects (reduced path length), similar to what Enfield and Bengtsson (1988) observed in laboratory columns with organic macromolecules. Penrose et al. (1990) found detectable amounts of plutonium and americium, 3390 m downgradient from a source, to be tightly or irreversibly associated with particles between 0.025 and 0.45 µm in size. Champlin and Eichholz (1976) demonstrated that previously "fixed" particles and associated contaminants may be remobilized by changes in the aqueous geochemistry of the system. Cerda (1987) demonstrated that the mobilization of kaolinite fines in laboratory columns was almost totally dependent upon the chemistry of the fluids present, with maximum mobility occurring under relatively high saline, weakly alkaline pH conditions. Repulsive colloidal forces promoting stability were in evidence up to 0.1 M NaCl (pH 9). Matijevic et al. (1980) studied the stability and transport of hematite spheres through packed-bed columns of stainless steel beads as a function of pH and the concentration of a variety of simple and complex electrolytes. Surface charge alterations of the hematite and stainless-steel beads by the different electrolytes was the dominant factor in colloidal deposition and detachment.

Recent estimates of colloidal concentrations in ground water range as high as 63 mg/L (Buddemeier and Hunt, 1988), 60 mg/L (Ryan and Gschwend, 1990), and 20 mg/L (Puls and Eychaner, 1990). Given the demonstrated high binding capacity of many of these particles, concentrations of this magnitude could have a significant impact on contaminant transport.

Dissolved vs. Particulate

Historically, 0.45 µm pore size filters have been used to differentiate between dissolved and particulate phases in water samples. If the intent of the filtration is to determine truly dissolved constituent concentrations for geochemical modeling purposes, the inclusion of colloidal material less than 0.45 µm in the filtrate will result in incorrect dissolved values. This result is often observed with iron and aluminum, where "dissolved" values are obtained that are thermodynamically impossible at the sample pH. Conversely, if the purpose of sampling is to estimate "mobile" species in solution, including both dissolved and particle-associated contaminants, significant underestimations of mobility may result, due to removal of colloidal matter by 0.45 µm filtration.

Kim et al. (1984), found the majority of the concentrations of rare earth elements to be associated with colloidal species that passed through a 0.45 µm filter. Wagemann and Brunskill (1975) found more than two-fold differences in total iron and aluminum values between 0.05 and 0.45 µm filters of the same type. Some aluminum compounds, observed to pass through a 0.45 µm filter, were retained on a 0.10 µm filter, by Hem and Roberson (1967). Kennedy and Zellweger (1974) found errors of an order of magnitude or more in the determination of dissolved concentrations of aluminum, iron, manganese and titanium using 0.45 µm filtration as an operational definition for "dissolved." Sources of error were attributed to filter passage of fine-grained clay particles.

Sampling Objectives and Recommendations

A common and overriding ground-water sampling objective is the acquisition of representative and accurate elemental concentrations for the purpose of risk assessment at hazardous waste sites. In addition to dissolved species, this should include contaminants sorbed to suspended (mobile) inorganic and organic particles. Disturbance of the subsurface environment is inevitable in the process of installing monitoring wells and collecting samples. Artifacts or contamination of samples can occur from the following: poor well design or construction; inadequate or improper well development; corrosion, degradation, or leaching of well construction materials; improper well purging, sampling, sample processing, transportation and storage. Intuitively, it makes sense to minimize disturbance of the sampling zone to obtain representative and accurate data. Excessive turbidity is the most common manifestation of disturbance. Turbidity results from stirred up or suspended sediment or foreign particles. Natural turbidity may exist where conditions are favorable for the production of stable suspensions (e.g., low ionic strength waters, geochemical supersaturation, high clay content), whereas excessively rapid pumping or purging relative to local hydrogeological conditions is the most common cause of artificial turbidity. Oxidation of anoxic or suboxic aquifer zones may result from high pumping rates which impact much larger segments of the aquifer than the interval of interest, causing the precipitation of iron oxyhydroxide and/or mixing of chemically distinct zones.

If a secondary objective is accurate "dissolved" elemental concentrations, then samples should be filtered in the field with in-line devices and using filter pore sizes ≤0.1 µm.

Sampling recommendations consistent with the above discussions and recommendations were summarized in a previous Environmental Research Brief (Puls et al. 1990; see Chapter 19). Briefly these recommendations included:

- Isolation of the sampling zone with packers to minimize purge volume,
- Low flow rate pumping to minimize aeration and turbidity,
- Monitoring of water quality parameters while purging to establish baseline or steady-state conditions to initiate sampling,
- Maximize pump tubing wall thickness and minimize length to exclude atmospheric gases,
- Filtration for estimate of dissolved species and the collection of unfiltered samples for estimates of contaminant mobility.

FIELD STUDIES

Sites

Between June 1988, and February 1991, three different field sites were used to evaluate the above sampling techniques and recommendations, emphasizing the impacts of different sample collection devices on sample turbidity and filtration effects on metals concentrations. The first site is at Pinal Creek, near Globe, Arizona, about 130 km east of Phoenix and 170 km north of Tucson. This site and sampling results were discussed in detail in Puls et al. (1990).

The second is a Superfund site near Saco, Maine, about 30 km south of Portland and 7 km inland from the coast. This site was used for chromium waste disposal by a leather tannery from 1959 to 1977.

Chromium wastes were dumped into 53 small unlined pits and two larger lagoons (each about 0.25 hectares). The site geology consists of glacial sediments, underlain by a sloping fractured bedrock surface. Sediment thickness ranges from 0 to 17 m. Analysis of ground-water flow is complicated by both the fractured nature of the bedrock and an apparent ground-water divide in the overburden. Upward gradients have been determined at some locations associated with ground-water discharge to surface drainages. Depth to water table ranges from 1 to 2 m below ground surface.

The third site is near Elizabeth City, North Carolina, about 100 km south of Norfolk, Virginia, and 60 km inland from the Outer Banks of North Carolina. A chrome plating shop, in use for more than 30 years, has discharged acidic chromium wastes into the soils and aquifer immediately below the shop. The site geology consists of typical Atlantic coastal plain sediments characterized by complex and variable sequences of surficial sands, silts and clays. Ground-water flow is generally to the northeast; however, in the immediate vicinity of the plating shop, flow appears to be directly toward the Pasquatank River about 90 m north of the shop. Ground-water flow is somewhat complicated due to wind tides. Depth to ground water is about 2 m. An estimated hydraulic conductivity value of 15 m/d was based on aquifer test data.

Site Sampling

The sampling set-up used at the Saco and Elizabeth City sites is depicted in Figure 20-1. This was similar to the arrangement used in Globe, where a laser light scattering instrument was used for tracking particle concentrations instead of a turbidimeter; and a bladder or submersible pump was used instead of a peristaltic pump (Puls et al. 1990). For comparison, a bailer was used in addition to the peristaltic pump at Saco and at Elizabeth City. A multiparameter instrument with flow-through cell was employed in all cases to monitor pH, temperature, specific conductance, redox potential, and dissolved oxygen during both purging and sample collection operations. Sample collection was initiated when all parameters, including turbidity, reached steady-state. Figure 20-2, for well MW101 at Saco, is typical of the trends for parameter equilibration during purging. Specific conductance, pH and temperature, although recommended by many sampling guidelines, were the least sensitive parameters, attaining steady-state values rather rapidly. Corresponding contaminant concentrations in addition to turbidity, redox, and dissolved oxygen, are also plotted in Figure 20-3 for well 1 at Elizabeth City. Chromate concentrations were shown to follow trends similar to those for equilibration-sensitive parameters.

Suspended Particles and Sampling Devices

At the Globe, Arizona site, comparisons were made between values of suspended particle concentration and particle size distributions using the following pumps: bladder (0.6–1.1 L/min), low speed submersible (2.8–3.8 L/min), and high speed submersible (12–92 L/min). Particle size distributions were measured with a laser light scattering instrument using photon correlation spectroscopy (Malvern AutoSizer IIC). Particles were captured on filters and identified by scanning electron microscopy with energy dispersive X-ray (SEM-EDX).

In well 105, more than 13 times more particles were mobilized by the low speed submersible pump compared to the bladder pump. This well is screened in the dense basin fill, where hydraulic conductivities are more than two orders of magnitude lower than those in the upper alluvium. Particles captured on filters were identified as iron-coated albite, gypsum and calcite. This lower region of the aquifer is saturated with respect to calcite, but unsaturated with gypsum. Gypsum particles were not present in the bladder pump samples, but were present in the submersible pump samples, probably due to mixing of the upper and lower aquifer waters caused by the relatively high pump rate. Differences in water chemistry from the bladder pump and high-speed submersible pump samples in June 1988, support this hypothesis (Brown, 1990). Interestingly, the calcite particles in the bladder pump samples were uniformly spherical and approximately 1 µm in diameter.

In well 452, screened in the alluvium, over 20 times more particles were mobilized by the high speed submersible pump compared to the bladder pump. These particles were captured on 0.1 µm filters and identified with SEM-EDX as predominantly smectite clays. Their presence was probably due to the fact that well 452 is screened in relatively fine grained sediment in the alluvium, and it is

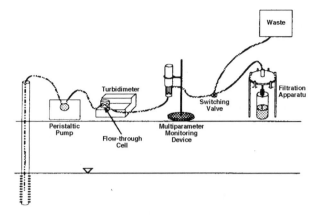

Figure 20-1. Sampling set-up for Saco, Maine, and Elizabeth City, North Carolina, sites (shallow wells).

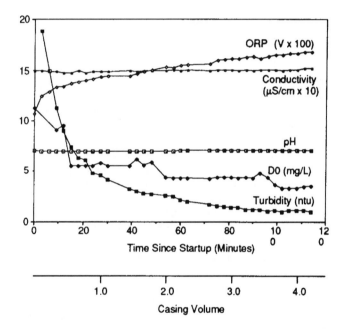

Figure 20-2. Equilibration of ground-water quality parameters during well purging (well MW 101, Saco, Maine, peristaltic pump (-0.2 L/min)).

near the leading edge of the acidic waste plume where pH is decreasing rapidly and iron oxide coatings on colloidal clay are dissolving.

In well 503, also in the upper alluvium, successive use of the bladder, and the low speed and high speed submersible pumps produced increasingly more numerous and larger particles in suspension. The two low-discharge pumps produced monomodal particle size distributions of approximately 500 nm. The high discharge submersible pump produced larger particles in a bimodal distribution centered around 800 and 2000 nm because of increased turbulence. The predominant mineral identified on the filters from well 503 was gypsum. The upper alluvial aquifer is supersaturated with respect to gypsum due to the dissolution of calcite by sulfuric acid-dominated wastes which have leached into the subsurface for over 80 years.

Even with the bladder pump, particles brought to the surface were as large as 10 μm, probably too large to be naturally suspended in situ, but there was clearly a significant difference in particle population and size between the three different pumps. Increasing pump rate generally resulted in

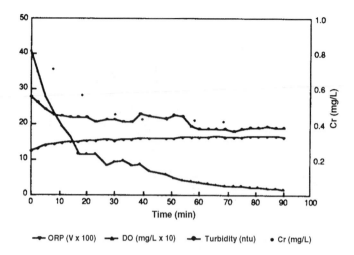

Figure 20-3. Equilibration of most sensitive ground-water quality parameters and chromate concentration during well purging (well 1, Elizabeth City, North Carolina, peristaltic pump (-0.2 L/min)).

increased turbidity with larger particles brought into suspension. Some anomalous behavior in this regard was caused by the sequence of pump comparison in a given well (Puls et al., 1990).

A peristaltic pump was used at both the Saco, Maine and Elizabeth City, North Carolina sites because of the shallow depth to ground water. As a result, lower pumping rates were possible (0.2–0.3 L/min). Turbidity due to suspended colloids was measured with a turbidimeter equipped with flow-through cell (Figure 20-1). Turbidity is commonly measured in nephelometric turbidity units (NTUs) and based on the comparison of the intensity of light scattered by a sample with the intensity of light scattered by a standard reference suspension under the same conditions. Formazin polymer is used as the reference. Formazin has been found to be more reproducible than clay or natural water (APHA, 1989). Jackson candle units (JCUs) were previously used with candle turbidimeters, and kaolin was a standard reference material. Table 20-1 lists correlations between NTUs, JCUs, and counts/1000/sec, as measured by two turbidimeters and a laser light scattering instrument respectively, using kaolinite as a common reference. Counts/1000/sec are photon counts recorded from laser light scattering measurements.

At Saco, most wells equilibrated at less than 5 NTUs; however, two wells equilibrated at 10 and 58 NTUs. The latter was an older well, and age or improper installation may explain the high turbidity value. At Elizabeth City, only 1 of 12 wells equilibrated at more than 5 NTUs. All of these wells were installed and developed by R.S. Kerr Laboratory personnel using best available technology and guidance. The well which had the highest equilibrated NTU value was well 8, the only well located (screened) in a clayey zone at the site (Figure 20-4).

A down-hole camera was used at Elizabeth City during purging and sampling to evaluate the disturbance caused by emplacement and pumping. Little impact was observed when the peristaltic pump was turned on after both the pump tubing and the camera had been left in the screened interval overnight. Emplacement of the camera itself created the greatest turbidity and required overnight re-equilibration in the absence of pumping. Purging at low flow rate produced approximately the same result, in terms of turbidity, as did overnight equilibration. These observations argue strongly for dedicated sampling equipment as the optimal and perhaps most efficient manner of collecting representative ground-water samples.

Filtration and Sampling Devices

Filtration differences among the different sampling devices used at the Arizona site were generally not significant. Greater than 10% differences were observed in some wells, particularly with the high speed submersible pump, due to artifacts from the excessive turbidity created down-hole by the pump compared to the natural hydrogeological conditions (Puls et al., 1990). Similar filtration studies at Saco and Elizabeth City produced much more dramatic results.

Table 20-1. Comparison of Nephelometric Turbidity Units (NTUs), Jackson Candle Units (JCUs), Photon Counts from Laser Light Scattering (cts/1000/sec) and Kaolinite Concentrations in Water (mg/L)

NTUs	JCUs	cts/1000/sec	mg/L
0.2	—	2.3	0.1
2.7	3.0	20.5	1.0
12.2	7.0	77.7	5.0
25.2	10.0	175.9	10.0
63.0	28.5	438.2	25.0
121.0	53.0	699.8	50.0
227.0	100.0	1412.2	100.0

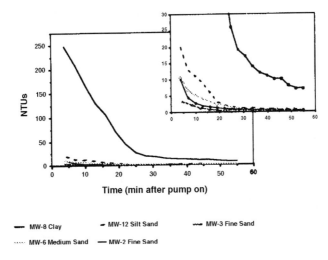

Figure 20-4. Equilibration of turbidity levels during well purging for several wells at the Elizabeth City site (peristaltic pump, ~0.2 L/min).

Figure 20-5 shows chromium levels in samples from well 1 at Elizabeth City where samples were collected both with a peristaltic pump (200 mL/min) and with a bailer. The purge time for water quality parameter equilibration using the peristaltic pump was 1.3 hr, or about two casing volumes (Figure 20-3). Bailed samples were collected after a standard three casing volumes had been bailed. There were no significant differences in chromium concentrations between unfiltered and 5.0, 0.4 and 0.1 μm pore size filtered samples with the peristaltic pump. The bailed samples were not only significantly different, but were also 2 to 3 times higher than the peristaltic pump values. A similar response was observed in well 8. In all twelve wells, there were no differences observed in metal concentrations over the entire range from unfiltered to 0.1 μm-filtered, when the samples were collected with the peristaltic using a low pumping rate (~200 mL/min) and the set-up depicted in Figure 20-1.

Although the Saco site is a chrome tannery waste disposal site, the inorganic contaminant of greatest interest in the ground water is arsenic. It is unclear at this time why the arsenic levels are elevated, and this is under further investigation. Figure 20-6 for well 113A shows arsenic levels for samples collected using both a peristaltic pump and a bailer. Results were similar to those for chromium at Elizabeth City. Once again, there were no differences observed in metal concentrations using the peristaltic pump and different filter pore sizes; but large differences were observed between filtered and unfiltered bailed samples. Also, these two sets of values were generally different from the peristaltic pump sampled values. The sampling set-up used with the peristaltic pump (Figure 20-1) consistently produced the most reproducible results, providing increased confidence that these samples were more representative of natural geochemical conditions and particle loading than those collected with the bailer.

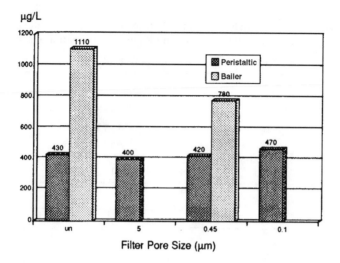

Figure 20-5. Differences in chromium concentrations for samples collected with peristaltic pump and bailer (well 1, Elizabeth City).

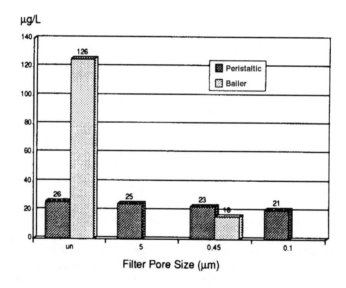

Figure 20-6. Differences in arsenic concentrations for samples collected with peristaltic pump and bailer (well 113A, Saco, Maine).

It was interesting to note that there seems to be no significant contribution to contaminant transport from suspended and mobile particles greater than 0.1 μm at either the Elizabeth City or the Saco site. However, this does not indicate that colloidal facilitated transport by smaller particles may not occur at these sites.

LABORATORY STUDIES

Particles with diameters of 0.1 to 2.0 μm may constitute the most mobile size fraction in porous media. This is because the efficiency of particle removal increases rapidly above 1 μm diameter due to sedimentation and/or interception processes; whereas for particles smaller than 0.1 μm diameter, removal occurs primarily by diffusion (Yao et al., 1971 and O'Melia, 1980). Although significant contaminant transport by colloidal material in this size range was not observed for the above three sites, repeated particle size analyses using laser light scattering with photon correlation spectroscopy (PCS) for aqueous samples and scanning electron microscopy (SEM) analysis for particles collected on filters at the Globe site indicated a preponderance of particles in the size range 0.5 to 2.0 µm at the lowest flow rates used for sample collection. Because of these and similar observations by Gschwend and Reynolds (1987), laboratory experiments using alluvium from the Globe site were performed to investigate specific aqueous chemical effects on the transport of environmentally realistic colloids, in the size range of 0.1–0.9 µm, through natural porous media under controlled conditions.

Iron oxide particles were synthesized to specific size and shape for use as the mobile colloidal phase in laboratory column experiments. The aquifer materials from Globe (wells 107 and 452) were used for the column packing or immobile phase. Arsenate was selected as a ubiquitous and hazardous inorganic contaminant, to study its interaction with both the porous immobile aquifer solids and the mobile inorganic colloids. Batch experiments were performed to evaluate colloid stability and assess the interactions between arsenate and colloidal Fe_2O_3, and arsenate and the aquifer matrix. Column experiments were performed to determine the extent of colloid transport and to compare retardation of aqueous and colloid-associated arsenate. Study variables included column flow rate, pH, ionic strength, electrolyte composition (anion/cation), colloid concentration and colloid size.

Characterization of Aquifer Solids and Colloidal Fe_2O_3

Core material from two locations at the site was used to pack 2.5-cm diameter, adjustable, glass columns. Prior to packing, the core sample was air-dried and sieved with the fraction between 106 and 2000 µm used in the columns. Subsamples were analyzed by X-ray diffraction. The predominant mineral phases, identified in order of intensity, were: quartz > albite >> magnesium orthoferrosilicate > muscovite > samsonite > manganese oxide.

The pH_{zpc}, or pH at which the net surface charge of a solid equals zero, is an important parameter affecting both colloidal stability and the interaction of the colloids with immobile matrix surfaces. Above the pH_{zpc}, minerals possess a net negative charge; while below this pH, the net charge is positive. Most sand and gravel type aquifer solids exhibit a net negative charge under most environmentally-relevant pH conditions, due to the predominance of silica ($PH_{zpc} \sim 2$) and other minerals such as layer silicates and manganese oxides which have pH_{zpc}'s < 4.

Spherical, monodisperse colloidal Fe_2O_3 (100–900 nm) was prepared from solutions of $FeCl_3$ and HCl using the method of Matijevic and Scheiner (1978). The method was modified by the addition of a spike of $_{26}Fe^{59}Cl_3$, prior to heating, to permit > detection of the colloidal hematite with liquid scintillation counting > techniques. The labeled colloidal Fe_2O_3 allowed unequivocal discrimination between injected particles and those mobilized within the column packing material.

Colloid concentration, in milligrams per liter (mg/L), was determined gravimetrically by both filtration and residue-on-evaporation techniques, coupled with solute analyses and mass-balance calculations. SEM and PCS were used to determine the particle size. PCS was also used to evaluate stability of the diluted colloidal suspensions and particle size in both influent and effluent column suspensions. The surface area of 200 nm diameter uniformly spherical hematite particles was calculated to be 5.72 m²/g using the equation,

$$A = \frac{6 \times 10^{-4}}{pd} \tag{1}$$

where A is the geometric surface area (m²/g), p the density (g/cm³), and d the diameter (cm).

The pH_{zpc} of the colloidal hematite was evaluated from acid-base titrations using varying concentrations of NaCl or $NaClO_4$ as the background (non-interacting) electrolytes. The plot in Figure 20-7a illustrates a distinct crossover in the titration curves at approximately pH 7.4 in NaCl. These titrations were performed in a nitrogen-filled glove box. Micro-electrophoretic mobility (EM) was used to evaluate the pH, (isoelectric point) of the particles. This technique was performed in $NaClO_4$. When only noninteracting electrolytes are present in solution, $pH_{zpc} = pH_{iep}$. Therefore, this mobility measurement served to support the titration pH_{zpc} data (Figure 20-7b). The EM measurements were made on the

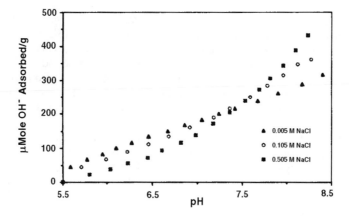

Figure 20-7a. Potentiometric titrations of Fe_2O_3 colloids as a function of pH in the presence of different concentrations of NaCl.

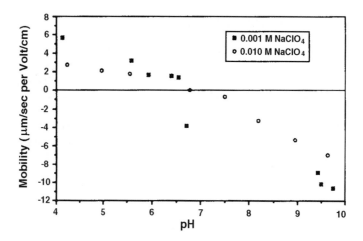

Figure 20-7b. Electrophoretic mobility of Fe_2O_3 colloids as a function of pH in the presence of different concentrations of $NaClO_4$.

bench in the presence of atmospheric CO_2. Colloid stability in both influent and effluent column suspensions as well as in batch studies was also evaluated using PCS to monitor coagulation. The colloidal suspensions were stable in dilute $NaClO_4$ and NaCl over the pH ranges 2.0–6.5 and 7.6–11.0 (Figure 20-8) respectively, with a region of instability corresponding to the estimated pH_{zpc}.

In this study, significant enhancement of colloid stability in suspensions of 0.01 M Na_2HAsO_4, and 0.01 M NaH_2PO_4 was observed at pH values as low as 4 ($\ll$ pristine pH_{zpc}) (Figure 20-9). This observation corresponds with work by Liang and Morgan (1990) who observed that hematite particles bear an overall net negative charge at pH $\ll$ pH_{zpc}, pristine in the presence of specifically sorbed anions (e.g., phosphate species). This phenomenon has the effect of increasing the stability region where the particles are negatively charged.

Arsenate Adsorption/Desorption

Adsorption of arsenate to the aquifer solids was performed to determine its affinity for these surfaces and to compare batch and column-derived solid-solution distribution values. Adsorption experiments with the colloidal hematite determined adsorption capacity and strength of arsenate retention. Adsorption data for arsenate on the aquifer solids were fitted to a Freundlich isotherm, defined by the relation

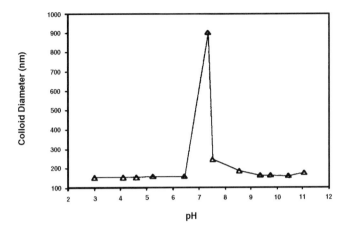

Figure 20-8. Stability of 150 nm Fe_2O_3, colloids as a function of pH in 0.005 M $NaClO_4$.

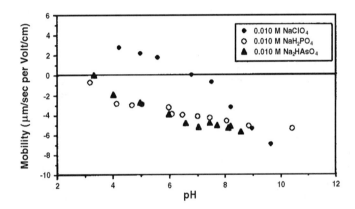

Figure 20-9. Electrophoretic mobility of Fe_2O_3 colloids as a function of pH in the presence of 0.01 M sodium electrolytes of different anionic composition.

$$S = KC_f^n \qquad (2)$$

where K is the empirical distribution coefficient or solid surface affinity term, S the steady-state concentration on the solids (mol kg), C_f the steady-state solution concentration (mol/L), and n is an empirical coefficient related to the monolayer capacity and energy of adsorption. Steady-state, as used here, represents the pre-determined batch equilibration times (24 hr) where no continued decrease in aqueous arsenate concentrations within analytical uncertainty were observed. Values of n < 1 imply decreasing energy of sorption with increasing surface coverage. The calculated K and n values using the logarithmic form of the above equation were 5.5 and 0.73, respectively. These values represent relatively weak interaction with the aquifer solids, with the interaction primarily due to the presence of iron oxide coatings on mineral grains as determined by sequential extraction techniques (Tessier et al., 1979).

Arsenate adsorption data for the Fe_2O_3 colloids were fitted to a Langmuir isotherm (Figure 20-10) defined by the relation

$$S = \frac{kbC_f}{1 + kC_f} \qquad (3)$$

where k is the Langmuir solid surface affinity coefficient, b the adsorption capacity, and S and C_f are defined above. An advantage of the Langmuir model is the incorporation of the capacity term. The

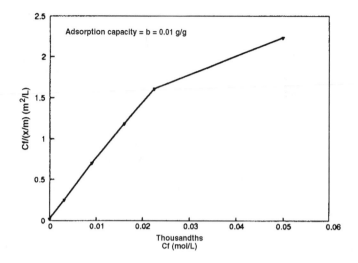

Figure 20-10. Langmuir isotherm data for arsenate adsorption on Fe_2O_3 colloids (pH 7, 0.01M $NaClO_4$, 4.5 mg:30 mL, 24 hr equilibration).

correlation coefficient for the linearized Langmuir form of the above equation was 0.97 and the adsorption capacity was estimated to be 0.01 g arsenic/g Fe_2O_3. There was very little difference in adsorption extent between pH 4–7. However, a gradual decrease was observed with increasing pH.

Desorption batch experiments were performed immediately following arsenate adsorption to simulate passage of an arsenate plume with subsequent contact by low-arsenate or arsenate-free water. An equivalent volume of arsenate-free 0.01 M $NaClO_4$ was added to replace the extracted supernatant from adsorption batch reactors. The pH was the same pH used in the prior adsorption experiments (pH 7). Samples were equilibrated for 48 hr. Strong retention of the arsenate on the hematite was observed, since only about 2–6% of the adsorbed arsenate fraction was released (Figure 20-11). Percent desorption was directly proportional to the initial arsenate concentration, indicating a decline in the energy of adsorption as the surface became increasingly saturated with arsenate. This phenomenon could have important implications for pump and treat remediation of highly contaminated sites. The easily desorbed arsenate will result in high initial efficiency of dissolved arsenate removal which may significantly decline once concentration values are reduced below the plateau portion of the adsorption isotherm and desorption becomes less energetically favorable.

Dissolved Arsenate Transport

Column studies of dissolved arsenate transport were performed to compare distribution coefficients (K_d) with those derived from the batch tests and for comparison to Fe_2O_3 colloid-facilitated transport of the arsenate. Arsenate concentrations used in both sets of experiments were comparable. The column K_d roughly corresponds to the K value calculated from the batch tests and is determined by:

$$R_f = 1 + \frac{p_b K_d}{n} \qquad (4)$$

where R_f is the retardation factor or ratio, v/v_c, of the velocity of the ground water to the velocity of the solute, p_b is the bulk density, and n is the porosity. Tritiated water was used for estimating the average water velocity.

As the flow velocity was decreased, the column K_d values approached those of the 24-hr equilibrated batch K values, indicating rate limited adsorption onto the aquifer solids at the higher flow velocities (Table 20-2). These results demonstrate the importance of generating comparative data and not relying solely on batch sorption static equilibrium data, especially for specific site assessment purposes. When ground-water flow velocities are relatively rapid, assumptions of local equilibrium may be invalid.

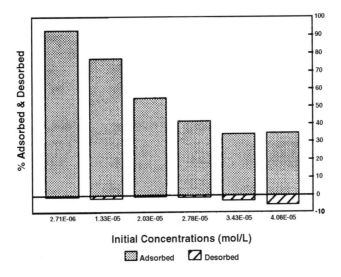

Figure 20-11. Adsorption-desorption data for arsenate on Fe_2O_3 colloids (pH 7, 0.01 M $NaClO_4$, 4.5 mg:30 mL, 24 hr equilibrations).

Table 20-2. Comparison of Distribution Coefficients (K_d, L/kg) for Arsenate Using Globe, AZ Aquifer Material in Batch and Column Tests (P_b = 2.65 g/cm^3, n = 0.4)

	Column		Batch
	3.4 m/d	1.7 m/d	Steady-state
	1.4	3.0	5.5

Following the arsenate transport experiments, the columns were flushed with deionized water (~zero ionic strength). This significantly increased turbidity in the column effluent due to dispersion of the colloidal aquifer fines. When the effluent was analyzed, the recovered arsenate was determined to be almost entirely colloid-associated and approximately equal to the influent arsenate concentration, demonstrating the potential importance of this transport mechanism (Figure 20-12).

Colloidal Transport

Column flow rates used were comparable to estimated ground-water velocities in the Globe alluvium (0.8–3.4 m/d). The injected colloidal hematite generally broke through at the same time or prior to tritiated water (Figure 20-13). In this case, the rate of colloid transport through the columns was over 21 times faster than the dissolved arsenate. A summary of column results for the colloidal transport experiments has been compiled in Table 20-3. No colloid transport occurred when the particles were net positively-charged indicating significant electrostatic interaction with the net negatively-charged matrix material. In low ionic strength suspensions of NaCl and $NaClO_4$, breakthrough exceeded 50% of initial colloid concentrations. These electrolyte suspensions were perhaps the most representative of natural conditions in uncontaminated ground water. There was substantially lower colloid recovery of sulfate-based suspensions, due to difficulties in maintaining colloid stability, and apparent nonspecific interactions of the sulfate with the hematite surface.

Maximum percent breakthrough occurred with phosphate and arsenate-based suspensions and appeared to be unaffected by the range of flow velocities or column lengths used. Likewise, no significant differences were observed due to colloid concentration. The specific adsorption of the predominantly divalent phosphate and arsenate anions onto the hematite surface caused a charge reversal on the initially net positively-charged surface. The consequence is a lowering of the pH_{iep} below the pH_{zpc} value and an increase in net negative charge near the particle surface over a wider pH range. The

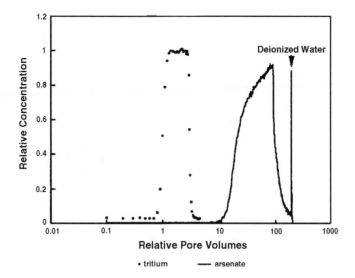

Figure 20-12. Breakthrough curve for dissolved arsenate versus tritium, and mobilization of colloidal-associated arsenate by deionized water.

Table 20-3. Column Results of Colloidal Fe$_2$O$_3$ Transport Through Natural Aquifer Material

Size (nm)	pH	Velocity (m/d)	Part. Conc. (mg/L)	Ionic Strength	Anion	%C$_0$ thru	Col. Length (cm)
200	3.9	3.4	10	0.005	Cl$^-$	0	3.8
125	8.9	3.4	10	0.005	Cl$^-$	54	5.1
150	8.1	3.4	5	0.001	ClO$_4^-$	57	3.8
250	8.1	3.4	10	0.03	SO$_4^{2-}$	17	3.8
150	8.9	3.4	5	0.03	SO$_4^{2-}$	14	3.8
100	7.6	3.4	5	0.03	HAsO$_4^{2-}$	97	2.5
100	7.6	1.7	5	0.03	HAsO$_4^{2-}$	96	2.5
100	7.6	0.8	5	0.03	HAsO$_4^{2-}$	93	2.5
125	7.6	3.4	10	0.03	HPO$_4^{2-}$	99	5.1
100	7.6	1.7	5	0.03	HPO$_4^{2-}$	99	2.5
100	7.6	3.4	5	0.03	HPO$_4^{2-}$	99	2.5
900	7.0	3.4	50	0.03	HPO$_4^{2-}$	33	3.8
900	7.0	3.4	50	0.03	HPO$_4^{2-}$	30	3.8

increased negative charge increased repulsion between the mobile, negatively-charged particles, and the immobile, net negatively-charged, column matrix solids. As a result, the colloids were stable at a greater distance from the pore walls in the column matrix, where fluid velocity is higher.

Particle size had an inverse effect on percent breakthrough; that is, increasing colloidal transport was observed with decreasing particle size. While the larger particles were still transported there were significant differences between the 100 nm and 900 nm size classes. A complicating factor in resolving these differences was the use of a different aquifer solid sample (well 452) for the larger hematite particles. Sieve analyses of the two samples reflected differences in particle size (Figure 20-14), although XRD analyses showed no significant differences in mineralogy. The high density (5.3 g/cm^3) of the hematite may have contributed to gravitational settling of the larger particles.

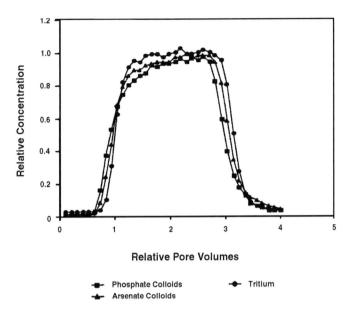

Figure 20-13. Breakthrough curve for Fe_2O_3 colloids suspended in 0.01 M NaH_2PO_4 and in 0.01 M Na_2HAsO_4, pH 7.6, 3.4 m/d, 5 mg/L.

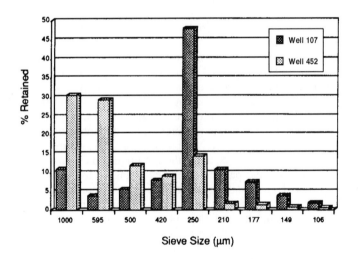

Figure 20-14. Sieve size fractionation of well 107 and well 452, Globe aquifer material.

Densities of secondary clay minerals which are more representative of colloids in natural systems are on the order of 2.69/cm³.

All of the parameters (Table 20-3 headings) or variables were explored in detail with the SAS program JMP, using %C_o breakthrough as the response variable. Only colloid size and anion significantly impacted the %C_o breakthrough. Combining these two parameters into a two-way main effects analysis of variance (2-way ANOVA) model accounted for 98.4% of the variability in the colloid breakthrough results. All other factors tested gave no significant correlation over the parameter ranges utilized in this study.

Given a ground water containing 10 mg/L suspended colloidal material, of surface area and reactivity comparable to these hematite particles, 0.1 mg/L of arsenic could be colloidally transported under some hydrogeochemical conditions. This is twice the maximum contaminant level (MCL) currently set for drinking water. It should be noted that these Fe_2O_3 model colloids are relatively nonreactive and have low surface area compared to the more ubiquitous subsurface colloidal minerals (e.g., clays, goethite). In addition, the suspended solids concentrations of these experiments were about one-half of those observed at the Arizona site and one-sixth the concentration observed at some other sites (Buddemeier and Hunt, 1988; Ryan and Gschwend, 1990).

SUMMARY AND CONCLUSIONS

Field results from three distinctly different sites indicate that the most representative and reproducible elemental concentrations are obtained by following the recommendations proposed previously by Puls et al. (1990). The selection of sampling devices, purging and sampling flow rates and filtration procedures is particularly important. There is a strong inverse correlation between turbidity and representativeness of samples. The greatest differences, both in terms of suspended colloids and inorganic contaminant concentrations, were observed between the bladder pump and the high speed submersible pump, in the deep wells, and between the peristaltic pump and the bailer in the shallow wells.

Steady-state turbidity levels observed at the three sites ranged from 1–58 NTUs; and in the case of one site, turbidity differences were strongly related to clay mineral content. Screened intervals with higher clay and silt contents had higher turbidity values. While artifacts of well construction and sample collection cause ground-water turbidity, there are indications that high levels of turbidity may occur naturally due to geology and geochemistry.

The down-hole camera indicated little artificial colloid generation or disturbance due to the low flow rate pumping action of the peristaltic pump. Emplacement of the camera, which is similar in size and shape to bladder pumps and submersible pumps, created the greatest disturbance (turbidity). While there has been no concrete evidence of significant colloidal-facilitated transport of inorganic contaminants at any of the three sites, the down-hole camera documented the existence of significant concentrations of suspended colloidal material in the flow field at Elizabeth City. Additional research in this area continues.

Laboratory experiments using natural aquifer material and realistic inorganic model colloids indicate that the transport of colloidal material through sand and gravel-type aquifers may be significant under certain hydrogeochemical conditions. Due to the strong reactivity of many inorganic colloids in natural subsurface systems, the potential exists that this form of contaminant transport may be important at certain sites. Its significance depends on a number of chemical and physical variables, including but not limited to ionic strength, ionic composition, flow velocity, quantity, nature, and size of suspended colloids, geologic composition and structure, and ground-water chemistry. The most significant of these factors, under the conditions investigated in these column experiments, were ionic composition and particle size. Neglecting colloidal mobility in our predictive contaminant transport models may underestimate both the transport rate, maximum transport distance, and mass. Chemical parameters affecting colloidal stability and transport must be included in transport modeling along with physical parameters (such as pore size distribution colloidal density and size, and flow velocity). Field sampling procedures must account for the possibility of colloidal transport and provide correct model input data. These concerns must be addressed during site characterization and assessment monitoring if colloid transport is deemed possible for the site.

ACKNOWLEDGMENTS

The authors wish to recognize and thank Dr. Terry F. Rees of USGS, San Diego, CA, for SEM-EDX analyses; Bert Bledsoe, RSKERL, for field assistance and much helpful technical assistance and guidance; Terry Connally and Dick Willey, U.S. EPA, and Frank Blaha and Jim Vardy, USCG.

REFERENCES

American Public Health Association (APHA). 1989. Standard Methods for the Examination of Water and Wastewater, 17th Edition. American Public Health Association, Washington D.C. [Editor's note: the 19th edition was released in late 1995.]

Brown, J.G. 1990. Chemical, Geologic, and Hydrologic Data from the Study of Acidic Contamination in the Miami Wash-Pinal Creek Area, Arizona. U.S. Geological Survey Open File Report 90-395.

Buddemeier, R.W. and J.H. Rego. 1986. Colloidal Radionuclides in Groundwater, FY85 Annual Report. UCAR 10062/85-1. Lawrence Livermore National Laboratory, Livermore, CA.

Buddemeier, R.W. and J.R. Hunt. 1988. Transport of Colloidal Contaminants in Ground Water: Radionuclide Migration at the Nevada Test Site. Applied Geochemistry 3:535–548, 1988.

Cerda, C.M. 1987. Mobilization of Kaolinite Fines in Porous Media Colloids and Surfaces 27:219–241.

Champ, D.R., W.F. Merritt, and J.L. Young. 1982. Potential for Rapid Transport of Pu in Groundwater as Demonstrated by Core Column Studies. In: Scientific Basis for Radioactive Waste Management, Vol. 5. Elsevier, New York, NY.

Champlin, J.B.F. and G.G. Eichholz. 1968. The Movement of Radioactive Sodium and Ruthenium through a Simulated Aquifer. Water Resour. Res. 4(1):147–158.

Champlin, J.B.F. and G.G. Eichholz. 1976. Fixation and Remobilization of Trace Contaminants in Simulated Subsurface Aquifers. Health Physics 30:215–219.

Eichholz, G.G., B.G. Wahlig, G.F. Powell, and T.F. Craft. 1982. Subsurface Migration of Radioactive Waste Materials by Particulate Transport. Nuclear Tech. 58:511–519.

Enfield, C.G. and G. Bengtsson. 1988. Macromolecular Transport of Hydrophobic Contaminants in Aqueous Environments. Ground Water 26(1):64–70.

Gschwend P.M. and M.D. Reynolds. 1987. Monodisperse Ferrous Phosphate Colloids in an Anoxic Groundwater Plume. J. Contaminant Hydrol. 1:309–327.

Harvey, R.W., L.H. George, R.L. Smith, and D.R. LeBlanc. 1989. Transport of Microspheres and Indigenous Bacteria through a Sandy Aquifer: Results of Natural- and Forced-Gradient Tracer Experiments. Environ. Sci. Technol. 23(1):51–56.

Hem, J.D. and C.E. Roberson. 1967. Form and Stability of Aluminum Hydroxide Complexes in Dilute Solution. U.S. Geological Survey Water Supply Paper 1827-A.

Kennedy, V.C. and G.W. Zellweger 1974. Filter Pore-Size Effects on the Analysis of Al, Fe, Mn, and Ti in Water. Water Resour. Res. 10(4):785–790.

Kim, J.I., G. Buckau, F. Baumgartner, H.C. Moon, and D. Lux. 1984. Colloid Generation and the Actinide Migration in Gorleben Groundwaters. In: G.L. McVay (ed.), Scientific Basis for Nuclear Waste Management, Vol. 7. Elsevier, New York, NY, pp. 31–40.

Liang, L. and J.J. Morgan 1990. Chemical Aspects of Iron Oxide Coagulation in Water-Laboratory Studies and Implications for Natural Systems. Aquatic Sciences 52(1):32–55.

Matijevic, E. and P. Scheiner. 1978. Ferric Hydrous Oxide Sols. J. Colloid Interface Sci. 63(3):509–524.

Matijivec, E., R.J. Kuo, and H. Kolny. 1980. Stability and Deposition Phenomena of Monodispersed Hematite Sols. J. Colloid Interface Sci. 80(1):94–106.

Means, J.C. and R. Wijayaratne. 1982. Role of Natural Colloids in the Transport of Hydrophobic Pollutants. Science, 215(19):968–970.

Nelson, D.M., W.R. Penrose, J.O. Karttunen, and P. Mehlhaff. 1985. Effects of Dissolved Organic Carbon on the Adsorption Properties of Plutonium in Natural Waters. Environ. Sci. Technol. 19:127–131.

Nightingale, H.I. and W.C. Bianchi. 1977. Ground Water Turbidity Resulting from Artificial Recharge. Ground Water 15(2):146–152.

O'Melia, C.R.. 1980. Aquasols: The Behavior of Small Particles in Aquatic Systems. Environ. Sci. Technol. 14(9):1052–1060.

Penrose, W.R., W.L. Polzer, E.H. Essington, D.M. Nelson, and K.A. Orlandini. 1990. Mobility of Plutonium and Americium through a Shallow Aquifer in a Semiarid Region. Environ. Sci. Technol. 24:228–234.

Puls, R.W. and J.H. Eychaner. 1990. Sampling Ground Water for Inorganics—Pumping Rate, Filtration, and Oxidation Effects. In: Proc. Fourth Nat. Outdoor Action Conf. on Aquifer Restoration, Ground Water Monitoring and Geophysical Methods. National Water Well Association, Dublin, OH, pp. 313–327.

Puls, R.W., J.H. Eychaner, and R.M. Powell. 1990. Colloidal-Facilitated Transport of Inorganic Contaminants in Ground Water: Part I. Sampling Considerations. Environmental Research Brief EPA/600/M-90/023. [See Chapter 19.]

Reynolds, M.D. 1985. Colloids in Groundwater, Master's Thesis, Mass. Inst. of Tech., Cambridge, MA.

Ryan, J.N. and P.M. Gschwend. 1990. Colloid Mobilization in Two Atlantic Coastal Plain Aquifers: Field Studies. Water Resour. Res., 1990.

Saltelli, A., A. Avogadro, and G. Bidoglio. 1984. Americium Filtration in Glauconitic Sand Columns. Nuclear Technol. 67:245–254.

Sandhu, S.S. and G.L. Mills. 1987. Kinetics and Mechanisms of the Release of Trace Inorganic Contaminants to Ground Water from Coal Ash Basins on the Savannah River Plant, Savannah River Ecology Lab. Aiken, SC. DOE/SR/15170-1.

Sheppard, J.C., M.J. Campbell, and J.A. Kittrick. 1979. Retention of Neptunium, Americium and Curium by Diffusible Soil Particles. Environ. Sci. Technol. 13(6):680–684.

Stumm, W. and J.J. Morgan. 1981. Aquatic Chemistry. John Wiley & Sons, New York, NY.

Takayanagi, K. and G.T.F. Wong. 1984. Organic and Colloidal Selenium in South Chesapeake Bay and Adjacent Waters. Marine Chem. 14:141–148,.

Tessier, A., P.G.C. Campbell, and M. Bisson. 1979. Sequential Extraction Procedure for the Speciation of Particulate Trace Metals. Anal. Chem. 51(7):844–849.

Tillekeratne, S., T. Miwa, and A. Mizuike. 1986. Determination of Traces of Heavy Metals in Positively Charged Inorganic Colloids in Fresh Water. Mikrochimica Acta B:289–296.

Wagemann, R. and G.J. Brunskill. 1975. The Effect of Filter Pore-Size on Analytical Concentrations of Some Trace Elements in Filtrates of Natural Water. Intern. J. Environ. Anal. Chem. 4:75–84.

Yao, K., M.T. Habibian, and C.R. O'Melia. 1971. Water and Waste Water Filtration: Concepts and Applications, Environ. Sci. Technol. 5(11):1105–1112.

DISCLAIMER

QUALITY ASSURANCE STATEMENT

Index